A LIGHT IN
DARK TIMES

A LIGHT IN DARK TIMES

THE NEW SCHOOL FOR SOCIAL RESEARCH
AND ITS UNIVERSITY IN EXILE

JUDITH FRIEDLANDER

Columbia University Press

New York

COLUMBIA
UNIVERSITY
PRESS

Columbia University Press gratefully acknowledges the generous support for this book
provided by Publisher's Circle member Anya Schiffrin.

Columbia University Press
Publishers Since 1893
New York   Chichester, West Sussex
cup.columbia.edu
Copyright © 2019 Judith Friedlander
Paperback edition, 2023

The font Neue, which means "new" in German, is a bespoke version of the font Irma,
designed by Peter Bil'ak. The proprietary font was created for and named
in honor of The New School and is used with permission.

Library of Congress Cataloging-in-Publication Data
Names: Friedlander, Judith, 1944– author.
Title: A light in dark times : the New School for Social Research and its
University in Exile / Judith Friedlander.
Description: New York : Columbia University Press, [2018] |
Includes bibliographical references and index.
Identifiers: LCCN 2018021894 (print) | LCCN 2018033610 (ebook) |
ISBN 9780231180184 (cloth) | ISBN 9780231180191 (pbk.) |
ISBN 9780231542579 (e-book)
Subjects: LCSH: New School for Social Research (New York, N.Y. :
1919–1997)—History. | Johnson, Alvin Saunders, 1874–1971.
Classification: LCC LD3837 (ebook) | LCC LD3837 .F75 2018 (print) |
DDC 378.747/1—dc23
LC record available at https://lccn.loc.gov/2018021894

Cover design: Elliott S. Cairns
Cover image: Thomas Hart Benton, *America Today*, 1930–31,
panel B, "City Activities with Dance Hall." The Metropolitan Museum of Art,
Gift of AXA Equitable, 2012 (2012.478a–j) © The Metropolitan Museum of Art.
Image source: Art Resource, NY.
(Benton originally painted his ten-panel mural, *America Today*, for the New School for
Social Research. On the lower right corner of "City Activities with Dance Hall," we see the
painter and the New School's president Alvin Johnson having a drink in a speakeasy.)

In memory of my husband, Erwin Fleissner.

The son of German intellectuals, he shared my deep attachment
to the history of the New School for Social Research
and its University in Exile.

CONTENTS

Prologue: In the Archives   ix

PART I: A SCHOOL OF SOCIAL RESEARCH

1 The First Founding Moment   3

2 Alvin Johnson and *The New Republic*   9

3 Columbia University   20

4 The Idea Takes Shape   34

5 The New School Opens   44

6 Alvin Johnson Takes Over   60

PART II: THE UNIVERSITIES IN EXILE

7 The Founding of the German University in Exile   85

8 The University in Exile Opens   116

9 Ring the Alarm   137

10 Ecole Libre des Hautes Etudes   152

PART III: THE MIDDLE YEARS

11 Alvin Johnson Retires   167

12 The Red Scare   178

13 The Orozco Mural   203

14 "The New School Really Isn't News Any Longer"   215

15 "Save the School"   237

PART IV: "BETWEEN PAST AND FUTURE"

16 The "New" New School   255

17 Three Doctoral Programs at Risk   283

PART V: RENEWING THE LEGACY

18 Rebuilding the Graduate Faculty   299

19 Rekindling the Spirit   320

Epilogue: Extending the Legacy   343

Appendix A: Extended Notes and Commentary for Chapter 6   355

Appendix B: Extended Notes and Commentary for Chapter 7   359

Appendix C: Extended Notes and Commentary for Chapter 9   365

Appendix D: Extended Notes and Commentary for Chapter 18   367

Acknowledgments   371

Notes   375

Index   441

Photo section follows page 214

PROLOGUE: IN THE ARCHIVES

As I was nearing the end of many months of research in the New School's archives, I opened a box filled with bulletins and announcements, a miscellaneous collection spanning over ninety years.[1] In a folder labeled Early History, I found a typed memo, ragged and discolored, with no date or author's name. The paper looked old enough to belong in this file with other documents going back to the interwar period, but the memo itself referred to events that took place at a much later time.

Unable to make sense out of what I was reading, I was about to give up and turn to something else when I noticed a few faded words penciled in at the top of the first page: "Memo to A. J. who proposes writing a history of the School." A. J. was, of course, the legendary Alvin Johnson. An economist and journalist, he founded the New School for Social Research in 1919, together with other prominent intellectuals and philanthropists of the day, including the historians Charles A. Beard and James Harvey Robinson, and the editor in chief of *The New Republic*, Herbert Croly. Champions of academic freedom, they opened the New School as an act of protest against university presidents across the country who had forbidden professors to express themselves freely. Their primary target was Nicholas Murray Butler of Columbia University, who had fired two faculty members in 1917 for speaking out as pacifists during World War I while U.S. soldiers were fighting overseas. Several years later the two historians and Croly resigned from the New School, leaving its fate in the hands of Alvin Johnson.

If the memo I found was intended for Johnson, then its author was Agnes de Lima, his old friend and publicity director of the New School. Her style was unmistakable, an engaging blend of authority and charm, almost breezy at times, but never losing sight of the task at hand—in this case, to provide Johnson with an outline for his book. She promised to follow up with the necessary documentation.

De Lima had material going back to the early 1920s, with vivid examples of how Johnson had taken a failing "independent school of social science" and turned it into the country's preeminent school of adult education—to provide what he liked to call "the continuing education of the educated." By 1927, the New School had become *the* place to go to hear famous people lecture on politics and the arts, or recent developments in new fields of inquiry such as anthropology and psychoanalysis. In 1933, when Hitler rose to power, Johnson created within the New School the University in Exile, offering lifesaving visas and academic positions for nearly two hundred refugees. With this heroic achievement, he followed through with the founders' original idea of building a strong research faculty in the social sciences. Known officially, after 1934, as the Graduate Faculty of Political and Social Science, the University in Exile became a magnet for students interested in studying with eminent scholars who had fled the great universities of Europe.

Attached to the outline were fragments of a proposal, still in draft form, that Johnson had apparently written. Neither he nor de Lima ever finished the book.[2] The only evidence I have that one of them, at least, was planning to do so was a notice published on November 23, 1959, in the *New School Bulletin* informing its readers that Agnes de Lima had just retired "in order to devote all her time—24½ hours a day—to the completion of a book describing the history of the New School."[3] The announcement appeared during the final weeks of the university's year-long celebration of three milestones: the fortieth anniversary of the New School for Social Research, the twenty-fifth anniversary of the University in Exile, and the eighty-fifth birthday of Alvin Johnson.

Despite his advanced age, Johnson was still going strong in 1959, and the university he had built was finally bouncing back after a long and rocky transition following his retirement. Honored guests stepped forward at every event to toast the first president, aspiring to match the eloquence of earlier tributes made by luminaries such as Thomas Mann, the German novelist and Nobel Prize laureate, who sang Johnson's praises in 1943 during Europe's darkest hours:

> We are met to do honor to a man known wherever liberty is cherished, a man consecrated to the cause of intellectual freedom and dedicated to the principle of creative endeavor, a man who through his effort has made the New School for Social Research a place of abiding faith in liberal thought. Alvin Johnson, by his foresight and perseverance, has given refuge, hope, and home to hundreds

of exiles now privileged to participate in the fight for freedom. . . . Long live Alvin Johnson!

Long live the University of Both Hemispheres.[4]

Alvin Johnson continued to lead an active professional life well into his nineties, writing prodigiously and keeping an eye on university affairs. What prevented him, therefore, or de Lima for that matter, from finishing the much-anticipated book? I believe they backed away six months after the big celebration, when the New School faced a serious crisis in leadership, making it difficult to complete the uplifting story they had started to tell on the few yellowed pages they had left behind.

Things began to deteriorate in June 1960, soon after the man Johnson had chosen to replace him stepped down as president. A political scientist and policy analyst, Hans Simons belonged to the generation of refugee scholars the New School had rescued "from the claws of fascism." Although they had their disagreements, Simons remained faithful to Johnson's vision of the school and consulted with him regularly. The next president, Henry David, was less solicitous. He preferred doing things his own way and, in the process, he nearly bankrupted the institution.

Johnson died in 1971 at the age of ninety-six; de Lima three years later at eighty-seven. Although they never followed through with their history of the school, de Lima spent the final years of her life organizing Johnson's papers for future researchers to use, filling dozens of boxes with hundreds of letters, speeches, and publications. She preserved countless newspaper articles and announcements as well that recorded the university's many accomplishments and those of its first president.

Over the years, Johnson maintained an active correspondence on the major issues of the day with politicians, jurists, intellectuals, and artists. He also wrote thousands of letters to raise money for the university, continuing to do so long after he retired. A master of the genre, in 1952 he playfully promised the New School's faithful friends that, with their next gift, they would receive a bound volume of his fund-raising letters, called *The Compleat Beggar*.[5]

Johnson published widely on economics, politics, and the role of education in a democratic society in scholarly journals and for the general public. He tried his hand at fiction as well. In his popular writing, he often used a deliberately folksy style that dripped with irony when he described his political opponents—for example, in his autobiography, written at the height of the McCarthy period, where he defiantly took aim at the "Philistines" in Washington.

Although the New School has preserved many boxes of letters and other pertinent material, Johnson sent his official papers to Yale, a decision he tried to explain diplomatically, but the message was clear. In a mass mailing dated "spring 1967," Johnson wrote:

> Recently, the Yale University Library has invited me to place [my] papers in the Beinecke Rare Book and Manuscript Library in New Haven, which is specially equipped to care for archives entrusted to it. This I am very glad to do since the New School for Social Research, where my papers might properly belong, has no archival facilities at present and is growing so fast that any space that becomes available is promptly pre-empted for classrooms and offices.
>
> I am therefore calling on my friends and colleagues to help me gather the material together. If by any chance you have preserved any of the letters or articles with which I was wont to afflict you, won't you send them to my friend, Agnes de Lima, whom I have asked to organize and classify the material and then send it on to Yale.[6]

Others followed Johnson's example. Joseph Greenbaum, dean of the Graduate Faculty, sent the papers of the New School's refugee scholars to a special archive in Albany, at the State University of New York.[7] And the political philosopher, Hannah Arendt, who joined the faculty after the war, sent her papers to the Library of Congress. By the mid-1980s, whatever documents remained in the New School's archives were in tatters, the predictable result of years of neglect and the object today of a major campaign to preserve them.

Johnson wrote with exuberant pride about the early years at the New School. His descriptions literally jumped off the page, often teasing readers with an irreverent anecdote but never letting them forget that he was writing about some of the most significant scholars, politicians, and artists of the day. At the end of his proposal for the book he never completed, Johnson attached a short sketch of life at the New School during the late 1920s, signaling, in a few sample paragraphs, that he planned to write an unconventional history of his decidedly unconventional school. The incidents he described took place in Chelsea, where the New School held classes before moving to Greenwich Village in 1931:

> In *The New York Times* of April 3, 1927, we find an item on Senator [William] Borah, who "often pictured as Jovian and cloud wrapped, seemed entirely human

here the other night when he attended a meeting of the New School for Social Research in a small back room of a basement bookshop. He was cloud wrapped at that, but the clouds were only tobacco clouds. He sat smoking . . . while a group of kindred spirits plied him with questions."

The New School lecturers in those days included names still well known today. A sampling: Clarence Darrow, John Dewey, Walter Lippmann, [Zachariah] Chaffee . . . taking part in a series on "Freedom in the Modern World." . . . Eva Le Gallienne gave benefit performances of "The Master Builder" in Feb.'27.

One incident disturbed the scholarly calm of the little courtyard or campus on West 24th Street. Horace Kallen in his bachelor days had rented from the New School an apartment on the top floor of one of the houses. One night an intruder broke in. It was a hot summer night and Horace Kallen's feet protruded beyond the sheets. The intruder with a strange sense of humor, the press reported, stopped and tickled the professor's toes. Horace Kallen, alarmed, less for himself than for the safety of his sister lying ill in the adjoining room, leaped on the burglar, grappled with him, and triumphantly threw him out of the third-story window. By that time, the place was in an uproar. Fred Grote, the superintendent, summoned the police, who came in droves to search for the culprit, who was nowhere to be found. But Fred's little fox terrier set up a frightful din outside some shrubbery planted against the wall of the courtyard. The police drew out the shrinking fugitive who was bleeding profusely from a severed ear. A German newspaper, reporting the incident declared, "Der Herr Professor biss dem Dieb das Ohr ab" (The distinguished professor bit the thief's ear off).[8]

Ending the sketch playfully with a quote in German permitted Johnson to note, as if only in passing, that his "Herr Professor" had an international reputation, a distinction Kallen shared with other scholars and artists who lectured regularly at the New School. Johnson could safely assume in 1959 that his readers would recognize Kallen's name. The philosopher was widely known for having introduced the term *cultural pluralism* into scholarly and popular debates during the first quarter of the twentieth century. According to Kallen, ethnic diversity strengthened democracy in the United States by replenishing the nation's cultural and economic resources. His own biography was a case in point: The son of an Orthodox Jewish rabbi, his family emigrated from Silesia in 1887, when he was five years old, following the expulsion of Jews and Poles from the expanding German Empire. Raised in a strictly religious home where the family spoke and read several languages, Kallen went on to become a major figure in American philosophy and in the nation's growing community of secular Jews.

In the outline itself, Johnson described the New School as "a center where the intelligent layman and the specialist were able freely to examine together the vast and frequently bewildering issues of the time." It attracted people, he explained, who wanted to learn about the complexities of contemporary society and culture from different perspectives. The New School was one of the few places where they could do so:

> In the days when the teaching of the social sciences was languishing in universities and colleges throughout the country, the New School boldly pursued those studies, including the revolutionary discoveries in psychology, psychoanalysis, and anthropology. Similarly, in the fields of modern art, modern music, modern dance, the New School was among the pioneers in offering courses and workshops directed by leading artists and critics.

And it taught these courses during the evening, making it possible for working people to attend.

But that was not all. What defined the New School above everything else was "its continuing struggle," Johnson proclaimed, "against discrimination in education, signalized both by its dramatic rescue of foreign scholars from the hands of dictators and its stated charter provisions that no consideration whatever be given in the appointment of faculty members to race, creed, or other irrelevancies. The dramatic story—one of national significance—of the University in Exile will be here given in illuminative detail!"

Johnson planned to open each chapter with an overview of the period, and then show how the New School organized debates around the important issues of the day with leading intellectuals, artists, and politicians who dared challenge conventional wisdom from the left and the right—like the "Jovian" Senator Borah. In addition to describing the rise of fascism in Europe and the founding of the University in Exile, Johnson intended to focus on the events following each of the two world wars, when "Red scares" threatened democratic institutions throughout the nation. The proposal spoke of comparing the impact on the New School in the early 1920s of New York State's Committee to Investigate Seditious Activities, popularly known as the Lusk Committee, with that of the House Un-American Activities Committee in the late 1940s and 1950s. On both occasions, government agents sat in on classes and interviewed members of the administrative staff about the political activities of the faculty.

The book, Johnson continued, would describe the changing "spirit of the times" between 1919 and 1959 and the ways the New School responded. After World War I, during the first Red scare, students lost interest in "social issues."

They preferred courses in psychology, modern literature, modern art, and modern music, "all reflected in the New School curriculum." But the faculty did not abandon social issues entirely. They continued offering courses on such provocative subjects as the Communist Revolution. Did the Lusk Committee try to close these classes down? And if so, how did the New School respond?

With the Great Depression, interests changed. During the 1930s, students clamored for courses on the failing economy and the rise of dictators across Europe: "The New School's answer was the founding of the University in Exile [which gave] great impetus . . . to social science teaching throughout the country." When the United States entered the war, the New School "not only continued its rescue of foreign scholars, strengthening its function as a center of international scholarship, [it also] opened up new courses and workshops in international affairs."

After Germany fell and the Soviet Union gained control over Eastern Europe, a new wave of hysteria swept across the United States and into the nation's universities. Few academic institutions distinguished themselves during the McCarthy period, and the New School was no real exception. Although it weathered those years honorably when compared with many others, it too bowed to political pressure. Had Johnson spoken frankly about the period, he would have had to discuss the compromises his successors made over his vigorous objections.

Finally, Johnson planned to include portraits of some of the "dominant personalities" who had taught at the New School, among them such "world famous figures" as the French philosopher Jacques Maritain and the British political theorist Harold Laski. He also intended to quote from editorials "reflecting the school's philosophy," reconstruct faculty seminars and class discussions, and draw on other "human interest material." As Johnson envisioned it, his history of the New School would "truly [be] a mirror of the times and throw fresh light on contemporary American culture"—but the light it would throw, he must have been thinking, would not always be flattering.

Johnson could have ended his book with his retirement in 1945 when the New School was still at the height of its fame, praised the world over for having saved the lives of nearly two hundred scholars and with them the humanistic traditions of Europe. But that would not have been very generous. As his contribution to the anniversary celebrations, he would bring the story up to date. Or at least so he intended, until he abandoned the project entirely, for reasons I hope one day to discover. In the meantime, I can only speculate.

The first book-length history of the New School was published in 1986. Written by Peter Rutkoff and William Scott, the study focused on the heyday of the university when Johnson was president. It then moved briskly over the post-Johnson years and stopped in the early 1980s. A second book, by Claus-Dieter Krohn, came out in West Germany in 1987 and was translated into English in 1993. Written for scholars interested in the Weimar and Nazi periods, Krohn looked exclusively at the University in Exile. Since the 1980s, a number of other works have appeared on intellectuals in New York during the interwar period and the Hitler years that also include extensive discussions of the social scientists, philosophers, and artists who taught at the New School.[9]

A Light in Dark Times offers a fresh look at the early history of the New School for Social Research without shying away from moments that complicate the familiar narrative. It then turns to the post-Johnson years, which others have essentially ignored, taking the story up to the beginning of the twenty-first century. In these later chapters, I focus primarily on the precarious fate of the Graduate Faculty in an institution that lacked the resources it needed to support it adequately.

The New School for Social Research has changed a great deal since the end of the twentieth century, symbolized, in part, by its decision to change its name, first to New School University, then to the New School *tout court*, at which point the Graduate Faculty adopted the institution's original name. Known today as NSSR, the old University in Exile sees itself as embodying the ideals and values that gave the New School its historic place in American higher education as a champion of academic freedom and human rights and as scholars of engaged social research. Colleagues affiliated with other parts of the university firmly lay claim to the New School's legacy as well, adding pointedly that the university owes its place in history primarily to the role it has played as a pioneer in adult education.

A Light in Dark Times examines these overlapping narratives through the "incidents and stories" that hide behind the idea of the New School. To quote Hannah Arendt:

> I have always believed that, no matter how abstract our theories may sound or how consistent our arguments may appear, there are incidents and stories behind them which, at least for ourselves, contain in a nutshell the full meaning of whatever we have to say. Thought itself ... arises out of the actuality of incidents, and incidents of living experience must remain its guideposts by which it takes its bearings if it is not to lose itself in the heights to which thinking soars, or in the depths to which it descends.[10]

In the spirit of Johnson's book proposal, *A Light in Dark Times* unfolds against the backdrop of the political upheavals that marked "the short twentieth century":[11] World War I and the first Red scare; the rise of Hitler and World War II; the McCarthy years; the student protests during the Vietnam War; and the downfall of communism in Eastern Europe. At times, colleagues' stories take us beyond the walls of the institution itself: to Washington, D.C. during the First and Second World Wars, to Germany and England in 1933, to Nazi-occupied Europe during World War II, and to Soviet-dominated Eastern Europe during the Cold War period.

The people who appear on the pages of this book are formidable figures, with strong opinions about what the New School stands for and how or whether the university should change. Johnson, however, towers over everyone else. Without his vision and entrepreneurial imagination, the New School would have folded in the early 1920s, its impact reduced to a footnote in history.

In moments of reverie, I imagine Johnson still inhabiting the walls of the New School's buildings, like the *lares* and *penates* he read about as a boy, those legendary house gods of ancient Rome who protected the occupants of family dwellings. An avid student of Latin and Greek, Johnson drew on his classical education regularly to strengthen an argument or to entertain. It takes only a small leap of faith to believe that he continues to watch over the New School family and to meddle, when necessary, to keep his idea of the university alive as he persisted in doing long after he had retired.

A LIGHT IN DARK TIMES

PART I

A School of
Social Research

(1919—1933)

1

THE FIRST FOUNDING MOMENT

The New School opened with "éclat" on February 10, 1919, bursting onto Manhattan's cultural scene with an exciting program of Preliminary Lectures delivered by leading social scientists of the day.[1] A full set of courses would follow in October. As Alvin Johnson described it in his autobiography, "Every liberal in the city was excited by the novel venture of an institution headed by . . . such dynamic figures as James Harvey Robinson and Charles Beard." Fiercely committed to academic freedom, these widely acclaimed historians had already caused a media sensation by resigning from Columbia University. "Self-disfrocked from . . . conventional academic life," they turned their backs on New York's most prestigious educational institution after the university's trustees fired two pacifist professors who had continued to campaign against taking up arms after the United States had entered the Great War.[2]

The fired professors were James McKeen Cattell, a nationally renowned psychologist, and Henry Wadsworth Longfellow Dana, a young literary scholar and grandson of the poet. Neither man had any illusions about what would happen to him if he persisted in speaking out. Columbia's president, Nicholas Murray Butler, had made things perfectly clear in a widely circulated speech delivered on June 6, 1917, during a commencement luncheon for students who were graduating that year:

What had been tolerated before was intolerable now. What had been wrongheadedness was now sedition. What had been folly was now treason. . . . [T]here is and will be no place in Columbia University, either on the rolls of its faculties or on the rolls of its students for any person who opposes or who counsels opposition to the effective enforcement of the laws of the United States, or who acts, speaks, or writes treason.[3]

Beard and Robinson were not pacifists; on the contrary, they fully supported America's decision to enter the war. But they refused to remain at Columbia or affiliate with any other academic institution that fired colleagues who disagreed. Now, in the winter of 1919, admiring New Yorkers were rushing down to Chelsea in lower Manhattan to take courses with the two historians and other members of the New School's star-studded faculty, all of them known for their bold ideas and firm commitment to academic freedom.

Two weeks after the New School opened, Beard wrote to his good friend Lucy Salmon, a professor of history at Vassar College, describing triumphantly how he and his colleagues were going to "unhorse the autocrats who are blocking the advancement of learning in American institutions!"[4] In another letter to Salmon, he described himself as "a man with a six-shooter in each boot."[5] The economist Wesley Clair Mitchell used similar language as he tried to capture the excitement of the moment.

Like Beard and Robinson, Mitchell too had left Columbia—at least temporarily—to join the new venture. Twenty years later, while reminiscing about his decision to do so, Mitchell spoke of the rapid-fire exchange he had had with Johnson in 1918 that persuaded him to perform his "civic duty" by joining the faculty of the New School. The two men, Mitchell explained, had settled their "moral issues on the spot, with a six-shooter, after the best traditions of the old West, in which both of us had been dipped"[6]—of the old Middle West, to be more precise, which still looked like the wild frontier during the last quarter of the nineteenth century when he and Johnson were growing up.

Mitchell's allusion to their gunslinging past was not entirely in jest. He did not want anyone to forget that he and Johnson hailed from the other side of the Appalachians. People might associate them—and rightly so—with New York's circle of progressive intellectuals, but the two men grew up in homes on the open prairie that had little in common with those of the scions of East Coast families, whose names had made their group so famous.

Nor were they the only ones. Their circle of progressive intellectuals had attracted other midwesterners as well, several of whom became founding members of the New School: Beard, like Mitchell, was from Illinois; Johnson, from Nebraska; Robinson, from Indiana; Thorstein Veblen, from Wisconsin. And they were proud of it, as they reminded their readers now and again with a folksy aside—the cornier the better. Although most of them came east to study and settled down in New York, they still enjoyed seeing themselves as cowboys ambling into town, loaded with arguments they were ready to fire at anyone who stood in the way of social reform and academic freedom.

Thorstein Veblen was the sharpest shooter of them all, and the most infamous after he published *The Theory of the Leisure Class* in 1899—a wicked satire on the economic and social behavior of wealthy Americans. Among the economist's other books was *The Higher Learning in America*, an extended essay aimed mercilessly at university presidents and boards of trustees. Appearing in bookstores a few months before the New School opened, this slender volume made a timely case for abandoning "conventional academic life" and building something radically new.

In *The Higher Learning in America*, Veblen called on colleagues at universities across the country to rebel in precisely the way the founders of the New School were doing: seize control of an educational institution, do away with the office of the president ("the academic executive"), and minimize the role of the board of trustees ("the board of governors"). Several members of the New School's organizing committee had been publishing articles along the same lines in *The New Republic* and other liberal periodicals, but Veblen's rhetoric was the most explosive:

> As seen from the point of view of the higher learning, the academic executive and all his works are anathema, and should be discontinued by the simple expedient of wiping him off the slate; . . . the governing board, in so far as it presumes to exercise any other than vacantly perfunctory duties, has the same value and should with advantage be lost in the same shuffle.[7]

The problem, Veblen explained, was structural, not personal. It had less to do with the way one individual ran a particular institution than with the widespread practice by university trustees of appointing academic leaders to protect the political and economic interests of their own social class. Leaders, in other words, who prevented reform-minded professors from taking initiatives that might threaten the status quo.

Structural, not personal? In theory yes, but the examples Veblen gave to support his arguments drew on the exploits of a specific academic leader and his board of governors, an individual so famous that he did not have to name names and risk being sued for libel. Everyone recognized Nicholas Murray Butler in Veblen's masterful "dissection of the species' most pernicious traits."[8]

Butler responded in kind. Without naming names either, he described Veblen and his New School comrades as "a little bunch of disgruntled liberals setting up a tiny fly-by-night radical counterfeit of education."[9] Columbia's president, we know, had scores to settle with two other members of the founding faculty (Beard and Robinson), both of whom had caused him and the university a great deal of embarrassment by resigning in protest. And that was not all. Butler was still digesting the fact that his distinguished economist, Wesley Clair Mitchell, had taken a leave of absence to help launch the New School and his best-known philosopher, John Dewey, had chastised the trustees in *The New York Times* right after Beard resigned—doing so not only in the name of a renowned member of Columbia's faculty, but as the founding president of the American Association of University Professors (AAUP) and author in 1915 of the association's "Declaration of Principles on Academic Freedom and Academic Tenure."[10] Finally, although Dewey never took a leave of absence the way Mitchell did to join the New School, his name appeared on the faculty list in 1919–1920.

Butler expected this "fly-by-night counterfeit" of an institution to fold quickly. And it probably would have had Johnson not taken over in 1922 when Beard and Robinson abandoned their new venture in higher education. Although finances remained rocky after the two men resigned, the New School, under Johnson, mounted a popular new program in continuing education with a singularly New York feel about it. A curious development, some might say, given the faculty. But perhaps that was the point. In a city famous for the geographic and ethnic diversity of its residents, the New School offered students the opportunity to study with scholars and artists who came from different parts of the country and overseas, just like the people they met on the street and read about in Horace Kallen's essays on cultural pluralism.

Although foreign visitors and immigrants had been teaching at the New School from the very beginning, their numbers increased significantly under Johnson. The proud son of Danish immigrants, he was well on his way toward creating an international faculty by the early 1930s, with scholars and artists not only from Europe, but from Latin America. Among them were the muralists José Clemente Orozco from Mexico and Camilo Egas from Ecuador, who together with the American Thomas Hart Benton paid tribute to the institution's commitment to cultural pluralism on the walls of the New School's new building, itself the achievement of the Austrian architect Joseph Urban. Then when Hitler rose to power in 1933, Johnson turned his intellectual predilection into a political imperative.

⊷⟐⊶

In 2009, as the New School celebrated the seventy-fifth anniversary of the University in Exile, the political scientist Ira Katznelson marked the occasion in his keynote address by comparing what he called the two "founding moments" in the history of the New School: 1919 and 1933. A much-admired scholar of American politics and history, Katznelson served as dean of the Graduate Faculty of Political and Social Science in the 1980s, during what some New School colleagues now call the third founding moment.[11] Katznelson's use of this evocative term brings to mind the kinds of landmark events scholars usually refer to when they speak of founding moments—political acts "that break ties with the *ancien régime* and lay the foundation for the establishment of modern states"[12]—for example, the Constitutional Convention in 1787 when the fathers of the American Revolution came together in Philadelphia and drafted the U.S. Constitution.

When the New School opened in 1919, the faculty broke with an *ancien régime* "to unhorse the autocrats who [were] blocking the advancement of learning in American institutions." That goes without saying. But Katznelson's allusion went deeper than that. The founders of the New School in 1919 were recognized scholars of political institutions and constitutional theory.[13] So were the founders of the University in Exile in 1933, some of whom helped draft the constitution of the Weimar Republic, while others held influential government positions in interwar Germany until Adolf Hitler rose to power, dismantled the constitution, and fired them for being enemies of the Reich.

As evocative as the term may be, founding moments, Katznelson reminds us, only become founding moments after eyewitness reports of the events themselves go through an editing process. In the case of the New School, the revised version of these events describes "a seamless consistency" from one founding moment to the next—perhaps "too seamless":

> Separated by a tumultuous decade and a half, the fears, the insecurities, and the orientations to liberty in 1919 and 1933 were not identical. Though joined by many shared commitments, each founding was dedicated to goals and nourished by explicit and tacit understandings that diverged, sometimes sharply, with respect to the standing of democracy and the status of intellectual authority, and with regard to how free scholarship should responsibly conquer fear and advance liberty. Those differences were not superficial.[14]

After cutting open the stitches and revealing the seams, Katznelson wove more textured accounts of the two founding moments back into their historical periods. Or rather he began the process, arguing persuasively that future historians needed to pay attention to the "incidents and stories," to quote Hannah Arendt again, that pulled at the seams of the 1919 narrative before moving on to

1933—and again, to 1983, Katznelson's own period, when the university renewed its commitments to academic freedom and human rights, under the leadership of Jonathan Fanton.

As Katznelson described the historic circumstances surrounding the first founding moment, he spoke of the courage it took to open the New School in 1919. It was "audacious," he explained, because "the repression of dissent at Columbia was not exceptional":

> The wartime quest for security had generated fear, and fear had justified author-itative violations. In 1917, Congress passed an Espionage Act that mandated sen-tences of up to 20 years for individuals who encouraged "disloyalty" in wartime. The year 1918 witnessed the passage of an Alien Act that authorized Washington to deport members of anarchist organizations. That same year, a Sedition Act made it illegal to use "disloyal, profane, scurrilous, or abusive language" about the flag, the armed forces, and the country during the war. And 1919, of course, was the very year Attorney General Alexander Mitchell Palmer initiated wide-spread raids on some 10,000 suspected radicals, and infamously deported 249 individuals to the Soviet Union on the SS *Buford*, where they did not meet a happy fate.[15]

The founders of the New School in 1919 were what we would call today public intellectuals. Journalists, academics, and philanthropists, they all belonged to *The New Republic* crowd. Prominent among them was Herbert Croly, the magazine's editor in chief and a major force behind this "novel venture" in higher education. Thanks to Croly, *The New Republic* served as the base of operations for the plan-ning committee. It was also thanks to Croly that Alvin Johnson joined the group and took part in these early conversations.

As Johnson tells us in his autobiography, the New School was not his idea. He just happened to be at *The New Republic* as things were taking shape, having just been hired as Croly's new senior editor. Yet a few years later he was fully in charge: "I had myself made Director," he told the anthropologist Elsie Clews Parsons.[16] How did he do it? With "the gentleness of the dove and the wisdom of the serpent," replied Wesley Clair Mitchell, and with a "remarkable combination of good will, imagination, shrewdness, humor."[17]

2

ALVIN JOHNSON AND
THE NEW REPUBLIC

Born in 1874, Alvin Johnson grew up on a small farm in northeastern Nebraska. Although "it was taken for granted," he wrote, "from the day of my birth, that I would develop the hunger for scholarship that had characterized my mother's family since time immemorial," he never lost his love of farming or his desire to do something about the "the decadence of rural life" that was destroying family farms like the one his family was forced to abandon.[1] In 1906, the year he accepted a professorial position at the University of Nebraska, Johnson did policy research for the U.S. Department of Agriculture, under the direction of Elwood Mead, on a federal irrigation project.[2] He also conducted research for state governments on the many problems facing small-time farmers, the findings of which led him to recommend the creation of "communities of family farms." During the Hitler years when he was famously rescuing scholars and artists fleeing Nazi-occupied Europe, Johnson helped establish an agricultural community in Wilmington, North Carolina, that saved the lives of refugee Jewish farmers.[3]

Johnson attended college during the 1890s at the University of Nebraska, where he majored in classics and philology. After finishing his BA in 1897, he received a master's degree in Greek without taking his final exams, he confessed, a gift from the State of Nebraska for having enlisted in the army during the Spanish-American War. The government, Johnson explained, had fallen "into a frenzy of patriotism and decreed that all students who would have come up for degrees in June 1898, but had been unable to complete their work because of their enlistment, should have their degrees nevertheless." After finishing the final draft of his MA thesis on "the influence of the Peloponnesian War on the conceptions of Euripides," Johnson left school precipitously to join the army, without taking

his final exams, not out of "a frenzy of patriotism" or enthusiasm for this particular war but with a sense of urgency about the one that would follow, which he
expected to break out any day. When the time came, he wanted to have the military training he would need to help "destroy the reactionary empires of Europe
and complete the liberation of peoples that had been begun by the American and
French Revolutions."

The Spanish-American War ended before Johnson ever saw combat. He
spent four months instead in Chickamauga, Georgia, doing "obsolete" military
exercises and "observing the steady progress of typhoid, dysentery, and malaria
through the susceptible ranks from the Nebraska prairie." Although he was
deeply disappointed, he conceded that the experience changed his life:

> The four months [between May and October 1898] gave me abundant leisure for
> reflection. Who made that war for us: the democracy, or the official romanticists
> and the practical business adventurers? Why was it necessary to have gross inef-
> ficiency in everything connected with the war—enlistment, supplies, transporta-
> tion, medical service? Was it really inevitable that a world war must come, and if
> it came, what would be the outcome for civilization? The classics and comparative
> philology were irrelevant to such problems. As soon as I could get my discharge
> from the army, I set off for Columbia University to study political science.[4]

Johnson arrived during a transformative period in the history of New York's
oldest academic institution, as Columbia was in the process of remodeling itself
after the great research universities of Europe. Founded in 1754, it opened its
first research doctoral program in 1880, four years after Johns Hopkins University had established the very first of its kind in the United States.[5] Known as the
School of Political Science, Columbia's program required PhD students to take a
series of core courses in a broad new field of inquiry known as the social sciences,
after which they conducted doctoral research in either economics, history, politics, or sociology. Johnson did his in economics and wrote a dissertation on the
theory of rent. The American Economic Association published his thesis in the
fall of 1902, a few months after he had received his PhD—the association itself
had only been founded in 1885.[6]

While finishing his dissertation, Johnson began teaching at Bryn Mawr
College, but he returned to Columbia the following year. Although he enjoyed
teaching at Bryn Mawr and remained good friends with its president, M. Carey
Thomas, Johnson could not resist an invitation to go back to Columbia from
the eminent economist Edwin R. A. Seligman. Not that the appointment itself
was very glamorous. Seligman hired the newly minted PhD at the rank of tutor,

assigning him to teach undergraduates and to work as an assistant editor on several academic journals (*The Political Science Quarterly, The Columbia Series in History,* and *Economics and Public Law*). From that point on, Johnson wrote many years later, he would never again be entirely free "from what is generally described as the drudgery of editing," a task he characterized as "whipping manuscripts into shape; reducing involved and confused composition to direct statement; substituting the better word for the dull one." But for Johnson, this was not "drudgery." He considered it "one of the elementary duties of the scholar to advance the cause of clear exposition wherever he can."[7]

Not drudgery, perhaps, but Johnson grew restless. As the youngest member of the faculty, he felt "cramped." Even after his colleagues promoted him to instructor, then to adjunct professor of the Faculty of Political Science—which gave him the privilege of teaching a graduate course—he felt stuck in a boring routine, with little hope of earning tenure in the near future. And so he began looking around. In 1906, he received two job offers, both at the rank of full professor: one from Thomas, who wanted him to return to Bryn Mawr, and the other from the University of Nebraska. He decided to return to his alma mater.[8]

But once again, he grew restless. Johnson remained at Nebraska for only two years before moving on to the University of Texas in 1908, then to the University of Chicago in 1910, by which time he had earned the reputation for being "one of the most peripatetic of American professors." A year later, in 1911, Johnson moved to Stanford, then to Cornell in 1912, where the university gave him a professorial chair in the Department of Economics. This time he remained on the faculty for four years, but he escaped Ithaca as often as possible, making no secret of his low opinion of the university. In reply to one of Johnson's tirades, Amherst College's president, the philosopher Alexander Meiklejohn, concurred with glee:

> Your study of Cornell thrills me. . . . My impression is that the essential evil grew from the words of Ezra Cornell. "A place where you teach anybody anything" is by implication a place where nobody knows anything, and so there is nothing to be taught. I judge that your experience of occupying a chair is just about that which one might expect to have when occupying a chair made of sawdust without any cohesive material.[9]

Meiklejohn at the time was fighting an uphill battle at Amherst where entrenched members of his own faculty were successfully resisting his efforts to expand the liberal arts beyond the classics and philosophy and introduce students to the social sciences. As part of his campaign to open up the curriculum,

Meiklejohn had made Johnson an offer in the spring of 1916, which he had to rescind three weeks later, bowing to faculty pressure: "It isn't easy for me to say that we are not ready, but I think it is true. I hope it will not be true much longer and when it isn't, I shall be on your trail—only to hear you tell me then that I missed what part of a chance I was ever destined to get."[10] After twelve embattled years (1912–1924), Meiklejohn was forced to resign.

When Meiklejohn wrote to Johnson in the spring of 1916, the economist was on leave from Cornell and working happily in New York as a visiting editor at *The New Republic* magazine. He loved the life of a journalist and being back in the city, but he still turned Herbert Croly down when the editor in chief offered him a job as a full-time member of the editorial staff. With a wife and several children to support, he could not take the risk of giving up tenure at an established academic institution for a job as a junior editor at a recently founded weekly magazine that was not even two years old. Returning to Cornell, however, was out of the question. Since Amherst was no longer an option, Johnson accepted an invitation to move back to Stanford as professor of economics and politics. He did so, however, with a heavy heart. Palo Alto was too far away.

Taking advantage of Johnson's ambivalence, Croly refused to let go. He hounded the economist with letters throughout the fall semester of 1916, hoping to change Johnson's mind. With the United States threatening to enter the war, he had a "moral obligation," Croly proclaimed, to return to the magazine. An obligation Johnson finally assumed when Croly agreed to make him a senior editor.

Over the summer of 1917, the peripatetic professor abandoned Stanford for the second time and drove back east with his family. He arrived in New York a few weeks after the United States sent its first expeditionary forces to Europe.[11]

In July 1918, Johnson received an invitation from Wesley Clair Mitchell to join him in Washington D.C. for a few months to work on the War Industries Board. As Johnson tells the story, "Of course I accepted eagerly," to which Mitchell added playfully he had little choice: This was Johnson's side of the bargain the two men had struck when they settled "their moral issues with a six-shooter."[12]

Columbia University had granted Mitchell a leave of absence the summer before so that he might move to Washington temporarily and volunteer his services as an economic consultant to the war effort—something hundreds of other economists and businessmen were also doing at the time. "Dollar-a-year men," people called them. They "swarmed to Washington," Johnson wrote, where things were so chaotic at first that they "flew around in circles." President Wilson turned these dollar-a-year men over to the financier Bernard Baruch, whom he had appointed to lead the newly established War Industries Board. As originally conceived, the board was supposed to advise the administration on the purchase of supplies, but in ways so vague, Johnson added, that this "outstanding body of professional men [was] clothed only with the power of discussion and advice."[13] Finally, Wilson gave Baruch the authority he needed to make a real impact on economic policy, at which point the financier drafted a group of specialists from his larger team of volunteers to work with him on several targeted projects. Among those selected was Mitchell, whom Baruch made chief of the Price Section in the Statistical Department.

Baruch asked Mitchell and his staff to recommend limits on imports and to help the government fix prices on all commodities. To do so effectively, Mitchell replied, he needed to create "a Central Bureau of Planning and Statistics as a clearing house of statistical activities" staffed with "the best of all possible men to design and supervise a monthly summary of statistics." When Baruch gave him the green light, Mitchell "wired Alvin Johnson,"[14] who in turn asked Croly to let him divide his time between New York and Washington until the end of the war.

As Mitchell had predicted, Johnson flourished in the nation's capital. Baruch took to him right away. Reminiscing in 1949 about their time together in Washington, the financier recalled how Johnson "gained the admiration and affection of all the hard-bitten politicians, army, navy, and air force men, as well as the businessmen who were associated with me in an undertaking which was sailing an uncharted sea."[15] In his memoir, published eleven years later, Baruch referred to Johnson as "my dear friend . . . who later established the much-esteemed New School for Social Research."[16]

Johnson worshipped Baruch. When he wrote about him in his autobiography, he expressed deep admiration and gratitude in subdued, reverential tones. But in his personal correspondence, he afflicted the financier with bursts of emotion that knew no bounds. Addressing him affectionately as "my dear Chief," Johnson showered him with praise in ways that must have made Baruch squirm, particularly when he was also asking him for money. During World War II, for example, the director of "the much-esteemed New School for Social Research" took his effusive epistolary style to shameless extremes:

> Mrs. Roosevelt—God bless her, if there were such an office as democratic Queen, it would be hers by right—has talked to you about the New School. And You, Mr. Baruch, by Clemenceau's wise decree, Prince of Israel, could not refuse the Queen of Democracy her request that you read a letter I write, and if it does not bore you too much will, on your trip to Washington, let me ride with you as far as Philadelphia, to put the case of the New School as well as I can.[17]

Did Johnson need to drop Mrs. Roosevelt's name to get an audience with his "dear Chief"? And why, on top of that, mention Clemenceau? No doubt to remind Baruch that he had invited Johnson to join him on a trip to Europe in the early 1920s to bear witness to the financial crisis that was crippling the economic recovery of Germany. "Do you remember," Johnson wrote less elliptically in another fund-raising letter, "the thrill we shared when we left the Majestic and landed at Cherbourg under the golden sun of France? . . . Where [upon arriving] in Paris you promptly set off to call on your good friend Clemenceau, the Tiger, who as usual greeted you with the splendor of French cordiality, as the Prince of Israel?"[18] After which, Baruch and Johnson left for Germany.

Baruch opened many doors for Johnson during World War I and the early interwar period, and the economist was eternally grateful. The financier also educated him on the nuances of Washington's political culture. What Johnson learned from Baruch would serve him well when he returned to the nation's capital in 1933 with the hope of persuading "hard-bitten" politicians to authorize visas for refugees fleeing a country with which the United States still had diplomatic ties. Johnson's experiences on the War Industries Board further educated him in the intricacies of doing policy research for government agencies during times of war, lessons he put to good use when he opened a policy institute at the New School in the early 1940s. Staffed with refugee scholars from occupied Europe, the Institute of World Affairs did research on highly sensitive matters for a number of U.S. agencies during World War II.

In the summer and fall of 1918, Johnson led a hectic life commuting between Washington and New York. At *The New Republic*, Croly expected him and the other senior editors to publish approximately three thousand words per week and to play an active role on the editorial board.[19] During his days in New York, Johnson also participated in meetings Croly hosted with the planning committee for what came to be known as the New School for Social Research, but whose name at the time was still a matter of debate. The Columbia crowd preferred the Free School of Political Science to distinguish their bold venture in higher education from that other School of Political Science, which was anything but free.[20]

⊰≡⊱

It is difficult to disentangle the early history of the New School from that of *The New Republic*. Those who taught at one were contributing articles to the other. The financial backers, for the most part, were the same people as well. Even after Croly resigned from the New School and Johnson from *The New Republic*, writers associated with one continued teaching at the other, and in impressive numbers, well into the 1930s.[21]

Founded five years earlier than the New School, the editors of *The New Republic* called their publication a "journal of opinion." Identifying themselves on the political spectrum as liberals, they saw their new weekly magazine as a forum for the free and open exchange of ideas. As they told their readers, they looked forward to publishing vigorous debates that exposed engaged citizens to serious analyses from opposing points of view. The first issue appeared on November 7, 1914, a few days after the midterm elections, during which, the editorial stated bluntly, "progressivism of all kinds fared badly." The time had come to do something about it. In their opening statement, the editors explained that *The New Republic* was "frankly an experiment":

> It is an attempt to find a national audience for a journal of interpretation and opinion. Many people believe that such a journal is out of place in America; that if a periodical is to be popular, it must first of all be entertaining, or that if it is to be serious it must be detached and select. Yet when the plan of *The New Republic* was being discussed it received spontaneous welcome from people in all parts of the country. They differed in theories and programmes; but they agreed that if *The New Republic* could bring sufficient enlightenment to the problems of the nation and sufficient sympathy to its complexities, it would serve all those who feel the challenge of our time.[22]

As historian Thomas Bender noted, *The New Republic* hoped to appeal to self-proclaimed "young Intellectuals," whom the editors saw as an emerging "strategic elite." Positioning themselves as the voice of this up-and-coming generation, they hoped to persuade the White House to take them seriously and provide them with access to President Wilson. This was particularly true of Walter Lippmann, Croly's second-in-command.

With the arrogance of youth, Lippmann concluded that Wilson was floundering and needed his advice. The president had only won the election in 1912 because Theodore Roosevelt had turned his back on the Republican Party, which had elected him president twice (1901–1909), and ran instead on the ticket of the Bull Moose Party, dashing the hopes of President William Howard Taft of winning a second term. Because Wilson had served as president of Princeton University and had ties to young intellectuals like him, Lippmann assumed that the Democrat would welcome the counsel of *The New Republic*, even if the magazine's founding editor and financial backers were closely tied to Roosevelt.[23]

━━◆━━

By the time *The New Republic* published its first issue, Europe had been at war for three months and Germany had just won a major victory in Belgium. Although the editors had promised to follow no party line, the magazine echoed Roosevelt in its early issues on whether the United States should enter the war. At the time, Roosevelt had been writing a series of articles for *The New York Times* on "What America Should Learn from the War." In the last one, published November 1, he criticized Wilson for remaining neutral on both moral and political grounds. With the Allied forces retreating in humiliating defeat, abandoning Belgium to the Central Powers, Americans had to respond by sending troops overseas. Its current policy of neutrality was not only "evil" but exposed the United States to the "most frightful risk of Disaster."[24]

The New Republic made the same argument a month later, warning: "A nation does not commit the great sin when it fights. It commits the great sin when it fights for a bad cause or when it is afraid to fight for a good cause. Peace is one of those good causes on behalf of which fighting continues to be necessary."[25] But as Roosevelt's rhetoric grew increasingly bellicose, Croly broke away, a decision he did not make lightly, considering how much he owed the former president. Had it not been for Theodore Roosevelt, he might never have become the editor in chief of a new progressive magazine.

When Roosevelt had run for president in 1912, he had asked Croly to serve on his team of campaign advisors, inspired to do so after reading the journalist's widely acclaimed book, *The Promise of American Life*. Roosevelt told Croly that he borrowed ideas from the journalist's book for the Bull Moose Party's platform. A curious claim, Thomas Bender observed, given the fact that Croly offered no concrete program. Published in 1909, *The Promise of American Life* argued that Americans should go through "an intellectual awakening" first, before building a new political movement.[26] Roosevelt may have missed the point, but Croly accepted his invitation all the same to work on the campaign.

After losing the election, Roosevelt sent a copy of *The Promise of American Life* to his good friend, the investment banker Willard Straight, who, as the story goes, thought the book was so important that he wanted to meet Croly right away. A few weeks later, Straight asked Croly to serve as the editor in chief of a new progressive magazine that he wanted to publish together with his wife, Dorothy, a well-known advocate of progressive causes, perhaps even more so than her husband, and the heiress of the Payne Whitney fortune.[27] As *The New Republic* took its distance from Roosevelt, Straight registered his disapproval, but he honored his promise not to intervene.

In July 1915, Croly asked Johnson to write an article "for us on the probable effect of the war (in case it should last another year or two)." Turning the task over to the economist, who had voted for Wilson in 1912, Croly confirmed that *The New Republic* had turned its back on Roosevelt's muscular patriotism and calls for vengeance against the Central Powers. Johnson's piece avoided the question of whether the United States should enter the war and focused instead on laying the foundation for peace. Neither side, Johnson argued, should walk away from the peace table with "a taste for easy victory" or "an abiding sense of shame." He then ended provocatively with the question: "What if the coming peace shall be inconclusive?" To which he replied: All the better! A treaty that recognized everyone's losses and pain had a greater chance of producing "a lasting peace."[28] As the hostilities dragged on for several more years, Croly relied on Johnson numerous times to represent *The New Republic* on the economic implications of the war and, subsequently, on the disastrous outcome of the Paris Peace Conference.

Johnson was exactly the kind of liberal intellectual Croly wanted to have write for *The New Republic*. In September 1914, two months before the first issue appeared on the stands, Croly sent the economist a special letter of invitation to subscribe to the magazine that went only to people Croly hoped would contribute articles as well. Would Johnson join him, Croly asked, in an open exchange of ideas? *The New Republic* would "respect no taboos . . . play no favorites; . . . be confined to no set creed and tied to no political party. Its philosophy will be a faith rather than a dogma. Its editorial attitude will be good-natured, open-minded, eager to find and accept facts."[29]

Croly sent a second letter in October asking Johnson to contribute an article for the first issue of the magazine, which was due to appear on November 7. Pleased to accept, Johnson submitted a piece on the current "cotton crisis" that was threatening the economy of the American South in ways similar to the coffee crisis in Brazil. Overproduction, he argued, was the problem in both cases.[30] From then on, articles by Johnson appeared regularly in *The New Republic*, some signed, others unsigned, depending on the subject and the journal's specific editorial needs. Croly thanked Johnson "for allowing us to use our own discretion."[31]

When Johnson worked at *The New Republic* during the 1915–16 academic year as a visiting editor, Croly had him writing articles, book reviews, and editorials on a wide range of topics, among them tax and tariff issues, the economic implications of the war in Europe, the Mexican Revolution, and educational reform in the United States.[32] In early September, after Johnson had returned to teaching, Croly complained bitterly that *The New Republic* was managing badly without him: "I knew that I should miss you after you had gone," Croly wrote, "but I did not realize how much I should miss you. It would have been an enormous help during the last few weeks with all these labor problems on hand to have had your counsel and assistance."[33] By January Croly was beside himself. He needed Johnson "to handle the prohibition matter," which had been assigned to another member of the editorial staff, the renowned essayist Randolph Bourne, who "will not be capable of it . . . he has not shown any indication of being able to grasp the matter in all its political as well as in its more special bearings."[34]

On February 1, the day after Germany announced its intention to resume submarine warfare against merchant ships traveling on the Atlantic, Lippmann sent Johnson a desperate telegram, after which he finally agreed to return:

AS THE CHIEF QUESTIONS ARISING OUT OF THE CRISIS WILL BE ECONOMIC WE DO NOT SEE HOW WE CAN RUN THE NEW REPUBLIC WITHOUT YOU. WE ALL WANT TO KNOW WHETHER YOU CANNOT BE RUTHLESS TO RESIGN AT ONCE AND COME EAST. IF BY ANY CHANCE THIS IS OUT OF THE QUESTION WE DEPEND ON YOU TO DO MAJOR WORK ON ECONOMIC CONSEQUENCES.[35]

In the weeks leading up to Germany's latest aggression, Croly and Lippmann, in large part influenced by their British friends, had reached the conclusion that the United States would have to enter the war. More than a dozen English academics had been writing for *The New Republic*, including the political theorist Harold Laski and economist John Maynard Keynes. As Johnson thought about what these British contributors had to say, he appreciated "the openness and wide reach of their minds." While they described the war as "a ghastly atrocity," they did not see the Germans as "more atrocious" than any other nation would have been, caught as they were "between formidable enemies on the East and the West: . . . But in spite of this British fairness of mind, or perhaps because of it, our English friends were utterly resolute in defense of the British war policy, wholly prepared for any sacrifice to be borne on the way to victory."[36]

As *The New Republic* moved slowly and reluctantly toward accepting the inevitable, it continued to resist the blood-thirsty drumbeat that was sweeping the country. Picking up on the arguments Johnson had made in 1915, the editorial board urged Wilson to ignore the warmongers and continue focusing his efforts on building a lasting peace. If the United States entered the war, the president would have a seat at the peace table, where he could use his influence to persuade the Allies to abandon their imperialistic designs. Instead of vengeance, they should lay the foundation for a true league of nations that respected not only the interests of those who had won but of the vanquished as well.

On April 3, 1917, *The New Republic* congratulated Wilson for making "The Great Decision":

> Mr. Wilson is to-day the most liberal statesman in high office, and before long he is likely to be the most powerful. He represents the best hope in the whole world. He can go ahead exultingly with the blessings of men and women upon him.[37]

Two years later the editors withdrew their endorsement. They were furious with Wilson for having embraced the vindictive terms of the Versailles Treaty, thereby betraying his earlier commitment to seek a "peace without victory." A bitter Croly asked Johnson to respond for *The New Republic*. Drawing on his classical education, Johnson opened the editorial with these words: "Not since Rome punished Carthage for Punic faith has such a treaty been written."[38]

3

COLUMBIA UNIVERSITY

The editorial board of *The New Republic* may have waited until 1917 before urging the United States to enter the war, but some of its regular contributors had been publishing articles in favor of doing so since 1914. These included Columbia University professors of history Charles A. Beard and James Harvey Robinson. In her biography of Beard, Ellen Nore noted that the historian "never supported President Wilson's policy of neutrality in the conflict." Although he did not advocate military interventions indiscriminately, he had "no deep aversion to war." Warfare, Beard explained, had led to the "origin of the State and the progress of mankind."[1] As for Robinson, he started warning readers in *The New Republic* as early as December 1914 that "Germans of all classes" were marching lockstep behind the Kaiser and his imperial army. Germans truly believed that they were "inherently a superior race who [had] developed a civilization (*Kultur*) of unprecedented perfection, of which their military organization, with its marvelous discipline and applications of modern science, is the essential safeguard against the jealousy of decadent nations, like France and England, and the barbarism of the Slavs." They based these unforgivable claims on "older notions of race" that anthropologists, biologists, and historians had rejected long ago.[2]

The best-known pacifist at Columbia was none other than Nicholas Murray Butler, widely recognized in 1914 for the prominent role he had been playing in the U.S. peace movement. A proud champion of pacifist causes, Butler gave himself credit for having persuaded the steel magnate Andrew Carnegie to create the Carnegie Endowment for International Peace. Although scholars have disputed his claim, Butler was part of the group that founded the endowment in 1910.[3]

Butler came through the war years with his pacifist credentials intact, as did the trustees of the Carnegie Endowment, who had also supported Wilson's decision to enter the war. In 1925, these same trustees appointed Butler president of the endowment, a position he would hold until 1945 when he retired from Carnegie and Columbia at the age of eighty-three. In 1931, while serving as president of both institutions, Butler received the Nobel Peace Prize for his "lifelong commitment to international arbitration and conciliation"—the irony of which was not lost on everyone. As Butler's biographer Michael Rosenthal observed, letters poured in from around the world, but one "stood out" from among all the others:

> On December 11, Henry Wadsworth Longfellow Dana, the young assistant professor whom Butler had dismissed in 1917, produced one sublimely cutting sentence: "Let me be the first to congratulate you on receiving the Nobel Peace Prize."[4]

Dana waited fourteen years to take revenge against the man who had fired him, confronting him in a personal letter with a stinging rebuke but in a way that attracted no attention. Beard had taken revenge right away and had done so in the media. Even more striking, whereas Dana had accused Butler of being a warmonger, Beard accused him of being a pacifist. For Dana, Butler was a wolf in sheep's clothing. How dare he accept the Nobel Peace Prize! For Beard, he was a hypocrite and a coward who paid lip service to a war he did not believe in to save his own skin, and in doing so destroyed the careers of two men who had the courage of their convictions. What is more, and this was hardly incidental, Beard accused Butler of being a pacifist at a time when Red-baiting congressmen were demanding that peace activists be arrested and thrown into jail.

Newspapers began covering stories about Beard's accusations against Butler in October 1917, immediately after the historian resigned, and they continued doing so over the next two years, most spectacularly in the winter of 1919, two weeks before the New School opened. On January 26, *The New York Times* published a copy of the letter Beard sent to Senator Lee Slater Overman of North Carolina in which he described Butler's pacifist leanings in some detail. Overman was chairman of an infamous congressional committee—the precursor of the House Un-American Activities Committee—established to root out and discipline pro-German and Bolshevik sympathizers in the country.[5] Beard's name had recently appeared on a list of "Who's Who in Pacifism and Radicalism" that New York state's firebrand attorney Archibald Stevenson had sent to the committee. Incensed by the accusation directed at him, Beard asserted, "I am not and never have been a pacifist," which he then proceeded to prove with "the facts in my case," comparing his impeccable pro-war record with that of people who qualified for recognition as bona fide pacifists, for example, the president of Columbia University, and other notables whom he also identified by name:

> When Nicholas Murray Butler, Assistant Secretary of War Keppel and Elihu Root were manipulating the Carnegie peace millions, issuing pacifist pamphlets by the thousands, organizing pacifist societies in our colleges, employing Columbia instructors and professors to write pacifist tracts and to engage in pacifist agitation, I was teaching the truth that war has been one of the most tremendous factors in the origin of the State and the progress of mankind. My old students will bear witness to that fact. I never advocated war for war's sake, but I was never "too proud to fight."[6]

A great admirer of German culture, Butler had difficulty accepting the possibility that Kaiser Wilhelm had become an enemy. As late as 1912, he was still referring to the king as the Carnegie Endowment's greatest ally in advancing world peace. When war broke out in Europe two years later, Butler worked with the endowment to devise a plan for a lasting peace and a new world order, assisting a campaign that put him at odds with the more militant members of Columbia's Board of Trustees. As Rosenthal describes it, these trustees did not find Butler's "alleged 'pacifism' endearing." Beard put it more bluntly, noting that "some of the trustees [had been] 'after' President Butler for his pacifist writings and affiliations."[7]

But once the United States entered the war in April 1917, Butler fell in line with the trustees and became a militant patriot—at least in public—making it a matter of university policy that faculty and students do the same. In an effort, no doubt, to reassure them, we see Butler two months later submitting a draft of his lunchtime commencement speech to his critics on the board for their editorial assistance and approval before he announced to the university community—in whose words precisely?—that "what had been tolerated before" would not be tolerated any longer.[8] Butler's public proclamation set off a chain of events that prompted Beard to resign in October and galvanized "a group of public-spirited patriotic citizens" to use Robinson's words, to open "a novel type of school for men and women."[9]

⟨⬦⟩

Beard's resignation came at the end of a long and complicated power struggle that had been going on for years at Columbia and other universities across the country. As Thorstein Veblen characterized it provocatively in *The Higher*

Learning in America, since the beginning of the twentieth century, boards of trustees had been slowly refashioning the governance structure of academic institutions to resemble business corporations—strengthening the authority of their hand-picked presidents at the expense of faculty autonomy. Professors resisted these changes on their own campuses and organized nationally. With the active participation of distinguished members of Columbia's faculty, the nationwide campaign led to the creation of the American Association of University Professors and the election of John Dewey as its first president in 1915.

Beard had his first run-in with Columbia's trustees in 1912 after the retirement of John Burgess, the university's renowned Ruggles Professor of Political Science, whose area of expertise was U.S. constitutional law. In addition to his scholarly accomplishments, Burgess had played a prominent role nationally during the last quarter of the nineteenth century in establishing political science as an independent discipline and, more locally, in persuading the trustees to open a School of Political Science at Columbia, a decision that turned the institution into a research university. Replacing Burgess with a scholar of comparable distinction was understandably important to the faculty, in particular to Beard given his own interests in the field. After much back and forth, Butler had assured the faculty, Beard reported, that he would honor their recommendation on this and other academic appointments, but in the end he betrayed them and offered the position to a law partner of one of the trustees.

As Beard described the incident in *The New Republic*, when Butler selected William D. Guthrie over the scholar the faculty had recommended, he gave the new Ruggles Professor a very light teaching load, assigning him only "one lecture a week for one semester a year." Guthrie did virtually nothing else: "Of his contributions to learning," Beard added sarcastically, "I shall not speak, but I can say that he did not attend faculty meetings, help in conducting doctors' examinations, or assume the burdens imposed upon other professors." The faculty's candidate, Frank Johnson Goodnow, whom Beard identified discretely as "Mr. X," had written a controversial book that "justified criticism of the Supreme Court as a means of bringing our constitutional law into harmony with our changing social and economic life." It was for this reason, Beard maintained, that the trustees had refused to hire him.[10]

Beard's second run-in with the board occurred in the early months of 1916 when the trustees' Committee on Education summoned him to appear before them and answer recent charges leveled against him in the press. A newspaper had reported that Beard had defended a man who had proclaimed "to hell with the flag" at a meeting taking place in a public school. Beard denied having done anything of the kind. What he had said about the unfortunate incident, in a speech given at the National Conference of Community Centers, was that "the intemperance of one man should not drive us into closing the schools" to community organizations.

The trustees accepted Beard's explanation. But as the historian rose to leave, assuming that the interview was over, two board members hounded him, he recalled, with questions about what he was teaching: "When the inquisitors satisfied themselves, the chairman of the committee ordered me to warn all the other men in my department against teachings 'likely to inculcate disrespect for American institutions,'" an allusion, clearly, to the arguments Beard had made in his controversial *Economic Interpretation of the Constitution of the United States*, published several years earlier. Loaded for bear, Beard "reported my order to my colleagues who received it with a shout of derision, one of them asking me whether Tammany Hall and the pork barrel were not American institutions!"[11]

Between April 1916 and March 1917 there were a few more skirmishes between the faculty and the trustees that resulted in the board's passing a resolution to form a special committee of their own "to inquire and ascertain" whether members of the faculty were teaching unpatriotic doctrines at the university. As *The New York Times* summarized it in the headline for the story, the intent of the resolution was "aimed at the pacifists."[12] The faculty in the School of Political Science responded immediately:

> Whereas the resolution of the trustees by its very terms implies a general doctrinal inquisition, insults the members of the Faculty by questioning their loyalty to their country, violates every principle of academic freedom, and betrays a profound misconception of the true function of the university in the advancement of learning, *Be it resolved* that we will not individually or collectively lend any countenance to such an inquiry.[13]

The trustees quickly backed down and appointed an academic committee to conduct these inquiries. Chaired by the widely respected Edwin Seligman, the Committee of Nine consisted of four professors, representing the various faculties at Columbia, one of whom was Dewey, and five deans, including Seligman, who was serving as dean of the School of Political Science. Moving forward, the trustees promised to keep their hands off any future investigation— a commitment they did not keep.

A few weeks later, after the United States had entered the war, the trustees fired Leon Fraser, a young instructor of politics at Columbia College. The official excuse was retrenchment: "On the assumption that the war would reduce materially the number of students in the college," the trustees had decided to let several untenured faculty members go. But Fraser's case, Butler admitted, was more complicated than the others. He would never teach at Columbia again, even if the university hired back some of the assistant professors. Why? Because in 1916, after accepting an invitation from Butler to teach a class for the Association for International Conciliation, Fraser spoke critically about a military camp in Plattsburg, New York—"in a moment of youthful enthusiasm," added Beard. Columbia's president had been serving at the time as director of the U.S. branch of the association and in that capacity had asked Fraser to help organize "courses in colleges throughout the country on pacifism and international conciliation." Twelve months later, Beard continued, seething with moral outrage, Butler fired the young man![14]

Unlike Fraser, James McKeen Cattell was anything but a vulnerable assistant professor. When he and Dana were fired in October 1917, Cattell was recognized nationwide as a leading figure in the field of experimental psychology.[15] Over the years, he had served as president of the American Psychological Association and as editor of four research journals.[16] As befit a man of his stature, he had been elected to the National Academy of Sciences, but Cattell was also a troublemaker. Identifying himself as a "radical democrat," he had systematically burned bridges with almost everyone at Columbia. And he had a particular disliking for the president and trustees of the university.

Cattell began teaching at the university in 1891, eleven years before Butler became president. According to the psychologist, when Butler took over, he moved quickly to consolidate the institution's administrative structure, a maneuver that cost the faculty its autonomy and decision-making authority on such critical matters as the appointment of academic deans. Previously, the different faculties had elected their own deans, following the European model.

In 1913, Cattell published an edited collection of articles that included two lengthy essays by him, one essay each by nine other scholars who had the courage to identify themselves by name, and 299 anonymous letters "by leading men of science holding academic positions." One of the first exposés of its kind, *University Control* accused presidents of academic institutions of working in collusion with their boards of trustees to usurp faculty prerogatives.[17] Even before the book came out, the trustees had been looking for a good excuse to let Cattell go. Now they thought they had one, but in the end they listened to the dean of graduate studies and a group of faculty members, who recommended against it. Although Cattell's colleagues also found him very difficult to deal with, they did not want to set a dangerous precedent of "retiring" a professor whose ideas the university did not like.[18]

The trustees accepted defeat this time around, but they were not giving up. Moving forward, they would try to find a less controversial reason for getting rid of Cattell and, while they were at it, Beard as well. *An Economic Interpretation of the Constitution of the United States* had also come out in 1913 and it caused a national scandal in the press. *The New York Times* accused Beard of having "sought to show that the founders of this Republic and the authors of its Constitution were a ring of land speculators who bestowed upon the country a body of organic law drawn up chiefly in the interest of their own pockets."[19]

Beard had many friends on the faculty; Cattell did not. Both men had reputations for being difficult, but Cattell knew no limits. Witty and acerbic, he enjoyed taking potshots at Butler and the trustees in ways so embarrassing that he eventually lost the support of outspoken defenders of academic freedom on campus, some of whom had intervened on numerous occasions to defend the irascible psychologist.

Few struggles over academic freedom illustrate more vividly than the one over Cattell how messy celebrated cases can be before sympathetic historians remove inconvenient details from the narrative. In this particular case, not only did Cattell wander off script but so did Seligman and Dewey, complicating the story for those of us focused on the history of the New School, where the economist and philosopher played heroic roles. Although Seligman and Dewey redeem themselves in the Columbia story, Cattell succeeded in pushing them to act in ways that were out of character.

Seligman declared war on Cattell four months before Columbia fired the psychologist. On June 18, the renowned economist and champion of academic freedom sent a letter to the Board of Trustees recommending that the university let Cattell go—for disciplinary reasons only, he stressed, that had nothing to do with academic freedom. Seligman was writing, he explained, in the name of seven members of the Committee of Nine who had not yet left for the summer. He promised to reconvene the entire group in September and send a follow-up letter after everyone had a chance to vote. In the meantime, he wanted to share with the trustees the unanimous "opinion" of those who had attended the first meeting. Seligman also wrote to Cattell:

> I desire to state emphatically that in my opinion academic freedom has nothing to do with your case. Instead of helping the principle of academic freedom, you have done more than anyone else to discredit the principle.... [Y]ou have shown that it is impossible for you to respect the ordinary decencies of intercourse

among gentlemen. . . . I regret to have to come to the conclusion which is shared by not a few of your colleagues that your usefulness in the University has come to an end.[20]

Seligman, like Cattell, was a founding member of the AAUP, but he had turned against his colleague over what started out as a trivial incident in January 1917 but turned into a full-blown crisis by June. A few weeks after the faculty returned to Columbia from their Christmas holidays, Cattell sent a "confidential" memorandum to three hundred members of the university's Faculty Club that was deeply offensive to Butler. Seligman agreed with the president that what the psychologist had written was puerile, but advised Butler to ignore it: The interest of the university "would best be advanced by taking no official notice of the incident." In early March, however, a colleague leaked the childish memo to the press, which caused considerable embarrassment for the university.[21]

As *The New York Times* told the story, Columbia had decided to tear down the building that members of the Faculty Club had been using for years. Although the university intended to move the club to new facilities, Cattell warned his colleagues that the replacement would not be good enough. The faculty should ask for something better, for example, he suggested provocatively, Butler's costly new residence: Columbia's "many-talented and much-climbing" president would probably be leaving Columbia very soon, Cattell wrote, "swept away by a reactionary wave into the national Vice Presidency"—an ironic reference to the 1912 presidential elections when the Republicans had nominated Butler to serve with Taft on the party's losing bid for a second term. When Butler left for the nation's capital, Cattell chortled on, the next president of Columbia "would not likely care to live in such a mausoleum."[22]

On the day these insulting words appeared in the press, Seligman sent the psychologist a letter of reprimand—signed by twenty-three other members of the Faculty Club, among them, Dewey and Wesley Clair Mitchell, expressing the group's collective disapproval of the psychologist's memo. Had passages from Cattell's adolescent prank not appeared in the newspapers, the matter would have "scarcely seemed to require serious consideration." Now, however, "we feel that, in justice to ourselves and without intending to magnify the importance of the subject, we are obliged to advise you that we do not share the sentiments of the memorandum and that we regard with entire disapproval the terms in which it is expressed."[23]

In his capacity as chairman of the Committee of Nine, Seligman urged the trustees to resist the temptation to fire Cattell. In exchange for their leniency, the psychologist, he promised, would sign a letter of apology to President Butler that Seligman himself would write to make sure that the tone was appropriate.

Although Cattell was not enthusiastic about the terms of the compromise, he agreed to cooperate as long as Seligman did not share his letter of apology with anyone but Butler, the trustees, and his fellow committee members.

Seligman did not keep his word. He bowed instead, he later confessed, to pressure from members of the Faculty Club. When the psychologist learned that Seligman had betrayed him, he lashed out with a vengeance. The economist responded to the verbal abuse by calling an emergency meeting of the Committee of Nine and gaining the support of the seven members still in residence to urge the university to sever ties with their colleague. He then informed Cattell and the Board of Trustees of the group's recommendation.[24]

After hearing from Seligman, Cattell upped the ante. Since he was going to lose his job anyway, the psychologist came up with a more dignified reason for being fired than his Faculty Club caper—one that had everything to do with his rights as a U.S. citizen to express his political opinion. On August 23, Cattell sent letters on Columbia University stationery to several members of Congress who had vigorously campaigned for the United States to enter the war:

> I trust that you will support a measure against sending conscripts to fight in Europe against their will. The intent of the Constitution and our consistent national policy should not be reversed without the consent of the people. The President and the present Congress were not elected to send conscripts to Europe.[25]

Cattell succeeded in getting a rise out of several legislators, including Representative Julius Kahn, a Republican from California and a militant patriot. Kahn alerted Butler immediately: "I do not think that you will approve of the action of this man Cattell in sowing seeds of sedition and treason with the apparent sanction of the Institution of which you are the honored head."[26] Finally, the board had the excuse it needed to fire Cattell. Trustee John B. Pine could hardly contain himself, "We have got the rascal this time and must leave him no loophole." Butler agreed, but they had to move quickly and decisively: "Words without deeds are futile."[27]

As the news leaked out around campus, Cattell's enemies on the Faculty of Applied Science urged Butler to fire the psychologist. On September 24, following a discussion with the Board of Trustees during which Seligman learned that Cattell would be dismissed, the economist drafted a carefully worded resolution on behalf of the full Committee of Nine calling instead for Cattell's retirement. Columbia should not fire the psychologist, but let him go with his honor intact and with all the benefits due a distinguished scholar who had taught at the institution for many years. Addressed to Trustee George L. Ingraham, chairman of the board's Joint Committee, the resolution recommended "the retirement from active service of Professor J. McKeen Cattell under the provisions of Section 67 of the Statutes." According to those provisions, members of the faculty who had worked at Columbia for at least twenty-five years could retire with a pension, even if they had not yet reached the age of sixty-five.[28] Cattell, at fifty-seven, had just completed twenty-six years. The resolution did not refer to the reasons Columbia should retire him; nobody needed an explanation. It dwelled, instead, on the specific terms of his dismissal: Cattell had served Columbia long enough to retire with benefits. The trustees disagreed and in doing so created political problems for Seligman, which they then further exacerbated by firing Dana without consulting anybody on the faculty.

Seligman had worked hard to convince all the members of the Committee of Nine to support the resolution to retire Cattell. Dewey had personal as well as political reasons for resisting. As Dewey's biographer Alan Ryan reminds us, Cattell had "been more responsible than anyone else in bringing Dewey to Columbia."[29] But in the end, even Dewey reluctantly signed the resolution, at least for twenty-four hours.

The next day Dewey withdrew his endorsement and resigned from the committee. He had just learned that the trustees had fired Dana, and done so without discussing the matter with "any representative body of the Faculties." Dewey urged Seligman to resign as well and dissolve the committee, which Dewey added, had always been problematic but had now become "inconsistent with professional self-respect":

My dear Mr. Seligman,

In view of the fact that the President has asked for the resignation of Professor Dana under penalty of dismissal without securing an inquiry by or hearing before any representative body of the Faculties, there seems no reason for the continued existence of the Committee of Nine, and I herewith present my resignation.

You are aware that I have felt from the first that the Committee was in a delicate position in that it would be easy for conditions to so shape themselves that we should become an inquisitory body without corresponding power of defending our colleagues against arbitrary action. . . . I wish my resignation to be construed retroactively so far as to disassociate myself entirely from the action taken yesterday.[30]

Two weeks later, Dewey, Robinson, and a colleague from the law school, Thomas R. Powell, wrote to the AAUP "respectfully" requesting that the association conduct an investigation into the circumstances surrounding the dismissal of both Cattell and Dana. Anticipating the possibility that the cases might end up in court, they urged the association to make an independent investigation for the sake of everyone involved, including Columbia: "We believe such an investigation highly desirable in order to protect the name of the University in case the procedure of dismissal was justifiable and to protect not only the repute of these men but others against arbitrary action in case the action in substance or form was unjustified."[31] The "Professors' Union," as *The New York Times* disparagingly called the AAUP, took a year to say anything, and when it did, the response was disappointing.[32]

In the winter of 1918, the AAUP published a report on academic freedom during times of war, which came out in favor of Columbia and other universities that had disciplined pacifists who persisted in speaking out once the United States had entered the war. But the association also cautioned academic leaders against doing anything that might "abrogate the ordinary right of the citizen to make his voice heard with respect to pending questions of legislation." Tucked away near the end of the report, the AAUP noted that the governing body of "an important university" (it did not mention Columbia by name) had punished "a distinguished man of science" for exercising his constitutional right to lobby congressmen about a bill that was before them at the time.[33]

Cattell, in other words, had committed no act of treason or sedition when he wrote to members of the House of Representatives and urged them to support alternative military service for conscientious objectors. A fact that Butler and the trustees learned the hard way when Cattell successfully sued Columbia and won a handsome settlement. But that was as far as the AAUP would go—nothing more than a gentle rap across the knuckles for the unnamed institution that had fired one of the founders of the association for having exercised his constitutional rights. As for Dana, the AAUP ignored his case entirely, implying by its silence that it agreed with Columbia—the literary scholar got what he deserved.

Had Dewey still been president of the AAUP, would he have succeeded in persuading the association to defend the rights of pacifists during times of war? Perhaps, but not necessarily. What we know for sure is that Dewey waited until Beard resigned before taking a public stand, at which point he told *The New York Times*: "I regard the action of Professor Beard as the natural consequence of the degrading action taken by [Columbia's] Board of Trustees last week."[34] A month later he apologized in *The New Republic*, blaming himself for not having spoken out sooner against the hysteria sweeping across the nation over the imagined dangers of pacifism. He ended his "In Explanation of Our Lapse" by urging liberals like himself, who supported the war effort, to defend the rights of those with whom they disagreed:

> I believe—though it may be my hope is the source of my belief—that some of our intolerance at diversity of opinion and our willingness to suppress civil liberties of democracy in the name of loyalty to democracy is merely a part of our haste to get into the war effectively. . . . Meantime it behooves liberals who believe in the war to be more aggressive than they have been in their opposition to those reactionaries who also believe in war—and who believe that loud denunciation of treason on sight is the best way to regain a political prestige of hate badly discredited. Let the liberal who for expediency's sake would passively tolerate invasions of free speech and action take counsel lest he be also preparing the way for a later victory of domestic Toryism.[35]

These were admittedly confusing times. Americans, Dewey acknowledged sympathetically, were "unused to the ways of war and like every eager and energetic beginner we are pressing our stroke." But that was still no excuse for remaining silent, for himself or anyone else.

⸻

When Columbia fired Cattell, the trustees dropped their earlier disciplinary charges against him and focused only on his alleged acts of sedition, a decision that helped secure the psychologist's place in history as a hero in the early struggles for academic freedom. At the time, however, Cattell's reputation for being a troublemaker had spread well beyond Columbia, which may explain why the psychologist never held another academic position.[36] Did the New School, for example, try to recruit him? Cattell never taught there, despite the institution's early interest in psychology.

By all accounts, Dana performed his academic duties at Columbia quietly and responsibly. But he was also a committed pacifist and had no intention of hiding his beliefs after the United States had entered the war—no matter what Butler threatened to do to colleagues who refused to censure themselves. Defying Butler's new policy, Dana actively campaigned against the draft over the summer of 1917 with the People's Council, a socialist group he had been affiliated with for some time.

Dana continued doing his political work during the early weeks of the new semester. In September, the People's Council sent him to Washington with the hope that his family's name and academic affiliation might persuade the

White House staff to let the young literary scholar meet with Wilson and make the group's case for peace. The strategy failed.

When the trustees learned about Dana's trip for the People's Council and his other activities over the summer, the board's disciplinary committee concluded that the young professor had stepped over the line:

> As a prominent member of that association, Assistant Professor H.W.L. Dana has been exceedingly active. He has participated in their proceedings and has given to them the benefit of his name, his reputation, and his connection to the university. These activities of Professor Dana are in express disregard of the warning given by President Butler and a violation to his duty to the university.[37]

Given his good conduct at Columbia before the summer of 1917, the trustees offered Dana the dignified option of resigning. The young man refused. He preferred to lose his job with his head held high, in the company of Cattell. Five year later, after Alvin Johnson expanded the New School's curriculum to include literary studies, Dana joined the faculty and eventually made a name for himself as a critic of modern European drama, known for his work on George Bernard Shaw and several Soviet writers.

Beard resigned seven days after Columbia fired Cattell and Dana. *The New York Times* covered both events on the front page of the paper, describing them in dramatic detail. The first article reproduced in full the trustees' resolutions to fire the two professors; the second, Beard's letter of resignation.[38] To this day, Beard's letter remains one of the most forceful and principled statements ever written in the name of academic freedom. Addressed to Butler, Beard warned Columbia's president that the university was "under the control of a small and active group of trustees who have no standing in the world of education, who are reactionary and visionless in politics, narrow and medieval in religion." If these had been normal times, Beard continued, he would have paid little attention to this power grab on the part of the board, but these were anything but normal times. The United States, he proclaimed, was engaged in a life-and-death struggle against forces that threatened to plunge the world into "the black night of military barbarism":

> I was among the first to urge a declaration of war by the United States, and I believe that we should now press forward with all our might to a just conclusion. But thousands of my countrymen do not share this view. Their opinions cannot

be changed by curses or bludgeons. Arguments to their reason and understanding are our best hope.

Such arguments, however, must come from men whose disinterestedness is above all suspicion, whose independence is beyond all doubt, and whose devotion to the whole country, as distinguished from any single class or group, is above all question. I am convinced that while I remain in the pay of the Trustees of Columbia University, I cannot do effectively my humble part in sustaining public opinion in support of the just war on the German Empire or take a position of independence in the days of reconstruction that are to follow. For this reason, I herewith tender my resignation as Professor of Politics, to take effect on the morning of Tuesday, October 9, 1917.[39]

In an editorial the following day, *The New York Times* congratulated Butler and the board of trustees on "Columbia's Deliverance." The university, it said, was "better for Professor Beard's resignation,"[40] an opinion shared by trustees and alumni in letters the paper published as well. None of this silenced the historian.

As the weeks went by, Beard's campaign gained momentum. In late December, *The New York Times* reported that Beard was publishing an article in *The New Republic* that gave a detailed account of his conflicts with Columbia over the years. Although the journalist's tone was insulting, his article provided welcome publicity for advocates of academic freedom, well beyond what *The New Republic* could have done on its own.[41]

Beard's description of the events leading up to his resignation made a persuasive case for why New Yorkers needed a new kind of academic institution. Five months later, Herbert Croly picked up where Beard had left off, announcing in *The New Republic* that a school of social research would soon open in New York. Here the "faculty would enjoy full control over the appointment and dismissal of professors and over the educational policy of the institution." Only then would progressives like Beard have the freedom to challenge the status quo and prepare students to meet the ever-growing demands of modern society.[42]

4

THE IDEA TAKES SHAPE

Herbert Croly started thinking about creating an independent school to train "social experts" as early as 1910.[1] He then developed his ideas further at *The New Republic* with Alvin Johnson and British academics who were writing for the magazine, including the political theorist Harold Laski.[2] James Harvey Robinson had also been thinking about opening a school since the early 1900s and had been discussing the possibility more recently with colleagues at Barnard College and Columbia Universtiy, a number of whom, like himself, were writing for *The New Republic*.[3] After Charles Beard resigned from Columbia, the two groups came together.

While they were still meeting separately, Johnson remembered listening to Laski compare academic life in the United States and England. At the time, the political theorist was teaching at Harvard. Despite the occasional high-profile scandal back home—Oxford fired the philosopher Bertrand Russell in 1916—leaders of British universities, Laski maintained, were considerably more tolerant during the war than their American counterparts. As Laski described his English colleagues enjoying "unchallenged liberty" at the London School of Economics (LSE), Johnson could not stop thinking about the way academics in the United States were routinely being fired if they departed "by a hand's breadth from the prevailing war doctrine." Tabloids reported on these dismissals almost every day under the same taunting headline: "Another Professor Goes Pop." Why the difference? LSE was not "handicapped," Laski explained, "by mobs of beef-devouring alumni, passionate about football and contemptuous of scholarship. . . . It could address itself to real problems, even the most contentious of the time. It could train leaders for the Labour Party and for the labour movement in general."[4]

During the war years, most of *The New Republic*'s British contributors were affiliated with the recently founded London School of Economics—a number of whom later taught at the New School.[5] A group of Fabian socialists opened LSE in 1895, with the hope of giving "benevolent experts" the skills they needed to build, as Ralf Dahrendorf described it in his history of the institution, "an organized, well-run society." LSE's faculty wanted to train social scientists how to "find out the facts" through good empirical research. Facts, they believed, would emancipate society. The leading voice at the school was the labor historian and social reformer Sidney Webb. Inspired by "research-driven institutions" in other countries, Webb modeled LSE on the Ecole libre des sciences politiques in Paris, which "was the object of much interest in London in the early 1890s," Dahrendorf explained, "and to whose name only 'London' and 'Economics' had to be added."[6]

Croly followed suit. On June 8, 1918, he announced in *The New Republic* that a "school of social research" would open in New York that was "analogous, if not similar" to the Ecole libre des sciences politiques—popularly known today as Sciences Po. As Croly outlined what he planned to do, he described the history of this French institution in some detail.

The founder of Sciences Po was Emile Boutmy. A journalist like Croly, Boutmy opened his school in 1872, the year after France had surrendered to Germany in the Franco-Prussian War. The son of a well-known family of intellectuals, Boutmy blamed France's humiliating defeat on the poor education of its political elite in government-funded schools. Moving forward, the nation needed to train future generations of public servants in independent institutions, free of the political and economic control of the state.[7]

In his announcement in June 1918, Croly proclaimed that France was finally reaping the benefits of Boutmy's experiment. The French were going to win the Great War thanks to the excellent preparation a new generation of leaders had received at the Ecole libre des sciences politiques, where they had learned "to apply scientific methods to the subject matter and the problems of politics." The Free School of Political Science in Paris owed its success, Croly continued, to its financial and intellectual independence. The faculty governed itself, and that was how it would and should be in New York. The American analog would also "pursue its work without fear of interference from those class and official interests whose social behavior it would necessarily investigate."[8]

"Analogous, not similar," Croly's Free School of Political Science would not limit itself to politics alone as the one in Paris was doing. Following the example of LSE, which Croly curiously did not mention, it would offer courses in all the social sciences "because political science can no longer be profitably isolated from anthropology, psychology, economics, and social organization." Multidisciplinary in approach, the Free School in New York—also referred to as the Independent School before everyone settled on the New School for Social Research—would draw on the theories and methodologies from across the social sciences, while remaining focused on its one and only political goal: "to make social research of immediate assistance to a bewildered and groping American democracy."[9]

Progressives hailed the idea. A month before Croly announced the opening of the Free School, articles had already appeared in *The New York Post* and *The Nation* enthusiastically endorsing the idea, about which their authors already knew a great deal from friends on the organizing committee who "will not permit the use of their names for the present in order that attention may not be distracted from the merits of the scheme."[10] Both articles claimed that the founders had a guarantee of $150,000, which they expected would largely cover the school's expenses for ten years.

The Nation predicted that this exciting new experiment in higher education would face hostile criticism from the "privilege mongers and all their parasites, whether the latter be found in the pulpit, the university, the press, or the legislature." But many others, the editors continued, would welcome the school warmly, including "far-sighted business men . . . [who] realize that the salvation of this country depends on its ability to utilize to the full expert brains in the service of democracy." Ending on a high note, *The Nation* expressed its "gratitude to those who have conceived and made possible such a bold and far-reaching plan."[11]

The Free School's organizing committee needed all the support it could get to keep "the privilege mongers and their parasites" at bay. But its members also had to deal with internal disagreements, a specter Robinson publicly alluded to in 1920 after the school had opened. Now that the founders had done away with university presidents and reactionary boards of trustees, they had nobody to blame but themselves if they failed: "*L'école c'est nous.*"[12] And fail they did, in 1922.

Looking back on the experiment, Johnson admitted that the odds had been against them from the very beginning:

> If you want to live at ease in the political world, be a practical reactionary. . . . You can all win together, following the politician's Golden Rule: "Scratch my back and I'll scratch yours."
>
> It is much harder to live at ease, or even in peace, as a liberal. For liberalism is by nature uncompromising, intransigent. I have my ideal of the public interest.

You have yours. I can't get you to support my ideal in return for my support of yours. Ideals don't cooperate. They fight.[13]

As Johnson saw it, part of the problem was a conflict in leadership styles. Croly was an east coast Hamiltonian, whereas he was a prairie-bred Jeffersonian.[14] Although the two men usually agreed on practical matters, Croly liked "finding out what was good for the people and doing it for them," whereas Johnson preferred the more egalitarian approach of letting the people decide on their own, without any interference—or so he said. Not everyone would have agreed with the portrait he drew of himself. In the end, neither Hamilton nor Jefferson had very much to do with why the collaboration failed. What really pulled the founders apart were the different educational goals that Croly and Robinson had for the New School and the founders' inability to sustain both of them.

Although Croly and Robinson came together to build a school for adults that specialized in the social sciences, they did not agree on what that entailed, or even who those students should be. Robinson envisioned a school for adults who were "eager to extend, elaborate, and elucidate their personal experiences by studying matters which have aroused their curiosity, shown up their ignorance or puzzled them." In other words, a school for mature students who had a passion for learning: "No one comes to the New School because he is sent, or hopes for a degree or diploma, or even for the momentary relief that comes from pleasing teacher by matching a series of questions with acceptable answers."[15]

At Robinson's New School, college graduates, primarily, would learn about "mankind and his present predicament . . . in the light of man's history and nature as now understood." At Croly's New School, public servants and labor organizers would acquire the skills they needed to become effective "social planners"—or as his critics characterized them, "social engineers." One envisioned an institution where mature adults would attend lectures by distinguished scholars of "history, anthropology, psychology, public law, and the rest of the disciplines which have man, his nature, and social organization, for their theme." The other a school with a clear social purpose.

Eager to reach a more targeted audience, Croly invited Robert Bruère to open a labor research bureau and annex it to the New School. Bruère was just the right man to run a program like this. An advocate of vocational education, he was also the brother of Henry Bruère, the former head of New York City's Municipal Bureau of Research, with which several members of the founding faculty had strong ties. Charles Beard, for example, had served as director of the Municipal Bureau's training school to prepare people going into public administration. Reinforcing family ties, Croly appointed Henry Bruère's wife to the New

School's Organization Committee. Now, under the leadership of Robert Bruère, the New School would have its own research bureau that would recruit students from New York chapters of labor unions—an idea that did not please everyone. Although the unions would pay a substantial fee for these courses, Johnson was not enthusiastic: "I didn't like this project. It was chaining one of our organs to a particular group. But I wasn't looking for trouble and presented my objections merely for the record."[16]

Although Robinson also wanted the New School to help society bring about political and social change, he expected the faculty to contribute to this goal in diffuse ways, not by training social engineers but by introducing mature students to new ways of thinking about human society; in his case, through the teaching of history. Robinson had developed his vision in two highly regarded books, *The New History*, published in 1912, and *The Mind in the Making*, in 1921. The latter, based on lectures he had given at the New School, was a huge critical success that sold over one hundred thousand copies.[17] With these two books Robinson "exerted a profound and beneficial influence on the thought of his generation" observed his former student, the American historian Carl Becker.

In 1937, a year after Robinson died, Becker described the importance of his teacher's work for other historians. Robinson had challenged the discipline, Becker explained, to answer "two quite different questions: . . . What has happened here and there from time to time? . . . How is it that we now do as we do, feel as we feel, and know what we know?" According to Robinson, Becker continued, late nineteenth- and early twentieth-century historians had been "commonly satisfied to ask and answer the first question, whereas it is the second that was important":

> Robinson's quarrel with historians was not that they took history seriously but that they took it without discrimination, studied it objectively, that is to say without object. He insisted that it should be studied with an object. That object should be to throw some light on the nature of man and thereby enable him to understand better what he is doing and should do.[18]

Taking his intellectual vision and applying it to the New School, Robinson saw himself and his colleagues transforming the social sciences in twentieth-century America the way Francis Bacon, Galileo, and Descartes had transformed the natural sciences in seventeenth-century Europe: The New School's mission, Robinson wrote, was to emancipate the social sciences from "academic traditions and popular prejudices which suspect and resent any fair statement of the actual terms and conditions of human life."[19]

Beard had more sympathy than Robinson for the idea of developing educational programs for members of labor unions. He had been active for years, together with his wife the historian Mary Beard, in supporting a number of different initiatives to provide educational opportunities for working-class people. In 1906, he served on the founding board of directors of the Rand School of Social Science, established by the American Socialist Party to teach "social science from the standpoint of socialism," a fact his critics used against him to prove that he was a radical subversive. Beard, however, did not like Croly's plan to create a labor research bureau at the New School.[20]

Having studied, taught and coauthored books with Robinson, Beard sided with his former teacher's vision of the New School. But if the truth be known, Beard had lost interest in both. Although he was a popular lecturer, he no longer believed in the efficacy of classroom teaching. He preferred imparting knowledge on the printed page. [21] What he wanted to do more than anything else was to train a few student assistants to help advance his research.

Johnson was probably Robinson's most enthusiastic supporter, but he too had reservations. The historian, Johnson wrote, had taken a very good idea to risible extremes. Caricaturing the plan, he described Robinson's New School as a place where "cultivated gentlemen could present their ideas informally to cultivated gentlemen and ladies."[22] Not that Johnson wanted anything much different. As he imagined the New School, a similar group of cultivated scholars would deliver lectures for "the continuing education of the educated."

Were Johnson and Robinson only interested in attracting adult students from the privileged classes? Not exactly; everyone was welcome. But they pitched their appeal in 1919 to college graduates who belonged to the upper reaches of society. As Johnson wrote in his autobiography, if educated adults continued to study—the subtext, of course, was with scholars like themselves—their ongoing engagement with the world of ideas would lead them to reject the self-serving "waves of dominant opinion" in favor of assuming their "social responsibility" and using their influence for the benefit of the wider society.[23]

Robinson began publishing articles about educational reform in 1900 while he was serving as acting dean of Barnard College. A liberal arts education, he wrote, had to incorporate the new sciences, by which he meant the social as well as the natural sciences.[24] With the outbreak of the war in 1914, he felt a real sense of urgency about the issue.

Robinson began meeting with like-minded colleagues and wealthy friends to see what it would take to break away from Columbia and build an independent school of social science. With the help of Barnard professor of history Emily James Putnam and their mutual philanthropist friend Charlotte Hunnewell Sorchan, he drafted a set of by-laws for the new institution in January 1916, which Putnam described proudly in a note to him as a "revolutionary conception of the academic polity." But it was still not ready for circulation. Before sharing it with their wider planning committee, she recommended consulting with Beard on a number of points, including Sorchan's controversial idea that they do away with having a permanent faculty. Putnam signed off with a conspiratorial, "Yours for anarchy, EJP."[25]

When Beard resigned from Columbia in October 1917 and Croly and Robinson officially joined forces, they brought together a group of friends who had known one another for years. According to Johnson, their first meetings took place in the home of Caroline Bacon, whom he identified as the wife of the wealthy businessman George Bacon and "a scholar in her own right" who had taught at Smith College. Robinson reported that they first met in the home of Sorchan. Both women, along with Putnam, continued to play important roles at the New School after Beard, Croly, and Robinson had abandoned the project.[26] This enlarged group of friends quickly evolved into the Organization Committee and moved its base of operations to *The New Republic.*

In the spring of 1918, the Organization Committee published "A Proposal for An Independent School of Social Sciences for Men and Women." Nineteen individuals identified themselves publicly with the project (ten women and nine men), all of them major figures in New York progressive circles.[27] More women than men sent a clear message. Although the United States would not ratify the Nineteenth Amendment for two more years, the proposal was already predicting that "the granting of the suffrage to women and the extension of women's interest into new and important spheres of public life will lead them to seek a better equipment both for power and service."[28]

The women whose names appeared on the proposal were independently wealthy. Although some of the men had money as well, it was the women who pulled out their checkbooks to launch the New School. The two most important contributors were Dorothy Whitney Straight, who had been financing *The New Republic* since 1914, and Charlotte Hunnewell Sorchan, Putnam and Robinson's good friend, who was also underwriting a major urban renewal project at the time on the east side of Manhattan (Turtle Bay Gardens). When *The New York Post* and *The Nation* reported that the independent school had raised $150,000, they were referring to the pledges made by these two women—a gift from Straight for $100,000 and another from Sorchan for $50,000.[29]

Not only were the women on the Organization Committee wealthy, they also held important positions in educational, labor, and social activist institutions. Putnam, for example, was a scholar of ancient Greece and women's history and had served as the first female dean of Barnard College. Ruth Standish Baldwin was president of the National Women's Trade Union League and one of the founders of the National Urban League.[30] Then there was Mary Harriman Rumsey, who had founded the Junior League for the Promotion of Settlement Movements, a volunteer organization of society women who supported the settlement house movement and other progressive causes. Rumsey had also opened and was running the University Settlement House. Straight had been active in the Junior League as well and was serving as its president when the New School opened.

Most of these women represented what feminist scholars of the period call "New Women." Politically active, they used their financial independence to walk away from the "outgrown customs and standards" still imposed on women in early twentieth-century America. A number of them belonged to Elsie Clews Parsons's circle of friends and embraced the anthropologist's radical critique of conventional marriage. Parsons's bold books and essays on the subject, some of which had been published by *The New Republic*, confirmed the choices these women were making in their personal lives.[31]

The nine men on the Organization Committee included the best-selling novelist Winston Churchill and five members of the legal profession: Felix Frankfurter, professor at Harvard Law School and a regular contributor to *The New Republic*; Emory Buckner, a prosecutor from Nebraska and a good friend of Frankfurter's; Charles Burlingham, a noted legal reformer; Thomas Chadbourne, the "radical capitalist"; and Joseph P. Cotton, the future under secretary of state in the Hoover administration. The remaining three men were Charles Beard, Herbert Croly, and Alvin Johnson. Curiously missing was James Harvey Robinson. Although he had been actively involved from the very beginning, he wanted his identity "to be kept secret" because "it would queer me in various ways as long as I am connected with Columbia."[32]

Unlike Beard, who resigned right away after Nicholas Butler fired James Cattell and Henry Dana, Robinson dawdled. It took him nine months to let Columbia's president know that he was leaving, and when he finally did in July 1918, he wrote that he would not resign for another year, until the summer of 1919. Robinson sent a second letter a few months later to ask whether the university might do him the favor of letting him retire amicably, with his full pension, rather than having him walk away in protest. His request, he understood, would require the trustees to bend the rules slightly, giving him his pension after twenty-four, not twenty-five, years. The board turned him down.[33]

After writing to Butler, Robinson came out of the shadows and agreed to serve informally as the chairman of the Board of Directors, the newly established governing body, consisting of six women and six men, that had replaced the Organization Committee of nineteen. In assuming the job, he saw himself as the first among equals, with very little authority over the other members of the board. The founders had firmly rejected the idea of having a hierarchical administrative structure.[34]

As the independent school's spokesman, Robinson published an article in *The Nation* in September 1918 updating earlier descriptions of the school with "fuller information in regard to [the plan] and the spirit in which [the school] is being received." Six responses followed, the most enthusiastic coming from the historian's faithful student Carl Becker and board member Mrs. Learned Hand, wife of the distinguished judge and a noted figure herself in feminist circles. Two others acknowledged "its advantages" but had serious reservations: in one case, about whether the social sciences were truly sciences; in the other, about the choice of name—what made this institution independent? Still another questioned the wisdom of creating a school in the first place. Why not a foundation instead?

The most nuanced of the comments came from Johnson's old friend, Amherst College president Alexander Meiklejohn, who expressed real enthusiasm for the idea in the abstract but raised "some anomalies which torment a mere administrator." The founders would have spared themselves a great deal of grief had they listened more carefully to what Meiklejohn had to say. Quoting from the proposal itself, Meiklejohn demonstrated how confused the founders were on such fundamental matters as fund-raising, faculty governance, curricular issues, and the role of administrators. Instead of emancipating themselves, they were tying themselves into knots. The problems, Meiklejohn suggested, were not only structural but ideological. How could the school remain "free from bias," he asked, when it limited its courses to the social sciences? Although the founders claimed that they wanted to train the next generation of leaders, "literature and philosophy—the appreciations, the values, and the intellectual presuppositions—are alike ignored. Can the programme with this deliberate mutilation be kept free and fundamental?" Nevertheless, despite all his reservations, Meiklejohn endorsed this "new educational adventure":

Why, then is the venture so full of promise? It is not because of its form of organization. This is a protest rather than a plan. It is not because of its freedom and independence. The school is radical rather than free, in the academic sense. It appeals to men who wish to know how society should be changed rather than to those who wish to know that it should be.

But the real strength of the school is that of the persons who are making it and of the compelling quality of the cause which they serve. It is whipping us all with the last of its protests, and that we surely need. It will set a group of good students at work with fine enthusiasm in a great cause. It may be that in time it will even learn to whip itself.[35]

The exchange in *The Nation* took place two months before the end of the war. Everyone knew by then that the Germans were going to surrender, but nobody was rejoicing. They had too much to do to repair the devastation of the past four years. As Robinson proclaimed, "Never in the history of the world, has there been a time when it was so essential as now for thoughtful people, conscious of their obligation to humanity, to combine in novel and efficient ways the single-hearted consideration and criticism of existing ideals and institutions in the hope of suggesting practical betterments and readjustments." The school's "high ambition," Robinson wrote (sounding a bit more like Croly), was to train new political leaders, teachers, journalists, and others, all of whom, in their different capacities would shed light on society's problems and work in the "real interests" of the people they represented.[36]

5

THE NEW SCHOOL OPENS

When the New School opened in 1919, it welcomed students to "seductive if modest" facilities, as Alvin Johnson described them, two blocks from the offices of *The New Republic*. Thanks to the generosity of Dorothy Straight and Charlotte Sorchan, the Board of Directors had "acquired" six townhouses in London Terrace, between Ninth and Tenth Avenues; three of them on the north side of West Twenty-Third Street, and the other three on the south side of West Twenty-Fourth. Together the houses shared a "set of ashcan and alley-cat backyards." Under the direction of Sorchan, "an amateur architect of great talent,"[1] the directors converted these old Victorian homes into what one student described as "a charming garden court with bits of old sculpture, work offices, improvised classrooms, some residential space, a large assembly hall, and a few special rooms, typical of the best of Victorian New York."[2]

All of this was over the fierce objections of Charles Beard: The idea of creating a gracious home for the New School went against everything the founders had set out to do. He had no interest in reproducing the genteel comforts of a conventional university. What Beard had in mind, wrote James Harvey Robinson's biographer disparagingly, was for them to find "humble quarters located over a livery stable, garage, or brewery where even the olfactory stigmata of conventional education would be effectively obscured." Johnson described Beard's posturing with less pungent language, but with equal disdain, as did Herbert Croly who also pulled rank. As the former editor of *Architectural Review* and the current editor of *The New Republic*, Croly defended their decision to design an aesthetically pleasing space to house their progressive institution. Apparently, nobody on the committee sided with Beard.[3]

On February 18, 1919, one week into the New School's trial semester, the Board of Directors' secretary, Emma Peters Smith, reported that students "showed such interest in the new enterprise that we were greatly encouraged." During that first term, they attracted "about 500 persons," not only for the lectures delivered by famous professors but for the technical and fieldwork courses staffed by members of the Labor Research Bureau.[4] When the New School opened officially the following fall, 549 students enrolled in thirty-nine lecture courses, seminars, and workshops, all of which, the founders noted proudly, were pitched at a high academic level.[5] They had no interest in wasting their time with weak students or recent high school graduates who were just going through the motions, whether they had an intellectual calling or not. As Robinson put it in his article for *The Nation*,

> In every educational institution, the problem always arises whether the instruction and methods of study are to be adapted to the most gifted and promising students or the mediocre and poor. The New School proposes to meet this difficulty fairly and honestly. In the first place, it is not designed for boys and girls, who often find their way to and through college with no honest interest in study or capacity to think carefully or write clearly. It will have no attractions for anyone who is not intent on real study and the acquisition of knowledge and insight for their own sakes.[6]

The 1919–20 announcement of courses made the same point, but more diplomatically. The New School invited anyone who was interested, with or without a college degree, to sign up for "open courses" as an "auditor" and listen to leading scholars lecture at a level comparable to what people hear at the best graduate schools in the country. At the end of every class period, students would have the opportunity to ask a few questions. But they should expect nothing else: no outside consultations, no grades, no exams, no paper assignments. A professor may occasionally agree to run additional discussion sections for highly motivated auditors.

The New School also offered "closed courses" for a select group of "regular students." Like the auditors, regular students would receive no grades, but they would have the opportunity to work closely with their professors on individual research projects. To qualify as a regular student, candidates had to go through a special application process to demonstrate that they had the necessary background and level of expertise through "previous training or experience."[7] What precisely did that mean? Robinson did not mince words: "Just as in the Ecole des Beaux Arts, only those could expect the attention of the instructor who had some artistic gift, so in [the New School] regular students must have gone far enough to exhibit the capacity to interest themselves scientifically in social problems, and to express themselves intelligently in discussion and writing."[8] As intended, very few students qualified.

At the end of the fall semester, an unnamed colleague, presumably Emma Smith, prepared a detailed report for the Board of Directors in which she confirmed that the New School had made the right decision to schedule its courses at the end of the day. As anticipated, they had attracted students with full-time jobs. Among those employed in the professions, seventy-two identified themselves as school teachers, fifty-eight as "philanthropic and social workers," followed by a modest number each of lawyers, judges, engineers, chemists, writers, editors, journalists, bankers, and trade union officials. Among those in business, thirty-four identified themselves as secretaries, clerks, and stenographers, thirty-three as "officials of business companies and merchants," followed by a handful of accountants, bookkeepers, and salesmen. Out of the 549 students who had enrolled in the fall, 230 identified themselves as having no occupation, 149 of whom were "married women."[9]

The report did not identify students by gender, but it is safe to assume that most of them were women, and so they remained, at a ratio of two to one, throughout the early years.[10] The New School did not report ethnicity either, but what records we have of the names of the students during the interwar period suggest that Jews were well represented, comparatively speaking. This was hardly a surprise given the New School's policy of opening its doors to people of all ethnicities and races, at a time when other universities had imposed a *numerus clausus* on the number of Jews they admitted.[11]

Although the faculty was overwhelmingly male, gentile, and entirely white, it too was more diverse than mainstream institutions. Of the twenty-four instructors whose names appeared in the announcement of courses for 1919–20, two of them were women (Emily James Putnam and Elsie Clews Parsons). Another five of them were of Jewish origin.[12]

The faculty divided their lectures and seminar classes into three categories: (1) descriptive and historical, (2) development of thought and ideals, and (3) special contemporary problems.[13] During the fall semester of 1919, the most popular course across the three groups was Graham Wallas's Social Inheritance with an enrollment of 226 students—a tribute to the eminence of the visiting scholar and to the effectiveness of the New School's publicity campaign. For those who did not know who Wallas was, the course bulletin included a brief biographical sketch, printed prominently on the first page:

> Mr. Wallas, who has come to this country for the purpose of giving his time to the work of the school, has taught for a number of years in the London School

of Economics and has been Professor of Economics in London University since 1914. He is a member of the Fabian Society and has been active in the London County Council and on various educational commissions. He is the author of *The Life of Francis Place*, *Human Nature in Politics*, and *The Great Society*. His lectures at the school will cover courses on Social Inheritance and English Administrative Experiments in Central Executive and in Local Government.[14]

Next in popularity, was Robinson's course on the History of the Human Mind (117), followed by Historic Background of The Great War (49) that Robinson was teaching with Harry Elmer Barnes, a promising young historian who would rise to infamy after World War II.[15] Then came Robert Bruère's Modern Trade Unionism (46), Beard's Problems of American Government (35), Barnes's Modern Industrialism and the Rise of Radical Programs of Social Reconstruction (30), Thorstein Veblen's Economic Factors in Civilization (28), Alexander Goldenweiser's The Groundwork of Civilization (21), and Horace Kallen's Typical Theories of Life (18).

Among the more poorly enrolled courses was Parsons's Sex in Ethnology. Only seven students registered to study with her, but they included the writer Signe Toksvig, who, like Parsons, contributed regularly to *The New Republic*, and Ruth Benedict, an "unhappily married woman . . . who was looking for something to do with her life."[16] As Parsons's biographer Desley Deacon writes, Parsons urged Benedict to continue studying anthropology at the New School with Goldenweiser who, in turn, encouraged her to do doctoral work with Franz Boas at Columbia. By the early 1930s, Benedict had become one of the nation's most distinguished anthropologists. Her best-selling *Patterns of Culture*, which remains a classic to this day, drew on philosophy and psychology as well as anthropology, very much in the multidisciplinary tradition of the New School.

The low numbers in Parsons's course did not worry the founders as much as the weak enrollment in Wesley Clair Mitchell's The Business Cycle. Economics, after all, was the main focus of the New School's academic program, a point *The New York Times* had stressed in an article announcing the opening of this "new school of research." Quoting faithfully from the founders' own press release, the *Times* explained that the New School "varies from the average college and university in confining its work almost entirely to economics and maintains a graduate standard for all." Yet only eight students had registered for Mitchell's demanding course. The same happened repeatedly over the next three years, persuading the distinguished economist that he was wasting his time at the New School.

Most accounts of the early years rely heavily on Johnson's autobiography, the most comprehensive reconstruction we have in the words of one of the founders. By the time Johnson published *Pioneer's Progress* in 1952, Beard, Croly, and Robinson had all passed away, as had Mitchell and Veblen. Would they have accepted Johnson's version of the story? Their biographers did not challenge it in any significant way, implying that their subjects would not have objected either, at least not on the substance. Johnson's barbed editorial asides were another matter. Sparing only Mitchell, he skewered everybody else.[17]

Thanks to Mitchell's wife, Lucy Sprague Mitchell, a major figure in childhood education, we have another account of the early days at the New School in the words of a founding member of the faculty. In *Two Lives*, Sprague Mitchell pieced together Clair Mitchell's record of the events as they were unfolding from his diary entries, letters, and lecture notes, most of them written between 1918 and 1920.[18] These fragmentary descriptions have been woven into Sprague Mitchell's vivid account of the couple's professional lives and circle of colleagues and friends. Their group included members of the faculty at Columbia University who were also activists in the education reform movement; among them, needless to say, was John Dewey. The philosopher had not only written major theoretical works on education but had offered his support to Sprague Mitchell and other pioneers in the reform movement. In 1916, Sprague Mitchell opened the Bureau of Educational Experiments, later known as the Bank Street School for Children.

The founders of the New School had been participating actively in a nationwide campaign for educational reform. Although the movement's leaders focused primarily on early childhood education, everyone recognized the New School as part of the same cause and relied on its founders for intellectual and material support. When, for example, Sprague Mitchell opened a "cooperative school to train student teachers" in the early 1930s, Johnson gave her classroom space at the New School until she had acquired facilities of her own. By that time, Sprague Mitchell was also a member of the New School's Board of Trustees.[19]

When the New School launched its trial semester in February 1919, Clair Mitchell was still in Washington, closing down his office at the War Industries Board. Although he could not move back to New York for another year, the economist understood that his friends needed him right away to help silence critics such as Nicholas Murray Butler, who were trying to dismiss the faculty as consisting of little more than "a bunch of disgruntled liberals." February was out of the question but he could make time in the third week of March to give a series of lectures on The Price System and the War.[20]

After Mitchell joined the faculty full time, he, Beard, Robinson, and Veblen established themselves as the "Big Four."[21] Dividing curricular responsibilities among them, Mitchell took charge of organizing the courses in economics, Veblen in sociology, Beard in politics, and Robinson in history, psychology, and anthropology. Mitchell also served as an ambassador to the wider community.

During the summer of 1920, the economist gave an informal talk about the New School to a group of friends. The New School, he explained, "aims to supplant guesswork, however brilliant, by genuine knowledge, however laborious." Inspired by the "hope that the social sciences may be developed into serviceable instruments of social progress," the founders opened a school "where professors could express themselves freely without fear of retribution." This was rarely the case at conventional private and public universities at the time, where reactionary trustees at one and state legislators at the other interfered with academic freedom.[22]

According to Sprague Mitchell, despite her husband's outspoken commitment to academic freedom, he would never have joined the New School in its name alone. What excited him about the project was the opportunity it would give him to work with mature students who had hands-on experience and were now eager to come back to school to learn how to do sophisticated analytical research. Clair Mitchell was convinced that the best graduate students in economics had already worked in business or on the floor of the stock exchange. Although his young students at Columbia learned statistics quickly and mastered the other tools they needed to do good analytic work, they lacked the practical experience needed to make significant contributions to ongoing debates about business cycles, his area of expertise.

But much to Mitchell's disappointment, the New School appealed less to a student body with specialized skills than to "the intelligent man or woman," as he characterized them, "who wishes to keep abreast of the times in social matters, but who, for various reasons, cannot or will not follow university courses." Although Mitchell respected the idea of keeping broadly educated people informed about the latest findings in the social sciences, this was not what he had signed on to do. Students like these were "less important" to him. When he agreed to join the faculty, he fully expected to find a sufficient number of well-trained businessmen equipped with the skills necessary to do serious research. Johnson and Robinson had assumed he same. The New School, they thought, would attract students capable of doing advanced work in economics and in the other social sciences.

Although things did not work out the way Mitchell had expected, the econo-mist still preferred Robinson's vision of the New School over Croly's. He did so, in part, out of the deep respect he had for the intellectual historian, whom he described as, "Erudite—very broad knowledge." Robinson, he added, revealing his biases, was "a man of ideas, which is not orthodox in an historian." He thought less of Beard in this regard, as did Johnson.[23]

In July 1918, Mitchell wrote to his wife that he had just met with Johnson, who once again was trying to persuade him to join this new academic institution that some people were still calling the Free School of Politics to distinguish it from that other School of Politics at Columbia. Johnson, Mitchell reported,

> [had] brought up the Free School, or whatever it is called, again and asked my advice—I am to see some of the people the next time I am in New York for a day. He says there is no leading spirit—certainly Charley Beard does not play that role. On the contrary the group is now large enough to have developed two cur-rents of policy. Herbert Croly wants to make the school primarily a concern for "social engineering." James Harvey on the other hand would make it primarily a scientific body, though one alert to current developments of a social sort and eager to promote movements in which it believes. Needless to say, Johnson and I are temperamentally addicted to Robinson's bias.[24]

Given all the uncertainties, Mitchell hedged his bets. Before leaving Wash-ington, he asked Edwin Seligman, who was still serving as dean of Columbia's School of Politics, to extend his leave of absence a little longer so that he might help their mutual friends launch their experiment in higher education. Three years later, Mitchell was back at Columbia having decided after all that his grad-uate students there "would have more influence than the students at the New School on the development of economics as a science."[25] And he would have more of them!

Mitchell never abandoned the New School, however. After he resigned in 1922, he remained on the Board of Directors for several more years and served as its treasurer.[26] Then in 1933, he worked closely with Johnson to recruit an outstanding group of refugee economists to the University in Exile. During his three years at the New School, Mitchell also cofounded two other experimental institutions: the National Bureau of Economic Research, which he directed from 1920 to 1945, and the Social Science Research Council.

Charles Beard and Mitchell resigned from the New School in 1922, in Beard's case from the board as well as from teaching. Robinson stopped teaching that year but he remained on the board until 1923. As for Croly, he did not step down until 1926, at least not officially, but he essentially turned his back on the institution in 1922, paying little attention to future developments at the school.

As Johnson describes these defections in his autobiography, he suggests that Croly abandoned the experiment before everyone else and took his donors with him. An assertion not supported by the New School's announcements of course offerings, published every semester with an updated list of board members. Croly's name finally disappeared in 1926, the same year Johnson's disappeared from the masthead of *The New Republic*.

After Johnson took over the direction of the New School, he became increasingly uncomfortable at *The New Republic*. Croly, he said, was very angry about what had happened to his educational venture: "a failure, he regarded it, a pernicious failure." They both knew that the situation was beyond repair, but neither one of them resigned for another three years, until things finally became so "untenable" that Johnson picked a fight with his old friend: "a quarrel in which I was in the wrong." [27]

Although the founders had different reasons for resigning, or in Johnson's case for soldiering on, everyone agreed that the New School had failed to recruit enough auditors to pay the bills. Nor had it attracted a sufficient number of regular students with the skills needed to do advanced social science research. Between 1919 and 1922, enrollment figures remained essentially the same—about eight hundred students a year, spread over two or three semesters—an impressive number, in all fairness, and higher than they had originally predicted. But they had underestimated the cost of running an ambitious research program and the difficulty they would have in raising additional funds. If the New School had to rely more heavily on tuition dollars than the founders had anticipated, how many students would they have to enroll? Nobody had done the math, but the number was considerably higher than eight hundred. Between 1925 and 1929, with Johnson at the helm, the New School enrolled, on average, two thousand five hundred a year. But even this was not high enough to cover the cost of a serious research program. [28]

In addition to the enrollment problems, Beard had lost what little interest he still had for classroom teaching, some suggested because he was going deaf, but that was not the main reason. As the historian had been saying for years, he believed he would reach more students—and do so more successfully—on the written page. All he wanted to do at this stage of his life was devote himself to doing research and publishing his work. [29] As for Croly, he had grown tired of listening to the academics on the board accuse the Labor Research Bureau of costing too much money. He had also taken a particular dislike to Robinson, Johnson reported, and accused him of having turned a serious research institution into a cheap lecture bureau. By 1921, Croly "detested" the intellectual historian to such a degree that he refused to publish *Mind in the Making*, a regrettable decision, Johnson added, that cost *The New Republic* a best-seller.[30] Although Robinson had no more sympathy for Croly than Croly had for him, he agreed that his lecture courses were a disappointment. The founders probably should have waited longer before opening the New School. Having rushed into the project without the resources they needed, they had lowered their standards with the hope of attracting enough students to pay the bills. In the end, Robinson agreed with Mitchell, conceding that the New School would never appeal to stronger students if it did not offer an accredited academic program.

Barnes offered empirical evidence to support Robinson's conclusion:

While a lecturer at the New School during its first year, the writer [Barnes] was on numerous occasions assured by graduate students from Columbia that the New School offerings were much more attractive than most of the courses then offered by the Faculty of Political Science at Columbia, but that they simply could not attend the New School regularly because they had neither time nor money to invest in an educational enterprise which would produce nothing more than increased erudition, intellectual development and improved cerebration. Professional ambitions and conjugal responsibilities or aspirations forced upon these students diligent and solemn devotion to those courses which would ultimately secure for them the magic doctor's degree.[31]

The New School also had trouble attracting students from labor unions, particularly from those that had educational programs of their own. When, in February 1921, the founders offered twenty-five tuition scholarships to members of the International Ladies' Garment Workers Union (ILGWU), the educational committee's secretary replied crisply that "we appreciate" the New School's interest in the ILGWU, but "we find it more advisable to concentrate our activities within two types of institutions which we developed—the Unity Center and the Workers' University, upon which we place all of our attention."[32]

The Teachers Union of the City of New York was more receptive to the idea of collaborating, in part no doubt thanks to Dewey's intervention. But what they wanted more than anything else was a place to run classes of their own that spoke directly to the interests and needs of schoolteachers. In a letter to

Beard, an organizer of the Teachers Union asked whether Marietta Johnson, "founder of the School of Organic Education in Fairhope, Alabama," might give ten lectures at the New School in October and November 1920 as part of a series of courses that the union hoped the New School would run for its members: "Dr. Dewey thinks very highly of her work, as you probably know, and devotes quite a bit of his *Schools of To-morrow* to a description of her school."[33]

Given the high intellectual quality of the courses they offered during their first academic year, the founders did not understand why they had failed to attract enough students to cover their expenses. In addition to the full-time faculty, they had lined up an impressive group of visitors for 1919–20, including Roscoe Pound and Felix Frankfurter from Harvard Law School, both of whom had participated in a course on law reform with Charles Beard and several other eminent scholars. Visiting as well, as previously noted, was England's Graham Wallas, whose course on social inheritance had indeed attracted a huge crowd. But the numbers overall were not strong enough.

Unwilling to change direction after only two semesters, the founders remained true to their original mission for another year. The purpose of the New School, they repeated in the announcement of courses for 1920–21, "is to carry on research with a view of increasing our knowledge of human nature and social institutions, to establish and measure social facts, to create in students a scientific attitude toward present political, social, and economic problems, and to make known through open courses and publications the results of investigation in the social sciences." For students interested in doing social research, they could compete for three $2,000 fellowships. To hold on to the same program, however, for another year, the Board of Directors had to reduce the faculty from twenty-four instructors in the fall of 1919 to twelve in the fall of 1920: six economists, two historians, two philosophers, one anthropologist, and one psychologist.[34] The courses that remained represented the minimum core for a serious curriculum in the social sciences: classes on social science methods and theory and contemporary economic and social problems.

By the second semester of the second year, everyone accepted that an academic program with a heavy emphasis on economics was not appealing to the kinds of students whom they had expected to attract and now needed to help pay the bills: "It was altogether impossible to float a course in economics," recalled Clara Mayer. A recent graduate of Barnard, Mayer had followed her favorite professor

Robinson to the New School. Several years later she became an indispensable member of the New School's administrative staff and her family, major donors.

Reminiscing about the early 1920s, Mayer dismissed the lack of interest in economics as simply a matter of bad timing: "In the pre-1929 boom . . . everyone felt they knew just about all the economics they needed to know."[35] This false sense of security may have contributed to the problem, but Mitchell, Robinson, and Barnes had a more persuasive explanation: students wanted to receive academic credit. Whatever the reason, they reluctantly agreed that they would have to change course. If it was going to survive, the New School would have to expand the range of courses it offered the following year and open its doors, at least temporarily, to outside groups that wanted to use the New School's facilities to run their own programs.

The mission statement prepared for the 1921–22 announcement of courses reflected the new reality:

> The object of the New School is to develop the vital relation between recent scientific discoveries and our conception of human nature and of social problems. . . . Our aim is to break down the barriers between the so-called natural and social sciences and show that they are really closely interrelated. Chemistry, physics and biology have an essential bearing on the condition of life, thought, and progressive readjustments. We can no longer expect to understand mankind without their help. The new and startling discoveries and theories in fields of psychology, anthropology, and history have a still more direct significance in the revision of political economy and politics.

In an effort to expand the curriculum, the New School welcomed the National Committee for Mental Hygiene to mount a series of lectures in psychology for the fall semester of 1921. These lectures would "introduce the study of the human mind as revealed in disease" and demonstrate how research in this new area of scholarship would enhance the work going on in sociology. Individual sessions would cover such topics as Arteriosclerosis and Senility, General Paresis and Syphilis, and Psychiatry and Eugenics.[36]

Determined to fill all the seats, the New School's business manager tried to interest the National Girl Scouts in the new lecture series, but the organization's education secretary turned him down, for reasons that must have made him shake his head in despair: "So far as the Girl Scouts are concerned," the secretary wrote, "this would not be a topic of immediate interest as our work is entirely with normal girls who are for the most part rather advanced types mentally. Our Leaders need, therefore, work in normal psychology."[37] In spite of this demoralizing response, the lecture series attracted such a large crowd that the New School invited the National Commission to teach again the next year, and again throughout the 1920s.

＝◆＝

As Alexander Meiklejohn had predicted, the decision to rely on an egalitarian administrative structure did not simplify matters for the New School's founders. Although the academic members of the board had enthusiastically supported the plan, nobody, it turned out, had the time or patience to do the work. When Robinson agreed to serve informally as the school's director, he warned that he would only be "available for consultation for some hours each week." With the board's agreement, he hired Emma Smith to take care of the daily business of running the school. As secretary, Smith also assumed the duties of treasurer, registrar, and publicist. A year later Robinson added a business manager and a librarian. And the year after that he turned the job over to Beard, who lasted about nine months. Not only did Robinson and Beard have little interest in running the institution, they did not like fund-raising either—nor were they any good at it, Johnson added in one of his acerbic asides.[38]

Although Johnson had been playing a minor role on the board during those first three years, he was paying enough attention to see that the founders did not have a viable financial plan to let the institution grow and become self-sufficient. As Beard envisioned things, after Straight, Sorchan, and a few other friends made the final payments on their ten-year pledges, the New School should live "on a hand-to-mouth plan" with no endowment. If they had a deficit at the end of an academic year, they would turn to their wealthy friends to bail them out—that is, as long as the New School was worth the investment.

Johnson warned the founders that Beard's plan was flawed, particularly if they wanted the New School to have an active research program: "I believed that the adult educational program could in the end approach self-support. But research . . . earns nothing." When Beard fiercely disagreed, Johnson let the matter drop. The board's wealthy friends easily could have provided the funds to seed a modest endowment, but after Beard made his "passionate renunciation," the committee voted "to let us take our annual chances of solvency."[39]

Robinson made an equally impassioned case against establishing a Board of Directors. As Johnson summarized his position, no matter how progressive the members of their board might be, they would eventually "thrust thick blunt fingers into the delicate texture of intellectual policy." Robinson eventually gave in after learning that no legal authority would provide the New School with an official charter if it did not have a board. Without a charter incorporating the New School, they would not be able to recruit students.

New York State denied them a charter all the same. Johnson gave no explanation for the rejection, stating only that "the New York educational authorities were cold to our petition for a charter."[40] Was it for political reasons? Red scare hysteria was sweeping through Albany at the time, and several members of the New School's proposed Board of Directors were under surveillance, including Beard and the editors of *The New Republic*. In the months preceding their attempt to get a charter, Johnson reported having had "the great privilege of being attended by some of the stupidest of mankind then drawn into the secret police." Rejected by the Board of Regents of the State of New York, they turned to the District of Columbia, which "would charter anything," Johnson added playfully.[41]

This, however, was no joking matter. The Board of Regents may have rejected their petition because they did not have enough money, as historians Peter Rutkoff and William Scott have suggested, but we cannot dismiss the possibility that it rejected them for political reasons as well.[42] No sooner did the New School open in February 1919 than state agents began sitting in on classes and newspapers started spreading rumors about "Who's Who" on the faculty and Board of Directors, suggesting ominously that Beard, Croly, Johnson, and Veblen might possibly be engaged in "shadow Hun, shadow Bolshevist, or other Un-American Propaganda."[43]

Even Dorothy Straight appeared in the tabloids and on the front page of *The New York Times*. When the New School opened in 1919, the heiress of the Payne Whitney fortune was still serving as president of the Junior League where, together with the League's founder, Mary Harriman Rumsey, she was recruiting wealthy women to support the settlement house movement and similar social welfare causes. On February 17, one week after classes began, the city's newspapers reported that a militant faction within the Junior League had staged a "revolt" against their president, after she had allegedly told them that they would have to attend lectures at the New School given by Charles Beard, James Harvey Robinson, and Thorstein Veblen. In a resolution sent to all twelve hundred members of the organization, the leaders of the rebelling faction proclaimed that "these men are not suitable teachers for the members of the League" and urged them not to go. The article in the *Times* made no mention of the League's progressive reputation, identifying it only as "a social organization composed of young women from families prominent in society."

A second article appeared the next day, after the officers of the League had met, "voted down the protest," and issued a statement of their own "dispelling the apprehension of some of the members that rules might require their attendance at lectures given in the New School of Social Research." A special Committee on Training Courses had been appointed, they explained, "at the request of the League to recommend a course of study and field work 'to increase the power of service to its members.'" The committee's members, which included Eleanor Roosevelt, had identified five possible schools to host the effort, one of which had indeed been the New School, but in the end, they had settled on Barnard College "in co-operation with the Department of Extension Teaching of Columbia University."[44]

The smear campaign against the New School continued into the next academic year. During the spring semester of 1920, at the height of the Red scare, New York State's Joint Legislative Committee Investigating Seditious Activities officially branded the New School as a radical institution. Popularly called the Lusk Committee after its chairman, State Senator Clayton Lusk, it issued a four-volume report in April under the title "Revolutionary Radicalism: Its History, Purpose and Tactics," in which it identified so-called subversive institutions across the state, including the New School. After conducting a thorough investigation, the Lusk Committee concluded that "The New School for Social Research . . . has been established by men who belong to the ranks of the near Bolshevik intelligentsia, some of them being too radical in their views to remain on the faculty of Columbia University."[45]

Needless to say, publicity of this kind did not help the New School recruit students. The founders, however, did not flinch. Despite the obvious risks, they continued to offer classes that "would neither attack nor defend Socialism, but explain its doctrines and principles and then leave the mind of the student open for freedom of action."[46] These included lectures in 1919 and 1921 on the Russian Revolution by the radical intellectual Moissaye J. Olgin, openly described in the announcement of courses as having played an active role in the revolutionary movement in Russia from 1900 to 1914. Olgin would teach again at the New School in the 1930s, by which time he was a prominent member of the National Committee of the Communist Party of the United States of America (CPUSA) and a translator into English of the works of Lenin. Among Olgin's other claims to fame, he founded and edited the Yiddish communist newspaper, *Morgen Freiheit.*[47]

⸺⬦⸺

The New School paid dearly during the early years for remaining true to its political convictions, weathering blistering attacks from critics who wanted to close the institution down. But the biggest threat came from the founders themselves in the spring of 1922 when Beard, Croly, Mitchell, and Robinson announced their intention to resign. Mitchell would leave at the end of the term. The others left the date open.

Before giving up entirely, Croly and Robinson tried to settle their differences a final time. Although they had lost their enthusiasm, they each presented a possible plan for moving forward. Carolyn Bacon did as well.[48] The board rejected all three of them, after which Croly recommended that they ask Johnson to play a mediating role. A good choice, potentially, given his temperament and strong ties to members of both factions. He had also wisely remained neutral during this latest struggle over the soul of the institution.

As Johnson tells the story, after the board appointed him to the task, Bacon, Putnam, and Sorchan invited him for tea and filled him in on the back story. The time had come, they told Johnson, for him to do more than referee. They wanted him to take over. As Johnson recorded what they said, "Nearly half the board was threatening to resign." Mitchell had already announced that he was returning to Columbia. Then, as if that were not enough,

> Robinson and Beard were [also] talking about resigning, and the rest of the faculty were at sixes and sevens. . . . It was my duty, Caroline Bacon asserted, to go into the whole problem of the school and work out a plan by which it could be saved. Any plan I might propose they would back up.[49]

Although Johnson never had any illusions about the financial health of the institution, what he discovered was much worse than he had anticipated. After examining the books, he interviewed the faculty. Angry and disaffected, the instructors had little to offer in the way of constructive advice. Having given up on the New School, Veblen wanted Johnson to find money for him alone, so that he might go off to England with a few research assistants "to show how the British Kingdom and Empire were just the publicity façade of British business." A project Johnson tried to support, in spite of himself, but he failed.[50]

About a week later, Johnson called the board and faculty together and presented them with two proposals for how they might proceed. One favored Robinson's model: expand the number of lecture courses and maintain a small group of researchers. The other leaned in the direction of Croly's: turn the New School into a research institute and build the infrastructure necessary for doing serious social research. Croly's faction rejected the lecture-friendly proposal out of hand, at which point several members of Robinson's camp agreed to switch sides. But Croly and his followers refused to accept the other proposal as well.

Why? As Croly's biographer David Levy explains it, the editor had lost hope. He "had placed so much importance on social education, the fact that a group of the country's leading progressives could not carry off harmoniously an experiment in advanced education for progressive purposes was a tragedy heavy with depressing implications." But Levy also admitted that Croly had another reason for pulling out—*The New Republic* had serious financial problems of its own and needed his full attention.[51]

After Croly's faction rejected Johnson's research-friendly proposal, Robinson's group reunited behind the lecture model only to have their plans upended several weeks later when Robinson and Beard resigned.[52] By this time, Croly had closed down his Labor Research Bureau, even though he remained on the New School's board for another four years.

6

ALVIN JOHNSON TAKES OVER

A lvin Johnson's description in *Pioneer's Progress* of how and when Charles Beard, Herbert Croly, and James Harvey Robinson resigned differs in significant details from what we read in the surviving documents of the period. Most surprising of all is his claim that Croly quit before the others, taking the school's most generous donors with him, in particular, Dorothy Straight. Beard was the first to leave, in 1922, followed by Robinson in 1923. Croly left in 1926 and Straight in 1930. Finally, although Johnson complained, before Straight stepped down from the board, she had made all outstanding payments on her pledge of $100,000.[1]

Johnson never forgave Straight for leaving the New School. In a confidential letter to a donor years later, he even accused the heiress of being an anti-Semite. In her defense, Straight had understandable reasons for resigning from the board. First and foremost, *The New Republic*, her primary commitment, was in serious financial difficulty. Second, her life circumstances had changed. Willard Straight had died of the Spanish flu in 1918. In 1925, Dorothy remarried Leonard Elmhirst, who was English, and left the United States to join her husband. Even so, she remained on the board four years longer than Croly.[2]

Johnson's account of Beard's and Robinson's resignations deserves closer attention as well. As he tells the story in his autobiography, after Croly rejected his proposals for restructuring the New School's academic programs, the nonteaching members of the Board of Directors called an emergency meeting for everyone but Robinson and Beard. Now that Robinson's faction was fully in charge of the academic side of things, the others decided to take control of the administration of the New School and this included making personnel changes in the office. The secretary and business manager whom Robinson had hired would have to go.

Since Johnson was the designated mediator, the board asked him to inform the historians: "I didn't like the job of breaking the news," Johnson confessed, but he fully agreed that the time had come to strengthen the management side of the school, adding defensively that Emma Smith and Lawrence Frank "could easily find other employment." Beard and Robinson were furious, in particular about Smith, who had left a secure job at Barnard to follow them to the New School.

A few hours later Robinson returned with Smith:

"Johnson, I'm quitting. I'm tired of the vexations the board has put me through. We were to be free; no interference in academic matters by the board. I've had to suffer more interference in these two years than in my entire career in the conventional institutions. I'm through."

"Beard is leaving too," said Emma Smith, the secretary. "So that's the end of the New School."

"Oh, I don't know," I [Johnson] said, trying to sound calm."

"Whom will you get to run the school?"

"If I can't get anyone else, I'll run it myself."[3]

Johnson had no regrets about letting Smith go. Describing her in *Pioneer's Progress* as "a determined young woman . . . [with] totalitarian attitudes," he found her very difficult to work with. Smith's personality, however, was not the only issue. He had somebody else in mind for her job, and that somebody was not an incidental detail, The departure of Beard and Robinson was another matter. Nobody had a bigger following than they. Johnson would have to win over the students to keep the New School running without them.

When the founders discussed the New School's governance structure, they imagined having students serve on the Board of Directors and on other major committees. Proceeding accordingly, they appointed two students to the board in 1920, but they lasted only a year. No one replaced them until 1924 when a reticent Clara Mayer finally accepted Johnson's invitation to serve.[4] Johnson did not expect to have so much trouble recruiting students to the board. He assumed, naively, that the students would choose their own representatives. Nobody, however, or so it seemed, had the authority to organize elections, largely because the New School had no campus life outside the classroom. Johnson set out to change that.

In the fall of 1922, Johnson invited students to take advantage of the opportunities the New School offered them inside and outside the classroom: "It is hoped," he wrote in the announcement of courses, "that the Students Association to which every person registered for a course is eligible may be strengthened and constitute itself as an active agency for the continuous expression of student opinion." Three students responded to his call and asked Johnson to tea: W. W. (William Warder) Norton, Mary Ely, and Mayer. These were precisely the kinds of people Johnson and Robinson had dreamed of attracting to the New School: upper class, politically progressive, and committed to strengthening the fledgling adult-education movement. In 1923, Norton established a publishing house to make available in print lectures delivered at Cooper Union's People's Institute, an adult-education program for the working classes and immigrants. Three years later Norton helped Johnson open a teacher training program in collaboration with the People's Institute to prepare instructors to work with adult students. As for Ely, she founded the American Association for Adult Education (AAAE), which remained closely tied to the New School. In 1938, the AAAE published a collection of Johnson's writings on adult education; and in 1939, it elected him president. But most important of all for the future of the New School was Mayer, Robinson's former student and the youngest daughter of a powerful real estate family—a fact that had not escaped Johnson.[5]

After meeting Mayer in the fall of 1922, Johnson recommended to the board that they appoint her as their student representative. Mayer demurred. Had members of her family cautioned her against it? All she said by way of explanation was that it took her "a couple of years to recover from the shock and consummate the deal."[6] When Mayer joined the Board of Directors, skeptics conceded that the New School might survive after all without Robinson and Beard. Following her appointment in 1924, the board attracted other new members, growing from an all-time low of ten in 1923 to eighteen in 1927, and twenty-nine in 1928. Mayer not only helped Johnson recruit new trustees but provided him with much needed administrative support, rising quickly through the ranks over the next seven years to become his second in command.

In 1931, Johnson made Mayer his assistant director. A few years later he promoted her to associate director and then dean. After he retired, Mayer became vice president, a position she held until 1961 when the New School's fourth president made the fateful decision to fire her, precipitating a financial crisis that led Johnson, now eighty-eight years old, to stage a palace coup.

Thanks to Mayer, Johnson gained entry into New York's community of wealthy German Jews, a number of whom gave generously to the New School for many years. Mayer also played a critical role in helping Johnson expand the original mission of the New School, turning it into a magnet for students interested in learning about the latest developments in psychoanalysis, literature, and the arts. As Johnson put it in a letter to Mayer many years later, "The New School is our child, yours and mine." Paying public tribute to her in *Pioneer's Progress*, he confessed that he could have (should have) written "a whole chapter on C.W. M, as she appears on reams of New School stationery. . . . It would have been hard for the New School to survive without the true friendship and the staunch support of the Mayer family."[7]

After Beard and Robinson resigned, Johnson added literature courses to the curriculum, a decision he highlighted in the 1922–23 announcement of courses: Although the "original purpose of the School" remained essentially the same, "no scheme of social instruction can be complete unless it makes a place for the study of the main tendencies in literature and the other arts." With that goal in mind, he invited Henry Wadsworth Longfellow Dana to join the faculty. Since losing his job at Columbia in 1917, Dana had been teaching part time at a number of progressive institutions, from the elite Bryn Mawr College to the socialist Rand School. In his first course for the New School, Dana introduced students to Social Forces in Modern Literature. Johnson also hired the playwright and *New Republic* theater critic Stark Young to host a lecture series on The Art of the Theatre. A year later he welcomed the noted architectural critic Lewis Mumford to the faculty.

During Johnson's first semester without Beard and Robinson, the New School ran more courses in psychology than in any other discipline, including one by the widely acclaimed behaviorist John Watson. The number and diversity of classes in philosophy expanded as well, including one by Horace Kallen, Beauty and Use, that explored the role of the arts in society. In this course, Kallen explained, students would explore "the connection between the fine arts and the other interests of the community." Remaining faithful to his friend, John Dewey stepped forward in the fall of 1922 and taught a class on The Significance of Modern Philosophy, as did other notable philosophers, including Bertrand Russell, who attracted the most attention, and Harry Overstreet, who went on to become a regular member of the faculty four years later. City College's legendary philosophy professor Morris Raphael Cohen gave a class the following spring and continued doing so for many years to come. Once again, almost every one of them wrote for *The New Republic*.

Although most everyone knew that Beard and Robinson had stopped teaching after the spring semester of 1922, the fall announcement still listed their courses, noting only that they would not be lecturing that year. Filling in for them were Harry Elmer Barnes and Carl Becker, with courses in European and

American history. Kallen helped out as well by offering a course in intellectual history on the Dominant Ideals of Western Civilization.

Rounding out the curriculum for the 1922–23 academic year, Johnson added a number of courses in the physical sciences, reminding students that these disciplines were as critical as the arts to a "scheme of social instruction." As part of this second initiative, Cohen gave a course that spring on Science and Contemporary Thought. Johnson never seriously considered creating a rigorous program in the hard sciences the way he had in psychology and the arts, but he invited internationally renowned scholars to lecture on cutting-edge subjects in their fields. In 1924, for example, the British biologist Julian Huxley lectured on Some Aspects of Evolutionary Biology.

As Johnson expanded the range of courses, he also tried to strengthen enrollment across the social sciences, especially in anthropology and economics. When Alexander Goldenweiser left the New School in 1926, Johnson invited Columbia University's Franz Boas to fill in for a couple of years. In economics, although he had lost Wesley Clair Mitchell, Johnson made sure he did not lose Frederick Macaulay, who, along with Mitchell, was a founding member of the National Bureau of Economic Research. He held onto Leo Wolman as well, the head of the Research Department of the Amalgamated Clothing Workers of America, and, of course, Thorstein Veblen, the most famous of them all. In 1922, Veblen even created a new course for Johnson to support his efforts to expand the curriculum on the Industrial Arts as a Factor in Human Behavior. The syllabus included a section on the "growth of the handicrafts" as an early example in the history of industrialization that transformed "the conditions of life and enforced new habits of conduct."[8]

Veblen, however, was a notoriously poor teacher, a reputation he assiduously cultivated at the New School. Having determined early on that adult students did not interest him, every semester he tried to discourage those who showed up by refusing to speak above a whisper. The irascible economist drove students away and Johnson around the bend: "I was so ungenerous," Johnson recalled, "as to regard this expiring voice as an affectation, for I had heard Veblen's strong, clear voice through the eucalyptus grove on the Stanford campus." Tired of Veblen's shenanigans, Johnson hid a microphone on the lectern, but to no avail. A stunned Veblen found the contraption and tossed it into the wastebasket, reporting triumphantly to Wolman a few days later: "Johnson thought he would make me popular. But I fooled him."

Veblen stopped teaching after the fall of 1924 for health reasons, he explained, but he did not retire officially until 1926. With the financial support of Mitchell and other loyal friends, he continued to receive a salary to do research, which was administered through the New School, but in the end, he did not have the strength to pursue his scholarship either. A broken man, he moved to California to live with his stepdaughter and died there in 1929. [9]

Before Johnson saddled himself with running the New School, he tried to find a seasoned academic administrator to take the job. When "no established scholar was willing to consider so precarious a venture," he hunted down his old English professor from the University of Nebraska, who had gone on to build a strong English department at the University of Iowa. By 1922, Clarke Ansley had abandoned academic life and was living on a farm in Michigan. Johnson promised Ansley that he would "hold the reins" until his fellow midwesterner "could adjust to the educational ways of the East"—something Ansley failed to do. Accepting his losses, Johnson "bid him farewell" at the end of the academic year and assumed the job himself.[10]

In 1925, Johnson launched his first fund-raising drive. In an attractively designed pamphlet, he proclaimed that the New School had established that it had "the right to live." Now it was "seeking the right to grow." The pamphlet urged students and friends to ensure the future of this innovative academic institution that offered high-level courses in vocational training to ambitious professionals looking to advance in their careers.

The New School's enrollment had nearly doubled since its founding, Johnson continued, and a "noteworthy and appreciative" student body was taking "courses of constructive value" taught by "distinguished" scholars and artists. Who were these students in 1925? They included 69 executives; 59 doctors and lawyers; 189 social workers and nurses; 162 teachers; 142 office workers and librarians; 42 research workers, accountants, and statisticians; 24 engineers and draftsmen; 8 artists; and hundreds of others who did not identify themselves by their professions. In the spirit of the founders' commitment to offer courses that addressed the challenges facing postwar America, Johnson described how every course analyzed contemporary issues from the disciplinary perspective of the instructor. Students, he continued, put together their own individualized course of study based on their specific interests and professional needs, choosing from a rich array of classes in psychology, political economy and labor movements, modern science and philosophy, literature and the theater, educational reform, and research methods. Finally, the pamphlet listed recent publications by some of the New School's most distinguished scholars, including works by Julian Huxley, Horace Kallen, Lewis Mumford, and John Watson.

After celebrating what the New School had already accomplished, the fund-raising document laid out what the institution could do if it had the resources it needed to expand. First, it would increase the number of professional training courses. Second, and most important, it would create a center of research as it had originally set out to do— a place where faculty and students would "make contributions of immediate practical importance to the literature of labor, agriculture, banking, applied psychology, education, religion."[11] The resources, however, did not materialize.

By 1927, Johnson had accepted the fact that the New School would not have the money any time soon to build a center of social science research. It did not even have the funds to subsidize the work of a handful students: "Special scholarship funds were urgently needed," he pleaded. Finally, in the fall 1929 class bulletin, he proudly announced that the New School could now offer twelve research fellowships and encouraged students to apply. But then the stock market crashed, putting an end to any thought about building a research program at the New School until Johnson opened the University in Exile in 1933.[12]

In 1927, Johnson also abandoned the idea of offering vocational courses with one major exception, the new program he had launched in 1926 with the Cooper Union's People's Institute to train adult education teachers.[13] The New School, he concluded, should focus instead on recruiting the kinds of students Robinson had envisioned from the very beginning. In the announcement of courses for the 1927–28 academic year, Johnson described the institution's ideal students as professionals who were seeking "cultural rather than vocational" enrichment. Having already found "their economic adjustment to life," or being well on their way to doing so, they came to the New School "primarily to satisfy purely intellectual needs." But that did not mean they were wasting their time, Johnson hastened to add. As students expanded their intellectual and cultural horizons, the courses they took would inspire new and innovative practical applications. Drawing loosely on the educational philosophy of his good friend Dewey, he explained how lawyers signing up for a course in psychology and physicians for one in the fine arts would "find values that are applicable at unexpected points to their professional work."[14]

Between 1926 and 1928, the New School began to offer an extraordinary range of courses in psychology and psychoanalysis. Leading figures representing almost every major faction in these dynamic new fields were lecturing at the school, preferably on different days of the week, Mayer added, to keep the warring parties apart. Among the instructors were former and current members of Freud's Vienna circle: Alfred Adler, Sándor Ferenczi, and Fritz Wittels. Teaching as well were distinguished U.S. psychologists identified with equally combative camps, among them the pioneer in behavioral psychology John Watson.[15]

The diversity of courses in psychology, Johnson wrote, reflected "the policy of the New School. It is a policy of freedom of instruction, analogous to that which prevailed in the European universities in the period of their greatest vigor." Mayer agreed, noting with pride that "a broadminded psychiatrist" had told her: "How lucky Dr. Johnson is not a psychologist. No psychologist would have dared to attempt such a thing."[16] Johnson continued welcoming controversial figures in these areas well into the 1930s, when, for example, he added the German psychoanalyst Karen Horney to the mix. Together with Adler, Horney had challenged orthodox psychoanalysis—most famously, in her case, Freud's theory of female sexuality.

The New School also expanded in the arts. In the fall of 1926, it offered a course on the motion picture—the first of its kind ever taught in an academic institution and the subject of enthusiastic notices in the press.[17] Other courses raised hackles, for example a series of lectures on modernism. Two days before Modern Art was scheduled to meet for the first time, an article appeared in *The New York City Telegraph* telling students to stay away.

Johnson had asked the novelist and critic Waldo Frank to host the course. A regular contributor to *The New Yorker* and *The New Republic*, Frank had lined up an impressive roster of critics and artists to lecture in the class over the course of the semester, among them the literary critic Edmund Wilson and the music critic Paul Rosenfeld, both of whom wrote for *The New Republic* as well. Frank had also invited Alfred Stieglitz, the photographer and owner of the Intimate Gallery, famous for exhibiting the best avant-garde painters in the country, including the work of his wife, Georgia O'Keefe. But for the journalist in the *Telegraph*, the course would be a sham: "Not only do we suffer the bores gladly, but we are willing to pay them for the suffering that they inflict on the rest of the world."[18]

In 1927, Johnson asked Gorham Munson, the literary critic and contributor to *The New Republic*, to run a new series of workshops for aspiring writers, beginning with a course on Style and Form in American Prose. Those accepted into the class would have the unique opportunity of publishing some of their own work in *The Figure in the Carpet*, a new literary magazine the students would edit themselves.[19] Over the course of that academic year, the New School also offered an outstanding selection of classes in the fine arts and literature, including Art and the Actual, with the art critic and collector Leo Stein. The poet Alfred Kreymborg lectured on modern poetry in the United States. Then, most exciting of all, singled out for special billing, was the "talented young composer Aaron

Copland," who gave a course on contemporary music "followed by six concerts of modern music arranged by Edgar Varèse and Aaron Copland."[20]

—◆—

According to music historian Sally Bick, the New School made a significant contribution to the development of "a strong national musical culture in the United States" during the 1920s and 1930s. Its impact went unacknowledged for years, she explained, because anticommunist witch hunts succeeded in silencing leading figures in American modern music well into the 1960s and 1970s. When people such as Copland and Charles Seeger finally opened up, they recalled how Johnson had provided them with "classroom and concert space for musical activities sponsored by CPUSA [Communist Party of the United States of America] or Marxist-influenced organizations."[21] Reminiscing in 1984, Copland wrote, "Looking back at my lecture notes fills me with renewed wonder and respect for the New School for the opportunity it gave me to explore such topics," by which he meant musical ideas that gave shape to the "American School of Composers."[22] In 1927, Copland persuaded Johnson to invite Henry Cowell, an exciting young composer, to teach at the New School.

Three years later, Johnson decided that the New School should open a program in modern music. Following the same model he was using for creative writing, he asked Cowell, not Copland, to direct it, a decision that probably explains, Bick suggests, why Copland stopped teaching at the New School for five years (1930 to 1935). Johnson chose Cowell because the young composer had an innovative idea about how to put the program together that diverged significantly from what other universities were doing in music at the time and in ways that spoke to the social sciences. Instead of focusing on modern American and European music alone, Cowell proposed offering courses in non-European traditions, including the music of "indigenous" peoples. To help him run the program, Cowell persuaded Johnson to hire Charles Seeger, his former teacher at Berkeley. Cowell also asked Johnson to offer a visiting position to the German ethnomusicologist Erich von Hornbostel, with whom Cowell had studied in Berlin in the late 1920s. Although the German scholar turned down the New School in 1930, he gratefully accepted Johnson's second invitation three years later to join the University in Exile.

—◆—

When Cowell approached Johnson about Hornbostel, he knew that the New School's director was deeply immersed in the new scholarship coming out of postwar Germany—in the social sciences primarily, but for Johnson the social sciences encompassed the arts. The same was true for Johnson's former colleague and dear friend Edwin Seligman, with whom he had been collaborating for several years on the publication of a fifteen-volume *Encyclopaedia of the Social Sciences*.

In 1926, Seligman asked Johnson to serve as the associate editor of the *Encyclopaedia*, a project that included contributions from "2,000 workmen," most of them scholars from the United States and Europe.[23] Defying the skeptics, Seligman and Johnson succeeded in publishing all fifteen volumes between 1930 and 1935, admittedly to mixed reviews, but even their critics conceded that this ambitious work, which had the financial backing of the Carnegie Corporation, Russell Sage, and Rockefeller Foundations, would make a significant contribution to the advancement of knowledge in the social sciences.[24] As associate editor, Johnson visited Germany to recruit social scientists to write articles for the different volumes. Most of them were economists, but he also met Max Wertheimer, one of the founders of "Gestalt" psychology. At the time, Wertheimer was doing research with Hornbostel on the psychological impact of music.[25]

It took courage during the late 1920s to identify the arts as an important subject of inquiry for the social sciences. The academic societies sponsoring the *Encyclopaedia* wanted to see social scientists conduct empirical research that met the rigorous methodological and theoretical standards of the "hard" sciences.[26] The two editors agreed, at least in principle, but Seligman concluded his brief introduction to Volume 1 with a statement defending the inclusion of the arts that was reminiscent of the one Johnson had written in 1922 for the New School's announcement of courses:

> Finally, we come to the realm of art. It goes without saying that art as creative activity stands in contrast with science, whose objective is analysis and understanding. But artistic creation is dominated by values and these are, at least in part, of social origin. In the history of art there is much that helps explain social institutions and vice versa. No one who wishes to understand the operation of social laws in the modern world can afford to overlook the evidence offered by the arts.[27]

For the entry on music, Johnson recruited Seeger, Cowell, and Helen Roberts. He asked them to use the concept of "social function" as the "guiding thread," then apply the "developmental and comparative method" to analyze how music served different social functions across time and space, beginning with primitive societies—"insofar as the material was available"—moving next from Antiquity to the Middle Ages, and from the era of absolute monarchies to liberal democratic states. "We'd also like some account taken of the initially parallel, later divergent streams of folk music and 'art' music."[28] A tall order, but very much in line with what Cowell and Seeger had already been doing at the New School.

—◆—

The New School's art programs continued to grow during the late 1920s and early 1930s as Johnson added new courses in music, theater, architecture, and the plastic arts, all of them taught by leading figures in their fields. By the early 1930s, almost every significant figure in the avant-garde had lectured, performed, or given studio courses at the New School—or so it seemed. In 1931, Johnson asked Frank Lloyd Wright to lecture on American architecture and decoration; in 1934, he invited Berenice Abbott to open a studio art program in photography. And the following year he appointed the Ecuadoran painter Camilo Egas art director, accepting the fact that he needed someone to coordinate all the courses the New School was offering in drawing, etching, painting, sculpture, photography, and crafts.[29]

Johnson did not forget his earlier commitment to the writing program either. In addition to expanding the number of classes in the craft of writing—some of which he taught himself—Johnson invited internationally renowned writers and critics to lecture and read from their work, among them the poets Robert Frost and T. S. Eliot, *The Nation*'s drama critic Joseph Wood Krutch, and the expatriate sensation Gertrude Stein, who lectured on Poetry and Grammar at the New School in November 1934 as she set off on her six-month tour across the United States.[30]

But the greatest expansion took place in the performing arts. In 1931 Johnson persuaded Doris Humphrey to take over the school's fledgling program in modern dance. During her first semester as director, Humphrey gave demonstration lectures in Dance Forms and Their Developments in conversation with her guest artist Martha Graham. She also began technique classes for selected New School students.[31] In 1933, Harold Clurman, the founder of the Group Theatre, taught a course on The World of Theatre, while other members of his company offered A Critical Analysis of Contemporary Plays. Then, in 1940, the New School established its own Studio Theatre and Dramatic Workshop under the direction of the German refugee dramatist Erwin Piscator. Over the years, Piscator recruited an outstanding faculty to work with him, including Clurman's legendary colleagues Stella Adler and Lee Strasberg, whose classes famously trained students in Konstantin Stanislavsky's "method acting" techniques.

During the late 1920s and early 1930s, the New School gave performances of avant-garde music, theater, and dance. In addition to the annual concerts organized by Cowell and Seeger, in 1927 Johnson persuaded Eva Le Gallienne to give benefit performances of Henrik Ibsen's *The Master Builder*, featuring the actors of her new repertory company. In 1931, he invited the Fortune Players to stage innovative productions of eighteenth-, nineteenth-, and twentieth-century plays. Former apprentices of Eva Le Gallienne ran open rehearsals of ten European plays in 1933. And, most exciting of all, Martha Graham and her modern dance company gave a series of "revolutionary" concerts at the New School during that same year.[32]

With the exception of *The Master Builder*, all of these performances took place in an ultramodern egg-shaped auditorium, designed by the Austrian architect Joseph Urban for the New School's sensational new home in Greenwich Village. Located on Twelfth Street between Fifth and Six Avenues, the building opened its doors on January 1, 1931, in the depths of the depression.

As Johnson waited on New Year's Day for the first group of visitors to arrive, he dashed off a letter to Agnes de Lima, boasting triumphantly about what he had managed to pull off. "Out of our poverty has risen far and away the most interesting building that has been erected in New York in many a year." Boastful? Perhaps, but others agreed: "at least 10,000 people visited the School . . . some of them stayed for hours."[33] Yes, Johnson conceded, they had taken a huge financial risk, one that he knew would plague the New School for years, but he never regretted the decision. Nor did it stop him from sinking the New School further into debt two years later when he opened the University in Exile. Despite all the headaches, the new building only made him bolder.

So much for the rhetoric. How did Johnson finance Urban's architectural triumph at a time like this? The New School was already facing serious financial difficulties in the months leading up to the crash on Wall Street. By December 1928, Dorothy (Straight) Elmhirst and other members of the original Organizing Committee had made the last payments on their ten-year pledges. Without their annual contributions, the New School would have a big hole in its operating budget for the coming year. Then during the spring of 1929, Johnson learned that they would have to leave their townhouses in Chelsea by the fall of 1930. The owners had sold the land to a big developer. Although the timing was bad, Johnson was delighted with the news. He had been trying to persuade the board for a year already that they needed to move. Now, they had no choice.

When Johnson informed the board of directors that they had lost their lease, one recalcitrant member suggested that they "hibernate for a year." Johnson objected. Gathering his old friends around him, he asked them, Mayer recalled,

> whether in their judgment the New School still had its contribution to make to the future or whether the time had come to terminate this ten-year experiment and call it well done. It was an unpleasantly close call, but his old friends stood by—as they have ever since. Caroline Bacon was enlisted to solve the building problem—a *New York Times* photograph which we still have, shows her studying the plans with Alvin and their gifted designer, Joe Urban.[34]

Johnson had approached the Board of Directors for the first time in the spring of 1928. In order to survive financially, he explained, the New School had to increase enrollments significantly, something it could not do if it remained on the far west side of Manhattan. He based his argument on the results of a survey he had recently commissioned that confirmed what he had been suspecting for a long time. Students who relied on public transportation had difficulty getting to the New School unless they lived along the route of the Ninth Avenue elevated trains. "Vast areas of the Greater City were a desert, as a source of students." Although students also had the crosstown bus on Twenty-Third Street, those interviewed complained that the service was too "slow, uncertain, and uncomfortable, especially in stormy weather."

Even at their current location, Johnson continued, the student body had tripled in size, forcing the New School to rent additional classroom space at Rumford Hall on West Forty-First Street for the coming fall semester. Clearly, the New School could grow significantly bigger if it moved to a more central location. Johnson then presented the directors with a proposal that outlined what this would entail, which they promptly rejected.[35]

When they learned, however, in the spring of 1929 that the New School had lost its lease, they agreed to give Johnson a chance. Even though they were still dubious, they authorized him to form a committee to look for a site, find an architect, and draw up a plan for financing a new building. At the end of the meeting, Johnson's good friend Maurice Wertheim spoke on behalf of the others, summing up only partially in jest what his fellow board members were thinking: "You can't do it, Alvin. But if you do succeed, you'll belong either in the penitentiary or in Wall Street."[36]

Johnson's account in *Pioneer's Progress* about what happened next reads like a fairy tale. Had he not told the same story in January 1931 as he welcomed students to the new building, we could have dismissed it as a classic example of his mixing fact with fiction for literary or rhetorical purposes. This time, however, he recorded the events faithfully.

With the skeptical blessings of the board, Johnson approached Daniel Cranford Smith, a retired businessman and one of the New School's most devoted students. Everyone called him "Uncle Dan." Smith owned a row of town houses on Twelfth Street between Fifth and Sixth Avenues, two of which he rented out. He and his wife lived in the third. Johnson told Uncle Dan that his three properties were ideally situated for the New School. If he agreed to sell, the Board of Directors would build him and his wife a large, sunny apartment on the top floor of the new building, with a spectacular view of the city, high above the other houses in the neighborhood. They would also provide him with an outside terrace for a garden, in a space far superior to the one he now had in his shady courtyard. Instead of giving Smith cash for his properties, the New School would purchase bonds at a price determined by an "honest appraiser" of what the land and houses were worth. These bonds, Johnson admitted, "won't be a gilt-edge investment, but neither are your real-estate equities."

After consulting with his wife, Smith agreed. The New School then purchased a fourth lot next door to the other three, financing it with "a tissue of equities and mortgages" woven together, Johnson added, with the help of some of "the most experienced and resourceful real-estate operators in New York":[37] Clara Mayer's brothers Charles and Albert Mayer; William Taylor of the Taylor Construction Company; and Joseph Milner, a New School trustee and a member of Johnson's subcommittee. Charles Mayer introduced Johnson to the internationally renowned architect and stage designer Joseph Urban. The two men hit it off right away. As Urban told *The New York Times*, he and Johnson had a great deal in common: "We talked the same language, in philosophy, in art, and in our attitude toward modern life. When I left him after our first conversation, I had the architectural vision of the New School."[38]

Urban had come to the United States from Vienna in 1911 to design stage sets for the Boston Opera, after which he received commissions from other opera houses and theaters and decided to remain in the country. Before long, he was also working in Hollywood. When Johnson met Urban in the spring of 1929, the architect was at the height of his fame, having recently completed the Ziegfeld Theatre in midtown Manhattan, designed in the Art Deco style. His next big commission was from the Metropolitan Opera Company—the blueprints for which he had just completed when the stock market crash put an end to the project.[39]

Urban agreed to design a building for the New School for far less money than he usually charged and to begin working right away before Johnson had even begun his fund-raising campaign. By the end of the summer, the architect delivered his plans for the building, which the New School's director shared with the board in early September. The response was disappointing, Johnson reported, until Emily Putnam, "our recognized arbiter of good taste and good sense," helped sway the others. Everyone had signed on just before Wall Street collapsed a few weeks later.

The timing "was unpropitious," Johnson conceded, but he convinced the board to let him proceed. Even though the "financial collapse" had ruined, or seriously compromised, the fortunes of many, friends stepped forward to help Johnson organize a benefit dinner at the St. Regis Hotel for February. *The New York Times* announced the gala in the same issue that it ran a long article about the new building and Johnson's pioneering ideas about continuing education. The New School, the *Times* reported, offered adults the opportunity to "pick up the culture that had to be missed" during their college years, when they understandably focused on courses that would "equip [them] with quick progress in a vocation." Quoting Johnson, the article explained that the human mind, like the body, needed constant exercise throughout an individual's adult life. Hence the importance of the New School's program in continuing education.[40]

The New School hoped to raise $500,000 at the benefit dinner in addition to the $100,000 the Mayer family had already contributed. To make the event a success, Johnson leaned not only on members of the Board of Directors to invite their rich friends but also on the special advisory committee he had formed in 1925 to help the school with fund-raising. The committee included well-known figures in art, education, politics, philanthropy, and business, some of whom were mentioned by name in *The New York Times*, for example, Eleanor Roosevelt, already a well-known activist for progressive causes and the wife of New York State's governor, and the novelist Willa Cather, whom Johnson had known since his student days at the University of Nebraska. Did the benefit succeed in reaching its goal? What we know for sure is that by the time the building opened in January 1931, the New School had spent a little over $1 million, money raised through a combination of bonds, mortgages, and gifts. An impressive sum, given the times, but it was still not enough. As he welcomed students to the building that winter, Johnson asked them to step forward again and help the New School raise the final $50,000.[41]

——◆——

On January 4, *The New York Times* published a detailed article on the building with photos of the New School's "spacious quarters" on Twelfth Street, which it described as having "discreet originality":

The façade is dignified, thoroughly modern without being freakish, and "functional" in the least wabbly sense of that rather elastic term. . . .

The most conspicuous feature of the interior is the auditorium, of ample dimension and oval-shaped, rising to an oval-shaped dome of minutely patterned perforated metal. The dome is arranged in layers, and . . . suggests an interesting method of lighting.

The author of the article was the art critic Edward Alden Jewell, who had already written a long and enthusiastic piece about the building in November, highlighting the fact that Johnson had asked world famous artists to decorate the walls of several interior spaces. In his earlier piece, Jewell noted, "Modern architecture calls for modern murals. . . . American buildings of 1930 must be decorated, if at all, in a spirit expressing harmony with both the architecture of this period and with the life of which this architecture is an increasingly logical expression. The New School for Social Research . . . has responded handsomely to the call."

Johnson persuaded the American Thomas Hart Benton and the Mexican José Clemente Orozco to paint murals in time for the grand opening for no compensation other than the cost of materials. When Jewel wrote his first article in November, Benton had nearly completed his sweeping panorama of "America Today" on ten individual canvas panels using a thick, gluelike medium called gesso. Enthralled by what he saw, Jewell described the images so vividly that they seemed to walk off the canvas and onto the floor of the artist's studio.

In two of the panels the artist mirrors the life of a great American city. We find fitted into a powerfully constructed mosaic the feverish struggle of Wall Street, the jazz of cabarets, the unending grist of the movies, the soda fountain, the child welfare clinic, the allure of the circus, the evangelist drawing in hysterical converts, the rest and the romance of the city parks, the prize-fight, the night life of a city's streets, the stoical packed patience of the subway.

In other panels we see men and machines: men building cities: tapping a great blast furnace at night, pouring molds, with a Bessemer converter looming mightily in the background; miners bend to their task; we see men refining oil, piping, drilling, herding sheep and cattle—responsible for the "changing west"; we see the aviator winging on his way, carrying mail, carrying passengers, conquering a new and tricky element; we explore the realms of agriculture and of the woodsman with his saw; wheat is reaped and threshed; corn, pork, and timber are prepared for the use of man; power: here are the locomotive and the Diesel engine, the dynamo, the dam, the spillway, all in full operation, all requiring the perpetual labor of man; great rivers with their traffic carry us up and down a land of ever-changing horizons, a land full of men who are building a young nation toward unglimpsed future goals.[42]

When the building opened on January 1, Orozco had still not completed his mural, giving Jewell an excuse to reserve judgment until he had. The art critic returned to Benton's mural instead, reporting that "America Today," looked even better "than one dared hope....This ought to prove one of the most interesting modern rooms in America." When Jewell finally reviewed Orozco's frescoes several weeks later, he panned them mercilessly, as did almost every other critic.[43]

⸺⬥⸺

Despite the disappointing reviews of Orozco's mural, the building was a huge critical success. Not surprising, perhaps, given the architect, but for those involved with the construction process it was a miracle. As Clara Mayer tells the story, in the fall of 1929, the board asked her brother Albert to supervise the work. In no time, he and Urban were no longer talking to one another, forcing Johnson and Clara to serve as go-betweens, which placed the two of them in the impossible position of trying to mediate between an irate architect who insisted on maintaining the integrity of his design and a stubborn contractor determined to keep the costs down.[44] The New School, in the meantime, was strapped for money, obliging Johnson to make draconian cuts in the academic programs.

During the spring of 1930, Johnson reduced the size of the faculty from twenty-six to sixteen. Over the summer his staff packed up everything and vacated the Chelsea townhouses, even though the Twelfth Street building would not be ready for another six months. With the school homeless and nearly broke, Johnson put together a skeletal program for the fall semester in rented classroom space at 66 Fifth Avenue, between Twelfth and Thirteenth streets, in the same building as Martha Graham's dance studio.[45]

For the grand opening in January 1931, Johnson pulled out all the stops, putting together an outstanding semester of courses, taught by forty instructors, including such luminaries as Harold Laski, Julian Huxley, Robert Frost, and Thomas Hart Benton, on a wide range of subjects that promised to attract many more students than they could have ever accommodated on West Twenty-Third Street. The strategy worked, at least up to a point. "Twice as many" students registered for courses as "in a similar term in the old place," but the school needed "five times as many."[46]

Everyone was understandably worried. Two months into the term, the Mayer brothers and Joe Milner suggested that Johnson let go of the business side of the New School. Seething with rage, he vented to Agnes de Lima:

They wanted a business man to take care of the business side, I to confine myself to the job of dean of the faculty. The fact that starting out with $20,000 my business manipulations had set up a plant costing a million, and a kind of plant which had given us vastly more publicity and general discussion than Al Smith's $60,000,000 Empire State building, appeared to my conspiring friends as no evidence of business capacity. Nor that my overriding them at every point has given us something of enduring excellence, which has won the enthusiastic interest of all the architects that are worthwhile. Nor that we have become the natural center of any liberal interest. . . . We have twice as many registered for courses as in any winter term in our history, three times as many people paying single admissions. The whole enterprise set up and put through by me and paid for by my anguish: yet I have no business ability. Well, I took an ax, and the Mayers are reduced to abject submission. I'm looking for Joe Milner.

I was once a mild and gentle person wasn't I, Agnes? I was patient with everybody, little disposed to put my will into my arguments. I seem to have been sent back to the foundry and recast into something with much harsher lines.[47]

Two years later Johnson set the New School on a course that would sink it further into debt, but this time Milner and the Mayers applauded.

As we turn now to the founding of the University in Exile, the best account we have are the letters Johnson wrote to de Lima during the spring and summer of 1933. Invaluable as well are the press releases de Lima wrote in later years, after she joined the New School in the early 1940s, about the next wave of émigré scholars who arrived from Belgium and France. She also saved boxes of news clippings, letters, and other documents, all carefully cataloged for the New School's archives and for Yale, where Johnson's official papers reside.

De Lima served as director of publicity from 1940 to 1959, during which time she worked for three presidents. "Respected and beloved," to quote the *New School Bulletin*, she had a great deal in common with the women who supported the New School during its first ten years, both financially and intellectually. A respected journalist, feminist, and political activist, she was best known for her articles on early childhood education. She was also the mother of Johnson's eighth child. The two never married, but they remained very close friends until the end of their lives.

Like the women affiliated with the New School during the early days, de Lima came from a wealthy family and had the financial independence she needed to defy the social conventions of the day. As a journalist and activist, she belonged to the same circles of progressive women whose names appear on various New School documents dating back to the interwar years—Dorothy Straight, Emily Putnam, Charlotte Sorchan, Elsie Clews Parsons, Caroline O'Day, Willa Cather, Eleanor Roosevelt, and Clara Mayer. Each of these women struck out on her own, freeing herself from society's constraints in different ways. In de Lima's case, she embraced the radical teachings of Parsons, taking great pride in the fact that she had chosen to live an emancipated life, in both her professional work and her intimate relationships.

Agnes de Lima was the daughter of a prominent Sephardic Jewish banking family from Curaçao that came to the United States before she was born. Raised in New Jersey, she attended Vassar College, where she majored in English. She also studied history with Lucy Salmon, Charles Beard's good friend, whom de Lima credited with having radicalized her. After graduating from Vassar in 1908, she moved to New York City and did a graduate degree in social work. Before long she had become an activist in the school reform movement and a journalist.

Johnson met de Lima in 1916 through his *New Republic* colleague Randolph Bourne. Although many remember Bourne for his articles on pacifism, he also wrote on education for *The New Republic*. De Lima and he got to know one another in 1914, while they were covering a famous controversy in New York over whether the city should adopt the Gary (Indiana) Plan for its public schools. Popular among education reformers, the plan's supporters argued that it would provide students with smaller, more specialized classes and administrators with increased efficiency.

Bourne and de Lima became good friends, and through de Lima Bourne met the woman he hoped to marry, the beautiful and "bewitchingly provocative" Esther Cornell. A Bryn Mawr graduate and aspiring actress, Cornell shared an apartment in Greenwich Village with de Lima. When Bourne fell madly in love with the aspiring actress, the young woman welcomed his attention, but he "never really conquered her," de Lima wrote to a friend. "No man ever did," she continued, "which accounts for the extraordinary hold she always held over them." By 1922, that included Johnson.

Between 1916 and 1918 Bourne spent a lot of time with Cornell and de Lima, a detail often recorded by his biographers. Over the summer of 1916, they rented a house together on the Jersey Shore, and Johnson, among other friends, visited on the weekends. The following summer they went to Woods Hole, Massachusetts, by which time the United States had entered the war, and Bourne's pacifism was arousing suspicion. In John Dos Passos's trilogy, *USA*, the novelist repeated the frequently told story of a policeman stopping the three friends while they were dancing on the beach and accusing them of signaling German submarines.[48] In December 1918, Bourne died of the Spanish flu in de Lima and Cornell's apartment on Eleventh Street.

Bourne knew that Johnson and de Lima were having an affair and had been thinking about having a baby together. The child's "possible advent interested him deeply," de Lima wrote to a mutual friend. During this same period, de Lima became a frequent visitor in the Johnsons' home, often babysitting for the children. By all reports, she was treated like a member of the family.

How did Johnson's wife cope with the affair? We do not have her side of the story, but she too was an independent spirit. The daughter of a wealthy Nebraska family, Edith Henry had defied her parents' wishes and married Johnson, her college sweetheart, in 1904, two years after he had finished his PhD and was teaching at Columbia. Although the family was not enthusiastic about the union, there is no evidence that the Henrys ever cut their daughter off. She probably had the means to leave Johnson if she had chosen to do so. She did not.

Was it the times? As difficult as it remains today for a wife to leave a philandering husband, it was considerably worse then, even for women belonging to Edith Johnson's social class. But not everyone put up with husbands having multiple affairs. Nor did every academic institution disregard wagging tongues, something Thorstein Veblen learned the hard way. Mrs. Veblen's bitter complaints about her husband's alleged dalliance cost him his job at Stanford.

In 1909, the president of Stanford University forced the economist to resign because Veblen "seems unable to resist the 'femme mécomprise' [sic]," David Starr Jordan wrote in confidence to Harry Pratt Judson, the president of the University of Chicago. Jordan learned about Veblen's alleged indiscretions from, among others, the economist's wife: "The university cannot condone these matters, much as its officials may feel compassion for the individual." Jordan shared his decision with Judson because Veblen had resigned from Chicago three years earlier for reasons that historians continue to debate.[49]

The New School left Johnson alone even though he stirred things up plenty for the institution as well as his wife and de Lima, when, in 1922, he hired his latest lover, Esther Cornell, to work as his secretary. In spite of it all, Johnson remained the esteemed director of the New School and devoted companion—at least in his fashion—of the two most important women in his life. By all reports he was also a loving father and grandfather. Although things must have been complicated between Edith Johnson and Agnes de Lima, we know that they shared many interests, including a deep commitment to new experiments in primary- and secondary-school education. In Edith's case, she was a pioneer in the home-schooling movement.

Since Johnson bounced the family around a great deal between 1906 and 1917, during his period as a peripatetic professor, Edith decided to educate their children at home, a practice she continued even after they settled down permanently in New York. According to Johnson and their children, Edith was a wonderful teacher and brilliant scholar. As an undergraduate at the University of Nebraska, she, like Alvin, had majored in the classics. After they married, she studied philosophy at Columbia with John Dewey. Her dissertation, "The Argument of Aristotle's Metaphysics," was published in 1906.[50]

When de Lima gave birth to Sigrid in December 1921, Edith knew that her husband was the baby's father. Although she certainly could have made things difficult, she did not stand in the way of Agnes and Sigrid visiting the family regularly. She did, however, keep her children from learning that Sigrid was their half-sister until after they were grown.

Johnson played an important role in Sigrid's life, but he did not recognize his daughter officially, a decision de Lima fully endorsed. On the child's birth certificate, de Lima identified the Scottish folklorist Andrew Lang as Sigrid's father, an unlikely candidate had anyone bothered to check, given the fact that Lang had died nine years earlier. "That was a family joke," explained Sigrid's daughter, Alison de Lima Greene:

> When my grandmother went to the hospital to deliver my mother, she didn't want to reveal who the father was. So, on my mother's birth certificate (which is public record) she said it was Andrew Lang, who was famous for collecting various volumes of Fairy Tales (in other words, a fictional/fairy tale "father"). However, the fact that she named my mother "Sigrid" with its Nordic connotations points pretty directly to my mother's heritage.

Alvin and Edith Johnson gave three of their children Nordic first names as well: Thorold, Ingrith, and Astrith. They also changed the last name of their seven children to Deyrup, the patronymic Johnson's Danish father had given up when he entered the United States. Counting Sigrid, Johnson had six girls and two boys: Dorothy, who died young, became a painter; Thorold, a chemist; Alden, a lawyer; Natalie, a doctor; Ingrith, a zoologist; Felicia, an economist; Sigrid, a novelist; and Astrith, a painter.

Three of the children taught or studied at the New School: Felicia joined the Graduate Faculty in 1949 and retired in 1969. She also gave courses in Continuing Education on U.S. economic history. Astrith taught batik and fabric painting in Continuing Education between 1960 and 2001, and Sigrid participated in the New School's writing workshop that Hiram Haydn had taken over from Gorham

Munson. In 1953, while still studying with Haydn, Sigrid won the prestigious Prix de Rome, giving the illustrious program a winning streak—her classmate William Styron had won the prize the year before. Five of the eight children married, but only three of them had children: Thorold, Alden, and Sigrid.

══◆══

Several months after Sigrid was born, Robinson and Beard resigned from the New School because, Johnson explained in *Pioneer's Progress*, the board had decided to fire Emma Smith and Lawrence Frank. Although Johnson described the incident in surprising detail, he skipped briskly over the fact that he—not the board—had replaced the "totalitarian" Smith with "the bewitchingly beautiful" Esther Cornell. The board apparently ignored the scandal—they had enough on their hands with Beard and Robinson storming out. But Johnson's friends in the wider feminist community did not give him a free pass. Not because they objected to him "cheating" on his wife and on the mother of his out-of-wedlock child—sexual fidelity was passé—but because they did not approve of the way he treated women.

Elsie Clews Parsons confronted Johnson directly in 1923, about a year after he and de Lima had broken up. She accused him of "lacking candor" in the way he communicated with women. This upset Johnson a great deal. In an effort to plead his case, he wrote an eloquent, if not entirely persuasive, letter in response that went on for four pages. There was a difference, he proclaimed, between being "candid," which he did "not want to be," and being "honest," which he firmly believed he was.[51]

De Lima responded to Johnson's "lack of candor" by getting on with her life. She renewed her relationship with the Canadian journalist Arthur McFarlane, to whom she had been engaged before taking up with Johnson. They married in 1925. Between 1922 and 1927, she wrote regularly for *The New Republic* and *The Nation* on education, republishing a number of those articles in 1926 in a volume dedicated to her three-and-a-half-year-old daughter, "from whom I have learned more about education than from any pedagogue or book." *Our Enemy the Child* remains a classic in the literature on school reform to the present day.[52]

Johnson's passionate affair with Cornell burned out quickly, we are told, even though Cornell remained his secretary for eight years—until the New School moved into the new building on Twelfth Street and Johnson appointed Mayer his assistant director.[53] For the sake of the child, de Lima and Johnson kept in touch, but communications remained strained until the late 1920s, at which point they resumed their close friendship, if not their affair. The rapprochement occurred around the same time that de Lima divorced her husband and left New York, first for Mexico to see her ailing father, then, after he died, to Palo Alto, where Johnson's sister lived. A practicing physician, Johnson's sister, also named Edith, welcomed mother and child warmly and helped de Lima get work in the progressive Peninsula School. During the summer months, mother and child drove back to New York to see Johnson and the family.

Johnson wrote to de Lima about the founding of the University in Exile while she was living in Palo Alto. In 1937, de Lima moved back to New York with her sixteen-year-old daughter and settled down in a house that Johnson helped her find near his family's home in Nyack. For the first few years, she worked as a freelance writer; then Johnson hired her as his director of publicity. In addition to her press releases for the New School, she continued writing about education reform, attracting critical attention in 1942 for *The Little Red School House*, an extended essay on the well-known progressive primary school in Manhattan.

The full story of de Lima's relationship with Johnson will soon appear in Andra Makler's biography of the education reformer. Let us turn now to the founding of the University in Exile, reconstructed in part with the letters Johnson wrote to the woman he called his "soul mate" to the end of his life.[54]

PART II

The Universities in Exile

(1933–1945)

7

THE FOUNDING OF THE
GERMAN UNIVERSITY IN EXILE

lvin Johnson went to Germany in the summer of 1932 to meet
with colleagues contributing to *The Encyclopaedia of the Social
Sciences*. He had visited the country before, the first time with
Bernard Baruch in the early 1920s, where he witnessed the punishing impact
of the Versailles Treaty on the German economy. During that earlier trip, the
two men observed how the National Socialists and other parties critical of
the governing Social Democrats were exploiting the crisis for political gain.
Not that anyone seemed particularly worried about the Nazis at the time, not
even in Munich where party thugs had succeeded in staging their "Beer Hall
Putsch" in the fall of 1923. Government forces crushed the coup easily and threw
Hitler in jail for nine months—time he used productively to write *Mein Kampf*,
the foundational text of the Third Reich.

The German economy was still in tatters in the summer of 1932, but Hitler
had moved by then from being a political outcast to having a significant
following.[1] On July 31, the National Socialists won 37 percent of the seats in the
Reichstag, the lower house of parliament, giving them a considerable lead over
the other parties.

When Johnson got to Berlin in the days following the election, he went to see
the economist Emil Lederer. Things were changing so rapidly that he needed to
speak to someone right away whose opinion he valued to help him make sense of
what was happening. Originally from Austria, Lederer moved to Germany just
before the Great War, where he quickly made a name for himself at the University of Heidelberg, a major center of social science research. Now he was living in
the nation's capital, having recently accepted a prestigious chair at the University
of Berlin.

Lederer did not mince words. Hitler, he warned, would soon take over the country; and when he did, his "regime would be mob rule, the most terrible in history." At the time, Johnson confessed, he still believed that National Socialism was little more than "a passing popular aberration, like so many wild political crusades in our own country." Perhaps, Johnson suggested, Lederer was "painting the picture too black." Had history not given examples of tyrants as threatening as Hitler who, after seizing power—even by "abominable means"—became "sober" leaders of their countries? The Austrian economist dismissed Johnson's optimism: "How about Nero?" he countered. Hitler "was madder and more cruel than Nero."[2]

The city planner, Werner Hegemann, agreed. He was leaving Germany "at the first news of Hitler's triumph." So was Johnson's old friend, the economist Moritz Bonn, who had already lined up an invitation for himself at the London School of Economics. But that was about it.

With the exception of a handful of colleagues who were writing for *The Encyclopaedia of the Social Sciences,* Johnson spoke to almost nobody in Germany that summer who took the Nazis very seriously. Historians of the period concur: The German people not only underestimated Hitler, they misperceived him entirely; and that included major figures in the academic community.[3]

The astonishing speed with which Hitler gained dictatorial power bears retelling. As the noted historian Fritz Stern described it, in less than two months the new chancellor "coerced and cajoled a people to give up what for so long they had taken for granted: the formal rule of law, a free press, freedom of expression, and the elementary protection of habeas corpus. Bogus legality covered his action."[4] On January 30, 1933, Paul von Hindenburg, president of Germany, appointed Hitler chancellor of a coalition government, gambling that he and his conservative allies in the Reichstag could control the dangerous political ambitions of the Nazi Party's leader while they used his popularity to advance their own legislative agenda. Politicians on the left were equally naive. After years of fighting with the Social Democrats, the German Communist Party saw Hitler, to quote Stern's chilling words, as "a tacit ally in wrecking Weimar." With little compunction, they turned their backs on "the all too weak Social Democrats" who were trying to hold a fractured opposition together.

During Hitler's first weeks in office, he faced little resistance, not even from religious leaders and university professors who still had the legal and moral authority to sway public opinion. By the end of February that was no longer the case: On February 27, a fire broke out in the Reichstag building, destroying its main plenary chamber and providing the Nazis with the pretext they needed, to quote historian Benjamin Hett, "to gut the democratic Weimar constitution through the emergency 'Reichstag Fire Decree.'" While everyone agrees that the fire played right into Hitler's hands, widely respected historians continue to blame a deranged immigrant whom the police arrested on the night of the crime as the sole perpetrator—rejecting new evidence that Hett published in 2014 that suggests otherwise.[5]

On the night of the twenty-seventh, the police arrested Marinus van der Lubbe, a stonemason from Holland and accused him of setting fire to the Reichstag in the name of the Communist Party. Within twenty-four hours, Hindenburg had signed the Reichstag Fire Decree, outlawing the party and authorizing mass arrests. The president's decree succeeded in crippling the weak opposition even further, destroying any lingering hope that warring parties on the left might rise above their differences and form a coalition large enough to block Hitler's next move. On March 23, the majority of those who still had the right to vote granted Hitler dictatorial power for four years. Only the Social Democrats—and not even all of them—opposed the so-called Enabling Act, "the Communists having already been imprisoned or debarred."[6]

Now fully empowered, Hitler moved quickly. On April 1, he placed a ban on Jewish shops and businesses. A week later he introduced the Civil Service Restoration Act (*Gesetz zur Wiederherstellung des Berufsbeamtentums*), which called for the immediate dismissal of university professors who failed to meet the new "racial" or political criteria required of those holding positions in state-run institutions. A significant number failed on both counts.

Over the next two years, German universities fired 16 percent of their faculty, and that proportion rose to 24 percent by the end of 1938. In departments of economics, the toll was much higher, particularly at institutions in which professors and researchers leaned to the left. Between 1933 and 1935, Heidelberg lost 63 percent of its economists; Kiel, 50 percent; and Frankfurt, 40 percent.[7]

It took Johnson less than a week to come up with a response to the April 7 Civil Service Restoration Act: The New School, he told the Board of Trustees, should open a university in exile. The German scholars who were losing their jobs were "to an extraordinary proportion" the very same people *The Encyclopaedia of the Social Sciences* had identified as "the best scholars in the field of the social sciences." Entire schools of thought were being wiped out: "The traditions and methods that had been the glory of the German university were [being] eclipsed or exiled from [their] own soil."[8] Americans, he proclaimed, had to oppose this outrage in ways that would have a real impact. Sending petitions to Washington and Berlin was a waste of time, even though he continued to sign them. They had to do more.

On April 14, Johnson wrote to Agnes de Lima: "I am setting out to find money, if I can, to get ten or a dozen [German professors] to the U.S. to set up a German university in exile."[9] On April 24, he officially launched his campaign to raise $120,000, enough to cover the cost of as many as fifteen social scientists for two years. He then charged ahead at a furious pace, making sure that nothing stood in the way of opening the doors of his new university by the beginning of the fall semester.

As the days flew by, Johnson gave de Lima a running account of his progress, at times writing every week. These letters captured the frantic rhythm of his life, recording his trip to Washington in April to talk to immigration officials about issuing visas right away, the endless meetings in New York throughout the spring, and his trip to London over the summer, during which he tried to persuade eminent scholars with other options to choose from to throw in their lot with his new university that had no reputation to speak of.

When Johnson described these early days in his autobiography, he slowed the narrative down. The idea, he wrote, of creating a university in exile did not come to him right away. His first response was to contact the presidents of other universities and urge them to invite a single refugee scholar to teach at their institutions, as he himself was planning to do at the New School. The replies were disheartening. Everyone "agreed in principle, but university budgets were suffering severely under the depression." The New School had even less money to spare, but surely, Johnson said to himself, he could find $5,000 to sponsor a single scholar. And so, he tells us in 1952, he set out to raise money for Emil Lederer alone, the number one man on his list.

Three weeks later he gave up, having only scraped together $450:

> Reflecting on these disappointing results, I began to cudgel myself for my stupidity. This is New York . . . and New York can't see anything so minute as the fate of a single man, however great a man. If I had set out to finance a whole faculty, New York would at least have taken note of the fact.
> The idea excited me.[10]

At which point the story picks up speed: After wasting three weeks looking for $5,000 to save the life of a single man, it took him only a few days to collect

$120,000 to save the lives of fifteen.[11] An exaggeration clearly, but he did raise the money quickly.

Yet why did Johnson play with the facts in the first place? What he recorded in 1933 was far more exciting than the version he gave in 1952. Even if he began with the idea of saving Lederer alone, something he repeated on numerous occasions, it took him less than a week to change his mind. By the time he wrote to de Lima on April 14, he already had the approval of the Board of Trustees to open his University in Exile. So what was going on? Johnson must have had a reason for replacing a riveting story with a corny anecdote about how New Yorkers could only think big.

Johnson enjoyed slipping into the voice of a prairie yokel who still needed a lesson or two about the ways of city folk. But when he did, it was rarely innocent. He switched registers strategically to ridicule critics or ideas he opposed—the more urbane and sophisticated the better.[12] In the yarn about Lederer, Johnson was targeting several leaders in the philanthropic community who had given him a hard time in 1933 when he refused to abandon his University in Exile and work exclusively with them on their national campaign to send refugee scholars, one-by-one, to institutions across the country.

By adding several weeks here and stretching the truth there, Johnson suggested in 1952 that he not only joined the national campaign from the very beginning but had actually launched it himself. The University in Exile, he tells us in *Pioneer's Progress*, was an afterthought, a plan he came up with when the other idea failed. With playful irony, he even blames himself for what was, in his eyes, the "stupidity" of those who came up with the other idea. His message, however, was dead serious: Nobody should think he had turned his back—even for a few weeks—on this wider rescue effort, which had the potential of saving many more lives than what he could have done at the University in Exile.

But who could possibly care anymore in 1952 about a squabble Johnson had in the spring of 1933? By July, he had buried the hatchet and was working with the national campaign, sponsored by the Institute of International Education (IIE) and the Rockefeller Foundation, while he simultaneously moved ahead with the University in Exile—a fact that remained a sore point between Johnson and his critics for many years to come, so much so that Johnson was still defending himself twenty years later.

After changing the chronology in 1952, Johnson had to tinker with other details as well. For example, he reported having "urgent correspondence" in the spring of 1933 with the presidents of other American universities, asking them to welcome a German professor to their campus. These letters, however, between April and June, consisted exclusively in efforts to solicit their help for the University in Exile. Could anyone blame him? His critics apparently did.

Even after Johnson had raised enough money to launch the University in Exile, he campaigned cautiously for the other cause. In July 1933, he published an article in *The American Scholar* urging American academics to welcome persecuted German professors to their own institutions: "There is not a university," he wrote, "that does not owe this duty to German scholarship." But he made this appeal to faculty members alone, giving a pass to university presidents because, he wrote, academic institutions could not "stretch their budgets to meet this emergency need." Professors, he said, should respond to the crisis instead by imposing a voluntary tax on themselves:

> What I urge is that American scholars as individuals should consider seriously whether they care enough about academic liberty to tax themselves 1 per cent, 2 per cent, or 5, to succor their fellow scholars who are victims of political oppression. Is liberty worth a price?[13]

A similar campaign already existed in Great Britain—a detail Johnson left out of his article—and members of the British academic community were responding generously. Those in the United States never did, with the singular exception of the émigré scholars themselves. Putting the Americans to shame, the faculty at the University in Exile taxed their meager salaries so that they could help other refugees.[14]

The explanation Johnson gave in *The American Scholar* for letting university presidents off the hook was not persuasive. Yes, budgets were tight during the depression years, but every institution could have found $5,000, as Johnson himself noted pointedly in his autobiography nineteen years later. But in July 1933, Johnson left the presidents alone because he was still leaning on them at the time to lend their names to the University in Exile. In the end, a number of universities opened their doors to refugee scholars, but they never responded as generously as they could, not even after the Rockefeller Foundation volunteered to subsidize the salaries of the exiled professors for one to three years. Given the reticence of presidents of academic institutions across the United States, the Rockefeller Foundation and IIE collaborated with the New School far more closely than they had intended. But they did so while remaining critical of Johnson's competing idea of building his University in Exile.[15]

Since the late 1920s, Johnson and the Rockefeller Foundation had been following the work of the same group of German social scientists. This was no coincidence. The foundation, after all, was one of the financial sponsors of *The Encyclopaedia of the Social Sciences*. Rockefeller also had ties of its own to German academic institutions. After the United States signed the Versailles Treaty, condemning a defeated Germany to financial ruin, the foundation made several generous grants to German universities with the hope of strengthening social science research in the war-torn country. The scholars affiliated with these institutions were the ones most aggressively targeted by the Civil Service Restoration Act for both political and "racial" reasons.[16]

During the summer of 1933, the Rockefeller Foundation joined forces in the United States with the Emergency Committee in Aid of Displaced German Scholars. Founded in May by the Institute of International Education (IIE), the committee had taken the lead in trying to persuade U.S. universities to sponsor refugee scholars. Now, with the help of the Rockefeller Foundation, it could also offer participating institutions a stipend for up to three years. Over that same summer, Stephen Duggan, the director of IIE, tried to get Johnson to "give up my University in Exile and throw in my resources with his plan." Johnson refused: "We would always be ready to cooperate, but we could not merge." And cooperate he did, "with the aid of the Rockefeller and other foundations." Between 1933 and 1945, Rockefeller spent $1,410,778 on the refugee scholars program, $540,000 of which came to the New School. During this period, the foundation sponsored 303 scholars, 214 of whom came to the United States.[17]

Between 1933 and 1945, the New School helped nearly two hundred refugee scholars and their families, an impressive number but a painfully small percentage of the thousands of requests that poured in every year. As Johnson told Albert Einstein, he had received more than five thousand letters in 1935–36 alone.[18] Needless to say, the selection process was brutal. Johnson only looked at the applications of scholars who were making outstanding contributions to their fields. He turned everyone else away. The Rockefeller Foundation and the Emergency Committee did the same. Within that smaller group, Johnson focused exclusively on candidates who had lost a professorial or research position from a recognized academic institution and were fifty-five years of age or younger. Occasionally Johnson lobbied for an older colleague, for example, the French physicist Paul Langevin about whom Einstein had written passionately, but very rarely.[19] Finally, candidates had to prove that they had lost their jobs as a result of the Civil Service Restoration Act or, after 1938, similar acts in occupied countries.

The State Department imposed additional restrictions. The United States had essentially closed down immigration in 1924, and the government reviewed very carefully the political histories of candidates applying for special visas as refugee scholars to weed out individuals with ties to the Communist Party. Those who passed could enter the country with their wives and dependent offspring. Older children or other members of the family had to apply for their own visas, which were rarely forthcoming.

The situation grew worse with the outbreak of World War II. When France surrendered in June 1940, Johnson contacted the Rockefeller Foundation and it responded right away. Joining forces once again, the New School, Rockefeller, and the renamed Emergency Committee in Aid of Foreign (no longer just German) Displaced Scholars worked alongside the young journalist Varian Fry and his Emergency Rescue Committee (ERC). Together these campaigns helped over 2,000 intellectuals and artists get out of France before the Germans closed down that border as well.

Fry went to Marseille in August 1940 and remained for about a year. During that time, he provided visas and boat passage, via Lisbon, to the United States for a star-studded group of refugees whose names still resonate today. They included André Breton, Marc Chagall, Marcel Duchamp, Max Ernst, and Albert Hirschmann. Fry also rescued two unknown but promising young scholars who ended up at the New School, the French anthropologist Claude Lévi-Strauss and the German philosopher Hannah Arendt.[20]

══◈══

Historians may quibble over the precise number of refugees Johnson welcomed to the New School, but everyone agrees that he took in many more scholars and artists than any other academic institution in the United States. The most frequently cited figure is 182.[21] Most of them taught in Continuing Education for brief periods of time before finding more permanent positions elsewhere. Committed as he was to saving as many refugees as possible, Johnson's top priority remained the University in Exile, a model he hoped other academic institutions would adopt.

In Johnson's grand scheme of things, Americans should do more than save the lives of individual scholars, as important as that was. They should also rescue the institution that gave rise to German scholarship. At stake, he proclaimed, was the future of civilization. No piecemeal solution would do. If Americans dispersed the exiled professors across the country, they would save the lives of valued members of the German academic community but deprive them of the intellectual support they needed to maintain the great humanistic traditions of Europe.

Johnson had another reason for wanting to create a university in exile. For years, he had been trying unsuccessfully to add a graduate division in the social sciences to the New School, but he did not have the resources to do so. As he explained in *Pioneer's Progress*, he knew of lawyers, bankers, and businessmen taking courses in Continuing Education who wanted to understand the theories behind legal systems, finance, and market economies and to do empirical investigations of their own: "These men had something important to say but did not know how to say it." Johnson firmly believed that the New School could "mobilize the disorderly mass of lay ability if we had a group of graduate instructors." Now, with the growing crisis in Germany, he would be able to raise the money he needed to build an outstanding social science faculty while he championed a cause he believed in deeply and that spoke directly to the founding principles of the New School.[22]

As the associate editor of *The Encyclopaedia of the Social Sciences*, Johnson had spent many hours reading the work of European social scientists. The more he read, the more interested he became in what they were doing, particularly the Germans, who he believed were head and shoulders above their counterparts in the United States. Johnson explained what he meant in a letter to Columbia University sociologist Robert MacIver: The Germans saw economics as "a mighty historical force . . . [not] just a calculus of utilities and disutilities." They saw political science as "not just a speculation on the rights and wrongs of man, but a record of the adjustment of man to the complications of political living; sociology, not a desperate attempt to be enrolled in the physical sciences, or to escape into social work, but an interpretation of the mass feelings and mass actions of men."[23]

Johnson acknowledged that the United States had also produced a number of great social scientists whose work showed the same kind of theoretical breadth as that of the Europeans he admired—Thorstein Veblen for one, but he was an "epiphenomenon," easily dismissed by Americans in ways Europeans did not dismiss their own. In Germany, "everybody had to know Max Weber." If Johnson succeeded in creating his University in Exile, the faculty would be "capable of retaining the continental academic values and adapting them without mutilation to the American tradition." To retain those values meant recognizing the centrality of philosophy to all the disciplines: "In the continental universities," Johnson wrote, "the base of all instruction, even in the physical sciences, was philosophy. . . . Here [in the United States] philosophy is a course among other courses, and seldom the really attractive course. You could get a Ph.D. on the architecture of haystacks without ever being able to distinguish between Aristotle and Eugene Field," he added sardonically, referring to the popular nineteenth-century humorist and poet of children's verses.[24]

Excited by his idea, Johnson wanted to give it a name that would capture the imagination of funders; one as compelling as Saint Peter's in Chains, the famous church in Rome whose name nobody forgets. When he came up with the University in Exile, he knew he had found what he was looking for because it was "the university itself that was being exiled."

Given his long-term plans for building a permanent graduate faculty, Johnson was going to have to raise additional funds beyond this emergency campaign to support his refugee scholars for the first two years. To do so, however, would create "a permanent financial burden for the New School."[25] When he asked the trustees to endorse his idea, he promised to recruit a second board of trustees to oversee the new initiative. The existing board would have no additional financial responsibilities. This of course meant that Johnson was committing himself to a project that would demand an enormous amount of his time for many years to come—not exactly what he had been planning to do before Hitler passed the Civil Service Restoration Act: "I am going in the wrong direction, since my goal [was] ease, and the leisure to write and reflect." But there was no turning back. "One gets an idea and has to see it through."[26]

By the middle of April, the trustees had endorsed Johnson's plan to raise $120,000 to support up to fifteen scholars for two years at $4,000 per year or twelve at $5,000. Once he had their blessing, Johnson asked his old friend Edwin Seligman to help him raise the money by reaching out to his colleagues and wealthy friends, many of whom were of Jewish origin. Johnson delivered one hundred copies of this fund-raising letter to Seligman, in which he explained the urgent need for establishing a university in exile.

Dear Professor Seligman:

I am writing to ask for your help in a matter which deeply concerns both of us. . . . I refer to the case of the German university professors who have been ruthlessly dismissed in the mad anti-Semitic rage of the present German government. You have seen some of the letters that are coming to the Encyclopaedia from them. . . . It is still incredible to me that any government, however fanatic, would cashier men like these whom all the world regards as among the ablest and most creative scholars anywhere to be found.

But to the point. Merely vocal protest will help these men little if at all. I therefore propose a protest which will arrest the attention of every person interested in scholarship, namely the prompt establishment of an institution to be known as "The University in Exile." Because everything turns on prompt action, if the protest is really to count, I propose to confine it to the social sciences—broadly interpreted—a field which is also the center of the battle. . . .

I propose to invite fifteen of the proscribed professors to the New School. They will select their own Dean, arrange their own curricula and establish here a center where German university methods may be taught as efficiently as they were in any German university. With all the resources we have on the Encyclopaedia staff, we can select as brilliant a group as were ever brought together. . . .

It must be done promptly. The world is quick to forgive invasions of academic liberty by a forceful government. It long ago forgave Mussolini. It will never forgive Hitler so long as we have a working University in Exile. . . .

I am not asking for money for the project unconditionally. Unless we can have enough to put the whole program through, for fifteen men, I do not want any money at all. The project must be big enough to stand out from obscurity, or there is nothing in it. What I want are pledges contingent upon the whole $60,000 a year being raised. Even a sceptic in point of practicability could afford to subscribe on these terms.[27]

Seligman attached a cover note to the letter and mailed it off.

Johnson then left for the nation's capital. From Washington he wrote to de Lima, describing how he had "been working so furiously" that he had little time to do anything else: "There may be some difficulty in getting the professors out of Germany and into the United States. That is why I am trying to see the State and Labor departments. They are hard to get at, but I think I'll manage it."[28]

Back at the New School colleagues started gathering the names of scholars whom they knew needed help. Everyone understood that the New School would only recruit social scientists, but for Johnson that could easily include a scholar who specialized in the arts, particularly someone such as the musicologist Erich von Hornbostel, who was doing collaborative research with the Gestalt psychologist Max Wertheimer. Even though Hornbostel had turned down the New School three years earlier, Clara Mayer predicted that he would accept this time. On May 4, she informed Henry Cowell that Hornbostel had contacted Franz Boas at Columbia to let the anthropologist know that he had lost his job and was eager to find work in the United States: "Dr. Johnson will certainly invite him if the money can be found."[29]

On May 6, Johnson wrote to de Lima:

> My head spins so hard with my University in Exile. I write letters and letters, have interviews, arguments from morning to night, interminably. But I am taking one fortification after another, and as things look now I'm going to get that university. There are alternative plans to fight with—Einstein's Jewish University in London and plans for a committee to insinuate these exiles one by one into the various universities. I've taken Einstein's key man away from him and invited Einstein into my camp. I've started to dissolve it by capturing some of its keys. So my hopes are looking up. . . .
>
> You may wonder what drives me on into a venture that has so much possibility of perplexity and labor in it. Hanged if I know. It's a brilliant idea, isn't it? A University in Exile. The conception of such an idea is a delight: the parturition follows by a law of nature.[30]

In the same letter, Johnson boasted that he had already raised $7,500 despite the fact that he had "hardly begun to try." On May 11, he reported having $17,000 and gaining the endorsement of the American Jewish Committee, which had previously distanced itself from anti-Nazi campaigns out of fear of stirring up anti-Semitic passions in the United States. Now that he had the support of the committee, it was time to go to the press: "I am going to talk with Arthur Sulzberger, son-in-law of Ochs and supreme authority on the *Times*."[31]

When Johnson wrote to de Lima on May 11, he said nothing about the huge anti-Nazi demonstration that had taken place in New York the day before. Had he participated? *The New York Times* covered the story on the front page of the morning's newspaper: one hundred thousand people had marched from Madison Square Garden to Battery Park in a "six-hour protest over Nazi policies." Sponsored by the American Jewish Congress—not to be confused with the American Jewish Committee—the demonstration had attracted a wide range of political and religious leaders. Among the speakers were Mayor John O'Brien, Major General John O'Ryan, and members of the Protestant Episcopal Diocese.

Rabbi Stephen Wise, president of the American Jewish Congress, had scheduled the demonstration to coincide with the day Nazi students began their national book burning campaign. In Berlin alone they destroyed more than twenty thousand "anti-German" and "anti-Aryan" volumes. When Wise spoke at the protest, he proclaimed that May 10 would "stand as a tragic day in the annals of the German people for they have done an ignoble deed, which after a time they will choose not to remember, but which history will not let them forget."[32]

On May 13, *The New York Times* announced that the New School was going to open the University in Exile: "Faculty of Exiles Is Projected Here." The article explained that Johnson would sponsor "fifteen Jewish and liberal professors recently ousted from German universities"—adding that he would publish the names of the professors once arrangements had been finalized. Johnson told the reporter that "several German professors of world-wide fame in their fields" had already expressed "a willingness to come." Given their stature, they would attract students "who might otherwise be tempted to go to Germany for their education." Finally, the article described Johnson's fund-raising campaign, publishing the names of distinguished Americans who had joined his outreach committee. In addition to Seligman and John Dewey, the members included a former Supreme Court justice (Oliver Wendell Holmes), a future Supreme Court justice teaching law at Harvard (Felix Frankfurter), the governor of Connecticut (Wilbur Cross), and the president of the University of Chicago (Robert M. Hutchins).[33]

Johnson also told de Lima, in his letter of May 11, that he planned to return to Washington later in May to "take the German ambassador [Hans Luther] by the beard and make him promise either to let the men out of Germany or give me a publicity handle that will be worth grabbing." If he could get "anything like a consent from [Luther]," he would send a representative to Germany right away and begin recruiting faculty.[34] Needless to say, Johnson did not get what he wanted, nor did he follow through with his threat. Luther had many friends in Washington and in the wider academic community.

While the director of the New School was calling on academics to join his protest, Hitler's ambassador was giving speeches at U.S. universities to reassure faculty and students that professors in Germany were doing just fine—with the exception of an occasional troublemaker. Luther urged members of the academic community to ignore the alarmist propaganda they were reading in the press and maintain their strong ties to German universities.[35]

Johnson spent most of May sending letters to colleagues and wealthy friends around the country, asking them to contribute whatever they could to his protest. One of these letters, modeled on the one he had written for Seligman, was cosigned by Horace Kallen and addressed to the philosopher's extensive network.[36] Johnson also reached out to university presidents, asking them to lend their names to his fund-raising committee. On May 29, he wrote to Joseph Ames, president of Johns Hopkins University, describing the University in Exile as "a protest against invasions of the principles of educational freedom to which we all adhere," adding that the "protest will count much more effectively if it commands the approval of educators like yourself." To which Ames replied two days later: "I have had to make it a rule not to allow the use of my name in connection with any project, however much I may approve of it."[37]

Johnson had more success with Robert M. Hutchins, president of the University of Chicago. Hutchins joined the fund-raising committee right away and expressed interest as well in Johnson's more ambitious idea of establishing universities in exile on campuses across the country, each with a different academic focus but all affiliated under a "federal charter of incorporation." As Johnson imagined it, the New School would take the social sciences, Chicago the physical sciences, and together he and Hutchins would try to persuade the presidents of other universities to build faculties of refugees in the arts, philosophy, and psychology. "We could work out a plan," Johnson wrote, "for the government of such a delocalized institution which would make clear its cooperative character." Hutchins replied that he thought the idea "is a good one and shall endeavor to follow it through," but he was not optimistic. He had just "received a setback [which] may be fatal to our plan in Chicago."[38]

When Hutchins proposed opening a university in exile to a wealthy German Jewish friend of the institution, the "key-man here . . . was entirely opposed to bringing any Jewish professors to America, on the ground that it might lead to the development of anti-Semitism in this country. . . . He is opposed to your project and also to mine."[39] Johnson urged Hutchins not to give up. He would find the money for him in New York. If Chicago made a commitment, other universities would follow. Together he and Hutchins had the influence to "center popular attention where it belongs, in the acquisition by the United States of new and valuable intellectual resources, under an institutional form that emphasizes cooperative rather than competitive considerations." Untenured faculty would stop worrying about losing their jobs, university boards of trustees would not have to veto the idea for fear that the cost of supporting these refugees would divert money allocated for other priorities. Finally, Johnson argued, the plan would minimize the risk of anti-Semitism: "The Jew as Jew would drop out of the picture."

In another letter to Hutchins, dated May 27, Johnson added that although he had raised only 25 percent of the $120,000 he needed for the New School, he was confident that he would soon have the rest for himself and also funds for Hutchins:

> At dinner the other evening I sat next to a very rich man, who is doing something rather substantial for the New School project although his own interest is in the physical sciences. What has attracted him is the very name, University in Exile, and the possibility it offers to side-stepping all sorts of complexities. I told him

I was hoping to see realized a scientific faculty of the University in Exile, to be organized independently but to enjoy the hospitality of some great university like the University of Chicago. He became very much excited and thought the funds would flow very quickly. It is my own conviction that we could raise every dollar you would require right here in New York.

[In a postscript, Johnson added] If I can get your group in science underwritten to the extent say of $120,000, would you be willing to come in? This is not a rhetorical question, but a dreadfully confidential one.[40]

Chicago never opened a university in exile, but Hutchins welcomed an impressive group of refugee scholars during the 1930s and 1940s, including the economist Jacob Marschak and the philosopher Leo Strauss, both of whom came to the New School first. In the end, no one signed on to Johnson's second idea, but several other academic institutions recruited clusters of European scholars who worked in the same fields, as Johnson had done, most famously Abraham Flexner at the Institute for Advanced Study in Princeton. Flexner shared Johnson's high regard for German universities and set out in parallel fashion to recruit an outstanding group of mathematicians and physicists, beginning with Albert Einstein.[41] Max Horkheimer's legendary Institute of Social Research moved to Columbia University, where in rented facilities philosophers, psychoanalysts, and social scientists continued working together on their interdisciplinary projects, as they had been doing in Frankfurt before Hitler rose to power. Several members of that group, including Franz Neumann, joined the faculty at Columbia. The Mannes College of Music opened its doors to refugee artists. And still others, most significantly historically black colleges.[42] No institution, however, came close to welcoming as many refugee scholars as the New School.

It took Johnson only three weeks to raise $120,000, but he was not boasting. When he wrote to Hutchins in the last week of May about having dinner with a "very rich man," he already had the money. No doubt Hutchins assumed as much, even if Johnson had maintained otherwise. This "very rich man" was Hiram Halle, president of Universal Oil Products (UOP), a position he had held since 1919. Based in Chicago, UOP controlled the patents for scientific processes used to transform crude petroleum into marketable gasoline.[43] By 1933, the company had amassed a fortune leasing its patents to Standard Oil and other major refineries. According to Halle's business diary, the president of UOP tried to reach Johnson on May 9. Johnson returned the call on May 11 and the two men met in person the next day.[44] The details of the gift were worked out at that meeting or shortly thereafter.

A few years later Johnson thanked Louis Halle for having told his brother Hiram about the University in Exile. A friend of Seligman's, Louis had apparently received a copy of Johnson's fund-raising letter and passed it on to his brother. But Halle also could have learned about the rescue effort from his nephew, Joseph Halle Schaffner, whose own ties to the New School went back to 1925 and would continue for many years to come.[45]

Johnson kept Halle's gift a secret for as long as he could. He did not even share the good news with de Lima for nearly a month. In a letter dated June 9, he confessed that he had been "making a profound secret of the fact that [he had] a guaranty of the whole $120,000 from a single man" because he wanted to raise as much money as he could for what he knew would be a very expensive undertaking. Then Halle spilled the beans "in confidence" to thirty men at a luncheon. Among the guests, was a friend of Johnson's who had been planning to donate $5,000 but decided against it after hearing about Halle's gift. Although Johnson still hoped to raise additional funds, his benefactor's indiscretion would "certainly" cost the University in Exile $20,000. Johnson was so upset that he gave into his bitterness, describing Halle to de Lima in a surprisingly mean-spirited way as "a rich and close-fisted man . . . who was captivated by the name, University in Exile."[46] Before long, he and Halle had become the best of friends, and Halle continued making gifts to the New School until he died.[47]

Johnson paid tribute to his friend's generosity on countless occasions, at times outdoing himself even by his own effusive standards. In the spring of 1952, eight years after Halle had passed away, Johnson told his benefactor's sister:

> Hiram was to me a brother, a big brother who took me to the shelter of his great coat when I was shivering with cold fear. . . . There are hundreds, indeed thousands of people who live and breathe the air of freedom, who owe their lives to Hiram. Most of them are unaware of their debt. That fact never meant anything to Hiram.[48]

Johnson wrote these words to warn Julia Halle that he might break down and cry when he spoke at the upcoming dedication ceremony for the new Hiram Halle Library in Pound Ridge, New York. The town was honoring the memory of their prominent citizen who had played a leading role in the community on a number of projects, including the restoration of more than thirty "vintage homes."[49] In his formal remarks, Johnson repeated what he had written in his autobiography about how Halle had stepped forward in the spring of 1933, making it possible for the New School to open the University in Exile the following fall. He also described how Halle had financed the New School's unabridged translation of Hitler's *Mein Kampf*, a fascinating, if controversial, chapter in the history of the institution, about which Johnson rarely spoke.[50]

⟐

Johnson was among the first in the U.S. academic community to respond to what was happening in Germany, but he was not the only one. Flexner got right to work on his Institute for Advanced Study. As did Joseph Schumpeter, Harvard's distinguished émigré economist, who reached out to American colleagues in April on behalf of the "victims of Hitlerian ardors," many of whom he knew personally.[51] Born and educated in Austria, Schumpeter moved to Germany after World War I. In 1925, he accepted a professorial chair at the University of Bonn, but he had his eyes on a more prestigious chair in Berlin. When that position became available in the early 1930s, the department chose another economist over him. Infuriated by the slight, Schumpeter accused the Social Democratic Party of conspiring against him and influencing the vote, after which he accepted a job at Harvard and moved to the United States, arriving several months before Hitler rose to power.

This incident may explain why Schumpeter acknowledged having sympathy for the rise of National Socialism in Germany—any party, he thought, would be better than the Social Democrats. But he never endorsed the Nazis' racial laws. When he heard about the Civil Service Restoration Act, he wasted no time in looking for ways to help former colleagues who had lost their jobs.[52]

On April 19, Schumpeter asked Wesley Clair Mitchell to assist him in finding teaching or research positions for nine "Hebrew colleagues," eight economists and one sociologist, who had just been dismissed from their academic positions in Germany. He was making this request not only for them personally, Schumpeter explained, but for the future of the social sciences. The scholarship of these men was "more than competent . . . I did on purpose not include any distinctly weak brothers." Schumpeter listed the scholars from one to nine, according to his frank opinion of the quality of their work. Those who had achieved the rank of professor were still receiving their salaries, he added, but nobody expected that to last for very much longer: "I have had a letter from Lederer which, although perfectly dignified, displays pathetic anxiety and despair."[53] The more junior scholars were no longer receiving anything.

Mitchell responded right away. He would do his best to help the nine social scientists, but could he do anything more? Yes, Schumpeter replied. He was also setting up a committee of about ten economists to serve "as an employment agency" for the many other German economists who were going to need help. Would Mitchell work with him on that as well? Its members, Schumpeter added, should have "as few Jews among them as possible" to avoid attracting the attention of anti-Semites. As he envisioned it, the committee would survey departments of economics in colleges and universities across the country and in other institutions that did economic research "with the view of finding suitable employment" for those who had lost their jobs. He hoped economists with major reputations would volunteer to serve because their recommendations would have more sway than those from administrators no matter how well-intentioned these other people might be. Schumpeter also wanted the committee to raise money for individual stipends and for an emergency fund "should it happen that any of those Germans should one day land without any means." Finally, to be effective, the committee needed a strong chair. Would Mitchell agree to head it? Schumpeter could not do it himself because he was a foreigner. He had already approached Reverend Harry Fosdick, the founding minister of Riverside Church, but he turned him down.[54] Mitchell agreed.

In late April, Schumpeter asked the economist Edmund Day to join the committee in his capacity as director of the Social Science Research Division of the Rockefeller Foundation. Day declined. The foundation, he said, had made it a matter of policy not to engage in any activity that might be construed as unfriendly toward the German government—a policy Rockefeller did not honor for long. Schumpeter replied to Day that he fully understood, adding, "I know something of the government which preceded Hitler's, and I can only say that I am quite prepared to forgive him much by virtue of comparison." But would it be possible all the same for Day to lend "a helping hand in the way of advice and personal support?"[55] Apparently it would not.

On May 2, the same day he replied to Day, Schumpeter contacted Mitchell again to let him know that he had just heard about Johnson's plan to create the University in Exile: "My first impulse was to heave a sigh of relief." What were the chances of it succeeding? If they were good, Schumpeter would feel "justified in stopping our own activities [but] only if we think Johnson and Seligman have a fair chance of success."[56]

Schumpeter also wrote to Johnson. He began his letter with a detailed description of what he had been doing in collaboration with Mitchell, adding that they had planned to ask Johnson to join their committee: "Of course, you figure on the list of members." But having heard about Johnson's "excellent plan," Schumpeter was happy to step back and let the New School take over. If "there [were] any chance of realizing" the University in Exile, Schumpeter would disband his committee right away. The only caveat, he added, was that he would not lend his name to the New School's campaign "because of the strong emphasis placed on the element of protest":

> Although I do disapprove just as much as you do of any injustice or harshness, I cannot feel about the Hitler government as many people do because I know the one that went before. If I do not approve of the reaction I could not say with truth that I do not understand it.

Schumpeter attached the same list of nine scholars that he had sent to Mitchell, singling out Gustav Stopler and Jacob Marschak, whom he had ranked numbers one and two. They were both relatively young, so Johnson may not have heard of them before, but Schumpeter urged Johnson to look at their work seriously. "As far as scientific talent and originality of work goes, [Marschak was] far above the rest." Schumpeter also recommended Hans Neisser and Karl Mannheim very highly. Even if "they were ever so comfortably lodged in Germany," it would simply be a matter of "business to try to get [all four of] them to this country."[57] The others too were "more than competent," but Schumpeter did not express the same level of enthusiasm for them, not even for Lederer, whom the Austrian economist had known since their student days in Vienna.

The overlap between the social scientists on Schumpeter's list and those who came to the New School is striking. All the more so given Johnson's close ties to Mitchell and Mitchell's promise to Schumpeter that he would help find jobs for the "Hebrew" scholars. Five of Schumpeter's nine ended up at the New School: Gerhard Colm, Emil Lederer, Adolph Lowe, Jacob Marschak, and Hans Neisser.[58] Johnson also tried to recruit Karl Mannheim, the one sociologist, but he failed.

In addition to the names on his list of top priorities, Schumpeter had also been trying to place a labor economist at a women's college. Her name was Frieda Wunderlich. As Schumpeter explained to colleagues at Smith and Bryn Mawr, this particular "case is still more difficult than that of the other economists who have been dismissed, because she is a woman, which fact very much restricts the range of possible employment."[59] When Johnson heard about Wunderlich, he hired her right away.

<hr />

After the New School's Board of Trustees authorized him to open the University in Exile, Johnson asked Lederer to serve as its first dean. Lederer had left Germany in the early days of April to attend a meeting in Paris, and he was still there on the seventh. When he heard about the Civil Service Restoration Act, he went straight to London and began writing letters to colleagues in the United States and Europe asking them to help him find a new job. The University of Manchester offered him a temporary position immediately. But after Johnson announced that he had raised $120,000, Lederer signed on with him, welcoming the opportunity to take a stand against National Socialism by creating a new academic institution for scholars fired from their university posts in Nazi Germany.

By the middle of May, Johnson and Lederer had settled on the people they wanted to invite and began tracking them down. At the top of their list were Adolph Lowe, Karl Mannheim, and Jacob Marschak, all of whom, Lederer told Johnson, had already moved to London. If the three men joined the University in Exile, others would quickly follow. Lederer urged Johnson to send a colleague to England to help answer any questions the refugee scholars might have about the New School.

Johnson asked Edwin Mims Jr., a member of his team at *The Encyclopaedia of the Social Sciences*, to go to London, but Mims returned empty-handed. As Johnson tells the story, although Mims was "profoundly impressed by the charm and intelligence of the three scholars and did his best to win them," the German refugees rejected the invitation, "and Eddie came home discouraged."[60] Johnson was less diplomatic in private. Clearly taken by surprise, he complained bitterly to de Lima about the way Lowe, Mannheim, and Marschak had responded to the New School offer. Dismissing them defiantly, on June 9, he wrote to de Lima:

> They have had a lot of nibbles from various institutions that will never come across and think they are heroes and can dictate terms. Naturally they want to dictate their favorites in and the others out. Fortunately, I'm in a position to reshape my plans and let any man go who gets too biggity. But isn't this a hell of a note?[61]

Johnson was not about to give up. By the time he wrote to de Lima to complain, he had already cabled Lederer and asked him to come to New York as quickly as possible. On June 16, he introduced the Austrian economist to Halle.[62] He then followed his friend back to London in July, but to no avail. Even Johnson, with all his powers of persuasion, could not convince Mannheim, Lowe, and Marschak to join the faculty and move to New York. All three of them accepted offers in England—Mannheim at the London School of Economics, Lowe at Manchester, Marschak at Oxford—preferring to remain on temporary appointments at established universities than to risk it with Johnson. In Lowe's case, he did not worry about signing on to a short-term contract. He expected to return home very soon. Surely the Germans would come to their senses and throw Hitler out. In the meantime, he explained, he did not want to move far away.[63]

Johnson could not believe what was happening. Even scholars with nothing lined up were hedging their bets. As he wrote to his twelve-year-old daughter, Sigrid de Lima, the arrogance of these German professors astounded him. Still, little by little, he was making progress:

Here I am far from home and my friends and my job, trying to make final arrangements with the German professors who are to make up my University in Exile. You'd think that would be easy. There are nearly a hundred professors of economics and social science who have been dismissed from Germany. The English universities are taking four or five of them and various American Universities are taking about the same number. My University in Exile will look after more of them than all the rest of the world put together. You'd think all I'd need to do would be to say, "Will you come?"

And they'd say "Ja" or "Ja gewiss." No: they think, here is somebody so simple minded he wants to help a stranger. Can't we get something more out of him? And so, I have to argue, plead, explain as if I were the beggar. That is the way of life, though. It is the principal reason why man is so reluctant to be generous to man. It is not so hard to find generous givers as generous takers.

Still, I have half my team signed up and those who have signed up are very ardent for it. And a host of outsiders are very ardent about it. After all, it stands out still as the most important undertaking in all the world to meet the outrage Hitler has committed against the universities. And it is going to be a grand working organization. I do not know who the students will be, but they will get better teaching and training than they could get in any German University or American.[64]

Years later, Johnson admitted that he had been "bitter about the resistance of the three professors" because he was convinced that his plan would be compromised without them. Feeling "down on my luck," Johnson allowed that he might have said some regrettable things when they turned him down. But if he had, Lowe forgave him and went on to become "one of my best-loved and most highly valued colleagues."[65] Johnson wrote these words long after Marschak and Lowe had reconsidered their earlier decisions and come to the New School, although Marschak did not stay very long.

During that frantic summer of 1933, Johnson refused to return to New York until he had signed on enough scholars to open the University in Exile. It took him three weeks.[66] Wth the help of Lederer, he contacted refugees now living in Switzerland, Czechoslovakia, and Austria. He also wrote to several non-Jewish scholars who had remained in Germany after losing their jobs. For those who could not get to London to meet him, Johnson sent an emissary to them—a young sociologist by the name of Hans Speier.[67]

Speier had studied with Mannheim in Heidelberg, then with Lederer in Berlin where he also worked as an assistant professor (*Privat Dozent*). Noted for his keen intellect, the sociologist rarely shied away from controversy, even when that meant criticizing the work of his own professors—as he famously demonstrated a few years later, in 1937, at the expense of Mannheim. When *Ideology and Utopia* came out in English, Speier gave this magisterial work a mixed review in the *American Journal of Sociology*, upsetting Mannheim a great deal.[68] But Speier remained deeply devoted to Lederer. When Lederer died in 1939, he published the work his professor had left behind, most significantly *State of the Masses*, one of the first book-length analyses of totalitarian societies to appear in English. Inspired by Lederer, Speier went on to become a leading specialist in the United States on totalitarian propaganda and spent the war years in Washington, working in the Office of War Information in the State Department's Occupied Areas Division.[69]

Since Speier was not Jewish, it was easier for him to go back and forth between Germany and England to meet with scholars Johnson and Lederer were hoping to recruit. Among the people he visited, was Arnold Brecht, a legal theorist who had taught at the Deutsche Hochschule für Politik and had held a number of important government posts before Hitler dismissed him in February of 1933. Over the years, Brecht had worked under seven Reich chancellors.[70]

Speier found Brecht in late July, hiding out in his family's retreat on an island in the North Sea. The legal theorist had been in trouble for several months after stunning the nation by lecturing Hitler on his constitutional responsibilities as chancellor of Germany. This astonishing spectacle took place in early February in the chambers of the Reichsrat—the upper house of parliament—where Brecht had been serving as the chief representative of the State of Prussia.

Every member of the founding faculty left Germany under difficult circumstances, Jew and gentile alike. Hans Staudinger, for example, an elected representative of the Reichstag, was imprisoned and badly beaten for political, not racial, reasons; he was a Social Democrat. Released in the fall of 1933, he came to the New School in 1934.[71] Mixing pride with bitter irony, Adolph Lowe liked to say that the Nazis had dismissed him for political reasons first, then because he was a Jew. He too was a Social Democrat.[72] In the days following the passage of the Civil Service Restoration Act, members of the Nazi party in Kiel stormed the Institute of World Economics and viciously attacked the economists Hans Neisser and Gerhard Colm, wounding Colm seriously. It mattered little that the families of both men had converted to Christianity two generations earlier.[73] And so on.

Brecht's story, however, stands out. He was neither a Jew nor a Social Democrat, even by Hitler's definition, nor was his wife. He could easily have played it safe. After he died, the political scientist Erich Hula, a New School colleague and fellow émigré, described Brecht's courage this way: "In the tumultuous years which presaged the downfall of the Weimar Republic, Brecht, without being affiliated with any political party, fought in the first ranks of German democracy for the preservation of freedom in his homeland. The role he played in those stormy years testifies to his personal courage as well as to his deep devotion to the ideal of constitutional democracy."[74] Harvard's émigré political scientist Carl Friedrich described Brecht in similar terms, in his review of Brecht's autobiography, as "a truly great man, whose depth of feeling, sincerity, and strength can be sensed on every page."[75] In his early years at the New School, however, Brecht's behavior made Johnson and other colleagues suspicious about where he stood politically.

Arnold Brecht was born in 1884 into an upper-class Prussian family. Raised in the city of Lübeck, he completed his university studies in Berlin and Göttingen and received a doctorate of law at the University of Leipzig. In 1910, he was appointed judge to a Prussian court; in 1918, counselor to the Reich Chancellery. With the establishment of the Weimar Republic, he held several other government positions at the national and state level.[76] In 1921, Brecht became ministerial director of the Division of Policy and Constitution in the Ministry of the Interior, a position that gave him the opportunity to work at the nuts-and-bolts level in strengthening democratic institutions in Germany—a task he embraced with such enthusiasm that he made his conservative colleagues in the government suspicious. In 1927, the new head of the Ministry of the Interior fired Brecht, allegedly at the request of Alfred Hugenberg, the leader of the German Nationalist Party who went on to serve in Hitler's cabinet. A few days after losing his federal job at the Ministry of Interior, the State of Prussia appointed Brecht director of its Ministry of Finance and one of its chief delegates to the Reichsrat.

Brecht was still serving in these last two positions in July 1932 when Chancellor Franz von Papen tried to topple the socialist government of Free Prussia.

As chief delegate of Prussia and a skilled lawyer, Brecht challenged the legality of the chancellor's coup before the Supreme Court and won. Furious with the outcome, Papen fired Brecht from the Reichsrat, but once again the Supreme Court stood behind him and reinstated him, at least for a few months. On February 6, 1933, Hitler fired Brecht and his fellow Prussian ministers, four days after Brecht's brazen performance in parliament during which he gave the new chancellor a lesson in constitutional law.

As Brecht tells the story, Hitler came to the Reichsrat on February 2 to make his first official speech as chancellor before a chamber packed with spectators. According to custom, when a chancellor addressed the upper house of parliament, a representative of the largest state (Prussia) responded on behalf of his colleagues. This dubious honor fell to Brecht. After Hitler made a few sober remarks about the importance of respecting tradition and the law, Brecht picked up on the same theme, reminding the chancellor that on January 30 he had taken an oath to uphold the constitution. He then expounded at length on what that oath entailed, quoting chapter and verse from the Weimar Constitution.

Long and didactic, Brecht addressed Hitler with the authority of an upper-class Prussian, describing the subtleties of German law to this Austrian upstart. In patronizing tones, he reminded Hitler that as chancellor he had the obligation to respect the rule of law and honor the nation's commitment to constitutional democracy. He was no longer "the leader of a movement grown in rigid opposition . . . [but] the responsible chief of the German Reich":

> We all feel that this has been an extremely serious decision for you personally. . . . For it means that you have taken over the grave duty and confirmed it by a solemn oath to use your strength for the benefit of the entire people, to uphold the Constitution and the laws of the Reich, to fulfill your duties conscientiously, and to conduct your office "impartially and with justice toward everyone." The entire Reichsrat will support you in the fulfillment of these duties and with understanding.[77]

That same evening Brecht received a call from the state secretary of the Chancellery, informing him that "the Führer was very indignant about the speech and the men who had accompanied him were furious." Why? Brecht asked. He had only assured Hitler that he had the support of the Reichsrat "in the fulfillment of his duties."[78] The next day the left-liberal press praised Brecht's speech, in particular the Social Democrats who described it as brilliant "political theater." The National Socialists called Brecht "outrageous," and the communists accused him of having prostrated himself before the Führer, humiliating both himself and the Social Democratic government of Prussia.[79]

When Brecht was fired, along with his fellow ministers, he appealed the decision, but this time the Supreme Court ruled against him. Two months later the Gestapo arrested him or, as the warrant read, took him into "protective custody because of the threatening attitude of the population." The police accused him of having committed three crimes while serving in the Reichsrat: supporting the rights of Jews to emigrate; supporting the rights of a Jewish prisoner who was on parole; and for having "participated in the propaganda campaign against National Socialism," during which he "spent public funds." In the end, the Supreme Court of Accounts dismissed the accusation that Brecht had "embezzled public money." When they released him, however, the Gestapo warned that the SS would be keeping close tabs on him.[80]

Brecht fled to his brother's house in Cologne. Since Gustav Brecht was a wealthy businessman and prominent in high society, it was risky for him to shelter Arnold and his wife, Clara. But he kept them for three months all the same, over the spring of 1933, and continued to welcome them on many other occasions throughout the 1930s. Gustav also welcomed their sister Gertrud and her Jewish husband, the violinist Ossip Schnirlin. In July, Arnold and Clara left Gustav's home for Wangerooge, the family's island retreat in the North Sea. It was there that Speier caught up with him:

> After mysterious telegrams, Hans Speier, an academic of about twenty-eight years, came by air from Berlin to visit us. He passed on an invitation extended to me from Dr. Alvin Johnson to join a newly established graduate faculty at the New School for Social Research. I had until then not thought of emigrating, knew little of America, and nothing about the New School for Social Research in New York. After long discussions I delayed answering, but returned to Berlin, where Speier introduced me in the Café Josty at Potsdam Square to Karl Brandt, to whom he had given a similar invitation.[81]

Brandt accepted Johnson's invitation right away and arrived in New York in time to appear in a photo with Johnson and eight other refugees that the *The New York Times* published on October 4, announcing the opening of the University in Exile at the New School.[82] An agricultural economist, he had been dismissed from his position as director of the Landwirtschaftlichen Hochschule in Berlin for political reasons only. Like Brecht, he was not a Jew. Although Brandt turned to the right politically in the United States, he had a reputation in 1933 for being a "critical leftist."[83]

Brandt's dismissal in April 1933 surprised many, including Hamilton Fish Armstrong, editor of *Foreign Affairs*. Armstrong was one of several American journalists covering economic matters in Germany, and he had been consulting with Brandt regularly. On his first visit back to Germany after Hitler came to power, Armstrong expected to see Brandt again, but the economist was gone. So were a number of other scholars he had been relying on. When Armstrong asked about them, "They had disappeared, I was told, and in any case, it was better for them that I should not try to look them up."[84]

Brecht did not accept Johnson's invitation right away because he continued to believe that he had enough influence in government circles to redeem his "insulted honor" and that of the other Prussian ministers, some of whom, he feared, were in grave danger. He was particularly concerned about the Social Democrat Carl Severing, the former head of the Prussian Ministry of the Interior. Even though he knew that things were rapidly deteriorating, Brecht refused to give up.

At the end of July, Brecht received a letter from Hermann Göring, the newly appointed minister-president of Prussia, which informed him that his "national loyalty was faulty." As a result, and "in accord with Section 4" of the Civil Service Restoration Act, Göring was dismissing him "definitively" from public service and reducing his pension by a fourth. Brecht appealed the decision, attaching letters of reference from distinguished jurists and politicians who attested to his character and distinguished record of service in Germany. On August 30, the appeal was denied.

Unable to work, Brecht decided to take a vacation in the lake country of northern Italy. But when he and his wife applied for a temporary exit visa, the Gestapo confiscated their passports. That was the last straw:

> I recalled Alvin Johnson's invitation to New York. I sent him a cable, veiled as family news to "Uncle Alvin," saying that I would like to visit him if he still wanted me. He cabled back on October 4, "Come immediately, Uncle Alvin."[85]

Brecht reached out to the few people he still knew in the Foreign Office and asked them to help him retrieve his and Clara's passports and clear the other bureaucratic hurdles that might stand in their way. His contacts told him that he would need to produce further documentation to assure the German government that the invitation to the New School was for "purely scientific" reasons— everyone had dropped the "Uncle Alvin" by this time. Johnson would have to confirm as well that the New School had not created a university in exile. Finally, Brecht would have to promise that he was only visiting the United States temporarily and would return to Germany after fulfilling his academic assignment. As Brecht tells the story,

Johnson understood immediately and sent a cable back on October 26, saying that the work was purely academic, that the term "university in exile" was not an official name, but a description thought up by the press, and that every member was at all times free to go wherever he wanted.[86]

The Foreign Office accepted Johnson's statement, returned the passports, and provided Brecht with the necessary exit papers. Then, a few days before he and his wife were supposed to set sail, Brecht received a letter from the Gestapo, informing him "politely" that the secret police "was unable to recommend" that they be allowed to leave the country. Brecht replied in the same civilized tone that clearly the Gestapo was mistaken because Minister-President Göring had given them permission. Leaving nothing to chance, he delayed mailing the letter, making sure it would only arrive after he and Clara had departed. On November 9, as the Brechts boarded *The Germany*, two SS officers examined their papers for a final time, flipping through a thick book to confirm that their names did not appear on the party's detention list. The Gestapo, apparently, had not updated their records in time. As the ocean liner pulled out of the harbor, the Brechts "scattered flowers on the North Sea, a symbol that we would return."[87]

Johnson had remained in London through the first week of August, working tirelessly to persuade German scholars who had lost their jobs to come to the New School. By the time he left, he and Lederer had put together a faculty large enough to begin classes in the fall. On August 19, *The New York Times* reported on its front page that the " 'University in Exile' with a faculty of German professors driven from their country by the anti-Jewish and anti-liberal stand of the Nazi government" would open at the New School on October 1:

> The announcement followed Dr. Johnson's arrival in New York on the United States liner *President Roosevelt* after three weeks spent in London. He has made arrangements to bring fourteen exiled German scholars to the United States. The first members of the group are to sail soon and all are expected to be here within the next few weeks.[88]

Johnson gave the names of only three of the fourteen to the *Times*, explaining that the others "could not be made known at present . . . but would be announced by September 1."

In the follow-up story that appeared on September 2, Johnson revealed the names of seven more, whose identities, he said, had previously been withheld "to permit them to wind up their affairs in Germany and to take such precautions as were necessary for the protection of their friends and relatives pending their official acceptance of posts in this country." Known as the "Mayflower" professors, this original group of ten consisted of six economists, one legal theorist, one musicologist, one psychologist, and one sociologist.[89] Brecht and the Italian legal theorist Max Ascoli, who had fled fascist Italy two years earlier, joined the faculty in November, as did Johnson and Kallen.

In his August interview with the *Times*, Johnson explained that he had selected his faculty from a list of nearly eight hundred scholars who had lost their jobs in German universities over the last few months. That number, he warned, would soon reach fifteen hundred, and every one of them would be looking to the academic community in Europe and the United States for assistance. In England, Johnson continued, colleagues had responded to the emergency immediately and established the British Academic Assistance Council, which by August had raised enough money to create temporary positions at their universities for about fifty German scholars. France had also "found many places," mostly in the applied sciences; the Hebrew University in Palestine had created special professorial chairs for a few more. Academic institutions in Switzerland, Holland, Belgium, Spain, Yugoslavia, Turkey, Egypt, and China were also doing something; as were others in the United States. Without mentioning the Rockefeller Foundation or the Emergency Committee by name, Johnson reported that "an extensive organization . . . is raising funds for the temporary placement of German scholars in the various universities." By conservative estimates, he continued, about one hundred scholars would be placed by early September—an impressive achievement, but hundreds more needed help.

As leaders of other American universities began opening their doors, Johnson hoped that some of them would follow his example and create entire faculties of refugee scholars. Hutchins may have abandoned the idea, but Johnson had not given up. As he told the *Times*,

> A single faculty, however able, does not make a university. There ought to be, in addition to the faculty in political and social sciences, a faculty in education, a faculty in the arts, a faculty in philosophy and psychology, a faculty of pure and applied sciences. . . . The extension of the plan, however, may come later. Most Americans will agree that a German "University in Exile," fairly covering the whole range of German academic culture, would offer an extraordinarily interesting contribution to our general intellectual life.

The University in Exile, Johnson continued, was not "a charitable venture." It had brought together a faculty of "such distinction and attainment that they would have done very well anywhere else and at a rate of compensation 50 percent above what we can afford to pay." Nobody, in other words, should reduce what he was doing to "anti-Nazi propaganda." The body of work produced by the scholars coming to the New School was "too serious to admit of political by-play." Nevertheless—and this was crucial—"the New School had established this center of academic excellence as an act of protest against Hitler's racist and politically discriminatory policies that were destroying intellectual life in Nazi Germany."[90]

When Johnson gave his interview in August to *The New York Times*, he reported that hundreds of scholars were losing their jobs in German universities because they were "Jews or Marxists":

> By "Jew" is meant anyone who has as much as one-quarter "Jewish blood," even though the Jewish ancestor was more purely blond and long-headed than the average Nazi German. By "Marxist" is meant anyone who voted for Social Democratic candidates for office, or who accepts the view held by Marx but also by most other competent historians that the forms of political and social life are heavily influenced by the economic conditions of the times.
>
> Never in the history of occidental education has there been any such "purification" of university life. Russia and Italy ousted men whose doctrines were objectionable to the dominant regime, but Germany has added to this category a whole race, and this a race which by tradition has always stood close to the centre of intellectual life.[91]

Even though Johnson had selected his faculty "entirely on the basis of scholarship and not on race," most of them were Jewish, at least as defined by the racial laws of Germany. This was not exactly a surprise, he added, because the vast majority of those who had lost their jobs between April and August had been dismissed precisely because they were Jews. Only one hundred and fifty of them were "Aryans." Of the ten Mayflower professors whose names Johnson had given to the press, two were Aryans (Brandt and Speier). The remaining eight were identified as Jews even though Colm came from a family that had converted to Christianity before he was born, Lederer had converted to Christianity as a young man, and Hornbostel had been raised a Christian by a gentile father of aristocratic descent and a mother of Jewish origin. Eduard Heimann identified so deeply with the work of progressive Protestant theologians that he converted to Christianity after settling in the United States. The remaining four—Arthur Feiler, Hermann Kantorwicz, Max Wertheimer, and Frieda Wunderlich—may not have been practicing Jews, but they had not formally abandoned the faith.[92]

Two years later, when the faculty had grown to eighteen, Johnson told the Board of Trustees that "rather more than one-third had no Jewish blood at all, and of the others several could be classed as non-Aryan only by virtue of the grandparent clause." Those identified as Jews, like those identified as Aryans, also qualified for dismissal because of their so-called "political unreliability." In other words, Johnson explained, "all the members of the faculty had supported the democratic government under the Weimar constitution, some of them had participated in it and were therefore unacceptable to the present government." A goodly number of them belonged to the Social Democratic Party, "whose position was virtually that of the present-day American progressive, whether Democrat or Republican."[93] Their decision to oppose "Nazi discipline and philosophy" made them enemies of the Reich. But for those identified as Jews, their race was reason enough. Johnson fully understood this, of course, even if he stressed the faculty's political leanings in his report to the trustees. The gentiles on the faculty understood it as well, several of whom were married to Jews.[94]

As Johnson liked to remind his readers, race was irrelevant to him personally, and he made sure that it had no impact on New School policy. But racial prejudice, to state the obvious, was deeply embedded in the nation's culture in 1933—as it sadly remains today—and Jews were identified as members of a separate race. Everyone knew that the best universities in the United States restricted the numbers of Jews they admitted and that exclusive clubs kept them out entirely.

Under the circumstances, it is hardly a revelation that high-ranking officers at the Rockefeller Foundation were "not always immune to anti-Semitism."[95] What made the foundation stand out in 1933 was the speed with which its leaders responded to the international crisis despite the predictable prejudices of members of its staff. By the end of the year, Rockefeller had withdrawn its financial support from German universities and taken the lead in helping displaced scholars find academic positions in other parts of Europe, the United States, and Latin America. Most of these scholars were Jews—at least according to the racial laws of Nazi Germany.[96]

In January 1944, Johnson explained how he became "so deeply involved in the problem of discrimination." He wrote these words to a New School donor a few months after Governor Thomas Dewey had appointed him chairman of a commission to combat racial discrimination against African Americans in New York

State.[97] Addressing a man of Jewish origin, he focused on anti-Semitism. Johnson explained to the donor that as a child growing up in a Danish immigrant family on a farm in Nebraska he learned that racial discrimination belonged to an evil time in the past, "fortunately buried deep in history." When he encountered anti-Semitism for the first time as a graduate student at Columbia University, he "fiercely" opposed it, "but my driving motive was only the sense of injustice." When he became a faculty member several years later, he added another driving motive: "scholarly public policy. I saw the colleges and universities selecting, not the best man but the best Gentile." In doing so, Johnson continued, they were weakening and corrupting the ideals of an "honest education." This was how he stood when he took over as director of the New School and "established the principle that no consideration of *race* should stand in the way of selecting the best man available. If this happened to involve a large proportion of Jews, this was no concern of ours." No trustee, he "stipulated, . . . would ever presume to suggest that we had too many Jews on the Faculty":

> The final phase in my development came with the advent of Hitler. It became clear that anti-Semitism not only heaped injustice upon many of our finest spirits, not only plugged our institutions with counterfeit standards, but threatened the life of democracy and civilization itself.[98]

8

THE UNIVERSITY IN EXILE OPENS

Alvin Johnson spent the final days of August 1933 welcoming his German scholars and their families to New York and helping them find temporary lodgings. This was no easy task, but despite the headaches he was very pleased with the way things were going. Nobody, he boasted to Agnes de Lima, was doing more than he was:

> Plautus said, "If a man is looking for trouble, let him get a wife or a ship. He'll never be through outfitting either." Plautus did not know what a faculty is like to outfit. I have so many perplexities. I'm in a daze. German families filtering in to be met at the ship and escorted to temporary shelter, advice as to the research for permanent quarters, question of schools, maids, English teachers. Mrs. Feiler, a nice middle-aged lady, says she looks on me like a father; that they all do.
>
> But after all they are signed up and coming. That is the first stage in the process. The second stage is getting them actually at work. We have already decided on a magazine to be called the International Journal of Political Science [*Social Research*]. . . . Of course, I have nearly a hundred people begging to see me every day, to talk about the possibility of my doing something for their German relatives. Publicity men, big and small . . . [and] every sort of new proposition for cooperation is cropping up. But so far matters go along rather triumphantly. It still remains true that I am taking care of more of the exiles than all of the notables organized under the Emergency Committee, even tho [*sic*] that committee does have the Rockefellers to cover dollar for dollar.[1]

On October 3, *The New York Times* reported that the University in Exile had officially opened, following up the next day with a photo of Johnson and nine members of the faculty. It opened, however, with very few students. Understandably so, Johnson told the trustees, given all the uncertainties. Enrollment that fall "was necessarily restricted."[2]

The course bulletin listed ten lecture courses and ten seminars. Although the descriptions of some of the lectures looked highly technical, others focused on problems that had broader intellectual and political appeal, for example, Eduard Heimann's The History of Economic Theory, Gerhard Colm's Public Finance and the World Crisis, and Max Wertheimer's Logic and Psychology. A similar mix appeared in the seminars. Among those of more general interest were Hans Speier's The Labor Movement, Frieda Wunderlich's The Family, and Emil Lederer's Technological Unemployment.[3]

True to New School tradition, the bulletin announced that every professor would "be absolutely untrammeled, teaching freely and fearlessly whatever he believes to be the truth"—in matters of science, that is. The faculty made a sharp distinction between the "scientific motive and the political," committing itself "exclusively to the scientific." Describing the university as "a non-political educational institution," they would "offer no comment on the political expediency or the justification of a policy pursued by a foreign nation." Curious words to read in the first course bulletin of an academic institution founded, as Johnson repeated many times, to "protest the reorganization of German university life under the National Socialist revolution."

Did Johnson publish this disclaimer under pressure, perhaps to protect the New School's tax-exempt status? Whatever the reason, he qualified his statement a few pages later: Although the university would "offer no comment" about the policies of a foreign nation, it had the "obligation," as an "American institution, . . . to express by word and act its own faith in the value of academic liberty":

Without freedom of inquiry and teaching in the higher educational institutions there can be no intellectual freedom in society at large; and without intellectual freedom the democratic system under which we live cannot long endure. Other peoples may prefer other systems but Americans expect no substantial human progress except through the institutions of democracy. . . .

In extending its hospitality to a group of the German professors who have been displaced the New School conceives itself as acting in the capacity of a representative of American institutions, in the first instance, and, ultimately, of American democracy.[4]

Johnson was even more explicit when he spoke at the inauguration of the University in Exile. The event filled the oval auditorium on Twelfth Street, attracting an audience of "more than 500 guests," a number of whom, Johnson noted with pride, had come from as far away as Harvard and the University of Pennsylvania:

> There are men who would end all political discussion, in the supposed interest of stability. There are others who ardently desire revolution and regard free discussion as a force that weakens the revolutionary impulse. The great majority of Americans, however, still believe in liberty. But belief unsupported by acts is not sufficiently effective in a time like the present. This is the meaning of the institution whose inauguration we are celebrating.[5]

Although Johnson loved the name, the University in Exile, the refugee faculty refused to keep it. When the Board of Regents of the State of New York granted the New School a provisional charter in 1934, authorizing the institution to grant graduate degrees, the émigrés officially changed the name to the Graduate Faculty of Political and Social Science (GF). The charter became permanent in 1941.

In the fall of 1934, the teaching faculty consisted of fifteen professors and four lecturers (ten economists, four political scientists, two sociologists, one philosopher, one psychologist, and one musicologist).[6] These included Alvin Johnson, Horace Kallen, and the Italian refugee legal theorist Max Ascoli. By 1941, the faculty had grown to thirty-one—"besides some 30 lecturers, tutors, research scholars, and assistants"[7]—all of them refugees with the exception of Johnson and Kallen.

In the fall of 1935, 150 students had registered to take graduate classes. Five years later that number had grown to 520, of whom 149 had signed up for a master's degree and 100 more for a doctorate. These encouraging figures dropped precipitously after the United States entered the war. Neighboring institutions faced serious losses as well, in some cases greater than the New School. When classes began in the fall of 1942, the GF reported having 192 students in its courses.[8]

The academic program at the Graduate Faculty looked radically different from that at other American universities. To begin with, the GF had no departments. Although students chose a disciplinary focus in either economics, philosophy, political science, psychology, or sociology, they all received the same master's and doctoral degrees—a master of science (MSc) and a doctor of science (DSc) in the social sciences. Given the small size of the faculty, this made practical sense. It also reflected the theoretical bias of the refugee scholars who approached their specific areas of expertise from a broad, multidisciplinary perspective—a curious fact, in the eyes of the wider academic community, since the majority of them were economists. Defying the stereotype, the New School's economists did not turn their backs on the "softer" social sciences, but taught their subject as part of an integrated field of knowledge.

The New School's émigré economists coalesced as a group in the early 1920s at several German universities and research institutes, A number of them also held government positions in the Weimar Republic, helping to build new economic institutions for their defeated country in the aftermath of the Great War. Their scholarship reflected those experiences As they looked for ways to minimize the punishing impact of the Versailles Treaty, they drew on insights they had gained from social and political theory. Calling themselves "reform economists," the group envisioned building an economic system that offered attractive incentives to free market capitalists but protected the social benefits enjoyed by salaried workers in planned economies. Rejecting rigid ideological solutions from the right and the left, they made the case for maintaining a balance between providing the conditions necessary for dynamic economic growth in the private sector and defending the interests of the laboring classes through government regulations.

The ideas put forth by the reform economists sounded very much like those of John Maynard Keynes, but the conclusions they reached diverged in significant ways. After the eminent British economist published his *General Theory of Employment, Interest and Money* in 1936, Lederer and Neisser explained where they disagreed in the reviews they published in *Social Research*. The GF's economists applauded Keynes's magisterial work, but they challenged his assumption that capitalist societies needed their governments to interrupt the natural flow of the free market only during brief and easily correctable periods of economic downturns.[9]

According to Lederer and Neisser, Keynes's analysis lacked historical depth. Having written *The General Theory* in response to the Great Depression, the British economist recognized the need for state interventions during a crisis of this magnitude. But he saw it as a temporary stopgap to stabilize the market and fix a short-term problem. Not so, cautioned the New School's economists; the state needed to regulate the market continuously. Had Keynes looked at the 1929 stock market crash in the context of cyclical swings over the last one hundred years, he would have seen that economic crises of this kind were "not aberrations" but predictable events that occurred like clockwork every time the economy in industrial societies switched to more efficient forms of technology. With every innovation, came structural changes and increased levels of unemployment. Given this predictable pattern, responsible governments of modern capitalist states needed to monitor their free market economies continuously and make adjustments as necessary along the way to minimize the disruption technological changes would cause in the lives of working people, while at the same time protect the conditions industrialists depended upon to stimulate economic growth. As governments proceeded to make these adjustments, economists needed to anticipate the social and political impact they would have on the lives of ordinary people. And this, in turn, required collaborating closely with colleagues in the other social sciences.[10]

⎯◆⎯

The European scholars who found refuge at the New School were broadly educated. Among the economists, Emil Lederer and Adolph Lowe had first studied law; Gerhard Colm, sociology. Several others, both economists and sociologists—Eduard Heimann, Jacob Marschak, Carl Mayer, Albert Salomon, Hans Speier, and Hans Staudinger—did their graduate work at the University of Heidelberg, famous since the late nineteenth century for its integrative approach to the social sciences, in large part thanks to the enduring influence of the sociologist Max Weber.

During the 1920s and early 1930s, students interested in studying economics from an interdisciplinary perspective went to Heidelberg to work with Lederer and Alfred Weber, the brother of the sociologist. The two economists had recently created the Institute of Social Sciences at the university to carry on the intellectual traditions of Max Weber, who had died in 1920. Heidelberg sociologist Karl Mannheim joined as well, together with his student Speier.[11] Even after Lederer moved to Berlin and Mannheim to Frankfurt, they all continued to collaborate and publish together in the *Archiv für Sozialwissenschaft und Sozialpolitik*, the journal Lederer had been editing for a number of years with Alfred Weber and Joseph Schumpeter.[12]

Another magnet for economists interested in collaborating with other social scientists was the Institute of World Economics at Kiel University. Lowe, who had worked in the ministries of demobilization, labor, and economics after World War I, served as the director of the institute between 1926 and 1930, and he recruited a talented group of like-minded economists, including Colm, Neisser, and briefly, Marschak. He attracted a number of talented students as well, among them Alfred Kähler.[13] In 1930, Lowe accepted an invitation to join the faculty at Goethe University in Frankfurt. Founded in 1914, this new university was rapidly becoming one of the most exciting centers of multidisciplinary scholarship in Germany, thanks in large part to its Kurator (head), the philosopher Kurt Riezler. Over the last several years Riezler had persuaded an eminent group of scholars to abandon their prestigious chairs at long-established universities and join him in Frankfurt. In addition to Lowe and Mannheim, these included the psychologist Max Wertheimer, the theologian Paul Tillich, and the philosopher Max Horkheimer, all of whom would lose their jobs after Hitler rose to power. With the exception of Mannheim, they all moved to New York as well, three of them to the University in Exile: Wertheimer in 1933, Riezler in 1938, and Lowe in 1941.

When Riezler arrived at the New School, the only other philosopher on the faculty was Johnson's old friend Horace Kallen. This was strange, given Johnson's deep appreciation of the role the discipline had been playing in the German social sciences and the dangers many philosophers now faced in Nazi Germany.[14] Philosophy, Johnson explained, "lay at the center" of the great scholarly traditions that Hitler had set out to destroy:

> There was indeed specialization in the German university, but the specialty was conceived of as a branch of the philosophical tree, not as an autonomous growth. The scholar, whatever his branch of the social sciences, felt himself responsible for the whole cultural system. And this gave the scholar a mission. Particularly after the debacle of the First World War, with the restlessness and disorders of the times, the scholar felt the obligation to help the student to think his way through to an inner order of the mind.[15]

So why did Johnson avoid hiring philosophers during the first five years? Perhaps, as he confesses in *Pioneer's Progress*, because "I am singularly unsuccessful in my relations with philosophers."[16] The exceptions were his two old friends, John Dewey and Kallen, and the former head of Goethe University, who had also had a distinguished career in government during the final years of Imperial Germany and again in the Weimar Republic.

When war broke out in the summer of 1914, Riezler was serving as Kaiser Wilhelm's speechwriter and the political advisor of Chancellor Theobald von Bethmann-Hollweg. Among his early tasks, Riezler drafted the 1914 September Program, outlining the war aims of his country. The chancellor also asked Riezler to track the progress of revolutionary movements across Europe and provide material support to rebel groups that were trying to topple the regimes of Germany's enemies—for example, the Russian empire. According to Riezler's biographer, Wayne Thompson, although no documents have surfaced to prove it, Riezler told several New School colleagues that it was his idea in April 1917 to help the exiled Lenin slip back into Russia in a sealed railway car—perhaps not his idea, cautioned Brecht, but he was certainly involved in executing the plan. After Germany lost the war and the imperial government fell, Riezler participated in drafting the Weimar Constitution, serving as a representative of the defeated government's Foreign Office. Then in 1927, he was appointed Kurator of Goethe University in Frankfurt, a position he held until the Nazis dismissed him in 1933. The scholars Riezler recruited to Frankfurt over those six years were outstanding figures in the social sciences. Many of them were also of Jewish origin.[17]

Reluctant to leave Germany, Riezler waited until the Kristallnacht pogroms in November 1938 before accepting that he had to get his family out of the country. Like other "Aryan" members of the Graduate Faculty, Riezler was married to a Jewish woman, at least by the standards of the new racial laws in Nazi Germany.[18]

⇒

Although Johnson liked to say that the Graduate Faculty was preserving the traditions of European universities, his faculty quickly learned that he expected them to adjust to the rhythms and customs of U.S. academic life. In addition to fulfilling their teaching responsibilities, he required them to participate in a faculty seminar. Known as the General Seminar, it met every week over the course of the entire academic year. Johnson also required them to write for and edit *Social Research*, the new international quarterly in political and social science that he had created with the aim of introducing the émigrés' work to the wider scholarly community. The General Seminar began right away, in October 1933, and the quarterly published its first issue in February.

Johnson acknowledged in *Pioneer's Progress* that the General Seminar imposed "a heavy burden" on the refugee scholars who had just arrived in the United States and were still getting used to lecturing in English. But it also served as an excellent vehicle for promoting "the unity of the social sciences" while providing exiled scholars with the opportunity to give academic papers in their adopted language before an audience consisting of émigré colleagues, graduate students, and professors teaching at neighboring institutions. Colleagues from Columbia University frequently joined the weekly seminar—as did other refugee scholars, such as the philosophers Paul Tillich and Ernst Bloch. Reminiscing many years later with the sociologist Robert MacIver, Johnson gratefully acknowledged:

> You of Columbia were wonderful to us and gave your time to joint meetings of members of your Faculty and ours. Nothing could have been devised better to acclimate the new Faculty to the American educational scene. Where the individual European scholar had felt himself at a disadvantage in a group of American scholars, this group met on terms of fair equality.[19]

Every semester the faculty chose a theme for the General Seminar that invited wide-ranging discussions across the social sciences. In the fall of 1933, they looked at the "Methods and Objectives of the Social Sciences." Later seminars focused on "The City," "Peace and War," "Labor in the United States and Abroad," and so on. In addition to the General Seminar, colleagues gave cross-disciplinary seminars of their own, occasionally adding an instructor from the adult division. The psychoanalyst Karen Horney, for example, cotaught a course with Wertheimer, Riezler, and Speier.[20]

Finally, Johnson asked the faculty to participate in "public seminars," or "symposia," that he was organizing to introduce the work of the refugee scholars to the wider New York community. In the early years, most of these events featured the reform economists. In December 1933, several of the seminars focused on the strengths and weaknesses of different economic policies: "Laissez-faire, Interventionism, Planned Economy." A month later they addressed the question, Has Capitalism Failed?[21] By the late 1930s, they had turned to totalitarianism and the impending war.

In addition to their renown as scholars and policy analysts, a significant number of the Mayflower professors had served as editors of major scholarly journals. Most prominent among them was the man Johnson had appointed as dean. Since 1922, Lederer had been the main editor of the *Archiv für Sozialwissenschaft und Sozialpolitik*, a position he filled with such distinction that colleagues referred to the quarterly as the "Lederer-Archiv." The journal first established a name for itself in the early 1900s when Werner Sombart, Max Weber, and Edgar Jaffé were coediting the publication at the University of Heidelberg. Focused primarily on scholarship in the social sciences and philosophy that reached across disciplinary divides, the *Archiv* had an outstanding record of publishing seminal works such as Weber's *Protestant Ethic and the Spirit of Capitalism*. When Lederer took over in the early 1920s, he published articles by his group of reform economists and by other pioneers of the interwar period, including Karl Mannheim, Karl Wittfogel, Herbert Marcuse, Otto Kirchheimer, and Georg Lukács.[22]

Among the first ten members of the University in Exile, six had served as editors of scholarly journals, and a seventh, Arthur Feiler, had been writing regularly for a leading German newspaper. In 1934, Johnson appointed two more refugee scholars with significant editorial experience.[23] Then, of course, there was Johnson himself who, after resigning from *The New Republic*, began serving on the editorial board of *The American Scholar*.

Given all this editorial experience, Johnson did not think twice about pushing his German colleagues to publish the first issue of *Social Research* in the early weeks of the second semester. The faculty disagreed. Speaking on behalf of the others, Lederer urged Johnson to reconsider. It took time, he protested, to do a good job. Before he and several colleagues launched a new journal in Germany, they spent six years planning it together. To which Johnson replied: "We hadn't six years at our disposal if we wished to become known to our American colleagues as a creative institution." Although he understood that this would not be easy, they were going to have to make it work. Otherwise, Johnson warned, the University in Exile would be forced to close down.[24]

Johnson prevailed. When *Social Research* appeared in February 1934, its inaugural issue consisted of a foreword by Johnson and seven articles by members of the Graduate Faculty—six economists and one sociologist.[25] Why, Johnson asked rhetorically in his introductory remarks, was it necessary to create a new journal at this time? Because this one was different: "In a world in which publications are already embarrassingly numerous," *Social Research* would focus almost exclusively on the work of refugee scholars and, in doing so, would have "a field of its own, won by circumstances and the wholesome disposition of scholarship to react positively to circumstances." Since the GF had gathered the "largest organic grouping of continental scholars found anywhere abroad, nothing could be more natural" than for them to step forward and give voice to those silenced by the "political revolution" taking place in Europe. Like the Greek scholars "expelled from Constantinople in the fifteenth century," the exiles today would give rise to "a new kind of thinking."

The contributors to the first issue were all members of the GF, but future issues would include the work of exiled scholars from other institutions in the United States and Europe and, occasionally, American-born scholars as well. "The subject matter," Johnson explained,

> will be drawn from interests that transcend the boundaries of a single country. It will include theory, political, social and economic; problems of social and political organization that are worldwide in their general character though national in specific characteristics, such as class differentiation, militarism, the labor movement, problems involving the interdependence of nations, like the phenomena of prosperity and depression, prices and currency, movements of international trade and investment.[26]

In closing, Johnson requested the "indulgence of the reader." The editors fully recognized that their first issue had "shortcomings." Most of the contributors "fell short of perfect English,"[27] as Johnson acknowledged in his autobiography, and that remained a problem for many years. Editing the articles of his German colleagues was murder, compounded by the fact that some of them were imperious. In 1946, Johnson wrote angrily to Brecht: "I acknowledge you, Dr. Brecht, as a better scholar than I am, but I do feel justified in asserting, I am a better editor than you."[28]

Johnson may have pushed his refugee colleagues harder than they liked, but he succeeded in publishing a first-rate journal. Despite the unmistakable German inflection to the writing, U.S. scholars praised *Social Research* throughout the Hitler years for the high quality of the articles.[29] During that period, almost every member of the faculty contributed at least one full-length article a year, often a book review as well. Several colleagues—Colm, Feiler, Lederer, Speier, and Wunderlich—appeared in almost every issue.

On the masthead of the journal, *Social Research* claimed that it had no editor in chief. It was a collective effort, "edited and published by the Graduate Faculty of Political and Social Science of the New School for Social Research" and, after 1944, "in cooperation with the Institute of World Affairs," a new policy center Johnson created after the United States had entered the war. Everyone knew, however, that Johnson was the one in charge.

When Johnson retired in 1945, the faculty established a small editorial committee "for efficient action" and asked Johnson to serve. Before long, however, the reputation of the journal declined, leading Johnson to conclude in 1950 that the time had come to close the quarterly down. The faculty disagreed. They asked the president emeritus to raise its quality by becoming its editor in chief, identified as such on the masthead of *Social Research*. Johnson agreed to give it a try, but only if he could rely on them to contribute to the journal regularly and share editorial responsibilities the way they used to do during the 1930s and early 1940s— a promise they made, but did not honor for very long.[30]

After Johnson took over, *Social Research* got better, at least for a while. But when he stepped down in 1960 at the age of eighty-five, the journal quickly deteriorated again and remained a mediocre publication for the next ten years, until a young cognitive psychologist, Arien Mack, took over as editor in 1970. As this book goes to press in 2018, *Social Research* continues to flourish under Mack's accomplished and enduring leadership.[31]

⭐

As the émigré scholars settled into their new lives, Johnson expected them to continue making a "persistent protest against the policy of the Hitler government in suppressing freedom of teaching and research." The future of the institution, he said, depended on their joining him in speaking out against Nazi Germany. Not everyone felt comfortable assuming this militant role, especially Brecht.

Although it was risky, since the Brechts were not Jewish, they could spend their summer vacations in Germany, ostensibly to see relatives and friends. To do so, however, they needed the help of the German Embassy, which in turn made it delicate for Brecht to participate publicly in anti-Nazi demonstrations. Although Johnson had never placed a travel ban on the faculty, he did not hide the fact that these summer trips disturbed him. Brecht was the only colleague at the GF still visiting Germany, and he continued to do so until war broke out in September 1939. At one point, Johnson suggested that Brecht might consider resigning: "From the beginning, your position with the Faculty was ambiguous because you alone of the group had not broken with Germany."[32]Johnson wrote these words after Brecht asked permission to slip out early from a benefit dinner.

On December 31, 1935, Brecht wrote to Johnson, requesting permission to leave the dinner before the formal speeches began. Johnson said no. The Board of Trustees was organizing the event on January 15 "with the purpose of consolidating moral support behind the institution."[33] He told Brecht that it would be better not to show up at all than to disappear early—"although neither is desirable":

> For after all, the Graduate Faculty came into existence solely as a protest against German policy with respect to race, religion and freedom of thought. It is maintained solely as such a protest. If all the members of the Faculty took the position that you do, that it would be personally unsafe for them to be present when that German policy is criticized, . . . no one in this country would feel that the Faculty had any claim to support whatsoever. . . .
>
> It is very painful for me to draw what seems the inevitable logical conclusion, because I have the greatest personal esteem and friendship for you. Logic, however, is inexorable. How is it possible for you, ethically, to remain a member of the Faculty, when your position is antagonistic to its existence and would be ruinous to its existence if publicly known? How is it possible for you, who can live and function in Germany, to occupy a chair that would maintain some other distinguished scholar who is desperately in need?
>
> These are painful questions to receive, painful to put. But I am sure that one with so high a sense of honor as you will wish them put definitely and answered as definitely, instead of seething in the minds of your friends.[34]

Brecht replied two days later on January 5, 1936. Although he had asked for a frank response to his question, he had not anticipated the answer he received.

Deeply offended by what Johnson had written, Brecht tried to explain why he did not want to sit through the after-dinner speeches. His "decisive reason," he said,

> had nothing to do with the German government but only with my personal feelings and my personal opinion about the ideal interests of the faculty in this country. I may be completely wrong in this opinion. But was I wrong . . . was it not rather my duty, to express such a serious point of view if I felt it so strongly?

Johnson was not persuaded. Although he did not fire Brecht and Brecht did not resign, relations between them remained strained for a number of years. On May 20, 1938, Johnson tried to get Brecht to admit that the Nazis were intimidating him:

> It is almost universally believed in this country that Germans here are subject to a pervasive espionage, and that if they say anything the Nazis might not like, it would go hard with them if they were caught inside Germany. If all our Faculty went back to Germany every year, this would be interpreted as meaning that they met all the requirements the Nazis chose to impose on them. Immediately the reason for existence of the Faculty would disappear. . . .
> [E]very member of the Faculty ought to feel absolutely free to criticize the Nazi regime as any other.

Johnson hastened to assure Brecht that he had "no doubt" that the legal theorist had maintained his "scholarly integrity and was expressing himself freely," but he also allowed that Brecht had finessed things by working now, since coming to the United States, on American political and economic institutions, not German. Johnson added that it was not "ruinous" for one member of the GF to return regularly to Germany, but these trips were having a negative impact on the faculty's "esprit de corps." He urged Brecht to keep them to a minimum and not to discuss them.

Brecht was furious. As he had told Johnson in 1936, when they first started having this difficult correspondence,

> I am here, as all my friends are, because I declined and refused to live in Germany in accordance with the present political situation. You say I am able to *function* in Germany. But such is not the case. I cannot function in Germany . . . either as an official or as a professor, either as an author or anything else. Formally the German laws do not exclude my writing articles or going into business. But practically these articles would not be accepted and no occupation [by me] could

be practiced. In this respect my situation is practically the same as with all the members of the faculty, and it is legally *and* practically the same as with all the so-called "Aryan" members of the faculty. We cannot function in Germany.

What is more, Brecht continued, he could not *live* in Germany for any period of time. He had tried that and failed. As for his pension, it had been "much curtailed" because he was considered "politically unreliable." How could Johnson possibly think that he was returning for mercenary reasons? He had, in fact, been giving most of what remained of his pension to the Jewish Committee in Germany; the rest he used to pay for his trips.

The correspondence dragged on for over two years. Finally, as a peace offering to Johnson, on May 29, 1938, Brecht wrote that he had decided to cancel his trip to Germany that summer—without mentioning that his wife would go without him. In that same letter, he added defensively that he had not switched to U.S. politics and political institutions, as Johnson had implied, "in order to evade the issue of fascism" but because he thought that this "was the best service I could render the Faculty." Brecht felt "absolutely free to 'criticize the National Socialist government as any other,' " and he had done so at length in his open classes for continuing education students and in his graduate seminars: "Every student of mine will assure you that I have lent frankest expression to my convictions on fascism." He then attached a list of the names of his students and invited Johnson to speak to them himself. Brecht ended this letter, as he did all his others, with a few amicable words about how he and Johnson shared similar views but diverged "with respect to their best application, as free men are allowed to differ." A friend, he conceded, can also adopt the other's point of view, "even if he is not convinced on all counts—and so I did," he added—by canceling his trip to Germany.

Despite his eloquence, it was difficult to side with Brecht. He was clearly holding something back. Many years later he revealed his secret in his autobiography: During their trips back to Germany Arnold and Clara Brecht met with people who were plotting against Hitler: "Any rash word would have jeopardized our lives and those of others."[35] He therefore spoke to very few people, not even to Johnson, about what he was doing.

But as Brecht cleared up the mystery surrounding his trips to Germany, he raised new questions about the cordial relations he maintained with Hans Luther, the Nazi ambassador to the United States. Brecht liked Luther, he wrote. He also owed him a great deal for having vouched for him to the Nazi authorities, adding weakly that the ambassador was "secretly opposed to the Hitler regime or at least its atrocities."[36] American journalists writing for newspapers critical of

Nazi Germany disagreed. They portrayed the ambassador as a faithful servant of Hitler; historians of the period have done the same.

Luther, at the time, had a great deal of influence in American academic circles. Although Johnson could not stand him and spoke disparagingly about him in letters to de Lima, he was in the minority. So was his good friend Felix Frankfurter, who tried, unsuccessfully, to block Luther from going to Harvard to give an honorary doctorate to Roscoe Pound, the dean of the Law School.[37] University presidents across the country hosted events in Luther's honor—and that included Nicholas Murray Butler—during which the ambassador spoke to audiences in packed auditoriums, reassuring them that Germany was still a "democratic" country with only "peaceful intentions." Then, in 1936, Luther succeeded in producing the largest delegation of university professors "by far of any foreign country" to participate in the five-hundred-fiftieth anniversary celebration of the University of Heidelberg.[38]

Brecht, however, had a soft spot for Luther. They had known each other since the Weimar period when the future ambassador held a number of important political positions. On the basis of these earlier associations, Luther agreed to write "friendly letters" for Brecht and his wife before they set sail every summer to Germany. These letters, according to Brecht, attested to "the purely scientific character of my activities and those of our Graduate Faculty and declared that I had stood up to the 'lies being spread about Germany.'" Technically, Brecht explained, Luther was telling the truth.

> [But] this was a highly ambiguous praise because the principal lies about Germany which I attacked emanated from the Nazis themselves, such as those claiming unanimous support of the German people, those concerning the Jews, and those on German history—loss of the war, revolution and Weimar Republic—a tissue of crude untruths which I constantly fought in my lectures on German history, democracy and dictatorship.[39]

During those summer trips, Brecht made contact with "many opponents to the Nazis," most of them former politicians who had represented a wide range of opinion during the Weimar period. Among them was Erwin Planck, the son of the famous physicist Max Planck and a conservative. In January 1945, Planck was hanged "after courageously enduring tortures without betraying his collaborators." Brecht also visited his brother, Gustav, who was fully aware of Arnold's political activities and supported them. Gustav also continued to welcome their sister, Gertrud, together with her Jewish violinist husband. In July 1939, on Arnold's last visit to Germany before the outbreak of the war, Gertrud committed suicide with the despairing Ossip Schnirin who could no longer take "the constant humiliation."[40]

Brecht said nothing in his autobiography about the conflict he had had with Johnson. Nor did he mention that after the war his brother ran into trouble with the U.S. military government. In 1945, the Americans forced Gustav Brecht to step down as chairman of the board of directors of the Rheinisches Braunkohlen, then froze all of his assets and accounts, together with his pension. On October 24, 1945, Arnold came to his brother's defense, appealing the case formally to Lieutenant General Lucius D. Clay. In his "legal deposition," Brecht first established his own credentials, summarizing the highlights of his career both in Germany before the Nazis dismissed him and subsequently in the United States. [41] He then turned to his political activities since the Nazis came to power, describing at length his visits to Germany between 1934 and 1939 and the work he had done there for the U.S. government:

> My wife and I masked as unpolitical voluntary exiles, who returned regularly to visit relatives and to spend our vacations in Germany, while actually we took up contacts with a number of liberal friends . . . [engaged in] the fight against the regime, e.g. Ernst von Harnack, hanged by the Nazis in March 1945 . . . and many others.[42]

Brecht told General Clay that members of the U.S. War Department knew about his summer trips and had enlisted his services. Then, after the United States entered the war, Brecht "cooperated" with the Bureau of the Budget in Washington "on matters of administrative organization" and with the War Department "on matters of psychological warfare." He consulted as well with the Social Science Research Council and the Council for Democracy, among other U.S. institutions in the private sector. Finally, he gave lectures to Army officers at Harvard and Yale, instructing them about the German government and its administrative bureaucracy and served as a supervisor of the German Area for the Army Specialized Training Program (ASTP) at City College.[43]

In his sworn testimony, Brecht claimed that Gustav, like himself, had been a member of the resistance. Among the many risks his brother had taken for him, Gustav hid subversive documents in his home that belonged to Arnold, including "a complete set of the violently anti-Nazi 'Blätter des Deutschlandbundes': There was never any doubt that my brother was as much opposed to the Nazi principles as I. Otherwise I would not have maintained close contacts with him, because fighting the Nazis was more important to me than family ties."[44]

In the end, Brecht succeeded in persuading the U.S. military government to lift the freeze on his brother's assets, which made it possible for Gustav to live out the rest of his life in relative comfort in war-ravaged Germany. As for Arnold, he stayed in the United States, became a U.S. citizen in 1946, and enjoyed a long and active professional life in his adopted country. In 1950, Brecht took a leave of absence from the New School for a year to help the U.S. military government draft a proposal for reforming the German Civil Service code.[45]

⋐═⟫═

When Brecht first arrived at the New School, he knew nobody. Wertheimer and Hornbostel had been collaborating for years, as had the economists and Speier, but Brecht had no prior history with the other members of the faculty. That quickly changed when Johnson appointed former colleagues of his from the civil service: the political scientist Hans Simons and the economist Hans Staudinger. Brecht met Simons in 1921 at the Reich Ministry of the Interior and Staudinger six years later when, after losing his job in the national government, he joined the Prussian Ministry, where the two men worked together on a number of assignments.[46]

Unlike Brecht, Simons and Staudinger threw themselves into campus politics, assuming major leadership roles at the New School. In 1950, Simons became president of the New School. Staudinger served as dean of the Graduate Faculty for more than ten years and, with Lowe, codirected the New School's Institute of World Affairs. Staudinger also shared his prodigious gifts as a fund-raiser. Working closely with Johnson, he helped save the New School from bankruptcy on at least two occasions. As for Brecht, although he remained aloof from university politics and avoided taking on major administrative duties, he established a revered place for himself as the GF's orator and poet.

By the time the war ended, Johnson and Brecht had become very good friends and enjoyed expressing their admiration for one another in poetry and prose. In the fall of 1949, Johnson wrote Brecht to congratulate him on his forthcoming article in *Social Research*. As a member of the journal's editorial committee, he routinely communicated with authors about their papers. But in this case, editorial matters were merely a pretext for sending Brecht a love letter. After praising his colleague for an excellent analysis of the new constitution of West Germany, Johnson added playfully, but with deep affection:

> The hours are so filled with small duties I never find time to present my love and admiration to my grand gallant colleague Arnold Brecht. But being clear sighted as you are, you must know, since first I exchanged letters with you in the difficult days of 1933, it has been my pride to be associated with Arnold Brecht, *chevalier sans peur et sans reproche*.[47]

Brecht outdid himself when he responded two months later on the occasion of Johnson's seventy-fifth birthday. At the university-wide celebration, the legal theorist spoke on behalf of his colleagues as he gave the New School's president emeritus an eighteenth-century edition of Virgil's works in the original Latin, "which we know you are able to read better than all of us." Abandoning academic conventions, Brecht recited a poem he had composed in the epic style of the great Roman poet. Taking a deep breath, he apologized for choking up, but the German people, he explained, came "from a sentimental heritage." In the opening verses of "December 1949" Brecht described how Johnson had stood up to the Nazi barbarians "with nothing but freedom to offer":

> When Hitler said: Lo, Providence wanted me and here I am
> When Goebbels said: (what we do not wish to repeat).
> When Goering said: I shall take command of the air and no
> foreign plane will ever throw bombs on Germany,
> And I want to be Reichsmarschall,
> Not to speak of Streicher, and of Ley, and of the rest of them;
>
> Then you thought, you, Alvin Johnson,
> You would defy Hitler, Goering and Goebbels.
> Having nothing to offer but freedom
> And an unbendable spirit,
> You would offer freedom
> And that brotherly spirit
> To those that would not bend theirs.[48]

The New School celebrated Johnson's seventy-fifth birthday with two fund-raising dinners: one hosted in New York by the philosopher John Dewey, the other in Washington by Supreme Court Justice Felix Frankfurter. By 1949, the university had already held countless events of this kind in honor of its first president, and it would continue to run many more through his ninetieth birthday. Occasions like these always attracted wealthy donors and the press. Respected scholars, writers, and statesmen made eloquent speeches. Presidents and first ladies sent telegrams; foreign ministers the same. In later years, especially during very difficult times, the trustees did not wait for a milestone year but used any birthday as an excuse to celebrate Johnson, as they did in 1963 when the president emeritus turned eighty-nine. The New School's own anniversaries provided other fund-raising opportunities, of course, but Johnson was always the main attraction. Taking his role seriously, he continued to micromanage these events until the very end.[49]

Johnson began running fund-raising events for the University in Exile almost as soon as it opened. Thanks to Hiram Halle's generous gift, he had a cushion for two years, but that was all. When Brecht asked in December 1935 whether he might skip the speeches at an upcoming dinner, he was referring to one of these early affairs at which Johnson planned to launch a campaign to raise the money he needed to underwrite the cost of the GF for the next five years. Scheduled for January 15, Johnson hoped to persuade the presidents of Johns Hopkins, Harvard, and the University of Chicago to speak at the event. As he explained to Isaiah Bowman, the new president of Johns Hopkins, "We believe we can find an endowment sufficient to maintain the institution, without drawing upon funds that would otherwise go to the maintenance of American scholars." But to succeed he needed the support of eminent educators such as Bowman to take a public stand and support the idea of the University in Exile against those who argued "that German professors would be more useful if distributed throughout our higher educational institutions."

The Emergency Committee, Johnson added, was having little success placing social scientists at other universities because it provided support for only a couple of years. "If it had been possible to offer universities permanent endowments for the professors placed with them . . . our effort might have been superfluous." With Bowman's support and that of others, the University in Exile would soon have a permanent endowment. Could Johnson count on him, please? Bowman accepted the invitation.[50]

On January 16, the day after the big event, Johnson wrote to de Lima that his "huge University in Exile dinner, to stir up the campaign funds . . . came off well. The speakers were good and the enthusiasm great." So great, in fact, that he almost got "shipwrecked" by the standing ovation he received, which was "enough to knock all the words out of my head."[51]

A year later Johnson staged an even bigger event to mark the fourth anniversary of the University in Exile. It extended over three days in April 1937 with a two-day academic conference that featured a star-studded cast of scholars and a black-tie dinner. The conference addressed three issues: "Intellectual Freedom," "The Interrelation of Cultures," and "The Bearing of Education." Each panel mixed émigré and American scholars from the New School and neighboring institutions. The talks were published several months later in *Social Research* together with of a series of forceful responses by faculty discussants.[52]

The highlight of the three days was the keynote address at the fund-raising dinner by Nobel Laureate Thomas Mann. The exiled German writer had made the trip to New York from his new home in Switzerland to pay tribute to Johnson and to the University in Exile. In his speech, Mann confessed that when he received the invitation, he thought about turning it down. The trip was long, he said to himself, and he was shy about speaking in public. Not to mention that the timing was bad—he was trying to finish *Joseph and His Brothers*. Looking for a way to decline gracefully, Mann turned to the biblical Moses: "I am not eloquent, but of a slow tongue. Let my brother Aaron speak." Instead of offering him solace, the famous verse shamed him, as it had Moses. How "false and selfish" that would have been. He had no choice but to come "such as I am [and] declare myself for you." Writers who refused to speak out at a time like this were "traitors."[53]

As he concluded his remarks, Mann described an incident that had recently been "inflicted" on the University of Heidelberg and "should put every German to shame." He mentioned it now, on this occasion, because it gave the New School, which "we are here today to celebrate and honor," the opportunity to establish an enduring bond with the University of Heidelberg, the oldest university in Germany: A beautiful inscription, engraved above the entrance of a new building had recently been altered by the Ministry of Propaganda. What had once read, "To the Living Spirit," now read, "To the German Spirit." The meaning was clear: "There is—for the time being—no home for the living spirit in Germany's universities." Turning to Johnson, the German writer proposed: "I suggest that your faculty take these words and make them your motto, to indicate that the living spirit, driven from Germany, has found a home in this country."[54]

Everyone listening to Mann knew about the incident. *The New York Times* had covered the story the year before in one of the many articles it had published on the five-hundred-fiftieth anniversary celebration of the University of Heidelberg. In that same article it also reported that the Nazi authorities had taken down the statue of Athena, which had been standing above "To the Living Spirit," and replaced the goddess of wisdom with a golden swastika and eagle.

As Mann noted in his speech, the building in question had been a gift to the university from a group of American alumni. Jacob Gould Schurman, the former ambassador to Germany and an alumnus himself, was the man behind the idea and organizer of the fund-raising campaign. The building opened in 1931. In recognition of Schurman's "long years of devoted service to Heidelberg," the university had planned to pay tribute to its "chief foreign guest of honor" during the five-hundred-fiftieth anniversary festivities. But Schurman declined. As the *Times* told the story, when he learned that the Propaganda Ministry had turned the original inscription into a Nazi slogan, he "informed the university authorities that he would be unable to attend the ceremonies." After which we might have expected American professors to do the same, but they did not.

Nothing, apparently, could dissuade distinguished representatives of academic institutions in the United States from participating in the first of two major propaganda events that took place in Germany that summer. The second was the Olympics. Twenty U.S. colleges and universities sent delegates to Heidelberg, and these included some of the nation's leading academic institutions. Five professors from the United States accepted honorary doctorates as well.[55] In addition to marching in solemn processions, American scholars respectfully listened to speeches delivered by high-level party functionaries such as Dr. Bernhard Rust, Minister of Science, Education and the People's Education, who had this to say about the future of academic research in Germany:

> The old idea of science based on the sovereign right of abstract intellectual activity has gone forever. The new science is entirely different from the knowledge that found its value in an unchecked effort to reach the truth.
>
> The true freedom of science is to be an organ of a nation's living strength and of its historic fate and to present this in obedience to the law of truth.[56]

No other nation sent as large a delegation of professors to Heidelberg as the United States. The British sent nobody thanks to a successful boycott campaign that *The New York Times* had been covering for months. As early as February 1936, the *Times* reported, Oxford, Cambridge, London University, and Birmingham University had already announced that they would not attend. England's leading scientific journal *Nature* had taken a public stand as well, exposing what it claimed was the real motive for the celebration: The date chosen, *Nature* informed its readers, had little to do with Heidelberg's history. "It is the anniversary of the clean-up [the Nazi Party purge, June 30–July 2, 1934] which established more firmly the present dictatorship in the German Reich and its dependent universities." The year 1936 did not even mark Heidelberg's five-hundred-fiftieth anniversary but the five-hundred-forty-ninth: "It has seemed curious to many of us that Heidelberg should have arranged for a half century celebration . . . but it is even more strange that the 549th anniversary was chosen."[57]

Nicholas Murray Butler ignored the British boycott and sent a delegation from Columbia to Heidelberg. He also paid little attention to the demonstrations on campus protesting his decision, which had been organized by members of the faculty and student body. According to Michael Rosenthal, the president of Columbia University and recent recipient of the Nobel Peace Prize could still not bring himself in 1936 to take a stand against Germany out of loyalty to the country's great cultural heritage. As Rosenthal explains it, Butler's decision to have Columbia participate in the University of Heidelberg's anniversary celebration was "a kind of last-ditch effort." He still wanted to believe "that the rich contributions of German culture could overcome the horrors of Nazi politics."[58] By the time Mann gave his speech at the New School a year later, Butler had finally joined the opposition. Although he did not attend the benefit dinner, he sent warm greetings through a New School trustee, parts of which appeared the following day in *The New York Times*.[59]

It may have taken the president of Columbia University until 1937, but Butler was finally acknowledging publicly the "seductive power" of National Socialism, echoing what the exiled faculty had been writing about since 1934 on the pages of *Social Research*. Hitler was not only dangerous, he was growing stronger every day.[60] By 1938, several colleagues had begun looking for ways to reach Americans beyond the academic community. Now that Hitler had annexed Austria and parts of Czechoslovakia, everyone had to know what the German leader was saying in his own words. The only edition of *Mein Kampf* available in English at the time was an abridged and sanitized version, authorized by the Nazi Party. The New School would produce a new and complete translation.

9

RING THE ALARM

lvin Johnson rarely spoke about the role the New School had played in the late 1930s in preparing the first unabridged translation of *Mein Kampf* for an American audience. Despite the importance of the project and the publicity it received at the time, he ignored the subject entirely in his autobiography. He did mention it, however, as we have already seen, at a ribbon-cutting ceremony for the Hiram Halle Library in Pound Ridge, New York that took place the same year *Pioneer's Progress* was published. The translation had been Halle's idea.[1]

When Halle suggested the project to Johnson, the only English-language edition available in the United States was Houghton Mifflin's 1933 abridged and sanitized version of *Mein Kampf*, endorsed by the Nazi Party for foreign consumption. After reading this cleaned up rendition, Halle got hold of the original German and asked Johnson to have the Graduate Faculty prepare a new and complete translation. Mimeographed copies could then be distributed to university libraries across the country. Halle would cover all the costs.

Hans Staudinger welcomed the idea and began working on the project immediately, in the early months of 1938, together with a few other New School colleagues and research assistants. Two years later he produced a critical analysis of *Mein Kampf*—as a companion piece of sorts—that quoted extensively from the New School's translation. But he quickly rejected what he had written, out of fear, he confessed, that he had made Hitler's ideas too appealing, even to someone as sophisticated as Johnson. Finally, Johnson reportedly told him, Americans would understand why the Germans found their Führer so persuasive. Staudinger should publish the text in *Social Research*. Absolutely not, the émigré economist recoiled: "The Nazis were our enemy. We hated them. It could not be permitted that my book might somehow gain that enemy any admiration." In 1981, a year after Staudinger died, Peter Rutkoff and William Scott published a posthumous edition of the work under the title *The Inner Nazi*.[2]

Staudinger wrote the book with the hope, initially, of helping Americans see the evil depths to which Hitler was prepared to go. "Knowing the enemy" meant understanding the "power of [his] idea." Americans should read the madman's "labyrinthine book . . . as properly expressing Hitler's system"[3]—a system whose evil intentions the German economist had experienced firsthand. As a well-known member of the Social Democratic Party and a vigorous opponent of National Socialism, Staudinger had been an early victim of those ideas.

During the final years of the Weimar Republic, Staudinger had held a number of important government posts in the Social Democratic government of Prussia, the last as secretary of the Ministry of Trade and Commerce in the administration of Minister-President Otto Braun. He had also occupied a seat in the Reichstadt as an elected representative of his party. After Franz von Papen dissolved Braun's government in July 1932, Staudinger earned a name for himself as an outspoken member of the opposition until the Gestapo arrested him in April 1933 in an effort to silence him. When Staudinger refused to cooperate, the police brutally beat him. Several months later the authorities released him and let him emigrate, in large part thanks to an international lobbying effort that included the King of Belgium and influential friends in the United States. Accepting an invitation to join the University in Exile, Staudinger arrived in New York in 1934 in the company of his wife, who was of Jewish origin. Trained in economics and social work, Else Maier Staudinger played a leading role in the United States helping exiled professionals find work. Between 1945 and 1966 she served as the executive director of the American Council for Emigrés in the Professions, an organization she and Hans had founded at the end of the war.[4]

In September 1938, a few months after Staudinger and his colleagues began working on the *Mein Kampf* translation, Reynal & Hitchcock, a young publishing company, heard about what the New School was doing. One of the founders approached Johnson to see if he would consider publishing the book with them. Johnson checked with Halle: "Let them have it," Halle said, "if it is annotated, to make clear the essential villainy of Hitler."[5] Johnson communicated the terms to Reynal & Hitchcock, and the publisher accepted them.[6]

Next, Johnson approached George Shuster, editor of the progressive Catholic magazine *Commonweal* and asked him to assume the enormous task of annotating the translation. Shuster had already published two books on Nazi Germany and had just returned from Europe where the U.S. Department of State had sent him on a sensitive research assignment. Now back in New York, he had "a few bucketfuls of experiences and notes," he wrote, including his own eye-witness account of the *Anschluss* in Austria. Although he would have to work quickly, and under a great deal of pressure, Shuster let Johnson "cajole [him] into supplying the desired comments on the text."[7]

To oversee the project, Reynal & Hitchcock appointed a high-powered committee of "editorial sponsors" and made Johnson the chair. Aside from Shuster, the other members included three historians from Harvard and Columbia and five leading journalists.[8] In their introduction to the " Complete and Unabridged" edition, the sponsors explained the urgent need for having the full text of Hitler's meandering screed available in English.

When Houghton Mifflin decided to publish an abridged edition in 1933, it "seemed most unlikely," the sponsors began, "that any large American public would care to read *Mein Kampf* as a whole." Everything changed after England, France, and Italy shamefully signed the Munich Agreement on September 30, 1938, acquiescing to Germany's decision to break international law and annex the mineral-rich Sudetenland of Czechoslovakia. Since that fateful day, Americans had to have access to the work in its entirety: *Mein Kampf* was "probably the best written evidence of the character, the mind, and the spirit of Adolf Hitler and his government."

This new, annotated translation identified all the "passages of great importance" that did not appear in the abridged edition: for example, key sections of chapter 5 in which Hitler shared his "wartime reflections . . . on propaganda and on methods for fighting Marxism." These passages, together with Hitler's endless repetitions, would let Americans see that *Mein Kampf* "above all [was] a book of feeling," and its powerful emotive appeal was sweeping across Europe. The editorial sponsors warned their readers that Hitler was "no artist in literary expression, but a rough-and-ready political pamphleteer often indifferent to grammar and syntax alike." Tempted though they were to render equivalent flaws in English, the translators concluded that "no purpose would be served thereby." They did, however, reproduce German-style grammatical constructions to avoid distorting what Hitler was trying to say.[9]

Most important, the sponsors wanted their readers to understand why they had appended copious notes to the new translation. "Few Americans," they explained, "are, in the very nature of things, so aware of the German historical background that they can surmise without help what the author is discussing." But that was not the only reason. The sponsors had a moral obligation as well:

"No American [editor] would like to assume responsibility for giving the public a text which, if not tested in the light of diligent inquiry, might convey the impression that Hitler was writing history rather than propaganda."

If the book offered nothing more than nearly seven hundred pages of poorly written propaganda, why should anyone bother to read it? Because *Mein Kampf* had become "the most startling phenomenon of our time":

> The engines of industry now spin round in trepidation, and the engines of war are piled giddily in higher and higher pyramids. . . . There is no stopping them until there are in the world ideas or ideals which are stronger than that contained in *Mein Kampf*. It is our profound conviction that as soon as enough people have seen through this book, lived with it until the facts they behold are so startlingly vivid that all else is obscure by comparison, the tide will begin to turn.

The publication of the unabridged translation quickly turned into one the most politically charged controversies in copyright law of all time, causing a great deal of embarrassment for the New School. Once Johnson and Halle had signed on with Reynal & Hitchcock, the firm requested "a contract lease" from Houghton Mifflin, the lawful holders of the copyright for any future edition of the book in the United States. After protracted negotiations, Houghton Mifflin (the lessor) agreed to give Reynal & Hitchcock (the lessee) a three-year lease to publish an unabridged edition "on a royalty basis" that required the lessee to pay a percentage of the book's earnings both to the lessor and the author.

The idea that Reynal & Hitchcock, and by association the New School, would pay royalties to Hitler enraged members of the Jewish community and led to threats of a boycott. It also served as political fodder for another publishing house, Stackpole and Sons, which was trying to break into the market by selling its own "unauthorized" edition of *Mein Kampf*. Johnson received letters from good friends urging him to reconsider what the New School was doing. In his reply to the Zionist leader Bernard Flexner, he wrote, "I hate as much as you do the idea of royalties going to Hitler." But he was staying out of it, he added weakly. Halle was in charge, and he had weighed the options carefully. They would stick with Reynal & Hitchcock. "It is a complicated business however you view it, and I am glad I am not standing in a position of quasi agency," Johnson confessed.[10] Meanwhile, the copyright case between the competing translations was making its way through the courts where it eventually took an ironic turn, vindicating Halle and Johnson not only legally but morally.

In addition to paying royalties to Hitler, Houghton Mifflin imposed another compromising condition on the New School's translation: The accompanying commentary had to treat Hitler's work with respect. As Shuster tells the story, since Hitler was "the Company's client," Houghton Mifflin had written into the contract that "nothing derogatory could . . . be said about him" in either the notes or introduction accompanying the translation. In the end, Houghton Mifflin let the editors publish pretty much what they wanted, although Shuster recalled that for a time "it looked as if we were in great trouble. But Alvin Johnson who was a past master of dealing with such matters and I . . . [only] agreed to striking out a passage dealing with Hitler's relations with his niece, Geli Raubal." The young woman had died mysteriously in 1931.[11] Shuster's remaining commentary survived, as did the editorial committee's introduction, the contents of which were anything but friendly.

The bigger threat came from the competing publishing house. According to Stackpole and Sons, Houghton Mifflin did not own the translation rights to the unabridged edition for two reasons. First, the publishers of the abridged edition never demonstrated any prior interest in bringing out a complete and uncensored version of Hitler's work. The only claim Houghton Mifflin might have had would have been over another abridged edition. But they did not even have the right over that because (reason number two): According to Section 8 of the Copyright Act of 1909, the law only protected the rights of authors who were American citizens or citizens of other nations. It did not protect the rights of "stateless people."

When Hitler's publishers requested copyright protection on behalf of their author in 1925 for volume one of *Mein Kampf,* and again in 1927 for volume two, the leader of the Nazi Party was a stateless person. His application should have been rejected. In the papers submitted in 1925 by Franz Eher Nachfolger Verlag, the publishers identified Hitler accurately as a "*staatenlöser Deutscher.*" In 1927, they must have realized the risk they were running and referred to him this second time as an Austrian. Hitler, however, had renounced his Austrian citizenship in 1925, the same year *Mein Kampf* was published, and he would not gain German citizenship until 1932. The courts should therefore nullify the "alleged copyright" of *Mein Kampf,* Stackpole and Sons argued, and release the work into the public domain where any publishing house could bring out its own edition with no obligation to pay royalties to Hitler.

In mid-December 1938, Stackpole and Sons announced that they intended to challenge Houghton Mifflin's claim that they alone had the right to authorize the publication of an unabridged edition of *Mein Kampf* in the United States. On January 28, one month before Reynal & Hitchcock and Stackpole and Sons were both scheduled to release their translations, Houghton Mifflin submitted a formal request to the Federal District Court asking the judges to place a "preliminary injunction" on Stackpole and Sons to keep them from selling their translation of *Mein Kampf* until the legal dispute between the two firms had been fully resolved.

On February 28, the day the two editions were supposed to appear in bookstores, Judge Alfred Coxe of the Federal District Court denied Houghton Mifflin its petition for a preliminary injunction. "Judge Coxe said in his opinion that as the facts were in dispute and the issues could not properly be determined on affidavits, he did not think the case was clear enough to warrant a preliminary injunction, although 'it may be that the plaintiff will succeed at the trial' at which a permanent injunction will be asked."[12] Both editions were released later that same day.

On March 12, *The New York Times* published a review of the two translations, mentioning the ongoing legal battle but focusing on the differences between the two editions: "On the whole the Reynal & Hitchcock edition leaves the impression of having been more carefully prepared, both as to format and editorial handling." The presentation would have been even better, however, if "the relation between the body text and the annotations had been more clearly indicated."[13] Something Shuster would no doubt have happily done had the conflict between Reynal & Hitchcock and Stackpole and Sons not put so much pressure on him to meet an unrealistic deadline.

In making its case against Reynal & Hitchcock, Stackpole and Sons raised the specter of Hitler making a fortune off the sales of the so-called authorized edition, something he would not do from the sales of their translation. Instead of sending money to an evil dictator, Stackpole and Sons planned to donate its profits to refugees fleeing Nazi Germany. Thirteen distinguished scholars and religious leaders had agreed to serve on the committee it had created to determine how these funds would be distributed. Adding insult to injury, Stackpole and Sons' committee included the names of Wesley Clair Mitchell and Horace Kallen, among other friends of the New School.

In response to this "dirtiest announcement in this whole messy business," Eugène Reynal accused Stackpole and Sons of having stolen his publishing house's idea. Reynal & Hitchcock were the first to announce that they intended to use the money they had earned from selling *Mein Kampf* to help refugees. They too had appointed a special committee to distribute their cut of the royalties, chaired by none other than Alvin Johnson. As Reynal explained to the court,

> Johnson's name is extremely important and the New School should be sufficient guarantee to anyone that the book is not pro-Hitler.... Stackpole have announced that they will donate 5 percent of their proceeds to a refugee fund after learning of our proposal. They are paying no royalties whatever. This amounts to little

more than one-sixth of what we are paying in royalties alone. . . . [W]e are turning over all our profits to the refugees after deducting our legitimate expenses.

Houghton Mifflin submitted a second petition in April to the Second Circuit Court of Appeals, this time for a permanent injunction. Over the next two months, three judges—Charles Clark, Learned Hand, and Augustus Hand—reviewed the case; the Honorable Learned Hand had a long association with the New School.[14] Meanwhile, the two translations continued to compete with one another for sales as well as with pirated abridged editions that cost considerably less than either one of them.

Finally, on June 9, Judge Clark delivered the court's opinion in favor of Houghton Mifflin. The headline in the *Times* read: "Rights of Hitler to Book Upheld." But with an interesting twist:

In an opinion regarded as a new landmark in copyright law and which ironically promised succor to Europe's literary refugees, the Federal Circuit Court of Appeals ruled yesterday that whether or not Adolf Hitler was a man without a country when he completed *Mein Kampf,* the German Chancellor and his publishers are secure in their title to the copyright of his autobiographical and political treatise.

Quoting directly from the court's opinion, the *Times* continued:

"Any other result than this would be unfortunate, for it would mean that stateless aliens cannot be secure in even their literary property. [Judge Clark then went on to explain]:

"True, the problem of statelessness has only become acute of latter years, but it promises to become increasingly more difficult as time goes on.

"The rule contended for by the defendants [Stackpole and Sons] would mean the United States, contrary to its general policy and tradition, is putting another obstacle in the way of survival of homeless refugees, of whom many have been students and scholars and writers."[15]

Still unwilling to give up, Stackpole and Sons took their case to the Supreme Court, where once again they lost.[16] When the justices announced on October 23 that they would not review the case, the publishers went back to the Second Court of Appeals with another copyright technicality. This last attempt dragged on until August 1941, after which Stackpole and Sons had no further recourse and accepted to defeat.

In the end, Hitler never saw his royalties. Once the case was settled, Houghton Mifflin charged Hitler's publishers for half the cost of the legal fees, which canceled out any royalties due Hitler up to that point. Four months later, when the United States declared war on Germany, all royalties due Hitler were set aside in a special government account, as required by the Trading with the Enemy Act and there the money remained until the end of the war, by which time Hitler was dead.

In 1942, Houghton Mifflin decided against renewing Reynal & Hitchcock's contract, preferring to publish a new translation of its own in a more fluid English than the New School's version and without George Shuster's running commentary. But before the New School's translation went out of print, it had sold more than 250,000 copies, making it possible for Reynal & Hitchcock to donate tens of thousands of dollars to organizations dedicated to helping refugees.[17]

On May 11, 1939, about a month before the Second Federal Court of Appeals had delivered its opinion, Eugène Reynal wrote to Johnson to confirm officially that the publishers had appointed him chairman of a committee of three "to handle the funds to be turned over to the refugees, resulting from the sale of our edition of *Mein Kampf*." To work with Johnson, the publishers had appointed Joseph Chamberlain, professor of law at Columbia University, who was serving as the U.S. representative on the Intergovernmental High Commission for Refugees, and James McDonald, chairman of President Roosevelt's Advisory Committee on Refugees. Reynal told Johnson that the firm had set up a special bank account in which he had just deposited a check for $20,000 from the Book-of-the-Month Club, designated specifically to help children.[18]

Even before Reynal made his appointment official, Theodore Newcomb, the chairman of the Bennington County Committee for Refugee Aid and a professor of sociology at Bennington College, wrote to Johnson to say that he had heard from one of his board members, Dorothy Canfield Fisher, that the Bennington program would probably receive aid from the *Mein Kampf* royalties fund to cover the cost of placing between forty and fifty refugee children in the homes of rural Vermont families for the summer. Writer, educator, feminist, and social activist, Canfield Fisher was Johnson's old friend from their student days in Nebraska. She was also a member of the editorial committee of the Book-of-the-Month Club and had no doubt influenced the club's decision to restrict the use of the money to children.

Johnson asked his committee to allocate $4,000 to the Bennington Project right away. Then, with the help of the American Jewish Joint Distribution

Committee, he put together a comprehensive list of the major agencies helping refugee children and reached out to them. Among the agencies and special projects that received contributions from the *Mein Kampf* fund—many of them in France and Palestine[19]—the most generous gift went to Canfield Fisher's Children's Crusade for Children. The fund covered all of the administrative costs of the program, making it possible for her to send every penny of the $140,000 she collected from American schoolchildren to organizations supporting the needs of young refugees.

Canfield Fisher made sure that everyone knew how grateful she was for the support she received from the *Mein Kampf* fund. But nothing, apparently, could persuade Johnson to discuss the translation project in *Pioneer's Progress*. Looking back on the incident, it is difficult to understand why he did not relish the ironic turn of events: Having stuck by their publishers' argument that Hitler had a right to earn royalties, the New School participated in a landmark decision that changed the nation's copyright law in favor of thousands of writers made stateless by the author of this heinous work![20]

In addition to working on the translation of *Mein Kampf*, colleagues at the Graduate Faculty were editing a collection of essays aimed at a more scholarly audience. Anticipating the inevitable, *War in Our Time* included analyses by seventeen colleagues about the impact the war would have on power politics and sovereignty, economics and labor, population growth and displacement, food distribution, political propaganda, and the role of the church. In his foreword to the collection, Johnson talked about the painful responsibility social scientists had to help Americans understand the implications of what was happening in Europe. Now that the leaders of democratic states had abandoned their friends to make "peace in our time," the contributors to this volume felt compelled to speak out, even louder than they had been doing, not with bombastic rhetoric but with careful analysis and empirical detail:

> We are living in what even the most cautious will describe as an epoch of tremendous changes in economics, in politics, in ethics, in law, in international relations. All things social-political appear to be in flux. There is no longer any validity in the most sacred of international contracts, as the betrayal of Czechoslovakia amply proves. That regard for the accepted rules of the game honored even by the red-handed conqueror of old has disappeared without a trace. What was once known as treason and betrayal of one's country to an implacable foreign enemy is now defended as conservative policy.[21]

Social Research published increasingly urgent articles as well on "the sources, meaning, and implications of persecution."[22] Although the contributions focused primarily on Germany, a few of them made comparisons between National Socialism and Italian Fascism, on the one hand, and Stalinist Communism, on the other, anticipating the arguments Hannah Arendt would make after the war in *Origins of Totalitarianism.* Although Arendt did not cite this earlier work, her analysis of mass movements in classless societies resonated with the arguments being made in the late 1930s by colleagues at the New School, most prominently by Emil Lederer in *State of the Masses: The Threat of the Classless Society.*[23] And like Arendt, but over a decade earlier, Lederer and his colleagues faced vigorous criticism from Marxist intellectuals for drawing parallels between Nazi Germany and the USSR. In the case of the New School's refugee scholars, they faced criticism from members of Max Horkheimer's Institute of Social Research, in particular the legal theorist and political scientist Franz Neumann.

In the early 1940s, Neumann described Max Ascoli in a private letter as a "puffed-up idiot of unmatched vanity." Speier, he wrote, was "a sly, highly intelligent, and formally extremely clever scoundrel." As for *Social Research*, he dismissed the journal summarily, claiming that it was publishing little of any significance.[24] More substantively and publicly, Neumann attacked Lederer's *State of the Masses* in his widely acclaimed book, *Behemoth: The Structure and Practice of National Socialism* that came out in 1942.[25] Speier had published Lederer's work in 1940, the year after his mentor died. In his foreword, the sociologist noted that Lederer had started writing his book in 1938, "after Czechoslovakia had been wiped off the map of Europe." By the time Germany invaded Poland eleven months later, Lederer was dead. *State of the Masses*, in other words, was a "testimony to the political acumen of the author, who never believed in the possibility of appeasing Hitler."[26]

As Lederer explained in the introduction to his book, Europe's dictatorships at the present time had nothing in common with what had come before. They represented "a modern political system which rests on the amorphous masses." The current crisis was not just another "manifestation of the class struggle, but the destruction of society at large, the substitution for society of institutionalized masses." For Lederer, the idea of analyzing the modern totalitarian state from a Marxian perspective was a mistake because it did not resemble what Marx had observed in the nineteenth century and then used as the basis for his theory: "There has never been a state which destroyed the social structure to such an extent, and there has never been a time which offered the technical opportunities of today to transform the whole people into masses and keep them in this state."[27]

Although Neumann conceded that "a little of the truth sifts into some of his formulations," he claimed that Lederer was basically wrong. He dismissed the economist's argument that the leaders of totalitarian states destroy social classes entirely. For Neumann, the "essence of National Socialist social policy"—and he limited his analysis to Nazi Germany alone—"consists in the acceptance and strengthening of the prevailing class character of German society." The ruling class consolidates its authority while it destroys the cohesion of "the subordinate strata" by suppressing "every autonomous group mediating between them and the state" and replacing these groups with a "system of autocratic bureaucracies [that] interfere with all human relations." According to Neumann, Lederer did not consider the possibility that some societies "may be divided into classes and yet not be socially differentiated in any other way," and that others may be "classless" but still "have sharp differentiations."[28]

A number of scholars have written about the disagreements individual members of the New School for Social Research had with members of the Institute of Social Research. Perhaps the best-known account is Martin Jay's *The Dialectical Imagination*, which came out in 1973. The German intellectual historian Rolf Wiggerhaus has written about the conflicts as well in his history of the Frankfurt School, which appeared in English in 1994. Both works described the Graduate Faculty as "anti-Marxist" and "anti-Freudian" and therefore, by definition, hostile to the institute.[29]

Speier may never have read Wiggerhaus's book. It came out in English after he died. But if he saw the German edition, he must have railed against it the way he did against Jay's, particularly when Wiggerhaus asserted that the New School had launched a campaign to "discredit the Institute in the eyes of grant institutions" by insinuating that members of the Frankfurt School had ties to the Communist Party.[30]

In his review of *The Dialectical Imagination*, the ever-combative Speier dismissed Jay's descriptions of the University in Exile as "distortions of the truth," adding that it "should have been easy for Professor Jay to get his facts straight." For example, in the case of Emil Lederer, the so-called anti-Marxist, he "had been close to the Austro-Marxists and identified himself as a socialist." The New School, what is more, "had a tradition," Speier continued, "of supporting radical and Communist Americans in New York"—a statement he knew perfectly well needed qualification.[31] In 1935, Speier and his fellow émigré scholars had written into the charter of the Graduate Faculty that they would not hire communists, a policy subsequently adopted by the entire New School even if its president interpreted it loosely.

Speier also rejected Jay's claim that Max Wertheimer and he did not socialize with members of the institute because they were skeptical about the way the Frankfurt School had applied Freud's ideas to the social sciences. That was ridiculous, Speier wrote. He conceded that he "was doubtful of the value of Freudian psychology for an analysis of social phenomena," but Speier pointed out that he had collaborated productively and amicably over the years with the psychoanalyst Ernst Kris. He had also taught a seminar with Karen Horney. "Apparently," Speier concluded, "Professor Jay believes that criticism must be equated with hostility."

Speier might have given other examples. Although Lowe and Horkheimer had serious intellectual and political differences, they became good friends in Frankfurt and reconnected in New York. Other members of the two institutions struck up friendships in exile. After Horkheimer arrived in 1934, he saw a great deal of Lederer, Colm, and Staudinger.[32] Less so of Speier, the sociologist admitted, but they socialized as well in Lederer's home. Speier's friends from the institute, he wrote, included Otto Kircheimer, Herbert Marcuse, and Neumann himself, "especially during the years we worked for the Federal Government."[33]

Even if we side with Speier, it is difficult to ignore the conflict that erupted between Neumann and several members of the GF in the spring of 1941. Both institutions had applied to the Rockefeller Foundation, seeking support for research projects to study totalitarianism. When Neumann learned that Rockefeller had turned down his proposal in favor of the one Johnson had written for the New School, he complained bitterly to the foundation. In an effort to appease the legal theorist, Rockefeller urged Neumann to sit down with the recipients of the New School grant to learn what they were planning to do and then submit a new proposal that did not duplicate their research. Neumann rejected the offer because, he told Horkheimer, he refused to serve as "a mere handmaiden" for others. At which point he severed what ties he had with the New School, encouraging his colleagues at the institute to do the same.[34]

As Claus-Dieter Krohn described the falling out,

Horkheimer tried repeatedly . . . to mend fences between the two camps. Out of a sense of intellectual isolation he begged the querulous Neumann to be a little more restrained in his attacks on others, for the Institute's circle of friends was getting smaller and smaller. He sent even clearer signals to Lowe. In spite of profound differences of opinion between them, he sought out contact with

Lowe because in him he found "that sense of liberality that is becoming rarer and rarer in the thinking of our own friends."[35]

Before he applied to Rockefeller for support, Johnson had proposed to the Board of Trustees that the New School establish a research institute. The GF, he explained in the spring of 1940, had the experience the U.S. government was looking for at this critical juncture in the country's history: "The era has begun in which the United States will be compelled to take active responsibility for the shaping of world affairs." Americans, however, did not have the background they needed to assume their new role in the international arena. Although a handful of independent organizations, such as the Council on Foreign Relations and the Carnegie Endowment for International Peace, were doing research on specific foreign policy issues, and although a number of universities had established professorial chairs for scholars of international affairs, "there does not exist any institution which can integrate this diffuse material into systematic studies." Given the nation's isolationist tendencies, the United States never saw the need to create a research institute specializing in foreign policy similar to the Institute of World Economics in Kiel, founded in 1910, or the Royal Institute of International Affairs in London, founded in 1920.

As Johnson explained it to the Board of Trustees, before 1933 the Kiel Institute had a reputation for being "the most competent source of sound information on economic and political conditions throughout the world." Now, sadly, "the sinister role" the institute was playing under the Nazis "in preparing the plans for the economic penetration of Europe [was] further proof of its efficiency." Similarly, the Royal Institute had been providing the British government with much needed research in support of the war effort: "The Royal Institute is serving the British Government as its main Intelligence Agency on all international questions, and at the same time as the preparatory body for British plans on international reconstruction."[36]

Johnson knew that the National Defense Commission had been looking for specialists since 1939 to do research on Germany's early military success,[37] and the New School had those specialists. By 1940 Johnson had recruited scholars from practically every occupied nation in Europe, many of whom had been working as policy analysts in various government ministries and research institutes until the Germans pushed them out.[38] Three years later, he boasted in a fund-raising brochure that the New School had the "largest body of international affairs experts of any institution in America . . . providing the government with considerable information—much of it confidential." He then listed the names of twenty-three federal agencies that were consulting with members of the GF and other researchers affiliated with the New School.[39] Three colleagues were also holding key positions in Washington, D.C.: Colm at the Bureau of the Budget, Ascoli at the Office of the Coordinator of Inter-American Affairs, and Speier at the Federal Communications Commission.

Although the Institute of World Affairs (IWA) did not open officially until 1943, colleagues were engaged in major research projects by 1941, largely thanks to the support they received from the Rockefeller Foundation. By 1942, Johnson had several projects going, all of which were producing confidential reports for the U.S. State Department and other agencies, as well as publications for the wider scholarly and policy communities. When IWA officially opened in November 1943, Johnson appointed Adolph Lowe as the institute's executive director, a position similar to the one he had held in the 1920s at the Institute of World Economics in Kiel.

In his inaugural remarks, Johnson noted that after Lowe fled Germany in 1933 he spent the next eight years in England where he "made [himself] intimately familiar with the operations of the Royal Institute." Nobody, in other words, was better qualified than Lowe to run IWA. Now that the institute had officially opened, it would give "definite form to the New School's research activities which presently consisted of "seven research groups, directed by fifteen members of our Faculty, employing sometimes more than twenty trained research assistants."[40]

During the war years, IWA ran on average four to five projects a year that focused on a wide number of critical questions, both local and international. The faculty recruited advanced graduate students to help with the research, providing them with "systematic training in research" as they worked side by side with their professors. Among the most significant research sponsored by IWA were two studies on totalitarian societies, one of which, directed by Speier and Kris, analyzed Nazi propaganda on the radio.[41]

The second project on totalitarianism, which the Rockefeller Foundation also funded in 1941—in this case for $40,000—looked at the "whole question of what is actually taking place in the internal economy of Germany and Russia, and what exactly is the status and condition of the working classes on whose behalf totalitarian propaganda claims the new regimes have been established." Known as the Social and Economic Controls in Germany and Russia Project, its collaborators included Frieda Wunderlich, Hans Staudinger, Arthur Feiler, Adolph Lowe, Jacob Marschak, and eight research assistants. This project produced a number of publications, among them a book on Russian industry and agriculture.[42]

During the 1940s, Johnson enjoyed telling his New School friends that members of the Roosevelt administration were consulting with the faculty regularly on highly sensitive matters concerning the economic and political reconstruction of Europe. Soon, he hoped, the government would also consult his colleagues on other parts of the world. From the very beginning he had also wanted the New School to do research in Latin America as part of Roosevelt's "Good Neighbor Policy," which was aimed at improving economic and political relations between the United States and their neighbors to the south.

With the hope of expanding the reach of the New School in international affairs, Johnson opened the Ibero-American Center in 1939 to explore ways to combine "scientific research and practical business experience" throughout the Americas. To direct the center, he appointed the "incomparable" Fernando de los Ríos, a Spanish legal scholar and diplomat who, in Johnson's eyes, was "almost a faculty in himself."[43] Before joining the GF, de los Ríos had been serving as ambassador to the United States from the Spanish Republic. When the nation's democratically elected government fell to Franco in 1939, de los Ríos resigned as ambassador and came to the New School, where he remained until he died in 1949.

When IWA opened, Johnson annexed the Ibero-American Center to the new institute. Then in 1945, he asked Sumner Welles to chair the center's "Board of Councilors." Welles had recently retired as undersecretary of state in the Roosevelt administration where before that he had served as assistant secretary of state of Latin America. In that earlier capacity, Welles had played a key role in developing the Good Neighbor Policy. As he announced these exciting new developments, Johnson added that the center would sponsor lectures in Spanish and English with the hope of producing a dynamic exchange of ideas among specialists in the region. The center would engage as well in new research that furthered "knowledge and understanding of the Latin American countries, particularly their economic structures and their meaning for intra-hemispheric economic relations." But the "ultimate aim" of the expanded center was to help the New School do a better job than it had been doing of attracting students from Latin America to study at the university's new francophone division, the Ecole Libre des Hautes Etudes.[44]

For generations, Johnson explained, members of Latin America's elites had been sending their children to France to complete their university education, a practice they had to interrupt in 1939 because of the war. Now, since 1942, a new opportunity had opened up for them in New York to study in an accredited French-language university that had the imprimatur of the exiled government of Free France Unfortunately, not very many were coming.

10

ECOLE LIBRE DES HAUTES ETUDES

When France fell on June 22, 1940, Alvin Johnson placed a call to Raymond Fosdick, president of the Rockefeller Foundation, and made an appointment to see him right away. He would worry about the details on the trip uptown.[1] As the Sixth Avenue bus made its way from Twelfth Street to Forty-Ninth and Rockefeller Center, Johnson decided to ask Fosdick to sponsor fifteen scholars. In the elevator, he raised the number to twenty-five, then to one hundred because, Johnson explained, Fosdick was being "so cordial." The foundation's president accepted Johnson's proposal and presented it to his executive committee: "A few days later Dr. Johnson had assurance that financing was available for 100 émigrés."[2] And with that, the president of the New School wasted no time in reaching out to scholars trapped in France and Belgium, assuming correctly that his contacts in Washington would come through once again with the necessary visas. Although it was too late for the new refugees to teach in the fall, the names of several of them appeared in the course bulletin for the spring.[3]

The Rockefeller Archives have preserved dozens of letters from members of this second wave of displaced scholars, many of which capture in vivid detail what these refugees were going through as they tried to get out of occupied France. Several letters describe the plight of the philosopher Jean Wahl. By the time Johnson's invitation reached him, Wahl was deathly ill, wasting away in an internment camp in Drancy, a small city on the outskirts of Paris. In one memo, a staff member from Rockefeller reported with disgust that "the camp physician recommended [Wahl's] release to save burial expenses." Despite his fragile condition, the philosopher somehow made it to Lisbon, but he still had to wait until his boat set sail for New York before he received any medical attention. After a brief stay at the New School, Wahl moved to Mount Holyoke College where he remained for many years.[4]

Johnson had less luck with Marc Bloch. By the time he heard from the Medieval historian, Bloch and his family had fled Paris and were living in the so-called Free Zone, which was under the control of the collaborationist government of Vichy. Jewish academics could no longer teach in the Zone Libre either, but the Ministry of Education had exempted Bloch from the "racial laws" and offered him a position in Montpellier, an exception it made very rarely for highly regarded scholars. Technically, therefore, Bloch did not qualify for a teaching position at the New School, reserved exclusively for deposed scholars, but Johnson made an exception for him as well and did what he could to help him get out of France together with his wife and six children.

Bloch was eager to leave, he told Johnson and the Rockefeller Foundation, not so much for himself, but for the sake of his family. He would only do so, however, if they could get him two visas, one for himself, his wife and four dependent children, and another for two sons who were over the age of eighteen. Miraculously, the U. S. Consulate agreed, but it would not release the second visa before June 1941, by which time, Bloch predicted, it would be too late. He was right. As they were waiting for the second visa to arrive, Vichy passed a new law "preventing every Frenchman, between the ages of 18 and 40, from leaving the metropolitan territory."

On July 31, Bloch wrote to Johnson to thank him for all he had tried to do for him and his family, and to apologize for having to decline his kind invitation to come to the New School. After the second visa arrived, he tried to persuade the Vichy authorities to let his two older boys leave with the rest of the family, but as he expected they denied his request. Although his sons, Bloch added, had urged him to go without them, that was out of the question. When the Germans occupied the Free Zone in November 1942, Bloch joined the resistance. Captured in the spring of 1944, he was tortured and killed by the infamous Klaus Barbie, the "butcher of Lyon."[5]

=◆=

As Johnson welcomed his new colleagues from Belgium and France, he realized that the New School could open an international university in exile:

> It had been my dream to build up in the New School an organization of international studies. The New School had never had resources enough to expand adequately the representation of foreign scholars of non-German origin. . . .

Now the opportunity for a great expansion appeared at hand. French and Belgian scholars of great renown had come under the New School roof. . . .

Professor Gustave Cohen had another plan. With the refugee scholars at the New School and the members of the French departments in nearby universities, he proposed to set up a regular French university, with all the conventional faculties, using French as the medium of instruction, giving certificates that would answer the requirements for Civil Service positions in the great African areas controlled by General [Charles] de Gaulle [*sic*]. . . .

I accepted Professor Cohen's plan with enthusiasm.[6]

When the Ecole Libre opened a year and a half later, the New School boasted a veritable "Who's Who of French and Belgian culture." The faculty included more than sixty scholars in the sciences, humanities, and social sciences, among them Jean-Baptiste Perrin, a Nobel Laureate in physics; mathematicians Jacques Hadamard and André Weil; philosophers Jacques Maritain and Alexandre Koyré; historians Gustave Cohen, Henri Focillon, and Henri Grégoire; legal scholars Henri Bonnet and Boris Mirkine-Guetzévitch; and the former prime minister of Belgium, Paul van Zeeland. Although Johnson paid little attention to them at the time, the Ecole had also welcomed the renowned linguist Roman Jakobson and the young anthropologist Claude Lévi-Strauss.

With this eminent group of francophone scholars, students who wanted to study in French had the opportunity to take a full program of courses in the sciences, social sciences, law, literature, and the humanities, all at a level comparable to the best universities in France and Belgium before the occupation. As Johnson proudly proclaimed to an overflowing crowd at the inaugural ceremony, the degrees and certificates conferred by the Ecole Libre would be treated as "fully legal French university diplomas" by General de Gaulle, the leader of Free France.

When Johnson founded the University in Exile, he did so, he claimed, to honor the New School's commitment to American democracy and to "express by word and act its own faith in the value of academic liberty." The financial support he received for his efforts in 1933 came only from American citizens who shared his convictions. But when Johnson opened the Ecole Libre in February 1942, he accepted gifts from foreign parties as well, most significantly from Charles de Gaulle and his Free France movement, the declared enemies of Vichy, with whom the U.S. government still had diplomatic ties. Johnson managed to keep the Department of Justice at bay for about two more years, maintaining that the Ecole Libre was not a political institution. The money it had received from resistance movements based overseas was for cultural, not political, purposes. In addition to Free France, it had also accepted gifts from Free Belgium and Free Czechoslovakia. Johnson's argument, needless to say, was not entirely persuasive.

The New School announced its plans to open a Free French School of Higher Studies on Armistice Day, November 11, 1941, a date loaded with political symbolism. Known today more inclusively as Veterans Day, November 11 at the time commemorated the end of World War I and the victory of the Allies over Germany. On this particular Armistice Day, New York's exiled French community was marking the occasion with a patriotic rally in support of Free France. For Johnson and his colleagues, the gathering provided an ideal opportunity to announce the opening of their French-language university.

The New York Times reported that "2,000 French men and women and their friends gathered at the Manhattan Centre to commemorate the anniversary of the only armistice with Germany recognized by them." The event, the *Times* continued, was "more a spectacle than an occasion for speeches," with old newsreels showing the French celebrating their victory over Germany at the end of the Great War. Before the evening broke up, the director of labor of Free France (Henry Hauck) interrupted the entertainment to read Armistice Day greetings from Charles de Gaulle and the governor and mayor of New York. Then Henri Focillon rose and addressed the assembled. Introducing himself as the director of the Ecole Libre, he announced "the organization of a 'Free French University,' . . . at the New School for Social Research," which General de Gaulle, he added proudly, had publicly endorsed.[7]

It is difficult to believe that Johnson did not understand what he was doing when he allowed the New School to associate itself with a political event organized by supporters of de Gaulle. Or what he continued to do over the next twelve months in spite of the fact that Roosevelt maintained diplomatic relations with France's collaborationist government until Vichy fell in November 1942, after which FDR still refused to recognize de Gaulle, allying the United States instead with Henri Giraud, the leader of a competing faction in the resistance. Roosevelt only accepted de Gaulle as the rightful leader of Free France in the fall of 1943, by which time the Ecole Libre had been open for over a year.

Johnson tried to finesse the situation by playing it both ways, and he expected the Ecole's faculty to do the same, but many of them resisted. The press was more cooperative. Journalists repeated Johnson's double-talk in their articles, but in doing so they revealed the weakness of his argument. Two days after Focillon made his announcement at the Armistice Day event, *The New York Daily News* published a full-page spread about the Free French School. Its author, Hal Lehrman, described the Ecole as the intellectual arm of de Gaulle's movement: "Free France," he proclaimed, "was opening a new front against Hitler on the battleground of ideas." Basing his description on Agnes de Lima's press release, Lehrman faithfully repeated that the Ecole Libre "has taken no formal stand against Vichy"; it "carried a big stick only for freedom." However, Lehrman continued, "there is no balm for Marshal Pétain on 12th Street. One of the university's most prized possessions is a cable of congratulations from the leader of Free France, Gen. Charles de Gaulle."[8]

The article caused Johnson a great deal of embarrassment. Worried about the fallout, he complained to the editor on the day it appeared (November 13, 1941):

> While the facts given by your reporter are essentially correct, the general effect of the article gives an impression that is misleading, and that I beg you to correct. The institution is made to appear as a part of the Free French movement and in opposition to Vichy. As a fact, it takes no political stand whatever. It would be highly improper for a group of foreign scholars to set themselves up to represent a foreign political party. This every member of the group recognizes.
>
> The New School entered this undertaking in the belief that America has much to gain from a more intimate understanding of the French culture of the great past and the great future. No political connections, no political propaganda, are possible under the settled policy of the New School. In this the group of French and Belgian scholars participating in the Ecole Libre is in complete agreement.[9]

Not everyone shared Johnson's confidence. At the Rockefeller Foundation, Tracy Kittredge, assistant director of the Social Science Division, informed his colleagues on November 24 that the Ecole's faculty "is predominantly composed of scholars who have adhered to the [Free] French movement." The organizers, he added, were counting on the U.S. State Department to recognize de Gaulle's National Council as "the de facto government of those parts of French territory under their military control." And when it does, the leading forces organizing the Ecole planned to seek "official designation as a French university in exile." All of this before the United States had even entered the war! [10]

As if this were not alarming enough, the same group of Gaullists had apparently warned two members of the faculty that they might lose their jobs after the school officially opened if they continued to complain about the Ecole Libre's political orientation. A threat, Kittredge reminded his colleagues at Rockefeller, that the Ecole's leadership had no right to make because "these stipends come from Foundation grants, [so] this pressure would appear to be unauthorized."[11]

Kittredge concluded his memo saying that the Ecole looked more like a "political manifestation" than an academic institution.

⸻◆⸻

The inaugural ceremony on February 14, 1942, confirmed Kittredge's assessment of the situation. Expecting a big crowd, Johnson gratefully accepted the offer of his old friend George Shuster, now president of Hunter College, to host the event in the college's new auditorium. Located on Park Avenue between Sixty-Eighth and Sixty-Ninth Streets, the space could hold three times as many people as the New School's theater on Twelfth Street. In the press release describing the inauguration, de Lima wrote,

> More than two thousand people prominent in educational and social circles crowded into the assembly hall of Hunter College last evening to celebrate the formal opening of the Ecole Libre des Hautes Etudes organized as a French university under the sponsorship of the New School for Social Research with a faculty of over sixty distinguished French and Belgian scholars in this country.
>
> A feature of the occasion was the reading of a congratulatory cablegram from General Charles de Gaulle welcoming the founding of the new institution on the free soil of America, as well as an additional message containing his official decree recognizing the certificate to be granted by the Ecole Libre as equivalent to those of French universities: "The diplomas and university certificates conferred after examination by the Ecole Libre des Hautes Etudes in New York are recognized as fully legal French university diplomas."

De Lima then quoted Focillon, who, embracing de Gaulle's message, added, "The Ecole Libre was founded primarily with the aim of serving disinterested knowledge. But under the present circumstances, its foundation takes on particular significance. By serving truth we also serve and are determined to serve, freedom." De Lima also quoted Gustave Cohen, whom she described as "formerly of the Sorbonne and now dean of the Faculty of Letters of the Ecole Libre." Grateful to the U.S. Government for its warm hospitality, Cohen announced that he and his colleagues "had telegraphed President Roosevelt that they were at his entire disposal" to work for the national defense of the American people. But nobody, de Lima continued, should draw the wrong conclusion. The Ecole Libre had no political program beyond "the noblest of all, freedom and free and creative scholarship." A distinction that did not prevent the assembled from singing the national anthems of the United States, Free France, and Free Belgium at the end of this triumphant evening.[12]

While Johnson insisted that the Ecole Libre had no "political program," he continued accepting financial support from Free France, Free Belgium, and Free Czechoslovakia. And while he chose his words carefully, what Johnson said, when he thanked his donors could only be interpreted as political endorsements. For example:

> Ever since the occupation of France by the Nazi barbarians, American scholars have pondered more and more deeply the importance of France to our modern civilization, the debt of America to French philosophy and culture. It was French philosophy that colored the thought of the writer of the Declaration of Independence and the framers of the Constitution. France will play a greater role than ever when the present error recedes into history.[13]

The city's newspapers echoed the same sentiment. In its article about the inaugural ceremony, *The New York Times* proclaimed:

> When Rome fell, the scholars fled to Constantinople. When Constantinople fell about a thousand years later, the scholars returned to Italy. Barbarian rule in various countries at various times has always benefited other countries to which the wise and thoughtful were exiled. So, in our own day.[14]

The first semester began on February 16, 1942. Five and a half weeks later, the Ecole Libre boasted an enrollment of more than four hundred students, who were attending fifty lecture courses, a few seminars, and special conferences divided among three different academic programs: science, letters, and law. In addition to building a strong curriculum of courses for undergraduates, the faculty created six research centers: the Center of Art, Drama and Cinema; the Institute of Sociology; the Institute of Comparative Law; the Center for the Study of International Relations; the Latin American Center; and the Institute of Philology and Oriental and Slavic History. The Latin American Center, under the direction of Claude Lévi-Strauss, established ties with Fernando de los Ríos's Ibero-American Center, an arrangement that provided the young anthropologist with additional resources and visibility. But the best-endowed center of them all was the Institute of Philology and Oriental and Slavic History, which came over "intact" from the University of Brussels. Thanks to a gift from the exiled Czech government, the Belgian institute welcomed the famous Prague School of Linguistics, directed by the eminent Russian linguist Roman Jakobson. After the invasion of Czechoslovakia in 1938, Jakobson had moved the imperiled school to the Sorbonne in Paris, only to have to move it again when the Germans occupied France. Several members of the Ecole Libre also taught at the Graduate Faculty and, after 1943, did research at the Institute of World Affairs.[15]

Finally, with the help of Alvin Johnson, the Ecole Libre launched a French-language academic journal in the winter of 1943 modeled on *Social Research*. The first issue proudly reproduced a letter from President Roosevelt addressed to the philosopher Alexandre Koyré, secretary general of the Ecole. Dated November 5, 1942, Roosevelt wrote to Koyré three days before American forces landed in French North Africa. Despite his antipathy for General de Gaulle at the time, President Roosevelt decided, apparently, to look the other way:

My dear Dr. Koyré:

It has given me great pleasure to read the report of the Ecole Libre des Hautes Etudes covering the work of its first term.

Wherever French and Belgian scholars maintain purity and the honor of French and Belgian thought, the spirit of France and Belgium is maintained.

The light of French culture has illuminated the world; so long as it is maintained, France cannot die. France is passing through dark hours. She has done so before, and has nevertheless arisen in strength and confidence. . . .

French thought was not made for slaves. Those who keep it alive work for the liberation of France and Belgium.

Very truly yours,
Franklin D. Roosevelt[16]

Despite the high quality of the faculty, the Ecole Libre did not succeed as an academic institution. Its rapid decline may help explain why it did not have the same impact on American scholarship as the New School's Graduate Faculty. There were, of course, some important exceptions. Claude Lévi-Strauss and Roman Jakobson's historic encounter at the Ecole Libre led to the founding of French structuralism. But even here, as Aristide Zolberg has pointed out, "unlike the German achievements, which quickly took root in the United States and radiated from that center, structuralism germinated in France in the 1950s, and returned to the country of its birth only a decade later."[17]

In other ways, the Ecole Libre was a huge success. Within a matter of months, it had become the most important center of French and Belgian intellectual and cultural life in North America. During the war years, it attracted large audiences, eager to hear professors lecture in French on a wide range of topics. And as word got out, the Ecole's faculty grew from sixty to one hundred. Most of them, however, had permanent positions elsewhere and gave only an occasional talk or a short series of lectures at the New School.

The biggest challenge facing the Ecole Libre was its inability to recruit students to register for academic degrees. Almost nobody had predicted the problem, either on the faculty or in the media. In his *Daily News* article, Lehrman spoke confidently about how the French school would "do much for the good neighbor cause."[18] But where were the children of Latin America's elites, or those of the francophone émigrés for that matter? Unable to go to France, the Latin Americans had apparently stayed home, and the sons and daughters of French-speaking émigés were attending U.S. universities instead. Having very few full-time students, the New School turned the Ecole Libre into the francophone annex of its adult education program.

As the months wore on, leading members of the faculty interrupted their teaching to work for their exiled governments, leaving the United Sates for extended periods of time. Paul van Zeeland, the former prime minister of Belgium, was almost never around. Henri Bonnet resigned in 1943 to head the French Comité de Libération in Algiers. When the Allies liberated Belgium and France in the summer of 1944, many more returned home, leading the press to conclude that the Ecole Libre would soon close its doors. On February 24, 1945, *The New York Times* bid the francophone faculty farewell, thanking them for the contributions they had made to American intellectual and cultural life. As the war was coming to an end, "members of the Ecole's faculty," the *Times* wrote, "are in the service of their country abroad or about to depart for such service":

> Technically, most of these eminent men were refugees, dependent on this country's hospitality. That is their debt to us. Actually, they brought us more than they received—their learning, their courage—above all their devotion to the principles of freedom. They taught us anew that the pursuit of knowledge is not drudgery but high adventure. If they do not return, the memory of their character and services will long remain with us.[19]

Not everyone departed on good terms. When Lévi-Strauss announced in 1945 that he was taking a leave to join de Gaulle, the New School asked him to resign. When he returned to New York a year later as the head of the French Consulate, the anthropologist initiated a series of difficult negotiations over how much the French government would subsidize the Ecole Libre now that the war was over and the size and distinction of the faculty significantly diminished. If Lévi-Strauss had had his way, he would have incorporated the Ecole into an international network of institutions similar to the Alliance Française. Complicating matters further, Johnson retired in 1945 and his successor, Bryn Hovde, had little interest in the collaboration.

══▷══

From the very beginning, Johnson had a number of run-ins with the leadership of the Ecole Libre. So did members of the francophone faculty, who never stopped fighting among themselves over political and academic matters. In the spring of 1942, secretary general Koyré and academc vice president Maritain called on their colleagues to take a stand against Vichy. As Koyré put it, "the strong scientific reputation of the Ecole Libre is of indisputable political value." In speaking out, they could sway public opinion in France and in the émigré community. Maritain went even further, urging the faculty to identify themselves as soldiers in the war against fascism. André Weil objected. He had made the choice to remain a civilian, and so, he added pointedly, had Maritain:

> You have asked all of us on the faculty of the Ecole Libre to call ourselves "camarades de combat." In all humility, I cannot accept the title. Whatever metaphorical meaning some of us may want to give to the term, I think, for the sake of clarity, we will serve the cause better by reserving "combat" primarily for the fight against the Nazis and their allies. And when it comes to that "combat," it goes without saying that I am not neutral, since I believe that the defeat of Nazism is a necessary (if not sufficient) condition for the survival of everything we hold most dear. . . . [But] given the work I do as a mathematician, . . . I would not be where I am if I did not believe that this is where I could do the most good in serving the interests of our civilization.[20]

And good science, Weil added on another occasion, did not serve a political cause![21]

Weil supported de Gaulle but refused to pose as a soldier fighting for Free France. Other colleagues sided with Henri Giraud's resistance movement; still others sided with Vichy, a position that cost them their jobs. The Belgians, too, were divided. Several continued to support Leopold III even after the king had signed an armistice with Hitler. Others sided with their colleague Paul van Zeeland, now the leader of the Belgian resistance.

As Zolberg observed, the faculty was further divided by a "spiritual cleavage" between representatives of independent Catholic universities and of state-sponsored secular institutions, which in France ranged from the govern-ment-controlled university system to the Collège de France and the Ecole Pra-tique des Hautes Etudes. Each of these institutions had different ideas about how to structure academic programs for students. Finally, colleagues took different stands on local administrative matters, lining up essentially according to whether they intended to remain in the United States after the war or return to Europe. Their postwar aspirations drove a wedge between Jewish colleagues in particular, some of whom came originally from the former Russian and Austro-Hungarian empires and had moved to Belgium and France during the interwar years; others came from families that had lived in Western Europe for generations. The East and Central Europeans saw a better future for themselves in the United States than as returning immigrants in war-torn Europe.[22]

During the summer of 1943, Maritain tried to keep the fractured faculty together and demonstrate to Johnson that he and his colleagues would be more careful than they had been about the way they expressed their political opin-ions in print. In August, the French Catholic philosopher offered a nuanced, if not entirely satisfactory, explanation of the Ecole's position on political engage-ment. As Emmanuelle Loyer summarized Maritain's position, when the Ecole denounced the Vichy government, it did so on moral not political grounds. When it evicted members of the faculty for supporting Vichy, it did so for the same reason. Moving forward, Maritain promised that the Ecole would avoid taking public stands for either de Gaulle or Giraud. And would not meddle in U.S. politics.[23]

Despite Maritain's efforts to contain the damage, things continued to deterio-rate to such an extent that the U.S. Department of Justice finally intervened. On March 20, 1944, the department invoked the 1938 Foreign Agents Registration Act and ordered the Ecole Libre to register as a foreign agent because the French university had been accepting money from foreign political parties. The offense, of course, was not new, but the authorities refused to ignore it any longer. After protracted negotiations, Johnson persuaded the department to rescind the order. The Ecole Libre, he argued, had never taken instructions from a political party, international or national, even if it had accepted a little money.[24]

Johnson's success did not please everyone, particularly the more militant members of the faculty. Lévi-Strauss, for one, wanted the Ecole to register with the U.S. government and openly proclaim that it had a political as well as an aca-demic agenda. If this meant leaving the New School, so be it. Johnson, however, would not let them go.[25]

A few weeks later, ongoing political tensions erupted on the editorial board of the Ecole's journal *Renaissance*. The Belgian historian Henri Grégoire had submitted an audacious article to the journal at a particularly sensitive time in the war as the Allies were making final preparations for the invasion of Normandy. In his paper, Grégoire criticized the plans Free France and Free Belgium had for their countries once the Germans were defeated. This upset several colleagues on the editorial board, and they voted against publishing the piece on the grounds that it was disloyal. Defying the board's decision, Grégoire managed to get his controversial piece into production for the next issue. Outraged by what he had done, Maritain, Mirkine-Guetzévitch, Koyré, and Lévi-Strauss resigned on the spot, embarrassing Grégoire into doing the same.

When Johnson got wind of the Grégoire scandal, he was furious but for entirely different reasons. The article had not only criticized proposals made by the exiled governments but offered unsolicited advice to the Allies as well about where they should draw the postwar boundaries between the Soviet Union and Poland. As far as Johnson was concerned, Grégoire was perfectly within his rights to discuss issues concerning Belgium and France. *Renaissance* did not belong to a political party, but offering advice on matters involving U.S. policy was off limits. The border dispute between the USSR and Poland was an explosive issue in 1944, involving high-level negotiations between Roosevelt and Stalin. As a foreign guest of the United States, Grégoire should keep his opinions on that matter to himself. Johnson felt betrayed. What Grégoire had done made it look as if the Ecole Libre was indeed the instrument of foreign political parties. And this, just after he had cleared the institution's name with the Department of Justice. Whether Grégoire meant to or not, he had turned Johnson into a liar.

The future of the New School depended on Johnson's ability to demonstrate that he was scrupulously, albeit creatively, obeying the letter of the law. All too often over the years he had to defend the integrity of the New School against accusations that it was harboring subversive foreigners and to endure such indignities as having government spies sit in on classes. Although Johnson had successfully managed to persuade the authorities to leave the New School alone in the past, he was not about to risk everything this time by letting a bunch of unruly French and Belgian colleagues do what they pleased—no matter how distinguished they were or how much he liked some of them personally. As far as he was concerned, they were abusing his hospitality and compromising the New School in the process. At the end of his long letter to the editorial board, Johnson laid down the law:

> I find a passage in one of Professor Grégoire's letters which if taken literally spoils the case I made with the Department of Justice as to our freedom from foreign governmental instructions. . . .

If this passage were to be taken literally, we are convicted of being foreign agents. We have taken foreign money, on condition that we treat foreign affairs according to the French and Belgian point of view. This is legally agency. I am personally sure that neither Dr. Grégoire nor any other member of the Ecole ever gave any such engagement. It would have been a shocking betrayal of the interests of the New School, which would thereby have been degraded to the rank of a foreign agent.

The moral is, however, that the Ecole Libre should keep in much closer touch with the Director of the New School, in every point of policy.[26]

Renaissance did not survive the crisis; it stopped publishing immediately. Three years later, in 1947, the New School severed ties with the Ecole Libre, and the francophone university moved to the Upper East Side near the Lycée de New-York. Considerably weakened, it hobbled along for another twenty-five years or so, finally closing its doors in the early 1970s.[27]

Had Johnson remained president for a few more years, things might have turned out differently, but even he had his doubts. Reminiscing in 1959 with his friend Max Ascoli, Johnson asked wistfully:

Do you remember the situation we were in when you joined our Faculty [1933]? I was depending for financing on the hatred of Hitler. I wanted an international, not just a German Faculty. It wasn't easy to convert our support to an international institution. . . .

You know how much maneuvering was necessary later. But we got [Alexander] Pekelis and Nino Levi, and ultimately an Ecole Libre [that] we might have kept if it hadn't been for the decentralizing Frenchmen.[28]

PART III

The Middle Years

(1945—1964)

11

ALVIN JOHNSON RETIRES

When Alvin Johnson stepped down in 1945, the New School lost its magic. This was hardly surprising. Filling the shoes of a legend was difficult. Accepting reality, Johnson's successors presented themselves as gifted managers, not mythic heroes. They would clean things up and ensure the future of this chronically underfunded university. Before long they uncovered a number of practices deeply embedded in the administration of the school that bordered on the unethical. Getting rid of them, however, was not easy, as two of the next three presidents learned, when they nearly bankrupted the institution trying to do so.

Hans Simons fared better than Bryn Hovde and Henry David, but the initiatives he took shook the New School to its core, particularly the Graduate Faculty (GF). Over a period of six years, he hired two academic consultants to help him find ways to strengthen the university's academic programs and recruit more students. On both occasions, the consultants recommended that the New School downsize the GF and concentrate its limited resources on Continuing Education. The old University in Exile, they argued, had run its course. The time had come to disband the division and absorb the faculty into the New School's adult education programs. Although Simons and the trustees rejected the consultants' recommendations, they studied the possibility very seriously and each time they did, they asked the émigré faculty to demonstrate why the GF was still critical to the life of the university.

In addition to all the administrative challenges, two of the next three presidents served during the nation's second Red scare and had to defend the university against charges that it was a hotbed of radical activity. These persistent accusations were similar to the ones the New School had faced after World War I. This time, however, the university's leaders bowed to the anti-Communist hysteria. And when they did, the president emeritus came out of retirement to oppose them.

=◆=

Johnson did not step down overnight. The process took nearly four years, with much jockeying back and forth. In 1941, he made the first move, more as a threat than anything else, when the Board of Trustees complained about the way he was managing the budget. The New School was at the height of its fame, earning international praise for its University in Exile, but it was also in serious financial difficulty, in large part due to the mortgage it carried on the Twelfth Street building. Relying loosely on Keynesian economic theory, Johnson made the case that the New School could survive carrying a substantial debt. It did not have to balance its budget.[1] The trustees disagreed. In an effort to settle their differences, they enlisted the services of a financial advisor by the name of James Causeway who, after weighing the options, recommended a high-risk solution: stop paying the mortgage immediately. The Central Savings Bank would initiate foreclosure proceedings and put the building up for auction. At which point, friends of the New School would step forward and make the winning bid. Although Johnson took risks all the time, Causeway's plan scared him. He offered to resign:

> Causeway vetoed my suggestion. I was a part of the merchandise he had to sell. I could not fly the coop until the business of putting the school through the wringer was finished. . . . Our friends would bid it in at the modest price such a building could command in time of depression and hand it back to us, all lily-whitened of its debts and sins.
>
> I felt very uneasy about so bold a procedure. All turned on our having friends who would fork over something like two hundred thousand dollars. In my opinion we hadn't such friends. I was wrong.[2]

The friend who stepped forward was Doris Duke, the heiress of a tobacco baron who was using her considerable fortune to support the arts and progressive causes. Although Johnson had met the philanthropist before, they did not know each other well. She belonged to Hans Staudinger's circle of admirers, not his. As Johnson tells the story, Staudinger met Duke through one of his students:

> Professor Staudinger had drawn to his class on population a brilliant and charming lady, Marian Paschal, friend and trusted secretary of Doris Duke. Marian introduced Staudinger to Doris Duke; they became good friends. . . . I too was

introduced to Doris Duke, a much more serious, intelligent, and public-spirited young woman than the press made her out to be. I did not succeed in establishing a solid friendship, for Doris Duke was shy, and I was diffident.

When our building was put up on the block, Doris Duke bid it in and presented it to us. We were debt free. The New School had been saved—by a miracle. It could go forward with a deeper breath of liberty.[3]

Duke came to the rescue just as the United States was entering the war, which in turn caused the New School to lose large numbers of students to the draft, particularly those in the GF. With registration figures plummeting, this was not the time to look for a new president. Nobody talked about retirement anymore. The trustees needed Johnson to recruit more students—women and men too old or infirm to serve in the army. While looking for short-term solutions, Johnson came up with the idea of designing a BA program within the adult division for returning soldiers who had interrupted their studies to fight overseas.

By 1944 the BA program was fully accredited and ready to welcome veterans coming back to school on the GI Bill. Carefully conceived to minimize competition with neighboring institutions, Johnson's program accepted only juniors and seniors. These older students, he predicted, would prefer the relative freedom and cosmopolitan atmosphere of the New School over the constraints of a traditional four-year college. Anticipating a spike in enrollment, Johnson split the adult division into two administrative units: the School of Political Science and the School of Philosophy, each with its own dean.

In the early months of 1945, student enrollments in Continuing Education reached an all-time high, and the numbers were climbing in the GF as well. Johnson could now retire in glory with his legacy intact. Not that he wanted to, but he accepted his fate and decided to move quickly before the trustees pushed him out. With Causeway still advising the board, sooner or later they would follow his advice and appoint a new president with a more conventional administrative style.

Johnson admitted that he never fit the mold of an administrator. His "Middle-Western democratic instinct had no place for giving and taking orders, the staple of administration." His way of running things—at least in his eyes—consisted of delegating responsibilities to highly competent people and then giving them the support they needed. In 1945, his administrative team included Hans Simons, dean of the School of Political Science; Clara Mayer, dean of the School of Philosophy; Horace Kallen, dean of the GF; Adolph Lowe and Hans Staudinger, codirectors of the Institute of World Affairs (IWA); Jacques Maritain, president of the Ecole Libre; and Erwin Piscator, director of the Studio Theatre and Dramatic Workshop.

"As for my own functions," Johnson added, "they lay largely in the field of public relations, within the institution and without. And if I ever seemed to be neglecting an issue, I had a succession of remarkably able secretaries to haul me up."[4]

Although Johnson characterized himself as a hands-off president "with the most self-governing faculty in existence," his colleagues described his management style as anything but: "We are completely self-governing," one colleague quipped, "and Dr. Johnson decides everything."[5] Those foolish enough to challenge his authority did not last very long. And this remained the case even after he retired, as future presidents of the New School soon discovered.

⇒

When Johnson finally announced that he would step down, he made light of his decision, dismissing it playfully, but with a touch of bitterness. It may have made sense, he said, in the early years of the New School to consider the university and its founding president inseparable, but "when the years sneak up on one, the question begins to be mooted: What will happen to the institution when the head of it drops dead? . . . I began to hear that too often. True, I was not in the habit of dropping dead. But the question was bad medicine for the fundraisers."[6]

To ease the transition, Johnson wanted the trustees to appoint his good friend Hans Simons as the next president. When he suggested his idea to Causeway, the trustees' advisor would not hear of it. Nor would Louis Weiss, the chairman of the board. No German, they said, could be president of the New School right after the war, not even a "good" German like Simons. Infuriated by their response, Johnson retaliated: "I sat on my job, sure that it would take an earthquake to dislodge me." In the end the trustees prevailed, and Johnson behaved. For weeks, however, he resisted, rejecting every candidate they asked him to interview. Finally, he met one he thought would be able to do the job—a Scandinavian American like himself by the name of Bryn Hovde. The candidate was serving at the time as chief of the Division of Cultural Cooperation at the U.S. Department of State. Before that he had worked in Pittsburgh, first in the Housing Department and later as director of Public Welfare. He also held a faculty position at the University of Pittsburgh, where he taught European history.

When Johnson announced his retirement in an open letter to the New School community, he congratulated the trustees on their choice of a successor, describing Hovde as

a man after my own heart, a man imbued with the ideals that have directed the New School from its beginning, a man who is interested in and experienced in the multiform related activities that compose the substance of the New School for Social Research. In my sober judgment, my successor-elect is better qualified to carry forward the ideals and activities of the New School than the present incumbent. I ask my friends, the friends of the New School, to rejoice with me in our good fortune.

In that same letter, Johnson asked the university's many friends to continue supporting the institution that "you and I have built up. . . . Do you not share with me pride in a work well done? And do you not see before us a work of expanding importance, through the exciting and confusing period our nation will enter upon when peace has been restored to the earth?" He urged them to send generous contributions in the coming weeks "to make Dr. Hovde's first year a success. He will make his second year a success, through his own energies. But this year is crucial. Can I count on you?"[7]

Hovde accepted his new job with humility. Taking over in December 1945, he spoke almost timidly about the task that lay ahead. "To succeed Dr. Johnson," he said, "is a great honor. But it is also a grave responsibility, to which I pledge my every effort."[8] But in no time Hovde changed his tune. After realizing what he had inherited, he began describing himself as the seasoned administrator that the university desperately needed. The New School finally had a president capable of cleaning things up and ensuring the future of this inspirational but financially fragile institution. Hovde promised that the university would free itself from the demeaning ritual of asking the trustees to cover its outstanding bills at the end of every academic year. Moving forward the New School would live within its means.

After three semesters, Hovde proudly reported to "contributors and friends" that he had begun to turn things around. As the New School completed its 1946–47 academic year, the adult division had enrolled six thousand students— 28 percent higher than four years earlier—and 90 percent of those were non-degree students, confirming the New School's enduring reputation as a leader in continuing education.[9]

When Hovde first arrived in December 1945, the new BA program had very few students, only twelve of whom were ready to graduate in the spring of 1946. Now, a year later, he noted with pride, the program had nearly two hundred students, an impressive increase for sure, which probably had more to do with the GI Bill kicking in than with any changes Hovde had made. Either way, it was gratifying to see.

Hovde also had good news to share about the Graduate Faculty. Over the last three semesters, the number of students registered for courses had increased by 31 percent: from 410 in the fall of 1945 to 541 in the spring of 1947. Those numbers,

Hovde predicted, would continue to grow now that the Board of Regents had granted the GF permission to offer master of arts and doctor of philosophy degrees in economics, philosophy, political science, psychology, and sociology, in addition to the master of science and doctor of science in the social sciences that the New School had been offering since 1934. Another factor that contributed to the rise in the number of graduate students, Hovde continued, was the greater visibility of the faculty, several of whom had produced significant research in recent years through the IWA. Six books had been published since 1943, all by Oxford University Press, and more were on the way. The institute had begun an Occasional Papers series as well.

The financial situation had also improved. Over the last three semesters, Hovde reported, the income from tuition, foundation grants, and gifts from donors, had increased by 78 percent, whereas the cost of running the institution had only gone up by 35 percent. Expenses, he cautioned, would rise again after the New School began its new building campaign, but this time in a carefully controlled manner. As the trustees had agreed, the institution's future depended on its being able to grow, which in turn meant expanding the campus. Even after factoring in these additional costs, Hovde assured everyone that the New School would still have fewer expenses than it had when he first took over.

Near the end of his report, Hovde added pointedly that when he arrived in 1945, he inherited a number of administrative policies that had no place in a progressive institution—for example, the New School's practice of paying instructors in Continuing Education on a sliding scale. Known as the split-fee system, the university gave them 50 percent of the tuition the registrar collected for their courses, encouraging them to hustle for students as if they were hawking merchandise in an open-air market. The full-time members of the GF received regular salaries, but at a rate far lower than that of their colleagues at neighboring institutions. Adding insult to injury, these distinguished professors had no pension or other benefits. Hovde promised to correct these embarrassments while remaining sensitive to budgetary constraints. By the spring of 1947, he had introduced a pension plan for full-time members of the GF and given modest raises to instructors in Continuing Education, while he persisted—unsuccessfully—in trying to ease the university off the split-fee system.

As Hovde ran down the list he had compiled of unacceptable practices, exposing Johnson to public humiliation in the process, he carefully avoided mentioning the controversial steps that he himself had just taken or was about to take, such as severing ties with the Ecole Libre in 1947 and the Studio Theatre and Dramatic Workshop a year later. The francophone university had been doing poorly, justifying his decision to bring an end to the relationship, but Piscator's theater program was flourishing, as Hovde had noted in his report, taking personal credit for its ongoing success. Yet behind the scenes the new president was making plans to get rid of the program because, he later explained, it had grown too costly. Johnson agreed, but money was probably not the only concern. The plays performed at the Studio Theatre leaned decidedly to the left, an image Hovde did not want to advertise on his watch during the late 1940s. As McCarthy was gaining influence across the country, the New School's president was making a name for himself as an outspoken critic of the Communist Party and other leftist groups, whose members he dismissed indiscriminately as fellow travelers.

In his concluding remarks, Hovde tried to imitate the soaring prose Johnson used in his annual reports during the Hitler years, but in Hovde's cumbersome style the words fell flat. In all fairness, the times had also changed. During the war, progressives of all stripes spoke in one voice as they railed against Nazi barbarism, but now, during the McCarthy period, these same progressives did not see eye-to-eye on how to respond to the so-called threat of the Red menace—even among those who identified themselves as virulent critics of the Soviet Union. Although Johnson, like Hovde, had harsh things to say about the Communist Party, he could not tolerate the position his successor had been taking in the name of the New School, a fact he did not keep to himself.

Nor did Johnson have much patience for the way Hovde was managing the university, especially after he insulted him publicly in his 1947 report. As far as Johnson was concerned, Hovde had to go, an opinion shared by others, including Clara Mayer and Hans Simons, whom the new president had kept on as deans. Had Hovde been stronger politically, he would have fired them both, but he was not. Faced with their growing hostility, Hovde was delighted when Simons received an invitation from the U.S. occupation forces to help the government complete the "democratization program in Germany."

Simons, too, was pleased by his good fortune. He needed a break from the New School. But he still complained bitterly to Agnes de Lima about the article published in the *New School Bulletin* announcing his appointment as chief of the Governmental Structures Branch of the U.S. Office of Military Government. Rightly or wrongly, Simons blamed Hovde for the lackluster piece, which was not only inadequate, but insulting:

I was somewhat disappointed by the announcement of my appointment here. If all I had to do were to prepare a German constitution my task would be both hopeless and unnecessary. If you read the letter which [Edward] Litchfield [director of the Civil Administration Division] sent to Dr. Hovde you will get a better idea of what I am really doing. Had I had an opportunity to make a suggestion I would have asked simply to quote from this letter which would have been the most correct and complete statement on my present assignment.[10]

During the remaining two years of Hovde's presidency, things deteriorated quickly. In December 1948, the Middle States Association of Colleges and Secondary Schools "declined to approve the New School" and recommended that it reapply for accreditation the following year.[11] Distinguished members of the faculty were abandoning the GF as well to accept positions at major academic and research institutions, among them Leo Strauss, who left for the University of Chicago, and Hans Speier, who went to the Rand Corporation. After having worked in Washington during the war years, analyzing the impact of Nazi propaganda for the Roosevelt and Truman administrations, Speier returned to the New School in 1947, only to resign the following year.

Despite Hovde's earlier optimism, by the winter of 1949 he had accepted defeat. Having failed to fix the university's budget problems, he began looking around for another job. In February, *The New York Times* announced that the Board of Higher Education had identified Hovde as the leading candidate in the search for a new president of Queens College, news that the New School trustees welcomed with enthusiasm. If he got the job, they would not have to fire him. As board member Max Ascoli put it in a letter he sent to Simons in Germany, when Hovde asked him whether he should accept the job, "God, said I, should you!" In the end, however, Hovde backed out of the race.[12]

By 1948, Johnson had become so confrontational that Hovde evicted him from his office on Twelfth Street and exiled him to his home in Nyack, where Johnson spent the next year plotting to replace him with Simons, an idea that had the enthusiastic support of Max Ascoli and other members of the board.[13] To Hovde's credit, he bowed out gracefully. When the trustees called Simons back from Germany in September 1949, Hovde warmly welcomed his rival home in the *New School Bulletin*, offering appropriate words of praise for the work he had done in Germany. Taking no chances this time, he also quoted at length from the letter of thanks he had received from the same Edward Litchfield:

> Now that Dr. Simons has departed, I want to write to thank you and the School for his outstanding work. During the two and a half years he has been here, Dr. Simons had made one of the greatest contributions thus far made in the Occupation. Not only did he provide a rich background of experience and unusually sound judgment, but he also served as a very great inspiration to the other members of the staff, with the consequence that he not only contributed directly through his own efforts, but indirectly through theirs.

I appreciate, and I believe General [Lucius] Clay appreciated, the fact that in making Dr. Simons available to the Government, the School made a very great sacrifice. While governments are slow to express their appreciation of the contributions that individuals make, I hope you will accept this letter of appreciation on behalf of all of the people who knew Dr. Simons as some recompense for the loss which you and your Faculty have suffered as a result of Dr. Simons' absence.

With very best wishes I am. . . .[14]

Over the next several months, the trustees managed the transition tactfully. In November, they made Dean Simons vice president. In February, they gave Hovde a leave of absence. In May, Hovde resigned. As the board "reluctantly disclosed to *The New York Times*," the reason for Hovde's "resignation lay in his distaste for fundraising as it must be done at this institution."[15] Simons became president in June 1950.

When Johnson published his autobiography two years later, he included a few measured words about Hovde, no doubt composed in his old office on Twelfth Street, which he quietly reclaimed after Simons took over:

> Bryn Hovde proved to be a distinguished administrator, true, human, intelligent, but not, alas, with a constitution up to his stature. He worked faithfully to do his job, but it is a terrible job for any man to carry a serious educational enterprise which has no endowment. After four years Hovde retired, to be succeeded by Hans Simons.[16]

When the New School announced the appointment of its third president, de Lima prepared a long biographical sketch as part of the university's press release. She did so, no doubt, to please the new president, whom she had learned could be prickly. But that was not the only reason. She also wanted to address any lingering concerns about making a German president of the New School.

Hans Simons, she wrote, was born in Velbert, Germany, in 1893 into an illustrious family. His father had served as foreign minister and chief of justice in Imperial Germany, and then as acting president of the new Weimar Republic at the end of World War I. As a young man, Simons attended the best universities in the country—Berlin, Munich, Tübingen, Bonn, and Königsberg—receiving his doctorate in law in 1921 at the age of twenty-eight, after having already distinguished himself as a soldier. Like many others in his generation, Simons had interrupted his studies in 1914 to join the army, where he served on the Russian and French fronts. Wounded in 1917, he was decorated with full honors for his bravery.

When the war ended, Simons cofounded the German Association of the League of Nations, and in that capacity he went to Versailles in 1919 as part of the German delegation. In the early 1920s, he was appointed to the Ministry of the Interior, "where he was in charge of constitutional matters and political problems." As part of his responsibilities, he represented Germany at the meetings of the International Institute of Intellectual Cooperation in Paris and the League of Nations in Geneva. He also participated in talks with Poland to discuss contentious border issues.

In 1924, Simons became director of the Hochschule für Politik in Berlin, a position he held until 1930. The Hochschule, de Lima explained, was "the first school of politics ever established in Germany. It served thousands of students who sought education in the social sciences, particularly in politics, which at that time was not available in universities." Then, between 1930 and 1932, Simons served as governor of two different districts on the German-Polish border, both of which—Stettin (Sczecin) and Liegnitz (Lengnica)—became part of Poland after World War II. De Lima referred to these posts as "semi-elected" positions: The national government named Simons as governor, after which the representative assemblies endorsed the appointment.

Simons's political career ended abruptly in the summer of 1932, after the July 31 legislative elections, when the National Socialists won 37 percent of the seats in the Reichstadt. He "was among the first six high officials forcibly removed from office." Eight months later, after Hitler had consolidated his power, Simons was officially blacklisted. Branded "politically unreliable," he quickly left Germany with his wife, Eva Haym, who was Jewish, a detail de Lima alluded to only indirectly by mentioning Mrs. Simons's maiden name. Simons joined the Graduate Faculty in 1935. Then in 1943, the same year Johnson made him dean of the School of Political Science, the Office of Strategic Services hired Simons as a part-time consultant. This in turn led to his appointment in 1947 to serve as chief of the Governmental Structures Branch of the Office of Military Government.

After describing Simons's role in Germany with the U.S. military, paraphrasing at length from Edward Lichfield's first letter and quoting in full from the second, de Lima concluded:

> The Board of Trustees chose Dr. Simons as president, it said, for three principal reasons: because of his long years of association with the New School and his familiarity with its purposes and problems; because he is widely known as a leading authority on international relations, a field of paramount importance at this time; and because his whole training and experience qualify him for the job of educating American adults for their new responsibilities as citizens of a world power.[17]

Simons became president as Joseph McCarthy and the House Un-American Activities Committee were in full swing, spreading fear and paranoia across the country and poisoning academic life. Given its unique profile, the New School was an easy target, criticized by groups across the political spectrum—by conservatives, predictably, but also by people on the left. In the eyes of progressives who had long admired what the New School stood for, both Hovde and Simons tarnished the reputation of the university.

12

THE RED SCARE

In *No Ivory Tower: McCarthyism and the Universities*, historian Ellen Schrecker mentions the New School twice, both times for having hired a blacklisted professor during the McCarthy years, something very few academic institutions were doing. The bar, admittedly, was not very high. Bryn Hovde welcomed nobody before he resigned in 1950, and Hans Simons very few, quietly burying the occasional ostracized professors in Continuing Education. The Graduate Faculty was out of the question.[1]

Did Simons maintain a low profile out of fear? In part, no doubt, but that was not the primary reason. He, like Hovde, was fiercely opposed to the Communist Party and the Soviet Union—an opinion he shared with almost every other émigré scholar at the University in Exile. By 1935, the refugee professors had imposed their ideological position on the institution's academic policy, inscribing it into the founding charter of the Graduate Faculty (GF): No colleague, they proclaimed, could belong "to any political party or group which asserts the right to dictate in matters of science or scientific opinion." No Communists, no Nazis, no Italian Fascists, or any other party that required its members to sign a loyalty oath, thereby obliging scholars to abandon their professional obligation "to follow truth wherever it may lead."[2]

Alvin Johnson fully agreed and adopted the language of the GF's charter for the entire New School. He did so, however, in his own idiosyncratic fashion, interpreting the injunction loosely, particularly when it came to famous artists whose political sympathies often leaned to the left. When questioned about this, Johnson assured his inquisitors that he screened every candidate very carefully before offering him a job at the New School. Johnson never hired anyone, he wrote in his autobiography, who could have posed a risk to the nation, something

he repeated in letters to friends and in response to inquiries by government officials. Given his many years of experience, Johnson told them, he could tell the
difference between a real "Commie" and a "crocus Communist" who would later
mend his ways. Not everyone trusted his judgment.

A number of exiled artists whom Johnson had hired during the Hitler years
were still raising hackles in the 1950s even though they had left the New School
and, in some cases, the country as well. Of particular concern was the Austrian
composer Hanns Eisler, whose history with the Communist Party was no secret.
On May 7, 1953, Agnes de Lima reported to President Simons:

> A student who works for the neighborhood paper of Murray Hill was quizzed
> by its editor for going to this "red" school. He indignantly denied the charge and
> she showed him a report of the Un-American Affairs Committee [*sic*] which he
> read and which he said was surprisingly favorable to the School, only scoring it
> and AJ for the Hanns Eisler business.[3]

Although the New School's detractors persisted in attacking the university
throughout the McCarthy period, they failed to undermine the institution, in
large part thanks to the GF's émigré scholars, whose political profiles and academic interests contradicted the ominous picture the university's critics were trying to paint. While "philistine" legislators, as Johnson liked to call them, accused
the New School of harboring European radicals, the White House was recruiting GF colleagues to work on confidential projects, something Roosevelt began
doing before the United States had entered the war, and Truman and Eisenhower
continued doing afterwards. Several colleagues took temporary leaves of absence
from the New School to assume U.S. government posts in Washington during the
1930s and early 1940s and, after 1945, in Germany also (Gerhard Colm, Arthur
Feiler, Hans Simons, and Hans Speier). Others provided much-needed research
for federal agencies through the New School's Institute of World Affairs (IWA).
In a letter to a donor in 1944, Johnson reported, "We have developed into an
institution so well manned, so well equipped for handling problems of world
affairs that every week Washington appeals to us to make a report on German
railways, on various economic problems of North Africa or Southern Italy, on the
ways in which Russia has developed industrial management, etc."[4] These appeals
kept coming well into the 1950s.

After Johnson retired, and much to his dismay, the next two presidents
defended the university's reputation by making the New School "politically
reliable" in humiliating ways, most dramatically in 1953. Bowing to the will of
the New School's trustees, Simons hung a curtain before the portraits of Lenin

and Stalin that appeared on the mural in the Twelfth Street cafeteria that José Clemente Orozco had painted in 1931. No chapter in the history of the New School brought greater shame on the university than this one. Although Johnson admired Simons and considered him a good friend, the Orozco scandal upset him a great deal.[5]

⟹

Since the day it opened in 1919, conservatives began raising questions about the political orientation of the New School, in part, perhaps, because it was founded in the same year as the Communist Party of the United States of America (CPUSA). Pure coincidence? In the eyes of many, it looked suspicious. By 1920, the New York State Joint Legislative Committee Investigating Seditious Activities (the Lusk Committee) had concluded that the New School had been "founded by men who belong to the ranks of the near Bolshevik intelligentsia."[6] A year earlier Horace Kallen recalled seeing "policemen taking notes on my lectures in philosophy" in a course he was teaching on the Evolution of the International Mind.[7] Incidents like these continued to occur now and again, reaching a new peak during the second Red scare, when once again the New School faced "unadmirable committees of investigation."[8]

Johnson had no more patience for members of the CPUSA than he did for McCarthy's henchmen. Speaking in the name of academic freedom, he dismissed the New School's Marxist critics as harshly as he did those on the right:

> The fact is that from the very beginning the New School has been what the Marxians call "bourgeois." We believed in free and untrammeled teaching. We wished to understand the other party's point of view as well as our own. . . . But to the Marxians there is no truth but their truth, and the whole duty of a teacher is indoctrination.

Looking back on the 1920s, Johnson bemoaned the fact that "Karl Marx had become fashionable among graduate students, especially among students of philosophy and ethics." As far as he was concerned,

> Marx was an intellectual convenience. He absolved the student from the necessity of attending to the problems of the actual economic system. Protection and free trade, the incidence and shifting of taxation, the development of standards of living, monopoly and competitive pricing, and the scores of other problems that occupy the "bourgeois" economist presented no difficulties to

the Marxian disciple. To him there was only one problem: how to get on with the revolution.[9]

In spite of his personal objections to Marxist ideas, Johnson honored the New School's commitment to academic freedom and continued to offer courses on the work of the philosopher, as the founders had been doing from the very beginning. But these lectures suffered the same fate as other courses in politics and economics during the 1920s—the New School's students were not interested. What made the institution radical at the time was the wide range of courses Johnson was offering in new disciplines such as psychoanalysis and anthropology and in avant-garde literature and the arts, often taught—and this was not incidental—by scholars and artists whose political sympathies leaned decidedly to the left. Johnson's outstanding new program in music was a case in point, with courses taught by Aaron Copland, Henry Cowell, and Charles Seeger, all of whom had ties to CPUSA, through which they recruited outstanding musicians to perform at the New School.

After the stock market crashed in 1929, the New School's students started clamoring for more classes on what Johnson described as "social issues." In response, he expanded the curriculum to include more courses in the social sciences, including several in the Marxist tradition. During the 1931 winter term, for example, students could attend a series of twelve lectures on The Philosophy of Karl Marx, delivered by John Dewey's disciple, Sidney Hook. Remembered today for his virulent opposition to the Soviet Union, Hook belonged to the Communist Party at the time and remained a member until 1933. Johnson also invited Moissaye Olgin back to give courses on Soviet Communism, something he had been teaching at the New School since it first opened.[10]

Johnson knew that Olgin and Hook were Communists. By the early 1930s, Olgin was a prominent member of the national committee of CPUSA, something the course bulletin reported openly. As for Hook, before inviting him to teach at the New School, Johnson had recruited him to write nine articles for *The Encyclopaedia of the Social Sciences*, including one on Materialism and another on Engels. Despite the school's firm policy on the matter after 1935, Johnson had no difficulty hiring Communists, he claimed provocatively in 1952, as long as they did not "slap a little Communist color on [their] work."

In *Pioneer's Progress*, Johnson described at length how he had also hired a former Communist to join the editorial staff of *The Encyclopaedia of the Social Sciences*. He recorded this story at the height of the McCarthy period to illustrate, he said, the difference between an anticommunist like himself and the fanatics on the House Un-American Activities Committee (HUAC). Although he protected the man's name in his autobiography, Johnson identified him in a private letter the following year. At the time, Louis Fraina (aka Lewis Corey) was fighting a deportation order that Johnson worried he was going to lose: "I'd like to have McCarthy quiz me on Lewis," he wrote to a friend. "But I learn from my friends on the FBI that orders have come down to let me alone. I'm sorry." Fraina died of a brain hemorrhage while he was still pleading his case.[11]

The incident Johnson described in his autobiography probably took place in the late 1920s:

> I had two assistant editors who asserted that they were Socialists. That was nothing to me; they were good and faithful workers. And one was so considerate of my reactionary bent as to inform me that a new editor I had taken on was a Communist. I sent for him.
>
> "Yes," he said. "I was once a Communist. The name by which I go is not my real name." He gave me his real name, which had figured in press accounts of rows in the Communist Party.
>
> "And so," he said, "you are going to fire me."
>
> "Certainly not". . . .
>
> Those were tolerant days. Intelligent Americans were no more hysterical about Communists than intelligent Europeans are today. We had not formulated the principle, "Once a Communist, always a traitor." We overlooked, with a smile, the excesses of the false spring of ardent youth. And a lot of crocus Communists developed into sound and reasonable scholars and businessmen, now a bit apprehensive that the McCarthyite goblins will 'git them ef they don't watch out.' "[12]

Ending the sketch with the words from "Little Orphan Annie," Johnson reduced the scare tactics of McCarthy and his henchmen to the familiar refrain of a popular children's poem. Outspoken and irreverent, he dared the "goblins" to silence him and the New School in the same ironic tone he had used on many other occasions from the 1920s through the 1950s, a fact that had not escaped the U.S. government.

In a report prepared for the FBI in 1943, a staff member confirmed that the bureau had an extensive file on the New School and Alvin Johnson:

> Numerous reports have been received by the Bureau from reliable informants indicating a close collaboration between the New School for Social Research and various prominent Communists and individuals known to be sympathetic with and advocates of Marxian Ideology. . . . In addition it will be recalled that Dr. Alvin Johnson, president of the New School for Social Research, and other individuals connected with this Institution, have upon occasion bitterly

criticized the Bureau for its investigative activity, including in one instance its investigation of a professor employed by the New School for Social Research who was being considered for employment by the Federal Communications Committee, which agency requested the Bureau investigation.

In view of the voluminous information available concerning the New School for Social Research and the clear indications of its questionable character, no complete summary has been prepared concerning it. However, it is believed that the above comments, taken from the main file on the New School for Social Research, clearly indicate the unreliability of this Institution.[13]

The "voluminous information" included reports about Johnson hiring Hanns Eisler to teach at the New School in the late 1930s, a decision that caused a media sensation in 1947 when HUAC summoned Eisler to appear before it.

By that time, the composer had been living in Hollywood for years. In 1943, the musical score he had written for Fritz Lang's *Hangmen Also Die* had been nominated for an Oscar.[14] When *The New York Times* asked Johnson in the fall of 1947 to explain Eisler's ties to the New School,

> Dr. Johnson said that in 1937 or 1938 he invited Eisler to lecture at the New School as one of the foremost experts of modern music. At the same time, he suggested Mr. Eisler to the Rockefeller Foundation as one well-qualified to undertake research into the subject of musical accompaniment for films.[15]

When Eisler gave his first lectures at the New School, the composer was in the country on a temporary visa. Hoping to acquire permanent residence, he left for Cuba and applied for a new visa, which was not forthcoming despite Johnson's endorsement. Upon hearing that Eisler had "encountered difficulty," as the *Times* put it delicately, Johnson wrote to Sumner Welles in the State Department, who, in turn, asked Eleanor Roosevelt to intervene on his behalf, which the First Lady agreed to do. Shortly thereafter, in the early 1940s, the composer moved to Hollywood, exchanging his New School's salary of $2,500 per year for $30,000—or so Johnson reported to a New School trustee.

Eisler continued collaborating with the New School from California for several more years on the Rockefeller-funded Film Music Project. He finally published *Composing for the Films*, coauthored with Theodor Adorno, in 1947, the same year he appeared before HUAC. In the preface to the book, the composer thanked Alvin Johnson, Clara Mayer, and John Marshall of the Rockefeller Foundation, "without whose active co-operation this study would never have come into being," an acknowledgment that nobody missed in Washington.[16]

As HUAC's witch hunts picked up steam in the early 1950s, critics of the New School returned to the Eisler affair. In addition to the editor of the Murray Hill newspaper, August Heckscher, chief editor of *The New York Herald Tribune* and a member of the New School's Board of Trustees raised the issue. *The Herald Tribune* had been a faithful friend of the university for years, singing its praises in articles and editorials, but Eisler was another matter. Writing off the record in December 1954, Heckscher alerted Johnson that someone had written to the newspaper to let it know that the "Communist" composer Hanns Eisler had taught at the New School. Although this was hardly a scoop, Heckscher asked why the university had hired the composer in the first place. The answer, Johnson replied, was simple:

> At the time, I was trying to develop courses on modern music at the New School. I had developed courses by Aaron Copland, Henry Cowell, Charles Seeger, [Edgard] Varèse, and had been so fortunate as to bring over [Erich] von Hornbostel, the world's foremost musicologist. Hanns Eisler was introduced to me, and I found him interesting. He was at the time the outstanding composer of singing music with a modern quality.

As for the composer's ties to the Communist Party:

> Naturally I inquired about his politics, because one of his airs had been adopted for the "Comintern," a song sung by millions. Eisler said he had not been a member of the Communist Party in Austria until the Nazis were rising to power, with the Communists [being] the only serious opposition. Then he joined the party but was dropped in six months for failure to pay his dues. He had no interest in the party in America.
>
> I have no reason to think that he was not telling the truth.[17]

Johnson did not waver. It did not matter that Eisler had appeared before HUAC in 1947 and then moved to East Berlin. As we see in this letter to Hecksher, written seven years after Eisler had left the country, he still believed what the composer had told him in the late 1930s.

Johnson also invited Bertolt Brecht to teach at the New School, even after he learned that the German playwright and poet was "at least a fellow traveler." While he was trying to persuade the U.S. Consulate in Sweden to give Brecht a visa, Johnson wrote to the poet Archibald MacLeish, the head of the Library of Congress at the time and a member of the New School's Board of Trustees:

April 29, 1940

Dear Mr. MacLeish:

I am trying to get the poet Bertholt [sic] Brecht out of Sweden, where he is in great danger from the progress of the Nazis. I have invited him to come over as a visiting lecturer at the New School.

The question has arisen whether he is a Communist, "fellow traveler," "Trojan horse." This needs to be cleared up if he is to get a visa. Do you know anything about Brecht's political views and activities?

MacLeish wrote back on May 2:

Dear Alvin Johnson:

I have the greatest admiration for Brecht, who I think is one of the great influences in the modern theater. Since you ask a direct question, however, I must answer it with equal directness. I met him on several occasions in New York three or four years ago. Although I do not know him well, I believed at the time that he was a Communist. Whether he is still a Communist I have no means of knowing. If I had to guess, I should guess that he is at least "a fellow traveler."

With little reason to doubt MacLeish, Johnson forged ahead, keeping in touch with Brecht and his friends as he fled Sweden and moved to Finland. Continuing his efforts to get the playwright a visa, Johnson wrote to the American Consulate in Helsinki: "You would place our institution under deep obligation by granting a visa to Mr. Brecht as promptly as possible."[18]

Brecht finally received his visa in the spring of 1941. From Finland, he went to the Soviet Union, crossing over the border a few weeks before Germany declared war on Russia. From Vladivostok he sailed to the United States by way of the Philippines. Arriving in California, Brecht decided to settle down in Los Angeles rather than continue on to New York, where Johnson had only offered him a six-month contract and $1,500.[19] In October 1947, Brecht was called to appear before HUAC. After a spectacular performance during which he named no names and admitted to nothing, he returned to Europe.[20] Two years later he settled down in East Berlin. In the end, Brecht's decision to remain in California spared the

New School the burden a few years later of having to explain the presence on the faculty of yet another "subversive" of international renown.

Of all the Communists, or former Communists, who received invitations from Johnson, Erwin Piscator had the greatest impact on the New School. The charismatic playwright and director belonged to Weimar Germany's flourishing avant-garde, which enjoyed the generous support of the German Communist Party until Hitler rose to power in 1933. During the 1920s, Piscator, like Brecht, was writing and producing epic dramas that were openly ideological and intended to inspire intellectuals and members of the working class to overthrow capitalism. In 1931, Piscator received an invitation from the Soviet Union to serve as director of the International Association of Revolutionary Theaters, a position he abandoned five years later when Stalin clamped down on agitprop drama and other forms of expressionist art. Since Germany had fallen to the Nazis by then, Piscator moved to Paris. Then, in 1938, he came to New York on a temporary visa, met Johnson, and soon began teaching at the New School, an arrangement that made it possible for him to reapply for a permanent visa.

In 1940, Piscator opened the Studio Theatre and Dramatic Workshop at the New School with the enthusiastic support of Johnson. This was a courageous decision considering what was happening at neighboring institutions during those years. While Piscator was producing works by Brecht and other controversial playwrights in 1941, City College was cooperating with the Joint Legislative Committee to Investigate the Educational System of the State of New York (the Rapp-Coudert Committee). Piscator continued undisturbed throughout World War II, even after the U.S. Department of Justice threatened to discipline the New School for harboring foreign agents at the Ecole Libre.

Between 1940 and 1951, Piscator and his faculty trained actors and playwrights who went on to become some of the best-known figures in theater and film in the postwar period, among them Harry Belafonte, Marlon Brando, Tony Curtis, Judith Malina, Walter Matthau, Arthur Miller, Rod Steiger, Tennessee Williams, Shelley Winters, and Philip Yordan. Not that the German director turned to any of them for help during the McCarthy period. As Piscator watched HUAC subpoena Brecht, Eisler, and other European friends, he spared himself the ordeal by leaving the country in 1951, before the committee contacted him. Warmly welcomed in West Berlin, he became the director of the city's Volksbühne Theater.[21]

Johnson remained Piscator's good friend throughout those difficult last years, even after Hovde severed ties with the Studio Theatre and Dramatic Workshop in 1948. Although Johnson apparently accepted the official explanation, telling Hecksher that the New School could no longer afford to subsidize the program, given the year and the personalities involved that may not be the entire story.[22] To ease the transition, Johnson agreed to serve as chairman of the board of Piscator's newly independent theater program.[23]

In an earlier gesture of friendship, Johnson wrote a letter of recommendation for Piscator when the dramatist reapplied for citizenship in 1946. The U.S. government had turned him down the first time. According to Johnson, Piscator had always played by the rules. He never engaged in any form of political activity that could have threatened the New School or the nation. As far as Johnson was concerned, Piscator would make a very good citizen. But the dramatist had never renounced his political past either, or said anything remotely critical in public about Marxism or the Soviet Union.[24] The authorities expected more.

Johnson went to extraordinary lengths to establish his credentials for recommending Piscator, revealing fascinating details about his own political activities over those years. He had, for example, been serving on an Enemy Alien Hearing Board, which required him "to report to the Federal authorities any alien of whose loyalty I had ever had the least reason to doubt":

August 19, 1946

Gentlemen:

I am writing to you in support of the application of Erwin Piscator for American citizenship.

Since 1938, when Dr. Piscator joined the New School to establish a Studio Theatre and Dramatic Workshop, I have been closely associated with him. I have been familiar with his most intimate ideas, as well as with all his public activities. I have known many scholars and artists of foreign origin, but I have never known any better qualified to become just a plain American, deeply appreciative of democracy as we define it in America and loyal to it.

May I add that as a member of an Enemy Alien Hearing Board, I felt myself bound by my oath to report to the Federal authorities any alien of whose loyalty I had ever had the least reason to doubt. I could not possibly have doubted the loyalty of Erwin Piscator.

As one of the greatest and most original figures in the theatre Erwin Piscator has an immense contribution to make to our democratic theatrical art. I am convinced that the public interest would be served by granting citizenship to Erwin Piscator.

Respectfully,
Alvin Johnson[25]

How was it possible for someone like Johnson to serve on an Enemy Alien Hearing Board? Did he do it for political cover? Did he ever turn anyone in? Clearly, he wanted the U.S. government to believe that he had.[26] Whatever his motivations, Johnson's credentials were not persuasive enough to convince the authorities to grant Piscator citizenship. But his service on the board may explain why the FBI and HUAC left him alone.

Did Johnson ever fire a colleague at the New School for being a communist? Sidney Hook reportedly said that he did on at least one occasion, but he "delegated" the task to Clara Mayer.[27] To date there is no corroborating evidence. By his own admission, however, we know that Johnson asked candidates about their political affiliations when he interviewed them for a job, at both the New School and *The Encyclopaedia of the Social Sciences*. Perhaps he refused to hire people occasionally for political reasons, but it is difficult to believe that Johnson actually fired colleagues, given how many high-profile communists and "fellow travelers" he welcomed to the New School and then continued to defend in later years, long after they had moved on. Johnson's successors did not follow his example.

⇒

On March 22, 1947, President Truman issued Executive Order 9835, transforming a "haphazard crusade" against communists and their friends into a systematic "loyalty-security program." As Ellen Schrecker reminds us, "No other event, no political trial or congressional hearing, was to shape the internal Cold War as decisively as the Truman administration's loyalty-security program."[28] With the authority of the president behind them, federal agencies moved quickly to fire "politically suspicious" employees—encouraging state agencies to do the same—and the Attorney General's office expanded its efforts to identify subversive organizations. Seven months later Hovde sent a memo to de Lima inquiring: "Do you keep a separate dossier or a cross-file on our alleged redness? It might be invaluable."[29]

De Lima created a "Red scare file" and began clipping articles from the mainstream media on the domestic war against communism and its impact on academic institutions. The file contained little on the New School itself, but it had enough to justify Hovde's concerns. Of particular interest were de Lima's handwritten notes, reproducing a few lines from an article published on January 20, 1948, in *The Chicago Tribune*: "The New School had been labeled a Communist Front by a New York State Legislative Committee." The *Tribune* was referring to a 1939 report prepared by the New York State Joint Legislative Committee on Law Enforcement, specifically to the section on popular fronts, which linked "politically suspicious" individuals with progressive institutions.

The main target of the article in *The Chicago Tribune* was not the New School but the United Nations, whose very presence, the journalist warned, threatened the security of the United States. In an effort to strengthen his case against the U.N., the journalist accused the international organization of collaborating with politically tainted institutions such as the New School. How? By offering a fifteen-week course on mass media and international relations at the university. According to an announcement made by the Department of Public Information at the United Nations, classes would begin in February and meet in the Twelfth Street building. Quoting its spokesman, the journalist reported disparagingly that the U.N. knew nothing about the New School's political leanings, but even if it had, "'we don't make any distinction,' he said, meaning that the U.N. does not distinguish between communist and non-communist outfits."[30] We might say the same, of course, about the journalist at *The Chicago Tribune* and the author of the 1939 legislative report, neither one of whom saw any difference, apparently, between a progressive institution like the New School and organizations working with the Communist Party. They were all identified as "popular fronts."[31]

The legislative report listed more than eighty so-called popular front organizations in Lower Manhattan, accusing them of participating in subversive activities; the New School was among them. After describing how "the memberships interlock pink and red" organizations, the report proclaimed in the same ominous tone: "The true nature of the interlocking membership is readily perceived upon an examination of the names of officials and prominent members, as follows, and it is important to note that the following are not merely members, but high-ranking leaders of the organizations listed beside their names."[32]

When de Lima got her hands on the report, she found that it "lists Heywood Broun on NSSR [New School for Social Research]!"[33] Broun was a newspaper columnist, not a New School official or prominent member of the faculty. His affiliation with the university consisted in having given a guest lecture in a course on journalism that Johnson ran during the spring semester of 1937. At the time, Broun had a regular column in *The New York World Telegram*. Seven years earlier he had run for Congress unsuccessfully on the Socialist ticket.

This, of course, was an old story. Johnson was no longer president of the New School, and the new president was far more consistent in his anticommunist rhetoric than Johnson had ever been; a fact that may have escaped the journalist in Chicago but was creating a great deal of tension on campus between the founding president and his successor. In retirement, Johnson had continued writing to colleagues and friends about politics and publishing opinion pieces

on the editorial pages of local and national newspapers, often in the name of the
New School, as he railed against what he considered to be an "un-American"
witch hunt, not only by McCarthy but by people like Hovde. Although Johnson
always identified himself as a confirmed anticommunist, he took great pains
to distinguish between his position and that of the man who had succeeded
him. In April 1949, Johnson published a blistering editorial on the pages of the
New School Bulletin that criticized the new president without identifying him
by name but in ways that nobody following the news of the day could have possibly missed.

Johnson's decision to publish his editorial in the April issue of the university's
bulletin was no coincidence. He wanted to make sure the New School community understood that he fiercely disagreed with what Hovde had said a few weeks
earlier in a keynote address at Freedom House before a huge crowd of virulent
anticommunists, most of whom identified themselves as liberal democrats. The
people who gathered at Freedom House had come together to take a stand against
those who were attending a three-day event taking place at the Waldorf Astoria
Hotel: The Cultural and Scientific Conference for World Peace.

Hovde described the sponsors of the peace conference as Soviet-backed
fellow travelers who, although they claimed to be calling for nuclear disarma-
ment and peaceful coexistence, were actually soldiers in the Russians' campaign
to destroy American democracy. Johnson was appalled. As president of the New
School, Hovde did not only represent himself when he spoke in public but the
entire institution. Switching into the voice of a folksy outsider, Johnson lunged
for the jugular:

> Someone asserts that the term fellow traveler was invented by John Bunyan.
> I do not know. All I know is that it was a good term, humane, sociable, until it
> was slicked over by venomous Communist and reactionary tongues. Now the
> worst you can say of a man is that he is a fellow traveler, a combination of dupe
> and scalawag.
>
> If it is your honest conviction that in the interminable debate between our
> own diplomats and the Russian, our side may sometimes be wrong, you are a
> fellow traveler. If you don't like "thought control" even in the interest of what
> you judge to be the Lord's side, you are a fellow traveler. If you inveigh against the
> newly invented "crime by association" you are a fellow traveler. . . .
>
> Hitler and Stalin needed thought control, orthodoxy. . . . But what made us
> import such a fantastic idea? We Americans, brought up to stand on our own
> feet, to do as we please so long as we harm nobody, to think as we please, to speak
> as we please, so long as we are not too boring. . . .

This is our America. . . . It is our privilege to play the fool. We have done that, time and again. But always we woke up, the morning after.

Wake up, America! The Philistines are upon us.[34]

On March 25, 1949, eight hundred people crowded into the Waldorf Astoria Hotel to attend the Cultural and Scientific Conference for World Peace.[35] The mainstream media covered the event in considerable detail, accusing the sponsors (as Hovde had done) of belonging to "Communist Front" organizations and the participants of being fellow travelers. Among the more spectacular articles, *Life* magazine produced a photographic essay that included mug shots of fifty luminaries who had attended the conference. The caption accompanying the photos read: "Dupes and Fellow Travelers Dress Up Communist Fronts."[36] Although New School colleagues attended the conference and, in some cases, helped to organize it,[37] the press identified the university with the protest rally taking place a few blocks away at Freedom House, where Bryn Hovde was giving the keynote address.

The people behind the protest included Sidney Hook and other outspoken anticommunists who called themselves Americans for Intellectual Freedom. They belonged to *The Partisan Review* crowd and the Congress of Cultural Freedom, an organization founded in 1939 by John Dewey and Hook. As Dewey's biographer Alan Ryan described it, the Congress of Cultural Freedom began as "an anti-Communist social democratic group of writers and others that swiftly gained the support of large numbers of intellectuals who had previously been members of one or other of the cultural front organizations set up by the Communist party."[38] Many believed that the Congress of Cultural Freedom was offering intellectuals on the anti-Stalinist left a welcomed alternative with no strings attached—until they discovered during the 1960s that they too had been "dupes," in their case of the CIA, which had been surreptitiously underwriting their journal *Encounter*.[39] Although Hook and his friends put the Freedom House rally together at the very last minute, they drew so many people that by the time Hovde spoke the audience was spilling out of the hall and into Bryant Park.[40]

The Conference for World Peace attracted Arthur Miller, Dorothy Parker, Lillian Hellman, and Henry Wallace, among others; the one at Freedom House, Mary McCarthy, Dwight McDonald, Max Eastman, and Arthur Schlesinger. One side focused on the threat of nuclear warfare; the other on the dangers of Stalinism and the Soviet Union. Accusing one another of ignorance and treason, those attending the conference at the Waldorf Astoria branded those at Freedom

House as red-baiting traitors who had abandoned the left and joined the extreme right, while the Freedom House crowd dismissed those at the Waldorf Astoria as fellow travelers and dupes of Soviet communism.

In the months leading up to the peace conference, Hovde had already established a big name for himself as an anticommunist liberal. During the summer of 1948, *The New York Times* covered Hovde's participation in Wroclaw (Breslau), Poland, at the International World Congress of Intellectuals. The chairman of the Union of Soviet Novelists, Alexander Fadeyev, welcomed everyone to the event in a keynote address aimed aggressively at the United States. Hovde responded in kind. Rising from the floor, he dismissed the arguments of the Russian novelist and vigorously defended American democracy before what the *Times* described as a generally hostile audience: "[Hovde] used blunt language and said things about the Russians that ordinarily are not spoken of in public in present-day [communist] Poland."[41]

Seven months later when Hovde gave the keynote address at Freedom House, *The New York Times* quoted the New School's president directly: "There is no more ruthless imperialism in the world today than that of the Soviet Union. Harboring designs to conquer the world for communism, its rulers impute motives of conquest and war to all who stand in the way." The *Times* also reported Hovde saying that he respected academic freedom and would reserve comment about those who were attending the so-called peace conference until he had heard what they had to say. If they criticized the Soviet Union, that would be one thing. If they did not, "we shall know how to classify the Americans at the Waldorf."[42]

Hovde did not deviate in his talk from the New School's long-standing position on the Communist Party, but he paid little attention to nuance. Johnson agreed that the New School had "no use for the Communists and never had," even adding that the university could take credit for being "the first educational institution in America to declare [in 1935] that no person following a party line can hold a place on its Faculty." However, and this was critical to him, the New School "does not interpret this principle wildly and unintelligently, as those who regard even abhorrence of war as a Communist idea, since Communists profess to abhor war."[43]

By the time Johnson published his April 1949 editorial attacking Hovde, everyone knew that the New School's second president was looking for another job. Two months earlier the press had announced that Hovde was a finalist in the search for a new president of Queens College of the City of New York. Hovde withdrew from that race when he became the target of a smear campaign that accused him, ironically, of having sympathy for communism. New York's mayor Bill O'Dwyer led the charge, with the hope of improving the chances of another candidate backed by the Democratic Party in the borough of Queens. Although the press fiercely criticized O'Dwyer's intervention, the damage was done. Hovde bowed out after the press reported the mayor describing him as " 'a political innocent' and a dupe of the communists who encouraged the New School's attack on received dogma."

O'Dwyer's faction had attacked Hovde not only for being president of the New School but for serving as vice chair of the Americans for Democratic Action (ADA), which in their eyes was even worse. Founded by New Deal Democrats in 1947, the ADA was more progressive politically than O'Dwyer's machine Democrats, but it was hardly soft on communism. As the party's platform clearly stated, "We reject any association with communists or sympathizers with communism in the United States as completely as we reject any association with fascists or their sympathizers."[44]

Hovde could satisfy no one. It mattered little what the New School's president said or with whom he associated. Critics on the right, from O'Dwyer Democrats to arch-conservative Republicans, called him a "dupe" and the university he led a hotbed of radical activity. Critics on the left accused him of having compromised the New School's reputation as a champion of academic freedom, and these critics included Johnson.

Even after Hovde stepped down as president, the New School continued to face vigorous criticism from both sides of the political spectrum. Within months of taking over as president, Simons was defending the New School from FBI and congressional investigations, as well as responding to complaints on the left that the university was bowing to McCarthyism. Although Johnson never criticized his old friend in public, he made it clear in private correspondence that he was furious. The New School, he complained, should not give in to political pressure. When he was president it resisted.

During the 1950s, administrators at the New School allegedly interviewed members of the faculty about their political affiliations. Among those allegedly questioned was the social realist painter Robert Gwathmey. Teaching full-time at Cooper Union, the painter began giving lectures at the New School in 1947. In 1979, Gwathmey reported to Peter Rutkoff and William Scott that Clara Mayer had interrogated him in Central Park in the early 1950s about his "previous party membership." Gwathmey "refused to answer but was so upset he immediately resigned from the New School."[45] There is no corroborating evidence that Mayer ever cornered Gwathmey in Central Park, but we do know that the painter resigned in the spring of 1952, causing the New School a great deal of embarrassment.

Students demanded an explanation. Why did Gwathmey decide to quit? On June 9, President Simons appeared before the Executive Council of the New School Associates and read a lengthy statement describing the university's policies on academic freedom in great detail. The associates were members of the Continuing Education student body who paid an annual membership fee of $100. Simons said that he took the students' concerns very seriously, and he wanted them to know that he too regretted that the painter had resigned. Having concluded that Gwathmey was not a member of the Communist Party, Simons assured the associates that the New School would never have fired him. He was sorry, he continued, that the painter had decided to sever his ties with the university "simply because his private political activities were questioned by friends of the New School."

Simons then quoted at length from the university's bylaws on academic freedom, which he said were adopted in 1946 but they reproduced passages from earlier documents. The section dealing with policies on political party affiliations had first appeared in 1935 in the Graduate Faculty's charter. Every member of the Board of Trustees, administrative staff, and faculty shall:

(a) accept the obligation to follow the truth of scholarship wherever it may lead, regardless of personal consequences; (b) shall not be a member of any political party or group which asserts the right to dictate in matters of science or scientific opinion; (c) bind himself, both individually and when acting collectively with others, in all official action, especially in recommendations and elections to the faculty or in promotion of members thereof, to be guided solely by considerations of scholarly achievement, competence and integrity, giving no weight whatsoever to scientifically irrelevant considerations such as race, sex, religion, or such political beliefs as represent no bar upon individual freedom of thought, inquiry, teaching and publication.

Simons explained that "party membership," at the time of an individual's appointment was the "pivotal issue," not views expressed in the classroom or held privately. If a candidate applying for a position claimed that he was not a party member, the New School would take him at his word. Once appointed, he would be "entitled to academic freedom and bound by academic responsibility under our By-Laws." The New School, Simons added pointedly, was "not bound by any arbitrary loyalty standards established by private agencies or by haphazard lists of subversive organizations, [like the one] published by the Department of Justice,

[nor] by any concepts of guilt by association; it is solely bound by its educational policy as stated in Article I, Section 1(c) of its By-Laws." As far as those bylaws were concerned, Gwathmey "meets the requirements of our general policy." Although Simons disagreed with the painter's political opinions, he would never have asked him to resign.[46]

Gwathmey, in fact, was an active member of the Communist Party at the time and had been for years, so much so that the FBI had been keeping an extensive file on him that they only closed in 1969. When the painter described his cloak-and-dagger encounter with Mayer in Central Park, he may have been conflating the New School incident with the interview we know he had with government agents on Central Park West. According to Gwathmey's biographer, Michael Kammen, the FBI accosted the painter near his home in December 1953 and tried to persuade him to cooperate with a government investigation. They failed.[47]

According to Kammen, during the 1940s and 1950s, Gwathmey participated in a number of "subversive" activities, including the peace conference in 1949 at the Waldorf Astoria where his name appeared on the list of organizers. But despite his various political affiliations, he never appeared before HUAC. Nor did he lose his job at Cooper Union. With the exception of the New School incident, he seems to have come through the McCarthy period unscathed. His social realist portraits of African Americans appeared regularly during those years in the best galleries in New York.

So what do we make of the New School story? Even if we dismiss the report that Mayer threatened the painter in Central Park, we know that Gwathmey resigned in protest in the spring of 1952 after someone associated with the institution spoke to him about his political activities. Yet neither Gwathmey nor his biographer said anything about it. In a four-hour taped interview, recorded in 1968, Gwathmey talked about teaching at the New School and even mentioned that he had resigned in the early 1950s, but he gave an entirely different explanation:

> I was an art owl from five to seven. And [the New School] was for girls and boys who were working and they would rush down from jobs, two hours of work without even having eaten dinner. . . . Well, it was so limiting. And so, I just didn't want it.[48]

Not that we have to accept the painter's explanation at face value. Gwathmey said nothing in that interview about belonging to the Communist Party either. Kammen, however, spoke at length about Gwathmey's politics and the McCarthy years and yet he too said nothing about Gwathmey resigning in protest from the New School.

=====◆=====

When Hovde and Simons spoke about the Soviet Union, they sounded very much like other anti-Stalinist progressives of the period, including self-acclaimed socialists like Irving Howe, the literary critic and a founding editor of *Dissent* magazine. Although liberal democrats and socialists disagreed with one another on many issues, when it came to Stalinist Russia they held similar views. Consider, for example, the statement made by the editors of *Dissent* in their inaugural issue in the winter of 1954. Eager to publish provocative new work, Howe and his fellow editors invited writers of different political stripes to submit their manuscripts, promising to publish articles that "dissented with *Dissent.*" Describing themselves as political "radicals," they presented the magazine's editorial policy as follows, without the slightest hint of irony: "Our magazine will be open to a wide arc of opinion, excluding only Stalinists and totalitarian fellow-travelers on the one hand, and those former radicals who have signed their peace with society on the other."[49]

Another example is the political theorist Harold Laski, an early contributor to *The New Republic* and a founding member of the New School's faculty. Although Laski returned to England in 1920 to accept a chair at the London School of Economics, he continued to visit the United States regularly, until the war intervened in 1939. During those trips he gave lectures at the New School. Over the years, Laski had emerged as a major figure in British politics, serving as chairman of the British Labour Party between 1945 and 1946. In the spring of 1949, he returned to the United States for the first time in ten years to give lectures at seven universities across the country, from the New School to UCLA.

When Laski landed in New York in the third week of March, he learned that UCLA had canceled his invitation. Although the university never gave him an official explanation, Laski had good reason to believe that the decision was politically motivated. *The New York Times* announced the cancellation in an article published on March 24, one day before the opening session of the World Peace Conference at the Waldorf Astoria. Given the timing, the journalist asked Laski to comment on the political leanings of the organizers of the forthcoming event:

> I think it's a fellow traveler organization, but I am not afraid of fellow traveler organizations. I think it's traditional in the United States not to be afraid of men speaking their minds. I think that's why you passed the First Amendment. . . .

If there is fear of communism in universities . . . then you had better pack off, because you are the same breed that feared Galileo in the 17th century.[50]

True to his reputation for being outspoken, Laski was ruthless in his analysis of American politics in the talks he gave at the remaining six universities. But on other occasions he was equally harsh about the Soviet Union. As Laski reminded *The New York Times* reporter, he belonged to the British Labour Party, which strongly opposed the policies of the USSR. In that spirit, he published a withering attack on Marxist-Leninism in 1948 in the introduction to the Labour Party's centennial edition of *The Communist Manifesto*.

Laski began his magisterial essay by describing the historical circumstances that led Marx and Engels to call for world revolution, before turning to what later happened in the Soviet Union, where "the large and flexible outlook of the *Communist Manifesto* [was] applied in a narrow and dogmatically rigid way." Although Laski would never have supported a policy that excluded communists from teaching at the New School, or from publishing their articles in *Dissent*, he agreed entirely with those who claimed that members of the party could not think freely because they deferred to the "Politbureau" of the Soviet Union as "the guardian of universal truth."[51]

But Laski was still a Socialist, and that was enough in the United States to set off the alarms, even at educational institutions that claimed to respect academic freedom. When Laski died unexpectedly in 1950, the New School held a memorial for him over the vigorous objections of faculty and students. Hovde had just resigned, and the incoming president, Simons, stepped into the vacuum to defend the university's decision. In a statement in the *New School Bulletin*, Simons acknowledged that the talk Laski had given the year before did not represent the philosophy of the university, but the way he had lived his life embodied everything that the New School stood for: "His continuous quest for the truth, his eagerness to improve the lot of man, and his final firm resolve to seek change by consent only."[52]

The speakers at the memorial were less conflicted. Supreme Court Justice Felix Frankfurter reminisced about Laski as a great teacher. Johnson recalled his "gallant stand on freedom of speech." Laski's life, he said, offered an inspirational lesson on the meaning of British democracy:

> Harold Laski was with us in the meetings that organized the New School. We valued him greatly. Extremely young, he was slight of form, quick and bright, though deeply intellectual. He stood for a principle of the English tradition that we Americans accepted in form but not in fact, the principle of freedom of speech.

Centuries of brave struggle had established for the Englishman the right to say what is in his mind to say. If what he has to say is unpopular his hearers can heckle him, but no official nor any organization can bully him into silence.[53]

Laski's visit to the United States in 1949 coincided with a wave of dismissals on university campuses of professors accused of being members of the Communist Party. In May, *The New York Times* ran a two-part series on the subject. The first article reported that the American Association of University Professors (AAUP) was being " 'swamped' with teachers' assertions that they are ousted or held back for politics." The most widely publicized case involved two professors at the University of Washington who had lost their jobs in the winter of 1949. Alarmed by the dismissals, colleagues at other universities started organizing meetings in solidarity with the fired professors. UCLA was among them. This persuaded Laski that the Board of Regents of the University of California had canceled his visit because UCLA's provost, who was Laski's good friend, "had recently invited to the campus two professors who were released by the University of Washington for alleged Communist connections." The board, Laski suggested, was "retaliating."[54]

The AAUP had never reviewed a case before 1949 that involved faculty members losing their jobs for allegedly belonging to the Communist Party. Everyone, therefore, in the academic community was paying close attention to see how the AAUP would rule. As the *Times* put it, "Many college presidents have indicated that they are awaiting the association's verdict before they take action against suspected Communists on their campuses." The AAUP was expected to reach a final decision by the fall of 1949, the details of which they promised to publish in the AAUP bulletin.[55]

Then nothing happened for seven years. When the AAUP finally reached a verdict in the spring of 1956, it announced that it would not discipline the current administration at the University of Washington.

Since the events of 1949, the personnel of the Administration of the University of Washington has largely changed. In the light of all the facts, although the Administration of the University of Washington merited censure by the American Association of University Professors at the time, it would not be appropriate to censure the present Administration on the ground of the 1949 dismissals.[56]

After remaining silent for all those years, the AAUP decided not to press charges on any of its other pending cases either. It would be more productive, the leadership concluded, to find ways to make peace among warring factions and move on.

With that goal in mind, the AAUP published a set of general principles in 1956 to guide future cases. It also published a "joint statement" by Ralph Fuchs, the general secretary of the AAUP, and Sidney Hook, a critic of the association, to bring closure, finally, to the endless debate about "whether a college or university faculty member, who is a member of the Communist Party, is unfit to retain his position if he has *consciously committed* himself to practice deceit in furthering the Communist cause, or only if he has actually *practiced* deceit as an educator—assuming, in either case, that his misconduct is established by due process" [emphasis added].

Hook had been debating the subject in the mainstream media since 1949. When a person joined the Communist Party, the philosopher argued, he committed himself consciously to practice deceit. Party membership alone was therefore grounds for dismissal. The AAUP, in theory, disagreed. The association may not have reviewed any cases between 1949 and 1956, but the association's delegates had been meeting every year and recommitting themselves to the principle they had adopted in 1947: As long as it was legal to join the Communist Party in the United States—and it remained legal during the entire McCarthy period—a faculty member could not be fired for belonging to the party, only for engaging in subversive activities. In 1956, the association's delegates reconfirmed their commitment to the same principle. The Fuchs-Hook statement, however, was more nuanced. Although the general secretary agreed that the AAUP should have censured the University of Washington in 1949 for having fired colleagues because they belonged to Communist Party, this did not mean that the AAUP was entirely at odds with Hook. Quoting extensively from the convoluted language of AAUP documents, Fuchs demonstrated that the association and the philosopher "are in substantial agreement on all questions of the moment":

> The AAUP has never maintained, and its Committee does not now assert, that a commitment by a faculty member to use deception or concealment, whether the commitment is made through acceptance of organizational policies or otherwise, must be followed by actual misbehavior before his dismissal can be justified. Such a commitment is clearly inconsistent with professional objectivity and integrity. . . . Conspiracy thus stands condemned; and conspiracy is completed by agreement, whether or not it leads to further misconduct. There is thus no conflict between the view of Professor Hook and that of the Association as interpreted, concerning condemnation of a proved commitment to practice deceit.[57]

By the time the AAUP came out with its disheartening report and its general secretary had sharpened the pain by publishing a joint statement with Hook,

McCarthy was dead, and the Red scare hysteria was calming down. During the difficult years, the officers of the association had remained silent, leaving the field open to plain-speaking leaders of academic institutions who did not hide behind screens of impenetrable prose. In all fairness, in June 1949 the AAUP did take a stand against imposing a special loyalty oath on college professors, along with Phi Beta Kappa and "a vast majority of responsible university leaders, as well as spokesmen for education generally."[58]

At the height of the McCarthy period, the Association of American Universities (AAU) was not as tongue-tied as the AAUP. On March 31, 1953, *The New York Times* announced on the front page of the paper: "Colleges Vote Freedom Code Banning Reds from Faculties." The subtitle added: "37 Universities in U.S. and Canada Demand Staff Members Be Loyal Citizens and Fearless in Ideas and Teaching." Only top-ranked research universities in Canada and the United States belonged to the AAU. The New School was not among them.

The head of the AAU was Harold Dodds, president of Princeton University, and A. Whitney Griswold, president of Yale, chaired the committee that drafted the association's new academic freedom policy. Other signatories included Cal Tech, Chicago, Columbia, Cornell, Duke, Harvard, Johns Hopkins, McGill, MIT, NYU, Northwestern, University of Pennsylvania, Vanderbilt, and a good representation of state universities, among them the Universities of California, Illinois, Indiana, Missouri, Virginia, Washington, and Wisconsin.

The *Times* published the full text of the document, which took up almost an entire page of the newspaper. By way of introduction, the statement reviewed the role higher education had played in the United States, tracing the history of universities back to the 1600s: "No country in history so early perceived the importance of that role [of higher education] and none has derived such widespread benefits from it." The modern university, the statement continued, is not a corporation with a hierarchical structure. Its permanent members—those with tenure—are all equals. They represent many different fields of knowledge and different points of view, but they all share a common set of values: "loyalty to the ideal of learning, to the moral code, to the country and to its form of government."

After having "set forth the nature and function of the university" and outlined the "rights and responsibilities" of members of the faculty, the AAU statement asked: What are the implications under the "present danger" and "current anxiety over Russian communism and the subversive activities connected with it"?

We condemn Russian communism as we condemn every form of totalitarianism. We share the profound concern of the American people at the existence of an international conspiracy whose goal is the destruction of our cherished institutions. The police state would be the death of our universities, as of our Government. Three of its principles in particular are abhorrent to us: the fomenting of world-wide revolution as a step to seizing power; the use of falsehood and deceit as normal means of persuasion; thought control—the dictation of doctrines, which must be accepted and taught by all party members.

To protect American democracy, universities should only appoint and grant tenure to faculty members who demonstrate "professional competence" and their "loyalty" to the nation:

Above all, a scholar must have integrity and independence. This renders impossible adherence to such a regime as that of Russia and its satellites. No person who accepts or advocates such principles and methods has any place in a university. Since present membership in the Communist Party requires the acceptance of these principles and methods such membership extinguishes the right of a university position.

The text of the Academic Freedom Policy ends with a reconfirmation of the Association of American Universities' commitment to "freedom of thought and speech."[59]

Critics of the AAU's statement must have found it particularly disheartening to see the name of the University of Chicago among the thirty-seven academic institutions that endorsed it. Four years earlier Chicago's Chancellor Robert Hutchins had been one of very few leaders of an educational institution to question the dismissal of the two professors from the University of Washington. But by 1953 Hutchins had retired and Lawrence Kimpton had replaced him.

Hutchins had also spoken out in 1949 in defense of members of his own faculty when a special legislative committee in the State of Illinois accused several colleagues of his and at Roosevelt University of belonging to "Communist-front" organizations. The committee quickly backed down. As Schrecker observed, had other prominent academic leaders followed Hutchins's example, they might have minimized the damage inflicted on universities by outside—largely government—interventions.[60]

But even Hutchins did not publicly defend the right of university professors to belong to the Communist Party. His primary concern was to protect the rights of full-time members of the faculty to govern themselves—as these rights had first been defined in 1915 by the AAUP. The faculty alone should decide whether communists might teach at their university.[61]

In addition to Hutchins, another hero of the period was Johnson's old friend Alexander Meiklejohn, the former president of Amherst College. In the days following the dismissal of the two professors at the University of Washington, Meiklejohn squared off with Hook on the pages of *The New York Times Magazine*. Taking the argument further than Hutchins had, Meiklejohn made an unqualified case for allowing communists to teach, but he did so as a private citizen, not as the president of a college. The "primary task of education in our colleges and universities is the teaching of the theory and practice of intellectual freedom, as the first principle of the democratic way of life." You cannot teach freedom of thought, he continued, by suppressing the ideas of others:

> These men who advocate that we do to the Russians what the Russians, if they had the power, would do to us are declaring that the Russians are right and we are wrong. They practice suppression because they have more faith in the methods of dictatorship than in those of a free self-governing society.[62]

Finally, Johnson also attracted national attention in May 1949. As Benjamin Fine reported in *The New York Times*, the New School's president emeritus had accepted an invitation that year to become the first president of a new academic institution in the Middle West, founded in the name of academic freedom. Ten faculty members had recently resigned in protest from Olivet College, a small liberal arts institution in Michigan, after the president there had fired six professors and the college's librarian for being too "liberal" politically. Inspired by what these colleagues had done, a group of alumni announced that they were abandoning their alma mater and providing the funds to build a new college where Olivet's former faculty members would teach. The alumni named their new academic institution after John Shipherd, the enlightened founder of Oberlin College. Although Fine announced that Shipherd College would open in the fall, it never did.[63]

Back at the New School, the leadership was lying low, doing only the minimum to defend its reputation as a champion of academic freedom. Although Simons occasionally hired a blacklisted professor, he was not sticking his neck out for communists, as a matter of principle, he would have added, not out of fear. To his credit, he had been inviting outside organizations that were standing up to McCarthy to hold events at the New School. In March 1952, the American Civil Liberties Union (ACLU) used the university's facilities to give awards to institutions of higher learning that had defended the rights of controversial colleagues to express their opinions freely. The New School was not among the recipients.[64] Then in 1953, Simons lost his nerve.

13

THE OROZCO MURAL

When the Twelfth Street building opened in January 1931, New York's leading art critics panned José Clemente Orozco's "Struggle in the Orient: Slavery, Imperialism and Gandhi." Johnson never forgave them, even though they had written rave reviews about Joseph Urban's architecture and Thomas Hart Benton's "America Today." Like other intellectuals of his generation, he marveled at the work of Orozco, Diego Rivera and David Alfaro Siqueiros, Mexico's three famous muralists, whose bold depictions of their country's political struggles and rich cultural heritage decorated the walls of government buildings across the nation. Having written about the Mexican Revolution for *The New Republic*, Johnson had more than a passing interest in Mexico.[1] The idea that one of "*Los Tres Grandes*" might paint a mural for the New School's cafeteria excited him a great deal. And of the three, Orozco was his first choice, for aesthetic and political reasons—he alone did not belong to the Communist Party.

In the early 1930s, the three great ones received invitations to paint murals in the United States—Orozco by Pomona College (1930), the New School (1931), and Dartmouth College (1934). When Johnson spoke to Orozco about what he might paint for the Twelfth Street building, he asked the muralist to choose a subject "of such importance that no history written a hundred years from now could fail to devote a chapter to it." The Mexican settled on "the revolutionary unrest that smolders in the non-industrial periphery, India, Mexico, and Russia."

Johnson wrote about Orozco's frescoes twice, first during World War II, then again during the McCarthy period. In his first essay, he complained bitterly about the negative reviews Orozco had received. The critics, he said, had dismissed the work for both ideological and aesthetic reasons. As far as

Johnson was concerned, "political criticism of a work [was] seldom injurious," whether it came from Trotskyists on the left—as some of it did in the case of Orozco—or anticommunists on the right. Aesthetic criticism, however, was another matter.

If Johnson had written these words before 1933, they might have passed without notice. But what a strange observation to make in 1942, during a genocidal war, when Hitler and Stalin were taking political criticism to murderous extremes! And Nelson Rockefeller, less heinously but troubling all the same, had destroyed a mural by Diego Rivera in the heart of Manhattan. E. B. White memorialized the Rockefeller scandal in a bitter satire soon after the event, in the spring of 1933. When Johnson read "I Paint What I See," in *The New Yorker* magazine, he must have had a good chuckle. The style was right up his alley, and the message deeply gratifying: Two years after the New School unveiled Orozco's mural with its portraits of Lenin and Stalin, here was Rivera, in White's irreverent words, offering to paint over a "couple of people drinkin'" and replace them with "a picture of Abraham Lincoln. . . . But the head of Lenin has got to stay!"[2]

Johnson dismissed political criticism all the same because, he explained, political alliances kept shifting. And when they did, political criticism shifted along with them. He saw that happen with the Orozco mural in a matter of a few years. In 1931, the reviewers railed against the portraits of Lenin and Stalin. Ten years later, when the Soviet Union became an ally in the war against Hitler, the critics stopped complaining about Orozco's rendering of the Russian Revolution and objected instead to his depiction of Gandhi, in a yoga position, dignified and serene, obstructing "the purposes of the British Empire"

Although Johnson gave other examples of political criticism, he scrupulously stayed away from the incident at Rockefeller Center, no doubt to avoid offending the family of the philanthropic foundation that was generously paying the salaries of refugee scholars at the New School. But had Johnson not had to worry about insulting his friends, he could have used this scandal to support his argument: The wrath of American capitalism may have destroyed "Man at the Crossroads" in New York, but Rivera reproduced it in miniature at the Palacio de Bellas Artes in Mexico City.

Aesthetic criticism, Johnson proclaimed, was far more dangerous. History could not save great works of art from academicians the way it could from political ideologues. "Connoisseurs" were destroying "every innovation, all progress." Only the enthusiasm of everyday people protected art from the professional critic. Orozco's mural survived thanks to public opinion. As Johnson wrote in 1942:

> Several hundred thousand people have come to view the pictures, and after ten
> years the visits continue. Several thousand newspapers and magazines, not only

in the United States but in Canada, Latin America, Europe, and even in China have asked permission to reproduce photographs of parts of the murals. A reasonable calculation would fix the number of people who have seen the murals and reproduced photographs of them at over one hundred million.[3]

Orozco's agent and biographer shared Johnson's outrage. Remembering her conversations with art critics at the opening, Alma Reed wrote: "Even those who had gradually become Orozco's admirers intimated by their lukewarm attitude and irrelevant questions that their New School reviews would lack enthusiasm."[4] Among them was Edward Alden Jewell of *The New York Times*, the same critic who had written so effusively about Benton and Urban a few weeks earlier when the Twelfth Street building first opened, noting cautiously then that he would wait until Orozco had finished his mural before discussing it as well. On January 25, the *Times* published Jewell's scathing review: "One is bound to confess, and with genuine regret, that the Orozco frescoes in the dining room of the New School for Social Research are disappointing." Although Jewell conceded that the mural had "some virtues," the work as a whole lacked unity: "The walls are a mêlée of fragments without—from the standpoint of design—any relationship." He also objected to the way Orozco's mural stopped midway down the wall, without reaching the floor.[5]

Several days later the *Times* published three irate letters to the editor: two from artists—Orozco's assistant and a visiting artist from France, who was "brought up on the tradition of classical and modern painting"—and a third from a woman who identified herself as "one who sometimes dines at the New School":

> As one who sometimes dines at the New School, I was amazed at the suggestion of the art critic in last Sunday's *Times* that the slate wainscoting beneath the Orozco frescoes was too high. I cannot see how the frescoes could have been placed lower on the wall and have the room function at the same time as a dining hall, which accommodates many tables, chairs and diners, twice a day. A vista of the frescoes as seen through a maze of tables and chairs and human legs could hardly give a "more advantageous point of view" to the spectator....
>
> Fortunately, mural painting of this type is a public possession and, unlike works displayed in the brief exhibitions of commercial galleries, it is the public and not the art critic who gives the final verdict.

Orozco's assistant challenged the reviewer's artistic sensibility: "Seldom has criticism so completely missed the mark," she complained. The French painter literally screamed off the page: "'No cohesion!' 'No composition!' 'Lack of melodic line!' . . . If it were only for the privilege of seeing Orozco's frescoes, it was worthwhile for me to cross the Atlantic. It would be, in fact, worthwhile for any French painter, any European painter and I do hope that very soon Orozco will be able to do the same honor to France and other European countries that he has done to the United States."[6]

Johnson loved the idea that Orozco had revived the ancient art of fresco painting. The process fascinated him:

> Orozco would chalk with his one arm (he had lost the other in a childhood accident) an area of rough plaster he wanted covered with a final coat, on which he would work with his little hair brush, with pigments, while the plaster was dripping wet. I was fascinated. There had never been, so far as I knew, a piece of true fresco in all the United States east of the Rocky Mountains. Here a true fresco was growing under my eyes.

He then went on at some length about the technical challenges of fresco painting, complicated further in this particular mural because Orozco had applied the principles of dynamic symmetry "that the Devil may understand." Johnson clearly did not. The technique had captured the imagination of the Delphic Circle, a cultlike society of artists and intellectuals with whom Orozco and Reed spent a great deal of time. Dynamic symmetry, introduced to early twentieth-century painting by Jay Hambidge, was a technique that applied the same "principles of design in the architecture of man and of plants" that the Greek masters had used during the great classical period.[7]

When Johnson turned to the historical significance of the mural, he spoke with greater authority. Taking his readers on a virtual tour from panel to panel, he began with the "Universal Table of Brotherhood," the painting diners saw first when they entered the cafeteria. Located on the far south wall, it depicted ten men seated along three sides of a large white table, each one representing a different nation. Presiding at the head were members of the three most "despised races": a Mexican peon, an African, and a Jew. The Caucasian figures at the table were portraits of friends: the Jew was the Palestinian painter Reuben Rubin; the Europeans, the Dutch poet Leonard Van Noppen and the French philosopher Paul Richard; and the American, the art historian Lloyd Goodrich. Rubin, Van Noppen, and Richard all belonged to the Delphic Society; Goodrich was an art historian and curator at the Whitney Museum, which had just opened its doors a few months earlier. He would soon become the museum's director.

Many years later, Goodrich explained how he ended up in the mural: Orozco had originally wanted Johnson to represent the American, but when the president of the New School failed to show up at the appointed hour, Orozco asked Goodrich to take his place. Johnson had another story: Orozco, he said, suggested seating him at the head of the table, together with the Mexican and the African, but Johnson insisted that he put a Jew there instead.[8]

Turning next to the west wall were Orozco's "Allegories of World Revolution": the Russian Revolution with portraits of Lenin and Stalin and the Mexican Revolution, with Felipe Carrillo Puerto, the governor of Yucatan, assassinated in 1924, a few weeks before he was going to marry Alma Reed. On the north wall was a scene from daily life in postrevolutionary Mexico, with laborers returning home to their wives and children after a productive day of work; then, on the east wall, Gandhi's passive resistance to British imperialism. Finally, on the walls outside the cafeteria, Orozco painted his "Allegory to the Arts and Sciences."

We have several accounts of Johnson's conversations with Orozco and Reed about what the muralist would paint. The descriptions differ in style and length, but they all agree that Johnson did not interfere with Orozco's decision to paint portraits of Lenin and Stalin. As the Mexican muralist told the story in 1942, "I had been given absolute freedom in my work: It was a school for investigation, not for submission."[9]

Johnson waited until 1952, at the height of the McCarthy period, to give his version of their interview. Orozco had died three years earlier. Describing their exchange in taunting detail, it reads like an open invitation to the philistines in Washington to come after him. Johnson's main target, however, was the New School's Board of Trustees, members of which had recently proposed getting rid of the Orozco mural. The president emeritus was livid. If they succeeded, he wanted to make sure that nobody thought that he had anything to do with it:

> There was the old Red army, led by a poster of Lenin. . . . As I looked at the picture, my liver, to use the Homeric expression, dissolved to water. My God, what trouble was in store for me! My beloved country had not at that time sunk so low [in 1931], aesthetically and intellectually, as it has sunk since. But even then, it conceived of pictures as propaganda, good or bad.
>
> Orozco scanned my features, congenitally inscrutable. "A reporter of *The New York Times*," he said, "told me this picture will make much trouble for Doctor Johnson. I do not want to make trouble for my friend Doctor Johnson. I am willing to knock the picture out and put something else."

"Señor Orozco," I said. "You painted this picture on my promise that you should be free. If you know of some other picture that would better express your idea, we will knock this one out and substitute the other. But not on account of any trouble to Doctor Johnson. For Doctor Johnson, as a man, is of few days, and full of trouble."

A faraway, prophetic look came over Orozco's face. He offered me his creative hand—his true, sincere hand. Its pressure was the highest tribute that has come to me in all my life.[10]

When Reed published her version in 1956, she toned down the rhetoric and gave herself a more prominent role in the negotiations than Johnson had assigned to her. As she remembered it, Johnson raised a few questions at first, but in the end he agreed:

Dr. Johnson finally agreed with the painter that the Marxist idea and its leader could hardly be omitted from any realistic appraisal of political trends. He was of the opinion that Orozco would not be accused of propaganda since his murals gave equal space and impartial treatment to all three political philosophies [capitalism, socialism, and Gandhi's *satyagraha*]. He conceded that Orozco had the same right as the historian to evaluate the events of the past and to forecast from their impact "the shape of things to come."[11]

According to Orozco and Reed, the mural caused the New School to lose a lot of money. Donors, they claimed, protested vigorously and stopped support- ing the university. As Reed put it, "the rejection of the murals by the financial 'backers' was not wholly unexpected. Dr. Johnson had warned me of official opposition after he had received the first objections to the Lenin portrait."[12] Ridiculous, Johnson replied. As he told a journalist in 1949 who had made a similar claim:

Although I lived with the picture for fifteen years I cannot say that I ever met or heard of a single person who withdrew one dollar on account of the mural. On the other hand, to destroy a mural that the most competent French critic pronounces the most important work of art done in America in three decades would cost the School its name for freedom and tens of thousands of dollars in income. Hence its "stubbornness."[13]

✧

In March 1951, rumors began circulating in artistic circles that the New School had placed a curtain in front of an unspecified number of panels of the Orozco mural to hide controversial sections from view. If this were true, Artists Equity threatened to mobilize its eight hundred members at its next meeting in early April and urge them to take "vigorous action." But first the head of the association asked Reed to find out what was really going on.

Reed contacted Agnes de Lima, who invited her to stop by on either March 28 or 29, when the mural, presumably, would not have been hidden from view. Reed, however, showed up on March 30. In de Lima's notes of their meeting, she recorded that she had explained to Reed that the New School placed curtains in front of the mural only when the university used the cafeteria for other exhibits. After which, they removed them. Reed gave a similar account of their meeting, adding with relief that "Orozco's memory is revered and his work admired by the members of the administrative staff, and particularly by Miss De Lima." Before she left, however, Reed reminded the New School's director of publicity that Johnson had promised Orozco that the New School would never censure his work.[14] De Lima had not forgotten, and like Johnson she was worried. Although she did not say anything about it to Reed, she knew that the rumors were not entirely unfounded.

In addition to writing about Orozco in his autobiography, Johnson tried to persuade friends of the New School to leave the mural alone. He made his case privately on both the aesthetic and political merits of the work, noting that Orozco was not even a communist! In the surviving draft of a letter to Edith Bry, an artist and New School Associate, Johnson wrote the following:

> In our time, there are just two [*sic*] great mural painters, Orozco and Rivera. They hated each other. Rivera was [a] Soviet Russian Communist; Orozco hated Rivera and Russian Communism. Orozco had a dream, not of a League of White Nations but of all the peoples of the World, regardless of color. His friend Tom Benton had painted on the third floor the dynamic possibilities of modern technology. Orozco wanted to paint the insurgence around the periphery of the peoples of color, Hindus, American Indians, Asiatic. . . . Orozco's own ideals are the peace table at the south of the room, all the races of all colors working together. . . .
>
> We've had a lot of fuss about [the] veiling or unveiling of the picture. When I was President there was no fuss. It was a great picture, let those who didn't like it lump it.[15]

As Johnson defended the mural, he did so in the language of a virulent anti-communist. In the same letter to Bry, he added, American communists "are not guileless Utopians, but members of a conspiracy to promote the interests of our great national enemy Russia. . . . We at the New School have a principle. We will interfere with no man's liberty to teach what he truly believes. No Commie can teach with us because he has to teach, not what he truly believes, but is in fact Commie propaganda."

Although Johnson failed to persuade the trustees to "let those who didn't like it lump it," he saved the frescoes from the fate of Rivera's mural at Rockefeller Center. Listening to reason, the board asked René d'Harnoncourt, the director of the Museum of Modern Art, to assess the value of the work. After reading d'Harnoncourt's report, the trustees conceded in March 1953 that "it would be a desecration to destroy these murals," which, in light of their state of deterioration, removal would likely cause. But they firmly maintained that the mural had become a "divisive element and had caused considerable annoyance" within the New School community. Even the Graduate Faculty had "unanimously adopted a resolution that [the paintings] do not express the policy of the School." In Continuing Education, the faculty and students were "of divided opinion concerning the keeping or removal of the murals."

In the end, having accepted that there would be no justification for removing the mural in a way that would destroy the panels, the board passed a resolution to place a curtain before the entire western wall of the cafeteria where Orozco had painted his allegories of the Mexican and Russian revolutions. In a lame attempt to appease a furious Reed, they then modified the original resolution and uncovered the portrait of Carrillo Puerto.[16]

Not every trustee believed that the "problem of the deterioration" was serious. Eager to see the mural go, a group of them urged the board to find a way to get rid of it as quickly as possible. Camilo Egas protested. Still serving as director of the New School's art program, he persuaded the trustees on the mural committee to seek the professional opinion of Alfred Crimi, who had restored some of Diego Rivera's murals. As Egas had predicted, Crimi concluded that given "the rapid disintegration of the murals" the work could not be removed until someone had restored the panels properly, something the New School could not afford to do right away.[17]

In Reed's biography of Orozco, she bitterly recalled how in 1931 Johnson had predicted a more "enlightened future." Yet here they were in the 1950s, and things had only gotten worse:

> The intolerance of certain members of the School's government board took a more aggressive form than financial boycott. During the early '50s, when "McCarthyism" attempted to force thought control on the American people, even the New School—a recognized stronghold of liberalism throughout the Hitler era—succumbed.[18]

The left-leaning *National Guardian* published one of the first articles about the New School's decision to cover part of the mural, coyly announcing in the headline: "New School hangs curtain over Orozco mural: it has S . . . n and L . . . n portraits." The article quoted de Lima as saying that although the New School recognized the mural as "a great work of art by a great artist" it had to cover over the panel on the Russian Revolution because the portraits of Lenin and Stalin "had aroused so much 'vituperation.'" Furious with the way the paper had quoted her, de Lima marked up the copy she saved for the archives, underlining the passages that misrepresented what she had said.

The National Guardian reported having contacted the heads of the Metropolitan Museum of Art and the Whitney Museum (Francis Taylor and Herman More), and the curator of painting and sculpture at the Museum of Modern Art (Andrew Ritchie). Neither Taylor nor Ritchie agreed to comment. More made a general statement without taking sides in the New School controversy: "I don't know the particular circumstances, but as a rule I am against any sort of vandalism like that, public or private." Rank and file artists affiliated with the National Council of Arts, Sciences and Professions expressed outrage. They told the paper that they wanted to organize a protest.[19]

Nine students at the New School tried to mobilize the campus. In May 1953, they circulated an impassioned statement, which they urged their fellow students to sign, after which they sent it on to *The New York Times*:

> What seems to be the controversy in Orozco's Mural? The work in the cafeteria displays some prominent figures of the Russian Revolution and is "politically outdated."
>
> But, must we agree with the depiction of an historic event in a work of art in order to have this work displayed and evaluated? Must we agree with the work's outward manifestations in order to appreciate the work's artistic quality? Must we agree with another man's opinion in order that he enjoy the freedom to express himself?
>
> According to Dr. Simons, the Board of the New School decided that the mural be covered . . . to protect the interests of the "captive audience" eating in the lunch room.
>
> Students—do you feel more of a captive when you have the freedom of choice either to look, or not, at the murals, at your discretion—or, when someone decides for you that the mural is not to be viewed?[20]

On May 22, *The New York Times* published an article on the scandal, with a photo of an unidentified woman pulling back the curtain to reveal the portrait of Stalin. In addition to giving the students' point of view, the *Times* presented the university's official position in some detail:

> The New School for Social Research will keep indefinitely a yellow cotton cur-
> tain over the "Revolutionary Violence" section of a mural in the school's cafete-
> ria by the late Mexican artist José Clemente Orozco because the painting "does
> not express the philosophy of the faculty," Dr. Hans Simons, president of the
> school, declared yesterday. . . .
>
> On the authorization of the school's board of trustees, Dr. Simons ordered last
> March the concealment of part of the four-part study of "Mankind's Struggle"
> because "heavy protests" poured in against the display of what was seen as the
> glorification of Lenin and Stalin and the Red Army. . . .
>
> Dr. Simons said the mural dispute was a "problem of the school and did not
> concern the outside."[21]

Members of the student protest refused to give up. Over the summer, a group of them wrote a carefully worded letter to Simons and the Board of Trustees to plead their case. In November, Simons responded in the *New School Bulletin*, by which time Crimi had evaluated the condition of the mural panels and made it clear that they could not safely be removed. The Soviet section, however, would remain covered, the president said, until the room stopped serving as the univer-sity's cafeteria. Simons added that the trustees recognized the artistic value of the mural and the need to restore it. They had therefore formed "a special committee to look into that subject."

The Orozco mural controversy remained newsworthy over the next couple of years. In the winter of 1954, Irving Howe mentioned it disparagingly as an exam-ple of the "problem of civil liberties" in the United States:

> Last summer [*sic*] the New School for Social Research decided to hang a yellow
> curtain over an Orozco mural in its cafeteria, because the mural included por-
> traits of Lenin and Stalin. The mural, explained Dr. Hans Simons, president of
> the school, "does not express the philosophy of the faculty." (Did it express the
> philosophy of the faculty when it was first unveiled?) In reply to protests, Dr.
> Simons said that the mural was "a problem of the school and did not concern the
> outside." One is not shocked at this, the language is familiar enough, go a step fur-
> ther and you have the American Legion or the DAR [Daughters of the American
> Revolution] telling one to *go back where you come from*. But wait: the philistine
> reference to "the outside" comes not from the American Legion, but the New
> School, which has been a refuge for liberalism and freedom. Well, Dr. Simons,

one is sorry to say this, but the mural is not merely "a problem of the school"; and one would be delighted to go back where one came from: New York.[22]

These comments appeared, ironically, in the same issue of *Dissent* in which Howe had announced, together with his fellow editors, that the magazine looked forward to publishing articles that "dissent with *Dissent*," but did not welcome pieces by "Stalinists and totalitarian fellow-travelers" or those of "former radicals" who had gone over to the other side. In May 1955, *The New York Post* raised the issue again in what was otherwise a glowing article about Hans Simons:

> In the five years of his presidency, only one unhappy incident has sullied a record generally regarded as admirable. . . .
>
> The [Orozco] murals have been there since 1930; they survived the indigestion of the Nazi-Soviet pact. Libertarians who loathe communism as much as Simons does managed to admire art, swallow their food, and remember that in a democracy one can distinguish between art, politics, the right of the artist to be politically wrong, and the duty of everybody to be tolerant, not to say adult.[23]

Nobody seems to remember when the curtain came down or how. It just happened, without ceremony, at some point in either 1956 or 1957.[24] During the 1970s, the New School's president John Everett began exploring once again the possibility of selling the murals, this time Benton's as well as Orozco's—no longer out of fear but to pay off lingering debts. In 1982, with the help of Mayor Ed Koch, the New School finally succeeded in finding a new home for "America Today" on Sixth Avenue at the corporate headquarters of Equitable Life (now AXA Equitable). Benton's ten-panel mural remained in the company's possession until 2012, at which point AXA Equitable donated it to the Metropolitan Museum of Art; it is currently on view there in a space designed with the same proportions as the room on Twelfth Street.[25]

Almost lost as well was the three-panel mural Camilo Egas had painted for the New School's Dance Studio in 1932. The university took "Ecuadorian Festival" down in the early 1980s and stored it in the basement of the Twelfth Street building, where it deteriorated badly. Only one of the three panels was salvageable. Beautifully restored in 2011, this panel is now on view at 66 Fifth Avenue, in the galleries of Parsons School of Design, a division of the New School since 1970.[26]

As for the Orozco frescoes, the panels remain where the Mexican artist painted them in the Twelfth Street building, thanks again to the assistance of Mayor Koch. In 1988, the mayor's office stepped in to help New School President Jonathan Fanton persuade the Mexican government to contribute generously to the restoration of the mural with the understanding that the work would remain at the New School. The Mexican government had proposed restoring the panels and then sending them to Mexico. Koch understood that this would have been a great loss, not only for the New School but for the city.[27] Several years later, the New School renovated the room as well, again with the generous support of the Mexican Consulate.

In the end, Johnson may have been right not to worry about the impact of political criticism—at least when it came to the New School's Orozco mural. McCarthy is gone, the Soviet Union is gone, but the frescoes remain. Beautifully restored, they command the attention of everyone who visits the university's landmark building, and that includes a new generation of "connoisseurs" who are finally describing the mural with the kind of enthusiasm Johnson had predicted that one day they would.[28]

1 Artist's rendering of 66 West Twelfth Street Exterior, 1930.

Source: New School Archives and Special Collections, Digital Archives.

2 Alvin Johnson smoking a pipe, probably late 1920s/early 1930s.

Source: New School Archives and Special Collections, Digital Archives.

3 Agnes de Lima at the Peninsula School in Menlo Park, California, where she was teaching in 1933, when Alvin Johnson was sending her letters about the founding of the University in Exile.

Source: Photo by Josephine Duveneck, founding director of the Peninsula School.

4 University in Exile opens first semester in New York. Faculty of dismissed or furloughed German professors at the New School for Social Research. Left to right, seated; Emil Lederer, Alvin Johnson, director of the New School for Social Research; Frieda Wunderlich, Karl Brandt; Left to right, standing; Hans Speier, Max Wertheimer, Arthur Feiler, Eduard Heimann, Gerhard Colm, and Erich von Hornbostel.

Source: Times Wide World Photo, *The New York Times*, Redux, October 4, 1933.

5 Adolph Lowe and Hans Staudinger, probably in the 1940s.

Source: Fred Stein/Peter Stein.

6 Horace Kallen (*left*) and Hans Simons (*right*) present the first Louis. S. Weiss Memorial Award in Adult Education to New York Times education editor Benjamin Fine (*middle*).

Source: New School Archives and Special Collections, Digital Archives.

7 "New School Keeps Red Mural Hidden: Curtain to Stay over 'Soviet' Part of Work by Orozco Despite Student Protest": "Dr. Hans Simons, president of the school explains, 'It does not express the philosophy of the faculty.'"

Source: Neal Boenzi, *The New York Times*, Redux, May 22, 1953.

8 The Russian Revolution panel of José Clemente Orozco's mural at the New School: "poster of Lenin, silhouettes of the old Red Army, multi-raced Russian population going to work: Stalin in the foreground."

Source: Peter Juley & Son, December 12, 1950.

9 John Everett and Jacob Kaplan award violinist and conductor
Alexander Schneider an honorary doctorate in 1965.

Source: New School Archives and Special Collections, Digital Archives.

10 Hannah Arendt replying to challenges from her audience at
the New School seminar after her talk on violence.

Source: Neal Boenzi, *The New York Times*, Redux, February 21, 1969:
Israel Shenker, "Power and Violence Debate at New School Seminar," 45.

11 Joseph Greenbaum
chatting with Arnold Brecht
at the émigré professor's
ninetieth-birthday celebration
at the New School, 1974.

Source: Paul Seligman/New School
Archives and Special Collections,
Digital Archives.

12 Jonathan Fanton with Vera List and Dorothy Hirshon after graduation exercises in
the spring of 1985. Both women worked closely with Alvin Johnson.

Source: New School Archives and Special Collections, Digital Archives.

13 Ira Katznelson teaching, 1989.

Source: Jerry Speier/New School Archives and Special Collections, Digital Archives.

14 Aristide Zolberg in Berlin after being named University in Exile Professor at the fiftieth anniversary of the University in Exile, December 1984.

Source: Landesarchiv Berlin/Filipp Israelson, F Rep. 290 No. 0264624.

15 Left to right: Jeffrey Goldfarb, Adam Michnik, and Jonathan Fanton in Warsaw at the graveside of Rev. Jerzy Popieluszko, a pro-Solidarity priest who had recently been murdered. The photo was taken on December 10, 1984, after President Fanton gave the Polish dissident an honorary doctorate.

Source: New School Archives and Special Collections, Digital Archives.

16 Richard Bernstein with Hans Jonas after being named the Vera List Professor of Philosophy, 1989.

Source: Jose Luis Palaez Studios/New School Archives and Special Collections, Digital Archives.

THE CHRONICLE

of Higher Education.

June 23, 1993 • *$3.25*
Volume XXXIX, Number 42

Quote,
Unquote

News Summary: Page A3

"Education is undoubtedly the key
to the future of our country.
Period."
Walter H. Annenberg, on his giving
a total of $265-million to three
universities: A24

"All of us in one way or another are
reaching for a new understanding
of the racial situation in the
United States."
A professor of law at the University
of Colorado: A7

"Publishing in the public interest
means publishing books
because they are inherently
important not for
financial reasons."
André Schiffrin, founder of the New
Press: A8

"We have the basis for something
that could influence the
development of the network for the
next four or five years."
An EDUCOM official, on legislation
to set up a "national
information infrastructure": A15

"These are the desperate acts of a
government that cannot make a
legitimate case."
An official of People for the Ethical
Treatment of Animals, on
federal probes of her group: A19

"It is time to start thinking about
what really causes incivility on
the campus and to begin to attack
its roots."
A professor of religious studies: A36

"Academics, especially, should
expect to have their ideas
taken seriously."
A law professor, on the writings of
scholars who are nominated for public
office: B1

"We have had enough seminars.
What we really could use are
your scholarly journals."
A professor from Eastern Europe: A28

SECTION 1	PAGES A1-36
Athletics	A30
Business & Philanthropy	A24-26
Gazette	A31
Government & Politics	A18-23
Information Technology	A15-17
International	A27-29
Personal & Professional	A13-14
Scholarship	A6-12
SECTION 2	PAGES B1-44
Bulletin Board	B5-43
Opinion & Letters	B1-4

Rebuilding East Europe's Academic Libraries: A28

17 Arien Mack's Journal Donation Project was featured in 1993 on the first page of
the *Chronicle of Higher Education*: "Rebuilding East Europe's Academic Libraries."

Source: Don Hamerman, *The Chronicle of Higher Education*, June 23, 1993.

18 Robert Heilbroner giving a lecture at the New School, 1990s.

Source: New School Archives and Special Collections, Digital Archives.

19 Panel discussion commemorating the twentieth anniversary of 1989 at the New School, with from left to right: Ira Katznelson, Adam Michnik, Andrew Arato, and Elzbieta Matynia.

Source: Courtesy of Elzbieta Matynia.

20 Ágnes Heller featured in an article in *The Chronicle of Higher Education* and reprinted the next day in the international edition of *The New York Times*, under the title "A Scholar Is Back Home and Defiant in Hungary" (December 9, 2013).

Source: Zofia Palyi/Anzenberger Agency. (Article: Paul Hockenos, December 8, 2013.)

14

"THE NEW SCHOOL REALLY ISN'T NEWS ANY LONGER"

n June 1952, nine months before the trustees covered over the Orozco mural, Agnes de Lima complained to Hans Simons about her "failure to reach the national magazines with the New School story." She had turned to a number of writers and editors for help, including "our very good friend [Robert] Heilbroner," Adolph Lowe's famous student, who was finishing his PhD in economics. Heilbroner's best-selling *Worldly Philosophers* would only come out in 1953, but he already had a big name in journalism. Despite his many contacts at "*Harpers, Readers Digest*, etc. etc.," Heilbroner could not interest anyone in writing an article, and he had been trying for over a year. Others had contacted *Mademoiselle, Time, The Saturday Review*, and *Newsweek* with similar results. De Lima had also reached out to "all the high pressure and very efficient publicity people," but to no avail. "You see," she, explained, "the New School really isn't news any longer, nor is adult education. If we have some major new development, if we change the name of the school and expand its program, we can try again and probably succeed."[1]

Things had clearly hit an all-time low. Nobody was better or more persistent than de Lima in getting the New School's story into print. On June 16, 1950, for example, the very day *The New York Times* covered Simons's inauguration, de Lima wrote to the paper's education editor, Benjamin Fine, and urged him to follow up with an editorial. She thanked Fine for "all you are doing for the New School in so many uncounted ways" and asked him to do her this additional favor because "we hope to go forward even more bravely" now that Simons has taken over. Leaving nothing to chance, she attached a copy of the biographical sketch she had sent to the *Times* a few days earlier in preparation for the original announcement and provided some additional language for the editorial:

> There is dramatic color in his [Simons's] rise to leadership, a tribute both to his own exceptional abilities and to the unique opportunity which America has always given the stranger and exile within her gates. . . . In this international age, and with America being forced into a dominant role in the world arena, we need the kind of world outlook and international background and training which Dr. Simons possesses.[2]

Fine did not respond immediately to de Lima's request, but he did come through in September when the New School ran a fund-raising dinner in honor of their new president. The *Times* also published a letter from Alvin Johnson. Both pieces congratulated the trustees for having appointed a European with Simons's political and intellectual profile—an inspired choice for any U.S. university in the postwar period, but particularly appropriate for this one. Other articles appeared over the next few days, but then the media lost interest.[3] The great New School story had run its course.

Anticipating the problem, Bryn Hovde had done his best several years earlier to keep the old narrative alive by rescuing twenty-five scholars "from behind the Iron Curtain," including the Hungarian physiologist and Nobel Prize Laureate Albert Szent-Györgyi. The distinguished scientist lectured briefly at the New School, along with ten other colleagues from Hungary, before they all left for Woods Hole, Massachusetts, to join a world-famous complex of research laboratories.[4] Then Simons tried again, providing twenty-five scholarships for "non-Communist Chinese students stranded in this country."[5] But his effort, like Hovde's, attracted little attention at the New School or in the press, nor did it succeed in silencing McCarthy's minions who persisted in accusing the institution of being "politically unreliable."

With government agents sitting in on classes and monitoring other activities, fund-raising, needless to say, was murderous. Tuition dollars were evaporating as well. Ten days after Simons became president, the United States declared war on North Korea, forcing young men to abandon their studies to fight overseas. The impact of the draft on the number of students registering for courses was even more crippling this time than it had been during World War II.

Simons shared the grim news with the Graduate Faculty in May 1951 at a meeting of the Executive Faculty. He urged his colleagues to "see our present problems in the context of the world situation, and of the difficulties which educational institutions are facing as a result." The war, however, was not the main issue. It was just making things worse.

When Hovde resigned, he left the university in serious debt and on academic probation. To turn things around both financially and academically, the New School had to address the concerns raised by the Middle States Association of Colleges and Schools, which was overseeing the accreditation of academic institutions in the mid-Atlantic States. This highly regarded agency wanted the New School to make significant curricular changes across the divisions, but especially in the BA program that Johnson had created during the war. To meet these demands was going to cost money, presenting Simons with the unenviable task of having to persuade the New School's trustees to make new investments while they were still paying off bills that Hovde had not taken care of. Something would have to give and that something was the Graduate Faculty, the biggest drain on the New School's budget.

Although no decisions had yet been made, Simons wanted the GF to know that he and the board were exploring the possibility of downsizing the full-time faculty through retrenchment. Nobody, he assured them, wanted to go down this path, but the trustees needed to consider all the available options. Before taking such a dramatic step, they would try to solve the university's financial problems by placing a hiring freeze on new appointments for the 1951–52 academic year and delaying tenure for those who had just come through the review process successfully. The trustees were also considering the possibility of closing down *Social Research*.

If these other measures failed, the trustees would initiate retrenchment procedures in the spring of 1952, beginning with Philosophy—a decision based on the fact that two members of the department would have reached mandatory retirement age by then and would have to step down anyway. As Simons was laying things out in painful detail, several colleagues interrupted him: Why worry them about all of this now, while the trustees were still deliberating? To make sure, Simons replied, that there would be no surprises:

It must be emphasized that the board is fully aware of the grave disadvantages which any policy of retrenchment implies. It does not want to discontinue the Philosophy department, but it does not see any other alternative to its present plans. . . .

[I am] sure that the Graduate Faculty as an institution has to be maintained and will be maintained. A New School saved at its expense would not be saved at all. Therefore, saying that the New School undoubtedly will survive is saying that the Graduate Faculty will survive too.[6]

Not that anyone "should base his personal plans on it now"! The message was clear. Although Simons would accept no proposal to save the New School that sacrificed the GF, the old University in Exile would have to change in significant ways.

To help Simons plan for these inevitable changes, he asked the sociologist Arthur Swift to conduct a campus-wide review of all the university's academic programs and policies, beginning with the GF. Professor of church and community at the Union Theological Seminary, Swift had been teaching part time in Continuing Education since 1932 and at the Graduate Faculty since 1945. When Swift submitted his report to the trustees in the spring of 1952, he did not mention closing down Philosophy or any other academic department in the GF. Instead he recommended a far more radical solution: use the Graduate Faculty to strengthen the schools of Politics and Philosophy in the adult division. The university's future depended on improving its programs in Continuing Education, with whatever resources it had, not in propping up the fading reputation of the GF. The time had come for the Graduate Faculty to relinquish its privileged position within the New School and begin serving the academic mission of the entire institution. As far as Swift was concerned, the GF had lost not only its academic distinction but also its symbolic value for the university.

Despite the somber tone of his report, Swift urged the trustees to keep the faith. The New School was still worth fighting for. Although it faced formidable challenges, it continued to play a unique role among academic institutions. Over the years it had "grown and changed somewhat opportunistically, moved by the vast social upheavals it has survived." But it remained "essential to the educational life of New York" because it was "a university for adult education."[7]

Moving forward, the administration should focus on doing a better job of letting students know what made the New School so special. Echoing de Lima, Swift reminded the trustees that adult education programs had proliferated in recent years, making it difficult now for students to see why they should choose the New School over, for example, Columbia or NYU. Yet the differences among these neighboring institutions were significant.

Columbia's Extension Program, Swift explained, offered a less prestigious path to an Ivy League education for students who had failed to meet the college's restrictive admissions standards. Some were too old; others too weak academically. Extension students at Columbia essentially followed the same course of study they would have taken had they been admitted to the college. Although the program, Swift conceded, was academically rigorous, it was "stultifying." Good students saw how "often dry-rot saps the vitality of the educative process."

Learning becomes a "game played with words and other symbols and the winners receive degrees as prizes." This kind of education sheds little light on real life experiences that "creep in, even to the mustiest classroom."

As for NYU, Swift dismissed it out of hand. Their program treated adult education as an academic free-for-all, a place to take noncredit courses on frivolous subjects taught by unqualified instructors who received little to no supervision from the full-time members of the faculty. As a result, "one may find masquerading as adult education those snide and vulgar and easy 'short-cuts' to understanding which prove the adage 'a little knowledge is a dangerous thing,' especially when it smirks and poses as competence." And NYU was no exception. After conducting a survey of adult education programs across the country, Swift concluded that the majority of them were like NYU. They "are satisfied to remain on the level of *how* to do, rarely asking *why* or to what end."

Adult education at the New School resembled neither, Swift continued. Its programs offered students academically serious courses that shed light on real-life experiences: "The exciting thing about the New School, its real and growing contribution to our national life, is just that it has refused to accept this cleavage." While remaining intellectually rigorous, "it has insisted that adult education address itself directly to the pressing and urgent problems" of everyday life. Only a program like this "can safely be trusted to bring to confused and baffled folks the kinds of facts and insights that will help them toward self-mastery and the social control of this intricate culture called civilization."

Given the stiff competition, the New School had to do a better job of getting the word out. This entailed making a number of significant changes, beginning with the name of the institution. The New School for Social Research was a misnomer: "Education has been its chief emphasis, not social research, or even the teaching of it." Swift recommended inviting students and friends to help find another name, one that might not "convey a history" but would be "more descriptive of what the school has become—a university for adult education."

Swift was not the only one in 1952 to raise the possibility of changing the name. De Lima, as we saw, had mentioned it in her memo to Simons, suggesting that it might help attract media attention. Johnson raised it as well in his autobiography, but he firmly advised against it. Although the founders had chosen poorly, it was too late to change the name now. When discussed at the GF, the faculty adamantly opposed the idea. So did Simons, who reassured his émigré colleagues that he would not support the proposal.

In the end, the university remained the New School for Social Research until 1999, when the issue came up again, at which point, those in favor of changing the name to New School University met with little resistance, either from the faculty or members of the board, with the exception of the Graduate Faculty. In 2005, the trustees changed the name once again, this time to the New School *tout court*. The GF responded by adopting the New School for Social Research (NSSR) for itself, as the new name of the graduate division of political and social science.

In his autobiography, Johnson explained how the founders came up with the name in the first place, using the story to take another swipe at McCarthy:

> At first, I proposed to name it after some distinguished authority, Adam Smith, David Hume, James Madison. That idea met no response. It was too pedantic. After trying all sorts of names, we accepted as a compromise the New School for Social Research.
>
> [Wesley Clair] Mitchell claimed that it was I who invented the name. If that is true I deserve to be punished for it; and, indeed, I have been . . . whether the sin was mine or not. . . .
>
> The New School for Social Research looked somewhat like the Rand School for Social Science. Hundreds of thousands of New Yorkers, thirty years ago, assumed that the two institutions were the same. And as the Rand School was a Socialist institution—and a very distinguished one—it was assumed that the New School was Socialist. In time, it has come to be realized, except in Paleolithic circles, that the two institutions are different. But the delusion has persisted that they follow the same doctrine, a delusion that has cost us tens of thousands of students and hundreds of thousands in contributions.[8]

Swift made seven recommendations to the Board of Trustees for how the New School might make itself more competitive, most of them threatening the future of the GF and the New School's historic commitment to social research. In addition to changing the university's name and folding the GF into Continuing Education, Swift wanted the Institute of World Affairs (IWA) to focus on teaching adult students "the principles and methods of social analysis." It should serve as "a students' research center rather than an agency for the operation of professional research." Swift also proposed creating a special business program that might raise a little money for the university—an idea first suggested to the New School by a wealthy friend of the institution. The program would give businessmen and scholars the opportunity to collaborate "in a joint effort to find out what in Economics and Psychology and Sociology and History, in Philosophy and the Liberal Arts there is to enlighten business operations and to refresh and liberate its workers, and to find out as well what in business experience and insight might enlarge and inform scholarly knowledge in all these fields." A business program along these lines opened in 1953. By 1957 it had recruited twenty-five business firms, each of which was contributing at least $1,000 in scholarship funds.[9]

Finally, Swift urged the New School to build a proper endowment, repeating what Johnson had been saying for years. "It was quixotic to refuse creating an endowment at the time of its founding."

Swift's report set the tone for the 1950s. Nobody used uplifting prose any more to describe the New School, or accepted as obvious that the university needed an independent Graduate Faculty. Although Simons rejected Swift's idea of incorporating the division into Continuing Education, he insisted that the Graduate Faculty play a more integrated role in the academic life of the university. Informal arrangements that dated back to the 1930s now became firm policy. By the mid-1950s the GF had opened up a third or more of its courses to BA and non-degree students. Colleagues had begun working more closely as well with the schools of Politics and Philosophy, reluctantly accepting the fact that they were destined to become the center of a university-wide faculty.[10]

Simons defended the GF as best he could during this period, often under very difficult circumstances that the faculty may not have appreciated fully—in part, perhaps, because his style was withholding, leaving colleagues wondering whether he was really on their side. When, for example, he saved Philosophy from retrenchment, he still deprived the department of the resources it needed to replace colleagues who had recently retired. Although Simons apologized for doing so at an Executive Faculty meeting in the winter of 1953, he also offered his colleagues punishing advice, cautioning them against accepting new students in Philosophy for the coming year. He then concluded with a few desultory words of encouragement: "While tangible evidence of progress toward a more favorable financial situation is lacking, nevertheless the New School seems to have made progress during the year." Exasperated with Simons, the GF defied the president and passed a resolution that authorized Philosophy to continue accepting MA and PhD students for the 1953–54 academic year.[11]

The faculty in Philosophy appreciated the support they received from their friends in the other departments, but they were doomed, they warned, if the New School did not let them hire. Speaking on behalf of his colleagues, Alfred Schütz made the case to the Board of Trustees in an eloquent memorandum called "The Scope and Function of Philosophy within the Graduate Faculty" (May 22, 1953).[12] Reading Schütz's statement many years later, it is sobering to think that this highly acclaimed phenomenologist of the first half of the 20th century—the man who introduced the work of Edmund Husserl to the United States—spent the final years of his life justifying the importance of teaching philosophy at the New School. He died in 1959.[13]

In his memorandum to the trustees, Schütz relied on the logic Simons had used to explain the centrality of the GF to the New School. Just as the entire institution would lose its place in the wider scholarly community if it closed down the Graduate Faculty, so too would the GF lose its place if it eliminated Philosophy. The Graduate Faculty, Schütz explained, stood out among other MA and PhD programs in the social sciences because it approached the disciplines as an integrated whole and provided students with the historical and philosophical background they needed to think critically about human affairs. This integrated approach relied heavily on the Western philosophical tradition. Given the very small size of the faculty in every one of the departments, there was no way the Graduate Faculty could hold its own against much larger programs at other universities without preserving its distinctive approach to the social sciences, which was based on a deep theoretical understanding of the ways the disciplines intersected with one another. Students came to the GF because it offered this critical perspective.

The Graduate Faculty's approach to the social sciences was grounded, Schütz repeated, in theory: "In nearly all of our courses special emphasis is laid on problems of theory and the theoretical approach." This was its "unique contribution" to higher education in the United States; its "very raison d'être." At the GF a student learned that

> the social sciences did not start with *his* thinking on human affairs, or with that of his teachers. He must learn that the whole process of inquiry occurs within a great tradition, that our actual problems are new only as to their shape, and as old as mankind in their substance. He has also to learn that, in Dewey's words, all inquiry occurs within a given social matrix, and that for this very reason philosophy itself is a social science—perhaps *the* social science from which all the other disciplines originate.[14]

Schütz reminded the board that Johnson had wanted the University in Exile "to retain the values of the European university discipline." With the help of his refugee professors, he would give American students a foundation in the great humanistic traditions of continental learning. And at the very heart of those traditions lay "philosophy extending to the state and society." According to Johnson's plan, the exiled scholars would teach American students to approach contemporary problems in human affairs from a perspective deeply rooted in the philosophical and ethical traditions of Western thought. Every member of the faculty had a different area of expertise, but each speciality, Schütz explained, quoting Johnson directly, "was conceived of as a branch of the philosophical tree, not as an autonomous growth. The scholar, whatever his branch of the social sciences, felt himself responsible for the whole cultural system."[15]

Schütz acknowledged that there was a glaring hole in his argument: If every member of the GF recognized the centrality of philosophy in the teaching of the social sciences, why bother with a stand-alone department? Why not let the faculty in the other departments introduce students to the Western philosophical tradition through economics, political science, psychology, and sociology? In the early days, after all, the University in Exile consisted almost exclusively of economists, legal theorists, and sociologists. But in those days, Schütz added, there were no departments either. Once the Board of Regents of the State of New York required the GF to conform to the same administrative structure as other graduate programs in the United States, it had to create separate academic units. Now that it had departments, it would send an ominous message if the New School closed down the very one that made the Graduate Faculty of Political and Social Science unique! To do so would not only discourage graduate students from coming to the New School for their master's and doctoral degrees but turn away students enrolled at neighboring institutions who for years had been registering for "one or two of our purely theoretical courses, which they cannot find at their own institutions."[16]

Schütz's memorandum persuaded the trustees to let Philosophy make new appointments. In reporting the good news to the faculty in January 1954, Simons announced that the trustees had unanimously agreed to provide the department with the resources it needed "as soon as possible."[17] For Schütz, that was not soon enough, but he soldiered on, relying on a group of part-time instructors, some of whom had international reputations, to offer a serious course of study. The following November, Simons congratulated Schütz on having increased the number of students in Philosophy "against the general decline of registration in the Graduate Faculty."[18] In recognition of the department's accomplishments, the university was releasing the funds they needed to make a new appointment.

In January 1955, Philosophy named one of its outstanding part-time instructors to the full-time faculty. Hans Jonas had been teaching in the department since 1951. A former student of Martin Heidegger, Jonas left Germany in 1933 and moved to Palestine. In 1940, he returned to Europe to fight Hitler in the British Army, then went back to Palestine in the late 1940s to fight for Israeli independence. In the early days of the new State of Israel, Jonas taught philosophy at Hebrew University, where he made a name for himself as a scholar of Gnosticism and comparative religion. During his years at the New School (1951–1976), Jonas helped develop a new field of inquiry known today as bioethics.

⟨══⟩

Although most descriptions of the New School's émigré professors focus on the influence these scholars had on GF students, Europeans on the faculty played an important role in the lives of students in Continuing Education as well, particularly during the early postwar years. A goodly number of these other students were aspiring artists, who had come to the New School on the G.I. Bill, looking for "a blind date with culture." For these young Americans, just back from the war, the dark, intense teachings of the émigré professors fit the bill perfectly. In his memoir, *Kafka Was the Rage*, Anatole Broyard recalled taking classes with "angry" refugees who did their best to make students like him "feel like exiles in our own country":

> All the courses I took were about *what's wrong*: what's wrong with the government, with the family, with interpersonal relations and intrapersonal relations— what's wrong with our dreams, our loves, our jobs, our perceptions and conceptions, our esthetics, the human condition itself.
>
> They were furious, the professors, at the ugly turn the world had taken and they were the warders, the storm troopers of humanism. The building resounded with guttural cries: *kunstwissenschaft*, *zeitgeist* and *weltanschauung*, *gemeinschaft* and *gesellschaft*, *schadenfreude*, *schwarmerei*. Their accents were so impenetrable that some of them seemed to speak in tongues, and the students understood hardly a word.
>
> We admired the German professors. We had won the fight against fascism and now, with their help, we would defeat all the dark forces in the culture and the psyche.
>
> As a reaction to our victory, sensitive Americans had entered an apologetic phase in our national life and there was nothing the professors could say that was too much. We came out of class with dueling scars.[19]

Broyard and his fellow students studied psychoanalysis with Karen Horney and Eric Fromm, Gestalt psychology with Rudolf Arnheim, economics with Adolph Lowe, and philosophy with Alfred Schütz and Hans Jonas. In addition to these Europeans with their impenetrable accents, Continuing Education students took courses with some of the most exciting writers and artists of the day: literature with W. H. Auden, painting with Robert Gwathmey, sculpture with

Seymour Lipton, photography with Berenice Abbott, art history and criticism with Meyer Schapiro,[20] not to mention music with Henry Cowell and his famous disciple John Cage (who also taught courses on mushrooms).

Complementing its rich schedule of courses, the New School sponsored a wide array of special events every year, featuring leading figures of the day. In 1951, these included literary readings by Carl Sandburg, William Carlos Williams, Edith Sitwell, and e. e. cummings. Those who graduated in 1952 heard Supreme Court Justice William O. Douglas deliver the commencement address, in which he called upon New School graduates "to make common cause with the revolutionary struggles for independence and for equality that are now sweeping the world."[21] And so on.

Students made long-term friendships at the New School during those years, some of which evolved into professional collaborations that had a lasting impact on the cultural life of New York—for example, Dan Wolf and Edwin Fancher's *Village Voice*. Looking back in a recent interview on what led them to create a new "alternative weekly," Fancher still sounded like a New School student of the late 1940s and early 1950s: "The literary *Zeitgeist*, I guess you'd call it, or *Weltanschauung*, around the Remo [San Remo Bar] and the New School was the intellectual heritage of the *Voice*."[22] In an earlier interview, Fancher added:

> We [he and Wolf] were both on the G.I. Bill studying full time. We were part of that whole group of veterans that came flocking back, particularly at the New School. There was a lot of excitement and many writers, and lots going on. We remained good friends. I went on to become a psychologist and had various jobs in psychology. I was finishing up my psychology internship when Dan said, "Let's start a weekly newspaper in the Village because the *Villager* really doesn't represent the culture of the Village as we know it."[23]

With additional financial support from Norman Mailer, the two New School friends published the first issue of *The Village Voice* in October 1955. Fancher and Mailer each contributed $5,000 to launch the paper, and Wolf assumed responsibility for editing it. When they needed another investor, Fancher went back to his New School network of friends and invited Howard Bennett to join the team.

During the late 1940s, before Hovde severed ties with Erwin Piscator's Studio Theatre and Dramatic Workshop, the New School counted some of the nation's most gifted actors and playwrights of the mid-twentieth century among its students: Marlon Brando, Sidney Poitier, Judith Malina, and Tennessee Williams. It also attracted talented young novelists, some of whom gained critical acclaim.

They came to study with the editor and writer Hiram Haydn, who had expanded the original program that Gorham Munson had established in 1927. Haydn is credited with having launched the careers of a number of well-known writers, including William Styron and Sigrid de Lima, both of whom won the prestigious Prix de Rome, in 1952 and 1953, respectively.

Not every New School student was a budding artist, writer, or social scientist. Businessman Charles Lieberman recalled studying there during those same years with equal enthusiasm. A young refugee from Nazi-occupied Belgium, he came to the United States in the early 1940s and volunteered to fight in the U.S. Army. Thanks to the GI Bill, he enrolled in the New School's BA program after the war and received a priceless education, he recalled, studying Shakespeare with W. H. Auden.[24]

More persuasive than anecdotes are the findings reported in an empirical study published in 1953 by sociologist Robert Knapp and experimental psychologist Joseph Greenbaum. The study ranked the New School number three in the country among small institutions with BA programs that sent their students on to graduate school. Basing their analysis on data collected between 1946 and 1951, Knapp and Greenbaum followed the careers of recent college graduates who went on to do MA and PhD work, with or without funding.[25]

In 1957, Greenbaum joined the Department of Psychology at the Graduate Faculty. Nine years later, he became dean of the GF, a position he held for twelve years.

⟨━⟩

In May 1955, the New School announced an ambitious capital campaign to expand the size of the campus. This was the kind of news de Lima had been waiting for and, as she had predicted, the press responded generously. Among the articles was a full-page "Closeup" in *The New York Post* by Irwin Ross:

> This past week the New School for Social Research made news with the announcement of a large expansion program to cost $2,500,000. An eight-story annex that looks like a small version of the Lever Bros. building, a new four-story library and a tree-shaded campus in between the two buildings will give the New School a physical plant in keeping with its status as the leading center for adult education in the U.S.
>
> In the press announcements that greeted the plans, little mention was made, however, of the man largely responsible for their development—Hans Simons, president of the New School since 1950. He had the vision and energy—and no

small audacity—to embark on the most ambitious venture in the school's history. He also raised $1,500,000 to break ground and start building; he will need $1,000,000 more to finish both structures.[26]

But even a well-meaning journalist like Ross did not pass up the opportunity to remind his readers that the president of the New School had "sullied a record generally regarded as admirable" with the Orozco mural affair. In 1955, the portraits of Lenin and Stalin were still hidden from view.

Simons's admirable record augured well for the future of the New School, but nobody spoke in superlatives anymore and that included Johnson—no doubt because he was still having trouble letting go, but that was not the only reason. Even though things under Simons were finally looking up, the New School remained a shadow of what it had been, making it difficult to describe it the way people once did. When Johnson wrote about his old friend's accomplishments, he did so in subdued tones, damning with faint praise.

Off the record, he was less diplomatic. Although Johnson supported Simons most of the time, he did not spare him over the Orozco mural affair or when he disagreed with him about academic policies. A firm believer in restricting participation in seminar courses to advanced students, Johnson objected to Simons's decision in 1953 to open them up to everyone, reminding the New School's third president that "the discussion method presupposes a serious familiarity of the group with the subject matter, or the possibility of the student working up the subject matter before the meeting." Students who had no preparation needed "a series of lectures by one who really knows the subject."[27]

Although Simons disappointed Johnson in ways he had not anticipated, the New School's third president was a good fund-raiser, as Irwin Ross had indicated, and New York was paying attention. On February 11, 1956, Simons invited influential politicians and other public figures to participate in a groundbreaking ceremony. Mayor Robert Wagner helped lay a cornerstone on Twelfth Street to mark the beginning of the construction of an $800,000 annex to the Urban building. In addition to the annex, the university was building new classrooms on Eleventh Street, on a lot located behind the Twelfth Street building, making it possible to create an inner courtyard between the two reminiscent of the old campus in Chelsea.

In addition to the article in *The New York Post*, de Lima placed several stories on the groundbreaking ceremony itself in *The New York Times*, *The New York Herald Tribune*, and *The New York Daily Mirror*. National television (CBS and NBC) also covered the story, and the local radio station, WNYC, taped the event and aired it a few hours later. As the *Times* told the story, after laying the cornerstone, Mayor Wagner congratulated the New School and its officers at a private luncheon for two hundred guests. In his speech, he praised the New School for doing exactly what it had set out to do in 1919—keeping democracy strong by continuing the civic education of the citizens of New York through exciting programs designed for adults.[28]

⇐✦⇒

Simons wanted to complete the new buildings by the end of the decade, in time for a year-long celebration of three milestones: the fortieth anniversary of the founding of the New School, the twenty-fifth anniversary of the University in Exile, and Alvin Johnson's eighty-fifth birthday. As the New School paid tribute to its heroic past, Simons planned to use the occasion to open a new chapter in the history of the university, one filled with promise and opportunity. Thanks to the recent expansion of the campus, the student body could now double in size and grow to thirteen thousand.

In preparation for the big anniversary year, de Lima combed through the archives for words of praise by venerable members of the founding faculty such as John Dewey and Wesley Clair Mitchell. She solicited new tributes from distinguished personalities who had taught in Continuing Education more recently—academics, journalists, businessmen, psychoanalysts, lawyers, politicians, and artists. Among the dozens of people who responded warmly to her request for written comments were *The Nation*'s theater critic Joseph Wood Krutch and Thomas Hart Benton, whose mural still decorated the walls of a classroom on Twelfth Street. Particularly poignant were the observations of historian Hans Kohn, a renowned scholar of nationalism in modern Europe:

> My experience in adult education is naturally limited, but it extends to a number of American cities and projects. Of all those I know there is certainly none comparable to the New School which since its beginnings attracted the collaboration of a most varied and frequently distinguished group of scholars who besides their regular work in leading American colleges enjoyed the contact with the mature mind and with the alert and open intelligence of New School student groups . . . who come solely and uniquely for the purpose of intellectual pursuit and of mental growth. . . . To have created and maintained during so many years in the difficult postwar transitional period in New York a center like the New School seems to me a great contribution to the cause of education.[29]

De Lima collected dozens of quotes about the Graduate Faculty as well from widely recognized journalists and social scientists affiliated with foundations, research institutes, and prestigious universities. Some of these statements dated back to the Johnson years, such as this one by the anthropologist Franz Boas, who had died in 1942:

> I am inclined to consider the organization of your graduate school of an importance equal to that of the foundation of Johns Hopkins University which was the most important stimulus to graduate work in the United States.
>
> . . . In your organization, you have broken through the unfortunate isolation of departments which in my opinion is one of the great handicaps in the development of university life. The cooperation between representatives of various disciplines is a model which should set an example to all universities.[30]

As dean of the Graduate Faculty, Hans Staudinger understood that the twenty-fifth anniversary celebration of the University in Exile provided the GF with an excellent opportunity to demonstrate to skeptical trustees that the New School's graduate division remained critical to the academic mission of the university. In his annual report for the 1956–57 academic year, Staudinger announced that the GF would appoint a special planning committee to organize its participation. *Social Research*, he added, would mark the anniversary with a special issue of the journal.

Simons wanted to do even more. Why not find a "disinterested outsider" to produce a history of the University in Exile? Although the faculty endorsed the idea in principle, they did not think a book-length manuscript on the subject would have much appeal.[31]

Simons never found his disinterested scholar, but the *New School Bulletin* published a few sketches about the GF and the adult division, most of them written by de Lima and Clara Mayer.[32] The Graduate Faculty also followed through with its plan to publish a double issue of *Social Research* featuring articles by members of the founding faculty,[33] but these were not what Simons had in mind. Coming a bit closer, Heilbroner produced a short history of the New School that appeared in a beautifully designed fund-raising brochure.[34]

Heilbroner's sketch described the early days at the New School in the voice of the disinterested historian, whom Simons had hoped would write an entire book about the Graduate Faculty. But when he turned to the University in Exile, he abandoned any pretense of objectivity and championed the role the GF was playing in an institution dedicated to the education of adult students: they too, he pointedly reminded his readers, were adult students. Like those who registered for courses through Continuing Education, GF students attended classes after a full day of work. Nobody should forget, what is more, that the Graduate

Faculty was making a unique contribution to the scholarly community in the United States:

> It was the introduction into America of a European philosophy of knowledge—a philosophy which did much to counterbalance an American tendency toward the fragmentation of learning and research. This European philosophy sought not only a virtuoso mastery of a given subject but "an inner order of mind."

Heilbroner wrote these words in 1958 after another outside evaluator—the second in six years—had recommended to the Board of Trustees that the GF "be limited severely." The man Simons hired to conduct this new study was Earl James McGrath, former U.S. Commissioner of Education. McGrath had recently launched a national campaign to improve undergraduate education across the country, the future of which, he warned, was in serious danger because the academic community had shifted its priorities to graduate teaching and research. With the exception of a handful of flagship research universities, American institutions of higher learning should dedicate themselves solely to the teaching of undergraduate students, or in the case of the New School to continuing education for adults.[35]

On April 21, 1958, McGrath presented his report to the Board of Trustees. The New School, he told them, lacked the resources it needed to compete with serious graduate programs. Nor did it have an undergraduate program of any merit. It should dedicate itself to continuing education alone, as it first set out to do, and get out of the business of graduate and undergraduate education. Although McGrath admitted knowing very little about the New School's history, he believed that what he proposed would strengthen the institution's original mission, which he characterized as seeking to "provide a high-class adult education for students who were not looking for a degree."[36]

Furious with the report, Johnson, who was still a trustee, agreed that McGrath knew very little about the New School and accused him of not having bothered to learn very much about the important place it occupied in the history of higher education in the country. Although the trustees rejected McGrath's conclusion, Simons still sent the report to Staudinger and asked the dean to respond to it in writing by the end of the summer. Why? To have a record of the GF's thoughts on the matter in the New School's files. Staudinger, in turn, shared the report with the Executive Faculty and requested their input.

Nearly everyone wrote back, both the émigré scholars who had been teaching at the New School since the 1930s and younger American colleagues who had joined the faculty in recent years.[37] For the most part, they took the exercise seriously, describing politely and in painstaking detail why the GF was critical to the New School and the wider academic community. But they also gave Staudinger a piece of their mind about what they thought of the whole process. As the sociologist Carl Mayer put it, he "was somewhat disturbed by the content" of Staudinger's letter of July 14, in which he had asked his colleagues to help him explain to the Board of Trustees why the GF still mattered:

> I had—perhaps naively—assumed that there was no longer any need to ask the question which you are supposed to answer, that the answer to it had been given long ago, and that this answer was universally accepted by all concerned: Faculty, Administration and Board. But this is obviously not the case. I wonder why? . . . After all, there has been almost endless debate and consideration of the matter.[38]

Most everyone wrote that the GF was making a unique contribution to the American academic community by offering students an attractive alternative to what they would find at mainstream universities in the country. Repeating what they had said on countless other occasions, this alternative taught the social sciences in the European tradition with a focus on theory and from a broad, multidisciplinary perspective. But who would extend this tradition in the future? As Staudinger noted in his statement to the board, over the next ten years, "all Faculty members who were brought to this country during the Hitler persecution will become emeriti. In this time a complete transformation of the Faculty must be brought about, and thus the careful selection of new members is of the greatest importance."

By 1958, that careful selection was well under way. As members of the émigré faculty retired, the GF replaced them whenever they could with other Europeans, younger than themselves, who had come to the United States without Johnson's help, in some cases after the war, like Hans Jonas. But even these scholars would soon be too old. The next best solution was to hire their own students as their professors had done in Germany, but this was not the American way. Treading lightly, the émigré faculty began by appointing their disciples as lecturers, in positions that would not lead to tenure, for example, Gerhard Colm's student Haskell Wald. Then, little by little, they began to offer former students permanent positions, among them Leo Strauss's protégé Howard White in Political Science, Alfred Schütz's students Peter Berger and Thomas Luckmann in Sociology, and Adolph Lowe's student Robert Heilbroner in Economics.

There was, however, one dissenting voice. Although Hans Neisser joined his colleagues in rejecting McGrath's recommendations, he disagreed with almost everyone else about the intellectual direction the GF should take. The time had come, he said, to open up the curriculum to Anglo-Saxon approaches to the social sciences. With the exception of sociology, Americans were doing far more interesting work in virtually every other field than were the Europeans. There were, of course, "viewpoints" and "approaches" from Europe that American students should learn to appreciate, but nothing more. What the GF had to offer that remained unique was its commitment to teaching graduate school for adult students at night. No other graduate school in the New York metropolitan area, he said, offered a serious program for working adults in 1958 and this would remain true for many years to come.[39]

On September 17, Staudinger submitted his twenty-two-page "Statement Regarding the Graduate Faculty" to the chairman of the Board of Trustees. Two weeks later he wrote to Simons, "I have endeavored to present my own views in as concise a form as possible in order to meet the challenging and provocative opinions set forth in the McGrath report. I hope they will serve the purpose of the board's request." He then appended the short statements he had received from members of the faculty—did he include all of them? Ever the diplomat, Staudinger's response to the board did not reflect Mayer's expression of disbelief that the administration was still asking the GF to defend its existence. Nor did he address Neisser's disparaging remarks about the value of European social sciences. The dean simply repeated the arguments that he and the majority of his colleagues had made many times before about the value of the GF to the New School as a whole and to the U.S. academic community while assuring the trustees that there was "always room for improvement":

> This does not mean, of course, that we have reasons for complacency. The GF—both in itself and in its integration with the rest of the school—is no exception to the rule that there is always room for improvement. Like the rest of the school we have the constant responsibility of concerning ourselves "with the meaning rather than with the mechanics of human existence," as Hans Simons has put it. . . . In the words of T. S. Eliot, "Where is our wisdom which we have lost in knowledge; where is our knowledge which we lost in information?" As a faculty for the training of adults, we must do all in our power to counteract the trend toward memorized knowledge and unstructured information.[40]

In the concluding section of his statement, Staudinger outlined some of the ways the GF might improve if the trustees gave the division the resources it needed. First and foremost, it needed to replace the aging faculty with younger colleagues trained in the European tradition of the University in Exile—*pace* Neisser.

When the faculty returned in the fall of 1958, many of them were still indignant about having had to spend time over the summer responding to the McGrath report, but they quickly put the matter aside and focused on the upcoming anniversary celebrations. On December 15, the *New School Bulletin* announced the schedule of events organized to celebrate the fortieth anniversary of the New School for Social Research and the twenty-fifth anniversary of the University in Exile. The festivities would begin December 18, on Johnson's eighty-fourth birthday, and end on the same day twelve months later. At the opening reception, Senator Jacob Javits of New York and Executive Secretary (Emeritus) Clarence E. Pickett of the American Friends Service Committee spoke briefly, setting just the right tone for the occasion. After paying tribute to the pioneering role the New School had played in the history of adult education, they congratulated the organizers for having chosen "Continued Learning in a Changing Society" as the unifying theme for the year's conferences. As the *New School Bulletin* described it,

> the New School will look into its own future—by examining the changing society, by redefining the role of higher adult education within it, and by reconsidering its own role in conferences, seminars, lectures, and workshops.
>
> The formal closing of the Anniversary Year will be on December 18, 1959, the 85th birthday of President Emeritus Alvin Johnson. It will be devoted to a projection of the Anniversary theme into the future under the title, "1999—Forty Years Hence."

Over the course of the anniversary year, Continuing Education ran four academic conferences on the future of education and other timely subjects, providing ample opportunities for audience participation, the brochures proudly stated, in the time-honored New School tradition.[41] In addition, Alexander Schneider and his chamber orchestra gave weekly concerts in the Twelfth Street auditorium featuring pianist Rudolf Serkin and other world-class musicians. The university also opened its renovated art center to critical acclaim. Finally, the New School organized a number of fund-raising events for Continuing Education, the most important being a benefit dinner on February 5 to celebrate the anniversary of the New School, which had opened forty years earlier on the tenth of the month. The dinner followed a widely publicized panel discussion on whether Democracy could "be exported."

During graduation exercises in June, Simons granted honorary degrees to four exceptionally distinguished and courageous individuals, two of whom had not only dedicated their lives to what the university stood for but had given courses at the New School during the 1920s: Supreme Court Justice Felix Frankfurter and the Pulitzer Prize–winning journalist Walter Lippmann. The other two recipients were the Canadian historian and politician Lester Bowles Pearson, who had won the Nobel Peace Prize in 1957 for his leadership in helping resolve the Suez Canal Crisis, and the Hungarian journalist Edith Bone, who had been arrested in Budapest in 1949 and condemned to seven years of solitary confinement on charges of being a spy for the West.

The Graduate Faculty ran a series of anniversary events of its own during the first week of April, with a mix of informal social gatherings and traditional academic seminars. Hans Jonas gave one of these seminars on The Practical Use of Theory with the psychologist Solomon Asch, now of Swarthmore College. Erich Hula and Adolph Lowe served as discussants. Karl Brandt came in from Washington, D.C., where he was serving on President Eisenhower's Council of Economic Advisors, to give a second seminar on Population Capacity of the World's Agriculture. Over the weekend, Alexander Schneider and his chamber orchestra gave matinee and evening performances of Handel's "Concerti Grossi" in honor of the University in Exile.[42]

On April 6, the New School held a benefit dinner for the Graduate Faculty at the Waldorf Astoria. Hiram Halle's nephew, Joseph Halle Schaffner, agreed to serve as master of ceremonies. As Schaffner welcomed more than one thousand guests, he read a few of the dozens of telegram messages received by the New School over the last several days, including those from President Theodor Heuss of West Germany, Governor Nelson Rockefeller of New York, and former First Lady Eleanor Roosevelt. President Emeritus Johnson made some opening remarks, then turned the microphone over to Simons. After dinner the speeches continued, delivered by Henri Bonnet, a founding member of the Ecole Libre and French Ambassador to the United States between 1944 and 1954; Detlev B. Bronk, president of the Rockefeller Institute of Medical Research; and Carl Sandburg, America's revered poet and biographer of Lincoln.

The speakers all sang Johnson's praises and paid tribute to the refugee scholars, extolling them for the role they played in enriching the intellectual and moral spirit of the United States. In the words of Carl Sandburg, they were outstanding examples of "that mystic and hazardous thing called the American dream":

The ghosts of Roger Williams and Ben Franklin, of Thomas Jefferson and Abraham Lincoln, of Emerson, Thoreau and Whitman, of Galileo and Elijah Lovejoy—they could all be at home and at ease here tonight. We give our salutations and deep affection and profound esteem to Alvin Johnson, calling him a pioneer, a pathfinder, a lover of mankind ever seeking new horizons. We salute the "University in Exile" as an institution born of a passion for freedom and ever aware that freedom is inexorably bound to responsibility and discipline. The culture stream of American national life is richer and safer because of the arrival and infusion of these refugees and exiles, these great teachers, rare minds, extraordinary personalities.[43]

Dean Staudinger thanked the after-dinner speakers and made a few remarks himself on behalf of the Graduate Faculty before turning the microphone over to Ralph Walker, chairman of the New School's Board of Trustees. Walker, in turn, introduced Millicent C. McIntosh, president of Barnard College, and Ernest Gruening, U.S. Senator from Alaska, both of whom offered their "felicitations" in a final round of toasts. Why the senator of Alaska? Because, Johnson told Staudinger in his inimitable style,

> Gruening was a liberal journalist, an editor of *The Nation*, widely known and esteemed by liberals of every stripe. I invited him to join the Board of the University in Exile. He accepted and was our most intelligent and active member.
>
> But Roosevelt made him Governor of Puerto Rico, to liberalize the government of the island. There was a small part of intransigent *Independistas* who thought it would be a wonderful gesture to kill Gruening, to show the world that mere liberal administration was not enough. No offense was meant to Gruening as a person, whom all Puerto Rico admired. Gruening's was not a subtle mind which could distinguish between being loved as a person and killed as an official. He resigned, and Roosevelt, having a rich vein of humor, made him Territorial Governor of Alaska, an office he filled with distinction for eleven years, when the Republican Administration ousted him. What Alaska thought of that is indicated by their electing him one of their first two Senators.
>
> We have to invite him to our Graduate Faculty dinner. . . . He would make the best speech and draw the most publicity.[44]

As the anniversary year was winding down, the Committee for the Commemoration of French-American Scholarship organized a special event to thank Johnson and the New School for having saved the lives of francophone scholars during World War II. On November 15, 1959, *The New York Times* reported that the committee's president, Philip Courtney, had commissioned two abstract murals by the French painter Michel Cadoret for the New School "to celebrate twenty years of Franco-American scholarship cooperation" and "to commemorate the rescue of nearly 200 French and Belgian scholars who were endangered by the Nazi invasion in World War II. As Hitler's armies rolled across the Low Countries and France, the New School, under the leadership of Dr. Alvin Johnson . . . called public attention to the plight of the scholars."[45] Before the official unveiling of the murals in the new building on Eleventh Street, everyone gathered in the Twelfth Street auditorium to listen to speeches by members of the Committee for the Ecole Libre, the Committee for the Commemoration of French-American Scholarship and the New School. Adding to the solemnity of the occasion, his Excellency Hervé Alphand, Ambassador of France, attended the ceremony as well. The New School, for its part, paid tribute to their French and Belgian colleagues, and to the intellectual tradition they represented so admirably, by conferring the degree of Doctor of Fine Arts, *honoris causa*, on Jacques Maritain, now professor of philosophy at Princeton.[46]

Finally, as announced, the university marked the end of the anniversary celebrations on December 18, Johnson's eighty-fifth birthday. With this last tribute to the president emeritus, many assumed that the Johnson era would come to an end. And it probably would have had a group of trustees not betrayed the New School in 1963, pressing Johnson back into service:

> There is a well-known phenomenon that when governments are impotent to act in a crisis, good citizens form independent organizations to act. In the recent crisis, the government of the School was patently unable to act. The "Save the School" group was the informal citizens' organization.[47]

15

"SAVE THE SCHOOL"

As the anniversary celebrations were winding down, colleagues looked toward the future with mixed emotions. The Eleventh Street building made it possible now to double the number of courses in Continuing Education and increase them significantly at the Graduate Faculty (GF). But what had once been a dream had become an imperative. Filling those seats would not be easy. The university needed new leadership to succeed, someone with entrepreneurial skills and experience in a mainstream academic institution. Everyone agreed about this, including Hans Simons, who had announced over the summer that he was leaving the New School to join the Ford Foundation. He would wait until May 1960 to give the trustees plenty of time to find his successor.

In the same spirit, Hans Staudinger stepped down in the spring of 1959, making way for the GF to replace their émigré dean with the American labor historian Henry David. Before joining the New School, David had been teaching at Columbia University's School of Business and serving as executive director of the National Manpower Council.[1] He arrived in the fall of 1959. On September 30, Simons officially welcomed David to the New School in the GF's new facilities on Eleventh Street. As the outgoing president introduced the new dean at the first Executive Faculty meeting of the semester, he spoke optimistically about the future. He was leaving his colleagues in the hands of a respected academic leader in the American mold and at a time when the New School, with its newly expanded campus, was ready to meet the challenges that lay ahead.[2]

A no-nonsense kind of man, David thanked the president briskly and got down to business, outlining his "hopes and plans" for the coming years.

Without mincing words, he told his new colleagues that they would not be able "to compete in general terms with other graduate schools," at least not in the near future. He urged the faculty to focus on what they did "particularly well" and to make arrangements for their students to take courses at other universities in the city with scholars who specialized in areas that the New School did not cover adequately. He also recommended using the General Seminar to "serve fresh purposes," implying that it currently did little to address the methodological and theoretical weaknesses he saw in the research conducted by members of the faculty.

Simons had not expected David to speak so bluntly. Interrupting him politely, he cautioned the new dean about broadcasting "too much overt criticism of the Graduate Faculty" until the Middle States Association of Colleges and Secondary Schools had completed its evaluation of the New School. Why make the accreditation process more difficult than it already promised to be? With Simons stepping down in May, and the search for his successor just beginning, the timing was unfortunate, but there it was. Middle States held these reviews like clockwork at ten-year intervals. No one should forget, Simons added ominously, that the association had placed the New School on probation the last time when Bryn Hovde was still president. They could not let the same thing happen again.

A few months later, the evaluation team commended Simons for all that he had accomplished, but they still only gave the New School a conditional pass because their president was leaving. The university would lose its accreditation, they warned, if the next president did not support the changes Simons had made over the last ten years and honor his promises for the future.

In April, Simons submitted his final budget to the Board of Trustees, predicting that the New School would enter the next academic year with a little cash on hand—an exceptional achievement for this chronically strapped institution. Still, he cautioned, it was too early to rejoice. The year-long anniversary celebrations had failed to attract wealthy new donors to the New School.[3]

The man chosen to succeed Simons as president was Abbott Kaplan, a nationally acclaimed figure in continuing education. For the past twelve years he had been serving as the director of the Southern Division of the University Extension of the University of California. Recognized as the largest adult education program in the nation, the division offered classes to more than four hundred thousand students. Although Kaplan's reputation in this area made him a very strong candidate, the trustees worried about appointing a man with no scholarly credentials to speak of to serve as the next president of a serious academic institution. To reassure themselves, they contacted a wide range of people to determine whether he had the background and commitment necessary to maintain the high quality of the New School's programs in Continuing Education and to strengthen the Graduate Faculty.

Everyone gave Kaplan a rave review. Among the letters received from other leaders of adult education programs was a glowing endorsement from Paul McGhee, dean of NYU's Division of General Education. It ended with these words:

> Actually, my own view is that UCLA, which, together with the programs throughout Southern California, is under Abbott's sole direction, has set the pace for the entire country. In all honesty, I do not know of any other institution of higher education in this country where there is so much going on that is exciting, original, and high-level in programming for continuing education. It is no coincidence that this has happened under Abbott Kaplan's administration.[4]

Going beyond the adult education community, the board consulted Adam Yarmolinsky, a highly regarded talent scout in liberal circles. He too recommended the candidate enthusiastically. The only concern raised—and repeatedly so—was whether Kaplan would ever leave California. Apparently he convinced the trustees that he would, but not before Labor Day. Even though Simons was stepping down in May, Kaplan refused to begin earlier. The board accepted the delay and asked Clara Mayer, Henry David, and the New School's treasurer, Issai Hosiosky, to run the university in the interim.

Kaplan began on September 6 and resigned five days later "because of illness in the family," *The New York Times* reported.[5] Rumor had it that he literally fled after Hosiosky gave him the unvarnished version of the New School's economic challenges.[6] In a matter of weeks, Kaplan had accepted a new job at UCLA as the dean of the Division of Theater Arts. Left in the lurch, the disappointed trustees made Nathan Levin, vice chairman of the board, acting president, more as a figurehead than anything else, hoping that his ties to the financial sector and high visibility on the boards of several philanthropic organizations might attract strong candidates to apply for the New School presidency.[7] In the meantime, the same team of three continued to run the university.

Unable to identify another candidate of Kaplan's stature, the trustees accepted defeat a few months later and promoted from within, appointing Henry David the fourth president of the New School. Everyone seemed pleased with the decision, including Alvin Johnson, who sent David a personal note to say how delighted he was with the way things had turned out: "I am devoted to you. If there isn't a Providence there is some power equally beneficent that made Abbott Kaplan run away and open the road to you." The purpose of his letter, however, was to warn the new president that "I am not just a yes man." In the interest of everyone, he recommended that he be "eased off the board."[8] David apparently rejected the idea, a decision he must have regretted when he needed to get rid of the formidable old man but no longer had Johnson's cooperation or the political clout to force him to resign.

David was inaugurated in March 1961 and served for two stressful years, making a number unpopular, but much needed changes. Even his critics conceded that he had improved the working conditions of the faculty and the quality of academic programs across the university. Among David's significant accomplishments, he succeeded in demonstrating to Middle States that the New School had continued to honor the commitments Simons had made despite the unanticipated difficulties the institution had faced in finding a successor.

When Middle States gave the New School a conditional pass in 1960, it did so with the understanding that the university would submit progress reports over the next two years. The first one was due in April 1961, a few weeks after David had become president. Given "developments affecting the top administration of the New School," David made "a justifiable request for a postponement, which was graciously granted by the Commission," but only until May. In June the association congratulated the new president, reminding him, however, that he still had a lot to do. Attached to their letter of warm "felicitations," was a long list of lingering problems that the evaluators wanted David to address over the next academic year. The university, they acknowledged sympathetically, was not "a traditional agency of higher education," but they urged the new president to continue honoring the commitment his predecessor had made to raise academic standards. Thanks to David, the New School had already introduced a number of structural changes that "would serve to tighten the administration procedures, without destroying the nontraditional character of the New School."

Middle States praised David, for example, for having announced his intention to raise tuition and do away with the New School's persistent "split-fee" system. Although Bryn Hovde had tried to put an end to the system in 1946, the university had still not abandoned its degrading policy of paying part-time instructors 50 percent of whatever the registrar collected in tuition for their courses. The evaluators expected David to follow through with his promise that a "new system of remuneration [would] be in effect by September 1962."

In their remarks about the GF, the evaluators praised David for having begun to address the procedural irregularities the team had identified in 1960. Now, over the next academic year, they wanted to see "a solid record of accomplishment"— evidence that he had reduced the number of courses taught by emeriti professors, addressed the problematic way the GF handled "admissions . . . degree requirements, non-matriculated students, etc," and eliminated the split-fee system.

Finally, the evaluators commended David further for having made eight new appointments to the GF since February 1960, while serving in his various administrative roles as dean, senior manager, and president. Together, these additions had given "the faculty a transfusion of younger men."[9]

Two years later, in March 1963, the New School praised David in a press release for all that he had done for the university, acknowledging that "the changes affected by Dr. David . . . have served to expand and strengthen the New School in all of its educational and cultural programs and have prepared the institution for the increased enrollments and responsibilities which it expects in the years ahead." As president of the New School, David had introduced "a series of major innovations in policy and management [that] have resulted in a significant reshaping of the institution, educationally and organizationally." These words, however, appeared in an article that announced David's resignation, a decision motivated by "differences with the board of trustees over questions of educational policy."[10]

Shortly after his resignation became public, David met with his colleagues in the GF to explain what the trustees meant by "differences." He had asked them, David explained, to make a stronger commitment to the New School than they were prepared to do in order to ensure the "preservation of the integrity and stability of the institution." On behalf of the GF, Dean Howard White thanked their former dean and president for having improved "the material lot of your colleagues."[11] Although nobody challenged White on this solemn occasion, not everyone was sorry to see David go—a sentiment vigorously shared by many colleagues in Continuing Education. When Dean William Birnbaum expressed "appreciation for the work and accomplishments of Dr. David and wished him well for the future,"[12] he was speaking on behalf of a faculty that had openly declared war on the former president two years earlier.

David lost the support of the Continuing Education faculty in the early months of his presidency when he made the dramatic decision to fire Clara Mayer. Outraged by what he had done, colleagues reminded the new president that Mayer had been playing a prominent role at the New School since the early 1920s. Perhaps, David conceded, but the time had come for her to step down as dean and vice president.

With the support of the trustees, David had decided to consolidate the schools of Politics and Philosophy in Continuing Education and create a new College of Liberal Arts under a single dean, a position he wanted to fill with a seasoned academic administrator from another institution. The New School, he explained, needed fresh ideas. Simplifying his task, Arthur Swift had retired as dean of the School of Politics in 1960, a position he had held since 1956.[13] Mayer, however, refused to step down voluntarily, daring David to fire her—which he did.

Mayer's old friend Henry Cowell formed a protest committee with the writer Alfred Kazin and the psychologist Rudolf Arnheim. With Kazin serving as chair, the committee sent an eloquent letter to David, signed by many other colleagues, urging the new president to make Mayer dean of his new College of Liberal Arts. David responded collegially and agreed to meet with the faculty to discuss their differences. On June 1, 1961, the writer Don Wolfe opened the meeting by reading a statement composed in the form of a resolution. It began with these words:

> I am among those who have been on the faculty of the New School since 1946. With many others, I recently signed the letter sponsored by Mr. Kazin's committee protesting the dismissal of Clara Mayer as vice-president and [acting] dean of the College of Liberal Arts. I think this decision was tragically wrong. Should not the first action of a new administration be to bring into harmony, so far as possible, the strong personalities and viewpoints which have enriched the New School? . . . Where there is arbitrary action, the New School loses. Where there is authority not persuasion, the New School retreats. Where there is an action that creates a division among faculty members such as ours, the New School is terribly weakened. . . .
>
> Only a handful of people remains like Miss Mayer, who gave early loyalty to the ideals of Beard, Robinson, and Johnson. We cannot afford to weaken this school by removing one of the founding spirits. You have the legal and technical right to dismiss Miss Mayer. But in so doing, you are going against many of the principles of creative action exemplified in the life of our great President Emeritus, Alvin Johnson.[14]

When Wolfe finished, David ruled the resolution "out of order on the ground that it would be ill-advised to discuss the reasons which led the Board of Trustees to reach its decision on Miss Mayer and to act on it"—to put it mildly, Johnson might have added, given the problems David was having at the time with the trustees. When the majority of the board voted in favor of letting Clara go, Albert Mayer resigned on the spot. How dare they treat his sister this way after all she and her family had done for the university!

The New School community adored Clara Mayer. As Johnson had written in his autobiography a decade earlier, "it would have been hard for the New School to survive without the staunch support of C. W. M. [Clara Woollie Mayer] and the Mayer family." And this included having persuaded many of their wealthy friends in the German Jewish community to contribute generously as well.[15] When Albert resigned, several trustees worried about the financial fallout. Not a problem, the new president assured them; the time had come to stop running the New School like a "mom and pop" shop. Other donors would soon take the place of the Mayer family and their friends.

Johnson was not convinced. He believed that "our President was handicapped by his theory of education, illustrated by a recent statement of his that he had found the New School dominated by family psychology; he was supplanting it with institutional psychology." David's mistake, Johnson continued, was "to expect loyalty from institutional psychology which is soundly based on *quid pro quo*."[16] But did Johnson oppose David's decision to fire Mayer? It is not at all clear that he did.

Although his enthusiasm for David faded quickly, Johnson believed that the new president deserved the full support of the board while he was just getting started. Focusing on his strengths, he praised David for making the New School intellectually and administratively stronger.[17] The university was attracting a dynamic new group of students and in greater numbers than ever, even after David had raised tuition,[18] but it was also going deeper and deeper into debt.

In May 1962, David asked the trustees to approve his budget for the coming academic year. Several members of the board complained that he was asking for too much money. If it cost that much to run the university properly, then the time had come to face reality: The New School did not have the means to support itself properly as an independent institution. Others objected. They should wait to see whether David's new initiatives could solve the university's chronic financial problem of coming up short at the end of every academic year. Since he had only been in office for a little over a year, they should give their new president until the following January. With little enthusiasm, the trustees agreed to wait and accepted the budget for the coming fiscal year.[19]

When the board reconvened in January 1963, the development committee reported that the university's fund-raising efforts over the last several months had yielded very little. Between May 1962 and January 1963, the New School had collected less than $500 in its alumni campaign and received nothing at all from philanthropic organizations. The finance committee made a similarly disappointing report. Over the last several years, the New School's deficit had been increasing at an alarming rate and was now more than double what it had been in the early 1950s when the university had hit rock bottom and was on the brink of bankruptcy. What is more, under David's leadership expenses were rising quickly, while contributions from the wider donor community were decreasing, leaving the trustees in the unenviable position of having to pay a larger percentage every year themselves of an escalating debt. In 1957–58, more than half the money used to cover the deficit came from individuals who did not sit on the board. By 1961, outside contributions had dropped to less than a third, and since then even more, which in turn discouraged the trustees from giving more themselves. After David became president, only three members of the board continued to make significant gifts and one of them had subsequently resigned!

On a more optimistic note, student registrations had increased significantly over the last six months, but the overall situation remained dire. The university would not raise enough money to cover the deficit for the second year in a row, and this time it no longer had a safety net. In 1962, the New School had bailed itself out by using its reserve fund as collateral, making it possible to borrow the rest at a reasonable rate. Now the reserve fund was gone, leaving the board with no option other than to borrow money on short-term loans at exorbitant rates, or mortgage the property.

Still unwilling to give up, a majority of the board asked the chair to appoint an ad hoc committee and charge it with finding a solution by March. This would give the administration the time it needed to analyze the registration numbers for the current semester and determine whether the university had begun to pay for itself—as David had confidently predicted—now that it had raised tuition and regularized the way it paid the faculty. The old fee-splitting system was finally dead. But even if David's predictions were right, the New School would not have enough money from tuition to pay off its debts at the end of this fiscal year. The trustees needed to have a plan by March for how it would raise several hundred thousand dollars over the next several months.

In February, members of the ad hoc committee initiated secret meetings with New York University to explore the possibility of a merger. Although NYU has no record of these conversations, the New School has ample evidence that they took place. The main contact at NYU was Paul McGhee, the very same dean of General Education who had written so enthusiastically about Abbott Kaplan.[20] Staudinger got wind of the plot right away, most likely from members of the ad hoc committee who opposed the idea. Alarmed by the news, he wrote to Levin, informing the board's chairman that he had heard from reliable sources that the ad hoc committee was considering two possible "solutions" to the university's financial problems, both of which were disastrous: merge with NYU or close down the Graduate Faculty. The latter, Staudinger added impatiently, was proposed every time the institution ran out of money.

With Levin's permission, the former dean would like to propose a third option: launch an emergency fund-raising drive to mobilize the New School's wide circle of friends, many of whom had stopped contributing in recent years. But before these friends would return to the fold, the trustees had to face the real source of the problem:

> In my opinion, the crisis has its roots in the conflict between the president and board over budgetary policy, as became evident last summer. It is a crisis of personal relations and of differences of opinion about the financial responsibilities of the board and president. I believe that the board and president are both guilty. The president did not offer a far-reaching educational-action program that would spark the support of the board and other contributors; he did not concentrate on establishing new sources of income which could make possible his expanded administrative program; he failed to establish real working relationships with either the board or the teaching staff. Thus, the board became more and more critical of the president.... [The board] failed to give positive leadership in a situation in which it felt that such leadership was lacking in the president. It criticized, but it did not act. If the board's criticism is justified—and I believe it is—the board has to face up to the implications of this judgment. The life of the institution is more important than the persons involved.[21]

Staudinger wanted the trustees to fire David immediately. They could then look for a more suitable academic leader with ties to the foundation world. Although Levin did not like the idea, he agreed to call a special meeting of the board to discuss the recommendation two weeks before the ad hoc committee was scheduled make its official report to the trustees. Since Staudinger was not a member of the board, he would not be present, but he was not acting alone—Johnson would make the case for the two of them. The president emeritus had already discussed the matter with trustee Vera List and had her full support. At the meeting itself, however, they did not have a quorum, so Johnson said nothing.

Staudinger wrote to Levin the next day on behalf of the president emeritus. Given the poor turnout at the meeting, Johnson thought that it might "be more dignified and graceful" to send David a letter, signed by the majority of the board, asking him to resign immediately. Johnson would sign the letter first, followed by Mrs. List who had already agreed to sign it as well. If Levin wanted to discuss their proposal and the wording of the letter, a draft of which Staudinger had enclosed, Mrs. List would be happy to host an off-the-record meeting and invite other members of the board who also wanted to see David step down. The final decision, however, "should be left to you."[22]

Levin stuck by David and withheld his consent. As he put it to a generous donor of the New School, who was not a trustee, "I had to fight upstream with my members of the board and my [ad hoc] committee in behalf of Henry David."[23] In the end, Levin lost. After rejecting Johnson and Staudinger's recommendation, the two men broke ranks and launched their own, unauthorized, "Save the School" campaign.

⸺✦⸺

Before going public in March 1963, Johnson and Staudinger contacted Hiram Halle's nephew, Joseph Schaffner, the head of Hart, Schaffner & Marx, a famous clothing company for men in Chicago.[24] An old friend of the New School, Schaffner had ties going back to the 1920s. After Halle died in 1944, the New School frequently turned to Schaffner to represent the family at events commemorating the founding of the University in Exile—as it had in 1959 when it asked him to serve as master of ceremonies at the twenty-fifth anniversary dinner. But that was not all. Having recently lost his wife, Schaffner was courting Staudinger's daughter Ruth, whom he married the following December. The man was, in other words, a perfect example of what David had in mind when he referred to the New School as a "mom and pop shop."[25]

When Staudinger contacted Schaffner, his future son-in-law responded immediately. In consultation with Johnson, the three men agreed that Schaffner would pledge $200,000 over the next two years, with one nonnegotiable condition: The university had to promise that it would "not be merged with another institution prior to August 31, 1964." If a merger took place before that date, the New School would have to reimburse Schaffner in full and right away.[26]

Schaffner's commitment of $200,000 made it possible for Johnson and Staudinger to raise an additional $240,000 before the board met again on March 13, most of it at an emergency meeting of sympathetic trustees and other wealthy friends of the New School. Invited guests received telegrams from Johnson on March 6: "A merger with another university is under discussion to which I am opposed. Mrs. Elinor Gimbel has kindly extended an invitation to you and an important group to meet with me at dinner at her home on Monday evening, March 11, so I may give you the facts and have your counsel and hopefully support."[27] On the same day as the dinner, Johnson sent a "confidential" letter to hundreds of friends in the New School community, exposing the "plot" and asking them to make a contribution immediately. In his letter, he described the situation as "the worst crisis the school had ever faced."

Why go public at the last minute? In part, no doubt, to embarrass the trustees. But Johnson had other reasons as well: The crisis provided the New School with an excellent opportunity to raise much-needed funds beyond the initial short-fall. It also gave Johnson the chance to lead the charge once again in the name of the New School—probably for the last time. He was, after all, eighty-eight years old. There was no holding him back:

The existence of the New School is endangered. A merger with New York University is under discussion. That would be the end. I am opposed to it, and I know every devoted friend of the school will join me immediately to prevent it. I have written to you and others many times about the needs of the school, but this is the worst crisis it has ever faced.

I am going to be straightforward with you and explain the situation, which I hope, however, will not be made public. . . .

The situation became so serious that some members of the board, good friends of mine, who have stood with the school for years, became desperate and proposed that the New School be merged. New York University would no doubt be happy to get our buildings, and even put its general education division in our house, taking over the name of the New School. But that would no longer be the New School. In a time when all responsible citizens are deeply concerned about the need for more and better educational facilities, we of the New School cannot in good conscience look on passively at the dissolution of a living and developing institution. . . . What is immediately necessary is guaranteed support not only for the current year, but for two or three years ahead—a pledge from each friend of a contribution as sizable as he can afford. . . .

A form and reply envelope addressed to me are enclosed. We need your response at once.

Sincerely,

Alvin Johnson
President Emeritus[28]

When the trustees met on March 13, the first item of business was the much-anticipated report of the ad hoc committee, appropriately amended to reflect the recent turn of events. In his report to the board, the chairman confirmed that the committee had taken the idea of a merger off the table, at least for now. He then ran down the current state of the New School's finances, concluding that the university would have a deficit of nearly $490,000 by the end of the 1963 fiscal year, most of which they could cover, thanks to the efforts of many people—he did not mention Johnson or Staudinger by name. Between January 9 and March 13, the New School had raised $440,000. They now had six months to raise an additional $50,000, something they should easily be able to do, after which they needed to find a more permanent solution. Although the Save the School campaign had bought the New School a little more time, it had done little to address the university's chronic financial problems. With the immediate crisis averted, the ad hoc committee recommended giving the board one more year to find a long-term solution.

Before the trustees took a vote on the committee's report, David asked them to discuss in executive session an unsolicited statement he had written and sent to them two days earlier in which he laid out a set of conditions—as if he were still calling the shots—that the board was going to have to meet before he would agree to continue serving as president. The trustees rejected David's conditions and asked for his resignation. When they met again a week later, Levin informed them that David had not yet resigned but would do so in a few days. He also reported that Dean McGhee had contacted him to express his concern about what he was hearing. He wanted to make sure that nobody thought NYU had tried to steam-roll the New School into a merger. Fearing that the story would leak to the public, he urged the two institutions to draft a joint press release.[29]

Not that anything would hit the newspapers right away. Since early December, the New York Typographical Union had been on strike, effectively closing down the city's papers for three months. The blackout had spared NYU and the New School embarrassment for several weeks, but the strike was coming to an end. They needed to come up with a story that both institutions could live with.

The New School prepared two press releases, neither one of which mentioned anything about a possible merger with NYU. The first, dated March 25, announced Henry David's resignation, and the second, dated March 31, announced the appointment of Robert MacIver as acting president. Professor Emeritus of Columbia University in political science and sociology, MacIver was also a New School trustee and an old friend of Johnson's who, as many remembered, had warmly welcomed the exiled scholars at the University in Exile to the academic community in New York.

On April 1, *The New York Times* published a short article on the recent changes in leadership at the New School. It appeared on the day after the strike ended:

Dr. Robert M. MacIver was appointed acting president of the New School for Social Research yesterday.

The appointment follows last week's resignation of Dr. Henry David from the school's presidency as a result of "differences with the board of trustees over questions of educational policy". . . .

Although neither Dr. David nor the trustees elaborated on their policy differences, it is known that part of the conflict was over Dr. David's demand for a long-term budget. The trustees, insisting that they must raise each year's available funds annually, were reported to have refused to underwrite a three-year budget.

Despite the differences leading to the resignation, the trustees agreed that Dr. David had instigated significant reforms in the academic program and administration, including the abolition of "the split-fee system." Under this system faculty members had been paid on the basis of the number of students enrolled in their courses.[30]

After David resigned, the trustees voted to launch a $5 million endowment campaign, headed by Johnson, now referred to affectionately in press releases as "the grand old man of adult education." Bad feelings persisted, however, between the president emeritus and members of the board, a fact Johnson memorialized on March 27, in a stinging four-page letter to the board accusing unnamed members of the ad hoc committee of having tried to pack up the school and send it down "the road to Mandalay" (Washington Square). Although he never mailed it, he made sure a few copies survived.[31]

Two days later, Johnson sent a slightly toned-down version of the same, outlining the conditions under which he would serve as chair of the endowment committee. First and foremost he insisted on having complete autonomy from the standing committees of the board. Then, given his advanced age, he wanted to appoint Staudinger as vice chairman even though the former dean of the Graduate Faculty was not a trustee. Staudinger, as everyone knew, was an outstanding fund-raiser. He was also fourteen years younger than Johnson.[32]

The trustees not only accepted Johnson's terms but further demonstrated their good faith by electing a new slate of officers with whom Johnson was on excellent terms. In May, Jacob Kaplan took over as chairman of the board and List of the development committee. By the end of the calendar year, both Kaplan and List had made major gifts to the New School, leading other board members to do the same. The university renamed its arts center for Mrs. List and its center of urban affairs for Mr. Kaplan. At about the same time, Schaffner endowed three professorial chairs for the GF in honor of Johnson, Hans and Else Staudinger, and Adlai Stevenson. Finally, over the next two years the New School organized three fund-raising dinners—on Johnson's eighty-ninth and ninetieth birthdays, and on the thirtieth anniversary of the Graduate Faculty.

As the New School looked for a new president, the university entered a period of relative calm, attracting attention in the media for significant cultural events instead of internal political unrest. In the spring of 1964, the Vera List Center for Art and Politics mounted a widely reviewed exhibit of works by Robert Rauschenberg and Ray Kerciu, inspired by the assassination of President Kennedy and the racial violence that had taken the lives of James Meredith and other civil rights activists. Continuing Education ran a lecture course on the American Race Crisis featuring fifteen civil rights leaders and experts, beginning with Martin Luther King Jr., whose march on Washington the previous summer had made him a national hero. The course enrolled 236 students.

During that same spring, the GF celebrated its thirtieth anniversary, at which Acting President MacIver granted honorary degrees to four émigré scholars who had come to the University in Exile in the 1930s and early 1940s: Max Ascoli, Arnold Brecht, Gerhard Colm, and Adolph Lowe. Over those last thirty years, Dean White noted proudly, the GF had awarded 1,033 graduate degrees in economics, philosophy, political science, psychology, and sociology. Now it was stronger than ever, having just enrolled 842 students in the fall semester of 1963, an increase of nearly 13 percent over the previous year. How would the GF evolve in the next thirty years? It would "probably change in size," the dean continued, "but little in purpose":

> Yet there must be changes other than that of size....
>
> Whatever science offers to strengthen or to modify a field of study, that field of study must accept and cooperate. We must see that we help to increase the output of qualified professionals in vital fields and they must be trained as professionals are trained. On the other hand, we hope that they will still maintain the humanistic tradition given to us by the University in Exile.[33]

During the next ten years, the New School doubled in size. Continuing Education, in particular, grew exponentially, enrolling thousands of students eager to study with the university's star-studded roster of scholars and artists. Others came looking for lighter fare, a fact that inspired cartoonists to poke affectionate fun at one of Manhattan's most beloved institutions. Highlighting the fact that 70 percent of the student body was female, *The New Yorker*'s Lee Lorenz exploited the tired theme of the unhappy housewife, which still passed as amusing at the time. In one of his cartoons, we see a woman stretched out on the couch in her psychoanalyst's office complaining about her husband:

> Whenever we have a problem, he tells me to take a course at the New School. So, I signed up for Advanced Creative Problem-Solving on Mondays, Alienation

and Affirmation on Tuesdays, Sexual Roles in Contemporary America on Wednesdays, Love, Humanity and Aggression on Thursdays. Then he asks me, "So what about Fridays?"[34]

The New Yorker also ran haute couture ads that mentioned the New School to give their fashion designers a little extra cachet. For husbands looking to purchase an extravagant gift for their wives over Christmas, Hattie Carnegie suggested a pair of Carole Lombard satin dinner pajamas from her Cinema III collection, "should your darling have herself involved in politics, working at the New School two nights a week and running the house as well."[35]

Although the New School welcomed the playful publicity, its own ads described Continuing Education as a magnet for adults interested in the burning cultural and political issues of the day, like the crowds who attended Max Lerner's lectures on foreign affairs—it registered over five hundred students every time the journalist gave the class—or those who filled the Twelfth Street auditorium on Sundays to listen to performances by Alexander Schneider and his celebrated Chamber Orchestra. It was this more serious image of the New School that attracted a seasoned academic leader to serve as the university's fifth president.

PART IV

"Between Past and Future"*

(1964–1982)

*I have borrowed the title for part IV from Hannah Arendt, *Between Past and Future* (New York: Viking Press, 1961).

16

THE "NEW" NEW SCHOOL

John (Jack) Everett became president of the New School on October 19, 1964. In the press release announcing his appointment, the trustees described the university's new leader in unadorned prose, avoiding the usual embellishments associated with communications of this kind. Their subdued tone might have slipped by unnoticed had they not added that Acting President Robert MacIver, the "noted political scientist," had agreed to stay on in "the newly-created office of chancellor." The New School, in other words, was taking no chances. Its distinguished friend and valued trustee would look after "long-term planning and development."[1]

A native of Oregon, Everett moved to New York after college to study for the ministry at the Union Theological Seminary and then for a doctorate in philosophy at Columbia University. After receiving his PhD in 1945, he spent five years teaching at Wesleyan College and Columbia, during which time he published two books on the impact theological ideas have had on society and culture (*Religion in Economics* and *Religion in Human Experience*). At Columbia, he also served as chairman of the Department of Philosophy in the School of General Studies.

In 1950, Everett left New York to accept the presidency of Hollins College, a small liberal arts institution for women in Roanoke, Virginia. Ten years later he returned to become the first chancellor of the City University of New York (CUNY). With Everett's appointment, five public colleges scattered across as many boroughs were brought together under a single leader and administrative structure, making it possible to create a graduate center for doctoral studies staffed primarily by colleagues affiliated with these previously independent institutions. Four of the five presidents of these municipal colleges vigorously opposed the merger. Everett lasted two years.[2]

The New School gave Everett much needed relief. Despite the lackluster announcement, the trustees welcomed him warmly and provided him with a cooperative and talented administrative team. In addition to MacIver, his new colleagues included the widely admired Albert Landa, whom the trustees had brought on as director of Public Relations when Henry David was president— Agnes de Lima had retired in 1959. Perhaps more than anyone else, Landa helped Everett turn a financially fragile university into a flourishing academic institution, with ongoing woes to be sure, but with a far more promising future. *The New York Times* predicted that people would remember "the Everett era" (1964–1982) as a major turning point in the history of this "maverick institution." During those years, the physical plant nearly tripled in size and the annual operating budget grew from $2 million to $40 million. Student enrollments more than doubled as well. As Robert Heilbroner described it to the *Times* reporter, Everett "caught the demographic wave and rode it like a surfboard."[3]

Even the Graduate Faculty was bursting at the seams, justifying the decision to move the GF out of its cramped quarters on Eleventh Street and into spacious new facilities on Fifth Avenue that extended the full length of a city block. The acquisition of 65 Fifth Avenue, previously the home of Lanes Department Store, remains one of the great New School stories.

With the new building, Everett hoped to achieve what Henry David had set out to do: turn the legendary University in Exile into a mainstream academic university, "a kind of M.I.T. in the social sciences," was the way he put it.[4] Looking back on those years, the Graduate Faculty's dean, Joseph Greenbaum, praised both men for forging ahead with their bold plans for the division despite stubborn efforts to resist them. David, he said, had "pushed the door open and Jack Everett opened it wide."[5]

During his eighteen years as president, Everett swung the doors open across the university. The Kaplan Center for New York City Affairs became the fully accredited Graduate School of Management and Urban Professions. Alvin Johnson's two-year undergraduate program, which had faded away, eventually became a four-year Seminar College. Finally, and most significantly, Everett took over Parsons School of Design, which was going bankrupt in 1970, and absorbed it into the New School—a risky gamble at the time but one that did more to secure the future of the university than any other decision he made.

Despite Everett's many accomplishments, he retired under a cloud. In May 1982, several weeks before he stepped down, Edward Fiske published a two-page article on the New School in *The New York Times* with the eye-catching headline,

"New School Facing Need to Rebuild with Approaching Change in Leaders."[6] In Everett's defense, he had more than his share of challenges during his years as president, many of them familiar to academic leaders throughout the country during the 1960s and 1970s.

By the late 1960s, the GF had earned a reputation for being a center of Marxist studies, in large part thanks to a dynamic new group of American social scientists who had recently joined the faculty and to visiting scholars from West Germany. The programs these colleagues built attracted students identified with the New Left.

In "*Democracy Is in the Streets*," historian James Miller traced the origins of the New Left to a 1962 gathering of young activists in Port Huron, Michigan. After several days of heated debate, the group of sixty succeeded in drafting *The Port Huron Statement*, calling for a new kind of politics described as participatory democracy. The manifesto, Miller continued, "inspired many of the students involved in the protests that shook America in the late Sixties," and it played a crucial role "in catapulting SDS [Students for a Democratic Society] to national prominence." By the end of the 1964–65 academic year—Everett's first as president of the New School—the mobilization "had mushroomed into a mass movement"[7] with representation at universities across the country, including at the New School.

In the spring of 1967, the New School's chapter of SDS called on Everett to cancel classes in solidarity with a nationwide protest planned for April 13 against the Vietnam War. Everett refused. The New School, he explained, would not take sides in a political controversy except "when that issue concerns academic freedom." It would remain, instead, "a free market place for ideas," welcoming views from the left and the right:

> This is not a new position for the New School. It is as old as the school itself. Through the years the New School has lost millions in endowments and has suffered accusations that run from pro-Communist to pro-Fascist, from libertarian to puritan, from hawk to dove, and from and to a host of other positions. The cost, and the confusion, is inevitable because we are wholly, deeply, and completely committed to the right of the human mind to be free.[8]

SDS was not persuaded. During the year leading up to the historic upheavals in the spring of 1968, it kept pressuring Everett to meet new demands; so did other radical groups on campus. As the student movement gained momentum, Greenbaum urged the president to resist the temptation to call in the police—a mistake other university presidents had begun to make. To support his argument, he sent Everett an editorial that had appeared in *Science* in March 1968 addressed sympathetically to "Beleaguered Presidents." Signed by the journal's publisher, Dael Wolfle, the editorial recommended that academic leaders use their universities' own disciplinary measures if student protests got out of hand.

According to Wolfle, students had "disrupted activities on 62 campuses" during the fall semester of 1967. Academic leaders who responded by calling in the police only made things worse. Those who held back "risked damage to property, possible injury to students, and public criticism," but they maintained the values that universities stood for. In the name of protecting "the academic freedom of students and faculty," presidents should follow their own institutions' "procedures for self-government" and avoid ringing the alarm.[9]

Everett heeded Greenbaum's advice for two more years, until the students staged "what must have been one of the longest sit-ins in history," as two faculty members proudly characterized it. Demonstrations began on May 1, 1970, the day after President Nixon announced that he had ordered U.S. troops to begin their invasion of Cambodia. At first Everett supported the students' right to protest. He even joined their demonstrations three days later, as did the leaders of other academic institutions, after members of Ohio's National Guard opened fire on students at Kent State University, killing four and wounding thirteen.

But by the end of the month, Everett had called in the police and authorized the arrest of nearly two dozen protesters, a decision he made with the endorsement of a handful of GF colleagues but against the vociferous opposition of many others. Two members of the GF were so outraged by what had happened that they published an article in *The New York Review of Books* describing the arrest and the events leading up to it in astonishing detail. The authors were Stanley Diamond and Edward Nell, department chairmen, respectively, of Anthropology and Economics.[10] Relative newcomers to the New School, the two men had ambitious plans for radicalizing the GF.

⟨⇒⟩

According to Diamond and Nell's account of the occupation, the students took over the GF building right after the massacre at Kent State. As they entered the lobby, they "called for a moratorium on routine university business, including classes, in order to muster the student body for antiwar activities, using the school as their headquarters." The protesters' steering committee described their political action as "a university strike against the war, not a strike against the university," a formulation that demonstrated, Diamond and Nell explained, how much the movement had matured over the last two years. Student activists no longer limited themselves to local concerns, as they had done in 1968. Now they were mobilizing against the Vietnam War, a cause that spoke to millions of people across all social classes and political constituencies at home and overseas. In an effort to build a mass movement, New School students turned the GF building into a gathering place for representatives of groups from around the city.

For the most part, Diamond and Nell conceded, the students failed. Construction workers rejected them with real hostility. Although the university's blue- and white-collar workers were more sympathetic, they too stayed away out of fear of losing their jobs. High school students, on the other hand, descended on the New School in droves. Word traveled fast: "If you want to keep cool, go to the beach or the New School." More than a thousand teenagers showed up for rallies and antiwar meetings when they should have been in class, leading critics to blame the New School for encouraging kids to play hooky. Diamond and Nell dismissed the accusation. Quoting figures published by the Board of Education, they reminded their readers that half of the city's high school students had stopped attending classes in early May in solidarity with a nationwide strike against the Vietnam War and the massacre at Kent State. Those who came to the New School during that period were the serious ones, intent on continuing their studies in the teach-ins taking place in the lobby of the GF building.

On the first day of the strike, professors at the GF circulated a statement "expressing solidarity with the students and calling for voluntary cancellation of classes," a position Everett supported as well. The president agreed to suspend all "normal school operations through May 9th." The attack on Kent State had threatened academic freedom, he proclaimed, and demanded a strong response from the New School.

For the students, however, that was still not enough. The steering committee wanted the moratorium to continue until the end of the semester, a demand that activists were making on other campuses as well. Everett said no but agreed to let the students use the GF lobby and a few offices in the building, provided that they did not disrupt classes and other academic activities taking place at the same time. The administration also agreed not to penalize students in the occupation for skipping classes, if, once again, they respected the rights of those who wanted to finish the semester.

During the second week of the strike, huge crowds continued to show up for the events the students were hosting in the GF lobby. And this made some members of the faculty very nervous, according to Diamond and Nell. When they invited the lawyer William Kunstler, head of the American Civil Liberties Union and hero of the student left, he drew such a big crowd that the audience spilled out of the building and onto Fifth Avenue. Kunstler, at the time, was appealing the convictions of five members of the Chicago Seven, the leaders of radical groups who had been arrested in the summer of 1968 for disrupting the Democratic National Convention.

Even Diamond and Nell had reservations about Kunstler—not out of fear, they hastened to add, but for ideological reasons. The lawyer, they claimed, did not understand the students: "Enthusiastic and in some respects, demagogic," Kunstler tried to persuade the crowd to take to the streets in the spirit of 1968. But the students were not interested. They had replaced violence with a broader, more peaceful strategy for achieving their political ends.

Those who had been following the news over the last several months, must have wondered how two professors teaching in Greenwich Village could have said a thing like that in June 1970, when three members of the Weather Underground had died and two others had been wounded in an explosion on March 6 that had taken place around the corner from the New School, in a townhouse on 11th Street, while the group was making bombs. In his book on student radicals, Miller described the Weather Underground as having been "the original spirit" of SDS.[11]

The few students who spoke to Diamond and Nell about Kunstler's speech reported that they liked having the civil liberties lawyer on their side, but they "did not seem impressed" by what he had to say. The only people who took Kunstler seriously, the authors tell us, were "conservative" members of the faculty who had fled Nazi-occupied Europe. Convinced that the strike was getting out of hand, these émigré professors encouraged Everett to call in the police: Later that week "faculty talk of a 'clean,' 'sanitary,' 'pre-emptive' bust began to be heard."

On Wednesday May 13, a four-piece rock band performed in the lobby for about an hour. They were loud, Diamond and Nell conceded, and the music "echoed around the university," but they were "competent," a view not shared by members of the "old New School," who described the musical event as having a "carnival or Woodstock atmosphere." For the émigré faculty the rock concert was the last straw, the "final indignity," but for Diamond and Nell it was the high point of the strike, marking the "moment when the New School was no longer the preserve of the faculty":

> Anarchy seemed to have broken loose. The conventional idea of the academy was essential to the psychic survival of the faculty at large. The school, it turned out, was not just their arena for routine and scholarly business; it was the central symbol of their lives. Students suddenly loomed as strangers. Familiar surroundings

disintegrated. The electronic noise of rock, neither understood nor anticipated, amplified their feelings of disorientation. For most of the faculty part of the time and part of the faculty most of the time, the New School had dissolved into a nightmare. The response was a furious demand for order.

By the next day, Everett too had had enough. He informed the students that the New School was going to close down the GF facilities temporarily to clean the building. The strikers would have to clear the premises. The students responded by taking over the registrar's office. Insisting on their right to "strike against the war and to use the university as a base in so doing," they would leave the office, they said, only after the New School had rescinded its threat to force them out of the building.

Everett gave the students until the evening of May 17 to leave. When they refused again, he extended the deadline to May 25. After which, Diamond and Nell reported, he called in the police who "launched a slow, civilized bust on the grounds of criminal trespass," arresting twenty-one students:

> As the students walked out of the building to the waiting vans, through a cordon of police under the puzzled eyes of the faculty, an authentically conservative political science professor wept. One distinguished philosopher in exile said to no one in particular, "Now we've got the building back."
>
> They've got the building, but the conflict over the character of the university is just beginning and the struggle for the soul of the country goes on. As for the student strikers, they are moving their antiwar committees, seminars and meetings out of the New School. This declaration of independence is a healthy thing and they have made their point. The Graduate Faculty of the New School was conceived in one crisis. Will it be reconceived in another?

Under the leadership of Diamond and Nell, Anthropology and Economics attracted veterans of the student movement to study at a Graduate Faculty radically reconceived. Other students came to study at what Diamond and Nell described disparagingly as the old New School, with the few remaining émigré professors on the faculty. Both groups looked forward to studying as well with younger German scholars who began teaching at the New School as visiting professors in the mid-1960s.

With the help of Hans Staudinger, Everett concluded negotiations in 1965 with the Volkswagen Foundation to create the Theodor Heuss Chair of the

Social Sciences, in memory of the first president of West Germany who had died in 1963. As *The New York Times* reported, this was "the first American professorship supported by a German foundation."[12] Volkswagen endowed the chair for five years, after which the federal government took over and has continued subsidizing it to the present day. Given the strong bonds of friendship between Heuss and members of the University in Exile, naming the chair after the first president of West Germany made the gift particularly meaningful.

The idea of establishing the chair evolved out of earlier exchanges of mutual recognition and appreciation. President Heuss took the first step in December 1954, when he offered Alvin Johnson West Germany's Grand Order of Merit.[13] Hans Simons reciprocated in 1958 by giving Heuss an honorary Doctorate of Humane Letters. In the formal citation, Simons celebrated their common history: "A distinguished German journalist, university professor, and public servant, [Heuss] like many members of the original Graduate Faculty of the New School, had been dismissed from his teaching post and driven from government by the Nazis in the early 1930s."[14]

Simons, Brecht, and Heuss had been colleagues in Berlin at the Deutsche Hochschule für Politik. Although they lost touch during the Hitler years, Heuss and Brecht renewed their close friendship after 1945. Another good friend was Kurt Riezler, as Heuss noted with emotion in 1958, when he came to the New School to receive his honorary doctorate. Riezler had died three years earlier.

From the very beginning, the Heuss professors included sociologists and philosophers who had studied critical theory in postwar Frankfurt with the original founders of the Institute of Social Research, among them Jürgen Habermas, who taught at the New School during the fall semester of 1967. Habermas, in those years, was helping to renew the legacy of the old Frankfurt School, together with other German theorists of his generation, focusing in particular on rekindling an interest in the early writings of Marx.

As Habermas described it, he came to the New School at a time of "turmoil in the United States. The nation's black ghettos were in full revolt, and hundreds of thousands of Americans of all races were demonstrating against the Vietnam War." This was the time, the critical theorist continued, when students were fleeing to Canada to avoid the draft and when Lyndon Johnson announced he would not run for president in 1968. This was also the time when the East Village was a "flourishing center of counterculture" and the Upper West Side, people warned him, was on the verge of decline. "But how different was the New School!"[15]

Habermas saw turmoil at the New School too, but what struck him more than anything else was the sense of going back in time. Having been raised in postwar West Germany, he felt as if he had entered a time warp where the "clocks were ticking somewhat differently." During that memorable semester at the GF, Habermas met Arnold Brecht, Erich Hula, Adolph Lowe, and Hans Staudinger, all of whom except Lowe had retired by then, an irrelevant detail for the young German philosopher because they were all very much around. The four men, he noted,

> still provided an immediate link with the University in Exile, with that early period when Emil Lederer, Eduard Heimann, Max Wertheimer, Hans Speier, Albert Salomon, and all the others had created the non-mistakable image of the New School. Moreover, Aron Gurwitsch, Hans Jonas, and Hannah Arendt formed that unique Triple Alliance that for a long time stamped the philosophical profile of the school. And finally, in the Sociology department, the spirit as well as the theory of Alfred Schütz was very much alive—due to the influential teaching of one of his former students, Peter Berger.

Habermas recalled meeting the émigré professors for the first time at a cocktail reception that Everett had organized in his honor. They were not very friendly at first, which "irritated" him. Only later, when he "had been warmly adopted by everybody," did Habermas understand that this "shadow of distrust did not apply to me personally, it pertained to an ambivalent past still present in vivid memories." The fact that Habermas came to the New School from "Horkheimer's and Adorno's Institute of Social Research" reminded them of the bitter arguments that took place in Manhattan during the Hitler years between members of the two groups of exiled scholars.

But memories of this "ambivalent past" were rapidly disappearing among the students. By the early 1970s the GF was attracting aspiring scholars who wanted to study Marx through the lens of critical theory. And as their numbers grew, confusion set in about the historic relationship between the Frankfurt Institute of Social Research and the New School for Social Research. Many members of the New Left generation assumed that Alvin Johnson had welcomed Horkheimer and Adorno to the University in Exile. A convenient error, perhaps, for those promoting the idea that the Graduate Faculty had long been a center of Marxist scholarship.

<hr />

In 1966, Arthur Vidich, the chair of Sociology, recruited Stanley Diamond to the GF. Before long the two men were fighting with one another so badly that Diamond seceded from Sociology and established his own Department of Critical Anthropology in 1970. Over the next several years he hired a group of young scholars whose work drew on Marxist and feminist theory: Shirley Lindenbaum, Rayna Rapp, William Roseberry, and Bob Scholte. In keeping with the times, he also recruited Michael Harner, who studied hallucinogenic substances in horticultural societies.

Economics hired Edward Nell in 1969 to serve as the new chair of the department and encouraged him to build a program in Marxist economics (political economy) to complement the department's historical strengths in German reform economics, Keynsian/post-Keynsian theory, and the history of economic thought. Thanks to Nell, the GF became one of the only graduate schools in the country where students could study economics from a Marxist-Leninist perspective. Although Nell himself continued to work in the post-Keynsian tradition, he recruited several young Marxist economists who had rejected the mainstream neoliberal paradigm after having been rigorously trained at Yale, Columbia, and Harvard. They included Anwar Shaikh and David Gordon.

Psychology added a new program as well, for reasons that had little to do with the rising popularity of Marxist studies but everything to do with the strains of late capitalism on the discipline. In 1974, Greenbaum created a separate track in clinical psychology because, he explained, New York State had introduced a rigorous new licensing protocol for psychologists who wanted to open a clinical practice. The protocol required training that the department did not yet offer. Had Psychology not complied, it would have lost most of its students. Before long more than half the candidates for degrees at the GF were studying psychology, and the vast majority of them were training to become clinicians. Although everyone understood that the GF could not survive financially without these students, colleagues complained bitterly that the clinical track was turning the department into a "trade school." Perhaps, Greenbaum conceded, but he held his ground.

By the mid-1970s, the departments of Philosophy, Political Science, and Sociology were in serious academic trouble because, many assumed, the émigré generation was disappearing. Diamond and Nell disagreed. As far as they were concerned, there were still too many émigrés around. The departments would be better off without them.

※

Who, precisely, did they have in mind? Diamond and Nell did not name names in the *The New York Review of Books*. They invited their readers to decide for themselves by publishing the names of forty-eight refugee scholars who came to the University in Exile during the Hitler years—reproducing the names engraved on a bronze plaque hanging in the lobby of the GF's new building. Although nine of these professors still appeared in the 1969–70 catalog, only Adolph Lowe had not yet retired; the others had already stepped down, in some cases long ago.[16] The names of three other émigré philosophers also appeared in the catalog on the list of full-time faculty, but they came to the New School after the war: Hannah Arendt, Aron Gurwitsch, and Hans Jonas.

Did Diamond and Nell have anyone else in mind? Over the years, the New School had appointed former students of the refugee scholars, two of whom were émigrés from Europe. But one was already gone by the time their article appeared in *The New York Review of Books*, and the other was on his way out. Thomas Luckmann left in 1965, and Peter Berger resigned in the spring of 1970. What sounded like an army of émigrés, in other words, consisted only of Arendt, Gurwitsch, Jonas, and Lowe.

According to Diamond and Nell, the émigrés analyzed everything through the lens of their Nazi experience. Traumatized by what they had lived through, they supposedly turned their backs on politics—on "Socratic engagement"— and embraced the "Platonic mystique of academic scholarship." And as they made their case for a certain detachment from worldly affairs, they distorted the Western philosophical canon, ignoring the work of other thinkers, like Marx, who called for political action. The time had come, Diamond and Nell proclaimed, to set the record straight, a task that also entailed liberating GF students from the émigrés' imperious manner in the classroom.

Diamond and Nell accused their European colleagues of not being able to empathize with the concerns of students of the Vietnam War generation the way they and other Americans on the faculty could. The GF, they explained, had recently hired a new and younger group of "internal émigrés" who tended

> to be politically radical, egalitarian, disenchanted with the aridity of academic practice, and involved in efforts to revitalize their disciplines and redefine their intellectual roles amid the inescapable crises of the times. If the older generation represents exile, these younger exiles represent engagement. Each in the name of freedom opposes the other. The old guard looks back to its political event; the younger is trying to establish one. Each lays claim to the birthright of the institution.

The most famous émigré scholar at the GF in the spring of 1970 was Hannah Arendt. Although she was on sabbatical that semester, Arendt attended the emergency meetings called in May to discuss the occupation. She had also been following the student movement very closely for the previous several years, in both the United States and Europe. Nobody at the GF was writing more than she about student activism and the impact of the Vietnam War on American politics and society, some of which had appeared in *The New York Review of Books*. Under the circumstances, readers must have assumed that Diamond and Nell were referring to Arendt when they drew their faceless portrait of the New School's émigré faculty. If Diamond and Nell had wanted them to think otherwise, they would have had to say so. They did not.

In later years, colleagues who lived through the student strike with Arendt and the other émigrés on the faculty have confirmed the obvious: the Europeans did not speak with one voice about student politics or anything else. Hans Jonas, for example, may have said things similar to what Diamond and Nell recorded in their article, but he did not represent the opinions of everyone else, least of all those of Arendt. In *Hannah Arendt: For Love of the World*, the philosopher's biographer Elisabeth Young-Bruehl reported that "Arendt was adamantly opposed to allowing police on the premises. To one of her émigré colleagues who favored a police 'bust,' she said: 'You forget, these are not criminals, these are our children.' " The colleague in question was Hans Jonas.[17]

Diamond and Nell also reported that an émigré economist worried that the students did not understand how dangerous the U.S. government might be for them individually and for the New School as an institution. Nell later attributed the comment to Lowe, adding that "Lowe thought that the students were right about the war, and about the necessity to undertake political action, but he thought that their course of action endangered the New School, and endangered their own future as well."[18] Given what had just happened at Kent State, Lowe's reaction does not sound like the paranoid fantasy of someone reliving a personal trauma from the deep Nazi past but a realistic assessment of what was going on in the United States at the time. Whether students should have taken the risk all the same is another matter.

⟺

During the 1960s and 1970s, Arendt wrote prolifically about the student movement and the scandals taking place in the Nixon administration. Several of these works were published around the time of the students' occupation of the Graduate Faculty. [19] In the days following the upheavals of 1968, Arendt expressed genuine enthusiasm for what the students were doing and she remained supportive, but with serious reservations.

After the events of May 1968 in Paris, Arendt reached out to Dany Cohn-Bendit, the celebrated leader of the French student movement, who was also the son of deceased friends of hers: "I want to say only two things: First, that I am quite sure that your parents, and especially your father, would be very pleased with you if they were alive now. Second, that should you run into trouble and perhaps need money, then we [Arendt and her husband Heinrich Blücher] and Chanan Klenbort will always be ready to help as far as it lies in our power to do so."[20] France's president Charles de Gaulle had just thrown the radical sociology student out of the country on the grounds that "Dany le rouge," was an undesirable foreigner—a decision that led to mass demonstrations with protesters chanting "We are all German Jews."

During the summer of 1970, Arendt gave an interview to the German writer Adelbert Reif. When asked, "Do you consider the student protest movement in general a historically positive process?" she replied: "I assume you mean, am I for it or against it. Well, I welcome some of the goals of the movement, especially in America, where I am better acquainted with them than elsewhere; toward others I take a neutral attitude, and some I consider dangerous nonsense."[21]

Arendt shared Diamond and Nell's belief that universities had to change. A week before the historic events in France, she fully endorsed the attempt by students at Columbia to close down the university's Institute for Defense Analysis, which was doing research for the U.S. government's war effort.[22] Arendt even conceded that students might have to resort to what she called political violence to advance significant short-term goals as they had already done, and effectively so.

When Arendt spoke of "political violence," she did not mean acts of physical violence only, the way Diamond and Nell did, but also unauthorized or illegal acts like the "peaceful" occupation of a university building. "France would not have received the most radical bill since Napoleon to change its antiquated education system if the French students had not rioted; if it had not been for the riots of the spring term [1968], no one at Columbia University would have dreamed of accepting reforms." The same strategy worked for "dissenting minorities" in West Germany. "Violence pays," she concluded, but not for achieving long-term goals. Just look at the historical record. She then turned to the current situation at American universities, adding provocatively:

> [Violence] pays indiscriminately, for "soul courses" and instruction in Swahili as well as for real reforms. And since the tactics of violence and disruption make sense only for short-term goals, it is even more likely, as was recently the case in the United States, that the established power will yield to nonsensical and obviously damaging demands—such as admitting students without the necessary qualifications and instructing them in nonexistent subjects.[23]

Arendt's high-handed way of dismissing "soul courses" and Swahili as "nonexistent subjects" must have infuriated Diamond and Nell, not to mention the way she described open-admissions policies at institutions such as the City University of New York (CUNY), where, beginning in the fall of 1970 every graduate of a New York City high school would be eligible to enter a college at CUNY. Arendt knew full well that these were fighting words, but she did not waver. Although she continued to endorse the student movement, she worried about the impact it would have on universities.

> [The student movement's] success with the Negro question is spectacular, and its success in the matter of the war is perhaps even greater. It was primarily the students who succeeded in dividing the country, and ended with a majority, or at all events a very strong, highly qualified minority, against the war. It could, however, very quickly come to ruin if it actually succeeded in destroying the universities—something I consider possible."[24]

Arendt delighted in seeing how student activists "discovered what the 18th century called 'public happiness,' which means that when man takes part in public life he opens up for himself a dimension of human experience that otherwise remains closed to him." She considered this aspect of the student movement "very positive." But by the summer of 1970, she warned that the movement was already being "eaten away by fanaticism, ideologies and a destructiveness that often borders on the criminal, on one side, by boredom on the other." The students lacked the skills they needed to be real revolutionaries. They did not have "an inkling of what power means" or how to use it. Nor did they have an analysis to guide them in the struggle that lay ahead, the way radicals in earlier movements had:

> To be sure, even then these analyses were mostly very inadequate, but the fact remains that they were made. In this respect I see absolutely no one, near or far, in a position to do this. The theoretical sterility and analytical dullness of this movement are just as striking and depressing as its joy in action is welcome. . . . In America, where on certain occasions it has brought out hundreds of thousands to demonstrate in Washington, the movement is in this respect, in its ability to act, most impressive! But the mental sterility is the same in both countries [West Germany and the United States].[25]

As far as Diamond and Nell were concerned, "theoretical sterility and analytic dullness" characterized the old guard, not the students. Why bother with concepts like power in the first place? The students occupying the GF lobby had no interest in power, they claimed, nor did they.[26]

Arthur Vidich described the student activists from a third perspective. Born and raised in the Midwest, this son of Slovenian immigrants sided neither with Diamond and Nell nor with the so-called émigré faction. Vidich, like Arendt, had been on leave during the spring of 1970, but he knew these students well because he had served on a faculty-student committee that Greenbaum had assembled the year before in response to a threat by a group of activists to "shut down the entire educational operation at the Graduate Faculty." In addition to advancing their national political agenda, the students wanted "more courses that were 'relevant' to their immediate interests, more Marx instead of Weber, more Gramsci instead of Simmel. They also demanded a complete transformation of the governing structure of the university as a matter of student rights, using the by-then familiar rhetoric of 'participatory democracy.' "[27] The faculty gave in to some of their demands but held firm on to such "traditional prerogatives," as making faculty appointments and other personnel decisions.

As Vidich remembered it, after the strike ended, the "student revolt at the New School lost momentum." In his memoir, he reported triumphantly that one student leader—he did not give his name—became the head of a national bank in Latin America; another, David Gilbert, joined the Weathermen, he noted soberly, and played a role "in the ill-fated 1981 Brinks armored-car robbery in Nyack, New York." But in the end, the sociologist concluded, the New School's problems during the 1970s had less to do with the demands student radicals were making than it did with the conflicting goals of members of the faculty about the future of the GF. Although he had hired Diamond, Vidich had little sympathy for his and Nell's plans for the "new New School," and even less for what remained of the "old." Striking out on his own, he tried to rebuild the Department of Sociology in his own idiosyncratic image.

When we listen to the students themselves, many of them describe their years at the New School as an extraordinary intellectual and political adventure. For those on the left, the GF was one of the very few places in the United States where they could go to study orthodox Marxism and critical theory seriously, *even* in a department of economics! Robert Pollin, for example, remembered taking a course with the Marxist economist Paul Sweezy in the winter of 1975, which in his eyes was like "taking a course on the civil war with Abraham Lincoln":

There was a fever pitch at the New School when the course began. On the first day, probably 400 people or so showed up, and you couldn't get into the room. The next class, you had to show your proof of enrollment . . . as another 400 showed up. However, things calmed down very quickly once we really got into things. Paul was an amazingly clear and committed teacher. But he definitely wasn't into any kind of theatre of teaching or histrionics. So the course rapidly thinned down to 30–40 people who really wanted to hear Paul expound on Marx.[28]

The New School's program in economics was very different from what Pollin would have found in a mainstream department.[29] That was what made it attractive. To begin with, it welcomed students like him who had no prior background in the field. It also encouraged interdisciplinary work. During his first semester, Pollin wrote a paper for David Gordon from a "world systems" perspective, applying the ideas of the historical sociologist Immanuel Wallerstein to explain social and economic change.[30] The next semester, he studied with Robert Heilbroner and Anwar Shaikh, who introduced him to ideas and methodological approaches to the field rarely taught in economics departments elsewhere in the United States.

Reminiscing about his time at the New School, Pollin described Gordon and Shaikh as the "leading lights" on the full-time faculty. Although they both called themselves Marxists, they taught economics in very different ways. Gordon, Pollin said, did not let his students turn their backs on mainstream approaches to the discipline. If radical leftists wanted to challenge neoliberal economics in a meaningful way, they would have to master the statistical tools of the prevailing paradigm. Shaikh, on the other hand, urged his students to focus on Marx and his disciples. As Pollin summarized it, Gordon trained his students to make "statistics sing." They had to learn how to apply the methodologies of econometric modeling, for example, to demonstrate why the conclusions mainstream economists drew from their data were wrong, not only by the logic of Marxism but by the logic of neoliberalism as well. Shaikh, on the other hand, wanted his students to learn how to "quantify Marx." First, they had to "nail down" the theory. Then, working within the logic of the system, they had to find ways to address problems not anticipated by Marx that occurred in late capitalism. One important way to do this, Shaikh argued, was to adjust the theory through "the transformation of the Labor Theory of Value to Price."[31]

Most students took sides, Pollin continued, but he wanted to learn from both of them. Those who lined up behind Shaikh were the "heavy theorists, the really smart guys." They had little patience for anyone who rejected the possibility of adjusting Marx's theory to explain late capitalism. Those who preferred Gordon wanted to solve concrete economic problems in the late twentieth century. They were the "politicos" who analyzed questions of class, race, and gender from a Marxist perspective while turning the neoliberal paradigm on its head.

Pollin expected to do his dissertation with Shaikh, but ended up working with Gordon on the "financialization of corporations." He got the idea for his thesis after reading an article in *The Monthly Review* by Harry Magdoff and Paul Sweezy, where the authors complained that nobody on the left was paying serious attention to finance and the financial markets. Gordon, he discovered, had reached the same conclusion and agreed to work with him. Today, Pollin is Distinguished Professor of Economics at the University of Massachusetts, Amherst, and codirector of the Political Economy Research Institute (PERI), which was modeled, he says, on the New School's Schwartz Center for Economic Policy Analysis. He is also the founder and president of PEAR (Pollin Energy and Retrofits), a green energy company operating throughout the United States. In his own research, Pollin has contributed to policy debates about the importance of creating a living wage and the urgency of "greening" the global economy.[32]

Another enthusiastic student was Jean Cohen. She came to the GF to study sociology in the fall of 1970, arriving the semester after the student uprising. As Cohen remembers it, "the political scene among the organized students was very orthodox, ultra-leftist." Most of them belonged either to the Progressive Labor Party (PL) or one of several Maoist factions. There were feminist groups as well, who had broken away from the male-dominated radical groups and from the equally sexist moderates, such as Citizens for Local Democracy, the group Arendt was sponsoring.

Although the ultra-leftists made a lot of noise, they congregated in Economics and Anthropology, making it easy, Cohen said, to ignore them. The other departments also had their share of political activists, but they did not dominate class discussions. Prominent among them was a group of exiled students from the Shah's Iran. Cohen identified with the left as well, but she had little interest in Marxist-Leninism or Maoism. She came to the New School after leaving a job in publishing to study "class relations, labor relations, and politics." Having participated in a failed campaign to unionize Random House, she wanted to understand why people voted against their own self-interest:

> It was at the New School that I encountered critical theory and began to study Marx (in study groups). I had been active on the New Left and in the Civil Rights movement, protesting against racism in Boston and the Vietnam War, but had not been involved with critical theory or Marxism.

By the early 1970s, the GF had become "the center of classical critical theory in the U.S." largely thanks, Cohen continued, to visiting professors from Germany, such as Albrecht Wellmer, who arrived several years after Jürgen Habermas. Courses on critical theory were always packed—"you can't imagine the scene," Cohen recalled, adding that people from Columbia, NYU, and other universities around the city registered for them as well. The classes attracted students who were working in philosophy, sociology, and the arts.[33]

As Cohen described the appeal of the GF, she admitted that it was "odd." With the exception of a few Marxist professors in Economics and Anthropology, the full-time faculty were neither orthodox leftists nor critical theorists. But the GF welcomed visiting scholars who shared the political and intellectual interests of the students. It was "completely open." Then once the students arrived, they began to branch out and take courses in continental philosophy and European political and sociological theory offered by members of the full-time faculty. Like Marxism and critical theory, these other philosophical traditions were rarely taught at universities in the United States.

Cohen enjoyed studying with the GF's émigré professors in Philosophy—Hannah Arendt, Aron Gurwitsch, Hans Jonas. She never took a course in Economics with Adolph Lowe, but she did with the exiled professor's star student Robert Heilbroner. Even though she often disagreed with their politics, Cohen found their courses intellectually demanding and very exciting. They were exceptional scholars.

In addition to the three émigré philosophers, the scholars who influenced Cohen the most were the visiting professors from Germany, in particular Albrecht Wellmer, who introduced her to critical theory; and Heinrich Popitz and Wolfgang Schluchter, who led her back to Max Weber. Together with the American sociologist Benjamin Nelson, Popitz and Schluchter taught Cohen how to read the work of the great German sociologist in ways unimaginable during the 1970s at other universities in the United States. Most Americans at the time had been studying Weber through the eyes of Talcott Parsons, Harvard's leading sociologist, whose conservative interpretation of the German's ideas had persuaded left-leaning intellectuals of Cohen's generation to turn their backs on one of the most important theorists of the late nineteenth and early twentieth centuries. Thanks to Nelson, Popitz, and Scluchter, Cohen discovered a different Max Weber and a rich body of literature that suggested the possibility of a "Marx-Weber synthesis."

Looking back on her student years at the GF, Cohen noted with gratitude that this unique educational experience helped her develop the theoretical framework she used in her book *Civil Society and Political Theory*, coauthored with her husband Andrew Arato, which quickly became a foundational text for scholars writing on democratic theory and on transitions to democracy in the years following the downfall of communism in East and Central Europe.[34] Today, Cohen is the Nell and Herbert M. Singer Professor of Political Science and Contemporary Civilization at Columbia University.

⫸⫷

During Cohen's second semester at the GF, *Social Research* published an issue on "Critical Issues on the Social Sciences" (winter 1971), with articles by Jürgen Habermas, among other leading philosophers and political theorists of the day.[35] The journal had just changed hands and its new editor, Arien Mack, was very interested in precisely the kinds of questions that made the GF exciting for students like Cohen. Trained in philosophy and cognitive psychology, Mack joined the Department of Psychology in 1966, where she taught and conducted laboratory research on the processes underlying human visual perceptions. Mack is best known for having discovered, with her colleague Irvin Rock, the curious phenomenon of failing "to see what is before our open eyes." They called this phenomenon "inattentional blindness."[36]

While Mack was using *Social Research* to shake things up in the social sciences and philosophy, some of her older émigré colleagues were digging in their heels. Although Diamond and Nell had oversimplified the problem, several members of the faculty were indeed resisting change and mobilizing their students to do the same. Prominent among them was Aron Gurwitsch, who wanted the Department of Philosophy to limit itself to the study of phenomenology. With that goal in mind, he did everything in his power to block appointments of critical theorists, pragmatists, and analytical philosophers, even as visiting professors. When Habermas, for example, came to the GF as a Heuss Professor in 1967, Sociology, not Philosophy, hosted him. In the spring of that year, Gurwitsch actively campaigned against the candidacy of Arendt, even though she had studied with the great Martin Heidegger. Arendt, he complained, had not remained faithful to her teacher's orthodox approach to phenomenology. When the department forwarded a split vote to the dean on her candidacy, Greenbaum overruled Gurwitsch and his faction and hired Arendt all the same.[37]

After joining the department, Arendt tried to persuade her colleagues to recruit faculty with varied approaches to philosophy.[38] In 1972, she suggested they hire Richard Bernstein, a scholar of American pragmatism, whose book *Praxis and Action* had impressed her a great deal. Indulging their new colleague, the department invited Bernstein to give a talk, after which they delivered a split vote to the dean just as they had for Arendt five years earlier. This time, how-ever, Greenbaum sided with Gurwitsch and his faction. In a letter to Bernstein, Arendt tried to soften the blow by dismissing what had happened as typical of the way academics responded to new and original ideas:

> I don't think that the opposition is due to Byzantine intrigues—if there were intrigues, they certainly weren't Byzantine. The reason as I see it is very simple. I just reread your book [*Praxis and Action*] which I also use for a discussion of Marx in [my] seminar and I was again struck by the freshness and originality of your thought. The first reaction of the academic milieu to somebody who quite obviously strikes out on his own is always negative, and a number of doctoral students, though not all, are already quite fixed in their thought habits, and react the same way as the faculty. Glenn Gray was here who, as you probably know is a friend and an admirer of yours and very much in favor of this appointment. He told me that he found among the general reaction to your work either great enthusiasm or a certain hostility. I know the situation very well because I was for a very long time the object of similar reactions. And I must say that I find this only natural. One shouldn't get bitter about it and one should not acquire per-secution complexes. All academic thinking, whether right, left, or middle is con-servative in the extreme. Nobody wants to hear what he hasn't heard before.[39]

During the heyday of the Everett era, classes were packed in academic programs across the university, but most astonishingly at the GF, which had always had the most trouble attracting students. In 1972, the GF reported registering ten thousand students; in 1962 the number was 2,661.[40] Although the New School offered little in the way of financial aid to graduate students, the cost of tuition had always been comparatively low ($85 a credit in 1972), making it more afford-able than other graduate programs. It also had a very lenient admissions policy, accepting virtually everyone who applied. And now, more recently, its academic programs had taken a radical turn to the left, at a time when student activists were entering graduate school in record numbers. Thanks to these high enroll-ments, Greenbaum was able to persuade Everett to let him hire more faculty and to move the GF into a building of its own, where finally, the dean predicted, they would succeed in turning the old University in Exile into a modern, American-style graduate school.

Greenbaum was particularly eager to strengthen the academic programs at the GF by appointing social scientists who did empirical research of the kind that federal agencies funded. When colleagues received money from the U.S. government, their awards usually included financial support for graduate students, thereby providing additional scholarships for GF students. Federal grants also provided money to the university's administration to help cover overhead costs related to the faculty member's research, some of which went directly to the dean. Greenbaum planned to skim off part of his cut to offer additional scholarships to students specializing in disciplines such as philosophy, where the faculty did not do fundable research. Even though tuition was comparatively low, the GF would never be able to attract top students if it could not compete for them with other graduate schools by providing generous fellowships.

If Hans Simons had invested in the Institute of World Affairs, perhaps colleagues at the GF would have started applying for research grants in the 1950s as social scientists at other universities were doing. But he did not. Given the other challenges he faced at the time, Simons accepted Arthur Swift's unfortunate recommendation to close the institute down. By the time Greenbaum joined the faculty in 1957, he found himself surrounded by colleagues who had never considered the possibility of applying for grants to support their research and were openly hostile to those who did.

Before leaving Wesleyan College for the New School, Greenbaum had received a grant for $25,000 from the Ford Foundation to subsidize the work he was doing with a colleague at Swarthmore on the psychological impact on Hungarians of the 1956 uprising. When Greenbaum told Simons and members of the Department of Psychology that he wanted to transfer the money to the New School, they refused to accept it. They "did not want outside money that they could not control" going to individual members of the faculty. And so the grant went to Swarthmore.

According to the GF's catalog, when Greenbaum came to the New School, the division had about twenty faculty members, spread thinly across five departments. And these included President Simons and three retired colleagues, none of whom taught very much, if at all. The catalog also listed about thirty visiting or part-time instructors, teaching fellows, for the most part, who were finishing their degrees, but also a few recognized scholars, like the noted phenomenologist Dorion Cairns and Gestalt psychologists Rudolf Arnheim and Solomon Asch, Max Wertheimer's distinguished disciples.[41]

Members of the full-time faculty were expected to teach seven courses a year, six at the Graduate Faculty and one in Continuing Education. When Greenbaum became chairman of the psychology department in 1960, he dropped the course load requirement to five and eliminated the obligation that his colleagues teach in Continuing Education. Six years later, when Everett appointed him dean of the Graduate Faculty, Greenbaum reduced the workload for everyone across the division. He also tried to persuade Everett to let the GF teach graduate students exclusively, but the president said no. Master's-level classes remained open to everyone at the university.

Despite the occasional slap on the wrist, Greenbaum succeeded in gaining more autonomy for the GF than it had ever enjoyed before. This, he learned, was a mixed blessing. As Everett let Greenbaum go his own way, he encouraged the other deans to do the same, setting into motion a proliferation of new degree-granting programs across the university, staffed with part-time instructors who earned a fraction of what Greebaum paid his faculty at the GF. Before long, the deans of the undergraduate Seminar College and the new Graduate School of Urban Management and Policy were hiring full-time faculty as well—once again on the cheap, taking advantage of the glut of newly minted PhDs on the job market, many of whom had little choice but to accept contracts that paid poorly and offered no prospect of tenure.

As Greenbaum watched the number of these degree programs expand in the other academic divisions, he saw the writing on the wall. It would only be a matter of time before the trustees hired another consultant like Earl James McGrath who would recommend doing away with an autonomous Graduate Faculty. The idea of preserving the descendant of the University in Exile might still resonate with a few old-timers on the board, but the New School was doing a brilliant job of demonstrating that it could run respectable academic programs without investing heavily in costly faculty who did little for the rest of the institution.

In an effort to change its image and give the GF a dignified new role at the New School, Greenbaum suggested that the university create joint BA/MA programs in collaboration with the dean of the Seminar College. Accelerated five-year programs like these were popular at academic institutions around the country, why not at the New School? Everyone, he hoped, would embrace the idea with enthusiasm. But nobody did, not even Everett. Accepting defeat, he intensified his efforts to make the Graduate Faculty indispensable to the New School by packing classes with as many students as possible. By the late 1960s, the GF was bursting at the seams, persuading everyone that it needed new facilities.

⟨◆⟩

To find an affordable piece of property near the New School's campus for the Graduate Faculty was not going to be easy, even for a talented fund-raiser like

Everett. The task required the skills of a magician, someone in the same league with Alvin Johnson. Although the president emeritus was still alive in 1967, he had finally retired from active duty.

Albert Landa took Johnson's place. He had just the right mix of ingenuity and daring. Hired by the trustees to help Henry David, Landa earned everyone's admiration early on when he increased the number of Continuing Education students by the thousands with a new marketing plan that made it possible for busy adults to register through the mail. In the weeks leading up to a new semester, Landa published a supplement in the *The New York Times* that listed all the courses for the coming term and provided a detachable form for interested students to fill out and mail back to the New School. The first time he published the supplement it yielded six thousand responses. And those numbers kept climbing by 10 to 15 percent every year. After David resigned, the trustees asked Landa to stay on and work with Johnson and Staudinger on the New School's endowment campaign—an assignment Landa embraced enthusiastically. It was his idea to feature Johnson in their promotional materials as "the grand old man of adult education."[42] When Everett became president in 1964, he promoted the New School's director of Public Affairs and Information to vice president.

Everett was a hands-off kind of president, a style that suited Landa perfectly. With the blessings of his boss, Landa worked closely with the deans, several of whom turned out to be gifted fund-raisers. Greenbaum was not among them. By his own admission, the dean of the GF spent his time generating income for the New School by registering more students than the GF ever had before and by helping faculty win national research grants that yielded overhead funds for the university. As Greenbaum saw it, his job was to create the demand for a new building. He happily left the rest to Landa.

⸺⬦⸺

In 1967, the U.S. Office of Education, under the auspices of the Higher Education Facilities Act, invited academic institutions to apply for federal grants and loans of up to $5 million to help them build new facilities or renovate the ones they had. Successful applications would receive a gift of $1 million up front and a loan for another $4 million at very favorable interest rates. Landa wanted the New School to take advantage of this great opportunity.

The university owned two brownstones next to the Twelfth Street building. Several members of the administration wanted Everett to tear these houses down and replace them with a new seven-storey building. Landa warned his colleagues that the plan would never gain approval from New York City's Landmarks

Preservation Commission, a new city agency established in 1965 to protect historic buildings like these from urban renewal. Although he failed to persuade them to drop the idea right away, Landa convinced Everett to hire a real estate firm to see if the New School could identify another piece of property in the neighborhood that it could afford to purchase. When the firm came up with nothing, Landa objected. Why not take over the lease of Lanes Department Store on Fifth Avenue? To push the clothing store out was not going be easy, but surely it was worth a try. Landa suggested the idea to Vera List's husband, who took it from there.

Albert List was the kind of self-made man New Yorkers enjoyed reading about. In 1986, *The New York Times* described how this child of Romanian Jewish immigrants made his fortune. Born in 1901, he had to leave high school at the age of sixteen to help run the family's small grocery store in the Bronx, and he never went back to school. By the time List was thirty-six, he had become a very rich man. Twenty years later he "gained control of the Glen Alden and later the Hudson Coal Company, the principal hard-coal producers of the United States, turning them into a conglomerate that included the 47-theater RKO chain." As his fortune grew, so did his desire to give back to society, particularly to educational, medical, and artistic institutions. "What are you put on earth for, anyway?" asked List rhetorically in 1965. "To be productive—for yourself until you've got everything money can buy. After that it belongs to humanity."[43] The New School benefited in countless ways from Albert and Vera List's philanthropic philosophy.[44]

Without minimizing the value of their many other contributions, nothing quite matches the role List played in acquiring 65 Fifth Avenue for the New School. As Landa tells the story, one day he went to see List on university business that had nothing to do with the new building. List was finishing up a meeting with Meshulam Riklis, a controversial figure in the real estate world. Among the many properties Riklis managed was the lease for Lanes Department Store. The coincidence did not escape Landa.

When Landa got back to the New School, he tried to reach Everett, but the president was busy. Unwilling to wait, Landa broke protocol. Without speaking first to his boss, he called List and asked him to speak to Riklis on behalf of the New School. After a long pause, List hammered Landa with questions: "Why do you ask? Do you really need the building? Can you cover the cost? Do you have the students?" Landa told List about the government's invitation for proposals, about the huge increase in the number of graduate students at the GF, and about the doomed idea the university had of tearing down the townhouses on Twelfth Street. If the New School got the building at 65 Fifth Avenue, their problems would be solved. But only if they moved quickly—the deadline for submitting the application to Washington was rapidly approaching.

"Will you be in your office for a while?" Yes, Landa assured him, he would.

Four hours later: "Albert, it's done." Although Landa was short on details, we do know that List spoke not only to Riklis but also to Arthur Cohen, the owner of the property. When the *New School Bulletin* announced the good news in October 1967, the article explained that the university had "been aided . . . by the efforts of the Albert A. List Foundation and New York businessmen Meshulam Riklis and Arthur Cohen." Legend has it that List persuaded Cohen to "sell" both the land and the building to the New School for a dollar.[45]

After List called Landa, the vice president thanked him profusely, of course, but he still had a big problem on his hands. As part of the application, the New School had to enclose a check for $500,000 to demonstrate that it had funds of its own to invest in the project. After what List had just done for the university, Landa knew better than to ask him to write the check. But time was running out. The architects had delivered their plans for renovating the building. Landa had a good working draft of the proposal, but he still needed $500,000 in cash.

Two days before the deadline, Landa was in his office putting final touches on the proposal when Stella Sweeting Fogelman, the widow of Raymond Fogelman, a successful textile manufacturer and generous friend of the New School, knocked on his door. Mrs. Fogelman told Landa that she wanted to make a substantial gift in her husband's memory, perhaps endow a professorial chair, unless Landa had another suggestion. Indeed he did, he told her. If she wrote a check right away for $500,000—the going price for an endowed chair at the time—the New School would name its new library after her late husband. She loved the idea and pulled out her checkbook. The next day Landa sent his assistant to Washington to deliver the application in person.

Once again Landa acted alone, without speaking to Everett or to the trustees, several of whom accused him of throwing away a major naming opportunity for too little money. No he had not, Landa objected, Stellla Fogelman's gift in cash for $500,000 had made the New School eligible for a $1 million gift and a low-interest loan for $4 million.

Despite the booming enrollments, the GF continued to lose money, and increasingly so after 1969 when the new building opened. The cost of maintaining the facilities came out of the GF's budget. Although everyone understood that graduate programs always lost money, other universities could cover the deficit with the profits they made on their undergraduate colleges and professional schools. The New School had no comparable unit on which to rely. The Seminar College was still limping along; other programs were doing better, but none made enough money to support the GF without imposing austerity measures on themselves, which they complained about doing, particularly for the GF, given how little their privileged colleagues did for the rest of the university. The situation was not sustainable without finding a new source of income.

During the spring of 1970, Landa received a call from Harold Oram, a man he had known for years. Oram was New York's "Number One liberal fund-raiser." He came out of the labor movement, Landa explained, "and knew how to organize." The Parsons School of Design had just hired him as a consultant.[46]

"What do you know about Parsons?" Oram asked, in his characteristically raspy voice. "Not much, Landa replied. "I've seen their ads—something to do with fashion." They were also leaders in interior and graphic design, Oram added. Then he got down to business:

> What if I told you that in two days the Parsons board would hold its last meeting to dissolve the school? What would you say?
>
> Harold, I don't know enough to say anything about it. How many students?
>
> Four hundred. All full-time.
>
> If they have 400 full-time students, they must be paying some decent tuition. I'd have to say that I'd be surprised to hear that the school was going to be dissolved. What's the score?

Oram explained that Parsons had been relying almost entirely on the generosity of one donor, who had also been serving as chairman of the board. The man was Arthur Houghton, the owner of Steuben Glass. When Houghton became chairman of the board at the Metropolitan Museum of Art, he started cutting back on his support of Parsons. Landa rejected that explanation: "The problem is always the president, the CEO." Parsons's president, Landa subsequently learned, was "a very nice guy, Francis Ruzicka, but. . . ."

After they talked for a little while longer, Landa said to Oram: "There's a board meeting in two days. What the hell can we do?"

> Well we would still like to talk to you. Maybe the New School could give money.
>
> Forget it Harold. We're not rich. Also, President Everett is in Mexico and cannot be reached. He won't be back until next week, and this is not a decision that anyone but he could make. . . . If [Parsons's board] agrees to cancel the meeting, and not just for a few days, because if we get interested, we're going to

have to look into things. . . . It's a 100 to one shot. I'll pull together who I can from here, and we'll meet together with a group from your school. Call me back if they cancel the meeting.

Oram called back that same afternoon. "Of course, they canceled the board meeting," Landa said smiling. When the two schools met a couple of weeks later, the president of the New School did not attend. He asked Allen Austill, dean of Continuing Education and his old friend Harold Gideonse, whom he had made chancellor, to accompany Vice President Landa. Parsons sent members of the board, the president, Oram, and "a young administrator in his 20's whose name was David Levy, director of student recruitment and fundraising."

Landa ran the meeting:

I had a list of questions. Every time they answered, a cash register exploded in my head: Parsons charged $4,000–$5,000 less in tuition than its competition. It was the best school in the country in interior design, fashion design, and the graphic arts. So why did they charge so little?

Parsons' president explained, "Because our first interest is in the students." For years they had been able to maintain this bargain-basement price thanks to Houghton's generous support, but those days were over. Parsons now had "a deficit of $300,000, which was nothing even then," Landa noted, "but they couldn't raise the money." Even after spending $35,000 the previous year on a fund-raising drive, they only collected $9,000 in donations.

Before the meeting ended, Landa had convinced himself that the New School should take over Parsons. It would cost them almost nothing. All Everett would have to do was find a good dean, and they already had a promising candidate: Parsons's own David Levy.

Landa's heart was pounding. He wanted to move quickly, but neither Austill nor Gideonse showed any interest. Austill cautioned, "We have too much on our plate." Gideonse agreed, adding, "It's a trade school. What do we want with a trade school?" Landa reminded his colleagues that the New School had been looking into the possibility of developing courses similar to the ones Parsons offered, without having the benefit of the design school's name. This was not even a new idea. It dated back to the early 1920s when Johnson became director of the New School and expanded the curriculum to include the fine and applied arts. Johnson did it then without compromising the mission of the institution. Everett could do it now.

Landa worried that Everett might side with Austill and Gideonse if he did not get to him first. After all, it was two against one. Expecting the worst, he made his argument carefully, trying to anticipate every possible objection. But he had nothing to worry about. Everett jumped at the idea: "Get those schmucks in to see me immediately," he ordered. The merger "was accomplished within weeks."

In 1972, the New School acquired two more buildings on Lower Fifth Avenue, just across the street from the Graduate Faculty. They had belonged to Mills College of Education, a well-regarded school that had run into financial and academic difficulty, according to the official story reported in the press, but there was also talk off the record of a scandal. The article in *The New York Times* praised Mills College for its "pioneering work in early childhood education" over the last sixty-three years. Then during the spring, the journalist continued, New York State's Department of Education revoked the right of this venerable institution "to offer degree programs on the ground that they did not meet minimal standards." The decision led the president of Mills College to retire, after which the board of trustees let the faculty go and made arrangements for their students to take liberal arts courses at the New School and education at NYU. Looking ahead, the trustees told the *Times* that they hoped the college would "become a subdivision of the New School." The paper also reported that the "New School has agreed to take over certain of Mills's assets and liabilities, including mortgage charges on the college's two buildings at 66 and 70 Fifth Avenue. . . . One of the buildings will be used this fall by the Parsons School of Design, a New School affiliate."[47] Until then Parsons had remained in its old facilities in midtown.

The New School decided against making Mills College a "subdivision" of the university, but it kept the buildings, expanding its campus beyond anyone's imagination. Had Everett stepped down at that point, or shortly thereafter, he would have gone down in history as the New School's most successful president after Johnson. But he stayed on for another ten years, during which time the Department of Education of the State of New York threatened to close down three departments at the Graduate Faculty for reasons similar to the ones it had given in 1972 for revoking the right of Mills College to grant degrees in education.

17

THREE DOCTORAL PROGRAMS AT RISK

Between 1976 and 1978, the Commission of Higher Education of the State of New York threatened to close down the departments of Philosophy, Political Science, and Sociology at the Graduate Faculty, the academic stronghold of what Stanley Diamond and Edward Nell had described disparagingly as the "old New School." By this time, the émigré generation had virtually disappeared from the full-time faculty, but the intellectual legacy of the University in Exile lingered on in ways that made the three departments more vulnerable than they previously had been.

Philosophy, in particular, had recently suffered heavy losses: Aron Gurwitsch died in 1973[1] and Hannah Arendt in 1975. Then Hans Jonas retired in 1976, after which he refused to have anything more to do with the university. Although he remained active professionally, he turned his back on the New School because, he complained, the institution had treated him shabbily.[2]

John Everett was not sorry to see the émigrés retire. Although he did not share Diamond and Nell's disdain for the philosophical inclinations of their European colleagues, the University in Exile, he agreed, had run its course, at least in the classroom. Fund-raising was another matter. Since Alvin Johnson's heroic achievement still inspired individual donors and philanthropic organizations, Everett would do his best to keep the story alive. If he had any doubts about this when he first arrived in 1964, they disappeared after the Volkswagen Foundation established the Theodor Heuss Professor chair. Everett marked that occasion by giving Willy Brandt, the Mayor of West Berlin, an honorary doctorate.

Eight years later, when the New School celebrated the fortieth anniversary of the University in Exile, Everett recognized Willy Brandt again, no longer as mayor, but as chancellor of the Federal Republic of Germany. This time Everett gave Brandt a copy of the University in Exile's Founders Medal, newly minted in 1973. Engraved on a silver disc, the medal reproduced the New School's motto, "To the Living Spirit" that the university had adopted in 1937, at the suggestion of Thomas Mann, one year after the Nazis defaced an inscription with those words that once graced the entrance of a building at the University of Heidelberg. As *The New York Times* reported, Everett also gave copies of the medal to two founding members of the University in Exile, Arnold Brecht and Hans Staudinger, and to New School trustee Rodman Rockefeller in gratitude for the role his family had played in saving the lives of hundreds of refugee scholars during the Hitler years. When Joseph Greenbaum gave his speech, he paid tribute to several other émigré scholars sitting in the audience who had come to the New School during the 1930s and early 1940s—Hans Speier, Adolph Lowe, Alfred Kähler, and Erich Hula—and to the omnipresent Horace Kallen. Sorely missed, *The Times* added, on this joyous occasion, was the New School's first president. Alvin Johnson had passed away in 1971 at the age of ninety-six.[3]

Dean Greenbaum invited Robert Heilbroner to speak as well about his student days after the war at "Heidelberg on Twelfth Street":

> The University in Exile had no building of its own. I'm not even certain if it had rooms of its own. We seemed to meet in nooks and crannies of the then only building of The New School. . . . Yet, that crowded and inconvenient and in some ways casual school, was surely for me and the other students who jammed into its rooms, an incomparable educational experience, and the reason was, of course, the faculty. . . .
>
> Today the Graduate Faculty has [a] spacious building [and] many fewer European accents. Yet I think that something of the old spirit remains, not alone in a continuing dedication of the unity of social knowledge, the transnational reach of ideas, but in an awareness of the dangers as well as the delights of education; in an awareness that education is and should be a perilous adventure.[4]

Education was indeed "a perilous adventure" in 1973, but not for the reasons Heilbroner had alluded to in his speech. Two years later Arendt told Richard Bernstein that she feared that the GF was going to close down the Department of Philosophy: "The last conversation I had with Hannah Arendt was in the spring before she died. She kept returning to the same theme. She was very disturbed about the New School. She was convinced that they were trying to give Philosophy up and she felt this would be a terrible mistake."[5]

⟹

Arendt had reason to worry, as did her colleagues in Political Science and Sociology. By 1971, New York's Department of Education had already announced its plan to evaluate every doctoral program in the state—in both public and private universities—with the explicit intention of weeding out the weaker programs. The job market could no longer absorb the large number of graduates pouring out of institutions of higher learning every year. And that number was increasing rapidly, in part thanks to the success of one of Nelson Rockefeller's greatest achievements as governor: the creation of a statewide university system. When Rockefeller took office in 1959, he inherited twenty-nine public colleges and universities scattered across the state, some of them little more than normal schools and technical colleges. By the time he stepped down in 1973, he had built one of the largest public university systems in the country, with seventy-two different campuses, a number of which had PhD programs. Other four-year colleges also wanted to create doctoral programs, but it was too late. The state had run out of money and the job market out of jobs.

New York's Department of Education appointed a special Commission of Higher Education and asked it to evaluate the state's doctoral programs by a uniform set of criteria. When Greenbaum spoke to his contacts in Albany about what this would entail, they confirmed his premonition. The evaluation process was designed to compare the relative strength of discipline-based programs that trained students to do empirical research, not interdisciplinary programs that honed their students' skills as theorists.

Clearly, it made little sense to evaluate the GF's doctoral programs by this set of criteria. Despite Greenbaum's earlier efforts to change the academic profile of the division, Philosophy, Political Science, and Sociology had been resisting him for years. By the early 1970s, the dean had accepted their reasons for doing so and hoped that sympathetic evaluators would do the same. But nobody would ever forgive the Graduate Faculty for the way it ran those departments, encouraging them to accept as many students as possible, without providing the faculty with the resources they needed to accommodate them.

Given the size of the faculty, the three departments were teaching too many students, many of whom did not come close to having the academic preparation they needed to pursue serious graduate work. An embarrassing number of these students dropped out every year before completing their MAs, let alone their PhDs. Among those who received their master's, far too many failed their PhD qualifying exams, and of those who cleared that hurdle as well, a goodly number of them never finished their dissertations. Finally of those who made it through the entire process and received their doctorates, they rarely received offers from academic institutions—an old problem that had only grown worse by the mid-1970s with the surplus of PhDs flooding the job market. Employment opportunities outside the university were somewhat better, particularly for clinical psychologists, but they were still not good enough.

The Commission on Higher Education sent its first team of evaluators to the New School in the fall of 1976. Beginning with the Department of Philosophy, the commission asked two distinguished members of the discipline to conduct the onsite review, instructing them "to report the facts and, as far as possible, not to make value judgments." A second "rating committee" would take it from there. The onsite team arrived at the New School a few months after Jonas had retired.[6] Although the department had added Anthony Quinton and Albert Hofstadter to the faculty by then, both of whom were widely respected philosophers, the facts recorded in the evaluators' report pointed to serious problems with the program.

After reading what the onsite visitors had written, the rating committee delivered a series of brutally frank recommendations, without anticipating, apparently, the impact they might have on the future of Philosophy at the New School. Although they praised the department for being the most important center of phenomenology in the United States, the time had come, they proclaimed, to expand the program and expose GF students to other schools of thought, in particular American pragmatism and recent developments in West German philosophy. A few weeks after Greenbaum saw the report, he received a personal letter from one of the members of the committee, Princeton's Richard Rorty, who was "speaking now as a private citizen."

Although his committee had said nothing about closing down the department, Rorty still worried that their report might persuade the administration to do so all the same. He was "very distressed," he wrote,

> at the thought that the review process of the State Education Department might eventually prove a factor in leading the New School to phase out graduate instruction in philosophy. Certainly, I and all my colleagues on the rating committee for philosophy are horrified at the thought that we might have made more likely the end of a tradition which has been so valuable.

To which Greenbaum replied:

> I am afraid our president and others have interpreted the rating committee's report on our philosophy program as being negative. . . . I must confess that in reading the

report there is no way to escape such an unhappy conclusion. . . . The intention of the rating committee may have been to help our philosophy department broaden its staff and strengthen its scholarship, but the consequences of its recommendations and the general tone of its report may accomplish just the opposite. I am determined, though, to make every reasonable effort within the resources of my budget to rebuild the department so as both to continue and extend its traditions.[7]

The New School, Rorty persisted, had "a golden opportunity to form a link between American philosophers and the exciting work which is currently going on among German philosophers," some of whom, he noted approvingly, had already taught at the New School—and, as Greenbaum knew, attracted hundreds of students from around the city.

Alasdair MacIntyre, who had served on the first committee, wrote to Greenbaum as well. Speaking "only for myself," Boston University's philosopher explained, "I was extremely impressed both with the program's achievements and with its potentialities." Both men urged Greenbaum to do everything he could to save Philosophy at the New School. Given the sorry state of the discipline nationally, the GF's department had a unique role to play. As MacIntyre put it:

At this moment in the United States philosophy is to some degree in crisis, a not always recognized crisis. The main trends within analytical philosophy now seem increasingly sterile and the overproduction of Ph.D.'s trained in that tradition is a major factor in distorting the job market. It is therefore perhaps more important than ever before that the distinctive traditions of the New School's philosophy faculty should be developed and strengthened rather than weakened or even abandoned.[8]

The trustees, however, had lost confidence. They refused to invest in a program that had received such a negative review, at least not until the New School examined the problems more carefully. As Greenbaum predicted, they instructed Everett to declare a moratorium immediately on admitting new doctoral students for the fall semester of 1977—a decision that caused student numbers to drop precipitously.

⸙

During the spring semester of 1978, New York State reviewed the remaining departments in the Graduate Faculty with the exception of Psychology. Since the American Psychological Association (APA) planned to do its own evaluation of that department in a couple of years, the Department of Education decided to rely on the association's report and focus its attention on Anthropology, Economics, Political Science, and Sociology. The first two came through the evaluation process successfully, but Political Science and Sociology did even worse than Philosophy, with their rating committees recommending point blank that the Department of Education close them down. Adding insult to injury, this time nobody stepped forward as "a private citizen" from any of the committees to encourage Greenbaum to fight back.

Having anticipated the outcome, Arthur Vidich had tried to mobilize national support from the American Sociological Association (ASA). Even before the New School heard back from the rating committee he wrote to William D'Antonio, the chairman of the Committee on Freedom of Research and Teaching (COFRAT) at ASA, to warn him that the New York State review process was not designed to evaluate programs like the one at the New School. Would the national committee come to his department's defense? COFRAT's chair acknowledged that there might be a problem, but he did not think his committee should get involved. After all, he explained, "the outside reviewers are sociologists of good reputation; the reviewers must certainly be aware of the special role the New School faculty has in graduate sociology; and it would appear that the Commission [of the State of New York] has not exceeded its authority in establishing the particular criteria for the present evaluation." Although D'Antonio promised to raise the matter with the other members of COFRAT, Vidich should not count on them to step in.[9]

In early May, *The New York Times* reported on the outcome of New York State's academic review under the alarming headline: "New School for Social Research May Lose Three Doctoral Programs":

> During the last two weeks, administrators at the school—long known for its distinguished faculty of European-born intellectuals—have received copies of preliminary rating reports from the state that call for the elimination of the doctoral degree courses in political science and sociology. The reports cite, among other criticisms, a small faculty, limited course offerings, large number of part-time students, and the lack of academic "stars."

The article also mentioned the moratorium the New School had placed two years earlier on the Department of Philosophy "after all three senior faculty positions . . . were left vacant by deaths and resignations." Quinton and Hofstadter had both resigned. As Hofstadter told the *Times*, "They started with a jewel and have turned it into trash and thrown it away." The journalist added that "whenever [Hofstadter] sought to hire new senior faculty members, he was told there was no money available."

Several colleagues at the GF blamed the current crisis on the "rapid expansion of the school's adult education and urban studies programs," while Everett rejected the idea that there was a crisis at all. It was "unthinkable," he told the *Times*, that the New School would consider eliminating the doctoral programs. Nevertheless, he admitted, no hiring would take place until the university had studied the situation carefully and drafted a new plan for reconstituting the three departments. The article ended with the announcement that "several hundred students [had] met and organized 'The Committee to Save the Graduate Faculty.' They plan to organize a lobbying effort with state and city officials in an attempt to influence the doctoral-review process, which they view as much a political process as an academic one."[10]

The departments of Political Science and Sociology wrote forceful rebuttals to the Department of Education; Everett did the same. In his letter, dated May 12, the New School's president proclaimed imperiously to Commissioner Gordon MacKay Ambach, "I am not satisfied with the rating committees' reports, and I am not satisfied with the answers given by our departments." Toning down the rhetoric, he asked Ambach to postpone making a final decision, promising that if the commissioner kindly agreed, he world declare a moratorium on admitting PhD students to Political Science and Sociology, the way he had already done in Philosophy. He would also establish "a committee in each discipline [of outside scholars] to study our situation as completely and thoroughly as possible."[11]

Much to everyone's relief, Ambach accepted Everett's proposal, persuading the optimists that things would now move forward with a minimum of pain. But before long, heads began to roll. The first victim was Greenbaum. Without ceremony, Everett announced in December that the man who had served as dean for the last twelve years would step down at the end of the month; Allen Austill would take over temporarily until the New School appointed a new dean. Outraged by the news, the GF called an emergency meeting of the Executive Faculty. Arien Mack was among the first to speak. She accused the university of using Greenbaum as a scapegoat and urged her colleagues to call for Everett's resignation. Although it took them several months, on May 22, 1979, the faculty informed the Board of Trustees that they had "reluctantly concluded that the presidency must now pass to new hands."[12]

A few days after Everett fired Greenbaum, the Executive Faculty told the president that they had begun the search for a new dean, whom they expected the university to appoint "no later than September 1, 1979." If Everett wanted Austill to serve on the committee, that was fine with them, but he would not play a significant role. Although the memo was polite, the subtext was clear: How dare Everett replace Greenbaum, even temporarily, with the dean of Continuing Education! Austill may have gone to the University of Chicago, but he had never even finished his PhD. Determined to put an end to this insult as quickly as possible, the Executive Faculty told Everett that he would have their list of finalists within the next few weeks.[13]

The other matter of immediate concern was the actual rebuilding process. With the hope once again of limiting Austill's role, colleagues started circulating proposals to get the conversation going before Greenbaum had even stepped down. On December 12, Heilbroner sent a bold statement to Everett and the Executive Faculty. In his "Future of the Graduate Faculty," the economist raised the specter of rebuilding the GF with fewer than six departments. Although he began by "enthusiastically" affirming his preference for keeping all of them, he would only endorse doing so if the New School accepted the following conditions:

1. That the financial cost of rebuilding a six-department faculty be squarely faced, and a long-term commitment adequate to fund such a program obtained. This is a responsibility of the president and the board.
2. That the intellectual and scholarly purposes of a rebuilt faculty are clearly enunciated and win the approval not only of the faculty itself, but of the board and administration. This is a responsibility of the faculty.

Heilbroner described in detail what a commitment of this magnitude would entail. It was not enough to make an initial investment, which he estimated would come to about $2,350,000. The New School had to accept the fact that the GF would never have the means to support itself: "*Without a long-term commitment,*" Heilbroner warned, "*a faculty of six viable, high-quality departments cannot be built.*" It would be doomed "to expose [itself] to the humiliations and defeats of last year. Therefore, I strongly oppose any effort to move ahead on all six fronts *until a decision has been made to provide the necessary financial support*" [emphasis in the original].

Heilbroner was no softer on his colleagues. The GF had to "define the scholarly purpose for which it exists." For the most part, graduate programs at other universities were based on the "research-oriented model," which was fine. "There is nothing wrong with the research-oriented 'model.'" But the GF would never grow big enough to sustain it. "Therefore, we have long ago turned toward another model—the 'theoretical' model":

The work we do tends to be wide-ranging, sometimes speculative, careless of traditional boundaries. It is very different from the empirical, technical, and carefully specialized work characteristic of most scholars. Even the psychology department, our most research-minded entity, aims at large-scale problems rather than small-scale ones.

No other university, Heilbroner boasted—not Columbia or NYU, "as excellent as they may be"—could say as the New School does: "There is no other place like ours." But having a unique "intellectual orientation" was not enough. The GF needed "both distinction and definition," some of which, he admitted, had been lost in recent years. The time had come "for it to be regained. . . . I would suggest that support for each department be contingent on its articulating a purpose that not only gains the approval of the faculty, the administration and the board, but . . . meets professional approbation."

Although Heilbroner repeated several times that he preferred a Graduate Faculty with six departments, he asked everyone to face the very real possibility that the New School could not afford to support them properly. In which case, the GF would have to accept "smaller, less expensive, faculty arrangements." If it came to that, he recommended that the board and president develop plans for an alternative structure in close consultation with the faculty, and they should do so quickly: "This is obviously the most painful and difficult of all problems, but it is not without the possibility of fair solutions."[14]

The Executive Faculty rejected Heilbroner's proposal. Although nobody questioned the economist's commitment to the GF, retrenchment was not an acceptable solution. When Austill raised the specter again a few months later, the faculty considered it a declaration of war.

On March 29, 1979, Austill distributed a forty-two-page memo to the faculty, asking them to read it carefully before coming to the next Executive Faculty meeting scheduled for April 4. Austill began by reviewing the challenges the GF faced in grim detail, quoting at length from the documents the departments had drafted themselves and from the ominous reports the New School had received from the various rating committees. He then ran down the various ways the university might be able to save the GF, none of them very appealing. At the same time, he tried to assure the GF that the Board of Trustees had "affirmed, repeatedly, its support of the Graduate Faculty," a position he also shared: "I support [the GF] because I believe it is essential to the future success of the entire university. A rich and vital history should be continued." The New School, however, had "to be able to afford the Graduate Faculty" on its limited resources and without abandoning the rest of the university. Although this would not be easy, Austill continued, the trustees had made a promise: "If there is any question at all, it has to do with the shape and character of the Graduate Faculty rather than its continued existence."

Austill recommended changing the "shape," if not the "character," of the GF by closing down the weakest departments. As he developed his argument, he relied heavily on the words of the outside evaluators, quoting most extensively from the report of the rating committee for Sociology: The New School's department was "simply not needed in the state," the evaluators bluntly proclaimed, because "the distinctive mission of the New School's sociology program as a purveyor of European thought is being better fulfilled elsewhere." Austill agreed, as he did with the findings of the rating committee for Political Science, which had reached the same conclusion. Neither department was worth saving. In the case of Philosophy, Austill conceded that the evaluators had said nothing about closing it down, but they wanted to see major changes. The report, he added pointedly, was anything but favorable.[15]

Before the faculty met with Austill, Vidich circulated a lengthy response to the interim dean's memo, challenging Austill point by point on his command of the facts. A difficult man among difficult men, Vidich had few friends on the faculty.[16] This time, however, almost everyone endorsed his statement, voting formally to accept the two resolutions he had attached to the end of his memo: (1) The Graduate Faculty officially affirms its commitment to maintain its six departments. (2) The GF insists that Austill append Vidich's response to his damaging memo and send both of them to the Board of Trustees.[17]

In his memoir, Vidich wrote that his colleagues at the New School had always treated him like an outsider and in some cases with downright hostility. Members of the émigré faculty dismissed him out of hand, he reported, as did their protégés Peter Berger and Thomas Luckmann. The Americans were not very friendly either. A product of Harvard's Department of Social Relations, Vidich joined the GF in 1960, hired by Henry David as part of the new dean's campaign to turn the old University in Exile into a mainstream graduate school of the social sciences. Although David recruited seven other colleagues during his three years at the New School, Vidich remained a "minority of one" for over a decade, until he succeeded in hiring his good friend Stanford Lyman in the early 1970s, which then made him a minority of two.

Vidich's description of the hiring practices at the Graduate Faculty sounded very much like David's earlier observation that Johnson had run the New School like a "mom and pop" shop:

In an effort to preserve the past, the émigrés appointed their own graduates: Howard White in political science (Kurt Riezler's son-in-law); Mary Henle in

Gestalt psychology (Max Wertheimer's student); Thomas Luckmann (a student of Alfred Schütz); Felicia Deyrup (Alvin Johnson's daughter); and Bernard Rosenberg in sociology (a student of Albert Salomon); . . . Werner Marx and Murray Green in philosophy (students of Karl Löwith and Hans Jonas respectively).[18]

Although Mary Henle never studied with Max Wertheimer, Vidich's point was well taken. Henle had been a student of Wertheimer's colleague Wolfgang Köhler. After joining the GF in 1946, she dedicated her life to promoting the teachings of Gestalt psychology. Howard White not only married Kurt Riezler's daughter but he did his PhD at the New School with Leo Strauss. What is more, Vidich's own department had hired not one but two students of Alfred Schütz: Luckmann and Berger. In 1970, Berger tried to hire his own brother-in-law, Hansfried Kellner, yet another New School student, but Vidich blocked the appointment. Berger then resigned and Vidich replaced him with his good friend Lyman.[19]

Even though these "in-house appointments" offended Vidich, a number of them, he admitted, were exceptionally good. He especially enjoyed the excitement of being in the same department with Berger and Luckmann at the height of their careers, as they were calling for what Berger described as "a basic reformulation of sociological theory." When the two sociologists published *The Social Construction of Reality* in 1966, it was good for everyone.[20]

By 1978, when the site visitors arrived, Berger and Luckmann were gone, and Benjamin Nelson was dead, having passed away suddenly the year before. The only tenured members left were Vidich and Lyman, whom the rating committee described in excessively unflattering terms, noting that they had not received "any major national honors, nor would either be regarded as a major figure in the field."[21] Deeply offended, the two men mounted a national campaign to redeem their reputations and save the department, but almost no one came to their defense.[22]

After their confrontation with Austill, the Executive Faculty and the Interdepartmental Council of Graduate Students closed ranks against the interim dean and started sharing ideas among themselves about how best to rebuild the Graduate Faculty. A few weeks later David Gordon from Economics and Rayna Rapp from Anthropology stepped forward with a "bold solution to the current crisis." Politically skilled and academically accomplished, they had guided their departments through the state's evaluation process successfully. Now they had a

"Proposal for Reconstitution." In six and a half pages, they imagined rebuilding the GF with the same six departments, reconfigured around an integrated theme dedicated "to a *systematic* and *critical* investigation of the meaning and uses of the social sciences," both within and across the traditional disciplines. Gordon and Rapp were not simply describing "what many people called 'interdisciplinary' studies." They had something more ambitious in mind that involved examining seriously the "methodological basis for disciplinary divisions":

> In short, the Graduate Faculty would pursue the following general problem: Many people are interested in studying the lives of people in society and their ideas about those lives. Is it necessary that we pursue these interests by channeling our studies through the methods and concerns of the traditional disciplines in the social sciences? Or would it be more fruitful to pursue those interests by trying to break down the boundaries among the traditional disciplines and seek an integrated approach? If so, what might constitute such an integration?

A project like this would sustain and develop the historic mission of the New School and the GF "not simply along lines established by the University-in-Exile but also from its original founding." To proceed, Gordon and Rapp recommended that the GF recruit a group of sociologists, political scientists, and philosophers with overlapping interests who all "share this common concern." The success of their proposal, they repeated, "*hinges* on the idea" of identifying a group. After canvassing the academic community for "luminous faculty" who shared a similar vision of the social sciences and philosophy, they concluded that a number of excellent scholars might welcome the opportunity to move to New York and join the GF if—and this was critical—they were hired together. Was this a utopian dream? No, they argued. Although they did not have access to all the necessary financial information, they had seen enough to say with confidence that their proposal was not only "promising" but "practical."[23]

The Executive Faculty and the Interdepartmental Council of Graduate Students endorsed the Gordon-Rapp Plan and submitted it to the Board of Trustees. On May 9, 1979 the trustees discussed the proposal "in great detail" and concluded, Austill reported, that "the president should consult with a group of distinguished outside members of the academic community and solicit [the] views" of no fewer "than three such individuals."[24]

The department chairs took control of the process. With Everett's consent, they selected the outside evaluators themselves. On June 6, they informed the chairman of the Board of Trustees, Henry Loeb, that they had invited Professors Sheldon Wolin of Princeton University, Alasdair MacIntyre of Boston University, and Michael Walzer of Harvard University "to visit the Graduate Faculty for the purpose of assisting us in an examination of our problems and our proposal for reconstitution. We have asked them to place their emphasis in their evaluation on the intellectual and scholarly merits of our proposal."[25]

On June 19, the three scholars submitted their "Report to the Chairpersons of the Graduate Faculty of the New School for Social Research," essentially endorsing the Gordon-Rapp proposal. They warned the New School against reducing the number of departments and breaking tenure and took issue with the conclusions reached by the Commission on Higher Education's evaluation teams, in particular with "the rating committee's assessment of the tenured members of the Department of Sociology, both of whom are in our view highly distinguished and contributing members of the profession."

MacIntyre, Walzer, and Wolin encouraged the New School to invest heavily in the GF. As Gordon and Rapp had recommended, the university should rebuild Philosophy, Political Science, and Sociology by hiring a group of outstanding scholars whose work focused on different aspects of the same overarching themes. A proposal like this, they acknowledged, "invites an unusual degree of academic asceticism and altruism on the part of the members of the departments of Anthropology, Economics and Psychology."[26]

Although the trustees did not commit themselves immediately, Austill assured the faculty that they agreed in principle to support a plan for rebuilding the GF.[27] As part of their commitment, the board promised to establish "a priority capital fund drive to help underwrite the future of the Graduate Faculty." To guide them through the process, they appointed F. Champion Ward to work with a committee of three colleagues from the University of Chicago and Yale to come up with a plan. Ward had served for many years as dean of the College at the University of Chicago and vice president of Education and Research at the Ford Foundation. During the 1960s, he had also served as chairman of the White House Task Force on the Education of Gifted Persons and helped the MacArthur Foundation establish its famous "Genius Awards" program.

In May 1980, Ward and his committee submitted a plan for rebuilding the GF to the Board of Trustees, expanding on the ideas first presented by Gordon and Rapp.[28] The board endorsed the recommendations and appointed Ward chancellor of the New School and acting dean of the GF. He would start in the fall.

PART V

Renewing the Legacy

(1982–2000)

18

REBUILDING THE GRADUATE FACULTY

Although John Everett did not resign until 1982, he had significantly reduced his activities two years earlier, allowing F. Champion Ward to assume responsibilities usually reserved for the head of a university. Ward, however, had only stepped in temporarily to give the trustees the time they would need to recruit a new president—a position many agreed would not be easy fill. As Edward Fiske put it in *The New York Times*, "Characteristically, the new president of this maverick institution will be charged not only with shoring up finances and enrollment and recruiting new faculty members, but also with constructing what amounts to a whole new approach to the social sciences in the 1980s."[1]

In the fall of 1980, the trustees asked Ward to begin the process of rebuilding the Graduate Faculty while they started looking for a new president. Moving quickly, the chancellor appointed a group of scholars from neighboring institutions to serve on an "Enabling Committee" alongside members of the GF.[2] In his instructions to the committee, Ward asked them to identify pioneer figures in their fields whom they thought would have the vision it took to come up with this new approach to the social sciences. Ward also sought their advice as he prepared a revised budget for the "redevelopment of the Graduate Faculty over the next five years." Although the trustees had already endorsed the proposal he had given them in May, they now wanted a detailed implementation plan.[3]

Ward invited the Enabling Committee to work over lunch at the Century Club. As Arien Mack remembered those meetings, the tone he set was "elegant" and "civilized," offering much needed relief from life at the New School. On March 23, 1981, Ward presented Everett and the trustees with an updated recruitment plan, prefaced by a cautionary note: The New School, he warned, would never attract a strong dean if it did not announce right away that it was prepared to make a significant number of high-profile appointments over the next two years in the social sciences and philosophy. The committee recommended nine appointments in all, five of whom should be major figures in their fields. This would cost about $4,300,000, most of which, Ward knew perfectly well, the university still had to raise.[4]

Ward's memo persuaded the New School to go public. In early April, *The Chronicle of Higher Education* reported that "Amid Hard Times and 'Intellectual Crisis,' New School Bolsters Its Graduate Division: New York's 'University in Exile' is recruiting top scholars to flesh out depleted faculty ranks."[5] The article quoted several members of the faculty, including Stanley Diamond and Arthur Vidich, neither one of whom sat on the Enabling Committee, and Robert Heilbroner, who did. Although the three of them rarely agreed about anything, they all endorsed the rebuilding campaign enthusiastically, embracing the idea of creating something new without abandoning entirely the intellectual traditions that had made the GF famous—even if what they meant by those traditions was not exactly the same. As Diamond put it with uncharacteristic diplomacy, the émigré scholars may have all passed away or retired, but he and other members of the GF could renew that legacy with the help of a few more outstanding appointments. In his interview with *The Chronicle*, he identified himself and his colleagues as "internal émigrés," repeating the term he had used eleven years earlier in *The New York Review of Books*. Excited about the possibilities, he saw the New School recruiting scholars "with imagination, who understand that there are no boundaries in the social sciences. . . . People of stature, in the social sciences, have always been, almost by definition, interdisciplinary. Think of Max Weber—he was more than a sociologist. The most obvious example is Marx—he was not even an economist." Vidich looked forward to having new colleagues who would join him in casting "a critical eye on the assumptions of the traditional disciplines." As for Heilbroner, he predicted that the New School would succeed in attracting new colleagues of true distinction because "the Hannah Arendts of the world are few—few and lonely. . . . If we could get six of them under one roof it will give them greater visibility."

One such giant, Ward announced to *The Chronicle*, had already signed on. Jerome Bruner, a widely respected cognitive psychologist, was leaving Harvard and coming to the New School in the fall of 1981. But other appointments of similar stature would have to wait. Speaking now in the name of the university's administration, Ward chose his words carefully, avoiding the sense of urgency he had conveyed in his budget memo a few weeks earlier. For the public record, he allowed that "it may take longer than expected to finance all the new appointments."

Dampening the mood even further, *The Chronicle* described the many challenges facing the GF at the time. The New School may have a visionary plan for the future, but "the burden of waiting falls on the students and faculty members. Even in departments that have continued to thrive, the faculties have been understaffed and rely extensively on visiting and adjunct professors." Ward acknowledged as much: "There is bound to be tension between the students' interest in the short-term future of the faculty and the administration's long-term planning." And nothing much would change until the New School found a new president.

The trustees appointed Jonathan Fanton president of the New School in September 1982. He was thirty-nine at the time, unusually young for a position of this kind. During the previous four years he had served as vice president for planning at the University of Chicago. Before that he had spent seventeen years at Yale, first as an undergraduate and PhD student in history; then in a number of administrative posts, including associate provost and chief of staff to the university's president. Over those years he worked on a number of special initiatives to improve town-gown relations, which included developing targeted programs for minority students. After Fanton finished his doctoral dissertation on FDR's assistant secretary of war, Robert Lovett,[6] he taught American history to undergraduates in addition to his other responsibilities at the university.

Looking back over his early professional years, Fanton was grateful, he said, for having had the opportunity to work for two outstanding academic leaders at two of the best institutions of higher learning in the country: Kingman Brewster at Yale and Hanna Holborn Gray at the University of Chicago.[7] In *The New York Times* article announcing his new appointment, President Gray described her departing vice president as having "played a major role in the planning of the institution's objectives and in their realization."[8]

Fanton identified himself as "a Connecticut Yankee, a Protestant from a Republican family, educated at the Choate School and Yale University"—a curious profile, to say the least, for the next president of the New School. Most people assumed that the trustees would appoint someone with urban grit and firsthand experience with student radicals. Not only did Fanton come from the genteel world of the upper classes, his scholarly inclinations had little in common with the intellectual traditions associated with the New School: "I am an historian by training, and an old-fashioned one at that, interested more in narrative that tries to reveal what happened and why than in grand theories of human nature."[9] During one of his interviews with the board, a trustee raised the anomaly.

Describing Fanton as a "square peg in a round hole," he asked why the vice president for planning at the University of Chicago thought the New School should appoint him president? The question, Fanton agreed, was fair:

> On the surface [the trustee] was right. Although I was no longer a Republican, my brand of independent centrism seemed at odds with the leftist image of the New School. My narrative style of American history hardly seemed appropriate for a cosmopolitan faculty for whom theory was all important. My small-town Protestant upbringing seemed off-key for a tough urban university with strong Jewish roots. And my experience at Yale and Chicago, two elite research universities, seemed oddly matched to this institution with adult education at its core.[10]

But in other ways Fanton was a good fit. First and foremost, he embraced Alvin Johnson's vision of the New School and his brand of independent centrism. As an American historian, Fanton also had a deep understanding of the Progressive Era and the FDR years, critical periods in the history of the university. Over the years he had developed as well a keen interest in twentieth-century European history.

While still a student at Yale, Fanton took courses with Gray's father, Hajo Holborn, one of the country's leading specialists of modern Germany.[11] Holborn's work on Nazi Germany had a great impact on him, Fanton said, as did the insights his professor generously shared later on about his personal experiences fleeing Nazi Germany and coming to the United States as an exiled scholar. After learning about the challenges Holborn faced, Fanton had a better idea, he felt, than he would otherwise have had about what the New School's émigré faculty had gone through. Although most of them were gone by the early 1980s, Fanton reached out to those who were still alive, establishing cordial relations with them and their families, in particular with Adolph Lowe, even after he moved back to Germany, and Hans Jonas, whom he persuaded to renew his ties to the New School community.

Most important of all, Fanton shared Johnson's aspirations for the future of the university. The new president recognized that the New School could not live off its past indefinitely. It should try to address present-day problems instead that resonated with the institution's founding commitments to defend academic freedom and human rights.[12]

In addition to the Graduate Faculty, Fanton took on a number of other major projects to strengthen academic programs at the university. During his seventeen years as president, he turned the eclectic Seminar College into the Eugene Lang College, naming it after the famous philanthropist and university trustee who generously supported the New School's decision to create a traditional liberal arts college. By the 1990s—over the vigorous opposition of old-timers at the GF—Fanton made it a contractual requirement that newly appointed colleagues teach at the college as well.[13] He also created PhD programs at the Graduate School for Management and Urban Planning and renamed that division after Robert Milano, the trustee who had financed the new initiative

Continuing Education expanded as well during the Fanton years, taking its place in the wider academic community as a pioneer in distance learning. It also opened a number of new degree programs at the bachelor's and master's level, including Jazz and Contemporary Music, Media Studies, Teacher Education, and International Affairs. Building on old strengths, Continuing Education introduced a master's in Fine Arts in Creative Writing, renewing the reputation of what Johnson had started in the 1920s when the New School had one of the only writing programs in the city.

In another important initiative, Fanton persuaded the trustees to invest more heavily in Parsons School of Design, making it possible for the school to build a new program in Digital Design, offer a master's degree in Architecture, and recruit heavily in Korea and Japan—from where it continues to attract a significant number of students today.[14] Finally, Fanton expanded the New School's programs in the performing arts. In 1989 he annexed the Mannes College of Music, one of the great conservatories in New York City, which had also opened its doors to refugees fleeing Nazi-occupied Europe. Five years later he welcomed back the Actors' Studio, the descendant of Erwin Piscator's legendary theater program.

Changes of this magnitude predictably lead to controversy, and Fanton had his critics. Not only did they object to some of his major new initiatives, they also took issue with his "micromanaging style." Fanton intervened on everything, they complained, matters big and small, from setting new priorities for academic programs to selecting the fabric used in reupholstering chairs around a seminar table. But he also welcomed full-throated debates with students and faculty on a wide range of questions, including allegations of racism and sexism.

In the spring of 1997, a group of students demanded that the university offer a position with tenure to a visiting professor who specialized in feminist theory and postcolonial studies. Originally from Trinidad and Tobago, M. Jacqui Alexander was in her last semester of a two-year appointment at Lang College and the Graduate Faculty's MA program in Women and Gender Studies. Fanton replied that he would not grant tenure without a process. He would, however, create a new position in feminist/postcolonial studies and run a national search to which Alexander could apply. Rejecting his offer, the students staged a hunger strike, accusing the New School of racial and gender discrimination. Several members of the faculty supported the protest, setting off acrimonious confrontations that quickly attracted media attention.

One of the most detailed articles on the strike appeared in *Lingua Franca*—a short-lived but popular academic periodical. Its author, Eyal Press, described the "Nightmare on Twelfth Street" with ironic glee: "When the New School for Social Research refused to tenure a radical professor of color, it provoked a semester of discontent. As the proudly progressive institution endured hunger strikes, hostage takings, and accusations of racism against faculty, some saw a crusade for justice and others a case of 'Monty Python does PC.'"[15]

Before the dust settled, some of the protesters tried to turn their local struggle into a national campaign. Targeting the GF's eminent political theorist and feminist scholar Nancy Fraser, they accused her of being a racist because she allegedly criticized the quality of Alexander's published work. Reaching out to a multi-campus network of activists, they tried unsuccessfully to mobilize their political allies at the University of Wisconsin to disrupt the keynote address that Fraser was scheduled to deliver in Madison at a feminist conference. In the end, the strike at the New School petered out and Alexander moved on.[16]

When students organized protests on campus, Fanton tried to turn these fractious confrontations into teaching opportunities for the entire university community, often linking the current issue to the history of the New School and to the principles for which it stood. Following in the footsteps of Charles Beard, Herbert Croly, James Harvey Robinson, and Alvin Johnson, Fanton also used the New School as a platform for taking stands in national debates about freedom of expression—most dramatically in 1990 when he sued the National Endowment for the Arts, accusing it of having infringed on the constitutional rights of artists. Finally, Fanton took the lead, as Johnson had before him, in championing the rights of persecuted intellectuals, first in East and Central Europe, then in parts of the former Soviet Union and Africa.[17]

By the time Fanton stepped down as president in 1999, he had completed a $225 million capital campaign and set the New School on its way to becoming a more integrated institution instead of a confederation of individual programs. None of these achievements would have been possible without his strong, if at times controversial, leadership and the generosity of the Board of Trustees, whose membership and level of giving increased considerably while he was president. Among Fanton's most faithful supporters were several old-timers Johnson had recruited to the board during the 1930s.

The New School could not rely on generous gifts from college alumni the way other universities did. Some of the institution's most loyal donors may have taken a course or two in Continuing Education, but they earned their BA degrees elsewhere, or not at all. By the time Fanton arrived, the New School had thousands of alumni from its graduate programs, but only a few of them had the means to make significant gifts. The education they received had prepared them to enter honorable professions, but not lucrative ones. Occasionally, however, an alumnus came from a wealthy family, for example Strachan Donnelley, the devoted student of Hans Jonas. Donnelley's great-grandfather had made his fortune in the commercial printing business in Chicago during the second half of the nineteenth century. When Fanton made Donnelley a trustee, the philosopher gave generously to the New School, but not out of some deep sentimental attachment to his *alma mater*—he saved that for Yale. He gave because he firmly believed in what the institution stood for.[18]

As Alvin Johnson complained on many occasions, the founders of the New School had compromised the future of the institution by refusing to build an endowment. In later years, if a trustee challenged the wisdom of holding on to this misguided policy, he would summarily be voted down—until 1963 when Johnson and Hans Staudinger defied the trustees and launched their Save the School campaign. Having neither an endowment nor a strong alumni base, Johnson raised money by building a dedicated network of friends who embraced the New School like family—a practice that enraged Henry David, but it worked. Hans Simons, Jack Everett, and Jonathan Fanton all benefited from the enduring loyalty of trustees whom the first president had recruited.

Dorothy Hirshon was one of them. A well-known supporter of progressive causes, Hirshon accepted Johnson's invitation to become a trustee in 1937. By the time the New School appointed Fanton as its sixth president, Hirshon was chairman of the board. After which fate intervened, as Johnson might have added, turning what had quickly become a strong working relationship into a close friendship. In March 1983, Hirshon's daughter, Hilary Paley Byers, married Fanton's good friend Joseph Califano, the former special assistant to Lyndon Johnson and secretary of Health, Education and Welfare under Jimmy Carter. Given the coincidence, Fanton became a regular guest in Hirshon's home on family occasions—beginning on the day she met her son-in-law for the first time.[19] In his memoir, Califano described this awkward encounter, providing us with a vivid portrait of one of the New School's longest serving trustees:

> I went to her apartment at 911 Park Avenue with a miserable cold. Dorothy perpetually puffed on cigarettes, unleashing a steady stream of smoke in my face, as New School President Jonathan Fanton . . . struggled to keep from laughing.

Her first question to me was: "How could you ever have justified waging that disastrous war in Vietnam?"

This, I knew, was going to be interesting. Unlike most of her social set, Dorothy was a Roosevelt liberal before Roosevelt was a liberal. She cheered the New Deal battles for social justice. She was a fighter for equal justice for blacks, decades before Lyndon Johnson took up the cause. In 1943, Dorothy encouraged her second husband, Bill Paley, to have CBS radio broadcast a program entitled *An Open Letter on Race Hatred.*[20]

When Hirshon died in 1998 at the age of eighty-nine, she had been a trustee of the New School for sixty-one years. In the obituary published in *The New York Times*, Enid Nemy described her as "a glamorous figure in New York society from the 1920s through the '40s, who later became active in social, human rights, and political causes." Remembered as "one of the most beautiful girls in Southern California," Hirshon married three times: John Randolph Hearst in 1927, William Paley in 1931, and Walter Hirshon in 1953—she divorced them all.[21] Nemy ended the obituary on a nostalgic note, observing that Hirshon had belonged to the "Algonquin set—the playwrights, journalists, and other intellectuals whose ripostes during the 1920s became literary legend."

Hirshon was a faithful friend of the Graduate Faculty from the very beginning, responding warmly to Johnson's persistent pleas for support, requests he continued to make long after he had retired. In 1959, the president emeritus, now nearly eighty-five years of age, asked her to join the "dinner committee" for the twenty-fifth anniversary: "Dear Dorothy Hirshon, I have been assigned the privilege of collecting names for our dinner committee for the Waldorf Astoria dinner of April 6 in celebration of the twenty-fifth anniversary of the University in Exile. Your name is at the top of the list. May I have it?" To which she responded, "Of course—with pleasure."[22] In later years, Hirshon gave generously of her time and money to the entire institution and embraced its expansion. When Everett annexed the Parsons School of Design, she served as chair of the division's oversight or visiting committee.

Hirshon's primary commitment, however, remained the GF. As chair of the board in the early 1980s, she campaigned forcefully for rebuilding the old University in Exile, persuading reluctant trustees to sign on. A decade later she established an endowed chair in the GF, the first occupant of which was David Gordon, the dashing, curly-haired Marxist economist and coauthor (with anthropologist Rayna Rapp) of the initial proposal that made the case for the rebuilding campaign. Hirshon was delighted with the choice. She liked smart, good-looking, radical men.

Before 1933, the New School's most generous friends came from Hirshon's social set: wealthy, politically progressive, and, for the most part, white Anglo-Saxon Protestant. Thanks to the Mayer family, Johnson recruited a few wealthy Jews from New York's German-Jewish community, but they remained in the minority until he opened the University in Exile. By 1944, the membership of the board was evenly split. Ten years later, Jews outnumbered gentiles by a considerable margin. People like Hirshon had become the exception, not the rule.

In December 1952, Johnson revealed the reason Jews outnumbered gentiles on the board, describing the ugly truth in a letter to Leo Heimerdinger, a Jewish philanthropist whose financial support the New School sorely needed. He even named names, perhaps unfairly in some instances. Heimerdinger had been a close friend of the recently deceased Jacob Billikopf, former director of the Federation of Jewish Charities in Philadelphia and devoted trustee of the New School:

[Billikopf] was sold on the New School because it was the one educational institution in all America that didn't give a hoot whether a student or a professor or a trustee was Jewish or gentile. It doesn't to this day. And I think it is worth keeping alive.

Maybe you'll ask me, how much gentile money do we get for our anti-discrimination program? I will tell you, for you alone. . . .

I lost Mrs. Willard Straight who was giving $1,000 a year and could have given half a million, when I announced that in the New School there would be no distinction between Jew and gentile. I lost Mrs. Walton Martin, who had tens of thousands to give. I lost Mrs. Rumsey, Mr. Harriman's daughter, who had real money. I lost Mrs. Tiffany, a fool with a lot of money. I lost Judge Learned Hand, whose daughter had married a Jew who didn't work out. I lost George Davis, whose wife couldn't stand Jews. I lost George Bacon, a grafter who had a lot of money free.

But by the grace of God, I kept my honor and the convictions of my heart.

I will tell you, my beloved friend Leo, when Jewish friends demand of me: "How much money are you getting out of gentiles?" If I had played the anti-Semitic game I would not in my old age be appealing to Jews. "Don't let the child of my heart, the New School, die."[23]

By the 1960s, the biggest donors on the board were virtually all Jews—or of Jewish origin—and so they remained, with very few exceptions, throughout Fanton's presidency.[24] Among the New School's most loyal friends during the 1980s and 1990s was a group of trustees from prominent families who had fled Nazi Germany and other parts of occupied Europe. Identifying personally with the history of the University in Exile, they contributed generously to the rebuilding campaign.

One of the first émigrés from Hitler's Europe to join the board was Walter Eberstadt—he became a trustee in 1975. When Fanton took over seven years later, he asked Eberstadt to chair the nominations committee, a position he accepted enthusiastically and used, in part, to recruit other émigrés of Jewish origin with family histories similar to his. This inspired idea renewed the New School's ties to the world the Nazis had tried to destroy and that Johnson had tried defiantly to save by creating the University in Exile.

The family histories of Walter Eberstadt, Henry Arnhold, and Michael Gellert have become an important part of the history of the Graduate Faculty. Descendants of wealthy German and Czech banking families of Jewish origin, their parents were not intellectuals, but they belonged to the same cultural milieu as Johnson's refugee professors. And like most of the scholars of Jewish origin at the University in Exile, these three trustees came from families that had tenuous ties to any form of Jewish community life, either religious or secular, until Hitler came to power. The Nazis' racial laws had made them Jews more than any deep attachment to the heritage of their ancestors.

In Eberstadt's case, his grandparents had already converted to Christianity in the nineteenth century, as had the grandparents of Gerhard Colm and Hans Neisser. Gellert's parents only converted in the late 1930s after fleeing occupied Europe, as had Eduard Heinemann, but they had already abandoned the faith many years earlier—to such an extent that their son's most vivid childhood memory of life in Prague was of celebrating Easter with his family. Arnhold's parents never converted to Christianity, but they too only celebrated Christmas and Easter at home—that is until Hitler came to power, at which point they made it a matter of honor to practice Jewish traditions. They even sent their reluctant son Heinrich (Henry) to a rabbi to prepare for his bar mitzvah.

Having belonged to the same world as the émigré scholars and experienced similar losses, Arnhold, Eberstadt and Gellert felt a strong personal bond to the émigrés who taught at the University in Exile and to the academic institution that saved them. These ties, as Eberstadt had predicted, inspired them to give generously to Fanton's efforts to renew the legacy of the GF.[25]

⟺

Dorothy Hirshon called Fanton, in the spring of 1982, to inform him that he was a finalist in the search for the new president. After hearing the encouraging news, Fanton felt fairly confident that if the trustees offered him the job they would provide him with the resources he needed to rebuild the Graduate Faculty. But could they or anyone else at the New School help him find the right dean? Someone with an outstanding scholarly record—that went without saying—and exceptional powers of persuasion. To succeed, the new dean would have to convince a group of academic stars to abandon well-endowed chairs at mainstream universities and come to a place where the future was risky and the amenities few. He would also have to earn the trust at the New School of embattled colleagues who might not like the idea of having an ambitious outsider as their next dean.

During that first conversation, Hirshon told Fanton that the Enabling Committee had identified a political scientist who looked like an excellent candidate for dean. She had met this Ira Katznelson as well and shared their enthusiasm. At the time, Katznelson was known in progressive academic circles for his work on race and politics in urban America and the United Kingdom. Conveniently for Fanton, he was also on the faculty of the University of Chicago, where he was serving as chair of the Department of Political Science. There was only one catch. Although Katznelson had met with the committee several times, he refused to become a candidate, even after Ward and others had urged him to do so.

Had Horace Kallen still been alive, he would have found a kindred spirit, both intellectually and culturally, in the man Fanton persuaded to take the job. The appointment of Katznelson marked only the second time in the history of the GF that the dean of this fiercely secular institution had a serious education in Jewish thought and culture, as well as in the humanistic traditions of Europe. Kallen was the first (1944–1946). In their philosophical and political writings, both men drew on their understanding of Jewish communal life as they eloquently described the many ways cultural pluralism strengthened democratic societies. Like Kallen before him, Katznelson argued that recognizing the rights of minorities in multiethnic states was not only compatible with, but essential for, the political health of liberal democracies.

Katznelson was born in New York City in 1944 into a family of East European Jewish immigrants with strong ties to socialist Zionism. His father had immigrated first to Palestine from Minsk to work with the Poale Zion movement.[26] In the United States he taught Hebrew school. The couple raised their family in Brooklyn and sent Ira to the Yeshiva of Flatbush, a modern Orthodox school, where he received a rigorous education in Judaism and in secular subjects.

Like other members of his family's circle of left-wing Jewish intellectuals, Katznelson's parents knew about the New School. Although they never attended lectures there—at least not to their son's knowledge—they talked about the university enough for Katznelson to remember hearing as a child about this place in Greenwich Village that provided refuge for Jewish scholars fleeing the Nazis even though it was not a Jewish institution.

Katznelson went to college at Columbia University and majored in history. During his senior year, he had the privilege of taking a tutorial with Richard Hofstader, one of the nation's leading historians of American democratic thought. Looking back on that experience thirty years later, Katznelson wrote that the tutorial "had an impact more considerable than the usual set of supervisions, for it provided a window into a remarkable effort in which [Hofstadter], along with such close colleagues as Lionel Trilling and C. Wright Mills, had sought to make liberalism adequate to their time."[27] Katznelson would pick up where his professor left off and continue that effort, both in his own scholarly work and in the intellectual direction he gave to the GF.

Katznelson graduated from Columbia in the spring of 1966 and went to Cambridge University the following fall to begin doctoral studies in political science. During the events of 1968, he was still in residence at Cambridge, where things had remained relatively calm. Eager to participate in what had become a major international movement for members of his generation, Katznelson took the train to London and joined thousands of left-leaning students, many of them Americans like himself, as they marched before the U.S. Embassy chanting slogans against America's war in Vietnam.

Katznelson described 1968 as "an emotional and symbolic roller coaster." He remembered spending hours talking with friends about "the possibilities and limits of politics." At times he felt a real sense of optimism about the influence he and his peers were having on public opinion in the United States in solidarity with activists from other sectors. He felt similarly optimistic about developments in Communist Eastern Europe. The changes taking place in Czechoslovakia "signified the possibility of joining liberal understandings and norms to the Socialist/Communist experience." But he heard the warning bells as well.

On January 30, while the Czechs were enjoying their Prague Spring, the Polish government closed down a production in Warsaw of *Forefathers' Eve* (*Dziady*), a play by Adam Mickiewicz, the nation's revered nineteenth-century poet. When university students marched in protest from the theater to a statue of Mickiewicz located nearby, the authorities crushed their peaceful demonstration. This in turn led to more protests and, on March 8, mass arrests of university students across the country. On April 4, American civil rights leader, Martin Luther King Jr., was assassinated in Memphis and on June 5, Robert Kennedy was killed in Los Angeles, after winning the Democratic Party's presidential primary in California.

And the bells kept ringing. On August 21, Soviet tanks rolled into Prague, putting an end to a new kind of socialism "with a human face." A few days later, at the Democratic Party's national convention in Chicago, hundreds of American policemen attacked demonstrators with billy clubs and tear gas. With the Democrats divided, the Republicans' candidate, Richard Nixon, won the presidential election in November, defeating Hubert Humphrey, for whom many on the student left had refused to vote.

Deeply shaken by the escalation of violence at home and in Eastern Europe, and the relentless horror of the Vietnam War, Katznelson spent the academic year of 1968–69 finishing his doctoral dissertation on racial conflicts in American and British cities, a topic of intense political concern in the months following the murder of Dr. King. After receiving his PhD in the summer of 1969, he returned to Columbia as an assistant professor of political science, where he remained for the next five years, working closely with like-minded colleagues in an effort to find constructive solutions to the ongoing demands of student activists. In 1974, he left Columbia for the University of Chicago.

By the time the New School contacted him about its search for a new dean, Katznelson was not only serving as chair of Chicago's Department of Political Science, but as study director of the university's National Opinion Research Center. He had also published two books by then and *City Trenches: Urban Politics and the Patterning of Class in the United States* was about to come out. In the eyes of many, this third book would become his most important work in the early years of his academic career.[28]

Ward was the first person to speak to Katznelson about the GF. They met in the spring of 1981. As Katznelson remembered it, one day, while he was working in his office, someone knocked on the door. Ward introduced himself and explained that he had a few meetings in Chicago and decided to stop by to meet Katznelson in person. Did the chairman of Political Science know, Ward asked, that he too had ties to Chicago? Yes he did, Katznelson replied, "Nice to meet you."

Ward got straight to the point. He had recently made some recommendations to the New School's Board of Trustees about how it might rebuild the Graduate Faculty, which had fallen on hard times. Would Katznelson be willing to take a look at what he had written? He would be happy to do so, Katznelson replied, but he declined the invitation Ward made at the same time to become a candidate in the search for the next dean. By this time, Katznelson explained, the New School was "already part of my imagination for a number of reasons. As an assistant professor teaching at Columbia, I went to the New School from time to time to hear people lecture. . . . I heard Hannah Arendt. . . . It wasn't the main focus of my life, but it was part of the intellectual milieu of the city."

Several months later Ward contacted Katznelson again and asked him to come to New York during the fall semester to meet with members of the search committee: "I'm chairing a committee at the New School that has a funny name. It's called the 'Enabling Committee.'" Although he accepted the invitation, Katznelson had not changed his mind about the New School. Becoming dean of the Graduate Faculty was still "the farthest thing from my mind." Once again, he told Ward, he did not want to apply for the position, but he would be happy to meet with the Enabling Committee and give them any advice he might have. At the time, he knew nobody serving on the committee, not even the outside members from other universities, nor did he know anybody else at the New School, with the exception of David Gordon.

Katznelson found the meeting very interesting. He learned that the New School was looking for a dean who understood, in the language of the Ward Report, that there was "an emerging crisis within the entire social science enterprise," requiring "a kind of stocktaking that involves reexamining the historical traditions and philosophical foundations of the social sciences and a multidisciplinary critical appraisal of current practices in social science research and training"—someone, in other words, who would see "much need [in the early 1980s] for precisely the kinds of intellectual perspectives which have informed the Graduate Faculty's mission in the past."[29]

The Ward Report described the Graduate Faculty's mission in terms reminiscent of what Alfred Schütz had written in the late 1950s. The division, it said, had remained committed to its "unique approach" to the social sciences, which consisted essentially of five "distinctive features": (1) The Graduate Faculty analyzed the "historical dimension." It saw the social sciences as "specific human enterprises, rooted in European and American cultural traditions and historical circumstances." (2) It maintained "close ties with philosophy." There was still not another social science program of any significance in the United States that was doing the same in the early 1980s. Grounded in the continental philosophical tradition, the GF provided students with the opportunity to analyze "the epistemological and ethical foundations" of social research. (3) It had a "global outlook," "cosmopolitan," and open to "other intellectual approaches" in ways rarely found in mainstream programs. And through this global perspective, the GF confronted "the 'big' problems of modern society and the world community." (4) The GF was interdisciplinary. It trained students to work across the social sciences. (5) Finally, the GF offered a "critical approach to social research," and this above all gave the Graduate Faculty its "distinctive ethos."[30]

Later that fall Katznelson received a second invitation to come to the New School—this time to meet President Everett, who offered him the job within a matter of minutes. Katznelson thanked him. He was flattered, he said, and would think it over—even though he had still not submitted his name as a candidate.

A few weeks later, he learned that Everett was stepping down as president. "He had never told me he was about to leave."

When Katznelson met with Everett again in January 1982, he told him point blank, "Honestly, I'm sorry you're leaving, but there is no way I can think about even imagining taking the job unless I know with whom I'd be working." Everett conceded the point, but asked Katznelson to do him the favor of speaking to the chair of the Board of Trustees. Katznelson agreed to talk to Dorothy Hirshon, whom he met later the same day in the dean's office. "That was the first time I met Dorothy." Katznelson recalled. "She came in with her three dogs on a leash":

"Well, what can I do for you?" Hirshon asked.

"I have only one question for you," Katznelson replied. "If you were in my position, would you even think of taking a job without knowing who the president is?" Hirshon's answer, Katznelson smiled, "endeared her to me forever."

"You'd be a damn fool."

With that, Katznelson returned to Chicago, assuming that the matter was closed. But Hirshon did not let go: "She sent me postcards almost every other week, saying, 'Think about us when we have a president.' And so on."

In late March or April, Katznelson received a call from Jonathan Fanton. Although they had heard of one another, they had never met. Fanton opened by saying that he was a finalist in the New School's search for president: "I understand you know a fair amount about the New School, but you're not interested. Can we have lunch at the Quadrangle Club [the faculty house]?" Lunch lasted three hours. By the time they had finished, they had a tacit agreement that if Fanton got the job Katznelson would think seriously about joining him.

Fanton called again in July: "I got the job. Will you jump into the pool with me?" Katznelson replied, "I'd gladly do it, but I wonder how much water is in the pool." Not very much, they discovered, at least not right away.

So why did Katznelson jump? "I loved the University of Chicago. We had a nice life in Hyde Park." His wife Deborah, he added, "had a good job." Although they both missed New York, Columbia had also made him an offer: "I had another New York option that wasn't this cockamamie option. But there was something really astonishing about the opportunity. This was a great institution that had a remarkable heritage."

Katznelson said that he was "smitten by three things": the New School's legacy; the fact that the GF was "in deep trouble"; and the commitment of the trustees "to provide the assets to rebuild the institution." Hirshon, he knew, was fully on board—they had kept in touch throughout the long negotiation process—as were several others, he believed, with whom he had also spoken. The more he thought about what he might do, the more excited he became.

Here he was, only thirty-eight years old, being offered the opportunity to recruit "a gang of people . . . to resurrect this institution in a way that could be consistent with its best principles in the past, but which would be new . . . we couldn't just reproduce . . . we weren't German Jewish refugees . . . this wasn't the 1930s, but we could be consistent with the advantages and character of the place." As Katznelson saw it, the resurrected GF would remain a small institution,

> where boundaries, one hoped, between disciplines would not be as high as else-where; where social science could engage the American academy, but not be identical to it; where it could have more depth in philosophy and history than was common in most social science faculties. There was a side which intellectu-ally meshed well with what I cared about, but also with what I thought other people might care about and might be recruitable to. There was [in other words] an uncommon opportunity to build a deeply historical social science—a kind of social science history—that you didn't find anywhere else.

When Katznelson accepted the job, what he wanted to do was still "on spec." He arrived alone, with no firm commitments from anyone else. But he had spo-ken about his plans to Aristide Zolberg, his good friend and colleague in Politi-cal Science at the University of Chicago who specialized in comparative politics and the persistent plight of refugees forced to flee home. Zolberg's approach to social science research reflected precisely the kind of work Katznelson believed would help rebuild the GF. Although Zolberg knew very little about the Univer-sity in Exile, his research resonated with the history of the GF, as did his personal story. Born in Brussels to Polish Jewish immigrants, Zolberg spent the war in hiding in Nazi-occupied Belgium: "It was clear to me," Katznelson said, "that he and Vera [Zolberg's wife, and a sociologist of art] were potentially interested." But he had not yet even begun to reach out to any of the other scholars he had thought about recruiting to help him turn the GF into a center of historically informed social science.

Katznelson had no intention of trying to create a freestanding department of history. The New School would never have the resources to do that. History was frequently the largest department in a university, with specialists covering all the major periods and parts of the world. He was looking for scholars who could rebuild Political Science and Sociology while they also served on an inter-disciplinary committee of Historical Studies modeled on the committees he had seen at the University of Chicago. Colleagues in Chicago with appointments in different departments came together to explore broad themes and questions that transcended their individual disciplines. A political scientist such as Zolberg, for example, with expertise in West Africa, played an important role on the Committee for the Comparative Study of New Nations.

In addition to the Zolbergs, Katznelson would try to recruit Charles and Louise Tilly, widely admired scholars in historical sociology and women's history. Soon after Katznelson became dean, he received an invitation from the Tillys to give a talk at the University of Michigan, where they were teaching, in one of their legendary Sunday night seminars. This provided the new dean with a good opportunity to let them know what he was doing at the New School and to plant the idea that perhaps they might like to join him. After he finished his presentation and everybody else had left, the Tillys and Katznelson stayed up until three o'clock in the morning talking about the GF. Within a few months the Tillys had signed on, and through them the sociologist of world cities, Janet Abu-Lughod.

Next Katznelson contacted Eric Hobsbawm, to whom the New School had awarded an honorary doctorate in 1982 during the inauguration of Jonathan Fanton. Although Katznelson did not know Hobsbawm personally, they had a number of friends in common. Like Zolberg, Hobsbawm had been a child in Nazi-occupied Europe—in his case Austria. His family fled to England in 1938. And like Zolberg and the Tillys, he too was very interested in building a historically oriented program in the social sciences. For Hobsbawm, the New School offered an additional attraction: British academics had to retire at sixty-five. Having just stepped down from his chair at the University of London (Birkbeck College) in 1982, he was very pleased to receive Katznelson's invitation in 1983 to teach at the New School for one semester every year.[31]

Before long, Fanton and Katznelson were making similar arrangements with other scholars, primarily from Europe but also from other parts of the world. With these one-semester appointments, the new president and dean renewed the New School's historical ties to the United Kingdom and the continent beyond what the university had been doing since the mid-1960s with the Heuss Professorship.[32] The list of these visitors was truly impressive. Some of them, like Hobsbawm, came every year; others came more sporadically.[33]

Katznelson's plan to turn the GF into a center of historical social science had an impact not only on the future of Political Science and Sociology but on Anthropology and Economics.[34] It did little, however, to address the problems in Philosophy. By the time Fanton and Katznelson had arrived, the troubled department had only one full-time philosopher left, the phenomenologist Reiner Schürmann, who specialized in the work of Martin Heidegger.

Born in 1941 in Nazi-occupied Holland, Schürmann agonized over the fact that he came into the world at a time when "Aryan" Germans, including his parents, were actively supporting Hitler's genocidal war. He responded to what he experienced as an existential crisis by moving to France, where as a university student he abandoned the German language. When he finished his studies and began publishing works of his own, he did so only in French. Schürmann did not, however, abandon Germany's rich philosophical tradition, elements of which, in the eyes of some, had given rise to National Socialism—a position he fiercely rejected. As a young student of theology and philosophy in Paris, Schürmann specialized in German phenomenology, particularly in the work of the politically compromised Martin Heidegger.[35]

Schürmann was so committed to phenomenology that he resisted the idea of recruiting new faculty to the department who represented other schools of thought such as American pragmatism, British analytic philosophy, and German critical theory. Rejecting the recommendations of the eminent philosophers who had reviewed the department for the State of New York, Schürmann insisted that the GF should continue to specialize in phenomenology, *tout court*. Katznelson disagreed.

Although Schürmann objected bitterly, Katznelson appointed NYU's analytic philosopher Thomas Nagel to the department's search committee to help the GF recruit strong candidates to rebuild the faculty. Recalling their early meetings, Katznelson regretted, he said, not having recorded Schürmann and Nagel's "rich and redolent debate about what philosophy was." Siding with Nagel, Katznelson refused to let the department continue to isolate itself from current developments in American and British philosophy, or from debates going on in Germany among philosophers who had rejected phenomenology.

In the end, the two philosophers who did the most to rebuild the department were the Hungarian dissident Ágnes Heller, György Lukács's favorite student and a leading figure in the Budapest School, and Richard Bernstein, who had strong ties to American pragmatism and German critical theory. Heller came in 1986, and Bernstein in 1989, after having first served on Katznelson's Enabling Committee and chaired the search committee that hired Heller. With Bernstein's appointment, Philosophy earned the right to accept PhD students again.

━━◆━━

After Katznelson succeeded in making a number of significant appointments in Sociology and Political Science, New York State lifted its restrictions on the two departments in 1986 and 1987, respectively.[36] On July 15, 1987, *The New York Times* ran a lengthy article on the GF under the gratifying title "New School

Graduate Unit Rebounds."[37] The journalist, Deirdre Carmody, reported that the GF now had seventy-five faculty members, forty-five of whom had been hired since 1983. Seeking the opinions of scholars beyond the New School, she interviewed Michael Walzer, now at the Institute for Advanced Study in Princeton, noting that he had "been watching the rebuilding"—not only watching but actively advising. As Walzer told Carmody, "It's been the strength of Ira Katznelson to attract first-rate scholars, even bringing people of stature to teach half a year."

At the GF, Carmody spoke to Zolberg, who added, "Katznelson turns out to be a genius at doing this kind of thing," adding, only partially in jest, "He can talk very unlikely people into doing this foolish thing and coming here. . . . [T]here were crazy people around who were willing to take the risk." Why did he and his wife Vera do it? In their case, Zolberg explained, there was "the excitement of being able to set intellectual themes and approaches and the challenge of rebuilding something that was virtually defunct." Like others, Zolberg was particularly attracted to an institution dedicated to cross-disciplinary research. But the transition was not easy. In 1983, the year he left the University of Chicago where he had taught political science for twenty years, his former department ranked fourth in the nation in a survey sponsored by the American Political Science Association. The GF's department did not make it into the top forty—and with good reason, Zolberg added: "It had nothing to say. It had disappeared."

In the eyes of the wider academic community, the biggest coup for the New School was the successful recruitment of Charles and Louise Tilly. The *Times* article called their arrival "a milestone in the turnaround." The Tillys were providing "the core of teaching and research in comparative historical sociology . . . to train social scientists who were interested in applying historical analysis to their own fields." Carmody also mentioned that Louise Tilly, one of the nation's leading feminist historians, was serving as the chair of Historical Studies.[38] By 1987 the Tillys' famous pro-seminar ("Think and Drink"), carried over from the Sunday evening seminars in Ann Arbor, had become "the intellectual highpoint."[39] It attracted faculty and students from all over the New York metropolitan area. Charles Tilly's Center for Social Change was also sponsoring a number of research projects on social movements, state formation, and comparative studies of cities in historical and contemporary contexts, making it possible for participating faculty to subsidize the research of one or more of their graduate students.

For Fanton, one of the most important indications that the GF had made a comeback was the support it was now receiving from the Mellon Foundation. In the mid-1980s Mellon gave the GF $250,000 to rebuild the Philosophy program, and it had just announced its intention to make a second grant to the university for $275,000. As Fanton explained to the *Times*, "This told the corporate-foundation world that this most respected foundation believed in what we were trying to do." The GF had also received major grants in recent years from the Volkswagen Foundation, the government of Berlin, and Exxon, in addition to generous gifts from members of the Board of Trustees. Outside funding for faculty research had increased as well.[40]

Now that Political Science and Sociology had the right to admit PhD candidates again, enrollment numbers in the two departments began to rise, but only slightly. While Carmody put a positive spin on the modest improvement, she studiously avoided mentioning the precipitous drop in enrollment in the three departments that had continued accepting doctoral students during that same five-year period. Some might say that those numbers decreased for the right reasons—academic standards were going up—but the GF could not afford to lose the tuition revenue.[41] Complicating matters further, the GF was still not attracting in significant numbers the same quality of students that its faculty "stars" had been teaching at their previous institutions. Given the competition from other graduate programs, this was hardly surprising. The GF did not have the resources it needed to give generous fellowships to more than a handful of the best students who applied.[42] Their other strong applicants accepted fellowships elsewhere, refusing to go into debt when other institutions were offering them substantial support. Fortunately, the GF also attracted foreign students who came with financial backing from their home countries.

But the vast majority of their students received little—if any—financial aid. Forced to work long hours to make ends meet, they did not have the time they needed to do high-level doctoral work. And with the rising cost of tuition, the challenge only grew worse. There were, of course, a few exceptional students who soldiered on without much financial aid and still did extremely well.

Nobody denied that many problems remained. But there was also much to be proud of by the summer of 1987, as *The New York Times* article made clear. Two of the three threatened departments were up and running again—and the third would soon be as well. This was a real achievement when compared to what had happened to programs at other universities in New York State that had similarly been targeted in the late 1970s. According to the Commission of Higher Education, the state had 1,500 PhD programs in 1978. By 1987, the number had dropped to 1,300. The ones that survived, noted Donald J. Nolan, deputy commissioner of Higher and Professional Education, had found ways to sharpen their focus "in areas where Ph.D.'s [were] apt to find employment,"[43] by which he meant positions outside the academy. Nolan's description, however, did not explain the encouraging news at the GF in the rebuilt departments.

Economics and Psychology were the only two departments that fit Nolan's description. Enrollment numbers had dropped significantly in both of them since 1982, but they still remained considerably stronger than the other four departments. Even graduates of the GF's radical Department of Economics were apparently finding non-academic jobs, but not in numbers close to those with degrees in clinical psychology.[44]

This persistent imbalance between the clinical psychology program and the other departments caused a great deal of tension between the clinicians and the rest of the faculty. In the early days of the rebuilding campaign, members of the clinical program tried to secede from the GF entirely, arguing that they had little in common with the intellectual mission of the rest of the division—and that included their colleagues in experimental psychology, which had such giants on the faculty as Jerome Bruner and Leon Festinger. Nobody disagreed. The clinical program was a poor fit and had been from the very beginning, but the Graduate Faculty could not afford to let it go.

19

REKINDLING THE SPIRIT

Few university presidents have enjoyed a closer working relationship with their deans than Jonathan Fanton did with Ira Katznelson. During the early months of their collaboration, the new dean commuted from Chicago and stayed with Fanton during the week. The arrangement made it possible for the two men to talk late into the night about the social scientists and philosophers Katznelson was trying to recruit. Yet the more they talked, Fanton recalled, the more they realized that recruiting a group of distinguished faculty would not be enough. They also needed "some animating ideas and ideals to rekindle the spirit of the University in Exile."[1]

Although other presidents had tried to do the same—Bryn Hovde, by "rescuing twenty-five scholars from behind the Iron Curtain," and Hans Simons, by offering scholarships to twenty-five "non-Communist Chinese students stranded in this country"[2]—those earlier efforts had long been forgotten. Understandably so, their critics might have added. Had Hovde and Simons followed Johnson's example, things might have turned out differently. Fanton would not make the same mistake. Inspired by the New School's first president, he used his "animating ideas and ideals" to strengthen the New School's academic programs and provide opportunities to improve the quality of civic life on campus.

While Fanton was president, the New School took the lead in a nationwide effort to protect artistic freedom in the United States. It also played a significant role in an international campaign to defend the rights of persecuted intellectuals in Communist Eastern Europe. Both initiatives raised hackles among small groups of students and faculty: the first with activists identified with the New Left, who, in the name of "freedom from intolerance," asserted their right to silence people whose words and visual representations were, they claimed, not only offensive but politically unacceptable.

⇒

In March 1985, colleagues at Eugene Lang College invited several members of the U.S. Army War College to participate in a panel discussion about the role the U.S. military was playing in domestic conflicts in Latin America and the Caribbean.[3] Few topics were more contentious at the time. Of particular concern was the civil war in Nicaragua, where the CIA and Defense Department were actively assisting the campaign of the antisocialist "Contras" in their effort to topple the Sandinista government. The event attracted outspoken critics of the Reagan administration, some of whom caused such a ruckus that the guests from the War College never got a chance to speak.

Fanton responded immediately. In an open letter to the New School community, he wrote that the incident "reminds all of us of the fragility of the freedoms which are so essential to the university's fulfillment of its mission. It further reminds us of our communal responsibility to preserve and enhance academic freedom and, specifically in this case, freedom of speech."[4] He then convened an ad hoc committee to review and, if necessary, revise the university's policies on freedom of expression. Chaired by Katznelson, the committee produced a set of recommendations that persuaded the trustees to amend the university's bylaws. The recommendations stressed the importance of clarifying the difference between freedom of speech in the wider community and freedom of expression in an academic setting— something the New School had not previously done. This distinction, the committee explained, was easily blurred because there existed an irresolvable tension between the two: Advocates of free speech in the wider community did not insist that speakers back up what they said with verifiable evidence; whereas advocates in an academic setting did, despite the risks involved in making demands of this kind:

> Any attempt to extend free speech norms so far that they challenge standards of evidence and argument, threatens the university; any attempt to restrict speech in the name of standards, or to have a body of standard-keepers to monitor the diversity of speech, threatens to undercut the foundations of academic freedom. Universities must learn to live with this conundrum, even more so the New School for Social Research.[5]

The committee noted that the original policies of the New School were written by members of the faculty who had lived through "the horrors of war and fascism" and that these experiences had "marked the university in three ways beyond its unusually profound dedication to free expression." First, having fought against political repression themselves, the founders of the New School in 1919 and again in 1933 insisted on maintaining a position of political neutrality. The university must remain a "nonpolitical institution." As such, it "should stand on the grounds of tolerance" and reject any compromise "on questions of free expression." Katznelson's committee fully agreed. The revised policy should preserve the university's firm commitment to tolerance.

Second, and seemingly in contradiction with the first, the founding members of the University in Exile wrote into the bylaws in 1935 that the Graduate Faculty would not hire anyone who belonged to a political party that repressed freedom of expression, by which they meant Fascists and Communists. This injunction was "still embedded in Article I of the By-Laws" in the 1980s. The committee recommended deleting the passage, adding: "The chilling possibilities of this section of the By-Laws far outweigh any protection to free expression that it may have been written to provide."

Finally, the university's "unusual and vigorous engagement with public affairs" in the early days of its history resulted in blurring the distinction between academic freedom and freedom of speech. The committee therefore recommended that the university recognize the distinction, while acknowledging the irresolvable tension that existed between the two. Katznelson's committee concluded with a set of guidelines that were purposefully tentative because it was "impossible," the members cautioned, to address the complexities of individual cases in an abstract list of procedures. The committee hoped, all the same, that its suggestions would help the university understand the challenges involved in respecting the rights of freedom of expression "in ways most conducive to secure the university as a community of reason."

When the New School's trustees reissued its policies on freedom of expression, they incorporated the recommendations of Katznelson's committee. Carefully worded, the new policies guided Fanton over the next several years as he tried to resolve subsequent confrontations on campus among groups of faculty, students, and activists with no ties to the university. One such conflict involved members of the Palestinian Liberation Organization who wanted to silence a talk on campus by Yitzhak Rabin, who was serving as Israel's minister of defense at the time. Another involved a group of gay activists who wanted to close down an event sponsored by *The New York Times* because the newspaper had recently published an editorial that the demonstrators deemed "homophobic."[6]

But the most explosive conflict of all took place in the fall of 1989 over an exhibit at Parsons School of Design of three hundred fifty prints by the Japanese artist Shin Matsunaga, one of which was widely considered offensive. *New York Times* journalist Steven Holmes described the print as a picture of "a black man whose face is dominated by the whites of his eyes and white lips." The image, Holmes continued, resembled the kinds of caricatures of black people frequently seen in minstrel shows before the rise of the civil rights movement. In Japan, the picture had circulated widely as part of an advertising campaign peddling soft drinks.[7]

Three days before the exhibit was scheduled to close, Sekou Sundiata, a faculty member at Eugene Lang College, defaced the controversial image. A nationally recognized poet and musician who identified himself as African American, Sundiata told the *Times*, "Matsunaga can say or draw whatever he wants, but you don't have to invite him in." Another colleague, John Jeffries, associate dean of the Graduate School of Management and Urban Professions (now the Milano School), added, "Freedom of expression is no more sacred than freedom from intolerance or bigotry." Fanton held his ground. In a letter to the university community, he proclaimed:

> [W]e have an affirmative responsibility to one another to be sensitive to our diverse backgrounds and beliefs. . . . There is no question that the design work that was defaced contains . . . an insulting visual image. I find the image deeply offensive and racist. The issue of whether the university should have "done something" about the piece was not, however, one that could be decided only on the basis of the work's offensiveness. It is a question that also must take account of the university's obligations regarding freedom of expression.[8]

The Matsunaga exhibit at the New School coincided with a heated national debate over artistic freedom. As Holmes explained in the same *New York Times* article, the issue at hand was whether freedom of expression was an "inviolable right," or whether limits should "be placed on it when art or speech is offensive." And if so, who decides? According to legal scholars, the U.S. Supreme Court had already settled the matter in its landmark decision in 1973 (*Miller v. California*), at least when it came to questions of obscenity. What constituted obscenity was a matter to be determined at the state level; there was no national standard or definition.

In the fall of 1989, Congress challenged the Court's decision. North Carolina Senator Jesse Helms sponsored an amendment that gave the National Endowment for the Arts (NEA) the authority to determine whether a particular piece of art was obscene. The new legislation inflamed artists and millions of other Americans, including Fanton, who claimed it was unconstitutional. As Fanton told a reporter for *The Los Angeles Times*, Americans should interpret the passage of laws like this as an "early warning sign" similar to those leading up to the McCarthy period.[9]

⬅◆➡

Helms introduced his amendment to Congress in early September 1989, largely in response to a nationwide controversy over the work of photographers Andrés Serrano and Robert Mapplethorpe. In the eyes of many, the artists had pushed the limits of tolerance beyond the acceptable. Of particular concern was a retrospective of Mapplethorpe's work that had received a grant from the NEA. The exhibit first appeared at the Whitney Museum in New York in the summer of 1988 and had been scheduled to move to the Corcoran Gallery in Washington, D.C. Outraged by its homoerotic content, members of Congress threatened to defund the NEA entirely, prompting the director of the Corcoran to cancel the much-anticipated show. The Helms Amendment became law on October 23, 1989.[10]

While Congress was debating the amendment, the New School's trustees voted to strengthen the university's commitment to artists. On October 4, two weeks before the Matsunaga exhibit opened, the board issued a new policy for artists that went beyond the university's more general policy protecting freedom of expression. Having just reaffirmed the New School's commitment to artistic freedom, the trustees were not about to remove a print from an exhibit on campus because it offended the sensibilities of members of the academic community—including those of its president. Given what was going on in the nation's capital, it was more important than ever to defend the constitutional rights of artists.

Fanton's critics rejected his argument. As one student told *The New York Times*, the university was "using a very sensitive issue in America today and the whole Jesse Helms position to shield an act of racism." Others added that "university officials [were] using freedom of expression to mask an inept handling of the affair," by which they meant that the New School had not intervened after colleagues at Parsons appointed a sixteen-member selection committee to choose the works for the show that had no African American representation. Adding insult to injury, the art center's director openly admitted that he had "looked at the image along with everything else and it didn't dawn on me that it would be offensive."[11]

The incident was particularly painful, Fanton wrote in an open letter to the university community, because the exhibition committee had given so little thought to the feelings of others. Assuming part of the blame himself, he apologized for not having spoken out right away, after seeing the show, to let everyone know that he had personally found the drawing "offensive and racist." He also should have called a town meeting to discuss the impact the exhibit was having on the New School community. Although he was sorry he had not responded right away, he firmly stood by the university's decision to leave Matsunaga's print up. Nobody, he continued, had the right to deface a piece of art because he or she found it offensive. Fanton ended his letter with this request:

> Let us not frame the issue as if freedom of expression and freedom from intolerance are incompatible or are enemies. They are both cherished values, and we should not have to choose which one we hold more dear. The question I think is how to use freedom of expression more vigorously in pursuit of a society free of prejudice and intolerance of all kinds.[12]

Five months later Fanton turned those same arguments against the NEA. In April 1990, he learned that the NEA had awarded the New School a grant of $45,000 to help cover the cost of renovating the courtyard behind the Twelfth Street building and turning it "into a work of art."[13] The letter that he and every other recipient received included language from the Helms Amendment: Before the National Endowment would release the funds, Fanton would have to sign a statement promising that the money would not be used "to promote, disseminate, or produce materials which in the judgment of the National Endowment for the Arts . . . may be considered obscene."[14]

The NEA's letter caused a storm of controversy across the country. One by one award winners announced to the press that they had refused to sign "the obscenity clause." Among them, in Manhattan, were Joseph Papp, director of the New York Shakespeare Festival and the Public Theater, and Jonathan Fanton, president of the New School, who not only refused to sign, but pursued litigation. With the help of First Amendment lawyer Floyd Abrams, the New School sued NEA and sought "injunctive relief" from signing the statement because, Abrams claimed, it was unconstitutional.[15]

In May, Fanton issued a five-page public statement, "Saying No to the Obscenity Condition," in which he outlined the New School's case against the NEA. Reminding his readers of the history of the university, the New School, he wrote, had a responsibility "to defend the right of free expression when it is threatened and when we are in a position to act effectively and meaningfully in response to such a threat." They had been doing so since 1919 and were not about to stop now.

The national media covered the story in detail, interviewing Fanton and quoting at length from the statement he had prepared:[16]

> The New School for Social Research [Fanton explained] has concluded that it cannot accept a grant that carries with it a limitation upon free expression. . . . We do not believe that it is sound public policy or that it is consistent with the Constitution to attach to grants conditions that infringe upon free expression, visual or verbal. We recognize that obscenity as defined by the Supreme Court is not a form of protected expression and that it is appropriate for government agencies to assure themselves that grantees will abide by the law. But Congress is obliged to write constitutional laws, and the section of Public Law 101–121 purportedly dealing with obscenity can hardly be deemed constitutional. Our challenge is directed at that law only by implication since we are seeking to remove a condition which the NEA, not the Congress, attached to our grant of its own volition.[17]

About a year later, the NEA settled the case out of court and dropped its requirement that the New School sign the obscenity condition. Reporting the good news, *The New York Times* announced that Judge Louis L. Stanton in Manhattan's Federal District Court had dismissed the case on February 20, 1991, adding that the settlement had delivered the New School a major victory and, by extension, the 1,990 others who had also refused to sign the obscenity clause. Every recipient of a letter from the NEA in 1990 indicating that he or she had been selected for a grant would now receive the money. The controversial passage in the original letter was "replaced by one stating that the arts endowment intends to enforce the anti-obscenity stipulation mandated by Congress [only] after a grantee has been convicted of violating a criminal obscenity or child pornography statute and all appeal rights have been exhausted." An "inoffensive" compromise, Abrams told the journalist covering the story.[18]

Between May 1990 and February 1991, as Fanton waited to see if the New School would go to trial or settle out of court, he shared the university's legal arguments with two institutions in California that had filed similar briefs against the NEA. Both cases appeared before a judge in Los Angeles, who ruled in their favor, stating that "the anti-obscenity clause in the arts endowment's letter of agreement was 'unconstitutional' " in the State of California. Finally, and to the great satisfaction of artists across the country, Congress eliminated the obscenity clause from the 1991 appropriations bill that would extend funding to the NEA for three more years. With this new bill, the task of defining what constituted "artistic obscenity" was returned to the judicial branch of government, at least for a while.[19]

Several months later, Congress found new ways to limit the use of NEA funding, diminishing the impact of what the New School and its partners in California had accomplished. As disappointing as this was for everyone involved, the three institutions had won an important early battle in what legal scholars predicted would be a very long war.[20]

⊷

Shortly after Fanton and Katznelson came to the New School, the university stepped forward to defend the rights of dissident intellectuals in East and Central Europe. By 1982, the USSR and its satellite states were visibly crumbling. Defying government crackdowns, intellectuals and workers throughout the region had created liberal democratic movements in their countries to oppose Soviet domination. The leaders of these "velvet revolutions" had been in and out of jail since the "cataclysmic events" of 1968 had shaken Poland and Czechoslovakia.

When left-leaning intellectuals in the West looked back in the early 1980s on what they had accomplished during the radical sixties, they took pride in having liberated themselves at the time from mainstream social and political thought and embraced the teachings of Marx and his disciples. When their counterparts in East and Central Europe looked back, they took pride in having challenged "the very Communist idea itself." And they were still speaking out in 1982 at great personal risk to themselves. With the benefit of hindsight, British historian Tony Judt blamed himself and his friends in London, Paris, and New York for not having paid closer attention to what was going on in Warsaw and Prague in 1968:

> For all our grandstanding theories of history, then, we failed to notice one of its seminal turning points. It was in Prague and Warsaw, in those summer months of 1968, that Marxism ran itself into the ground. It was the student rebels of Central Europe who went on to undermine, discredit, and overthrow not just a couple of dilapidated Communist regimes but the very Communist idea itself. Had we cared a little more about the fate of ideas we tossed around so glibly, we might have paid greater attention to the actions and opinions of those who had been brought up in their shadow.[21]

Two colleagues at the New School had been paying close attention in the late 1960s and early 1970s and were still deeply engaged in the early 1980s. Since their graduate school days, Andrew Arato and Jeffrey Goldfarb had been working in Communist Eastern Europe, Arato in Hungary since 1969 and Goldfarb in Poland since 1973. When Fanton and Katznelson arrived, the two men were teaching in the Department of Sociology: Goldfarb was an untenured assistant professor giving courses in the sociology of art, and Arato was a visiting adjunct—with a full-time appointment at Cooper Union—teaching courses in critical theory. Together, they approached the new president and dean with a bold proposal: As part of the rebuilding campaign, the GF should consider renewing the legacy of the University of Exile by supporting dissident intellectuals in East and Central Europe.

Arato, in particular, had personal ties to some of the leaders. Born in occupied Budapest in 1944 to parents of Jewish origin, Arato survived the final months of the war with his mother in the so-called international ghetto, protected by the heroic efforts of the Swedish diplomat Raoul Wallenberg, who saved the lives of thousands of Jews in the country. His father survived in hiding after escaping from a forced labor gang. In 1956, after the Soviet Union crushed the Hungarian uprising, the family moved to New York. Arato was twelve years old. Thirteen years later, he returned to Budapest, now as an American citizen and graduate student of the University of Chicago, with the hope of meeting the Marxist critic György Lukács, the subject of his doctoral dissertation. He also wanted to meet Lukács's disciples, the founders of the Budapest School of Philosophy and leaders in Hungary's dissident movement. These "children and grandchildren" of the legendary critic became his lifelong friends.

Both Fanton and Katznelson liked the proposal. Well versed in the "grandstanding theories of history," Katznelson had been following the struggles of dissident intellectuals in the region since 1968; Fanton less so. He knew a great deal about the American civil rights movement—and had been active in it—but very little about East and Central Europe.[22] With the help of Arato and Goldfarb, Fanton educated himself quickly. Then thanks to Joan Davidson, the daughter of New School trustee Jacob Kaplan, he met the leaders of Helsinki Watch and joined the organization. Founded in 1978, Helsinki Watch had been tracking human rights abuses taking place in the Soviet Union and its satellite states in violation of the 1975 Helsinki Accords. Before long, Fanton realized that Helsinki Watch was championing the cause of the very same dissidents Arato and Goldfarb had urged the New School to support, a convergence that provided the GF with an exciting opportunity to join forces with a major international campaign.

Reminiscing about their early conversations in 2011, Goldfarb was still amazed by it all. The new president and dean easily could have said, "Out with the old, in with the new, but they realized that there was some part of the old that they ought to learn from." Katznelson had arrived with a specific intellectual project, Goldfarb continued, and he got started right away:

[He organized] seminars on social history, on urban public policy. Some met weekly, some monthly. There was this dynamism he brought with him. He had clear ideas about whom he wanted to hire—neo-Marxists interested in the problems of the state and of class. You know, leading left-wing social historians in sociology, political theory, and history. But Ira also realized that there was this deep Graduate Faculty story and people.[23]

As Katznelson moved forward with his plan to rebuild the GF around Historical Studies, he also recruited several scholars with direct ties to East and Central European politics and society who could serve as intermediaries between the New School and dissident intellectuals living in Poland and Hungary, then Czechoslovakia and Yugoslavia, and finally, after 1989, eleven countries of the former Soviet bloc. In Katznelson's first year as dean, he tenured Goldfarb and appointed Arato full time to the faculty, also with tenure, positioning the two men to play active roles in developing a new East and Central Europe project for the GF and in strengthening the Department of Sociology. Other appointments soon followed, most significantly those of the Hungarian philosophers Ágnes Heller and Ferenc Fehér, whom Arato first met in 1969, and the Polish sociologist Elzbieta Matynia, whom Goldfarb had met in 1973.

⊰⊱

In 1984, the New School made the cause of dissident intellectuals in East and Central Europe one of the major themes of its fiftieth anniversary celebration of the University in Exile. To mark the occasion, Fanton organized three high-profile events: the first in New York, the second in Berlin, and the third in Warsaw. At each celebration, he gave honorary doctorates to individuals who had devoted their lives to fight for academic freedom and human rights during the Nazi period, and more recently as well. In New York, the recipients included Hans Speier, the only living member of the 1933 "Mayflower" generation of the University in Exile, and Adolph Lowe, who had arrived in 1941. The other honorees had no direct ties to the history of the GF but had also distinguished themselves as human rights activists in the United States, Germany, South Africa, Latin America, and the USSR/Soviet bloc countries.

In preparation for the anniversary celebrations, Fanton asked Arato to serve on the nominations committee for honorary doctorates to help the New School identify exceptional candidates from East and Central Europe. After consulting with Goldfarb, Arato recommended Adam Michnik, a leading activist and theorist for the democratic opposition in Poland. Although Arato's own work focused mainly on Hungary, he had been following Michnik very closely since the late 1960s and had recently published a couple of articles about the Polish dissident's ideas on the "new evolutionism" and "self-limiting revolution."[24] At the time, Michnik was virtually unknown in the United States, but he had a major reputation in Western Europe among left-leaning intellectuals, particularly in France. Members of the Polish émigré community in Paris had been publishing translations of Michnik's writings, which they had smuggled out of Poland, much of it written behind bars. Between 1968 and the downfall of communism in 1989, Michnik would spend seven years in prison.[25]

Although the New School's recognition of the Polish dissident became the big story, the main event took place in Berlin and included participation by leading German intellectuals and political figures. As Katznelson remembered it, Jürgen Habermas spoke "on German academic culture and the impact of the absence of a once-vibrant Jewish intellectual and cultural presence." Expressing gratitude to the New School for the role it had played during the 1930s and 1940s, the City of Berlin created a University in Exile chair for the GF, the first occupant of which would be Aristide Zolberg, who had survived the war as a child in occupied Belgium. Zolberg spoke in Berlin as well, giving "a moving account," Katznelson reported, "of personal and scholarly duress and renewal." The "highlight," however, was Richard von Weizsächer, the newly elected president of the German Federal Republic. Weizsächer received an honorary doctorate from the New School for his commitment to "the ideals exemplified by the University in Exile: the freedom of intellectual inquiry, the defense of human rights, and the pursuit of international understanding as an avenue toward peace." In his remarks, Katznelson continued, the West German president paid "homage to the New School's legacy of courage and resistance" while humbly acknowledging the heavy burden he bore as the son of a high-ranking member of the Nazi Party.[26]

When the New School gave Michnik an honorary doctorate in April 1984, the dissident was back in prison, having been arrested in December 1981, together with hundreds of other activists in the democratic opposition, after Poland declared martial law. Although Arato could have suggested to Fanton that he recognize one of the better known leaders of the Solidarity movement, for example Michnik's mentor Jacek Kuroń, or Lech Wałęsa himself, both of whom were also incarcerated at the time, he understood that the younger dissident was a better choice for the New School at this particular historical moment. An inspirational writer, Michnik was the symbol of Poland's generation of 1968, the person European veterans of the student movement identified with and admired. As Dany Cohn-Bendit confessed to Michnik, "I don't know if I'd have the courage to act the way you do in Poland." The Polish dissident dismissed the compliment. Paraphrasing a famous line from Alexander Solzhenitsyn's *Gulag Archipelago*, Michnik told the hero of Paris 1968, "I thank God for my years in jail." Prison, he explained, had given him an education in "concrete communism," convincing him that he would never leave Poland and go into exile, no matter what they did to him. Prison not only strengthened his resolve, it also made him a writer "appreciated in Poland and translated in the West. What should I complain about?"[27]

Since Michnik was in prison, Fanton asked the Polish émigré poet and Nobel Laureate Czesław Miłosz to accept the honorary degree on behalf of the young dissident at the first event the New School held to commemorate the fiftieth anniversary of the University in Exile. The ceremony took place on April 25, in Manhattan's First Presbyterian Church on Twelfth Street. Speaking before an overflowing crowd, Miłosz read a translation of the letter Michnik had sent the previous December to the Polish minister of the interior, General Czesław Kiszczak, in response to the minister's offer to release him from prison in time for Christmas—provided he left the country immediately. Michnik refused. He preferred prison, he said, to a "Christmas vacation on the Riviera":

> You cannot believe that such people exist. . . . For me, General, prison is not such painful punishment. . . . For me, General, real punishment would be if on your orders I had to spy, wave a truncheon, shoot workers, interrogate prisoners, and issue disgraceful sentences. I am happy to find myself on the right side, among the victims and not among the victimizers. But, of course you cannot comprehend this: otherwise you would not be making such foolish and wicked proposals. . . .
>
> I know that I will have to pay dearly for this letter. . . . That is why I am asking you for no favors. Except one: I ask you to think again. Not about my fate, because I hope to endure whatever new ideas your colonels and majors may come up with.
>
> Please think about yourself. When you are sitting down to your Christmas dinner, take a moment to think that you will be held responsible for your actions. . . . It will be a grim moment for you. . . .
>
> I hope at that moment you will manage to retain your personal dignity. . . . As for myself, I hope that when your life is in danger, I will be able to appear in time to help you . . . [and] place myself once again on the side of the victims and not that of the victimizers.

Michnik's letter "swept us like a tornado," Robert Heilbroner told *The New York Times* reporter William G. Blair, who covered the story on the front page of the newspaper.[28] In the weeks following the New School's event, the Polish authorities released Michnik and several other high-profile dissidents—at least temporarily—long enough for Fanton to organize a second gathering in Warsaw to give Michnik his degree in person: "I well recall that cold December 10 [1984]," Fanton later told a group of East and Central European intellectuals, all of whom had played important roles in the velvet revolutions in their countries: "Of course, the police were outside taking names and pictures, and it won't surprise anyone that the lights went out just as the ceremony began. But fortunately, a battery -powered . . . television camera illuminated the room, with the ironic effect of capturing the whole ceremony on tape for broadcast around the world."[29]

The ceremony itself took place in the living room of the economist Edward Lipiński, one of the founding members of KOR, described by Goldfarb as the "grand old man of the secular opposition and a lifelong Socialist, then 96 years old." [30] Given his advanced age and international reputation, the Polish authorities left the economist alone, making it possible for him to offer hospitality and other forms of support to the growing dissident movement. As Michael Kaufman noted in *The New York Times*, Lipiński had also opened his home to Polish intellectuals in 1976 when they came together to create KOR. On this later occasion, in December 1984, about thirty people "including most of Warsaw's most prominent former political prisoners" crowded into the economist's apartment to witness Michnik receive his honorary doctorate from the New School. Among the guests were Jacek Kuroń and Bronisław Geremek, both of whom went on to play leading roles in government during the early days of post-communist Poland.[31]

For Michnik and other members of Poland's generation of 1968, Kuroń was the "godfather" of the Polish opposition. He had "challenged Communist rulers first as an ardent and ideological party member in the 1950s and then kept training generations of dissidents . . . to be active, critical, and creative."[32] Kuroń, not Michnik, the younger man demurred, was the one who deserved the New School's recognition. In thanking Fanton, Michnik expressed his gratitude "not only for the honor but also for 'our freedom.' " The New School, Michnik said, had exerted precisely the kind of pressure "that [had] forced Polish authorities to release him and his fellow detainees in an amnesty last summer." But the award, Michnik repeated, should have gone to his mentor and friend, Jacek Kuroń, because he "has sacrificed and lost more than any of us in the struggle."[33] In the eyes of Poland's dissident intellectuals, Kuroń was the great strategist of the democratic opposition.

When Fanton gave Michnik an honorary doctorate, he was paying tribute through him to the entire pro-democracy movement. Everyone assembled in Lipiński's apartment understood. In singling him out, Fanton may have embarrassed the younger dissident, but Arato had given the New School's president good advice. Michnik represented the future of a post-communist Poland. Before long, his eloquent essays calling for a peaceful transition to democracy would be known in the United States as well as in Western Europe.

Intellectuals in the West got to know Michnik personally in the mid-1970s, thanks to the intervention of the French philosopher Jean-Paul Sartre, who petitioned the authorities to let the young writer leave Poland for an extended period of time. During 1976 and 1977 Michnik spent eight months traveling around France, Germany, and Italy, making contact with veterans of 1968. Wherever he went he tried to persuade his counterparts to support the dissident movement in Poland, but he had little success. As he told Cohn-Bendit, they all shared his brazen antiauthoritarianism, but not the goals of the Polish opposition: "Those who'd been through 1968 understood me, but they weren't ready to take on the Eastern point of view; they wanted to fight American imperialism." When other dissidents had similar experiences with leftists in the West, they gave up, Michnik continued, and accepted the support of the anticommunist right. But Michnik refused. He wanted to engage the left: "I am a man of the left, and I demand that they take a stand."[34]

Fanton invited Goldfarb to accompany him to Warsaw and participate in the honorary doctorate ceremony, after which the sociologist stayed on for another week. He wanted to get better acquainted with Michnik, whom he had met only casually on earlier visits to Poland. Through Michnik, Goldfarb met other members of the opposition, from major figures in the Solidarity movement such as Kuroń to grassroots intellectual activists he had never heard of before but who were writing for Michnik's underground journal *Krytyka*.

One day, as he and Michnik were walking through the streets of Warsaw talking about thinkers they both admired, Michnik suggested to Goldfarb that they organize an international seminar to study the works of leading theorists of democracy and totalitarianism. He was particularly interested, he said, in focusing on the work of Hannah Arendt, which had been banned in Poland. As Michnik explained it, he wanted to use the occasion of his honorary doctorate to build something both concrete and symbolic. Dissident intellectuals in Poland were isolated and had few opportunities to exchange ideas with their peers in other countries. With a seminar like the one he envisioned, they would create ties not only to intellectuals in New York but to members of the opposition in other East European countries.[35]

Michnik already had strong ties to dissidents in Prague and Budapest. Since 1978, he, Kuroń, and other founders of KOR had been meeting clandestinely on the Polish-Czech border with Václav Havel and members of Charter 77.[36]

Michnik also had contacts in Hungary with Arato's good friends, the dissident philosophers György Bence and János Kis, the academic "grandchildren" of Lukács. Although the Czech seminar did not materialize right away, Bence ran a group in Budapest, Goldfarb in New York, and Michnik expected to do the same in Warsaw, but he was arrested again and sent back to prison. The Warsaw seminar met all the same under the direction of Jerzy Szacki, a distinguished professor of sociology at Warsaw University, who taught intellectual history and social theory. Szacki had also been one of several founders of the Warsaw School of the History of Ideas, along with the since exiled philosopher Leszek Kołakowski.

Although Szacki disapproved of the student dissidents' tactics—and he told them so on several occasions—he continued to support them. Early on, in the winter of 1968, he tried to persuade Michnik and his friends to find a less confrontational way to express their opposition to the government's decision to close down the production of *Forefathers' Eve*. Michnik refused to follow his professor's advice, but he deeply admired Szacki's sense of "integrity and independence of thought."[37] He could think of nobody better to sponsor the seminar than Poland's leading sociologist who, he later learned, had his own ties to the New School.[38]

How was it possible to run a seminar like this at the University of Warsaw? Although the harsh restrictions of martial law had been lifted by then, one still had to be careful. People like Szacki, however, had more leeway. As the Polish sociologist explained it, professors with international reputations were free, relatively speaking, to do what they wanted in their classes, at least in Warsaw and Krakow. Michnik's seminar would not be a problem as long as the discussion remained on a theoretical level and did not turn to current politics. Szacki had already tested the waters by giving a seminar on censorship. But that was about as far as he would go.

Szacki acknowledged many years later that he never published works that openly challenged the one-party state. Nor did he join organizations like KOR. And he was not alone. With the exception of scholars who went into exile, professors who supported the opposition waited until they retired, as Lipiński had, before they did anything more radical. A political strategy that made it possible for students such as the New School's sociologist Elzbieta Matynia to study with a man of his moral and intellectual integrity. Thanks to Szacki, Matynia said, she learned to think critically.

Michnik wanted the seminar to begin with Arendt's *Origins of Totalitarianism* because, he explained, the political philosopher represented the antitotalitarian left. He had discovered her work in the 1970s in an underground journal called *Temat*, published in Polish by political exiles living in the United States. The first piece of hers that he read was "Lying and Politics: Reflections on the Pentagon Papers." He then found an abridged version of *Origins of Totalitarianism* in French during his trip to Western Europe. For him, Arendt was a woman on the left, he said, who dared to oppose both National Socialism and Bolshevism in the early Cold War period. She had the courage to attack people on both sides of the political divide.

Michnik was not the only one interested in Arendt, Szacki noted. During the early 1980s, dissident intellectuals representing a wide range of opinion were all eager to read her. And what they found, Szacki added, was often very different, leading to lively debates about her work. As Szacki remembered it, most of the participants in the seminar were writing for *Krytyka* and shared Michnik's political views. But there were others, such as the philosopher Marcin Król, a Catholic intellectual.

Krol had been particularly interested, he said, in the articles Arendt had published on Catholic intellectuals in *The Partisan Review* during the late 1940s, including one on Jacques Maritain. When the seminar met, the *Krytyka* crowd dismissed Krol and his faction for being too conservative because, Krol explained, he and his friends rejected Marxism. At the time, Krol continued, dissidents of every stripe rejected Soviet-style communism, but Michnik and his friends followed the teachings of Kołakowski and Kuroń, who still believed in the mid-1980s that Poland could build the kind of socialist society described in the early writings of Marx. Krol did not.[39]

The seminars met between 1986 and 1989 in New York, Warsaw, and Budapest with varying degrees of frequency. When possible, Szacki and Bence sent reports summarizing what they had discussed to Goldfarb in New York, who then circulated them to the others along with his report on the seminar at the New School. Matynia described these exchanges as an "earnest dialogue . . . with a fleeting quality." Everyone understood that the seminars "would not advance academic careers or make political heroes or public celebrities of any members." But they still served an important purpose, she maintained, providing opportunities for "engaged intellectuals" to read works that were banned in their countries and then discuss together the "fundamental problems facing their respective societies"[40]— at least on the theoretical level.

During this same period, Arien Mack decided to dedicate two issues of *Social Research* to the scholarship of dissident academics in Poland and other communist countries.[41] With the financial support of the Central and East European

Publishing Project, she traveled to Warsaw and Budapest in April 1987, accompanied by Andrew Arato—who introduced her to members of the dissident communities there—and then later to Prague with the Hungarian philosopher György Bence. Mack also went to East Berlin, where she was closely followed by the secret police, as she no doubt had been in the other cities as well, but in this case she could prove it.

Mack's "official" reason for going to East Berlin was to attend a party in the home of the head of the American Consulate. After mixing with the guests for a while, she left the festivities and made her way to the apartment of Wolfgang Templin, the head of the democratic opposition. Templin lived with his wife on the shabby outskirts of East Berlin in what looked like an abandoned part of the city. Although the couple had lost their jobs and had visibly little to eat, they insisted on sharing a small piece of bread with Mack, a gesture that moved her deeply. After the reunification of Germany, the magazine *Der Spiegel* published selections of the *Stasi* files, including an entry about Mack's visit with Templin, which described the purpose of her meeting in impressive detail.[42]

By February 1989, Michnik was out of prison and taking part in a series of "Round Table" negotiations together with Wałęsa, Kuroń, and over thirty other members of the democratic opposition. Two months later, Poland's Communist government and the dissidents reached a historic agreement that led to new elections and a peaceful transition in Poland to a liberal democratic state. Hungary followed suit in September; the Berlin Wall came down in November; and communism collapsed in Czechoslovakia in December, a month after tens of thousands of citizens had marched in Wenceslas Square, an event Fanton witnessed in person. Having arrived in Prague on Helsinki Watch business a few days earlier, Fanton joined the demonstration in the company of the Czech sociologist Ivan Gabal.

In the euphoric months following the fall of communism, members of the New School's network of dissident intellectuals took on important responsibilities in their newly liberated countries in government, academic, and cultural institutions. The work ahead of them was enormous and they needed help. Major philanthropists including George Soros stepped forward. Although the New School had little to offer in the way of money, it responded quickly as well, assisting regional initiatives to revitalize "scholarly life within the social sciences, especially in the fields of sociology, political science, philosophy. and economics." To coordinate the New School's efforts, Fanton created the East and Central Europe Program at the GF and appointed Matynia its director. Before long,

Matynia recalled, "there evolved a whole roster of fully collaborative activities . . . [including] curriculum development, research projects, co-teaching initiatives, and programs of joint 'east-west' graduate study."[43] By 1996, the GF was reaching out to South Africa as well, and Matynia turned the East and Central Europe program into the Transregional Center for Democratic Studies, with two offsite institutes that met every year during the summer months: July in Krakow and January in Cape Town.

Between 1990 and 1995, the East and Central Europe program expanded Goldfarb and Michnik's original idea of running Democracy Seminars to fourteen cities, located in eleven postcommunist countries. Participants included former dissidents who were now fully engaged in rebuilding their countries.[44] During those five years, Fanton hosted a meeting every spring—each year in a different country—that brought together the chairs of these seminars, members of the GF, and a few other scholars whose work focused on the region or on building democratic states more generally.[45] The group spent several days together debating the works of classical and modern political and social theorists and the significance of those ideas to the changes taking place in postcommunist East and Central Europe. Looking back on those meetings in 2007, Marcin Król described them as providing a wonderful opportunity to exchange ideas with his counterparts in other post-Soviet countries and with a remarkable group of scholars from the GF. The contacts he made through the New School remained very important for many years, he said, a sentiment many others expressed as well.

Not everyone agreed that the Democracy Seminars should continue after 1989. When György Bence visited the New School in the late fall of that year, he told Arien Mack that Hungarians did not need any more seminars. They needed journals and books to help them catch up on what they had missed over the past forty years in philosophy, political theory, and the empirical social sciences. The same was true, he suggested, for colleagues in the other post-communist countries.

Having served as editor of *Social Research* for nearly twenty years, Mack "knew a lot of journal editors," she said. "So, I wrote to everyone I knew and asked them to donate subscriptions. The Berlin Wall had just come down; it was the 'end of the evil empire.' It [would be] easy to get money," she predicted, to cover the cost of mailing the journals to libraries overseas. And she succeeded, thanks to the enthusiasm and generosity of Anthony Richter at the Soros Foundation and Richard Quant at Andrew Mellon.

Within a very few months, the editors of dozens of academic journals printed in English had agreed to provide free subscriptions and back issues of their publications. With the help of Matynia, Mack contacted university libraries across Poland, Hungary, and Czechoslovakia. As the East and Central Europe program expanded throughout the region, the Journal Donation Project moved into those countries as well and then beyond. By the mid-1990s, it had extended its reach into Central Asia—to some of the former republics of the Soviet Union—as well as to parts of Africa and East Asia. Twenty years later the Journal Donation Project was working with two hundred fifty libraries in twenty-five countries.[46]

The reach of Matynia's East and Central Europe Program/Transregional Center for Democratic Studies has necessarily been more limited, but the ties Matynia developed over the years with individuals and academic institutions have had an enduring impact on students and colleagues in several countries in East and Central Europe, in particular Poland, and South Africa, not to mention at the GF itself. With the generous support of New School trustees and outside foundations, students from these new democracies have come to the New School for their doctoral studies and then returned home to join the faculties of universities in their countries.

In the summer of 1981, Matynia came to the New School on a postdoctoral fellowship, fully expecting to go back to Warsaw at the end of the academic year. But her plans changed abruptly in December when Poland declared martial law and arrested active members of Solidarity, including several of her friends. Given her strong ties to the movement, Matynia's family urged her to stay in the United States.

The GF had invited Matynia to New York on a special fellowship that Vera List had established in the late 1970s when John Everett was still president of the New School. The ever-faithful trustee made the gift after reading an article in *The New York Times* about Katarzyna Kalwinska, a Polish peasant woman who had risked her life to save Jews during World War II. The first Kalwinska scholar was a Communist Party hack, who had come through a selection process controlled by the Polish Ministry of Higher Education and Technology.

When Goldfarb met the individual, he saw that the visiting fellow had little interest in what was going on at the New School and even less in the history of the institution. Although, as Goldfarb put it, he was "a lowly assistant professor at the time," he contacted Vice President Albert Landa, who was administering the grant, to explain the situation and to urge him to find a better way to identify future candidates. Landa thanked Goldfarb for stepping forward and asked him to help the New School establish a different process that did not rely on Polish bureaucrats. Not an easy assignment before fax machines and email, but Goldfarb was eager to try.

During the year he spent in Poland as a graduate student, Goldfarb met Jerzy Szacki, the much-admired sociologist who had been supporting students in the opposition. With Landa's blessings, he wrote to Szacki, who responded right away with the recommendation that the New School invite his star student Elzbieta Matynia.[47] Goldfarb knew Matynia well, having met her through Szacki in 1973 when the two of them were doing their doctoral research on political theater. "I felt a little guilty," Goldfarb admitted, "that the person being recommended was my best friend, but on the other hand, I didn't write to her. I wrote to Szacki. It was clear to me what her qualities were."[48]

Matynia came from Starachowice, a small city located between Warsaw and Krakow. Since her parents did not belong to the Communist Party, she had to perform exceptionally well in school to gain access to the best universities in the country. Clearing the hurdle, Matynia entered Warsaw University in 1969, where, as an undergraduate and master's student, she studied philosophy and literature—with a seriously depleted faculty, she added bitterly. Although there were a few exceptions, most of the nation's leading professors in the humanities had lost their jobs in 1968 and left the country. It went without saying that those who remained did not teach the works of the great exiled dissidents such as Miłosz, Gombrowicz, and Kołakowski. Matynia and her friends read them on their own in pirated editions smuggled into the country, most often from Paris where émigrés had founded the Polish-language journal *Kultura*.

Since she was still in high school in March 1968, Matynia did not participate in the historic student protests. But when she began her university studies in Warsaw, she joined the democratic opposition, a decision she tried to mask at first by majoring in the humanities—the radicals majored in the social sciences. In the end, she abandoned her cover. After writing her master's thesis on the history of political theater, carefully limiting her analysis to the past, she switched into sociology, where she could do her doctoral dissertation on contemporary political theater.

By 1980, Matynia had her PhD and was serving as Solidarity's liaison between Warsaw University and the Ursus Tractor Factory. Harmless work, as far as she was concerned, but suspicious enough, apparently, that the authorities turned down her request for a passport, making it impossible for her to accept the New School's invitation to spend the 1980–81 academic year at the New School as the Katarzyna Kalwinska fellow. In the end, Matynia was grateful, she said. "Had I left Warsaw in the fall of 1980, I would not have lived through the amazing period of Solidarity," the triumphant victory of Lech Wałęsa and his dockworkers in Gdansk, who, after months of striking, won the right to form their own independent union. Matynia described that year as a "gift of hope, of joy, of amazement, of love towards others. Hate disappeared. Jealousy disappeared."[49] During those euphoric months, Matynia applied again for a passport, this time successfully.

When Matynia left Warsaw for New York in August 1981, she had no idea that four months later the Polish government would declare martial law, making it too dangerous for her to return home. Although she knew that she was lucky to be out of the country, "I was totally uninterested in America." She wanted to go back and join the struggle, but her family would not hear of it. Accepting her fate, she looked around for Polish dissidents in New York and discovered the Committee in Support of Solidarity. Through them, she met "this extraordinary universe of Poles in New York" who were actively supporting the movement in exile. She also met her future husband, the filmmaker Richard Adams, who was making a documentary about Solidarity at the time.

Matynia spent two years at the New School on the Kalwinska fellowship, after which she taught at Bard College and Sarah Lawrence, until the New School invited her back in the mid-1980s. When she returned, she began teaching in the GF's Master's program in Liberal Studies and eventually in the Department of Sociology as well. In recent years, Matynia has written extensively about the role the New School has played in helping to rebuild academic institutions in post-communist East and Central Europe and about Polish and Czech intellectuals during communist times. She has contributed as well to the literature on transitions to democracy, drawing her case studies from Poland and South Africa.[50]

In 1990, as the East and Central Europe Program and the Journal Donation Project were getting under way, Katznelson stepped down as dean and joined the faculty in Political Science. Fanton appointed the sociologist Alan Wolfe to replace him. Formerly dean of Social Sciences at Queens College of the City University of New York, Wolfe remained at the GF for three years before moving on to Boston University, then to Boston College. In 1994, Katznelson left as well to accept a position at Columbia University—the "other New York option" that he had turned down in 1982 when he agreed to join Fanton at the New School. As everyone understood from the very beginning, Katznelson would eventually return to Columbia.

As the New School bade him farewell, Fanton asked his first dean of the Graduate Faculty to deliver the commencement speech for the graduating class of 1994. Katznelson used the occasion to talk about the GF's deep involvement over the last decade with intellectuals in East and Central Europe. Looking back over those years, he spoke with characteristic modesty, paying tribute to Arato and Goldfarb, who had the idea in the first place, and to Fanton, who led the New School in championing the cause of dissidents throughout the region. Everyone listening, however, understood that Katznelson more than anyone else had helped frame the debates that took place at the New School during the 1980s and early 1990s about old democracies and new, between American intellectuals of the generation of 1968 and their counterparts in East and Central Europe.

In his speech, Katznelson suggested that the New School renewed its historic "concern for scholars in peril" when it created the East and Central Europe Program. By 1994, "the links fashioned between the New School and East European opposition intellectuals [had] taken on the illusion of inevitability." Because, he explained, fifty years after a group of progressive intellectuals had opened the New School for Social Research, another group of dissident intellectuals were meeting in secret to discuss the very same ideas that had motivated the New School's founders. One of these semi-clandestine groups in Warsaw, had an evocative name that Katznelson translated as the "Club of the Crooked Circle," Like the New School's founding faculty in 1919, these Polish dissidents spoke optimistically about "progressivism's experimental and pragmatic attempts to enlarge the scope of liberal democracy." But they also recognized, echoing Johnson's refugee scholars, that "the circumference of liberalism's circle is never smooth."

Katznelson ended his remarks on a somber note. The New School's European colleagues, he said—both those of the generation of 1933 and those of 1989— saw the weaknesses in liberal democracies more clearly than their American counterparts. Given their experiences with totalitarian regimes, the Europeans understood "that all liberal regimes are built on foundations of state violence and coercion, and that these instruments in the basements of the state can be used to topple the upper floors of open societies. At best, they remain in place as hidden instruments of rule."[51] A prescient warning for the graduating class of 1994.

EPILOGUE

EXTENDING THE LEGACY

By the time Ira Katznelson gave his 1994 commencement address, the New School's friends in East and Central Europe were playing important roles in their countries' new democracies as members of government, university professors, and journalists. After 1989, the Hungarian political theorist János Kis emerged as the leader in parliament of the Alliance for Free Democrats Party. In 1991, he left politics and joined the founding faculty of the Central European University (CEU). Subsidized by the Hungarian American philanthropist George Soros, the university had just opened that year "to spread the virtues of Western academic freedom to the whole of the post-communist world"—to quote CEU's president Michael Ignatieff.[1] Kis has written a number of significant works on democratic theory and constitutionalism.[2] In Poland, Adam Michnik served briefly in parliament as well before devoting himself full time to the *Gazeta Wyborzca*. As editor in chief, he quickly turned the newspaper into the country's leading daily, highly regarded for its rigorous reporting and editorial commitment to democratic values.

The 1990s were magical years throughout the region, particularly for the former dissidents. But not every new democracy looked like Hungary and Poland. Hence Katznelson's ominous warning about the instruments of violence lurking in the basement of the state. In 1991, Croatia and Slovenia broke away from Yugoslavia. Bosnia and Herzegovina followed a year later, which led to a brutal civil war and the eventual splintering of this multi-ethnic state into seven independent countries. In 1993, barely three years after triumphant demonstrations in Wenceslas Square, historic animosities between Slovaks and Czechs divided Czechoslovakia in two.

And the list continued to grow, even in states where ethnic conflict was not the issue. In Belarus, for example, its authoritarian president, Alexander Lukashenko, cleansed the country of fellow Belarussians who belonged to the democratic opposition. Among the victims was the European Humanities University, which was forced into exile in 2004.[3] Nobody, however, predicted what would happen in Hungary and Poland: In recent elections, the citizens of these countries voted to turn their governments over to political parties that reject the sanctity of fundamental rights protected in open societies. Once again the New School's friends are on the front lines of the opposition, this time against their former allies in the fight against communism who have since become leaders of "illiberal democracies."

In his concluding remarks to New School graduates, Katznelson was also thinking about the scholars he had recruited to the Graduate Faculty who had lived through the horrors of "state violence and coercion" during World War II, and in some cases under Soviet communism as well. Like the founders of the University in Exile, Katznelson's colleagues wrote extensively about "the hidden instruments of rule" and "the scope of liberal democracy"—their reflections guided by "the incidents of living experience," as Hannah Arendt would have added.[4] Aristide Zolberg and Ágnes Heller are prominent among them. Through their scholarly work and political commitments, both of them have extended the legacy of the University in Exile.

⊷⊶

Zolberg was the first person Katznelson invited to the New School to help him rebuild the Graduate Faculty: "More than any person I knew," Katznelson recalled, "[Zolberg] articulated the experiences, values, and intellectual project of the University in Exile tradition, which combined normative purpose, theoretical invention, historical imagination, and empirical precision."[5] Jonathan Fanton agreed and named Zolberg the University in Exile Professor.

Zolberg was born in Brussels in 1931 to Jewish immigrants from Poland.[6] In May 1940, a month before his ninth birthday, Belgium fell to the Nazis. A year later his parents hid their only child with a gentile family in a small Flemish village forty-five minutes away on the tram. "The cover," Aristide explained, was "that I was a distant relative who lived in Brussels and spoke French all the time. My parents wanted me to have a year's schooling in Flemish to really learn the ancestral language." The alibi worked, at least up to a point.

Aristide remained in Schepdaal for eighteen months and became fluent in Flemish, an experience that led him to write about bilingualism and language nationalism. His time in the village also led him to challenge the fashion after World War II of indiscriminately blaming members of specific ethnic groups for being complicit in the murder of six million Jews. Zolberg would never forget that he owed his life to a Flemish family—who belonged to a group frequently accused of collaborating with the Nazis—a German soldier, and a Catholic priest.

A few weeks after Aristide moved in with the De Dobbeleers, the local authorities ordered the family to provide housing for a German stationed in the village. Known to everyone as Herr Bittman, the soldier worked as a translator for the Nazis' counterintelligence unit. "We established rapport," Zolberg recalled, "and I always suspected that he had figured out that I was a Jewish kid." Many years later one of the sons in the family confirmed that "of course [Herr Bittman] knew."

Aristide spent a year in Schepdaal's primary school, then continued studying in Brussels at a Catholic secondary school, commuting back and forth on the tram. Until one day they told him not to come home: "I don't know what happened exactly, whether the German spy, Herr Bittman, warned them that there was going to be a checkup, or he just couldn't hold out any longer." Abbé Joseph Goossens, the head of the Institut Notre-Dame, did not press for details. He simply took Zolberg in. "So, for the rest of the war I stayed as a boarder in a Catholic school. My parents were paying for this initially, because my father was still alive and he had some money stashed away."

But by the end of 1943, Zolberg's father had run through their savings. Having no other option, he took the risk of reopening his small leather goods business and hiring back a few craftsmen whom he thought he could trust. Apparently, he was wrong. Several weeks later the police arrested Zolberg's father and sent him to Auschwitz. His mother survived, Zolberg explained, thanks to her false identity papers and to the fact, he added dryly, that Jews did not circumcise women.

After the war, Sabine Zolberg tried to get Aristide and herself out of Europe. In 1948, the American Consulate finally responded but gave her only one visa. The boy could enter the United States, a staff member told her in tortured legalese, under Belgium's immigration quota, even though the Belgians considered Aristide a "stateless person" born in Brussels to immigrant parents who had not been naturalized. Following the logic of U.S. immigration law, Aristide Zolberg still qualified because any child born in the United States was a citizen even if his immigrant parents were foreigners. Sabine Zolberg was another matter. The consulate identified her as a citizen of Poland, an enemy state since 1947 when it formed its first communist government. As such, she was not welcome.

Aristide came to New York alone at the age of seventeen and moved in with distant relatives. After finishing high school, he went to Columbia University on scholarship for his bachelor's degree, then pursued a doctorate in political science, receiving his PhD in 1961 from the University of Chicago. Two years later his professors invited him back to join the faculty, which included a number of distinguished émigré scholars, three of whom had ties or would have ties to the New School: Leo Strauss, Hannah Arendt, and Hans Morgenthau.

During the early years of his academic career, Zolberg worked primarily on party politics, nationalism, and development in postcolonial West Africa. Today he is best known for his landmark book on U.S. immigration policy, *A Nation by Design*, and for his many contributions to the literature on economic migrants and political refugees—much of it published after he came the New School where he also chaired the Department of Political Science for more than a decade.[7] In 1993, Zolberg founded the International Center for Migration, Ethnicity and Citizenship, which quickly became a magnet for scholars and students throughout the New York metropolitan area, some of whom were doing research on the victims of contemporary political upheavals reminiscent of those that had marked his life as a young boy.

When Zolberg died in 2013, his colleagues urged the university to invest in what he had left behind—an argument easily defended given the escalating crises in the Middle East, Africa and Asia that were forcing millions of people to flee their homes in numbers the world had not seen since the end of World War II. Generously endowed by Henry Arnhold and renamed in memory of its founder, the Zolberg Institute on Migration and Mobility is flourishing today under the leadership of its new director, T. Alexander Aleinikoff, a legal scholar and former Deputy High Commissioner for Refugees at the United Nations.[8]

◆

In the mid-1980s, Katznelson appointed the Hungarian dissidents Ágnes Heller and Ferenc Fehér to the faculty. The two philosophers were widely known as theorists of the New Left, particularly Heller. Both of them had studied philosophy in postwar Hungary with the legendary Marxist critic György Lukács. Then in 1963, they established the Budapest School of Philosophy, with two other disciples—György Márkus and Mihály Vajda—to continue working in the critical tradition of their mentor. By the middle of the decade, the Budapest School was attracting the attention of critical theorists in Western Europe, making the Hungarian government suspicious.[9]

In an effort, perhaps, to appease the authorities, Lukács described the Budapest School as "the renaissance of Marx." Not quite, responded Heller. She and her friends had set out to save "Marx from all his subsequent distortions and falsifications," which was nothing less than declaring war on communist Hungary's official ideology. To criticize Marxism-Leninism in the name of Marx cost Heller her job in the early 1970s and forced her into exile a few years later.

Born in 1929, Ágnes Heller "was touched personally by all the great, as well as all the tragic events of the last century," observed the Israeli philosopher Yirmiyahu Yovel:

> She lived them in close personal contact, both from within and from without: Nazism and Auschwitz; communism and Stalin; the modern experience of contingent existence; the collapse of historical traditions; the fall of the Soviet Empire and the wall of Berlin, which liberated her country Hungary; the ills of modernity in the West; and the transformations and vicissitudes of the modern Jewish situation. With all this she has coped both personally and philosophically. In fact, "both personally and philosophically," is one and the same for Ágnes, for this is the way she chose herself to be, and through this—through philosophy—she came into her own.[10]

Lukács, Heller wrote, made her a philosopher, but Pál Heller, her father, led her to ethics. He died in Auschwitz in 1944 when she was fifteen years old. Philosophers, Heller explained, do not invent a moral philosophy; they observe the way people around them have lived and then choose "the most exemplary." In her case, this was her father, who went through life, to the bitter end, as a "good person." In *A Philosophy of Morals*, she followed "the simplest choices [Pál Heller] made in everyday life up to the ultimate moral conflicts, the borderline situations. Not all men go this way up to the end. My father did."

When the Germans occupied Hungary in March 1944, Heller's father had no illusions about what would happen to him as a Jew and an active member of the resistance. What kept him going was the firm conviction that his daughter would survive and remain true to what he had taught her. "All you need," he wrote to Ágnes a few weeks before the Germans arrested him, "is a little more luck than your father had and everything will be all right. . . . Evil may be victorious for now—but goodness will prevail in the end. Every good person contributes a speck of dust to that final victory."[11]

Heller and her mother survived the war through a mixture of miracles and daring, like the time they avoided deportation by jumping onto a moving tram. Soon after the Nazis arrested Pál Heller, his wife and daughter were rounded up with thousands of other Jews, and marched through the streets of Budapest toward the city's railway yards where cattle cars were waiting to carry them to Auschwitz. When Ágnes saw that the city had not stopped the tram service, she urged her mother to walk by the tracks, reassuring her that the guards would not shoot, if they jumped onto a passing tram, out of fear of killing gentile passengers instead.

After making their escape, they returned to the "yellow houses" where Jews who had not yet been deported were forced to live while the Nazis finished building the walled ghetto. By the time the Soviet Army liberated them in the winter of 1945, Ágnes and her mother had defied death numerous times in similarly astonishing ways.

When Heller entered university in 1947, she was planning to study chemistry, but she changed her mind a few weeks later, after attending a lecture by Lukács, an experience so compelling, she recalled, that she switched majors right away. Recognizing the gifts of this enthusiastic new student, Lukács accepted to work with Heller and gave her the opportunities an ambitious student like her would need to have a successful academic career. After receiving her doctorate in 1955, he appointed Heller assistant professor and editor of a major philosophical journal, coveted positions that she lost the next year when she embraced the Hungarian Revolution—that "most beautiful and most enduring political experience of [my] life." From 1956 until the end of communist rule, the authorities barred Heller from entering the gates of the university: "I was considered poison for university students." They assigned her to a high school instead, where she taught literature for several years before Lukács succeeded in persuading the authorities to let her work in a research institute.

Ostracized at home, Heller started to attract a following abroad, "imperceptibly at first" was the way she described it, among New Left intellectuals in the West and dissidents in other communist countries. By the late 1960s, people were reading her work throughout Europe, Australia, and parts of the Third World in editions translated into multiple languages based on manuscripts pirated out of Hungary. Her most popular books in those days were *Everyday Life* and *The Theory of Need in Marx*, where she developed her ideas about creating a "revolution of everyday life"[12]

While Lukács was still alive, the authorities left Heller and his other disciples alone, at least by the standards of the day, limiting their opportunities without persecuting them aggressively. All that changed after the critic died in 1971. Two years later, the authorities staged the so-called Philosophers' Trial and stripped Heller and other members of the Budapest School of whatever privileges they still had, including, in her case, her research position at the Institute of Sociology. The situation became so intolerable that in 1977 she and Fehér went into exile—not that getting out was easy either—moving first to Melbourne, where they taught at La Trobe University, and then to New York at the New School for

Social Research, where Heller agreed to chair the crippled philosophy department and see it through the reaccreditation process.

After the fall of communism in 1989, Heller and Fehér returned home to a hero's welcome, moving back permanently in 1993. Fehér died a year later. As Heller reintegrated herself into Hungarian intellectual and political life, she continued teaching at the New School one semester each year. Her classes always filled to capacity. In Budapest, the academic community elected her to the Academy of Sciences and appointed her professor of philosophy at Eötvös Loránd University.

Heller officially retired in 2009, but that formality has not slowed her down. In 2018, at the age of eighty-nine, she continues to write prolifically and to give lectures around the world. At home she participates regularly in academic and political events, appearing frequently on whatever remains of independent radio and television.

By the time Viktor Orbán and his revitalized Fidesz Party returned to power in 2010, Heller was a revered symbol of the dissident movement, admired for the role she had played during communist times and her defense of liberal democracy in recent years despite persistent efforts to silence her. In 2011, the government accused Heller and other philosophers of having embezzled federal research funds. The police eventually dropped the case for lack of evidence, but the harassment of "Heller's Band" continued, with smear campaigns published by *Magyar Nemzet*, an influential paper on the extreme right. In 2013, András Doncsev, Orbán's deputy minister of Human Resources, dismissed Heller's importance in Hungary to an American journalist, observing impatiently that she was only "doing what she always does: complaining loudly abroad whenever there's an anticommunist government in power in Budapest. Hungarian universities are world-renowned and enjoy full academic freedom [*sic*]."[13]

In April 2018, Orbán won a politically transformative victory for a third consecutive term. Swept into office on an ethnic-nationalistic platform, he can now clamp down on freedom of speech even harder than he had been doing before, while he continues to keep the nation's borders closed to Syrian refugees and escalate his campaign against citizens with liberal and leftist affinities. Until her death in July 2019, Heller remained a target of vituperative attacks, but this time, she refused to leave home and go back into exile—a choice George Soros and the Central European University did not have. Anticipating the worst, a few days after the election, Soros announced his decision to open a satellite campus in Vienna.[14]

When Jonathan Fanton left the New School in 1999 to become president of the John D. and Catherine T. MacArthur Foundation, Hungary and Poland had flourishing democracies—as did the United States, not that anyone would have commented on that at the time. Andrew Arato by then was widely recognized for his work on civil society and was now writing about constitution making in new democracies. Inspired to do so by his friend János Kis, he was rapidly becoming a leading theorist in the field.[15] This recent turn in his scholarly interests led Arato back to the work of members of the University in Exile.

In 1999, Elzbieta Matynia's Transregional Center for Democratic Studies was running two summer institutes in Krakow and Cape Town, creating the rare opportunity for anticommunist intellectuals from the new democracies in East and Central Europe to study with socialist intellectuals from post-Apartheid South Africa. Her scholarly work at the time analyzed the ways nonviolent "performative" practices in political movements like Solidarity had turned authoritarian states into open societies. Now, more recently, given the rising threat to liberal democracies, she has founded The New School for Social Research–Europe Network to protect and advance scholarly freedom.[16] In the final year of the twentieth century, Jeffrey Goldfarb was still teaching regularly in Matynia's institutes and had recently published a book on the role of intellectuals in democratic societies. Fourteen years later, he launched an online Public Seminar, modeled on the Graduate Faculty's General Seminar as Alvin Johnson had first conceived of it. The Public Seminar blog provides a virtual platform for scholars to present their work on the burning issues of the day.[17]

Since Fanton's departure, nobody has been more persistent than Arien Mack in trying to extend the legacy of the University in Exile and Alvin Johnson's original mission "to educate the educated." She had, in fact, begun working on these projects a decade before Fanton arrived. Smart, strong-willed, and good looking—"profoundly beautiful," wrote theater director Harold Clurman—Mack faced her share of indignities during the early years of her career, of the kind French feminists describe as *"le sexisme ordinaire."* When Joseph Greenbaum made her editor of *Social Research* in 1970, he "mortified" her publicly by announcing with glee that he had chosen the "prettiest" woman on the faculty to replace Peter Berger, later adding to her list of qualifications that she was married to Irving Howe, the famous editor of *Dissent*. Hannah Arendt urged Mack to ignore the wisecracks and accept the position all the same. It would change her life, the philosopher predicted, and it did.[18] Several years later Mack had become one of the most influential members of the Graduate Faculty and a force to contend with in the university as a whole.

By the mid-1970s, Mack had restored the waning reputation of *Social Research* to its earlier distinction, framing each issue around a different theoretical or political theme that invited conversations across the disciplines. In 1988, she launched the *Social Research* conferences, high-profile events that take place twice a year "to enhance public understanding and influence ongoing debates about current social and political issues and to amplify the public voice of the *Social Research* journal." The range of scholars and public figures who have taken part in these conferences, and then appeared in the quarterly, recall the star-studded roster of speakers who lectured at the New School during the Johnson years.[19]

In 1990, Mack started her Journal Donation project, which remained active until 2017. In 2007, she added a special section to *Social Research*, "Endangered Scholars Worldwide," to call attention to the rising number of "endangered and imprisoned scholars around the world," one of whom had been a student at the New School and another a faculty member. And in 2009, on the occasion of the seventy-fifth anniversary of *Social Research*, she established a new program at the New School that assures a two-year stipend for a visiting University in Exile scholar. The stipend is generously funded by Henry Arnhold and the Institute of International Education's Scholar Rescue Fund—the descendant of Stephen Duggan's rescue campaign from the Hitler years.

Finally, on September 6, 2018, Mack opened the New University in Exile Consortium at the New School. Complementing the far-reaching work of the Scholar Rescue Program and Scholars at Risk, the consortium started with eleven academic institutions, each of which, like the New School, was sponsoring an endangered scholar. Membership has continued to grow. The consortium is the first group of universities to join together as academic institutions to defend freedom of expression and freedom of inquiry by assisting "scholars in need." Under the leadership of the New School, the consortium is building a cross-campus intellectual community for this latest generation of exiled scholars through a series of seminars and workshops, which meet regularly, culminating in an annual conference.

In 2001, the trustees appointed Bob Kerrey, the former governor and senator of Nebraska, to succeed Jonathan Fanton as president of the New School. An inspired choice, everyone agreed, given the senator's progressive political profile, his high visibility, and ties to the state where Alvin Johnson was born. But soon after the New School made the announcement, *The New York Times* and other media outlets published shocking details about a Navy Seal raid that Kerrey led during the Vietnam War, which ended up murdering unarmed women and children in the village of Thanh Phong. Kerrey did not deny the report. What happened, he said, was "a terrible tragedy and I had ordered it. . . . I have been haunted by it for 32 years." Despite the uproar on campus, the trustees stuck by their new president and continued to support him over the years, even after the faculty gave him a vote of no confidence. Kerrey resigned in 2010.[20]

Under Kerrey's controversial but effective leadership, the New School changed a great deal, symbolized most dramatically by the construction of a sixteen-story University Center on the site where the Graduate Faculty's building once stood. Designed by Roger Duffy, the new center opened in 2014 to great critical acclaim. Although Kerrey had stepped down by this time, the trustees hailed their former president at the ribbon-cutting ceremony for his bold leadership and formidable fund-raising skills.

The next president, David Van Zandt, stressed the "new" in the New School's name. A point driven home in 2018 on the opening page of the university's website with the words of John Cage, the avant-garde composer and former member of the faculty: "I can't understand why everyone is frightened by new ideas. I'm frightened of the old ones." Building on the New School's long-standing commitment to innovation and change, the campus has been transformed with its dramatic architectural statement on lower Fifth Avenue. The New School's academic profile has been reconfigured as well, with Parsons School of Design now playing a defining role in the intellectual life of the university. Although Parsons had been subsidizing the institution financially for over forty years and broadening its appeal to students in the arts, the university has only recently recognized the centrality of design to the curriculum. In the New School's Strategic Plan for 2013–2018, the vision statement reads:

> We are and will be a university where **design and social research** drive approaches to studying issues of our time, such as democracy, urbanization, technological change, economic empowerment, sustainability, migration and globalization. We will be **the preeminent intellectual and creative center** for effective engagement in a world that increasingly demands better-designed objects, communication, systems and organization to meet social needs.[21]

As the New School continues to change, the way every dynamic university should do, may its leaders, faculty, and students take to heart what Jonathan Fanton solemnly said in his farewell address: The New School, he reminded colleagues and friends, "stands for something." And that something calls on the institution to defend the rights of persecuted intellectuals at home and overseas, whenever circumstances demand it—as they do today. Given the current state of the world, it was gratifying to see the New School step forward again and launch its New University in Exile Consortium. All the more so on the eve of its centennial.*

November 2021

---

*David Van Zandt stepped down in the spring of 2020, and that November the New School welcomed its ninth president, Dwight McBride, the first African American to lead the university.

APPENDIX A

EXTENDED NOTES AND COMMENTARY
FOR CHAPTER 6

Extension of Note 49: On Thorstein Veblen:

Most scholars, including the archivists at the University of Chicago where Veblen's papers reside, say that Veblen retired from the New School in 1926, but Rutkoff and Scott write that Johnson fired him in 1925 because he refused to fulfill his teaching responsibilities.[1] Other scholars have revealed that Veblen was forced to resign from the University of Chicago and Stanford University during the first decade of the twentieth century because he was having adulterous affairs, a subject briefly alluded to in this chapter. Rutkoff and Scott limit their discussion to the New School and do not mention these other allegations.

According to the surviving records of the period, Veblen stopped giving classes at the New School after the fall semester of 1924, but he remained on the faculty throughout that academic year. Although his name disappeared from the published list of faculty members in the fall of 1925, other records indicate that he only retired "officially," at the end of the 1925–26 academic year. In January 1925, he wrote to his brother, "I am here [at the New School] as a transient, having quit lecturing, at least for the time, not having the necessary energy to do the work, but otherwise as well as usual."[2]

Joseph Dorfman, Veblen's biographer, tells us that the economist was disappointed by the quality of the students at the New School. He found them less interesting than the undergraduates he had taught elsewhere, concluding, as Mitchell had, that the New School could not attract strong students because it did not offer degrees.[3] Unlike Mitchell, however, Veblen had no Columbia to return to, nor did he have the financial means to stop working altogether as did Robinson and Beard. And so Veblen hung on after the other three had resigned.

Even after he had stopped teaching, the New School kept Veblen on salary through the 1924–25 academic year while Johnson and Mitchell tried to raise money for him to do research on British imperialism. By March, Johnson had raised about half the amount needed, but he stopped a month later after Veblen announced that he was physically not up to going to England to do the research. Mitchell and one other donor were still willing to help subsidize Veblen even after he abandoned his plans, but other donors withdrew their pledges. When the New School finally stopped paying his salary, Dorfman reported that the economist was strapped for money: "In desperation [Veblen] even expressed the desire to return to teaching in October 1925, but at his age of 68 there proved to be little prospect."[4]

According to Rutkoff and Scott, "Firing Veblen was probably the most difficult decision that Johnson ever made regarding the New School. He must have understood it as virtually patricide. He felt deeply torn, and on numerous occasions he jokingly, but defensively, justified his action."[5] Johnson did indeed complain that Veblen had refused to speak audibly in class and described how he tried to rectify this by planting a microphone on the lectern, but he said nothing about firing his old friend and colleague, nor did Dorfman.[6] The only person who did was New School's president, John Everett, who told Rutkoff and Scott that Johnson had fired Veblen in an interview he gave the two historians in 1978. Everett had reported the same six years earlier in a published interview in *Lithopinion*, without providing any documentary evidence.[7] Although Everett knew Johnson personally, the interview he gave to *Lithopinion*, was a free-wheeling account and inaccurate on a number of details.

In addition to Everett, Rutkoff and Scott refer their readers to two other sources to support their assertion that Johnson fired Veblen. One of them is Johnson's autobiography, the other Dorfman's biography of Veblen, neither of which supports their allegation. Nor does Robert Heilbroner's *Worldly Philosophers*, whose lengthy sketch about Veblen repeats the stories about the economist's difficulties at Chicago and Stanford, but says nothing about Johnson firing him.[8]

Was Johnson relieved to see Veblen go? No doubt. Veblen had been a headache. Did Johnson agree to take Veblen back when, "in desperation," he was looking around for a teaching position? We do not know whether they even discussed the possibility. Given Veblen's lack of enthusiasm for New School students, did he even ask Johnson to let him return? Dorfman implies that he was hoping to find work elsewhere.

What we know for sure is that Johnson kept Veblen on salary for a year after he stopped teaching, which was a generous gesture given the New School's chronic

budgetary problems. All of these details are amply documented in the correspondence reproduced in Dorfman's *Thorstein Veblen: Essays, Reviews and Reports,
Previously Uncollected Writings*, which came out thirteen years before Rutkoff
and Scott published their history of the New School. Nothing in the works by
Johnson and Dorfman says that Johnson fired Veblen.

Scholars have not spared Veblen when it came to his marital difficulties and
alleged extramarital affairs, even in short sketches focused on the impact Veblen's
work has had on economic and sociological theory.[9] Russell H. Bartley and Sylvia
E. Bartley have challenged these claims as scurrilous and largely unfounded.[10]
There is no doubt that Jordan fired Veblen from Stanford, accusing him of inap-
propriate behavior with women, but what happened at the University of Chicago
is less clear. The university's Board of Trustees "accepted" Veblen's resignation on
June 5, 1906. The next day *The Chicago Record-Herald* announced that Veblen
had resigned, together with four other colleagues; all but one of them were leaving Chicago for prestigious positions elsewhere, including Veblen who was going
to Stanford.[11] Why did Veblen leave? He had been complaining for several years
about not being paid enough.

In its article about the resignations, *The Chicago Record-Herald* quoted Wallace
Heckman, "counsel and business manager of the university," who added that one
of the five had been "let go," but he refused to say which one. Although the paper
assumed the fired professor was Veblen, neither the economist nor the trustees
confirmed the *Record-Herald*'s story. That said, the university did not hide the
fact that it was happy to see Veblen resign, as President Judson confirmed many
years later in a letter written in 1919 to Abraham Flexner: "Mr. Veblen was once a
member of our faculty, and we were quite willing to accept his resignation when
he tendered it."[12] Judson wrote those words in a note thanking Flexner for having
sent him an inflammatory review of Veblen's *The Higher Learning in America*.[13]
Veblen's *Theory of the Leisure Class* had caused a storm in Chicago in 1899, a fact
referred to by *The Chicago Record-Herald* in its article of June 6, 1906.

Was Veblen's behavior with women a matter of concern at the time? We do
know that the economist was having marital difficulties during his years at the
University of Chicago, which led to an affair with a student, whom he later married while he was at Stanford.

APPENDIX B

EXTENDED NOTES AND COMMENTARY
FOR CHAPTER 7

A. EXTENSION OF NOTES 15, 17, AND 21:
ON THE ROCKEFELLER ARCHIVES

The archivists at the Rockefeller Archive Center are in the process of updating and correcting the information they have published on their website about the refugees the foundation sponsored between 1933 and 1945, including those who came to the New School. Some of the scholars sponsored by the New School are identified on these charts as having gone to other institutions, which indeed they eventually did, but only after coming to the New School; for example, the philosopher Jean Wahl. Other documents preserved in the Rockefeller archives fill out the chronology. Then, some scholars do not appear on the charts at all, even though they came to the New School with money from Rockefeller. Once again there is documentary evidence in the Rockefeller archives to confirm this, for example, Leo Strauss and Jacob Marschak. Finally, there are people on the charts, like the philosopher Vladimir Jankélévitch who decided to remain in occupied France, even though they had received an invitation from the New School with funding from Rockefeller. Others who also declined invitations do not appear on the charts, for example the historian Marc Bloch.

In a frequently quoted document from the Rockefeller archives, an unnamed author, reporting in 1955 on the Refugee Scholars Programs, stated that Rockefeller subsidized the salaries of forty émigré scholars at the New School during the 1930s. When France surrendered in June 1940, it authorized the appointment of another one hundred scholars. Rockefeller's historians have not yet determined how many of these scholars actually came to the New School.[1]

In her edited book on the Rockefeller Foundation's Refugee Scholars' Programs, *The "Unacceptables,"* Giuliani Gemelli describes the New School as the foundation's "dialectical partner." In that same volume, Klaus-Dieter Krohn reports that the Rockefeller Foundation gave the New School $540,000, of which $300,000 paid the salaries of refugee scholars. In addition to paying the salaries of the scholars, the Rockefeller Foundation made several grants to the New School to subsidize the research of members of the émigré faculty. Thanks to this support, Johnson had the resources he needed to launch the Institute of World Affairs (IWA), which the New School opened in the early 1940s, after the United States had entered the war. Between 1933 and 1945 the New School also received major gifts from Hiram Halle, the Rosenwald family, the Lucius Littauer Fund, and Doris Duke.[2] The Halle story is discussed in some detail in this chapter.

B. EXTENSION OF NOTES 18 AND 19: ON THE SELECTION OF REFUGEE SCHOLARS

In addition to the examples given in chapter 7 of the difficult decisions Johnson had to make, see Johnson's letter to Thomas Mann (January 4, 1939) in response to the Nobel Laureate's request that the New School help secure a visa for the Czech novelist Max Brod:

> Unfortunately, I do not see any way by which [Brod] could emigrate except on a quota visa. A professorial visa is limited to persons who have held posts in recognized educational institutions during the last two years before emigrating and who have also received academic calls carrying a salary and tenure for at least two years. On the other hand, if a well-established institution like Princeton should invite him urgently, it is entirely possible that his quota number might be advanced. I have recently heard of such a case.[3]

C. EXTENSION OF NOTES 15 AND 21: ON THE REFUGEES WHO TAUGHT AT THE NEW SCHOOL

In his book on the University in Exile, *Intellectuals in Exile,* Claus-Dieter Krohn claims that Johnson welcomed 182 refugee scholars to the New School between 1933 and 1945, some of whom had arrived in the United States without Johnson's help. The official list circulated by the New School identified 167. Both lists need further attention.[4] Among the scholars mentioned as having been "expressly brought over by the New School" is Jacob Marschak, who had come to the United

States on funding from the Rockefeller Foundation that was not originally designated for the New School. Johnson had tried to persuade Marschak to come to the New School over the spring and summer of 1933, but Marschak remained in England until 1939, accepting an invitation from Oxford instead. Missing from both, is Bertolt Brecht, whom Johnson sponsored, even though he never actually taught at the New School; no doubt there are others.

Finally, both lists also include the name of the anthropologist Bronislaw Malinowski, even though he was not a refugee scholar. Born in Poland, Malinowski moved to England to study anthropology in 1910. He was then stranded in the South Seas during World War I, where he had been doing ethnographic fieldwork, after which he returned to England and went on to hold a prestigious professorial chair at the London School of Economics. Malinowski had been visiting in the United States during the summer of 1939. When England declared war against Germany in early September, he decided not to return and accepted a full-time position at Yale.

When Malinowski made an earlier trip to the United States in March 1933—before Johnson had even come up with the idea of founding the University in Exile—the director of the New Schoool held a dinner for the distinguished anthropologist to which he invited Franz Boas and Ruth Benedict, among others.[5] After joining the faculty at Yale in 1939, Malinowski lectured at the New School occasionally. He died in 1942.

D. EXTENSION OF NOTES 89 AND 93: ALVIN JOHNSON'S DESCRIPTIONS OF THE REFUGEE SCHOLARS WHO BEGAN TEACHING AT THE NEW SCHOOL BETWEEN 1933 AND 1935

In Johnson's "Report to the Trustees of The Graduate Faculty of Political and Social Science in the New School for Social Research," he provided the following thumbnail sketches of the first ten members of the University in Exile, NSA. Between 1933 and 1941, Johnson maintained a separate board of trustees for the Graduate Faculty:

KARL BRANDT formerly professor of agricultural economics in the Agricultural College in Berlin, director of the Institute for Agricultural Marketing, and editor of the *Blätter für Landwirtschaftliche Marktforschung*.

GERHARD COLM formerly professor at the University of Kiel and head of the research department of the Institute for World Economics, Kiel. Authority on public finance and world economics.

ARTHUR FEILER formerly professor of the College of Commerce at Königsberg, writer on world affairs for the Frankfurter *Zeitung*. Widely traveled and well known in the United States for his authoritative writings on international topics.

EDUARD HEIMANN formerly professor [of economics] at the University of Hamburg and editor of *Neue Blätter für den Sozialismus*.

HERMANN KANTOROWICZ formerly professor of jurisprudence at the University of Kiel. Dr. Kantorowicz was committed to the London School of Economics but joined the University in Exile for the initial year.

EMIL LEDERER [also mentioned in the *New York Times* on August 19, 1933] formerly professor [economics and sociology] at the Universities of Heidelberg and Berlin, and editor of the *Archiv für Sozialwissenschaft und Sozialpolitik*.

HANS SPEIER formerly lecturer in the Hochschule für Politik in Berlin. One of the most brilliant of the younger German sociologists. [Johnson's report to the trustees did not mention, as the *Times* did, that Speier had also been a *Privatdozent* at the University of Berlin.]

ERICH VON HORNBOSTEL formerly professor at the University of Berlin, anthropologist and the world' greatest authority on comparative music.

MAX WERTHEIMER formerly professor of psychology at the Universities of Berlin and Frankfurt; founder of the Gestalt school of psychology, which is now coming to play an increasing role in American educational and social psychology. Editor of *Psychologische Forschung*.

FRIEDA WUNDERLICH formerly professor at the Berlin Training College, and editor of *Soziale Praxis*, the leading German journal of social work.

By 1935, Hermann Kantorowicz had returned to England to honor his prior commitment to the London School of Economics, and Erich von Hornbostel had retired due to his failing health. Between November 1933 and October 1935 Johnson added eleven more scholars to the faculty and gave short biographical sketches of ten them as well in the same annual report. The eleventh scholar was Johnson himself:

MAX ASCOLI formerly professor of jurisprudence in several Italian universities; for two years, a Rockefeller Fellow in the United States.

ARNOLD BRECHT formerly lecturer in the Hochschule für Politik in Berlin, director in the Prussian State Ministry and Finance Ministry, earlier director for Constitution, Administration and Civil Service in the Imperial Ministry of the Interior. Member of the German Senate and Reporter on the Budget.

WERNER HEGEMANN leading German authority on town planning, formerly editor of the two most important architectural journals of Berlin, well known in the United States and throughout the world as an architectural authority and practitioner of town planning [he taught in Continuing Education].

ALFRED KÄHLER formerly director of the People's College in Harrisleefeld, Schleswig-Holstein.

FRITZ LEHMANN formerly assistant in banking in the University of Berlin, a brilliant writer on topics of finance.

RUDOLF LITTAUER formerly counselor to the Dresdner Bank at Leipzig, a rising authority on comparative commercial law.

CARL MAYER formerly assistant in the Institute for Social and Political Science in Heidelberg, an outstanding research worker in the field of the sociology of religion.

ALBERT SALOMON formerly professor at the Pedagogical Institute of Cologne, one of the leading sociologists in Germany, editor of *Die Gesellschaft*.

HANS SIMONS formerly director of the Hochschule für Politik, ministerial counsellor in the Prussian Ministry of the Interior; member of the Government Committee for Imperial Reform; editor of *Wiederaufbau*.

HANS STAUDINGER formerly Ministerialdirektor to the Prussian Ministry of Trade and Industry, responsible for the administration of transport and electric power. Worked out plan for the coordination of the state-owned power companies throughout the empire and the rationalization of the power of supply.[6]

APPENDIX C

EXTENDED NOTES AND COMMENTARY FOR CHAPTER 9

EXTENSION OF NOTE 23: HANNAH ARENDT AND THE
AMERICAN TRANSLATIONS OF *MEIN KAMPF*

When Hannah Arendt was writing *The Origins of Totalitarianism*, the most widely used English-language edition of *Mein Kampf* in the United States was Houghton Mifflin's 1943 translation by Ralph Manheim, which had replaced the one the New School had prepared. Instead of referring to Manheim's work, Arendt quoted from the "illegal" Stackpole and Sons version, which had been removed from U.S. bookstores in 1939—three and a half months after it had appeared on the shelves and two years before Arendt had arrived in the United States.

Was this purely coincidental? Arendt's biographer, Elisabeth Young-Bruehl, who died in 2011, did not discuss the matter. Nor has anyone else, says Jerome Kohn, Arendt's literary executor and editor of Arendt's posthumous works—at least not to his knowledge.[1]

Did Arendt even know about the controversy over the translations? The Court of Appeals made its final decision in the fall of 1941, several months after Arendt arrived in the United States, so it is possible that she had heard about the case. But if she did, it is difficult to believe that she would have sided with Stackpole and Sons, against a ruling that protected the rights of authors made stateless by Hitler, even if that meant protecting his rights as well. Finally, if Arendt had been following this controversy, she would have known that in the end Hitler never collected any of his royalties, nor did his publisher.

In *The Origins of Totalitarianism*, Arendt only gave the city and year of publication of the translation she used. She did not provide the name of the publisher, but she carefully noted that she was using the "unexpurgated translation" of *Mein Kampf*, which was the way Stackpole and Sons referred to their book. Reynal & Hitchcock called theirs "the complete unabridged." Both publishers were based in New York, and both translations were published in 1939.

Arendt's formal association with the New School started in 1954 when she began giving courses there on totalitarianism in the adult division.[2] She joined the Graduate Faculty in 1967.

APPENDIX D

EXTENDED NOTES AND COMMENTARY
FOR CHAPTER 18

EXTENSION OF NOTES 24 AND 25: BIOGRAPHICAL
SKETCHES OF WALTER EBERSTADT, HENRY ARNHOLD,
AND MICHAEL GELLERT[1]

Walter Eberstadt and Henry Arnhold could trace their ancestors back to the sixteenth and seventeenth centuries. Members of Eberstadt's family came from the ancient ghetto of Worms-on-Rhine, where they played an important role during the early nineteenth century in gaining citizenship for this Jewish community.[2] Arnhold's family came from the city of Dessau, the birthplace of Moses Mendelssohn, the father of German Jewish Enlightenment. During the early decades of the nineteenth century, his great-grandfather studied medicine in Berlin, an exceptional achievement for Jews at the time, which gave him the authority he needed to persuade the Breslau Rabbinical Conference to modify *halachic* prescriptions for performing the "covenant of circumcision." Thanks to Adolph Arnhold, the rabbis ruled in 1846 that moving forward they would only recognize medically certified *moehls* to enact this holiest of holy rituals.[3] In 1864, Henry Arnhold's grandfather founded the Arnhold Brothers' Bank in Dresden (Bankhaus Gebrüder Arnhold), which soon became one of the most important financial firms in Germany and, as a result, an early target for Aryanization after Hitler rose to power.

The wealth in Walter Eberstadt's family came from his mother's parents, the Flersheims, who had made their fortune importing ivory, mother-of-pearl, tortoise shell, and other natural products used in designing elegant ornaments. In the years following World War I, these in-laws helped Eberstadt's father go into

banking—a risky business in Weimar Germany, but he did extremely well, opening offices in Frankfurt and Hamburg. Then, of course, everything changed
when Hitler came to power in 1933, even for a man like Georg Eberstadt who
had been raised a Lutheran and decorated for his heroism during the Great War.
"What a blessing," Eberstadt wrote, that "Iron Crosses and baptismal waters did
not lull [father] into thinking he could survive under National Socialism!"[+] In
1935, a few months after the Reichstag passed the Nuremberg Laws, the Eber-
stadts moved to England. Walter was fourteen years old.

Eberstadt's parents arranged for their son to finish his gymnasium studies
at Tonbridge, a fashionable "public" school in Britain. Four years later, Walter
entered Oxford, arriving a few weeks after the outbreak of World War II.
Although his family had fled Nazi Germany, the British arrested Eberstadt in
1940, along with other "enemy aliens." When they released him a few weeks later,
he joined the British army and served for six years, rising through the ranks to
major. In 1945, the British sent their bilingual soldier to occupied Hamburg to
monitor the radio station of the city he had known as a child. Twelve months
later Eberstadt returned to civilian life and to his studies at Oxford. Graduating in 1948, he accepted a job on the editorial staff of *The Economist*, where
he remained for three years before moving to New York and beginning a long
and successful career in investment banking—first at Lehman Brothers, then at
Model, Roland and Stone, and finally at Lazard Frères. In 1975, Eberstadt joined
the New School's Board of Trustees. Among his many contributions to the New
School, he helped Jonathan Fanton raise money from other wealthy émigrés like
himself who had fled Hitler's Europe. In addition to those who eventually joined
the board, Eberstadt persuaded Peter Model, the son of his good friend and former boss Leo Model, to endow a professorial chair in economics in memory of
his father. Eberstadt died in 2014 after a long illness.

The wealth in Michael Gellert's family also came from his mother's side, who
was a descendent of the famous Petschek family. They made their fortune in coal.
The branch to which Mrs. Gellert belonged founded the Petschek and Co. Bank
after World War I in the newly established First Republic of Czechoslovakia. Gellert's father's family owned a successful paper business, which he abandoned when
he married Michael's mother and joined the Petschek bank. The Gellert family
left Czechoslovakia in May 1938, two months after the *Anschluss* and four months
before England and France signed the Munich Pact, clearing the way for the
Nazis to invade Czechoslovakia. The Gellerts fled first to England, then to Cuba,
and finally to the United States, where they arrived in 1941. Still a young boy at
the time, Michael spent the war years going to exclusive private schools on the

East Coast. In 1949, he went to Harvard to study for his bachelor's degree and to the Wharton School of Business in 1953 for a masters. After working for Drexel Burnham and Lambert on Wall Street, Gellert cofounded Windcrest in 1968, a venture capital and private equity firm. In 1987 he joined the New School's Board of Trustees and has since made significant gifts to the Graduate Faculty, Mannes School of Music, and the New School's building campaign. He died in August 2021.

Before the Nazis came to power, Arnhold's parents were prominent members of Dresden's secular elite, many of whom, admittedly, were assimilated/converted Jews. Among their many contributions to the cultural life of the city, every winter they hosted talks by distinguished artists and intellectuals in their gracious home. In the early 1930s, the speakers included, the expressionist painter Wassily Kandinsky and the Protestant theologian Paul Tillich. The family was also famous in Dresden for having one of Europe's finest collections of Meissen porcelain.

Soon after Hitler rose to power, Arnhold's father suffered a series of strokes and died in 1935. His mother then moved the family to Switzerland and sent Henry to a French-language lycée, where he studied with children from many different countries. Over the summer of 1939, one of his classmates invited him to visit his family in Norway. And that was where he was on September 3 when the Allies declared war on Germany, making it too dangerous for the teenage boy to return to Switzerland.

When the Germans invaded Norway the following spring, they arrested Arnhold and sent him to the Ulven labor camp for five months. After he was released, the boy acquired false identity papers and escaped Norway on foot, slipping across the border into Sweden, and eventually getting himself to Cuba. In the meantime, his mother and the other members of the family had fled to Brazil. In April 1942, the Arnholds were finally reunited in California.

Although Henry had never finished high school, he persuaded the director of admissions at UCLA to accept him as a college freshman, impressing her with his knowledge of modern art. Three months later the U.S. Army drafted him and sent him to Camp Ritchie, a military intelligence training center, where he spent the remaining years of the war interviewing German prisoners to determine whether any of them were reliable enough to serve as spies. When the war ended, he joined his uncle Hans Arnhold in New York at the family's reconstituted banking firm. He never went back to college.

Arnhold and Eberstadt met for the first time in New York, even though their families had known one another in Germany. In his capacity as chair of the nominating committee, Eberstadt arranged for Arnhold to have dinner with the newly appointed president, Jonathan Fanton, who then quickly followed up and invited Arnhold to join the board in 1985.

After accepting Fanton's invitation, Arnhold wrote to Eberstadt to thank him for having recruited him to the board, adding playfully that his friend had "enriched my life at the expense of my pocket." No trustee in recent years has been more generous to the New School than Henry Arnhold.

On August 23, 2018, three weeks before his 97th brithday, Arnhold died of a heart attack. He was still active until the very end.

ACKNOWLEDGMENTS

I served as dean of the Graduate Faculty of Political and Social Science (GF) between 1993 and 2000 and remained on the faculty until 2002. Yet I am curiously absent from my own history of the New School. As those who know me will certainly agree, I am no shrinking violet, so why did I leave myself out of the last chapters of the book when I was very much around? Because I wanted to focus on the collaboration of Jonathan Fanton, the New School's sixth president (1982–1999), and Ira Katznelson, his first dean of the Graduate Faculty (1983–1990). Fanton worked with two other deans after Katznelson stepped down—Alan Wolfe (1990–1993) and myself (1993–2000)—but the big story for the Graduate Faculty unfolded during the Katznelson years. Although I stand by my decision, in doing so I have regrettably ignored the valuable contributions of colleagues who joined the faculty after 1990.

To all those colleagues who do not appear on the pages of this book, please accept my apologies. I deeply cherish the years we spent together and wish I could have found a way to include you as well. Among the many people I would have liked to have written about, let me single out William Milberg, the current dean of NSSR, formerly known as the Graduate Faculty. When we met in 1993, Will was an assistant professor of economics and economic history. Three years later he coauthored *The Crisis in Vision in Modern Economic Thought* with the department's legendary professor emeritus, Robert Heilbroner—the first of two books they would write together. I salute you, Will, for your wise leadership in recent years and thank you for the support you have given me while I was writing this book.

I also want to recognize members of the New School's administration who played important roles during the Fanton years but do not appear in the book, a number of whom were very helpful to me. First and foremost, I thank Robert Gates, Ira Katznelson's associate dean, who later joined the offices of the provost and president. A German historian and gifted linguist (in German and Spanish), Bob accompanied me to Germany on my first trip to the reunified country to introduce me to the Heuss Professor Committee and to join me in meeting with the academic leaders of the Technical University of Dresden. The GF had just created a special scholarship program for East German graduate students to come to the New School—an initiative funded by trustee Henry Arnhold, whose family had fled the city in 1935. Bob remained an invaluable guide and good friend throughout my years at the New School, and since. Important as well were Provost Judith Walzer, Vice President Joseph Porrino, Associate Dean Dan McIntyre, the current Vice Dean Robert Kostrzewa, and Associate Director of Administration Sonia Salas.

Among other important members of the New School community whom I have regretfully left out of this book, I want to thank the following: Cynthia Greenleaf Fanton, who, while working full time as a lawyer, co-hosted memorable dinners in the president's residence for faculty and distinguished guests; Malcom Smith, chairman of the Board of Trustees and generous friend of the Graduate Faculty, who opened my eyes to Hiram Halle's other charitable endeavors beyond the University in Exile; Kenneth Prewitt, who served in multiple capacities, first as a member of Ira Katznelson's Enabling Committee, then on the Graduate Faculty's Visiting Committee/Board of Governors, where he helped me in more ways than I can count, and finally as Dean of the Graduate Faculty, under Bob Kerrey. I would also like to remember the late Alice Ginott-Cohn, alumna, Visiting Committee member, and generous supporter of the Graduate Faculty.

I could never have written this book without the help of dedicated librarians and archivists. At the New School I thank Carmen Hendershott and Wendy Scheir, whose assistance to me over the years went far beyond the call of duty. I also want to acknowledge Laura Miller at the Rockefeller Archives Center, as well as Debora O'Brien at the New Marlborough, Massachusetts Library. Finally, I want to thank my research assistants, Ellen Murray and Alejandro Nuñez Maldonado, and NSSR student Tara Mastrelli.

Many colleagues, family and friends have generously helped me advance my research and the writing of this book. These include Sara Adler, Peter Ascoli, Françoise Basch, Emily Braun, Paul Corner, Liliane Crips, the late Walter Eberstadt, Johannes Fabian, Merritt Fox, Paul Gottlieb, Nancy Green, Ulrich Hammerling, Peter Halle, the late Irena Hausmanowa, Benjamin Hett, Eva Hoffman, Jack Jacobs, Jonathan Kalb, Liliane Kandel, Richard Kaye, Bob Kerrey, Jerome Kohn, Lynda Klich, Mitchell and Gloria Levitas, Emmanuelle Loyer, Alasdair MacIntyre, Frank

Michelman, Edward Nell, Dmitri Nikulin, Amy Parsons, Michael Patullo, Marta Petrusewicz, Silvia Rocciolo, Mary Varney Rorty, Faye Rosenfeld, Leina Schiffrin, Anwar Shaikh, Susan Sawyer, Lori Singer, Sylvie Weil, David Van Zandt and, most generously, Harald Hagemann, who helped me understand the important role the New School's émigré economists played in Weimar Germany.

I also thank Alvin Johnson's grandchildren Mark Deyrup and Alison de Lima Greene, and his grandnephew Lee Rockwell for their generous help. In 2014, Lee Rockwell nominated Johnson to the State of Nebraska's Hall of Fame. I am grateful as well to Andra Makler, Agnes de Lima's biographer, and look forward the publication of her book.

To those I interviewed for *A Light in Dark Times*, I thank you for allowing me to tape our conversations and for the help you gave me in understanding the history of the New School, the Hitler years, and communist East and Central Europe: Andrew Arato, the late Henry Arnhold, Richard Bernstein, Jean Cohen, the late Strachan Donnelley, Jonathan Fanton, the late Michael Gellert, Jeffrey Goldfarb, the late Joseph Greenbaum, the late Ágnes Heller, Ira Katznelson, János Kis, Marcin Krol, the late Albert Landa, Arien Mack, Elzbieta Matynia, Adam Michnik, Robert Pollin, Jerzy Szacki, the late Aristide and Vera Zolberg.

As I prepared the manuscript for publication, I benefitted greatly from the editorial assistance I received from Pamela Dailey, Alyssa Wheeler, my patient editors at Columbia University Press, Philip Leventhal and Miriam Grossman, and my agent Georges Borchadt.

I also want to thank those who helped me acquire and prepare the photographs that appear in this book, creatively resolving unanticipated challenges: Richard Adams, Gonçalo Fonseca, Elzbieta Matynia, Jeffrey Roth, Wendy Scheir, Jerry Speier, Peter Stein, William Steele, Agnes Szanyi, and Erica Zolberg.

To Jennifer Raab, president of Hunter College, I thank you for the interest you took in this project from the very beginning and for your generous support over the years.

I save for last my heartfelt thanks to those who read through various drafts of the manuscript, offering precious support and advice along the way: Jonathan Fanton, Alice Kessler-Harris, the late Ágnes Heller, Ira Katznelson, Arien Mack, and Marie-Claire Pasquier.

NOTES

Archives and Special Collections

American Philosophical Society Library
Archives of American Art, Smithsonian Institution
Boston University, Howard Gottlieb Archival Research Center (BU)
Columbia University Archives and Special Collections (Columbia)
German and Jewish Intellectuals Collection at the State University in Albany
    (SUNY Albany)
Johns Hopkins Archives and Special Collections
New School Archives and Special Collections (NSA)
Rockefeller Archive Center (RAC)
University Chicago Archives and Special Collections (Chicago)
University of Nebraska, Lincoln, Archives and Special Collections (UNL)
Yale University, Manuscripts and Archives (Yale)

PROLOGUE: IN THE ARCHIVES

1. The New School is in the process of a major project to reorganize and digitize the archives. The head archivist, Wendy Scheir, has suggested that I not indicate boxes and folders, but just the archive itself (NSA).
2. Alison de Lima Greene (Agnes de Lima's only surviving heir who inherited all her papers) and Andra Makler (Agnes de Lima's biographer) have confirmed that Agnes de Lima did not leave behind a manuscript for a book on the New School. Makler's biography has not yet been published.
3. *New School Bulletin*, November 23, 1959, NSA.
4. Thomas Mann, "To Alvin Johnson: Great American, Citizen of the World," Daylesford, Philadelphia, 1943, copy preserved in NSA.

5.   Alvin Johnson, "The Compleat Beggar," *New School Bulletin* (March 17, 1952). Johnson rightly claimed that in 1952 the New School still had no endowment, but it was not for his lack of trying. In 1937 he wrote a little pamphlet called "The New School Catechism" in which he outlined a plan for creating an endowment, 7, NSA. The initiative apparently failed.

6.   In addition to Yale and the New School, the University of Nebraska has a large archive of material, which was donated by members of Johnson's family in the early 1990s.

7.   Vincent O'Leary to Joseph Greenbaum, November 16, 1977, NSA.

8.   Johnson's quote from *The New York Times* appeared in L.H.R., "Footnotes on Headlines: Briefly Examining Various Timely Matters," *New York Times*, April 3, 1927.

9.   See endnotes in Parts I and II for books and articles that discuss the New School during the interwar years and World War II. At this point, I will only mention Alvin Johnson, *Pioneer's Progress: An Autobiography* (1952; Lincoln: University of Nebraska Press, 1960); Peter M. Rutkoff and William B. Scott, *New School: A History of The New School for Social Research* (New York: The Free Press, 1986); Claus-Dieter Krohn, *Intellectuals in Exile: Refugee Scholars and the New School for Social Research*, trans. Rita Kimber and Robert Kimber (1987; Amherst: University of Massachusetts Press, 1993); and Thomas Bender, *New York Intellect* (Baltimore, Md.: The Johns Hopkins University Press, 1987).

10.   Hannah Arendt, *Thinking Without a Banister*, ed. Jerome Kohn (NY: Schocken Books, 2018), 200–201. Originally published in Politische. . . . Beck, 1962).

11.   Eric Hobsbawm, *The Age of Extremes: A History of the Short Twentieth Century, 1914–1991* (New York: Vintage Books, 1994).

1. THE FIRST FOUNDING MOMENT

1.   "The New School for Social Research: Preliminary Lectures," February–May 1919, NSA.

2.   Alvin Johnson, *Pioneer's Progress: An Autobiography* (1952; reprint, Lincoln: University of Nebraska Press, 1960), 278; Wesley Clair Mitchell, cited in Lucy Sprague Mitchell, *Two Lives: The Story of Wesley Clair Mitchell and Myself* (New York: Simon and Schuster, 1953), 334.

3.   Nicholas Murray Butler, cited in Michael Rosenthal, *Nicholas Miraculous: The Amazing Career of the Redoubtable Nicholas Murray Butler* (New York: Farrar, Straus and Giroux, 2006), 225, 226.

4.   Charles Beard to Lucy Salmon, February 25, 1919, Lucy Salmon Papers, Vassar College, cited in Ellen Nore, *Charles A. Beard: An Intellectual Biography* (Carbondale, Ill.: Southern Illinois University Press, 1983), 89n8.

5.   Charles Beard to Lucy Salmon, February 27, 1919, cited in Nore, *Charles A. Beard*, 89n8.

6.   Wesley Clair Mitchell, cited in Sprague Mitchell, *Two Lives*, 342.

7.   Thorstein Veblen, *The Higher Learning in America: A Memorandum on the Conduct by Business Men* (1918; reprint, Palo Alto, Calif.: Stanford University Academic Reprints, 1954), 209, www.elegant-technology.com/resource/HI_LEARN.PDF.

8.   Rosenthal, *Nicholas Miraculous*, 8.

9.   Nicholas Murray Butler, cited in Nore, *Charles A. Beard*, 89.

10. John Dewey, cited in, "[Beard] Quits Columbia, Assails Trustees," *New York Times*, October 9, 1917, p. 1. Although John Dewey's name appears on the list of faculty members when the New School opened in 1919–1920, he was on an extended research trip in Japan and China. He taught his first course at the New School the following year.

11. Ira Katznelson, "Reflections on the New School's Founding Moments, 1919 and 1933," *Social Research* 76, no. 2 (Summer 2009): 395–410.

12. Richard Albert and Menaka Guruswamy, "Call for Papers—Symposium on Founding Moments in Constitutionalism," *I-Connect* (blog), *International Journal of Constitutional Law*, November 13, 2015, www.iconnectblog.com/2015/11/call-for-papers-symposium-on -founding-moments-in-constitutionalism/.

13. Lecturers included Charles Beard, John Dewey, Felix Frankfurter, Horace Kallen, Harold Laski, Nathan Roscoe Pound, James Harvey Robinson, Graham Wallas, Wesley Clair Mitchell, Thorstein Veblen, and Leo Wolman.

14. Katznelson, "Reflections on the New School's Founding Moments," 399.

15. Katznelson, "Reflections on the New School's Founding Moments," 402.

16. Alvin Johnson to Elsie Clews Parsons, June 26, 1923, Elsie Clews Parsons Papers, American Philosophical Society Library.

17. Wesley Clair Mitchell, cited in Sprague Mitchell, *Two Lives*, 342.

2. ALVIN JOHNSON
AND *THE NEW REPUBLIC*

1. Alvin Johnson, "An Autobiographical Note," Author *Spring Storm*," (New York: Alfred A. Knopf, 1936), 4. For details on Johnson's childhood, see this pamphlet, which was published at the same time as Knopf published Johnson's loosely autobiographical novel *Spring Storm*. NSA has a copy of it. See also the early chapters of Johnson's autobiography: Alvin Johnson, *Pioneer's Progress* (1952; Lincoln: University of Nebraska Press, 1960).

2. Elwood Mead was a highly respected agricultural engineer. When Calvin Coolidge became president, he appointed Mead chairman of the U.S. Bureau of Reclamation.

3. Johnson, "An Autobiographical Note," 14; Alvin Johnson, *Pioneer's Progress: An Autobiography* (1952; Lincoln: University of Nebraska Press, 1960), 364–65; Alvin Johnson, "Van Eden, A Jewish Farm Community," *American Hebrew*, Agricultural Issue, November 1, 1940 (no page numbers). A copy of this article has been preserved in Alvin Johnson Papers, UNL. Susan Taylor Block, "Van Eden," *Lower Cape Fear Historical Society Bulletin*, XL, no. 1 (1995), no page numbers; Melissa Bently, "The Van Eden Settlement and Alvin Johnson's Attempt . . ." (senior BA thesis, University of North Carolina, Ashville, 2003).

4. Johnson, "An Autobiographical Note," 4, 6.

5. Founded in 1876, Johns Hopkins was the first research university in the United States. Next came Columbia, when it opened its School of Politics in 1880, then Harvard in 1890.

6. Alvin Saunders Johnson, "Rent in Modern Economic Theory: An Essay in Distribution," *Publications of the American Economic Association*, Third Series, vol. 3, no. 4 (November 1902), 1–129.

7. Johnson, "An Autobiographical Note," 7.

8. Johnson, "An Autobiographical Note," 7; M. Carey Thomas to Alvin Johnson, April 24, 1901, March 12, 1902, April 3, 1905, telegram April 5, 1905, box 4, Alvin Johnson Papers, UNL. For more on Johnson's early years at Columbia, see Joseph Dorfman, in R. Gordon Hoxie et al., *A History of the Faculty of Political Science* (New York: Columbia University Press, 1955), 189.

9. Alexander Meiklejohn to Alvin Johnson, January 16, 1916, box 3, folder 12, Alvin Johnson Papers, UNL.

10. Alexander Meiklejohn to Alvin Johnson, March 13, 1915, box 3, folder 12, Alvin Johnson Papers, UNL.

11. Alvin Johnson, "Curriculum Vitae," NSA.

12. Johnson, *Pioneer's Progress*, 252, 254; Wesley Clair Mitchell, cited in Lucy Sprague Mitchell, *Two Lives: The Story of Wesley Clair Mitchell and Myself* (New York: Simon and Schuster, 1953), 334, 342.

13. Johnson, *Pioneer's Progress*, 252.

14. Wesley Mitchell, cited in Sprague Mitchell, *Two Lives*, 296–97.

15. Bernard Baruch, "Honor to Alvin Johnson," *New School Bulletin* 7, no. 17 (December 26, 1949).

16. Bernard Baruch, *The Public Years: My Own Story* (New York: Holt, Reinhart and Winston, 1960), 53.

17. Alvin Johnson to Bernard Baruch, November 12, 1943, August 18, 1953, box 1, Yale.

18. Alvin Johnson to Bernard Baruch, November 19, 1941, NSA; cited in Aristide Zolberg and Agnès Callarmard, "The Ecole Libre," *Social Research* 65, no. 5 (Winter 1998): 931.

19. Herbert Croly to Alvin Johnson June 4, 1915, box 1, Alvin Johnson Papers, UNL.

20. Sprague Mitchell, *Two Lives*, 333.

21. In addition to Herbert Croly and Alvin Johnson, a sampling of the overlap of people affiliated with *The New Republic* who lectured and the New School included Charles Beard, Morris Raphael Cohen, John Dewey, Felix Frankfurter, Horace Kallen, John Maynard Keynes, Harold Laski, Walter Lippmann, Wesley Clair Mitchell, Elsie Clews Parsons, N. Roscoe Pound, James Harvey Robinson, Graham Wallas, H. G. Wells, and Judge Learned Hand. For excellent portraits of the contributors to *The New Republic*, see David W. Levy, *Herbert Croly of The New Republic: The Life and Thought of an American Progressive* (Princeton, N.J.: Princeton University Press, 1985).

22. "Opening Statement," *New Republic: A Journal of Opinion* 1, no. 1 (November 7, 1914): 3.

23. Thomas Bender, *New York Intellect* (Baltimore, Md.: Johns Hopkins University Press, 1987), 227.

24. Theodore Roosevelt, "The Peace of Righteousness," *New York Times*, November 1, 1914, Magazine Section 5.

25. Editorial, "Pacifism vs. Passivism," *New Republic* (December 12, 1914): 7.

26. Bender, *New York Intellect*, 225.

27. Levy, *Herbert Croly of The New Republic*, 205–8, 222–23.

28. Alvin Johnson, "An Inconclusive Peace," *New Republic* (July 24, 1915): 307–8; Editorial, "A Punic Peace," *New Republic* (May 17, 1919): 71–74. See Herbert Croly to Alvin Johnson, May 8, 1919, box 1, UNL, asking Johnson to write the unsigned editorial for the magazine on the Versailles Treaty for the May 17, 1919, issue; Levy, *Herbert Croly of New Republic*, 208.

29. Herbert Croly to Alvin Johnson, September 19, 1914, box 1, UNL.

30. Herbert Croly to Alvin Johnson, October 17 and 19, 1914, box 1, UNL; Alvin Johnson, "The Cotton Crisis" *New Republic* (November 7, 1914): 17–18.

31. Herbert Croly to Alvin Johnson October 26, 1914, box 1, Alvin Johnson Papers, UNL.

32. Johnson, *Pioneer's Progress*, 240–47. A small sampling of Alvin Johnson's articles published in *New Republic* follows. If unsigned, I have added Croly's requests to Johnson to write the articles: "The Cotton Crisis" *New Republic* (November 7, 1914): 17–18 (signed); "Economic Reserve in Peace," *New Republic* (May 29, 1915): 83–84 (unsigned, see Croly to Johnson, May 20, 1915, box 1, UNL); "An Inconclusive Peace," *New Republic* (July 24, 1915): 307–8 (signed); "The Democratic Revenue Bill," *New Republic* (August 26, 1916): 81–82 (unsigned, see Croly to Johnson, August 25, 19, 1916, box 1, UNL); "Democratic Intervention," *New Republic* (September 30, 1916): 207–8 (unsigned, see Croly to Johnson, September 26, 1916, box 1, UNL); "A Punic Peace," *New Republic* (May 17, 1919): 71–74 (unsigned, see Croly to Johnson, May 8, 1919, box 1, UNL); "Is Revolution Possible?" *New Republic* (November 26, 1919): 367–73 (signed). Johnson also published articles in *New Republic* under pseudonyms, Johnson, *Pioneer's Progress*, 242. Finally, he published a collection of fiction that included pieces he had previously published in *New Republic*, among them was "Carnegied," *New Republic* (September 29, 1917): 244–46 (signed). "Carnegied" was reprinted in the collection, Alvin Johnson, *John Stuyvesant and Other People* (New York: Harcourt, Brace and Howe, 1919), 184–193.

33. Croly to Johnson, September 8, 1916, box 1, UNL.

34. Croly to Johnson, January 26, 1917, box 1, UNL.

35. Walter Lippmann to Alvin Johnson, February 1, 1917, 4:58 PM, telegram; Herbert Croly to Alvin Johnson February 1, 1917, box 1, UNL.

36. Johnson, *Pioneer's Progress*, 243–44.

37. Editorial, "The Great Decision," *New Republic* (April 7, 1917): 280.

38. Johnson, "A Punic Peace," 71.

3. COLUMBIA UNIVERSITY

1. Ellen Nore, *Charles A. Beard: An Intellectual Biography* (Carbondale, Ill.: Southern Illinois University Press, 1983),72, 73; Charles A. Beard, cited in *New York Times*, January 26, 1919.

2. James Harvey Robinson, "War and Thinking," *New Republic* (December 19, 1914): 17.

3. Nicholas Murray Butler, *Across the Busy Years*, vol.1 (New York: Charles Scribner's and Sons, 1939), cited in Michael Rosenthal, *Nicholas Miraculous: The Amazing Career of the Redoubtable Dr. Nicholas Murray Butler* (New York: Farrar, Straus and Giroux), 164.

4. Rosenthal, *Nicholas Miraculous*, 377.

5. "Revolutionary Radicalism: Its History, Purpose and Tactics. . . . Being the Report of the Joint Legislative Committee Investigating Seditious Activities," filed April 24, 1920, 4 vols. (Albany, N.Y., 1920).

6. Charles Beard cited in "On Pacifist List, but Serve Nation," *New York Times*, January 26, 1919.

7. Rosenthal, *Nicholas Miraculous*, 225; Charles A. Beard, "A Statement by Charles A. Beard," *New Republic* (December 29, 1917): 249.

8. Rosenthal, *Nicholas Miraculous*, 218, 225.

9. James Harvey Robinson, "A New Educational Adventure," *Nation*, September 7, 1918, 264.

10. Charles A. Beard, "A Statement by Charles A. Beard," *New Republic* (December 29, 1917): 249. The controversial book by "Mr. X", to which Beard alluded, was: Frank Johnson Goodnow, *Social Reform and the Constitution*, (New York: Burt Franklin, 1911). Beard's account of why the trustees appointed W. D. Guthrie instead of Goodnow deserves closer scrutiny. Suffice it to say that the documentary evidence tells a different story: John Burgess, not the trustees, boycotted the appointment of "Mr. X." See John Burgess, "Letter to Editor," *New York Times*, January 15, 1917; R. Gordon Hoxie et al., *A History of the Faculty of Political Science* (New York: Columbia University Press, 1955) 105–6; Julius Goebel Jr. et al., *A History of the School of Law* (New York: Columbia University Press, 1955) 210–11; papers of John W. Burgess, central files, Box 318, file 1/1912–12/1917, Frank Johnson Goodnow, central files, Box 327, Rare Books and Special Collections, Columbia University.

11. Beard, "A Statement by Charles A. Beard," 230.

12. "Columbia to Sound Loyalty of Faculty. Aimed at the Pacifists; Trustees Want to Know if Any Professors Are Propounding Unpatriotic Doctrines," *New York Times*, March 6, 1917.

13. "School of Political Science Resolution," cited in Beard, "A Statement by Charles A. Beard," 250.

14. Beard, "A Statement by Charles A. Beard," 250.

15. See Rosenthal, *Nicholas Miraculous*, 226–36 for an excellent discussion of the Cattell affair, on which much of this summary is based.

16. Cattell founded the journal *Psychology Review* and owned and edited *Science*, which became the official organ of the Association for the Advancement of Science. See Ira Katznelson, "Reflections on the New School's Founding Moments, 1919 and 1933," *Social Research* 76, no. 2 (Summer 2010): 395–410.

17. James McKeen Cattell, *University Control* (New York: The Science Press, 1913).

18. Rosenthal, *Nicholas Miraculous*, 229.

19. Editorial, *New York Times*, October 10, 1919.

20. E. R. A. Seligman to James McKeen Cattell, June 18, 1917; E. R. A. Seligman to The Sub-Committee of the Trustees, John Dewey Papers, 1858–1970, vol. 1, 1871–1918, Special Collections of Southern Illinois University, electronic version.

21. E. R. A. Seligman to Nicholas Murray Butler, March 3, 1917, central files, box 338, folder 15, Columbia.

22. "Quest for Butler's Home. Members of Columbia Faculty Meet in Secret to Discuss It," *New York Times*, March 4, 1917.

23. E. R. A. Seligman + 23 other colleagues to James McKeen Cattell, March 3, 1917, central files, box 338, folder 15, Columbia.

24. John Dewey to E. R. A. Seligman, May 7, 1917, James McKeen Cattell to E. R. A. Seligman, June 13, 1917, E. R. A. Seligman to James McKeen Cattell, June 14, 1917, E. R. A. Seligman to James McKeen Cattell, June 18, 1917, E. R. A. Seligman to The Sub-Committee of the Trustees, June 18, 1917, John Dewey Papers, vol. 1, electronic version.

25. James McKeen Cattell to several members of Congress, August 23, 1917, cited in Rosenthal, *Nicholas Miraculous*, 234.

26. Hon. Julius Kahan to Nicholas Murray Butler, August 27, 1917, cited in Rosenthal, *Nicholas Miraculous*, 235; Butler's papers, cited in Rosenthal, *Nicholas Miraculous*, 235.

27. Trustee John B. Pine to Nicholas Murray Butler, September 17, 1917, Nicholas Murray Butler to F. S. Bangs, September 21, 1917, Butler's papers, cited in Rosenthal, *Nicholas Miraculous*, 235.

28. E. R. A. Seligman to George L. Ingraham, Chairman of the Joint Committee [of Columbia University's Board of Trustees], September 24, 1917, John Dewey Correspondence, vol. 1, Columbia University of the City of New York; Charters and Statues, 1916, Columbia, section 67, 21–22.

29. Alan Ryan, *John Dewey and the High Tide of American Liberalism* (New York: Norton, 1995), 198.

30. John Dewey to E. R. A. Seligman, September 25, 1917, John Dewey Papers, vol. 1, electronic version.

31. John Dewey, James Harvey Robinson and Thomas Reed Powell to Chairman of the Committee on Academic Freedom and Tenure of the American Association of University Professors, between October 10 and 19, 1917, John Dewey Papers, vol. 1, electronic version. The editors of Dewey's papers date this letter to the AAUP as having been written between the tenth and nineteenth of October; "To Sue Columbia, Cattell's Threat," *New York Times*, October 10, 1917.

32. "The Professors' Union" *New York Times*, January 21, 1916.

33. A. O. Lovejoy, Edward Capps and A. A. Young, "Report of Committee on Academic Freedom in Wartime," *Bulletin of the American Association of University Professors* 4, nos. 2/3 (February–March 1918): 29–47, at 44–45. In 1922, the AAUP finally published the case between Columbia and Cattell: "Columbia University vs. Professor Cattell," *Bulletin of the American Association of University Professors* 8, no. 7 (November 1922): 21–41. I would like to thank Hans-Joerg Tiede, senior program officer of the AAUP and author of *The Founding of the American Association of University Professors* (Baltimore, Md.: Johns Hopkins University Press, 2015), for helping me track down AAUP deliberations.

34. "Quits Columbia; Assails Trustees," *New York Times*, October 9, 1917.

35. John Dewey, "In Explanation of Our Lapse," *New Republic* (November 3, 1917): 28.

36. See Butler's correspondence with members of the Board of Trustees, Nicholas Murray Butler Papers, Columbia, during the late summer and fall of 1917.

37. Special Committee of the Board of Trustees of Columbia University, cited in "Columbia Ousts Two Professors, Foes of War Plans," *New York Times*, October 2, 1917.

38. "Columbia Ousts Two Professors"; "Quits Columbia; Assails Trustees; Professor Charles A. Beard Says Narrow Clique Is Controlling the University. Free Speech The Issue," *New York Times*, October 9, 1917.

39. Charles A. Beard, cited in "Quits Columbia."

40. Editorial, "Columbia's Deliverance," *New York Times*, October 10, 1917.

41. "Dr. Beard Attacks Columbia Trustees," *New York Times*, December 28, 1917; Charles A. Beard, "A Statement by Charles A. Beard," *New Republic* (December 29, 1917): 249–51.

42. Herbert Croly, "A School of Social Research," *New Republic* (June 8, 1918): 167.

4. THE IDEA TAKES SHAPE

1. Herbert Croly, "A Great School of Political Science," *World's Work* 20 (May 1910): 12887–88, cited in David W. Levy, *Herbert Croly of The New Republic: The Life and Thought of an American Progressive* (Princeton, N.J.: Princeton University Press, 1985), 270.

2. Alvin Johnson, *Pioneer's Progress: An Autobiography* (1952; Lincoln: University of Nebraska Press, 1960), 272.

3. Harry Elmer Barnes, "James Harvey Robinson," in *American Masters of Social Science*, ed. Howard Odum (New York: Henry Holt, 1927), chap. 10, 340; Luther Hendricks, "James Harvey Robinson and The New School for Social Research," *Journal of Higher Education* 20, no. 1 (1949): 1–11.

4. Johnson, *Pioneer's Progress*, 273.

5. Among these contributors was the eminent Graham Wallas, a founding member of the faculty at the London School of Economics. When LSE opened in 1895, Wallas served as its first lecturer of politics. Ralf Dahrendorf, *LSE: A History of The London School of Economics and Political Science* (Oxford: Oxford University Press, 1995), 9; Graham Wallas, "An Historical Note," *The Students Union Handbook 1922–1923*, LSE CF 116/C, cited in Dahrendorf, *LSE*, 4n6.

6. Dahrendorf, *LSE*, 5,7.

7. Herbert Croly, "A School of Social Research," *New Republic* (June 8, 1918): 167–71. Works on the history of the Ecole libre des sciences politiques include Pierre Rain, *L'Ecole libre des sciences politiques, 1871–1945* (Paris: Fondation nationale des sciences politiques, 1963); Richard Descoings, *Sciences Po. De La Courneuve à Shanghai* (Paris: Presses de Sciences Po, 2007); and François et Renaud Leblond, *Emile de Boutmy, Le Père de Sciences Po* (Paris: Editions Anne Carrière, 2013).

8. Croly, "A School of Social Research," 167, 168.

9. Croly, "A School of Social Research," 167.

10. "New York to Have a Free College," *New York Post*, May 9, 1918.

11. "An Independent College of Political Science," *Nation*, May 11, 1918, 559, 560.

12. James Harvey Robinson, "The New School," *School and Society* 11 (January 31, 1920): 130–31.

13. Johnson, *Pioneer's Progress*, 271.

14. For a contemporary gloss on the classic distinction between Hamiltonians and Jeffersonians, see George Packer's brilliant article on the 2016 presidential elections, George Packer, "The Unconnected," *New Yorker*, October 31, 2016, 55.

15. Robinson, "The New School," 2.

16. Johnson, *Pioneer's Progress*, 276.

17. James Harvey Robinson, *The New History; Essays Illustrating the Modern Historical Outlook* (New York: Macmillan, 1912); James Harvey Robinson, *The Mind in the Making: The Relation of Intelligence to Social Reform* (New York: Harper & Brothers, 1921).

18. Carl Becker, "James Harvey Robinson," *Nation*, January 9, 1937, 49.

19. Robinson, "The New School," 2.

20. Ellen Nore, *Charles A. Beard: An Intellectual Biography* (Carbondale: Southern Illinois University Press, 1983), 88, 93–94. In 1935 the Rand School became known as the Tamiment Institute and Library; in 1963 the library became part of York University.

21. Harry Elmer Barnes, "James Harvey Robinson," in *American Masters of Social Science: An Approach to the Study of the Social Sciences through a Neglected Field of Biography*, ed.

Howard W. Odum (New York: Henry Holt, 1927), 321–408; Charles A. Beard, "Letter to the Editor," *Freeman* 2 (July 20, 1921): 450–51. "Had not the printing press … made the university obsolete for all except those engaged in cramming candidates for degrees?" is Beard's clearest statement against classroom teaching and his preference for teaching with books, cited in Nore, *Charles A. Beard*, 91n15.

22. Johnson, *Pioneer's Progress*, 273.

23. Johnson, *Pioneer's Progress*, 274.

24. James Harvey Robinson, "On the Education of Women," *Columbia University Quarterly* 2 (June 1900): 229; James Harvey Robinson, "The Elective System and a Liberal Education, Historically Considered," *Proceedings of the Fifteenth Annual Convention of the Association of Colleges and Preparatory Schools of the Middle States and Maryland* (Albany: University of the State of New York, 1901), 21, cited in Hendricks, "James Harvey Robinson and the New School for Social Research," 2.

25. Emily James Putnam to James Harvey Robinson, January 26, 1916, Alvin Johnson Papers, UNL, folder 1 (1916–1918); On Putnam, see Rosalind Rosenberg, *Changing the Subject: How the Women of Columbia Shaped the Way We Think about Sex and Politics* (New York: Columbia University Press, 2003).

26. Johnson, *Pioneer's Progress*, 273, 280; James Harvey Robinson to his sister Sarah March 30, 1918 and April 7, 1918, cited in Hendricks, "James Harvey Robinson and the New School for Social Research," 6n10.

27. The full list of nineteen Organization Committee members was circulated in the spring of 1918 in "A Proposal for An Independent School of Social Science for Men and Women," NSA.

28. "A Proposal for An Independent School," 4.

29. "Independent School of Social Science Estimated Annual Cash Requirements to April 30, 1928 (Tentative and Preliminary)," June 4, 1918, NSA, 2. After the first trial semester of Preliminary Lectures, the New School reported that it had raised $218,250 of the $1,349,028 the founders thought they would need to cover cash requirements over the first ten years. The lion's share of the money pledged came from the two initial gifts of Dorothy Straight and Charlotte Sorchan, to be paid out over ten years. After 1921, Sorchan's name was listed on New School documents as Mrs. Walton Martin.

30. The National Urban League was established in the early 1900s to defend African American migrants fleeing from discrimination in the South and moving North.

31. Among Elsie Clews Parsons's most significant works about the constraints of marriage and other widespread customs that limited the freedom of women are *The Old-Fashioned Woman: Primitive Fancies About the Sex* (New York: G. P. Putnam and Sons, 1913) and *Fear and Conventionality* (New York: G. P. Putnam and Sons, 1914). For a contemporary review essay of Parsons's work, see Signe Toksvig, "Elsie Clews Parsons," *New Republic* (November 26, 1919): 17–18, 20. Toksvig wrote the article while she was taking a course with Parsons at the New School.

32. James Harvey Robinson to his sister Sarah, March 30, 1918, and April 7, 1917, cited in Hendricks, "James Harvey Robinson and the New School for Social Research," 5, 6n10.

33. Hendricks, "James Harvey Robinson and the New School for Social Research," 7.

34. The Board of Directors consisted of Mrs. George W. Bacon, Charles A. Beard, Henry Bruère, Herbert Croly, Mrs. Learned Hand, Alvin Johnson, Mrs. Thomas W. Lamont,

Wesley C. Mitchell (Treasurer), Mrs. Emily James Putnam, James Harvey Robinson, Mrs. Victor Sorchan, and Mrs. Willard Straight.

35. James Harvey Robinson, "A New Educational Adventure," *Nation*, September 7, 1918, 264–65. Brief comments followed Robinson's article by Jacques Loeb (Marine Laboratory, Woods Hole, Mass.), Ernst Freund (The University of Chicago), Carl Becker (Cornell University), Alexander Meiklejoun (Amherst College), Frances Hand (Windsor, Vt.), and Elisha M Frieman (Council of National Defense, Washington, D.C.), 265-267.

36. Robinson, "A New Educational Adventure," 264, 265.

5. THE NEW SCHOOL OPENS

1. The committee bought two of the townhouses and rented the other four. The purchase, however, did not include the land on which the buildings stood. The New School had to lease the land below the houses they had bought. "Independent School of Social Science Estimated Annual Cash Requirements to April 30, 1928 (Tentative and Preliminary), June 4, 1918," 8, NSA; Alvin Johnson, *Pioneer's Progress: An Autobiography* (1952; Lincoln: University of Nebraska Press, 1960), 276, 277; Emma Peters Smith to Albert M. Todd, February 18, 1920, box 45, folder 5, Alvin Johnson Papers, UNL. "The New School for Social Research: Work of the First Term," NSA.

2. Clara Mayer, 4, NSA, unpublished manuscript with no title, probably written in the 1940s, first sentence reads, "Social consciousness comes earlier to many of our young people."

3. Johnson, *Pioneer's Progress*, 276; Harry Elmer Barnes, "James Harvey Robinson," in *American Masters of Social Science*, ed. Howard W. Odum (New York: Henry Holt, 1927), 345.

4. Emma Peters Smith to Albert M. Todd, February 18, 1920, box 45, folder 5, Alvin Johnson Papers, UNL.

5. The New School for Social Research, "Work of the First Term," NSA.

6. James Harvey Robinson, "A New Educational Adventure," *Nation*, September 7, 1918, 264.

7. The New School for Social Research, Announcement of Courses October, 1919–May 1920, 7, NSA, http://digitalarchives.library.newschool.edu/index.php/Detail/collections /NS050101. All the course bulletins (Announcement) are posted online.

8. Robinson, "A New Educational Adventure," 264.

9. The New School for Social Research, "Work of the First Term," 2; Peter M. Rutkoff and William B. Scott, *New School: A History of the New School for Social Research* (New York: The Free Press, 1986), 26.

10. The report listed the names of students doing research projects, nine of whom were women (seven of them unmarried) and five men. The students mentioned were working with professors Horace Kallen, Wesley Clair Mitchell, Thorstein Veblen, and Leo Wolman. Professors Charles Beard and Alexander Goldenweiser had not yet reported on their students. The New School for Social Research, "Work of the First Term."

11. Rutkoff and Scott, *New School*, 26n29. The literature is vast on the subject of anti-Semitism in U.S. universities before World War II. New York City provided exceptional opportunities for Jews at City College and Hunter College during the period, but only at the

undergraduate level. See, for example, Sherry Gorelick, *City College and the Jewish Poor* (New York: Schocken, 1982); Judith Friedlander, "From Open Admissions to the Honors College: Equal Opportunities in the City University in New York," in *Higher Education and Equality of Opportunity: Cross-National Perspectives*, ed. Fred Lazin (Washington, D.C.: Lexington Press, 2010), 69–88.

12. Those on the faculty who would have been identified as Jews by the wider academic community were Alexander Goldenweisser, Horace Kallen, Harold Laski, Moissaye Olgin, and Leo Wolman. Had it not been for anti-Semitism, several of them would have maintained that their Jewish origins were an irrelevant detail. They did not identify themselves with either the religious or secular Jewish community. The New School for Social Research, Announcement of Courses October 1919–May 1920, 4.

13. The New School for Social Research, Announcement of Courses, October 1919–May 1920, 6.

14. "NEWS MATTER FOR USE IN THE MORNING PAPERS FOR TUESDAY SEPTEMBER 30 (THIRTIETH) AND EVENING AND MORNING PAPERS THEREAFTER," September 27, 1919, New School Press Release, NSA; "Research School to Open: Many New Members of Institution's Staff of Instructors," *New York Times*, September 30, 1919.

15. When Barnes taught at the New School during the interwar period, he was a widely respected historian, a reputation he seriously compromised after World War II. During the late 1940s, Barnes began to champion the work of the French revisionist historian Paul Rassinier who denied that the Nazis had exterminated six million Jews. See Harry Elmer Barnes, "The Struggle Against the Historical Blackout," 1947 http://palni.contentdm.oclc.org/cdm/ref/collection/archives/id/59463.

16. Desley Deacon, *Elsie Clews Parsons* (Chicago, Ill.: University of Chicago Press, 1997), 235.

17. Ellen Nore, *Charles A. Beard: An Intellectual Biography* (Carbondale: Southern Illinois University Press, 1983); David Levy, *Herbert Croly of The New Republic* (Princeton, N.J.: Princeton University Press, 1985); Lucy Sprague Mitchell, *Two Lives: The Story of Wesley Clair Mitchell and Myself* (New York: Simon and Schuster, 1953); Luther Hendricks, "James Harvey Robinson and The New School for Social Research," *Journal of Higher Education* 20, no. 1 (1949): 1–11. Barnes's biographical sketch in "James Harvey Robinson" does not challenge Johnson's later version either; nor does Joseph Dorfman's, *Thorstein Veblen and His America* (1934; New York: Augustus M. Kelley, 1966). Laski was a young colleague at the time and not one of the founders.

18. Sprague Mitchell, *Two Lives*, 333–45, 340–41.

19. Lucy Sprague Mitchell, "A Coöperative School for Student Teachers," *Progressive Education* 8, no. 3 (March 1931): 252, 254. There were many ties between the early childhood education reformers and the founding faculty at the New School. John Dewey, the most prominent example, was publishing widely on the subject of democracy and education during the period when the Bank Street School and the New School were founded. See, most significantly, the expanded edition of John Dewey, *School and Society* (Chicago, Ill.: University of Chicago, 1915); John Dewy and Evelyn Dewey, *Schools of Tomorrow* (New York: E. P. Dutton, 1915); John Dewey, *Democracy and Education* (New York: Macmillan, 1916). Dewey published regularly on the subject in *The New Republic*, as did Agnes de Lima and other education reformers with ties to the New School; Dewey also published in education journals such as *Progressive Education*, in which he had an article ("Democracy for the Teacher")

in the same issue carrying pieces by Lucy Sprague Mitchell ("A Coöperative School for Student Teachers") and Agnes de Lima ("Democracy in the Classroom"), *Progressive Education* 8, no. 3 (March 1931). Charles Beard made significant contributions as well. See, for example, Charles A. Beard, "Could Daniel Webster Teach in New York Schools?" *Nation*, August 2, 1919. So did Alvin Johnson did. See a collection of his essays in, Alvin Johnson, *Deliver Us from Dogma* (New York: American Association of Adult Education, 1934).

20. A pioneer in a new field in economics that focused on business cycles, Wesley Mitchell described his course as follows: "The role of prices in modern life. How the war raised prices. How the rising prices affected 'economic mobilization.' Price fixing. Rising prices and the distribution of income. The effect of peace upon prices, production, and wages." The fee for the six lectures was $8.00.

21. Dorfman, *Thorstein Veben and His America*, 449.

22. Sprague Mitchell, *Two Lives*, 340.

23. Sprague Mitchell, *Two Lives*, 333. Alvin Johnson had a lengthy correspondence with Howard Beale (Professor of History at the University of North Carolina) in 1948, providing excuse after excuse for refusing to contribute an essay to a Festschrift in honor of Charles Beard. Although he had weakly said yes at first, he then politely withdrew. But Beale persisted, provoking Johnson to respond bluntly, "I am personally devoted to Beard and could not write about his influence unless I could pronounce it significant. But I don't find it significant. His works have had much more influence upon journalism, particularly left wing—although he is rightest—than upon scientific writers. He has certainly influenced the historians, but I am not competent to appraise this influence. So I regretfully withdraw." Johnson to Beale, April 14, 1948, Alvin Johnson Papers, Yale.

Beard died on September 1, 1948. On the day following his death, Johnson wrote to Mary Beard:

> Dear Mrs. Beard:
>
> Permit me to share with you your sorrow over the death of your husband. Since I first met Charles Beard in 1902, I have recognized him as the most interesting and provocative scholar I have ever met. Because of him we are all more realistic, more intelligent.
> If I were asked what educator in our time has most influenced our minds I would say without hesitation, Charles A. Beard, or more likely Charlie Beard; for we all loved him.
>
> Sincerely,
> Alvin Johnson

24. Wesley Clair Mitchell to Lucy Sprague Mitchell, July 24, 1918, cited in Sprague Mitchell, *Two Lives*, 334–35.

25. Sprague Mitchell, *Two Lives*, 342–43.

26. After Wesley Mitchell resigned, Lucy Sprague Mitchell replaced him on the Board of Trustees.

27. Johnson, *Pioneer's Progress*, 284. For dates of resignation for Beard, Robinson, and Croly, see the list of members of the Board of Directors and the Instructors, published in the New School for Social Research Announcements of Courses for the academic years between

1919–20 and 1926–27. Even after Johnson resigned from *The New Republic* in 1926, he continued to write articles for the magazine.

28. Missing its title page, the surviving copy of this 1929 report announced a decision to construct a new building on West Twelfth Street. The document begins on page 3 with these words: "The New School for Social Research is primarily an institution for higher adult education. It has no entrance requirements, gives no examinations, and is open to all persons who are able to profit by its courses." The registration figures cited in the text come from page 3 as well. For a clear statement by Johnson about the New School's inability to support research, see Announcement of Courses 1927–1928, 7, NSA. These course bulletins provide an excellent record of the different ways the New School was changing during the 1920s.

29. See chapter 4, note 21 for a quote by Charles Beard on the question of teaching. Charles Beard, cited in Nore, *Charles A. Beard*, 91n15.

30. *The New Republic* had a publishing house as well.

31. Barnes, "James Harvey Robinson," 344.

32. Fania M. Cohn, Secretary of the Educational Committee of the ILGWU, to Lawrence K. Frank, Business Manager of The New School for Social Research, February 1, 1921, box 45, folder 8, Alvin Johnson Papers, UNL. Earlier, on September 17, 1920, Cohn had suggested that the ILGUW might be interested in Beard's course on the Role of the State in Modern Civilization. She would consult the committee. After more deliberation, the union apparently decided against collaborating with the New School. Fania Cohn to Lawrence Frank, Business Manager at the New School, September 17, 1920, box 45, folder 7, UNL.

33. Joseph Jablonower, Organizer, Teachers Union, to Charles Beard, August 27, 1920, box 45, folder 6, Alvin Johnson Papers, UNL. See letter from Lawrence Frank to Wesley Clair Mitchell, September 3, 1920, box 45, folder 7, Alvin Johnson Papers, UNL, urging the economist to recommend to the Board of Directors that they sponsor Marietta Johnson's course. Frank knew that Wesley Clair Mitchell, as the husband of Lucy Sprague Mitchell, was the obvious member of the faculty to approach about a course on education.

34. Economists/Business analysts: Thomas, A. Adams, Leon Ardzrooni, Wesley C. Mitchell, Ordway Tead, Thorstein Veblen, and Leo Wolman. Historians: Charles Beard and James Harvey Robinson. Philosophers: John Dewey and Horace Kallen. Anthropologist: Alexander Goldenweisser. Psychologist: Frederick W. Ellis. Announcement of Courses 1920–1921," NSA.

35. Clara Mayer, 10, NSA, unpublished manuscript probably written in the 1940s. Its first sentence reads, "Social consciousness comes earlier to many of our young people . . .".

36. Emily Martin, Secretary to Dr. Frankwood Williams, Medical Director of The National Committee for Mental Hygiene, to Lawrence K. Frank, June 23, 1921, box 45, folder 10, Alvin Johnson Papers, UNL.

37. Dr. Louise Stevens Bryant, Educational Secretary, Girl Scouts, to Lawrence K. Frank, Business Manager, September 9, 1921, box 45, folder 10, Alvin Johnson Papers, UNL.

38. Alvin Johnson, "The Compleat Beggar," *New School Bulletin*, March 17, 1952.

39. Johnson, *Pioneer's Progress*, 276–77.

40. Johnson, *Pioneer's Progress*, 277.

41. Johnson, *Pioneer's Progress*, 277. The New School archives has a document, identified in a file folder as the institution's charter, but the document itself does not say it is a charter and looks like a copy of the original. It is dated 1919. The day and month on the document are left

blank. In the 1920–21 Announcement of Courses, the Board of Directors reported that the New School was incorporated on January 9, 1919. All twelve members of the board signed the charter (NSA).

42. Rutkoff and Scott, *New School*, 21n9. The authors claim that the New School was rejected by the State of New York because it did not have an endowment of at least $500,000. The historians refer the reader to a file in the New School archives called "Early Documents," without identifying a particular document located in that file. No document confirming their claim has survived. What we do know, however, is that in 1910 the New York State Board of Regents published a set of *Rules and Standards for Incorporation*. In Section 61.0, the Board of Regents stated that "No institution shall be given power to confer degrees in this state unless it shall have resources of at least five hundred thousand dollars; and no institution of higher education shall be incorporated without suitable provision, approved by the regents, for educational equipment and proper maintenance. No institution shall institute or have any faculty or department of education in place or be given power to confer any degree not specifically authorized by its charter; and no corporation shall under authority of any general act, extend its business to include establishing or carrying on any educational institution or work without consent of the board of regents."

The New School had no intention of conferring degrees, so did it still need an endowment? In his account, Johnson said nothing at all about endowments. He only mentioned that the New School needed a board of directors. Would the Board of Regents in 1919 have given a charter to an educational institution that gave no degrees? All we know is that neither the New School's archives nor the archives in Albany have any record today of the New School having ever applied for a charter in the State of New York. But the New School archives does have a draft of the charter the board of directors submitted to Washington, D.C.

43. Everett Harré, "Who's Who in 'The New School': Did the 'New Class of Leaders' Specializing in 'The Reform of Social Evils' Ever Engage in Shadow Hun, Shadow Bolshevist or Other Un-American Propaganda?" *National Civic Federation Review*, April 10, 1919.

44. "Society League Starts a Revolt. Opposition Breaks Out Against Required Attendance at Research School's Lectures. Three Speakers Assailed," *New York Times*, February 17, 1919; "Explains Lecture Plan. Junior League Official Denies Arranging Course at New School," *New York Times*, February 18, 1919. Other New York city newspapers also carried the story, among them *Evening Telegram*, February 17, 1919 ("Junior League Split by Radicalism") and *Evening Sun*, February 17, 1919.

45. "Revolutionary Radicalism: Its History, Purpose and Tactics. . . . Being the Report of the Joint Legislative Committee Investigating Seditious Activities," filed April 24, 1920, 4 vols. (Albany, New York, 1920), vol. I, 1121.

46. James Harvey Robinson, cited in "Society League Starts a Revolt," *New York Times*, February 17, 1919.

47. Mossaiye Olgin's courses and lectures are listed in the course bulletins for the following years: 1919–20 ("Soviet Forces in Modern Russia"), 1921–22 ("Revolutionary Russia, 1917–1921"), Spring 1932 ("Russia 1931"), 1934–35 ("Reappraisal of the Soviet Scheme of Life"). In the spring of 1934, Olgin also gave a lecture on "The Workers and Peasants of Soviet Russia" in a course on "Soviet Russia Today." See obituary tribute to Olgin in 1939 by William Foster, chairman, and Earl Browder, general secretary, "Statement of the

National Committee of the Communist Party of the United States of America." This public statement mourning Olgin's death, November 22, 1939, is available at www.maristsfr .org/archive/olgin/obit.htm.

48. Johnson, *Pioneer's Progress*, 280; Rutkoff and Scott describe the two proposals Johnson presented at a meeting that took place April 26, 1922, referring the reader to documents they found in the New School archives. These documents have since disappeared, Rutkoff and Scott, *New School*, 28n38.

49. Johnson, *Pioneer's Progress*, 280.

50. Johnson, *Pioneer's Progress*, 280. Veblen's biographer notes that Johnson tried to raise money for Veblen, but failed in the end. Dorfman, *Thorstein Veblen and His America*, 487. Veblen proposed doing this research in 1924.

51. Levy, *Herbert Croly of The New Republic*, 271.

52. Beard's and Robinson's names do not appear on the list of instructors in the course bulletin for 1922–23. Descriptions of their courses, however, still appear, with a note indicating that they will not be given during that academic year. By 1923–24, their courses are gone as well.

6. ALVIN JOHNSON TAKES OVER

1. Alvin Johnson, *Pioneer's Progress: An Autobiography* (1952; Lincoln: University of Nebraska Press, 1960), 281; The New School for Social Research Announcement of Courses, 1922–23, 1923–24, 1925–26, 1926–27.

2. Johnson, *Pioneer's Progress*, 280; Alvin Johnson spoke bitterly about losing Dorothy Straight in a letter to a donor. The letter is reproduced on p. 307 of this book.

3. Johnson, *Pioneer's Progress*, 280.

4. Announcement of Courses between 1920 and 1924.

5. Johnson, *Pioneer's Progress*, 282. On W. W. Norton and the Cooper Union's People's Institute, see People's Institute's Records, 1883–1933, Humanities and Social Science Manuscripts and Archives Division, New York Public Library, iv; W. W. Norton.com, "Norton History," http://books.wwnorton.com/books/aboutcontent.aspx?id=4386. Announcement of Courses, 1927–28, also describes the collaboration between the New School and the Cooper Union's People's Institute. During the 1940s and into the 1950s, W. W. Norton published a number of works by Johnson's refugee scholars through the Institute of World Affairs. For more on this, see chapter 9 in this volume. For Mary Ely's ongoing involvement, see the collection of Johnson's essays she edited and published in 1934, together with Morse Cartwright. Alvin Johnson, *Deliver Us from Dogma* (New York: American Association of Adult Education, 1934).

6. Clara Mayer, unpublished manuscript, 3, NSA. See Note 2, chapter 5.

7. Alvin Johnson to Clara Mayer (Woolie), January 1, 1965, box 5, file Mag-Md 1935–1965, Alvin Saunders Johnson Papers, Yale; Johnson, *Pioneer's Progress*, 282. Much of what we know about Clara Mayer's direct influence on Johnson comes from hearsay and an unpublished memoir of an admirer who worked at the New School during the early 1940s: Kenneth Craven, *Greenwich Village and the Soul of a Woman*, 2001, NSA.

8. See Announcement of Courses, 1922–23, 1926–27, and 1927–28.

9. Johnson, *Pioneer's Progress*, 282–83; Joseph Dorfman, *Thorstein Veblen and His America* (1934; New York: Augustus M. Kelley, 1966), 452. Further details regarding Veblen's life, see note 49 in this chapter and Appendix A.

10. Johnson, *Pioneer's Progress*, 8, 283.

11. "The New School for Social Research, 465 West 23rd St., New York," 1925, NSA.

12. Announcement of Courses, 1927–28, 7. Johnson's announcement that he had raised scholarship funds for twelve students appears in Announcement of Courses 1929–30, 4.

13. For articles in newspapers about the new teaching program, see "Scrapbook 1926–1927," 4, 5, 7, digitalarchives.library.newschool.edu/index.php/Detail/objects/NS030101_PC_02 _OCR; New School Announcement of Courses 1926–27, 7–8, and 1931–32, 8.

14. Announcement of Courses, 1927–28, 5–8.

15. Announcement of Courses, 1926–27 and 1927–28; Clara Mayer, unpublished manuscript, 7ff, NSA.

16. Announcement of Courses, 1927–28, 7 Clara Mayer, unpublished manuscript, 7ff, NSA.

17. Clippings on the motion picture course in "Scrapbook 1926–1927," digitalarchives.library. newschool.edu/index.php/Detail/objects/NS030101_PC_02_OCR, 6–7. The New School claims this course on the motion picture was the first ever offered in an academic institution, newschool.edu/.

18. "Waldo Frank and Others," *New York City Telegraph*, October 4, 1926, preserved in "Scrapbook 1926–1927," 10; Announcement of Courses, 1926–27, 26.

19. Announcement of Courses, 1927–28, 7–8, 27.

20. The New School for Social Research, Report of the Director, 1927–28, 7, NSA.

21. Sally Bick, "In the Tradition of Dissent: Music at the New School for Social Research," *Journal of the American Musicological Society* 66, no. 1 (Spring 2013): 131–32.

22. Aaron Copland and Vivian Perlis, *Copland: 1900 through 1942* (New York: St. Martin's Press, 1984), 156–57, 133, 145n62.

23. E. A. J. Johnson, "The Encyclopaedia of the Social Sciences," *Quarterly Journal of Economics* 50, no. 2 (February 1936): 355–66, at 360. Edwin Seligman and Alvin Johnson, eds., *Encyclopaedia of the Social Sciences*, 15 vols. (New York: Macmillan, 1930–1935). It remained in print until 1967 and was then replaced by *The International Encyclopaedia of the Social Sciences*.

24. Johnson, "The Encyclopaedia of the Social Sciences," 366; Ellsworth Faris, "Encyclopaedia of the Social Sciences, Vol. 1, Aaronson-Allegiance," *American Journal of Sociology* 35, no. 6 (May 1930): 1112–13.

25. For a discussion of Erich von Hornbostel's work with Max Wertheimer, see D. Brett King and Michael Wertheimer, *Max Wertheimer and Gestalt Theory* (New Brunswick, N.J.: Transaction, 2005).

26. The ten sponsoring academic societies were the American Anthropological Association, American Economic Association, American Historical Association, American Political Science Association, American Sociological Society, National Educational Association, Association of American Law Schools, American Psychological Association, American Statistical Association, and American Association of Social Workers. Financial support came from the Rockefeller Foundation, Carnegie Corporation, and the Russell Sage Foundation.

27. Seligman and Johnson, *Encyclopaedia of the Social Sciences*, vol. 1, 7.

28. Alvin Johnson to Charles Seeger, November 6, 1931, Charles and Ruth Crawford Collection, Library of Congress, Music Division, Washington, D.C., cited in Bick, "In the Tradition of Dissent," 175n188. The article, commissioned by Johnson, appeared as Charles Seeger, Henry Cowell, and Helen Roberts, "Music," in *Encyclopaedia of the Social Sciences*, ed. Seligman and Johnson, vol. 11, 143–65.

29. Frank Lloyd Wright, Announcement of Courses 1931–32, 33; Berenice Abbot, Announcement of Courses 1934–35, 45; Harold Clurman, Announcement of Courses 1932–33, 32, 39; Clurman's Group Theatre, Announcement of Courses 1936–37, 43. From 1940 to 1944, Stella Adler taught in Erwin Piscator's program as did Lee Strasberg from 1946 to 1947. For a discussion of Piscator, see chapter 12 in this volume.

30. Alvin Johnson began teaching economics at the New School in 1923, Announcement of Courses 1923–24, 19–20. In addition to teaching economics, he participated in the writing program and offered a workshop called "Unpublished Review" for selected students: Announcement of Courses 1931–32, 15, 34. Robert Frost and T. S. Eliot, Announcement of Courses Spring 1933, 22; Joseph Wood Krutch, Announcement of Courses 1932–33, 34, and 1933–34, 31–32. Gertrude Stein gave a lecture at the New School in 1935, Ed Burns, ed., *The Letters of Gertrude Stein and Thornton Wilder* (New Haven: Yale University Press, 1996), 340; Mary McCarthy, *Intellectual Memoirs, 1936–1938* (New York: Harcourt Brace Janovich, 1992), 25.

31. Doris Humphrey and Martha Graham, Announcement of Courses 1931–32, 39.

32. The concert series became a regular part of the New School program. In 1933–34, Cowell and Seeger focused on Russian folk, Serbian/Yugoslavian folk, Irish folk, and modern American music. For Eva Le Galliene's production of *The Master Builder*, see Johnson's description of the early days in the Prologue of this volume; for the Fortune Players, see "The Alchemist Diverting," *New York Times*, June 5, 1931, and Announcement of Courses, 1931–32, 331–32. For a list of the open rehearsals for ten European plays by "apprentices" of Eva Le Gallienne, see Announcement of Courses, 1933–34, 31. One of the director-apprentices was May Sarton, who later became a widely acclaimed poet. For the Martha Graham's series of "evolutionary" dances, see www.newschool.edu/pressroom/pressreleases/2006/041106_elc_marthagraham.html.

33. Alvin Johnson to Agnes de Lima, January 1, 1931, and January 5, 1931, box 2, folder 27, Alvin Saunders Johnson Papers, Yale.

34. Clara Mayer, remarks she made in December 1944, presumably at Alvin Johnson's seventieth birthday celebration at the New School, 2–3, NSA.

35. Alvin Johnson, "The New School for Social Research, Report of the Director, 1927–1928," 13, NSA. Johnson, *Pioneer's Progress*, 316. See New School, Announcement of Courses, 1928–29, 7, for announcement that certain courses would take place at Rumford Hall.

36. Maurice Wertheim, cited in Johnson, *Pioneer's Progress*, 319.

37. Announcement of Courses, Spring 1931, 5–6; Johnson, *Pioneer's Progress*, 318–19. After the new building opened, Daniel Cranford Smith became a member of the Board of Directors and served as the treasurer of the New School.

38. Joseph Urban, cited in Clyde Beals, "Social Research School to Have a New Building," *New York Times*, February 16, 1930.

39. Joseph Urban had made a name for himself as an architect and set designer for the opera, theater, and film. He also enjoyed a major reputation as a painter and as an interior designer for private dwellings and was particularly well known for making furniture. Randolph Carter

and Robert Reed Cole, *Architecture, Theatre, Opera, Film* (New York: Abbeville Press, 1992); John Loring, *Joseph Urban* (New York: Abrams, 2010). Columbia University has Urban's papers and exhibited of his work in 2010. There are pictures on Columbia's website of his plans for a new Metropolitan Opera House, a grand project that had to be abandoned during the Great Depression: www.Columba.edu/ cu/ web/eresources/archives/rbml/uran /architect of dreams/text.html. Among the private mansions Urban designed in the United States is Mar a Lago in Palm Springs, Florida, currently owned by President Donald Trump.

40. Johnson quotes are from Announcement of Courses, Winter Term 1931, 6; and Beals, "Social Research School to Have a New Building."

41. "Social Research School Dinner," *New York Times*, February 16, 1930; Announcement of Courses, Winter Term 1931, 6–7.

42. Edward Alden Jewell, "Gesso and True Fresco: Artists Produce Work in the Modern Spirit for the New School for Social Research," *New York Times*, November 23, 1930; Edward Alden Jewell, "Discreet Originality, New School for Social Research Opens Its Spacious Quarters in Twelfth Street," *New York Times*, January 4, 1931.

43. For Jewell's discussion of Orozco, see chapter 13 in this volume.

44. Clara Mayer, "The Romance of Housing," manuscript, NSA.

45. The New School bought 66 Fifth Avenue many years later, after it had acquired Parsons School of Design. See chapter 16 in this volume.

46. Alvin Johnson to Agnes de Lima, January 29, 1931, box 2, folder 27, Alvin Saunders Johnson Papers, Yale. For information on the instructors between 1929 and 1931, see Announcement of Courses, 1929–30, 2; and Announcement of Courses, Winter Term 1931, 3. According to New School Archivist Wendy Scheir, there was no bulletin of classes for the fall of 1930 (personal communication, January 2017). The New School's digital archives have preserved an article titled "The New School Rooms," from an unidentified newspaper, indicating that courses were being offered in the fall of 1930 in rented facilities at 66 Fifth Avenue. The font suggests that the article came from *The New York Times*. The article reported that the New School would be sponsoring a series of lectures in French on the modern French novel by André Malraux beginning in October 1930, "Scrapbooks," 79, digitalarchives.library .newschool.edu/index/php/Detail/objects/NS030101PC_03_OCR.

47. Alvin Johnson to Agnes de Lima, March 29, 1931, box 2, folder 27, Alvin Saunders Johnson Papers, Yale.

48. John Dos Passos, *USA* (1930; New York: Random House, 1937), 105.

49. Dorfman, *Thorstein Veblen*, 252–54. David Starr Jordan to Harry Pratt Judson, October 6, 1909, President Judson's Papers, Special Collections and Manuscripts of the University of Chicago. See Appendix A, Extended Notes and Commentary for more on Thorstein Veblen.

50. Edith Henry Johnson, *The Argument of Aristotle's Metaphysics* (1906; Whitefish, Mont.: Kessinger, 2007).

51. Alvin Johnson to Elsie Clews Parsons, June 26, 1923, Elsie Clews Parsons Papers, American Philosophical Society Library.

52. Agnes de Lima, *Our Enemy, The Child* (New York: Arno Press & The New York Times, 1926), dedication.

53. On Esther Cornell, see New School Course Announcement of Courses, 1922–1930. Cornell's name is listed on those publications as Secretary. For descriptions of Esther Cornell, see Bruce Clayton, *Forgotten Prophet: The Life of Randolph Bourne* (Columbia:

University of Missouri Press, 1984), 180ff. He quotes Alyse Gregory, who found Cornell "provocatively bewitching." Also see Agnes de Lima's letter to Alyse Gregory, undated, Bourne Papers, Columbia University manuscripts. The relevant letter is the only letter from de Lima to Gregory that is five pages long.

54. In addition to the published and archival references cited, I want to thank Andra Makler, Agnes de Lima's biographer, for her assistance. As *A Light in Dark Times* goes to press, Makler has finished her biography, but has not yet published it. I also want to thank Alison de Lima Greene, Agnes de Lima's and Alvin Johnson's granddaughter, for her generous help. In particular I thank her for explaining why her mother's birth certificate claims, falsely, that Sigrid de Lima's father was Andrew Lang, Alison de Lima Greene to Judith Friedlander, June 30, 2016. Greene is Curator of Contemporary Art and Fine Art, Museum of Fine Arts, Houston.

I want to thank Alden Deyrup's son Mark Deyrup as well for sharing his memories of his grandfather with me. Mark Deyrup is senior research biologist at the Archbold Biological Station, Venus, Florida. Of all the grandchildren—two from Thorold, three from Alden, and one from Sigrid—Mark Deyrup probably knew his grandfather the best, having had the opportunity to live with him for six months during the last year of Johnson's life. Mark Deyrup to Judith Friedlander, January 16, 2017, email correspondence.

Finally, given the importance of Agnes de Lima's contributions to early childhood education and of her daughter Sigrid's to literature, readers might also be interested in: *The Little Red School House* (New York: Macmillan, 1942), which, together with *Our Enemy, The Child*, is still in print, For a published essay on the significance of de Lima's work, see James M. Wallace, *"Agnes de Lima and Progressive Education," Liberal Journalism and American Education, 1914–1943* (New Brunswick, N.J.: Rutgers University Press, 1991), chap. 8, 72–85, 195–96 (notes). Sigrid de Lima's novels include *Carnival by the Sea (1954), Praise a Fine Day* (1959), and *Oriane* (1968). For a brief appreciation of her work, see obituary "Sigrid de Lima, 77, Whimsical Novelist of the 50's," *New York Times*, September 25, 1999.

7. THE FOUNDING OF THE GERMAN UNIVERSITY IN EXILE

1. Alvin Johnson, *Pioneer's Progress: An Autobiography* (1952; Lincoln: University of Nebraska Press, 1960), 332.

2. Johnson, *Pioneer's Progress*, 337; Alvin Johnson, "Emil Lederer: In Memory," *Social Research* 6, no. 3 (September 1939): 313.

3. Fritz Stern, *Dreams and Delusions: The Drama of German History* (1987: New Haven: Yale University Press 1999), 125, 129.

4. Stern, *Dreams and Delusions*, 120, 130.

5. Benjamin Hett, " 'This Story Is About Something Fundamental': Nazi Criminals, History, Memory, and the Reichstag Fire," *Central European History* 48 (2015): 199. See also Benjamin Hett, *Burning the Reichstag: An Investigation into the Third Reich's Enduring Mystery* (Oxford: Oxford University Press, 2014); Richard J. Evans, "The Conspiracists," *London Review of Books* 36, no. 9 (May 8, 2014): 3–9.

6. Stern, *Dreams and Delusions*, 130.

7.   Claus-Dieter Krohn, *Intellectuals in Exile: Refugee Scholars and the New School for Social Research*, trans. Rita Kimber and Robert Kimber (1987; Amherst: University of Massachusetts Press, 1993), 13.

8.   Alvin Johnson, "An Autobiographical Note," *Spring Storm* (New York: Alfred A Knopf, 1936), 13.

9.   Alvin Johnson to Agnes de Lima, April 14, 1933, box 2, folder 27, Alvin Saunders Johnson Papers, Yale.

10.   Johnson, *Pioneer's Progress*, 338. Johnson published other versions of this story. In a biographical essay written in 1947 ("The Development of a Liberal"), Johnson described the anecdote this way: "With much effort I secured pledges of $450, and there my project balked. And then my inner voice spoke to me. 'Alvin Johnson, this is New York. New York has no spectacles, cartoons of Father Knickerbocker to the contrary notwithstanding. New York can't see small things. One professor no. But how about a whole Faculty?'" NSA.

11.   In his autobiography, Johnson writes that he received the call from Halle in less than a week from the day he had launched the April 24, 1933, fund-raising campaign. Johnson, *Pioneer's Progress*, 340.

12.   Readers today might think of Garrison Keillor and "The Prairie Home Companion," a popular program on National Public Radio that mixed political satire, music, and Americana corn (Keillor retired in July 2016). Johnson's inspiration was probably Mark Twain.

13.   Alvin Johnson, "Intellectual Liberty Imperiled," *American Scholar* 2, no. 3 (July 1933): 319.

14.   The British began imposing a tax on their own salaries in 1933. The refugee scholars at the New School may have begun a bit later, but they were clearly taxing themselves as well. Eduard Heimann, Karl Brandt, and Alfred Kähler, "Proposal for the Reform of Our Self-Taxation," Graduate Faculty Minutes, March 11, 1935, NSA, cited in Krohn, *Intellectuals in Exile*, 27. For more on the response of British academics to the refugee crisis, in particular the role of Oxford University, see Sally Crawford, Katharina Ulmschneider, and Jaś Elsner, eds., *Ark of Civilization: Refugee Scholars at Oxford University, 1933–1945* (Oxford: Oxford University Press, 2017).

15.   Scholars differ on the precise number of refugees who came to the New School with financial support from the Rockefeller Foundation. According to the website of the Rockefeller Archives, the Rockefeller Foundation sponsored 303 scholars, of whom 214 were invited to the United States; 52 of these received letters from Alvin Johnson. Some of those who received an invitation with funding from Rockefeller never left Europe for one reason or another and did not, therefore, come to the New School, for example, the philosopher Vladimir Jankélévitch: tables 1 and 2, RAC, rockarch.org/collections/rf/refugee.php. For further discussion about the Rockefeller Archives, see: Appendix B, Extended Notes and Commentary (A).

16.   Claus-Dieter Krohn, "American Foundations and Refugee Scholars Between the Two Wars," in *The "Unacceptables": American Foundations and Refugee Scholars Between the Two Wars and After*, ed. Giuliana Gemelli (Bruxelles: P.I.E.-Peter Lang, 2000), 42–43. Krohn tells us that Rockefeller gave $830,150 to Germany between 1928 and 1933. The largest amount ($125,000) sponsored anthropological research on German ideas about race. Other major grants went to the Institute of International Affairs at the Hamburg University ($20,000), the Institute of Social Sciences at the Heidelberg University ($60,000), the Institute of World Economics at Kiel University ($40,000), and Deutsche Hochschule für Politik in Berlin ($110,000).

The following members of the University in Exile faculty taught and/or studied at one or more of these institutions: Hamburg: Eduard Heimann; Heidelberg: Emil Lederer, Jacob Marschak, Carl Mayer, Albert Salomon, Hans Speier; Kiel: Gerhard Colm, Hermann Kantorowicz Adolph Lowe, Jacob Marschak, Hans Neisser, Hans Staudinger; Hochschule für Politik: Arnold Brecht, Hans Simons, Hans Speier.

17. See note 15 and Appendix B, Extended Notes and Commentary (A) on the matter of the number of scholars who came to the New School with support from the Rockefeller Foundation. See also Johnson, *Pioneer's Progress*, 344–45; Krohn, *Intellectuals in Exile*, 27ff; Krohn, "American Foundations and Refugee Scholars Between the Two Wars"; and Diane Dosso, "The Rescue of French Scientists. Respective Roles of the Rockefeller Foundation and the Biochemist Louis Rapkine (1904–1948), in Gemelli, *The "Unacceptables,"* 47–48, 202; Harald Hagemann, "European Emigres and the 'Americanization' of Economics," *European Journal of the History of Economic Thought* 18, no. 5 (2011): 660–61. For contemporary accounts, see the New School's brochure "To the Living Spirit," Spring 1943, NSA; and Editorial, *New York Times*, May 31, 1943. See also the report by the vice president of the Rockefeller Foundation, Thomas Appleget, "The Foundation's Experience with Refugee Scholars," March 5, 1946, RG 1.1, series 200, box 47, folder 545a, RAC. Appleget says the foundation saved 295 scholars, not 303. The website says 303. See Note 15 and Appendix B, Extended Notes and Commentary (A).

18. Krohn, *Intellectuals in Exile*, 77. See Appendix B, Extended Notes and Commentary (B).

19. See Alvin Johnson's correspondence with Albert Einstein and Stephen Duggan, head of the IIE and the Emergency Committee in Aid of Displaced Scholars, about the distinguished French physicist Paul Langevin. When the Rockefeller Foundation rejected Langevin because of his age, Johnson urged the IIE to seek funding elsewhere. Albert Einstein to Alvin Johnson, September 7 and 18, 1940, Alvin Johnson to Stephen Duggan March 10, 1941, and Alvin Johnson to Albert Einstein, March 18, 1941, Alvin Saunders Johnson Papers, Yale. In this last letter Johnson indicates that Duggan had responded positively and would most likely be able to help Langevin. For more on the criteria used to select refugees, see Appendix B, Extended Notes and Commentary (B).

20. Varian Fry, *Surrender on Command* (1945; Boulder, Colo.: Johnson Books, 1997). This updated edition includes a preface by Warren Christopher in which President Clinton's secretary of state describes the ceremony at Yad Vashem in which the State of Israel honored Fry's memory by recognizing him as one of "the Righteous Among the Nations." Fry also rescued the famous book editor Jacques Schiffrin; and a teenage boy, Georges Borchadt, who went on to become a literary agent in New York and has kindly agreed to represent this book.

There is a vast literature on Varian Fry and excellent documentaries. See Pierre Sauvage's film, *And Crown Thy Good: Varian Fry in Marseille*, and the Chambon Foundation website (www.chambon.org) for an excellent summary of the life and work of Fry and information about the film. Fry alone saved the lives of nearly 2,000 people. Some estimates are even higher.

21. For more about the scholars who came to the New School with funding from Rockefeller, see Rockefeller Archives, tables 1 and 2, rockarch.org/collections/rf/refugee.php; and Gemelli, *The Unacceptables*, 14. The most frequently cited list of European refugee scholars and artists sponsored by the New School between 1933 and 1945 can be found in the appendix of Krohn, *Intellectuals in Exile*, 205–10. Krohn's list includes 182 people. The original list

compiled by the New School in 1944 names 167 individuals, of whom 94 were "brought over expressly by the New School." The remaining 73 scholars and artists taught at the New School after getting to the United States by other means. See Appendix B, Extended Notes and Commentary (A and C).

22. Johnson, *Pioneer's Progress*, 339.

23. Alvin Johnson to Robert MacIver, April 10, 1957, box 5, folder 83, Alvin Saunders Johnson Papers, Yale.

24. Alvin Johnson to Robert MacIver, April 10, 1957. Among Eugene Field's poems for children were "Little Boy Blue" and "Wynken, Blynken and Nod."

25. Johnson, *Pioneer's Progress*, 339.

26. Alvin Johnson to Agnes de Lima, April 28, 1933, box 2, folder 27, Alvin Saunders Johnson Papers, Yale.

27. Alvin Johnson to E. R. A. [Edwin] Seligman, April 24, 1933, NSA.

28. Alvin Johnson to Agnes de Lima, April 28, 1933.

29. Clara Mayer to Henry Cowell, May 4, 1933, box 163, folder 13, New York Public Library, HCC, NYPL; cited in Sally Bick, "In the Tradition of Dissent: Music at the New School for Social Research, 1926–33," *Journal of the American Musicological Society* 66, no. 1 (Spring 2013): 166, 180.

30. Alvin Johnson to Agnes de Lima, May 6, 1933, box 2, folder 27, Alvin Saunders Johnson Papers, Yale.

31. Alvin Johnson to Agnes de Lima, May 11, 1933, box 2, folder 27, Alvin Saunders Johnson Papers, Yale.

32. Stephen Wise, cited in "100,000 March Here in 6-Hour Protest over Nazi Policies," *New York Times*, May 11, 1933. In the late fall of 1934, the Brooklyn Jewish Center opened the American Library of Banned Books. Although the university community had almost nothing to do with this effort, Johnson and Boas had both been asked to serve on the Advisory Committee. Boas's books had been among those burned by the Nazis. Stephen H. Norwood, *The Third Reich in the Ivory Tower* (Cambridge, Mass.: Cambridge University Press, 2009), 88.

33. "Faculty of Exiles Is Projected Here," *New York Times*, May 13, 1933.

34. Alvin Johnson to Agnes de Lima, May 11, 1933, box 2, folder 27, Alvin Saunders Johnson Papers, Yale.

35. Hans Luther had served as finance minister and chancellor (for forty days) in the 1920s before becoming head of the Reichsbank, a position from which Hitler made him resign. In the spring of 1933, Hitler appointed Luther Germany's ambassador to Washington, a position he held until 1937.

36. Alvin Johnson and Horace M. Kallen to Professor J [Jacob]. H. Hollander (professor of political science) at Johns Hopkins University, May 22, 1933, Record Group 02.001, Records of the Office of the President, Series 1, file #927.1 "Displaced German Scholars," Ferdinand Hamburger Archives, Sheridan Libraries, Johns Hopkins University.

37. Alvin Johnson to President Joseph S. Ames, Johns Hopkins University and Ames's reply, May 29 and May 31, 1933, Record Group 02.001, Records of the Office of the President, Series 1, file #927.1 "Displaced German Scholars," Ferdinand Hamburger Archives, Sheridan Libraries, Johns Hopkins University; "The Refugee Scholars: A Retrospect," October 1, 1955, RG1.1.S200, B47F42, RAC.

38. Correspondence between Alvin Johnson and Robert M. Hutchins, May 22, 25, 27, June 2, 1933, box 176, file 11, Robert M. Hutchins Papers, Chicago.

39. Robert M. Hutchins to Alvin Johnson, May 25, 1933.

40. Alvin Johnson to Robert M. Hutchins, May 27, 1933.

41. Abraham Flexner, *Universities: American, English, German* (Oxford: Oxford University Press, 1930); Franklin Parker, "Abraham Flexner, 1866–1959," *History of Education Quarterly* 2, no. 4 (December 1962): 199–209. Between 1933 and 1939 Brown University established the Graduate School of Applied Mathematics and New York University the Institute of Mathematics and Mechanics, dividing between them sixteen mathematicians from the University of Göttingen, all sponsored by the Rockefeller Foundation.

42. Roosevelt University in Chicago and Black Mountain College, located near Asheville, North Carolina, are two other examples.

43. Obituary for Hiram Halle, "Hiram J. Halle, 77, Oil Firm Executive," *New York Times*, May 31, 1944. See also Johnson's tribute to Halle, Alvin Johnson, "Hiram J. Halle—1867–1944," *Social Research* 11, no. 3 (September 1944): 265–67; Alvin Johnson, "In Memory of Hiram Halle," speech delivered at the dedication of Hiram Halle Pound Ridge Library, April 26, 1952 (draft dated April 25, 1952), box 35, folder 7, Alvin Johnson Papers, UNL.

44. Hiram Halle's business diary, May 9, May 11, and May 12, 1933, box 1LF6925, Honeywell UOP Archives. I want to thank Amy Parsons for leading me to the materials located in the archives of the Pound Ridge Library and at OUP. Parsons wrote a master's thesis on the homes of Hiram Halle in completion of her degree in the History of the Decorative Arts and Design, a program sponsored by Cooper Hewitt, the Smithsonian Design Museum and Parsons School of Design at the New School: "'To Good Use': The Life and Houses of Hiram Halle," 2016. I also thank John Simley at OUP.

45. See Alvin Johnson's letters to Louis Halle, thanking him for showing Seligman's letter to his brother Hiram, October 24, 1938, and March 11, 1940 (private collection of Titi and Peter Halle). Again, I thank Amy Parsons for putting me in touch with Peter and Titi Halle, the grandchildren of Louis, who have kindly given me permission to quote from these letters. In 1938, Johnson wrote: "if you had not been interested enough to show my letter to your brother the University in Exile might have died a-borning, or might have been born too feeble to live." But we also know that Hiram Halle's nephew, Joseph Halle Schaffner (his sister Sara's son), had been a member of the New School's Advisory Board since 1925: Announcement of Courses, 1925–26. Near the end of his life, after his first wife had died, Schaffner married Ruth Staudinger, the daughter of Hans Staudinger, a prominent member of the University in Exile, a brilliant fund-raiser for the New School, and a very good friend of Johnson. Ruth Staudinger had previously been married to the painter Michel Cadoret, a mural of whose was given to the New School in 1959 (see chapter 14 of this volume). In 1963, the year Schaffner announced his engagement to Ruth Staudinger, he also bailed the New School out of a major financial crisis (see chapter 15 in this volume).

46. Alvin Johnson to Agnes de Lima, June 9, 1933, box 2, folder 27, Alvin Saunders Johnson Papers, Yale.

47. In addition to his initial gift of $120,000, by 1940 Halle had given over $140,000, Archives of the Hiram Halle Library, Pound Ridge, New York.

48. Alvin Johnson to Miss Julia Halle, April 15, 1952, NSA.

49. The New School Archives and Special Collections have two 16mm films of lawn parties hosted by Hiram Halle with members of the Graduate Faculty ("Professors 1935" and "BBQ at Old Mill," undated but probably 1937) in his own vintage home. Halle also invited Einstein to join the Graduate Faculty at another lawn party in 1938; Archives of Hiram Halle Memorial Library, Pound Ridge, New York.

50. Johnson, "In Memory of Hiram Halle." For further discussion of the New School's translation project, see chapter 9.

51. For an excellent introduction to Keynes and Schumpeter's work for the nonspecialist, see Robert L. Heilbroner, *The Worldly Philosophers: The Lives, Times and Great Ideas of the Great Economic Thinkers* (1953; New York: Simon and Schuster, 1999), 248–310.

52. Krohn, *Intellectuals in Exile*, 76. After Emil Lederer moved to the University of Berlin in 1931, he campaigned for Schumpeter, but the faculty blocked the appointment. Harald Hagemann, "Emil Lederer: Economical and Sociological Analyst," *The Theory of Capitalism in the German Economic Tradition*, ed. Peter Koslowski (Berlin: Springer, 2000), 27.

53. Joseph Schumpeter to Wesley Mitchell, April 19, 1933, in U. Hedtke and R. Swedberg, eds., *Joseph Alois Schumpeter: Briefe/Letters* (Tübingen: Mohr Siebeck, 2000), 246–48. I am very grateful to Harald Hagemann for having led me to Schumpeter's correspondence. See Harald Hagemann, "Introduction," in "German Perspectives on the Social Sciences." Special issue, *Social Research* 81, no. 3 (Fall 2014), 505.

54. Schumpeter to Mitchell, April 22, 1933, Hedtke and Swedber, *Joseph Alois Schumpeter*, 249–51.

55. Schumpter to Edmund E. Day, May 2, 1933, Hedtke and Swedber, *Joseph Alois Schumpeter*, 251–52.

56. Schumpter to Mitchell, May 2, 1933, Hedtke and Swedber, *Joseph Alois Schumpeter*, 254–55.

57. Schumpeter to Johnson, May 2, 1933, Hedtke and Swedber, *Joseph Alois Schumpeter*, 252–54.

58. Lederer and Colm came in 1933; Marschak in 1939; Lowe in 1941; Neisser in 1943, after going to the University of Pennsylvania first. Of the five who came to the New School, Schumpeter ranked them as follows: Marschak #2, Neisser #3, Lederer #5, Lowe, #6, Colm #7. He ranked Karl Mannheim #4.

59. Schumpeter to Esther Lowenthal at Smith College and to Susan M. Kingsbury at Bryn Mawr, May 26, 1933, Hedtke and Swedber, *Joseph Alois Schumpeter*, 257.

60. Johnson, *Pioneer's Progress*, 342. Johnson wrote to Agnes de Lima that "the University in Exile is marking time, waiting for one of the German scholars to come over and talk over details of the plan," June 1, 1933, box 2, folder 27, Alvin Saunders Johnson Papers, Yale.

61. Alvin Johnson to Agnes de Lima, June 9, 1933, box 2, folder 27, Alvin Saunders Johnson Papers, Yale. Rutkoff and Scott wrote that Johnson accused Karl Mannheim of having "insisted that the New School create a school of social thought that revolved around his own ideas." Then claiming to quote Johnson directly, they added that Johnson was relieved when Manheim turned the New School down because the sociologist wanted to be "'the whole show.'" Peter M. Rutkoff and William B. Scott, *New School: A History of the New School for Social Research* (New York: The Free Press, 1986), 100n70. Rutkoff and Scott give as the source of that quote a letter Johnson wrote to Robert MacIver, April 10, 1957, box 5, folder 83, Alvin Saunders Johnson Papers, Yale. In that letter, Johnson's only mention of Mannheim reads: "I wanted to get Mannheim, Lowe and Marschak. I could not get them

at first, as they had found satisfactory posts in England. Later I got Marschak and Lowe." Other scholars have repeated what Rutkoff and Scott claim Johnson said about Mannheim, citing Rutkoff and Scott as their source. See, for example, David Kettler and Volker Mejia, *Karl Mannheim and the Crisis of Liberalism: The Secrets of These Times* (New Brunswick, N.J.: Transaction, 1995), 190n9; and Hans Speier, "Symposium: The University in Exile," *American Sociological Association* 16, no. 3 (May 1987): 278.

62. On June 1, 1933, Johnson told de Lima that he "was waiting for one of the German scholars to come over and talk over the details of the plan," box 2, folder 27, Alvin Saunders Johnson Papers, Yale. Hiram Halle's business diary indicates that Johnson phoned Halle on June 12, 1933, and paid a visit to him on June 13. Johnson returned for a second visit with Lederer on June 16. "Dr. Johnson and Professor Lederer," Honeywell, UOP Archives.

63. According to Harald Hagemann, who interviewed Adolph Lowe near the end of his life, Lowe frequently spoke about having wanted to stay as close to Germany as possible after being forced to flee the country in the spring of 1933. As Lowe put it in another interview that was published in 1979, "Wir sind 1933 nach England und nicht nach Amerika ausgewandert, letzthin aus einer utopischen Gläubigkeit meinerseits, dass der hitlerische Spaß doch nicht mehr als ein, zwei Jahre dauern kann, und ich wollte sozusagen nahe sein, wenn es vorbei war." ("We emigrated in 1933 to England and not to America due to my utopian belief that the Hitlerian 'joke' could not last for more than a year or two, and I wanted to be close by, you might say, when it was all over.") Interview with Adolph Lowe, "Die Hoffnung auf kleine Katastrophen," in *Die Zerstörung einer Zukunft. Gespräche mit emigrierten Sozialwissenschaftlern*, ed. Mathias Greffrath (Reinbek: Rowohlt, 1979), 147. Lowe fled Germany with his family on April 2, 1933, and went first to Basel, Switzerland, before emigrating to London. This was before Hitler announced the Civil Service Restoration Act, but it was after Lowe had heard that Hitler was planning to annul the passports of all Jewish citizens on April 3: Harald Hagemann, personal communication, 2017.

64. Alvin Johnson to Sigrid de Lima, July 24, 1933, written from Iddenino's Hotel, London, Agnes de Lima folder in Alvin Saunders Johnson Papers, Yale.

65. Johnson, *Pioneer's Progress*, 344.

66. "Exiles' University Opens Here Oct.1," *New York Times*, August 19, 1933.

67. Arnold Brecht, *The Political Education of Arnold Brecht: An Autobiography, 1884–1970* (Princeton, N.J.: Princeton University Press, 1970), 443.

68. Hans Speier, "Review of Karl Mannheim's *Ideology and Utopia*," *American Journal of Sociology* 43, no. 1 (July 1937): 155–66. Mannheim was furious about the review. Mannheim to Louis Wirth, July 3, 1930, Louis Wirth Papers, Chicago, cited in David Kettler and Volker Mejia, "Settling with Mannheim: Comments on Speier and Oestreicher," *State, Culture, and Society* 1, no. 3 (April 1985): 227.

69. Emil Lederer, *State of the Masses: The Threat of the Classless Society*, Forward by Hans Speier (1940; W. W. Norton; New York: Howard Fertig, 1967). Among Hans Speier's early work on propaganda, see "Morale and Propaganda," *War in Our Time*, eds. Hans Speier and Alfred Kähler (New York: W. W. Norton, 1939), 299–326.

70. Arnold Brecht's first publication in English was "Constitutions and Leadership," *Social Research* 1 (August 1934): 265–86. Among Brecht's most highly regarded work in English is *Political Theory: The Foundations of Twentieth-Century Political Thought* (Princeton, N.J.: Princeton University Press, 1959).

71. Peter M. Rutkoff and William B. Scott, "Biographical Afterword," in Hans Staudinger (with Werner Pese), *The Inner Nazi: A Critical Analysis of Mein Kampf*, ed. Peter M. Rutkoff and William B. Scott (Baton Rouge: Louisiana State University, 1981), 149–50.

72. As an old man, Lowe proudly bragged that the Nazis had dismissed him first for political reasons, then because he was a Jew: Harald Hagemann, personal communication, 2015. Lowe made a similar claim in the published interview: "Die Hoffnung auf kleine Katastrophen," in *Die Zerstörung einer Zukunft. Gespräche mit emigrierten Sozialwissenschaftlern*, ed. Mathias Greffrath (Hamburg: Rohwolt, 1979).

73. Krohn, *Intellectuals in Exile*, 65.

74. Erich Hula, "Arnold Brecht: 1884–1977," *Social Research* 44, no. 4 (Winter 1977): 601. In his autobiography, Brecht describes himself as a "liberal," but with close ties to the Social Democrats, in particular to important leaders on the more conservative side of the party, such as Carl Severing, under whom he had served when he was both Reich minister of the interior and Prussia's minister of the interior.

75. Carl J. Friedrich, review of Arnold Brecht, *"Aus nächster Nähe: Lebenserinnerungen 1884–1927,"* vol. 1 (Stuttgart: Deutsche Verlags-Anstalt, 1966), *American Political Science Review* 61, no. 1 (March 1967): 163. After Brecht published volume 2 in German, the book came out in an abridged English translation as *The Political Education of Arnold Brecht: An Autobiography, 1884–1970* (Princeton, N.J.: Princeton University Press, 1970). Krohn portrays Brecht as having been an outsider, even at the New School: Krohn, *Intellectuals in Exile*, 185–87. For further discussion of the reception of Brecht and other members of the University in Exile by the wider academic community in the United States, see Judith Friedlander, "In the Eyes of Others: The Impact of the New School's Refugee Intellectuals in the United States", *Social Research*, 84, no. 4 (Winter 2017): 873–93.

76. This biographical sketch draws on Brecht's autobiography (all quotes from the English edition), on contemporary newspapers that appeared in Germany in 1933, correspondence between Brecht and Johnson, and on a legal document that Brecht submitted to Lieutenant General Lucius Clay, October 24, 1945, as part of the successful case he made to the U.S. government on behalf of his brother that eventually persuaded the American authorities overseeing occupied Cologne to release Gustav Brecht's "assets and accounts, pension, etc., [that] have been blocked" and allow him to assume his position once again as chairman of the Board of Directors of the Reinische Braunkohlen A.G. (a copy of this legal document has been preserved at the NSA).

77. Brecht, *The Political Education of Arnold Brecht*, 408.

78. Brecht, *The Political Education of Arnold Brecht*, 409.

79. As Brecht wrote in his autobiography, his response to the speech Hitler delivered in the Reiechsrat, on February 2, 1933, was widely covered in the press. Although Brecht was not himself a Social Democrat, he was representing the Social Democratic government of Prussia, and the Nazis identified him as a member of the SPD. See the following articles reporting on Brecht's speech. Predictably, their descriptions of what Brecht said reflect the papers' ideological leanings: (1) The Social Democrats' *Vorwärts* "Brecht und Hitler: Kammerspiele in Reichsrat" ("Brecht and Hitler: Political Theater in the Chamber of the Reichsrat"), February 3, 1933, evening edition; (2) The left-liberals' *Berliner Börsen-Courier*, "Hitler stellt sich dem Reichsrat vor" ("Hitler Introduces Himself to the Reichsrat"), February 3, 1933; The National Socialists' *Der Angriff* (directed by Hitler's propaganda minister

Joseph Goebbels), "Die Rede des Führers vor dem Reicharat: Unverschämte Antwort dem Sozialdemokraten Dr. Brecht" ("The Führer's Speech Before the Reichsrat; Outrageous Response by the Social Democrat Dr. Brecht"), February 3, 1933; the Communists' *Die Rote Fahne*, "Fussfall Braun-Severings vor Hitler: Brechts Willkommensgruss an Hitler" ("The Braun-Severing [Government] Prostrated Before Hitler: Brecht's Welcome Address to Hitler"), February 3, 1933. I thank Alejandro Núñez Maldonado for helping me locate these articles.

80. Brecht, *The Political Education of Arnold Brecht*, 439–41; Arnold Brecht to Alvin Johnson, May 16, 1938, Ger024, box 6, folder 25, M. E. Grenader Department of Special Collections & Archives, SUNY Albany.

81. Brecht, *The Political Education of Arnold Brecht*, 442.

82. "Exiles' University Begins Term Here," *New York Times*, October 3, 1933; *New York Times*, October 4, 1933, photo of nine refugee scholars and Alvin Johnson with Brandt seated to the right of Frieda Wunderlich (see photo in this volume).

83. Krohn, *Intellectuals in Exile*, 183.

84. Hamilton Fish Armstrong, cited in Andrew Nagorski, *Hitlerland: American Eyewitnesses to the Nazi Rise to Power* (New York: Simon & Schuster, 2012), 114.

85. Brecht, *The Political Education of Arnold Brecht*, 443. Johnson writes that Brecht arrived after October 1 because "he was delayed for several months conducting the legal defense of the Social-Democratic leader Carl Severing, at great risk to himself." Johnson, *Pioneer's Progress*, 345. According to Brecht's autobiography, he had tried to defend Severing months earlier.

86. Brecht, *The Political Education of Arnold Brecht*, 444. See also Arnold Brecht to Alvin Johnson, October 13, 1933, Ger024, box 6, folder 25, SUNY Albany.

87. Brecht, *The Political Education of Arnold Brecht*, 444.

88. "Exiles' University Opens Here, Oct. 1; Faculty German," *New York Times*, August 19, 1933.

89. "10 Named to Staff of Exiles' College," *New York Times*, September 2, 1933. For names and short descriptions, see Appendix B, Extended Notes and Commentary (D), which reproduces the list found in Johnson, "Report to the Trustees of The Graduate Faculty of Political and Social Science," February 1935.

90. "10 Named to Staff of Exiles' College."

91. Alvin Johnson, cited in "Exiles' University Opens Here Oct. 1."

92. Of the first ten refugee scholars, Brandt and Speier had no "Jewish blood." They would soon be joined by other gentiles, including Arnold Brecht, Alfred Kähler, Kurt Riezler, Hans Simons, and Hans Staudinger. Although Gerhard Colm was a Jew according to Nazi Germany's racial laws, his grandparents had converted to Christianity.

93. For a list of members of the faculty by the winter of 1935, see Appendix B, Extended Notes and Commentary (D), which reproduces the list found in Johnson, "Report to the Trustees of The Graduate Faculty of Political and Social Science," February 1935.

94. Kurt Riezler, Hans Simons, Hans Speier, and Hans Staudinger were all married to women whom the racial laws identified as Jewish. Riezler came to the New School in 1938.

95. Krohn, *Intellectuals in Exile*, 23.

96. Krohn, *Intellectuals in Exile*, 37. Krohn, "American Foundations and Refugee Scholars Between the Two Wars," 47, 48. In a few cases, the Rockefeller Foundation continued to support the research of individual German scholars who had not been evicted from their

posts by the Nazis until Henry Fosdick became president of the foundation in 1936. Gunnar Take, "American Support for German Economists After 1933: The Kiel Institute and the Kiel School in Exile," *Social Research* 84, no. 2 (Winter 2017): 809–30.

97.   Between 1943 and 1944, Governor Thomas Dewey appointed Johnson chair of two New York State committees, the War Council Committee Against Discrimination and the Committee for the Equality in Education, tasked with drafting proposals for the legislature for bills that would end racial discrimination in employment and education in the State of New York. In his capacity as chairman of the first, Johnson helped write the 1945 Ives-Quinn Bill, which "barred discrimination in employment on account to race, color, creed or national origin." As chairman of the second, he led the way to the passage of "a law barring discrimination in student admissions to non-sectarian institutions of higher learning in New York State." See Alvin Johnson Papers, UNL, for excellent documentation on the work Johnson did and the controversies surrounding his effort to expand the mandate of the War Council Committee Against Discrimination. Johnson's role in drafting antidiscriminatory legislation for the State of New York was highlighted in the symposium and induction ceremony of Alvin Saunders Johnson into the Nebraska Hall of Fame. Johnson's grandnephew, Lee Rockwell, nominated Johnson and did the research. See also Johnson, *Pioneer's Progress*, 376–86.

98.   Alvin Johnson to Leo Heimerdinger, January 17, 1944, NSA.

8. THE UNIVERSITY IN EXILE OPENS

1.   Alvin Johnson to Agnes de Lima, August 31, 1933, box 2, folder 27, Alvin Saunders Johnson Papers, Yale.

2.   Alvin Johnson, "Report to the Trustees of The Graduate Faculty of Political and Social Science in the New School for Social Research," February 1935, 9, NSA. For more details, see Emil Lederer, "Report of the Dean of The Graduate Faculty of Political and Social Science in the New School for Social Research"(annotated and corrected copy), September 1936, 5, NSA.

3.   For lecture and seminar courses in the fall of 1933, see the online catalog, The Graduate Faculty of Political and Social Science ("The University in Exile"), Announcement of Courses, 1933–34, digitalarchives.library.newschool.edu/index.php/Detail/objects/NS050101 -gf1933ye.

4.   The Graduate Faculty of Political and Social Science ("The University in Exile"), Announcement of Courses, 1933–34.

5.   New School Press Release, October 14, 1933. The event took place on the evening of October 13, 1933. Other speakers included E. R. A. [Edwin] Seligman; William A. Neilson, president of Smith College; and Emil Lederer.

6.   For a list of members of the faculty by the winter of 1935, see Appendix B, Extended Notes and Commentary (D), which reproduces the list found in Johnson, "Report to the Trustees of The Graduate Faculty of Political and Social Science," February 1935.

7.   New School for Social Research, "To the Living Spirit," 1943, NSA. Although it was published in 1943, the title of the page of the section devoted to the Graduate Faculty reads 1941. See "Editorial," *New York Times*, May 31, 1943.

8. Johnson, "Report to the Trustees of the Graduate Faculty of Political and Social Science," February 1935; Hans Staudinger, Dean of the Graduate Faculty, to "Mr. Chairman" (presumably the chair of the board of trustees), December 7, 1942, NSA. Staudinger noted that although the overall registration numbers had predictably dropped after the United States entered the war, the number of students registered for degrees remained relatively stable. In the first semester after Pearl Harbor (spring of 1942), the number of students registered for a master's degree had dropped from 149 to 137; for a doctorate from 100 to 93. When the GF awarded its first doctor of science degree in 1937 to Etta Friedlander of Cleveland, Ohio (no relation to author), the event was reported in *The New York Times*, May 23, 1937.

9. Hans Neisser, "Commentary on Keynes I", Emil Lederer, "Commentary on Keynes II, *Social Research* 3, no. 4 (November 1936):459–487.

10. In my summary of the reform economists' disagreement with Keynes, in addition to the articles by Neisser and Lederer cited in note 9, I have drawn on the insightful analysis of Claus-Dieter Krohn, *Intellectuals in Exile: Refugee Scholars and the New School for Social Research*, trans. Rita Kimber and Robert Kimber (1987; Amherst: University of Massachusetts Press, 1993), 112–15. For other excellent discussions of the reform economists, see Claus-Dieter Krohn, "An Overlooked Chapter of Economic Thought: The 'New School's' Effort to Salvage Weimar's Economy," *Social Research* 50, no. 2 (Summer 1983): 452–68; "Refugee Scholarship: The Cross-Fertilization of Culture," Harald Hagemann and William Milberg, guest editors, *Social Research* 84, no. 4 (Winter 2017).

    I am grateful to William Milberg, New School economist and current dean of NSSR, for reviewing this section for me. Expanding on what I said, Milberg stressed the following: Two areas of research emerged as central to the work of the German reform economists at the New School and distinguished them from the Keynesians. Both research areas grew out of the group's conviction that capitalism was in a state of perpetual disequilibrium. The first looked at the problems caused by "technological unemployment," an issue that had concerned economists as far back as Ricardo in the early nineteenth century, and that the reform economists wrote about regularly during the Weimar period in Germany and then again in the United States. The second research area investigated ways to improve economic planning. Given the persistence of underemployment in capitalist societies, responsible governments, the reform economists argued, had to keep looking for new ways to connect existing resources to their potential uses, not only during periods of economic crisis, William Milberg, personal communication, April 2018.

11. Harald Hagemann, "Emil Lederer (1882–1939): Economic and Sociological Analyst and Critic of Capitalist Development," in *The Theory of Capitalism in the German Economic Tradition: Historicism, Ordo-Liberalism, Critical Theory, Solidarism*, ed. Peter Koslowski (Berlin-Heidelberg: Springer, 2000), 28.

12. Harald Hagemann, "Introduction," in "German Perspectives on the Social Sciences." Special issue, *Social Research* 81, no. 3 (Fall 2014): 505–8.

13. In addition to Lowe, Colm, Neisser, and Kähler, Johnson recruited another scholar to the New School who was affiliated with the University of Kiel, the legal theorist Hermann Kantorowicz.

14. In addition to Riezler, Johnson welcomed two other philosophers to the faculty in 1938, the Austrian epistemologist Fritz Kaufmann and Leo Strauss, political philosopher and classicist, who did not get a permanent appointment at the GF until 1941.

15. Alvin Johnson, *Pioneer's Progress: An Autobiography* (1952; Lincoln: University of Nebraska Press, 1960), 347.

16. Johnson, *Pioneer's Progress*, 221.

17. On Kurt Riezler, see Wayne C. Thompson, *In the Eye of the Storm: Kurt Riezler and the Crises of Modern Germany* (Iowa City: University of Iowa Press, 1980); Leo Strauss and Theodor Heuss, "Tributes to Kurt Riezler, *Social Research* 22, no. 1 (Spring 1956): 1–34. On the matter of Lenin, Thompson writes that when he interviewed Hans Staudinger in 1975 the New School's émigré economist reported that Riezler had told Alvin Johnson, Arnold Brecht, and himself that it had been his idea to hide Lenin in a sealed railway car as a way to sneak him back into Russia. When Arnold Brecht wrote about the incident in his autobiography, he suggested that the philosopher was merely following orders. Brecht wrote about this in volume 1 of the German edition of his autobiography: Arnold Brecht, *Aus nächster Nähe: Lebenserinnerungen 1. Hälfte 1884–1927* (Stuttgart: Deutsche Verlags-Anstalt, 1966), 76, cited in Thompson, *In the Eye of the Storm*, 135. Brecht's account did not appear in the abridged edition published in English. Also see Catherine Merridale, *Lenin on the Train* (New York: Metropolitan Books, 2017), 51, 52, 62. Merridale mentions Riezler, citing Thompson, but says nothing about the philosopher coming up with the scheme for smuggling Lenin back into Russia.

18. Riezler's wife Käthe, née Liebermann, was the daughter of the famous painter of Jewish origin Max Liebermann.

19. Johnson, *Pioneer's Progress*, 346; Alvin Johnson to Robert MacIver April 10, 1957, box 5, folder 83. Alvin Saunders Johnson Papers, Yale.

20. Hans Speier, "Symposium: The University in Exile," *Contemporary Sociology* 16, no. 3 (May 1987): 279.

21. Symposia on December 3, 1933, and January 7, 1934, *New School Bulletin* 3 (November 20, 1933) and *New School Bulletin* 5 (January 3, 1934), cited in Krohn, *Intellectuals in Exile*, 97n7.

22. Hagemann, "Introduction," 505, 508.

23. In his February 1935 report to the GF's board of trustees, Johnson claimed that ten of the twenty faculty members he had recruited by then had served as editors of academic journals or worked as journalists in the mainstream media, and he specifically identified eight. All of them had been hired by 1934: Karl Brandt (*Blätter für Landwirtschaftliche Marktforschung*), Eduard Heimann (*Neue Blätter für dem Sozialismus*), Erich von Hornbostel (*Sammelbände für vergleichende Musikwissenschaft*), Albert Salomon (*Die Gesellschaft*), Hans Simons (*Wiederaufbau*), Max Wertheimer (*Pyschologische Forschung*), Frieda Wunderlich (*Soziale Praxis*), and Arthur Feiler (*Die Frankfurter Zeitung*). Johnson, "Report to the Trustees of the Graduate Faculty of Political and Social Science," 6–9. See Appendix B, Extended Notes and Commentary (D) for a reproduction of the biographical sketches Johnson prepared for the 1935 report that include the names of these journals.

24. Johnson, *Pioneer's Progress*, 346.

25. See articles by Emil Lederer, Eduard Heimann, Karl Brandt, Arthur Feiler, Gerhard Colm, Frieda Wunderlich, and Hans Speier in first issue of *Social Research: An International Quarterly of Political and Social Science* 1, no. 1 (February 1934).

26. *Social Research* 1, no. 1 (February 1934): 4.

27. Johnson, *Pioneer's Progress*, 346.

28. Alvin Johnson to Arnold Brecht, February 7, 1946, box 1, Alvin Saunders Johnson Papers, Yale.

29. Lewis Coser, *Refugee Scholars in America: Their Impact and Experiences* (New Haven, Conn.: Yale University Press, 1984), 105.

30. Alvin Johnson to Members of the Graduate Faculty, September 21, 1951, NSA.

31. See Epilogue in this volume.

32. Alvin Johnson to Arnold Brecht, January 3, 1936, series 2, box 6, folder 25, Arnold Brecht Papers, 1865–1974, M. E. Grenander Department of Special Collections & Archives, SUNY Albany (hereafter referred to as Arnold Brecht Papers).

33. Johnson had invited the presidents of Johns Hopkins (Isaiah Bowman), University of Chicago (Robert Hutchins), and Harvard (James Bryant Conant) to attend the dinner in January. As he explained in the letter addressed to Bowman, "we are hoping . . . to stand out with the approval of the three University Presidents who represent in public opinion the newer, more vital trends in university education." Alvin Johnson to Isaiah Bowman, November 12, 1935, MS 58, series 2, box 23, Papers of Isaiah Bowman, Johns Hopkins University, Special Collections, Sheridan Libraries. Bowman accepted the invitation and spoke at the event at the Waldorf Astoria. When *The New York Times* reported on the dinner the following morning, it mentioned that Bowman had praised the sponsors of the University in Exile for organizing a single institution instead of trying to persuade other universities to "absorb more exiled scholars than they could." It also noted that Felix Frankfurter, Professor of Law at Harvard, criticized other universities for not having been more hospitable. Finally, the article also quoted from President Roosevelt's words of congratulations to the New School: "Roosevelt Hails University in Exile," *New York Times*, January 16, 1936.

34. Alvin Johnson to Arnold Brecht, January 3, 1936, Arnold Brecht Papers, SUNY Albany. Unless otherwise noted, citations from correspondence between Johnson and Brecht during the 1930s in this chapter come from this same collection of papers.

35. Arnold Brecht, *The Political Education of Arnold Brecht: An Autobiography 1884–1970* (Princeton, N.J.: Princeton University Press, 1970), 448–54. The shorter English edition draws from volumes 1 and 2 of *Aus nächster Nähe: Lebenserinnerungen* (the second volume, also published by Deutsche Verlags-Anstalt, came out in 1967 under the title *Mit der Kraft des Geistes: Lebenserinnerungen 2. Hälfte 1927–1967*).

36. Brecht, *The Political Education of Arnold Brecht*, 449.

37. Stephen H. Norwood, *The Third Reich in the Ivory Tower* (Cambridge, Mass.: Cambridge University Press, 2009), 56–57.

38. "Nazi Troops March in Heidelberg Fete," *New York Times*, June 28, 1936.

39. Brecht, *The Political Education of Arnold Brecht*, 449.

40. Brecht, *The Political Education of Arnold Brecht*, 454.

41. During this period, Oxford University Press published Brecht's *Prelude to Silence—the End of the German Republic* (1944) and *Federalism and Regionalism in Germany: The Division of Prussia* (1945). His articles appeared in the *Harvard Law Review*, *California Law Review*, *American Political Science Review*, *Social Research*, and other journals.

42. Arnold Brecht to Lieutenant General Lucius Clay, October 24, 1945, NSA.

43. Arnold Brecht to Lieutenant General Lucius Clay, October 24, 1945, 1, 3.

44. Arnold Brecht to Lieutenant General Lucius Clay, October 24, 1945, 4.

45. Brecht, *The Political Education of Arnold Brecht*, 462.

46. In 1921, at about the same time as Brecht began serving as the head of the Division for Policy and Constitution in the National Ministry of the Interior, Hans Simons was appointed the personal assistant to the Minister of the Interior, Adolf Köster. When Brecht was fired in 1927 from the National Ministry of the Interior and appointed ministerial director of the State and Finance of Prussia, he worked alongside Hans Staudinger, who was ministerial director of Prussia's Ministry of Commerce.

47. Alvin Johnson to Arnold Brecht, October 20, 1949, box 1, Alvin Saunders Johnson Papers, Yale. The article by Brecht that had inspired Johnson to write his letter was "The New German Constitution," *Social Research* 16, no. 4 (December 1949): 425–73.

48. Arnold Brecht, "December 1949," for Alvin Johnson's seventy-fifth birthday, NSA.

49. In 1963, after Johnson and Staudinger broke ranks with the Board of Trustees and ran an unauthorized but successful "Save the School" campaign, during which they raised enough money to thwart a plan to sell the New School to NYU, Johnson took charge of putting together the program for his eighty-ninth birthday. In a memo to Hans [Staudinger], November 7, 1963, he suggested that they ask Arnold Brecht to speak about Johnson's role in founding the University in Exile and Adolph Lowe about him as an economist, NSA.

50. Alvin Johnson to Isaiah Bowman, November 12, 1935, Isaiah Bowman to Alvin Johnson, November 14, 1935, MS58, series 2, box 23, Papers of Isaiah Bowman, Johns Hopkins University, Special Collections, Sheridan Libraries.

51. Alvin Johnson to Agnes de Lima, January 16, 1936, box 2, folder 27, Alvin Saunders Johnson Papers, Yale.

52. Anniversary Issue, *Social Research* 4, no. 3 (September 1937).

53. Thomas Mann, "The Living Spirit," *Social Research* 4, no. 3 (September 1937): 266–67. Reprinted in *Social Research* 82, no. 1 (Spring 2015): 6–7. Mann also gave three lectures at the New School in April of 1937 on Freud, Wagner, and Goethe, which were based on abridged versions of articles subsequently published in full in the United States: Thomas Mann, *Freud, Goethe, Wagner* (New York: Alfred A. Knopf, 1937).

54. Mann, "The Living Spirit," 272. The *New York Times* covered Mann's speech but did not mention his reference to the inscription: "Mann Denounces Christianity Foes," *New York Times*, April 16, 1937.

55. Among the twenty academic institutions that sent delegates to Heidelberg in June 1936 for the five-hundred-fiftieth anniversary celebration were Carleton, Carnegie, Columbia, Cornell, Harvard, Johns Hopkins, Michigan, Pennsylvania, Stanford, Vassar, and Yale. See Michael Rosenthal, *Nicholas Miraculous: The Amazing Career of the Redoubtable Nicholas Murray Butler* (New York: Farrar Straus and Giroux, 2006), 392; "Rust Says Nazism Precedes Science," *New York Times*, June 30, 1936; "Heidelberg's Aim Changed by Nazis," *New York Times*, July 1, 1936.

56. Norwood, *The Third Reich in the Ivory Tower*, 60ff.

57. Undated quote from *Nature* cited in "Ban on Heidelberg Extends in Britain," *New York Times*, February 28, 1936.

58. Rosenthal, *Nicholas Miraculous*, 394.

59. Nicholas Murray Butler to Governor Wilbur L. Cross of Connecticut (and Trustee of the University in Exile), cited in "Mann Denounces Christianity Foes."

60. Rosenthal, *Nicholas Miraculous*, 394.

9. RING THE ALARM

1. Alvin Johnson, "In Memory of Hiram Halle," April 25, 1952, box 2, folder 19, Alvin Johnson Papers, UNL.

2. Hans Staudinger (with Werner Pese), *The Inner Nazi: A Critical Analysis of Mein Kampf*, ed. Peter M. Rutkoff and William B. Scott (Baton Rouge: Louisiana University Press, 1981), 5.

3. Staudinger, *The Inner Nazi*, 12–30.

4. Peter M. Rutkoff and William B. Scott, "Biographical Afterword," in Staudinger, *The Inner Nazi*, 137–53. See New School Press Release, "Dr. Hans Staudinger of the New School Dies at 90; former Weimar Republic Official Fought Nazis," February 26, 1980, NSA.

5. Hiram Halle, cited in Johnson, "In Memory of Hiram Halle"; James J. Barnes and Patience P. Barnes, *Hitler's Mein Kampf in Britain and America: A Publishing History 1930–39* (1980; Cambridge: Cambridge University Press, 2008), 83.

6. The publication history of the U.S. edition of *Mein Kampf* has been thoroughly researched and presented in fascinating detail in Barnes and Barnes, *Hitler's Mein Kampf in Britain and America*. Unless otherwise indicated, the summary that follows, including quotes from primary sources, are from chapters 4–6 of this excellent work. Quotes from the "Introduction" to the translation are from Adolf Hitler, *Mein Kampf: Complete and Unabridged. FULLY ANNOTATED* (New York: Reynal & Hitchcock, 1939), vii–xii. In putting this story together, I have also relied on *Publishers' Weekly*, November 15, 1941; *New York Times*, March 1, 1939, March 12, 1939, and June 10, 1939; and Alvin Johnson's correspondence, UNL.

7. George N. Shuster, *The Ground I Walked On: Reflections of a College President* (New York: Farrar, Straus and Cudahy, 1961), 141.

8. The historians were Sidney Fay (Harvard), Carleton Hayes (Columbia), and William Langer (Harvard). The five journalists were Graham Hutton and Walter Millis of *The New York Herald Tribune*; John Chamberlain, editor of *Fortune*; John Gunther, freelance writer and former foreign correspondent for *The Chicago Daily News*; and Raoul J. J. F. de Roussy de Sales, foreign correspondent of *Paris Soir*, member of the French Consulate and president of the Association of Foreign Press Correspondents in the United States.

9. The translators of *Mein Kampf* are acknowledged in this note by the publishers: "Mr. Helmut Ripperger, on whom a heavy burden has fallen and various friends and helpers at the New School for Social Research have likewise given without stint of their time and energy to the translation."

10. Alvin Johnson to Ben [Bernard] Flexner, box 19, folder 2, Alvin Johnson Papers, UNL. The letter was written between December 1938 and February 1939, after Stackpole and Sons had announced that they planned to publish their own translation of *Mein Kampf* and before George Shuster, on behalf of the New School, had finished annotating the Reynal & Hitchcock edition. Bernard Flexner, brother of Abraham Flexner, the founder of the Institute of Advanced Studies in Princeton, was an eminent lawyer who played a major role during the Hitler years in settling refugees in farming communities around the world. At the time of this correspondence, he was vice president of the Refugee Economic Corporation. Together with Charles Liebman, the corporation's president, Flexner financed Johnson's farming community for refugees, Van Eeden, near Wilmington, North Carolina. See Alvin Johnson, *Pioneer's Progress: An Autobiography* (1952; Lincoln: The University of Nebraska Press, 1960), 364. Bernard Flexner had ties to the New School from its early days and is listed

as a member of the School's Advisory Committee in the brochure produced to celebrate the New School's eighth anniversary, February 1927, NSA.

11. Shuster, *The Ground I Walked On*, 141.

12. "Court Denies Writ in Hitler Row," *New York Times*, March 1, 1939.

13. "'Mein Kampf' in Unabridged Form," *New York Times*, March 12, 1939.

14. Learned Hand and his wife, Frances, were good friends of the New School from the very early days of the institution. A document dated June 4, 1919, lists Mrs. Learned Hand as a member of the School's Organization Committee and Chairman of the Sub-Committee on Finance. In February 1927, on the occasion of its eighth anniversary, the Hon. Learned Hand is listed as a member of the School's Advisory Committee, NSA. In a letter to Leo Heimerdinger many years later, Johnson speaks uncharitably about Learned Hand, describing him as an anti-Semite: Alvin Johnson to Leo Heimerdinger, December 30, 1952, NSA.

15. "Rights of Hitler to Book Upheld," *New York Times*, June 10, 1939.

16. Justice Felix Frankfurter recused himself from the deliberations at the Supreme Court. As the New School's good friend and outspoken advocate for the victims of Nazi Germany, he had conflicts of interest.

17. Stackpole and Sons sold nearly twelve thousand copies of their translation before they were forced to take it off the market in June 1939. When the case was finally settled in November 1941, Stackpole and Sons were forced to pay Reynal & Hitchcock $15,000 in damages: "'Mein Kampf' Copyright Case Settled," *Publishers' Weekly*, November 15, 1941.

18. Eugène Reynal to Alvin Johnson, May 11, 1939, box 2, folder 19, Alvin Johnson Papers, UNL.

19. Correspondence between Alvin Johnson and J. C. Hyman, executive director of the American Jewish Joint Distribution Committee, June 15, 1939, box 2, folder 19, Alvin Johnson Papers, UNL.

20. The administrative costs for the Children's Crusade for Children came to $35,000. In all, the Reynal & Hitchcock fund distributed about $50,000. Barnes and Barnes, *Hitler's Mein Kampf in Britain and America*, 123.

21. Alvin Johnson, "Foreword," in *War in Our Time*, ed. Hans Speier and Alfred Kähler (New York: W. W. Norton, 1939), 7–8.

22. For a good selection of these articles, see Ira Katznelson, guest editor, "Dark Reason: Reflections on the Early Years of *Social Research*." Special issue, *Social Research* 82, no. 1 (Spring 2015). To mark the eightieth anniversary of the journal, *Social Research* republished pieces written by members of the faculty of the University in Exile during the 1930s and early 1940s.

23. Harald Hagemann mentions these similarities in the "Introduction," in "German Perspectives on the Social Sciences." Special issue, *Social Research* 81, no. 3 (Fall 2014): 512. Krohn noted that Heimann and Lowe also identified the strategy of creating a classless society as one of the greatest dangers fascism and communism posed to democratic societies. Hans-Dieter Krohn, *Intellectuals in Exile: Refugee Scholars and the New School for Social Research*, trans. Rita Kimber and Robert Kimber (1987; Amherst: University of Massachusetts Press, 1993), 130. For a brief discussion of the criticism Arendt faced from intellectuals on the left for drawing out the similarities between National Socialism and Stalinist communism, see Elisabeth Young Bruehl, *Hannah Arendt: For Love of the World* (New Haven, Conn.: Yale University Press, 1982), 407. See discussion on Hannah Arendt's *Origins of Totalitarianism* and the New School's translation of *Mein Kampf* in Appendix C, Extended Notes and Commentary.

24. Franz Neumann to Max Horkheimer and Leo Löwenthal, July 20 and 26, 1940, and September 29, 1941, 6,30/15 and 111, Horkheimer Papers, Stadtund Universitätsbibliothek (SUB), Frankfurt, cited in Krohn, *Intellectuals in Exile*, 194n40.

25. Franz Neumann, *Behemoth: The Structure and Practice of National Socialism* (London: Oxford University Press, 1942).

26. Hans Speier, "Foreword," in Emil Lederer, *State of the Masses: The Threat of the Classless Society* (1940; W. W. Norton; New York: Howard Fertig, 1967), 15.

27. Lederer, *State of the Masses*, 18, 50, 46.

28. Neumann, *Behemoth*, 366.

29. Martin Jay, *The Dialectical Imagination: A History of the Frankfurt School and the Institute of Social Research, 1923–1950* (Boston, Mass.: Little Brown, 1973), 163; Rolf Wiggerhaus, *The Frankfurt School: Its History, Theories and Political Significance*, trans. Michael Robertson (1986; Cambridge, Mass.: MIT Press,1994), 254.

30. Wiggerhaus, *The Frankfurt School*, 255.

31. Hans Speier, "Review of Martin Jay, *The Dialectical Imagination*," *American Political Science Review* 70, no. 4 (December 1976): 1276–77.

32. Speier, "Review of Martin Jay, *The Dialectical Imagination*," 1276–77; "Review of Max Horkheimer, ed. *Studien* über *Autorität und Familie*," *Social Research* 3, no. 4 (November 1936): 503; Krohn, *Intellectuals in Exile*, 193.

33. Speier, "Review of Martin Jay, *The Dialectical Imagination*," 1276–77.

34. Franz Neumann, report to Max Horkheimer on the negotiations with T. B. Kittredge of the Rockefeller Foundation, May 6, 1941, 6, 30/81, Horkheiemer Papers, SUB Frankfurt, cited in Krohn, *Intellectuals in Exile*, 194, 242n41.

35. Max Horkheimer to Franz Neumann, August 2, 1941, 6, 30/52, Horkheimer Papers, SUB Frankfurt; Max Horkheimer to Adolph Lowe, August 14, 1941, 1/17/32, Horkheimer Papers, SUB Frankfurt, cited in Claus-Dieter Krohn, *Intellectuals in Exile: Refugee Scholars and the New School for Social Research*, trans. Rita Kimber and Robert Kimber (1987; Amherst: University of Massachusetts Press, 1993), 195nn44,45.

36. "An Institute of World Affairs: Proposal," 3, NSA, probably written at the end of 1942 or early 1943, and given its style, by Johnson.

37. Krohn, *Intellectuals in Exile*, 139.

38. Johnson spoke with pride about the ways the New School was conducting research for the U.S. government in his inaugural address, "An Institute of World Affairs," November 17, 1943, and in the fund-raising brochure "To the Living Spirit," which the university had published the previous spring: "The rich and varied experience of the New School's Graduate Faculty is completely at the disposal of the American government, which, in turn is availing itself of the opportunities for obtaining information from New School experts."

39. Unless otherwise noted, the information summarized in this section about the New School's ties to federal agencies during the war comes from the New School's fund-raising brochure, "To the Living Spirit," which Johnson sent out to potential donors in the spring of 1943.

40. Alvin Johnson, "The Institute of World Affairs: Aims and Organization," in *The Study of World Affairs: Two Addresses Delivered at the Inaugural Meeting on November 17, 1943* (USA: Oxford University Press, 1944), 4, 5.

41. Ernst Kris and Hans Speier, *German Radio Propaganda: Report on Home Broadcasts During the War*, Studies of the Institute of World Affairs (Oxford: Oxford University Press, 1944). With

Johnson's help, Speier and Kris received a grant from Rockefeller for $15,000 in 1941. Three years later, the results of their research were published by Oxford University Press thanks to a special arrangement Lowe had negotiated for the IWA that paralleled the one the Royal Institute had with the publishing house. The materials Speier and Kris analyzed in *German Radio Propaganda: Report on Home Broadcasts During the War* consisted of detailed transcripts of German radio programs that were originally recorded by BBC's media service and that Johnson helped them acquire. See: Alvin Johnson to Stephen Lawford Childs, at the British Embassy, Washington, D.C., April 20, 1941, NSA. Johnson asked for Childs's assistance in "speeding up as much as possible" the delivery to Speier of BBC's Daily Digest of Foreign Broadcasts. Yet in later years, Speier spoke ungenerously about the IWA, dismissing the support he had received for his research from Lowe and Johnson, and the value of the institute itself. See: Hans Speier, "Review of Peter Ruttkoff and William Scott, *The New School: A History of the New School for Social Research*," in "Symposium: The University in Exile," ed. Arthur Vidich, *Contemporary Sociology* 16, no, 3 (May 1987): 279.

42. The Minutes of the July 10, 1941, meeting of the Committee on Research (the group that became IWA) reported that the Rockefeller Foundation had made two research grants to the New School, one for the "Totalitarian Communication" project and the other for "Social and Economic Controls in Germany and Russia." The quote describing the aims of the Social and Economic Controls project appeared in: Agnes de Lima, Press Release, June 16, 1941, distributed to New York City's newspapers six days before the German army invaded the Soviet Union, NSA. This German/Russian project led to many publications, including Arthur Feiler and Jacob Marschak, ed., *Management in Russian Industry and Agriculture* (New York and London: Oxford University Press, 1944), with contributions by Gregory Bienstock, Solomon M. Schwarz, and Aaron Yugow.

43. Johnson, *Pioneer's Progress*, 347, 371.

44. Memo (no author but probably Agnes de Lima or Alvin Johnson), December, 7–10. The memo describes the ideals of the New School and its various programs (the document is ten pages long). See also Press Release, May 29, 1944, which describes the Ibero-American Center and announces that Sumner Welles would be giving a talk at the New School, NSA.

10. ECOLE LIBRE DES HAUTES ETUDES

1. For this chapter, in addition to my own archival research, I gratefully draw on the excellent work of Laurent Jeanpierre, "Des hommes entre plusieurs mondes. Etude sur une situation d'exil. Intellectuels français refugiés aux Etats-Unis pendant la deuxième guerre mondiale," 2 vols. (doctorat en sociologie, EHESS, 2004); Emmanuelle Loyer, *Paris à New York: Intellectuels et artistes français en exil 1940–1947* (Paris: Pluriel, 2005); Emmanuelle Loyer, *Lévi-Strauss* (Paris: Flammarion, 2015); and Aristide Zolberg (with Agnès Callamard), "The Ecole Libre at the New School," *Social Research* 65, no. 4 (Winter 1998): 921–55.

2. Alvin Johnson, *Pioneer's Progress: An Autobiography* (1952; Lincoln: University of Nebraska Press, 1960), 366–67, "The Refugee Scholars: A Retrospect," October 1955, 10–11, RG1.1, S200, B47F542, RAC.

3. New School Announcement of Courses, Spring 1941, NS050101_ns1941sp, NSA.

4. "The Refugee Scholars: A Retrospect," 12; Johnson, *Pioneer's Progress*, 368.

5. See correspondence preserved at the RAC and NSA concerning attempts to get Marc Bloch out of France, in particular letters written from Marseille by George Strode, a high-level member of the foundation's staff, and by Alvin Johnson, Marc Bloch, and Thomas Appleget, president of the Rockefeller Foundation, April 10, 1941, July 24, 1941, July 31, 1941, August 18, 1941. Bloch's letter to Johnson, dated July 31, 1941, speaks of Bloch's sons as the major impediment. The telegram from Strode, sent April 10, 1941, speaks of Bloch wanting to bring his mother over as well. Carole Fink's biography of Bloch mentions the fact that the United States would not give Bloch's mother a visa: Carole Fink, *A Life in History* (Cambridge: Cambridge University Press, 1989). In Johnson's letter "To Whom It May Concern," July 24, 1941, he confirms that the New School had invited Bloch to teach medieval history at the New School for two years, for $2,500 per year. A copy of Johnson's July 24 letter is located at NSA; the others are at the RAC. I want to thank Laura Miller, historian at the Rockefeller Archive Center, for her help.

6. Johnson, *Pioneer's Progress*, 371–72. While Johnson was discussing the possibility of setting up the Ecole Libre with French scholars allied with de Gaulle, a competing faction of the anti-Vichy resistance movement under the leadership of Henri Giraud was still in control of much of French North Africa. De Gaulle did not gain full control until 1943.

7. "French Here Mark First Armistice; 2000 Attend Ceremony of de Gaulle Adherents in Manhattan Center," *New York Times*, November 12, 1941.

8. Hal Lehrman, "Free French College Opens Here in January," *New York Daily News*, November 13, 1941.

9. Alvin Johnson, Letter to the Editor, *New York Daily News*, November 13, 1941. This is the date Johnson wrote the letter, a copy of which has been preserved in NSA.

10. Tracy B. Kittredge, Interoffice Memo, November 24, 1941, RAC, cited in Zolberg, "The Ecole Libre at the New School," 937–38. Zolberg added that there is no evidence that the Rockefeller Foundation ever tried to interfere with the Ecole's hiring and firing practices. Since the New School's charter made clear that it would not hire fascists or communists, Johnson had a ready explanation for not intervening should he have needed one, if the Ecole's leadership followed through with their threat to fire supporters of Vichy. I have not seen any correspondence on the matter between Johnson and the Rockefeller Foundation.

11. Kittredge, Interoffice Memo, November 24, 1941.

12. Agnes de Lima, two New School Press Releases, February 15, 1942, NSA.

13. Alvin Johnson, cited in Agnes de Lima, Press Releases (two), February 15,1942 (there were two that day), NSA.

14. "French Learning in Exile," *New York Times*, February 13, 1942.

15. Members of the Ecole Libre's faculty who also taught at the Graduate Faculty included Alexander Koyré, Claude Lévi-Strauss, Boris Mirkine-Guetzévitch, and Paul Schrecker. Their names appear on a bronze plaque that hung in the new GF building at 65 Fifth Avenue, which opened in the spring of 1969. See "The New School Salutes 'Exiles'; Plaque Honors the Faculty That Fled Totalitarianism," *New York Times*, April 26, 1969.

    In addition to welcoming several members of the Ecole Libre to teach at the GF, Johnson also invited Alexandre Koyré, Claude Lévi-Strauss, Jacques Maritain, Mirkine-Guetzévitch, and Paul van Zeeland to join the Institute of World Affairs. See Alvin Johnson to Jacques Maritain, May 25, 1943, NSA.

16. Letter from President Roosevelt, *Renaissance* 1 no.1 (January–March 1943).

17. Zolberg, "The Ecole Libre at the New School," 946. For descriptions of Claude Lévi-Strauss's encounters with Roman Jakobson, see Roman Jakobson, *Six Lectures on Sound and Meaning*, Preface by Claude Lévi-Strauss, trans. John Mepham (1976; Cambridge: MIT Press, 1978); Claude Lévi-Strauss and Didier Eribon, *Conversations with Claude Lévi-Strauss*, trans. Paula Wissing (1988; Chicago, Ill.: University of Chicago Press, 1991), Loyer, *Paris à New York*, and Loyer, *Lévi-Strauss*.

18. Hal Lehrman, "Free French College Opens Here in January, *New York Daily News*, November 13, 1941.

19. "Exiles Return," *New York Times*, February 24, 1945.

20. André Weil to Jacques Maritain, July 10, 1942, private collection, Sylvie Weil.

21. André Weil to Jacques Maritain, June 18, 1942, Jacques Maritain Papers, Jacques Maritain Center, University of Notre Dame, cited in Loyer, *Paris à New York*, 234n84.

22. See Zolberg, "The Ecole Libre at the New School," for an interesting discussion of the different political, cultural, and academic factions at the Ecole Libre.

23. Loyer, *Paris à New York*, 235.

24. Alvin Johnson to the Editorial Board of *Renaissance*, April 25, 1944, box 2, Alvin Saunders Johnson Papers, Yale.

25. Emmanuelle Loyer, "Autonomie scientifique et engagement politique," in *Paris à New York*, 234–38.

26. Alvin Johnson to the Editorial Board of *Renaissance*, April 25, 1944.

27. After the Ecole Libre closed its doors, a small group of French-speaking émigrés continued meeting informally under the name of the Ecole Libre, sponsoring lectures on subjects of common interest, primarily on themes in the medical sciences. The New School reestablished contact with this group in the 1990s and welcomed them to meet at the university.

28. Alvin Johnson to Max Ascoli, January 6, 1959, box 1, Alvin Saunders Johnson Papers, Yale. Between 1933 and 1945, Johnson hired at least thirteen Italian refugees, see NSA online at http://newschoolarchives.org/?p=644.

11. ALVIN JOHNSON RETIRES

1. Although Johnson, like the German reform economists, had reservations about aspects of Keynes's theory, he considered the British economist by "far the most creative economic thinker of our time." Alvin Johnson, *Pioneer's Progress: An Autobiography* (1952; Lincoln: University of Nebraska Press, 1960), 243.

2. Johnson, *Pioneer's Progress*, 401.

3. Johnson, *Pioneer's Progress*, 401. In the early 1940s, Duke made another gift of $50,000 to the Institute of World Affairs (IWA), codirected by Adolph Lowe and her friend Hans Staudinger. The announcement preserved in the NSA has no date, but it must have been made in late 1942 or early 1943, before the publication of a fund-raising brochure that devotes a page to the IWA. The gift covered the administrative costs of the institute for the first five years. In the announcement, Duke is identified as Doris Duke Cromwell.

   In later years, Duke also contributed money to a refugee scholarship fund at the New School. Recognizing her deep love of the arts, President Jonathan Fanton paid tribute to the university's generous benefactress in 1998, by creating a new jazz scholarship program in her name: "Knowing of her love of the arts, particularly Jazz, we thought Jazz scholars would be the most fitting way of recalling Doris Duke's critical role at the New School. Without her intervention, we would not be sitting here today." *New School Observer*, September, 1998.

4. Johnson, *Pioneer's Progress*, 403.

5. Cited in Peter M. Rutkoff and William B. Scott, *New School: A History of the New School for Social Research* (New York: The Free Press, 1986), 103.

6. Johnson, Pioneer's Progress, 403.

7. Johnson, fund-raising letter sent to one thousand friends of the New School on the occasion of his retirement, probably in the spring of 1945, NSA. It begins: "Most of the letters you have received from me have been strictly of a 'person to person' character. That is the only kind of letter I can write tolerably well. This letter I am writing to a thousand persons who have joined me in building up the New School."

8. Bryn Hovde, cited in Agnes de Lima, Press Release to City Editors, June 15, 1945, NSA.

9. Bryn Hovde, Report to Contributors and Friends, Spring 1947, NSA.

10. Hans Simons to Agnes de Lima, October 22, 1947, NSA. In a letter from Edward Litchfield to Bryn Hovde, August 25, 1947, NSA, the director of the Civil Administration Division requested Simons's services in 1947 for an extended period of time to help the U.S. Office of Military Government in Germany.

11. Frank H. Bowles, Chairman of the Commission on Institutions of Higher Education of the Middle States Association of Colleges and Secondary Schools to President Bryn Hovde, December 3, 1948, NSA. The New School remained on probation. See chapters 14 and 15 in this volume.

12. Max Ascoli to Hans Simons, March 24, 1949, box 206, BU; "O'Dwyer Attacked in College Stand," *New York Times*, February 21, 1949. See chapter 12 for more on Hovde's decision to bow out of the race for president of Queens College, Max Ascoli Papers.

13. Rutkoff and Scott, *New School*, 220.

14. Edward H. Litchfield to Bryn Hovde, August 26, 1949, NSA, and published in the *New School Bulletin* (September 9, 1949).

15. "Dr. Hovde Resigns New School Post," *New York Times*, May 9, 1950.

16. Johnson, *Pioneer's Progress*, 404.

17. Agnes de Lima, "Dr. Hans Simons, President, New School for Social Research: A Biographical Sketch," June 14, 1950, NSA; "Named to Succeed Hovde," *New York Times*, June 15, 1950.

12. THE RED SCARE

1. Ellen Schrecker, *No Ivory Tower: McCarthyism & the Universities* (New York: Oxford University Press, 1986), 288, 289. What is more, the New School made no secret of the fact that it did not welcome Communists. In this chapter, we look at the case of the painter Robert Gwathmey, who resigned after being questioned about his political affiliations. The experiences of others who, like Gwathmey, may have belonged to the Communist Party, deserve closer attention. The photographer Lisette Model, for example, taught at the New School between 1951 and 1953, until she "had a run in with McCarthy." She then taught there again in 1959. No evidence suggests that the New School ever fired Model. Ann Thomas, Curator of the National Photographic Archives of Canada, personal communication.

2. Thomas Jefferson's famous phrase became a popular refrain among anti-Communist progressives and conservatives during these years.

3. Agnes de Lima to Hans Simons, May 7, 1953, NSA.

4. Alvin Johnson to Lucius Littauer, January 6, 1944, NSA.

5. I discuss the Orozco mural scandal in detail in chapter 13.

6. "Revolutionary Radicalism: Its History, Purpose and Tactics . . . Being the Report of the Joint Legislative Committee Investigating Seditious Activities," 4 vols., filed April 24, 1920 (Albany, N.Y., 1920), vol. I, 1121. Also see chapter 5 of this volume.

7. Horace Kallen, cited in Murray Schumach, "$37-Million Expansion Planned by the New School," *New York Times*, December 12, 1968. In the New School's Announcement of Courses, October 1919–May 1920, 17, Kallen's course on the International Mind was described as "a survey of the psychological and social factors in the rise, development and subsidence of international ways of thinking and behaving: The relation of the state to society." NSA digital archives, digitalarchives.library.newschool.edu/.

8. Alvin Johnson to August Heckscher (Chief Editor of *The New York Herald Tribune*), December 29, 1954, NSA.

9. Alvin Johnson, *Pioneer's Progress: An Autobiography* (1952; Lincoln: University of Nebraska Press, 1960), 275.

10. For more about the new music program, see chapter 6 in this volume. For a list of courses taught by Mossaiye Olgin, see chapter 5, note 47, in this volume.

11. Alvin Johnson to Stacy May, May 27, 1953, box 8, folder 5, Alvin Johnson Papers, UNL. A major figure on the American left, Louis Fraina was one of the founders of the American Communist Party in 1919. When he left the party, he reinvented himself as Lewis Corey and was hired by Johnson at *The Encyclopaedia of the Social Sciences*. In the early 1950s, Fraina taught at Antioch for a year. He died of a brain hemorrhage in September 1953. At the time of his death, he was working for the Butcher's Union. See also, Esther Corey, "Lewis Corey (Louis Corey), A Bibliography with Autobiographical Notes," *Labor History*, 4 (Spring 1963): 105ff.

12. Johnson, *Pioneer's Progress*, 310–12. Johnson may have concluded that Fraina/Corey honored his request not "to slap a little Communist color on [his] work," but Daniel Tompkins suggests otherwise: Daniel P. Tompkins, "Moses Finkelstein and the American Scene," in *Moses Finley and Politics*, ed. W. V. Harris (Boston, Mass.: Brill, 2013), 14–15.

13. Federal Bureau of Investigation, February 11, 1943. The document was primarily concerned about research going on at the New School about the Hitler Jugend. An unnamed source is quoted as saying that somebody was " 'directing a research project at the New School for Social Research on a comparison of the ideology and actual practice of the Hitler Youth Movement and the Boy Scouts of America,' " http://homepages.stmartin.edu/fac_dprice /foia.docs/soc1.gif.

14. Sally Bick, "Political Ironies: Hanns Eisler in Hollywood and Behind the Iron Curtain," *Acta Musicologica* 75, facs. 1 (2003): 65–84.

15. "Johnson Explains Actions on Eisler; Former Head of New School Says Musical Authority Denied Link to Reds," *New York Times*, September 26, 1947. See also William S. White, "Eisler Plea Made by Mrs. Roosevelt to Sumner Welles," *New York Times*, September 25, 1947.

16. Theodor W. Adorno and Hanns Eisler, *Composing for the Films* (New York: Oxford University Press, 1947).

17.   Alvin Johnson to August Heckscher, December 29, 1954, NSA.

18.   Alvin Johnson to Archibald MacLeish, April 29, 1940, Archibald MacLeish to Alvin John-son, May 2, 1940, Alvin Johnson to the American Consulate in Helsinki, Finland, April 17, 1940, box 1, Bertolt Brecht folder, Alvin Saunders Johnson Papers, Yale. The Consulate in Helsinki took its time. Month after month during the summer of 1940 Johnson received letters from Brecht's friends pleading with him to do what he could to expedite matters, among them was Ernestine Evans of Barnard, Vermont.

19.   In addition to the correspondence preserved in the Alvin Saunders Johnson Papers at Yale, see James K. Lyon, *Bertolt Brecht in America* (Princeton, N.J.: Princeton University Press, 1980), 23–25, 28. I want to thank Jonathan Kalb for leading me to the relevant scholarship on Brecht.

20.   Brecht's appearance before HUAC was filmed. Part of the interview was reproduced in a documentary about producing *Mother Courage and Her Children*, with Meryl Streep, dur-ing the Public Theater's summer program in Central Park in 2006: *Theater of War*, directed by John Walter, 2008.

21.   In West Germany, Piscator continued to train gifted actors and playwrights, a consider-able number of whom, like their counterparts in the United States, went on to have bril-liant careers in the theater and cinema in the postwar years, among them Peter Handke. For excellent discussions of the impact of Piscator's work and his relationship to the New School, see Peter M. Rutkoff and William B. Scott, "Politics on Stage. Piscator and the Dramatic Workshop," in *New School: A History of the New School for Social Research* (New York: The Free Press, 1986), 172–95 and John Willett, "Erwin Piscator, New York and The Dramatic Workshop, 1939–1951," *Performing Arts Journal* 2, no. 3 (Winter 1978): 3–16. Scholars often refer to the Studio Theater and Dramatic Workshop as the Dramatic Work-shop only.

22.   Alvin Johnson to August Hecksher, December 29, 1954, NSA.

23.   Johnson, *Pioneer's Progress*, 403; Johnson's correspondence with Piscator, box 5, Alvin Saun-ders Johnson Papers, Yale.

24.   Willett, "Erwin Piscator," 3.

25.   Alvin Johnson to U.S. State Department on behalf of Erwin Piscator, August 19, 1946, box 5, Alvin Saunders Johnson Papers, Yale.

26.   Alvin Johnson to Edith Brie [*sic*], undated draft probably written in 1952, box 1, Alvin Saun-ders Johnson Papers, Yale. Edith Bry was a painter, a New School Associate, and a member of the Associates' Art Committee, *New School Bulletin* (May 21, 1951).

27.   Rutkoff and Scott, *New School*, 226.

28.   Schrecker, *No Ivory Tower*, 5.

29.   Bryn Hovde to Agnes de Lima, October 27, 1947, NSA.

30.   Chesly Manly, "Red Frontiers List U.N. Aids as Speakers," *Chicago Tribune*, January 20, 1948. See Agnes de Lima's handwritten notes in the Red Scare File, NSA.

31.   State of New York, Legislative Document (1939), No. 98: Report of the Joint Legislative Committee to Investigate the Administration and Enforcement of the Law, Pursuant to Resolution of May 7, 1937, Extended to March 1, 1939 (Albany, N.Y.: J. B. Lyon Printers, 1939), 205.

32.   State of New York, Legislative Document (1939), 205–6.

33.   State of New York, Legislative Document (1939); de Lima's handwritten notes.

34. Alvin Johnson, *New School Bulletin* (April 25, 1949).

35. Alice Kessler-Harris, *A Difficult Woman: The Challenging Life and Times of Lillian Hellman* (New York: Bloomsbury, 2012), 247. The conference was organized by the National Council of Artists, Scientists and Professionals (NCASP).

36. "Red Visitors Cause Rumpus," *Life*, April 4, 1949.

37. The leadership at the New School may not have participated in the conference, but a number of artists and academics with strong ties to the institution helped sponsor the event, according to a report by HUAC, including Stella Adler, Aaron Copland, Henry W. L. Dana, Robert Gwathmey, Thomas Mann, and Bernard Stern. Mug shots of three of them were published in the *Life* article (Aaron Copland, Henry W. L. Dana, and Thomas Mann). Former students of the New School were mentioned as well, including Marlon Brando. The HUAC report quoted from Bryn Hovde's account of the international culture conference in Breslau (Wroclaw), Poland: "Every speech insulting the United States and glorifying the Soviets was wildly applauded. . . . After the first speech by the Soviet novelist, Fadiejew [*sic*], a speech which for the vituperation was never excelled and which set the tone for the Congress . . . I wound up with a strong statement of democracy as the only basis for peace. No speaker at the Congress got a colder reception. . . . Speaking was like throwing flat stones on an icy lake." *Review of the Scientific and Cultural Conference for World Peace*, prepared and released by the Committee on Un-American Activities U.S. House of Representatives, Washington, D.C., April 26, 1950, 8.

38. Alan Ryan, *John Dewey: And the High Tide of American Liberalism* (New York: W. W. Norton, 1995), 330–31.

39. In the years following World War II, the CIA had quietly begun to subsidize the Congress of Cultural Freedom's journal *Encounter* as part of a wider effort to give progressives a way to express their opposition to mainstream U.S. politics other than through Soviet-sponsored outlets.

40. For more on the counterconference, see Richard Gid Powers, *Not Without Honor: The History of American Anticommunism* (1995; New Haven, Conn.: Yale University Press, 1998), 208.

41. Sydney Gruson, "Breslau Speakers Score Communists: New York Educator Says U.S. Wants No Secret Police—End to Attacks Asked by Huxley," *New York Times*, August 28, 1948. Fadeyev's speech enraged many others, not only Hovde, including important members of the Communist Party such as Jerzy Borejsza, Poland's Minister of Culture and the national organizer of the conference. Borejsza had wanted to use the occasion to welcome his five hundred foreign guests, coming from forty-five different countries, to an open and cosmopolitan postwar Poland. Infuriated as well were celebrated members of the French Communist Party such as Pablo Picasso, who theatrically stormed out when Fadeyev denounced Jean-Paul Sartre in his speech, referring to the philosopher as "that hyena writing on a typewriter, that vulture armed with a fountain pen." See Marci Shore, *Caviar and Ashes: A Warsaw Generation's Life and Death in Marxism, 1918–1968* (New Haven, Conn.: Yale University Press, 2006), 272.

42. *The New York Times* covered the story in several articles: Gruson, "Breslau Speakers Score Communists"; Sidney Gruson, "MANIFESTO ADOPTED: 'Handful' in America and Europe Charged with Seeking War," *New York Times*, August 29, 1948; and Sidney Gruson, "Hovde Returns Home After Defending U.S.," *New York Times*, September 12, 1948. Part of the speech Hovde gave at the World Conference of Intellectuals in Wroclaw was published in *The Saturday Review*, November 13, 1948. The complete text is preserved in NSA.

43. Alvin Johnson to August Heckscher, December 29, 1954, NSA.

44. Benjamin Fine, "O'Dwyer Attacked in College Stand," *New York Times*, February 21, 1949; "Board Defies Mayor, Bars Politics in Choosing Queens College Head, *New York Times*, March 4, 1949. Hovde was attacked by New York's mayor William O'Dwyer, by the Knights of Columbus, and by the Brooklyn *Tablet*. See Daniel Soyer, " 'Support for the Failed Deal in the Nation; Abolish the Raw Deal in the City': The Liberal Party in 1949" (unpublished manuscript, 2012). Soyer cites materials preserved in the Records of the Liberal Party of New York, "1949 Queens College/Hovde, Bryn," scrapbooks 21 and 23, box 8, Manuscripts Division of the New York Public Library. The quote establishing the official position of ADA on communism comes from Clifton Brock, *Americans for Democratic Action* (New York: Public Affairs Press, 1962), 52. For an excellent analysis of how the left saw the ADA at the time, see Kessler-Harris, *A Difficult Woman*, 238–40.

45. Robert Gwathmey was interviewed in 1979 by Rutkoff and Scott, *New School*, 228n30.

46. Hans Simons, "Statement about Communists on the faculty and staff," June 9, 1952, NSA. Gwathmey was a member of the Communist Party at the time, not a "previous member." See Michael Kammen, *Robert Gwathmey: The Life and Art of a Passionate Observer* (Chapel Hill: University of North Carolina Press, 1999), 53.

47. FBI Office Memorandum, December 15, 1953, no. 100–42001, cited in Kammen, *Robert Gwathmey*, 108–109n34. According to Kammen, Gwathmey taught at the New School part time, in addition to teaching at Cooper Union, from the spring of 1947 to the spring of 1952—with the exception of the spring of 1950 when he went to France to give himself a break from surveillance. He taught at the New School again in 1969–70, the year after he had retired from Cooper Union.

48. Interview of Robert Gwathmey with Paul Cummings, March 1968, Archives of American Art, Smithsonian Institution.

49. The Editors, "A Word to Our Readers," *Dissent* 1, no. 1 (Winter 1954): 3–4.

50. "University Bans Lectures by Laski," *New York Times*, March 24, 1949.

51. Harold J. Laski, "Introduction to the Communist Manifesto," *The Communist Manifesto of Marx and Engels* (1948; New York: Pantheon Books, 1967), 84.

52. Hans Simons, *New School Bulletin* 7, no. 36 (May 8, 1950): 1.

53. The memorial took place on May 16, 1950. Agnes de Lima made summaries of the speeches, NSA.

54. "University Bans Lectures by Laski," *New York Times*, March 24, 1949.

55. Benjamin Fine, "Charges of Freedom Curbs Rising in Nation's Colleges," *New York Times*, May 29, 1949.

56. "Academic Freedom and National Security," *Bulletin of the American Association of University Professors* 42, no. 1 (1956): 63–64.

57. Sidney Hook and Ralph F Fuchs, "A Joint Statement on a Matter of Importance," *Bulletin of the American Association of University Professors* 42, no. 4 (1956): 692, 693.

58. Benjamin Fine, "Education in Review: College Heads Resent Implication of Loyalty Oaths, Assail House Survey of Textbooks." *New York Times*, June 19, 1949.

59. Russell Porter, "Colleges Vote Freedom Code Banning Reds from Faculties," *New York Times*, March 31, 1953.

60. Schrecker, *No Ivory Tower*, 113.

61. Benjamin Fine, "Educators Insist on Ouster of Reds: Professors Would Drop Party Members, Saying Academic Freedom Has Limits," *New York Times*, May 30, 1949.

62. Alexander Meiklejohn, "Should Communists Be Allowed to Teach? Yes, Says Professor Meiklejohn, Who Argues That Democracy Will Win the Competition of Ideas," *New York Times Magazine*, March 27, 1949, SM 10, 64–66. At around the same time that this article appeared, Meiklejohn founded the National Committee to Abolish the House Un-American Activities Committee, together with Corliss Lamont, the Reverend William Howard Melish, and others. See "Dr. Alexander Meiklejohn Dead; Champion of Academic Freedom: Ex-President of Amherst was 92—Philosopher Received Medal of Freedom in '63," *New York Times*, December 17, 1964.

63. Fine, "Charges of Freedom Curbs Rising in Nation's Colleges."

64. "College Trustees Here Honored on Fight for Academic Freedom," *Herald-Statesman*, March 24, 1952.

13. THE OROZCO MURAL

1. Alvin Johnson (unsigned), "Democratic Intervention," *New Republic* (September 30, 1916): 207–8. See Herbert Croly to Alvin Johnson, September 26, 1916, box 1, Alvin Johnson Papers, UNL, asking Johnson to write on the subject.

2. E. B. White, "I Paint What I See," *New Yorker*, May 20, 1933, 29.

3. Alvin Johnson, *Notes on the New School Murals* (New York: International Press), 12–13. The pamphlet was produced during the early 1940s, after the United States had entered the war, probably around 1942. NSA has preserved a copy.

4. Alma Reed, *Orozco* (New York: Oxford University Press, 1956), 214.

5. Edward Alden Jewell, "The Frescoes by Orozco: Series Done at The New School for Social Research," *New York Times*, January 25, 1931.

6. Letters to the Editor, *New York Times*, February 1, 1931.

7. Jay Hambidge, *The Elements of Dynamic Symmetry* (1919; New York: Dover Books, 1968), xi.

8. Lloyd Goodrich, recorded interview with Harlan B. Phillips (unpublished and undated). A copy of the transcript had been sent to Jonathan Fanton, president of the New School (1982–1999). Johnson gave his explanation for why he does not appear in Orozco's mural, the way he does in Thomas Hart Benton's, in a letter to the painter Edith Bry, a New School Associate and member of the Associate's Art Committee, most likely written in late 1952. The letter also predicted that the trustees would vote in favor of covering over part of the Orozco mural, which they did in March 1953. Alvin Johnson to Edith Brie, [*sic* Bry], draft box 1, Alvin Saunders Johnson Papers, Yale.

9. José Clemente Orozco, *An Autobiography*, trans. Robert C. Stephenson (1942; Mineola, N.Y.: Dover, 2001), 144.

10. Alvin Johnson, *Pioneer's Progress: An Autobiography* (1952; Lincoln: University of Nebraska Press, 1960), 331.

11. Reed, *Orozco*, 207.

12. Reed, *Orozco*, 212.

13. Alvin Johnson to Frank Rasky, November 15, 1949, NSA. Rasky had recently written "The New School: Academic Enfant Terrible," which appeared in the Canadian journal *Liberty*.

14. Alma Reed, "Statement to Artists Equity," April 3, 1951. It begins: "The following is my brief report on the matter of Orozco's frescoes in the New School for Social Research." A copy of this statement has been preserved in the NSA.

15. Draft of letter to Edith Brie [sic Bry], probably late 1952, box 1, Alvin Saunders Johnson Papers, Yale. This letter was probably written just before the board voted to cover the murals. In his letter, Johnson said that there were two, not three, great Mexican muralists, Orozco and Rivera. That he ignored Siqueiros may not have been incidental. In 1940 Siqueiros had been part of the Stalinist plot to murder Trotsky in Mexico. Three years earlier Johnson's good friend John Dewey had headed up the American Committee for the Defense of Leon Trotsky. See Alan Ryan, *John Dewey: And the High Tide of American Liberalism* (New York: W. W. Norton, 1995), 303ff.

16. Minutes of Board of Trustees' meetings, taken by Agnes de Lima, March 4, 1953, and March 30, 1953, NSA. The board voted to cover over the murals between those two meetings, probably on March 23.

17. Alfred D. Crimi to Camilo Egas, August 6, 1954, NSA.

18. Reed, *Orozco*, 213. The biography was published in 1956, but the words quoted here were stated in 1953.

19. *National Guardian*, New York Edition, March 30, 1953, copy in NSA.

20. Student Statement, May 1953, NSA.

21. "New School Keeps Red Mural Hidden: Curtain to Stay over 'Soviet' Part of Work by Orozco Despite Student Protest," *New York Times*, May 22, 1953; "Curtain (Iron) Stirs School Art Row: Stalin Mural Covered Up," *World Telegram and Sun*, May 21, 1953.

22. Irving Howe, "Does It Hurt When You Laugh?" *Dissent* (Winter 1954): 5.

23. Irwin Ross, "Hans Simons: An Exile Finds a Home," *New York Post*, May 15, 1955.

24. The New School's archives have no record of when the curtain came down.

25. Carol Vogel, "Thomas Hart Benton Masterwork Goes to Met," *New York Times*, December 12, 2012; Karen Rosenberg, "Thomas Hart Benton's 'America Today' Mural at Met," and "Brother, Can You Spare a Wall?" *New York Times*, October 2, 2014. Between 1984 and 1996 the mural hung in the corporation headquarters of Equitable Life (now AXA Equitable) at 787 Seventh Avenue; then in the lobby of their new headquarters at 1290 Avenue of the Americas. In 2012 AXA Equitable gave Benton's mural to the Metropolitan Museum of Art. Although the Met announced in 2014 that it was going to move the Benton Murals to the Met Breuer annex on 75th and Madison Avenue (see citation above), the murals have remained on view in the Met's American Wing, on Fifth Avenue. The annex has since closed.

26. See chapter 16 in this volume for the story of the acquisition by the New School of the Parsons School of Design.

27. Mayor Edward Koch to President Jonathan Fanton, September 10, 1987, NSA.

28. See, for example, Diane Miliotes, "The Murals at the New School for Social Research, 1930–1931," in *José Clemente Orozco in the United States, 1927–1934*, ed. Renato González and Diane Miliotes (New York: W. W. Norton and Hood Museum of Art, 2002), 118–41; Anna Indych-López, *Muralism Without Walls: Rivera, Orozco, and Siqueiros in the United States, 1927–1940* (Pittsburgh, Penn.: University of Pittsburgh Press, 2009); and Anna Indych-López, "Making Nueva York Moderna: Latin American Art, the International Avant-Gardes,

and the New School," in *Nueva York: 1613–1945*, ed. Edward J. Sullivan (New York: New York Historical Society/Sacala, 2010), 234–55.

14. "THE NEW SCHOOL REALLY ISN'T NEWS ANY LONGER"

1. Agnes de Lima to Hans Simons, June 30, 1952, NSA.
2. Agnes de Lima to Benjamin Fine, June 16, 1950, NSA. *The New York Times* had published an article about Hans Simons's appointment the day before: "Named to Succeed Hovde As New School President," *New York Times*, June 16, 1950.
3. "The New School President," *New York Times*, September 20, 1950; "New School Puts Stress on Citizen," *New York Times*, September 24, 1950.
4. "Refugee Scholars and The New School," 3, NSA. Agnes de Lima saved this anonymous, undated document.
5. The precise numbers of Hungarian scholars and Chinese students were published in a document prepared in 1956, probably by Agnes de Lima, titled "Some Basic Information about the New School for Social Research," NSA. In addition to Nobel Laureate Albert Szent-Györgyi, the Hungarian scholars included other well-known scientists, for example, Bela Berend, Erwin Doroghi, and Barna Horvath. See also Robert Heilbroner, "Education in a New Dimension: The New School and the Challenge of the New Age," designed by Irv Koon, NSA. The brochure was published on the occasion of the joint celebrations of the New School's fortieth and the University in Exile's twenty-fifth anniversaries.
6. Minutes of the Graduate Faculty, May 23, 1951, 2, NSA.
7. Unless otherwise noted, all quotes by Arthur Swift come from his 1952 unpublished report to the New School's Board of Trustees on the academic programs at the university, "The New School Study," NSA. Four years later Simons appointed Swift "vice president in charge of educational planning and dean of the School of Politics." Agnes de Lima, Press Release, March 12, 1956, NSA.
8. Alvin Johnson, *Pioneer's Progress: An Autobiography* (1952; Lincoln: University of Nebraska Press, 1960), 275.
9. Samuel Feinberg, "Business Scholarship Plan," *Women's Wear Daily*, October 11, 1957; Samuel Feinberg, "Employers Underwrite Culture," *Women's Wear Daily*, October 14, 1957.
10. Over the next fifty years the GF quite successfully resisted several attempts on the part of the central administration to diminish the degree of autonomy it had from the rest of the New School. By the late 1990s, however, the GF had begun making joint appointments with other units and playing a more active role in the academic life of the whole university.
11. Minutes of the Executive Faculty Meeting, February 18, 1953. NSA.
12. Alfred Schütz, "The Scope and Function of Philosophy within the Graduate Faculty," May 22, 1953, NSA.
13. For a moving tribute to Schütz's contributions to philosophy, see Hans Jonas, "Alfred Schutz 1899–1959," *Social Research* 26, no. 4 (1959): 471–74.
14. Schütz, "The Scope and Function of Philosophy," 6.

15. Johnson, *Pioneer's Progress*, 347 (cited by Schütz, "The Scope and Function of Philosophy," 7).

16. Schütz, "The Scope and Function of Philosophy," 3.

17. Minutes of the Graduate Faculty's Executive Faculty Meeting, January 13, 1954, NSA.

18. Minutes of the Graduate Faculty's Executive Faculty Meeting, November 3, 1954, NSA.

19. Anatole Broyard, *Kafka Was the Rage* (New York: Carol Southern Books, 1993), 15–16.

20. See Broyard, *Kafka Was the Rage*, 56–61, for a portrait of Meyer Schapiro teaching at the New School.

21. Agnes de Lima, Press Release, June 2, 1952, NSA.

22. Edwin Fancher, cited in Louis Menand, "It Took a Village," *New Yorker*, January 5, 2009, 39.

23. John Berman and Roberta Gratz, "Edwin Fancher: An Oral History," January 26, 2000, Greenwich Village Society for Historic Preservation. GVSHP archives are available online at gvshp.org/_gvshp/resources/index.htm.

24. Charles Lieber, Mill River, Mass., personal communication August 2010. Auden's famous lectures have been reconstructed in Arthur Kirsch, *Lectures on Shakespeare by W. H. Auden* (Princeton, N.J.: Princeton University Press, 2001).

25. Robert H. Knapp and Joseph J. Greenbaum, *The Younger American Scholar: His Collegiate Origins* (Chicago, Ill.: University of Chicago Press, 1953).

26. Irwin Ross, "Hans Simons: An Exile Finds a Home," *New York Post*, May 15, 1955.

27. Alvin Johnson to Hans Simons, February 25, 1953, NSA.

28. "School Expansion Aided by Wagner," *New York Times*, February 12, 1956.

29. Hans Kohn, cited in "The Nature of the New School: Opinions of Former Lecturers," NSA.

30. "Opinions of the Work of the Graduate Faculty," NSA.

31. The Graduate Faculty's Executive Faculty Minutes, October 23, 1956, NSA.

32. Short historical pieces were published in the *New School Bulletin* and in countless press releases throughout the anniversary year. As mentioned in the Prologue of this volume, in 1959 Alvin Johnson and Agnes de Lima were planning to write a history of the New School from an insider's perspective, but they never followed through. About a year after the anniversary, Clara Mayer discussed the possibility of writing a history of the New School's Continuing Education programs with a group of her colleagues: Carlos Gutierrez, "Exchange of ideas concerning the possible publication of a book about the New School's adult division," Minutes of a meeting on the subject, November 12, 1961, NSA.

33. "Anniversary Issue," *Social Research* 26, no. 2 (Summer 1959).

34. Robert Heilbroner, "Education in a New Dimension: The New School and the Challenge of the New Age," 1959, NSA.

35. Earl James McGrath, "The Graduate School and the Decline in Liberal Education," Special publication of Columbia Teacher's College, 1959, cited in Jürgen Herbst, "Liberal Education and the Graduate Schools: An Historical View of College Reform," *History of Education Quarterly* 2, no. 4 (December 1962): 244. For the opinion of a member of the Board of Trustees regarding McGrath's report, see Robert MacIver, "The Graduate Faculty: Retrospect and Prospect," *Social Research* 26, no. 2 (Summer 1959): 202–3. Although MacIver does not mention McGrath by name, the context is clear.

36. Informal minutes of special meeting of the Board of Trustees of the New School for Social Research, Monday, April 21, 1958, Board of Trustees Papers, NSA. I am grateful to then

President Bob Kerrey for having let me look at the Informal Minutes of the New School Board of Trustees between 1958 and 1963.

37. Among the letters from colleagues about the McGrath report that Staudinger received, are communications from: Arnold Brecht, Adolph Lowe, Carl Mayer, Hans Neisser, Alfred Schütz (émigrés); Saul Padover, Irvin Rock, and Howard White (American born). NSA has preserved these letters.

38. Carl Mayer to Hans Staudinger, July 21, 1958, NSA.

39. Hans Neisser to Hans Staudinger, July 28, 1958, NSA.

40. Hans Staudinger, "Statement Regarding the Graduate Faculty," dated September 18, 1958, but submitted with a cover note to Ralph Waker, Chairman of the Board by the Dean of the Graduate Faculty, September 17, 1958. Hans Staudinger to Hans Simons, October 1, 1958, NSA.

41. Programs of all the fortieth anniversary events have been preserved in NSA.

42. The Alexander Schneider String Quartet performed an all Handel concert to celebrate the twenty-fifth anniversary of the University in Exile on April 5, 1959, NSA.

43. Carl Sandburg, cited in Robert M. Friedburg, New School Press Release, April 6, 1959, NSA.

44. Alvin Johnson to Hans Staudinger, September 24, 1958, NSA.

45. Sanka Knox, "The New School to Show Murals: Cadoret Art to Be Unveiled Tomorrow to Mark Aid to France During War," *New York Times*, November 15, 1959.

46. Citation for Jacques Maritain on the occasion of receiving an Honorary Doctorate from the New School, November 16, 1959, and the gift on behalf of the French government of the Cadoret murals were printed in the "Program 1940–1960 The Unity of Scholarship: A French–American Commemoration," NSA.

47. Alvin Johnson, Report on the "Save the School" fund-raising, March 27, 1963, NSA.

15. "SAVE THE SCHOOL"

1. Henry David's books include *The History of the Haymarket Affair* (New York: Farrar and Rinehart, 1936); and Henry David and Harry Elmer Barnes, *The History of Western Civilization* (New York: Harcourt Brace, 1935). At the time of his appointment, David was editing an eight-volume series on the economic history of the United States.

2. Minutes of the Graduate Faculty of Political and Social Science Executive Faculty Meeting, September 30, 1959, NSA. The words spoken by Hans Simons and Henry David cited in the text are recorded in the minutes of the meeting.

3. New School for Social Research Budget 1960–61, 1–2, NSA.

4. Paul A. McGhee to Hans Simons, January 11, 1960, NSA.

5. "New School Gets Head, Economist Named as Acting President in Kaplan's Place," *New York Times*, October 7, 1960.

6. Albert W. Landa, 2007, personal communication.

7. "New School Gets Head"; *New School Bulletin* (October 11, 1960): 1. A summary of this turbulent period has been recorded in the New School's Progress Report for the Middle States Association of Colleges and Secondary Schools, May 1, 1961, NSA.

8. Alvin Johnson to Henry David, January 11, 1961, box 2, Alvin Saunders Johnson Papers, Yale.

9. Henry David, Introduction to first interim report to Middle States Committee, "Progress Report for the Middle States Association of Colleges and Secondary Schools: Submitted by New School for Social Research," May 1, 1961," 1. Finla G. Crawford responded on behalf the Middle States: "The New School for Social Research: Comments on 1961 Report," June 4, 1961, NSA.

10. Albert W. Landa, Office of Information, New School for Social Research, "Dr. Henry David Resigns as New School President," Press Release, March 25, 1963, NSA. A short newspaper article followed several days later: "New School Names M'Iver President," *New York Times*, April 1, 1963.

11. Minutes of the Executive Faculty Meeting of the Graduate Faculty, March 20, 1963, NSA.

12. Minutes of the General Meeting of the New School Faculty, April 5, 1963, NSA.

13. Agnes de Lima, Press Release, March 12, 1956, NSA.

14. Minutes of the General Meeting of the New School Faculty, June 1, 1961, 6–7, NSA.

15. Alvin Johnson, *Pioneer's Progress: An Autobiography* (1952; Lincoln: University of Nebraska Press, 1960), 282.

16. Alvin Johnson, Report on the "Save the School" Fund Raising, March 27, 1963, NSA.

17. Informal Minutes of the Board of Trustees, January 9, 1963, 12, NSA.

18. Alvin Johnson, fund-raising letter, March 11, 1963, sent to hundreds of friends of the New School as part of Johnson's "Save the School Campaign," NSA.

19. A summary of the decisions made in May 1962 was presented to the New School Board of Trustees in the Report of the Development Committee, submitted and discussed at the meeting of the Board of Trustees, January 9, 1963, Board of Trustees Papers, NSA.

20. I want to thank the archivists at NYU's Bobst Library for having done their best to help me find a record in NYU's archives of conversations between President James Hester and/or Dean Paul McGhee and trustees of the New School. They found nothing in the files made available to outside researchers.

21. Hans Staudinger, "Memo on the 1962–1963 Crisis in the New School," February 1963, NSA. Although the copy in the archives is a draft and is not addressed to Levin, Staudinger refers to such a memo in his letter of May 2, 1963, to Eva and Hans Simons, NSA.

22. Hans Staudinger to Nathan Levin, March 1, 1963, NSA. Enclosed with Staudinger's letter to Levin was a draft of a letter, addressed to David, that Johnson and the former dean had written with the hope of persuading the Board of Trustees to sign it. The letter asked for David's resignation. Johnson had also drafted another letter to David that he planned to send on his own to urge the beleaguered president to take the initiative himself. The handwritten draft that survives in the New School files is undated. It is unclear whether Johnson ever sent that second letter.

23. Nathan Levin to Joseph Halle Schaffner, May 10, 1963, NSA.

24. Hart, Schaffner & Marx was such a well-known firm that novelist Saul Bellow famously complained that Americans tended "to turn [Bernard] Malamud, [Philip] Roth and me into the Hart, Schaffner & Marx of American literature," which he found "ridiculous": cited in Sam Munsen, "The Jewish Saul Bellow," *Jewish Ideas Daily*, November 3, 2010. Schaffner's name appeared on the New School for Social Research's Advisory Committee beginning in the 1925–26 academic year: digitalarchives.library.newschool.edu/ index.php/Detail /objects/NS050101_ns1925fa.

25. Schaffner and Ruth Staudinger married on December 9, 1963, eight months after Schaffner made his $200,000 gift to the New School.

26. Joseph Halle Schaffner to the New School's Board of Trustees, March 7, 1963, NSA.

27. Alvin Johnson to Dr. and Mrs. Max Ascoli (telegram), March 6, 1963, box 205, Max Ascoli Papers, BU.

28. Alvin Johnson, March 11, 1963, on Graduate Faculty stationery, prepared for a mass mailing, NSA.

29. Informal and Abbreviated Minutes of Special Meeting of the Board, March 19, 1963, 10, NSA.

30. "New School Names M'Iver President," *New York Times*, April 1, 1963.

31. Alvin Johnson, "Report on the 'Save the School' Fund Raising," March 27, 1963, NSA. Johnson never sent this draft of the memo because, as Hans Staudinger explained in a letter to Eva and Hans Simons, May 2, 1963, NSA, "it would have deepened the rift in the Board if the memo (signed by A.J.) had been distributed." The one he sent two days later, however, was forceful as well (see note 32).

32. Alvin Johnson, "To the Members of the Board," March 29, 1963, NSA.

33. Howard White, cited in "Saluting the Graduate Faculty on Its Thirtieth Anniversary," in "From the 'University in Exile': Three Decades of Growth and Service." Special issue, *New School Bulletin* (April 1964): 2. The article was unsigned but probably was written by Albert Landa.

34. Lee Lorenz, *Lithopinion*, 7, no. 2–26 (Summer 1972): 76 (Publication of the Amalgamated Lithographers, Local No.1); see also Lee Lorenz, *New Yorker*, November 16, 1968, 193. In the cartoon published in *The New Yorker*, a wife seated on the living room couch complains bitterly to her husband who is looking at her impatiently from the other side of their room: " 'A course at the New School'—that's your answer to everything!"

35. Advertisement, *New Yorker*, December 1, 1962, 35.

16. THE "NEW" NEW SCHOOL

1. Press Release from the Office of Albert W. Landa, Director of Public Information, "Dr. John R. Everett Named President of New School for Social Research," October 19, 1964, NSA.

2. As Arthur Vidich tells the story, when Everett became the first chancellor of the recently consolidated City University of New York, with one exception, the presidents of the city's colleges banded together against him and effectively threw him out. Arthur Vidich, *With a Critical Eye: An Intellectual and His Time*, ed. Robert Jackall (Knoxville, Tenn.: New Found Press, 2009), 439. The president who remained faithful to Everett was Harold Gideonse, president of Brooklyn College, who went on to become Everett's chancellor at the New School.

3. Edward Fiske, "New School Facing Need to Rebuild with Approaching Change in Leaders," *New York Times*, May 13, 1982. Title for continuation of the article is "The New School, a Maverick, Gets Ready to Rebuild." During the early days of Everett's presidency, he received positive press for his ambitious building campaign. See, for example,

Murray Schumach, "$37 Million Expansion Planned by the New School," *New York Times*, December 12, 1968.

4. "A Home for the Graduate Faculty," *New School Bulletin* 25, no. 3 (October 2, 1967): 1.

5. Joseph Greenbaum, spring 2010 New York, personal interview. Unless otherwise noted, when I quote or paraphrase him, my source is this interview. Joseph Greenbaum died in 2011.

6. Edward Fiske, "New School Facing Need to Rebuild with Approaching Change in Leaders," *New York Times*, May 13, 1982.

7. James Miller, *"Democracy Is in the Streets": From Port Huron to the Siege of Chicago* (Cambridge, Mass.: Harvard University Press, 1994), 14, 15. By the time Miller published this book, he had joined the Graduate Faculty, as director of Liberal Studies and professor of Political Science.

8. John Everett, Speech to the New School's chapter of Students for a Democratic Society (SDS), April 13, 1967, NSA.

9. Dael Wolfle, "Beleaguered Presidents," *Science* 159 (March 22, 1968): 1309.

10. Stanley Diamond and Edward Nell, "A Special Supplement: The Old School at The New School," *New York Review of Books*, June 18, 1970, 38–43. Unless otherwise noted, the detailed description of the student strike at the New School comes from this article.

11. Douglas Robinson, "Townhouse Razed by Blast and Fire," *New York Times*, March 7, 1970. For a description of the relationship of the Weathermen to SDS, see Miller, *"Democracy Is in the Streets,"* 311.

12. "Chair Is Dedicated at New School," *New York Times*, February 17, 1965; Press Release from the Office of Albert W. Landa, February 16, 1965, NSA.

13. Alvin Johnson to Theodor Heuss, December 28, 1954; Arnold Brecht to Alvin Johnson, December 19, 1954, NSA.

14. Press Release from the Office of Albert W. Landa, February 16, 1965, about the creation of the Theodor Heuss Professor, February 16, 1965; Agnes de Lima, Press Release, June 20, 1958, about Theodor Heuss receiving an honorary doctorate from the New School, June 20, 1958, NSA.

15. Jürgen Habermas, "On the German-Jewish Heritage," Commencement Address at the New School for Social Research, June 4, 1980, on the occasion of receiving an honorary doctorate, *Telos* 44 (Summer 1980): 127. Other quotes by Habermas in this chapter come from this same commencement speech.

16. The names of these retired émigré colleagues appeared in the GF catalog in 1969–70: Arnold Brecht, Erich Hula, Alfred Kähler, Adolph Lowe, Carl Mayer, Julie Meyer, Hans Neisser, Richard Schüller, and Hans Staudinger.

17. Elisabeth Young-Bruehl, *Hannah Arendt: For Love of the World* (New Haven, Conn.: Yale University Press, 1982), 530n82. After Arendt died, Robert Heilbroner reported the same incident to Jerome Kohn, the philosopher's literary executor, identifying the émigré colleague who had supported the "bust" as Hans Jonas: Jerome Kohn, July 2011, personal communication.

18. Edward Nell to Judith Friedlander, July 3, 2011, email communication.

19. Hannah Arendt, *On Violence* (New York: Houghton Mifflin Harcourt, 1970); Hannah Arendt, "Reflections on Civil Disobedience," *New Yorker*, September 12, 1970, 70ff; Hannah Arendt, "Lying in Politics: Reflections on The Pentagon Papers," *New York*

Review of Books, November 18, 1971, http://www.nybooks.com/articles/1971/11/18/lying-in-politics-reflections-on-the-pentagon-pape/.

20. Hannah Arendt to Dany Cohn-Bendit, June 27, 1968, cited in Young-Bruehl, *Hannah Arendt*, 412. Cohen-Bendit reports that Arendt's letter never reached him. He only learned about it many years later, Claus Leggewie and Daniel Cohn-Bendit, "1968: Power to the Imagination," *New York Review of Books*, May 10, 2018, 6

21. Hannah Arendt, cited in Adelbert Reif, "Thoughts on Politics and Revolution: A Commentary," interview of Hannah Arendt, trans. Denver Lindley. The interview took place in 1970 and was republished in Hannah Arendt, *Crises of the Republic* (New York: Harcourt, Brace, 1972), 201.

22. Young-Bruehl, *Hannah Arendt*, 415.

23. Arendt, *On Violence*, 79, 80.

24. Arendt, cited in Reif, "Thoughts on Politics and Revolution," 207–8.

25. Arendt, cited in Reif, "Thoughts on Politics and Revolution," 203–4, 206.

26. Diamond and Nell, "A Special Supplement: The Old School at the New School," 42.

27. Arthur Vidich, *With a Critical Eye*, 446.

28. Robert Pollin, "Remembering Paul Sweezy," *CounterPunch*, March 6–7, 2004, a political newsletter edited by Alexander Cockburn and Jeffrey St. Clair, www.counterpunch.org/pollin 03062004.html.

29. Robert Pollin, summer 2010, personal interview. Unless otherwise noted, quotes from Pollin come from this interview. Pollin named a lecture hall at the Political Economic Research Center at the University of Massachusetts in memory of his New School professor David Gordon, the first director of the New School's Center for Economic Policy Analysis (CEPA). Founded in the mid-1990s, CEPA was renamed the Schwartz Center for Economic Policy Analysis in the early 2000s.

30. Immanuel Wallerstein, *The Modern World System I: Capitalist Agriculture and the Origins of the European World-Economy in the Sixteenth Century* (Berkeley: University of California Press, 1974).

31. Anwar Shaikh, "Marxist Theory of Value and the Transformation Problem," in *The Subtle Anatomy of Capitalism*, ed. Jesse Schwartz (Santa Monica, Calif.: Goodyear, 1977), 108–39; Anwar Shaikh, *Capitalism: Competition, Conflict, Crises* (New York: Oxford University Press, 2016).

32. Robert Pollin's most recent book is *Greening the Global Economy* (Cambridge, Mass.: MIT Press, 2015).

33. Jean Cohen, summer of 2012, personal interview. Unless otherwise noted, quotes from Cohen come from this interview.

34. Jean Cohen and Andrew Arato, *Civil Society and Political Theory* (Cambridge, Mass.: MIT Press, 1992).

35. "Critical Perspectives on the Social Sciences." Special issue, *Social Research* 38, no. 4 (Winter 1971).

36. Arien Mack, "Invisibility or Blindness? On Attention, the Unseen and the Seen," *Social Research* 83, no. 4 (Winter 2016): 801; Arien Mack and Irvin Rock, *Inattentional Blindness* (Cambridge, Mass.: MIT Press, 1998).

37. Gurwitsch's efforts to block the appointment of critical theorists, pragmatists, and analytical philosophers were well known. Joseph Greenbaum shared this anecdote with me.

38. Young-Bruehl, *Hannah Arendt*, 80.

39. Hannah Arendt to Richard Bernstein, October 31, 1972. Library of Congress Collection, Washington, D.C. and NSA. Thanks to Richard Bernstein and the Mellon Foundation, electronic copies of Arendt's papers at the Library of Congress are available in the New School's archives.

40. Allen Austill, Memo to the Executive Faculty of the Graduate Faculty, March 29, 1979, NSA.

41. Graduate Faculty Course Catalog, 1957–58, 2, digitalarchives.library.newschool.edu/index .php/Detail/objects/NS050101_gf1957ye. Although the 1957–58 catalog does not include Joseph Greenbaum's name, he is identified in the 1958–59 catalog as having joined the faculty the year before at the rank of associate professor.

42. Albert Landa, fall 2007, personal interview. Landa died in January 2008. Unless otherwise noted, the quotes from Landa come from this interview. I rely heavily on Landa's account of the purchase of the GF building in 1967. At the time of the purchase, Landa was vice president of the New School.

43. In addition to Albert Landa's observations, the sketch of Albert List draws on Elizabeth Neuffer, "Albert A. List, 86; Industrialist Who Supported Many Causes," *New York Times*, September 12, 1987.

44. Roberta Smith, "Vera G. List, 94, Is Dead; Philanthropist and Collector," *New York Times*, October 13, 2002.

45. "A Home for the Graduate Faculty," *New School Bulletin* (October 2, 1967): 1, 4; Arien Mack, personal communication.

46. Albert Landa, personal interview fall 2007. I have relied exclusively on Landa' account of the New School's acquisition of Parsons in 1970. At the time of the acquisition, Landa was serving as vice president of the New School.

47. William K. Stevens, "Merger Planned by Mills College," *New York Times*, September 3, 197.

17. THREE DOCTORAL PROGRAMS AT RISK

1. In 1969, four years before he died, Aron Gurwitsch fulfilled his promise to Alfred Schütz and acquired a copy of Husserl's unpublished writings for the New School. See Joseph G. Herzberg, "Husserl Archives Are Dedicated; German Was Father of Phenomenology, 'Meaning Me,' " *New York Times*, April 6, 1969.

2. Jonas did not hide his bitter feelings about the New School. He talked about it to many people, including the Hungarian dissident philosopher Agnes Heller, who met him in 1986 when she joined the faculty.

3. Editorial, *New York Times*, September 25, 1973, Gene I. Maeroff, "Respect History, Brandt Asserts, *New York Times*, September 26, 1973. See also the many documents preserved in the New School archives of the fortieth anniversary of the University in Exile, most important: "Remembering: Fortieth Anniversary Convocation, Graduate Faculty, New School for Social Research", September 25, 1973, NSA. Among the many obituaries, announcing Alvin Johnson's death, see: "Dr. Alvin Johnson of New School Dies," *New York Times*, June 9, 1971, which appeared on the front page of the newspaper.

4. Robert Heilbroner, Speech at Convocation of the Fortieth Anniversary of the University in Exile, cited in "Remembering: Fortieth Anniversary Convocation, no page numbers.

5. Richard Bernstein, cited in Judith Friedlander, "A Philosopher from New York," in *Pragmatism, Critique, Judgment: Essays for Richard Bernstein*, ed. Seyla Benhabib and Nancy Fraser (Cambridge, Mass.: MIT Press, 2004), 344.

6. Jonas described Philosophy at the New School as having been embattled even before the Commission for Higher Education sent its evaluation team to the New School. See "Der Zeitgeist kann mir den Buckel herunterrutschen," July 2, 1991, on the occasion of his receiving an honorary doctorate at the University of Konstantz.

7. Richard Rorty to Joseph Greenbaum, June 10, 1977; Joseph Greenbaum to Richard Rorty, June 17, 1977, NSA.

8. Alasdair MacIntyre to Joseph Greenbaum, June 16, 1977, NSA.

9. William V. D'Antonio, chairman of the Committee on Freedom of Research and Teaching at the American Sociological Association (COFRAT/ASA) and Professor of Sociology, University of Connecticut, to Arthur Vidich, April 19, 1978, NSA.

10. "New School for Social Research May Lose Three Doctoral Programs," *New York Times*, May 7, 1978.

11. John R. Everett to Gordon MacKay Ambach, May 12, 1978, NSA.

12. Executive Faculty of the Graduate Faculty to the New School's Board of Trustees, May 22, 1979, NSA.

13. Executive Faculty of the Graduate Faculty to President Everett, December 20, 1978, NSA.

14. Robert Heilbroner to President Everett and Members of the Graduate Faculty, "*The Future of the Graduate Faculty*," December 12, 1972, NSA.

15. Allen Austill to the Executive Faculty, March 29, 1979, NSA.

16. In his autobiography, Vidich spoke openly about the way his colleagues at the GF treated him as if he did not belong: Arthur Vidich, *With a Critical Eye: An Intellectual and His Time*, ed. Robert Jackall (Knoxville, Tenn.: New Found Press, 2009). In my interviews with members of the faculty who knew Vidich, a number of them confirmed that he did not fit in.

17. Arthur Vidich, Chairman of the Department of Sociology to the Executive Faculty, April 3, 1979, NSA.

18. Vidich, *With a Critical Eye*, 395–96.

19. Vidich, *With a Critical Eye*, 450; Peter L. Berger, *Adventures of an Accidental Sociologist: How to Explain the World Without Becoming a Bore* (Amherst, N.Y.: Prometheus Books, 2011), 104.

20. Berger, *Adventures of an Accidental Sociologist*, 81–82. Peter L. Berger and Thomas Luckmann, *The Social Construction of Reality: A Treatise in the Sociology of Knowledge* (New York: Anchor Books, 1966). Berger and Luckmann's book came out the year after Luckmann left the Graduate Faculty.

21. New York State's Commission for Higher Education's Rating Committee for the GF's Department of Sociology, cited in Vidich, *With a Critical Eye*, 455.

22. Seven years later Vidich and Lyman offered a pointed "critique of the discipline of sociology born directly from the experience of the external review of 1978." Arthur Vidich and Stanley Lyman, *American Sociology: Worldly Rejections of Religion and Their Directions* (New Haven, Conn.: Yale University Press, 1985), 462.

23. David Gordon and Rayna Rapp, "A Proposal for Reconstitution," April 1979, NSA.

24. Allen Austill to the Executive Faculty of the Graduate Faculty, May 10, 1979, NSA.

25. The Executive and Budget Committee of the Graduate Faculty (the committee of department chairs) to H. Loeb, Chairman and Members of the Board of Trustees, June 6, 1979, NSA.

26. Alasdair MacIntyre drafted the "Report to the Chairpersons of the Graduate Faculty of the New School for Social Research" in June 1979. Michael Walzer and Sheldon Wolin submitted additional reports. The one dated June 19, 1979, was addressed specifically to Arien Mack.

27. Allen Austill to the Executive Faculty of the Graduate Faculty, October 31, 1979.

28. F. Champion Ward (chairman) et al., "A Distinctive Future for The Graduate Faculty of Political and Social Science," May 1980, NSA. The other authors were Alan Gerwith, Professor of Philosophy, University of Chicago; Donald Levine, Professor of Sociology, University of Chicago; and James Tobin, Professor of Economics, Yale University.

18. REBUILDING THE GRADUATE FACULTY

1. Edward B. Fiske, "New School Facing Need to Rebuild with Approaching Change in Leaders," *New York Times*, May 13, 1982.

2. The membership of the Enabling Committee changed over the years. In the early days, it consisted of the following outside consultants: philosopher Richard Rorty (Princeton), historian Carl Schorske (New York Institute for the Humanities), political theorist Michael Walzer (Institute of Advanced Studies), psychologist George Miller (Princeton), and sociologist Robert Merton (Columbia University). Committee members from the Graduate Faculty were anthropologist Rayna Raap, economist Robert Heilbroner, philosopher Reiner Schürmann, and psychologists Leon Festinger and Arien Mack. After psychologist Jerome Bruner joined the faculty in 1981, he joined the committee as well. This list was printed in *The New School Observer*, November 1982.

3. F. Champion Ward et al., "A Distinctive Future for The Graduate Faculty of Political and Social Science," May 1980, NSA. This was later referred to as the Ward Report.

4. F. C. Ward to John R. Everett, "A Memorandum: A Revised Plan for Funding the Redevelopment of the Graduate Faculty over the Next Five Years," March 23, 1981, NSA.

5. Janet Hook, "Amid Hard Times and 'Intellectual Crisis,' New School Bolsters Its Graduate Division; New York's 'University in Exile' is recruiting scholars to flesh out depleted faculty ranks," *Chronicle of Higher Education*, April 2, 1981.

6. Jonathan Fanton, "Robert Lovett: The War Years" (PhD diss., Yale University, 1978).

7. Jonathan Fanton, summer 2008, personal interview. Unless otherwise noted, biographical information and quotes come from this interview.

8. Hanna Gray, cited in Gene I. Maeroff, "University of Chicago Official to Be the New School's Head," *New York Times*, May 23, 1982. Fanton had also served as Gray's associate provost when she was provost at Yale.

9. Jonathan Fanton, *The University and Civil Society* (New York: The New School for Social Research, 1995), 2.

10. Fanton, *The University and Civil Society*, 6.

11. German historian Hajo Holborn came to the United States in 1934 with the help of Edward R. Murrow, secretary of the Emergency Committee for the Relief of Displaced Foreign Scholars. Hanna Gray, February 14, 2012, personal communication.

12. Fanton, *The University and Civil Society*, 20.

13. After Fanton stepped down, the New School started hiring faculty with dual affiliations between the GF and other divisions as well.

14. Of particular interest in recent years is the revival of Parsons in Paris, which had languishd after Parsons joined the New School. Albert Landa's efforts to create a presence for Parsons in Los Angeles as well has not been revived.

15. Eyal Press, "Nightmare on Twelfth Street, *Lingua Franca* 8, no. 5 (August 1997): 34–44; "A Haven for Oppressed Scholars Finds Itself Accused of Oppression," *Chronicle of Higher Education*, July 11, 1997.

16. During the student strike in the spring of 1997, I was in my fourth year as dean of the Graduate Faculty. Having given a course in the Women and Gender Studies program a few years earlier, I knew from experience what other colleagues had told me: The program was in serious academic difficulty. With the hope of offering support to the embattled MA program, I enthusiastically welcomed the idea in 1995 of offering M. Jacqui Alexander a two-year visiting joint appointment between Eugene Lang College and the GF's master's program. After leaving the New School, Alexander spent the 1997–98 academic year on a prestigious Guggenheim research fellowship and then joined the faculty of Connecticut College, where she remained for several years. After the strike ended in 1997, I made the controversial decision to close down temporarily the Women and Gender Studies program until the university could rebuild and subsidize it properly.

17. See chapter 19 for a detailed discussion of Jonathan Fanton's efforts to renew the New School's legacy as a champion of academic and artistic freedom on the national stage and the rights of persecuted intellectuals in Europe.

18. Soon after Jonathan Fanton became president, he invited Strachan Donnelly to join the Board of Trustees. Before Fanton came to the New School, Donnelley had taught philosophy in the Seminar College. In 1969, he contributed generously to the founding of the Hastings Center Institute of Bioethics, which became Hans Jonas's academic home after the German philosopher retired from the New School. From 1996 to 1999, Donnelley served as the institute's president. He died in 2008. Other generous GF alumni during the Fanton years included Alice Ginnott-Cohn, Robert Heilbroner, Edith Kurzweil, Robert Pollin, and Frank Roosevelt.

19. Fanton met Joseph Califano in 1977 through Yale's president Kingman Brewster. After President Jimmy Carter appointed Califano secretary of Health, Education and Welfare, the new secretary asked Brewster to "lend" him a member of his administrative staff for a few months to help him recruit and build a capable team to run his office in Washington. Brewster sent Fanton. The two men hit it off and became lifelong friends. In later years, Fanton thanked Califano for having shown him "how to be compassionate and tough, fair and demanding, romantic and practical in fruitful tension." Fanton, *The University and Civil Society*, 8.

20. Joseph A. Califano Jr., *Inside a Public and Private Life* (New York: Public Affairs, 2004), 396–97.

21. Enid Nemy, "Dorothy H. Hirshon, 89, Dies; Socialite and Philanthropist," *New York Times*, January 31, 1998. For a vivid portrait of Hirshon, see Sally Bedell Smith, *In All His Glory: The Life of William S. Paley* (New York: Simon and Shuster, 1990).

22. Alvin Johnson to Dorothy Hirshon, January 19, 1959, NSA.

23. Alvin Johnson to Leo Heimerdinger, December 30, 1952, NSA. The people named in this letter as anti-Semites included some of the most generous donors to the New School in 1919. In addition to Mrs. Willard Straight, who gave $100,000, Mrs. Walton Martin, formerly Mrs. Victor (Charlotte) Sorchan, gave $50,000, the two largest gifts.

24. Not all the major donors in Fanton's period were of Jewish origin. There were important exceptions, such as Robert Milano, after whom the New School named its Graduate School of Management and Urban Planning. See Saxon Wolfgang, "Robert J. Milano, 87, Self-Made Man," *New York Times*, February 3, 2000.

25. See Appendix D for additional biographical details about Henry Arnhold, Walter Eberstadt, and Michael Gellert.

26. Ira Katznelson, fall 2011, personal interview. Unless otherwise indicated, quotes come from this interview.

27. Ira Katznelson, *Liberalism's Crooked Circle: Letters to Adam Michnik* (Princeton, N.J.: Princeton University Press, 1996), ix, xv–xvi.

28. Early works by Ira Katznelson include *Black Men, White Cities; Race, Politics, and Migration in the United States, 1900–30 and Britain, 1948–60* (Oxford: Oxford University Press, 1973); with Mark Kesselman and Alan Draper, *The Politics of Power: A Critical Introduction to Government* (New York: Liveright, 1975); *City Trenches: Urban Politics and the Patterning of Class in the United States* (New York: Pantheon Press, 1981).

29. Summary based on Ward et al., "A Distinctive Future," 18.

30. Ward et al., "A Distinctive Future," 3, 4.

31. For a description of Hobsbawm's time at the New School, see Eric Hobsbawm, *Interesting Times: A Twentieth Century Life* (New York: The New Press, 2005), 299–300.

32. Among the Heuss Professors who came to the New School during Katznelson's deanship, was the critical theorist Albrecht Wellmer (fall of 1985), who had also taught at the New School in the 1970s and early 1980s.

33. In addition to the Heuss Professors, a number of whom returned on other arrangements as well, the distinguished group of international faculty who taught on a part-time basis at the Graduate Faculty, during the Fanton years, included economist John Eatwell, historians Perry Anderson,* Robin Blackburn,* Pierre Birnbaum, and Eric Hobsbawm*; philosophers Jacques Derrida and Yirmiyahu Yovel*; political scientists Sergio Aguayo and Shlomo Avinieri; psychologists Shlomo Breznitz* and Serge Moscovici*; sociologists, Janos Kis, Ernesto LaClau, and Claus Offe; and feminist theorists Chantal Mouffe and Renata Solecl. (Those with an * next to their names became regular part-time members of the faculty, teaching one semester every year.) Some of these scholars arrived after Katznelson had stepped down but while Fanton was still president. Serge Moscovici started teaching at the New School in the late 1970s. Claus Offe also served as a Heuss Professor. The British economist John Eatwell taught full-time for several years.

34. In the late 1970s, Anthropology hired the Latin Americanist William Roseberry, whose work on coffee-growing peasants used the same kind of historical analysis that others on the committee used as well. Then after Katznelson became dean, the department hired Talal Assad, a widely recognized scholar of colonialism and Islam. In Economics Robert Heilbroner, John Eatwell and, after 1991, the department's newly appointed economist and economic historian William Milberg all contributed to Historical Studies.

35. Reiner Schürmann, *Les Origines* (Paris: Fayard, 1976).
36. "Self-Study Report of the New School for Social Research, Middle States Association of Colleges and Schools," January 1991, 34–36, NSA.
37. Deirdre Carmody, "New School Graduate Unit Rebounds," *New York Times*, July 15, 1987. All quotes and paraphrases in this section come from this article.
38. Charles Tilly resigned from the New School in 1996, after having a falling out with the administration. See Bruce M. Stave, "A Conversation with Charles Tilly," *Journal of Urban History*, 24, no. 2 (January 1998): 184–225. Tilly spent the last twelve years of his life teaching at Columbia University. "Charles Tilly 78, Writer and a Social Scientist Is Dead," *New York Times*, May 2, 2008.
39. Aristide Zolberg, fall 2008, personal interview.
40. By 1987, the GF's budget had grown by $1.3 million since 1982–83 (adjusted for inflation) and now stood at $6.8 million, NSA.
41. The numbers Carmody published are confusing when compared to the official information provided in the 1991 "Self-Study Report of the New School for Social Research," 45.

GRADUATE FACULTY: ENROLLMENT TRENDS (HEAD COUNT), FALL TERM: 1982–1990

Program	1982	1983	1984	1985	1986	1987	1988	1989	1990
Anthropology	120	99	61	71	70	61	62	46	39
Economics	294	256	229	150	117	121	138	133	97
Philosophy	22	30	26	33	35	47	51	68	62
Political Science	66	89	79	63	61	60	73	89	69
Psychology	488	432	383	368	324	305	279	252	225
Sociology	33	30	44	29	42	54	62	72	69
Historical Studies	0	0	0	0	0	2	7	11	14
Liberal Studies (MA only)	65	49	53	39	43	32	41	29	26
Total Degree	1,088	985	875	753	692	682	713	700	591
Total Non-Degree	115	85	113	123	113	87	51	31	74
Grand Total	1,203	1,070	988	876	805	769	764	731	665

42. By 1987, many academic institutions with whom the New School was competing were only accepting students into their PhD programs with full funding. The GF that year was offering financial aid to 22 percent of its students, up from 13 percent in 1982–83, but it only had thirteen Prize Fellowships (tuition + stipend) and five Dean's Fellowships (tuition) to distribute among the six departments, something it did unevenly, favoring the newly rebuilt departments: "Self-Study Report of the New School for Social Research," 47. Charles Tilly's Center for Social Change had additional funding for students as did Aristide Zolberg, with funding from a grant he had for doing research on refugees. In Psychology, too, a few members of the department had grants that provided funding for students, but not enough to be competitive with other universities. By 1990–91, 31 percent of the student body was on financial aid and it was offering twenty-four Prize Fellowships and twenty-one Dean's Fellowships. Between 1986–87 and 1990–91, however, the overall enrollment of degree

students dropped from 692 to 591, which forced the New School to increase the cost of tuition: "The most serious consequence of the enrollment shortfall has been the necessity to raise tuition several points higher than we planned. By 1990–1991, we had planned to normalize tuition increases at 1 to 1.5 points above inflation. Instead, the 1990–91 tuition increase for degree students was 9.25 percent, or more than four points above inflation": "Self-Study Report of the New School for Social Research," 14.

43. Donald J. Nolan, cited in Deirdre Carmody, "New School Graduate Unit Rebounds," *New York Times*, July 15, 1987.

44. See the chart in note 41. Of the 682 students enrolled for a graduate degree in the fall of 1987, 305 of them were in Psychology, the vast majority specializing in the clinical track. The next highest was Economics with 121, followed by Anthropology with 61 and Political Science with 60. Sociology with 54 and Philosophy with 47.

19. REKINDLING THE SPIRIT

1. Jonathan Fanton, summer 2008, personal interview.

2. See chapter 14, notes 4 and 5.

3. As noted in chapter 18, the Seminar College became Eugene Lang College during Fanton's presidency. It was renamed in 1985.

4. Jonathan Fanton, cited in Ira Katznelson, "Report of the Committee on Freedom of Expression," August, 1986 (draft), 1, NSA.

5. This and all other quotes from the report are from Katznelson, "Report of the Committee on Freedom of Expression," 6–9.

6. Jonathan F. Fanton, *The University and Civil Society* (New York: The New School for Social Research, 1995), 121.

7. Steven Holmes, "Debating Art: Censorship or Protest?" *New York Times*, December 6, 1989.

8. Jonathan F. Fanton, "The Matsunaga Exhibit and Freedom of Expression," November 1989 (letter to the University Community,), cited in Fanton, *The University and Civil Society*, 105–6.

9. Jonathan Fanton, cited in Allan Parachini, "Lawsuit Filed Over Pledge in NEA Grants: Funding: A New York School calls anti-obscenity language a restraint on artistic freedom of expression. Litigation adds a new dimension to controversy," *Los Angeles Times*, May 24, 1990.

10. There is a vast literature on the Helms Amendment. See, for example, Richard Bolton, ed., *Culture Wars* (New York: The New Press, 1992); and New School's sociologist Vera L. Zolberg, "Censorship in the United States: Politics, Morality, and the Arts," in *Social Problems*, ed. Craig Calhoun and George Ritzer (New York: McGraw-Hill, 1993), 828–41. Five months after Christina Orr-Cahill, director of the Corcoran Gallery of Art, canceled the Mapplethorpe show, she was fired. The next director was David C. Levy, founding dean of Parsons School of Design at the New School in 1970, whom Fanton had promoted to chancellor of the arts in 1989. In the article announcing Levy's appointment as director of the Corcoran, the *Washington Post* described him as an art historian, photographer, and jazz saxophone player in the band of painter Larry Rivers. "Corcoran to Name Director" *Washington Post*, November 19, 1990.

11. Holmes, "Debating Art: Censorship or Protest?"

12. Fanton, "The Matsunaga Exhibit and Freedom of Expression," 110.

13. The New School had applied to the NEA for help covering the costs of hiring sculptor Martin Puryear and landscape architect Michael Van Valkenburgh.

14. The Helms Amendment to Public Law 101–121 gave the National Endowment for the Arts the authority to withhold federal funding from artists whose work the agency deemed obscene. Fanton discussed his concerns about the amendment to the New School community right after it passed. Fanton, *The University and Civil Society*, 159–60.

15. New School v. Frohnmayer, No. 90–3510, S.D.N.Y. (1990).

16. Allan Parachini, "Lawsuit Filed Over Pledge in NEA Grants: Funding: A New York School calls anti-obscenity language a restraint on artistic freedom of expression; Litigation adds a new dimension to the controversy," *Los Angeles Times*, May 24, 1990. The newspaper article covered the story at length, noting that a branch of Parsons School of Design, the Otis/Parsons Art Institute, was located in Los Angeles. It also quoted extensively from Fanton's statement, Jonathan F. Fanton, "Saying No to the Obscenity Condition," reprinted in full in Fanton, *The University and Civil Society*, 159–65.

17. Fanton, "Saying No to the Obscenity Condition," 160, 161.

18. Floyd Abrams, cited in William H. Honan, "Arts Agency Voids Pledge on Obscenity," *New York Times*, February 21, 1991.

19. The NEA settled with the New School after the agency lost its case against the two artistic institutions in California. NEA's defeat in California led Congress to drop the obscenity clause from the 1991 appropriations bill. Although the New School never got to court, it rightly claims credit for having taken the lead in the case. Thanks to Floyd Abrams, the New School provided the legal arguments that helped win the court cases for the Bella Lewitzky Dance Foundation and the Newport Harbor Art Museum. The Judge in the U.S. District Court for the Central District of California was John G. Davies.

20. Michael Wingfield Walker, "Artistic Freedom v. Censorship: The Aftermath of the NEA's New Funding Restrictions," *Washington University Law Review* 71, no. 3 (January 1993): 951.

21. Tony Judt, "Three More Memoirs," *New York Review of Books*, February 25, 2010, 19. Reprinted in Tony Judt, *Memory Chalet* (New York: Penguin Books, 2010).

22. Influenced by William Coughlin, the legendary Presbyterian minister who inspired a whole generation of students at Yale, Fanton took part in weekend freedom rides to the East Shore of Maryland where he joined black civil rights activists affiliated with churches in the area and marched with them into segregated restaurants and demanded to be served. During the years he was doing administrative work at Yale, Fanton ran a tutoring program for African American teenagers in local high schools (Ulysses S. Grant Program). He also created a Transitional Year program, which identified very bright African American students from poor high schools and gave them a postgraduate year at Yale. Finally, he worked with the Upward Bound and Intensive Studies programs that Yale, Columbia, and Harvard had organized together to offer students at historically black colleges opportunities to spend summers at these Ivy League institutions to help prepare them for admission to the top graduate schools.

23. Jeffrey Goldfarb, personal interview, spring 2011. Unless otherwise noted, in addition to my interview with Jeffrey Goldfarb, I have relied on personal interviews with Jonathan Fanton, summer 2008, Ira Katznelson, fall 2011 and Andrew Arato, fall 2012 for reconstructing the

early conversations these colleagues had about renewing the GF's legacy around the dissident movements in East and Central Europe. For my descriptions of the fiftieth anniversary celebrations of the University in Exile that took place in 1984 in New York, Berlin and Warsaw, I have also relied on: William G. Blair, "Drama Marks 50 Years of University in Exile," *New York Times*, April 26, 1984, Michael Kaufman, "Pole Without Honor in Own Country Is Honored," *New York Times*, December 12, 1984, Jeffrey Goldfarb's *After the Fall* (New York: Basic Books, 1992), Adam Michnik, winter 2007, Princeton, N.J., personal interview, and Ira Kaztznelson, "Reflections on the New School's Founding Moments, 1919 and 1933," *Social Research* 76, no. 2 (Summer 2009): 396–97.

24. Arato's first articles on Michnik were written in the early 1980s and published in *Telos*. They were later collected in Andrew Arato, *From Neo-Marxism to Democratic Theory: Essays on the Critical Theory of Soviet-Type Societies* (Armonk, N.Y.: M. E. Sharpe, 1993).

25. See, for example, Adam Michnik's widely cited article, "Une stratégie pour l'opposition polonaise," in *La Pologne en dissidence*, ed. Z. Erard and G. M. Zygier (Paris: François Maspéro, 1978), 99–111; and Adam Michnik, *L'Eglise et la gauche. Le Dialogue polonais*, trans. Agnès Sonimski and Constantin Jelenski (Paris: Le Seuil, 1979).

26. Katznelson, "Reflections on the New School's Founding Moments, 1919 and 1933," 397.

27. Interview of Adam Michnik with Dany Cohn-Bendit, in Warsaw, 1987. The interview was first published in French by Cohn-Bendit; then in English translation, "Anti-Authoritarian Revolt: A Conversation with Cohn-Bendit, " in Adam Michnik, *Letters from Freedom: Post-Cold War Realities and Perspectives*, ed. Irena Grudzinska Gross (Berkeley: University of California Press, 1998), 48, 66, 67.

28. Robert Heilbroner, cited in William G. Blair, "Drama Marks 50 Years of University in Exile."

29. Jonathan Fanton, "Opening Remarks," Sixth Annual Democracy Seminars Conference, May 27, 1995, Mała Wieś, near Warsaw, cited in Elzbieta Matynia, ed. *Grappling with Democracy: Deliberations on Post-Communist Societies 1990–1995* (Prague: SLON, 1996), 13. Jonathan Fanton reported that ABC Television lit up Edward Lipiński's living room, but Jeffrey Goldfarb claimed it was a Scandinavian company: http://www.publicseminar.org/2018/05/the-democracy-seminar-then-and-now/.

30. Jeffrey Goldfarb, *After the Fall*, 21.

31. Born in 1934, Jacek Kuroń is remembered as the "godfather of the Polish opposition." Although he did not become president or prime minister of Poland, among Polish dissidents he had the stature of Valclav Havel in Czechoslovakia. See Michael Kaufman, "Jacek Kuroń, of Solidarity, Dies at 70," *New York Times*, June 18, 2004. Bronislaw Geremek, a distinguished medieval historian of France, served as Poland's foreign minister (1997–2000). See Nicholas Kulish, "Bronislaw Geremek, 76 Dies; Helped End Communist Control of Poland, *New York Times*, July 14, 2008.

32. Elzbieta Matynia, "Introduction," in *An Uncanny Era: Conversations Between Václav Havel & Adam Michnik*, ed. and trans. Elzbieta Matynia (New Haven, Conn.: Yale, 2014), 216n7.

33. Michnik cited in Michael Kaufman, "Pole Without Honor in Own Country Is Honored," The New School's citation for Michnik was also cited in this same article.

34. Interview of Adam Michnik with Dany Cohn-Bendit, 54, 55.

35. Adam Michnik, personal interview.

36. Matynia, *An Uncanny Era*.

37. Jerzy Szacki, spring 2007, Warsaw, Poland, personal interview; Michnik, personal interview.

38. On Jerzy Sazcki see Matynia, *Grappling with Democracy*, 13. Szacki has written on social thought and the history of ideas. Two of his books have been published in English: *History of Sociological Thought* (Westport, Conn.: Greenwood Press, 1980) and *Liberation after Communism* (Budapest: Central European University, 1993). See also Jerzy Szacki, "Polish Democracy: Dreams and Reality," *Social Research* 58, no. 4 (Winter 1991): 711–22.

39. Marcin Krol, April 2007, Warsaw, Poland, personal interview. To understand the ideological differences between Michnik and Krol, compare articles each of them published before 1989 in their underground journals *Krytika* and *Res Publica*.

40. For a record of what went on during the Democracy Seminars before 1989, see Matynia, *Grappling with Democracy*, Introduction and Prologue.

41. "Central and East European Social Research," Parts 1 & 2. Special issue, *Social Research* 55 (Spring/Summer 1988). See, in particular, Timothy Garton Ash, "An Introduction to Special Issue," Part 1, 5–12. Arien Mack, winter 2018, personal interview.

42. Stasi Report on Arien Mack's visit to Wolfgang Templin's home in East Berlin, July 3, 1987: Stasi-Akte, "Verräter, [Erich] Honecker reist nach Bonn," in "Bürgerrechtler Dokumente einer Verfolgung, Teil." Special issue, *Der Spiegel* 3 (January 1993): 4, 79.

43. Matynia, *Grappling with Democracy*, 16. Mack, personal interview.

44. Democracy Seminar groups were established in Armenia (Yerevan), Bulgaria (Sofia), Czechoslovakia (Prague and Bratislava), Estonia (Tallin), Hungary (Budapest), Latvia (Riga), Lithuania (Vilnius), Poland (Warsaw), Rumania (Bucharest and Cluj), Ukraine (Kiev and Lviv), U.S.A. (New York), and in former Yugoslavia (Belgrade). The groups in Prague and Bratislava were both created before 1993 and the breakup of Czechoslovakia into the Czech Republic and Slovakia. The Belgrade seminar was formed in 1990 just before war divided that country.

45. The Democracy Seminars after 1989 regularly included colleagues from the New School and scholars from outside the region, including Israeli political scientist Shlomo Avineri, of Polish origin, and sociologist Claus Offe and legal theorist Ulrich Preuss, both from Germany. The first seminar took place in Budapest in 1990, and seminars were held in other cities/countries over the next five years.

46. By 2014 the Journal Donation project had reached 246 libraries in twenty-five countries. In the early days, journal subscriptions were totally free. Participating libraries now pay a reduced fee for each subscription. In 2017, its final year of operation, two hundred fifty publishers were participating in the program, and the value of the journals distributed since 1990 came to $14 million. In addition to Soros and the Andrew Mellon Foundation, which helped launch the project in 1990, the Journal Donation project has received funding from four other foundations, including the Ford and Eurasia Foundations. Mack, personal interview.

47. Elzbieta Matynia, "Sociology and Theater: A Sociological Study of Political Theater in Inter-War Poland, 1918–1939" (PhD diss., defended at the University of Warsaw with distinction, 1980).

48. Jeffrey Goldfarb, personal interview.

49. Elzbieta Matynia, spring 2009, personal interview.

50. See, for example, Matynia, *Grappling with Democracy*; Elzbieta Matynia, *Performative Democracy* (New York: Routledge, 2009); and Matynia, *An Uncanny Era*.

51. Ira Katznelson, Commencement Address at the New School, May 12, 1994, NSA.

EPILOGUE: EXTENDING THE LEGACY

1.   Michael Ignatieff, "The Role of Universities in an Era of Authoritarianism," *University World News*, April 13, 2018. Ignatieff became president of the Central European University (CEU) in 2016.

2.   János Kis, *Constitutional Democracy* (Budapest: CEU Press, 2003); János Kis, *Politics as a Moral Problem* (Budapest: CEU Press, 2009).

3.   Founded in Minsk in 1992 under the direction of Anatoly Mikhailov, the European Humanities University was exiled in 2004 and reestablished itself in Vilnius, Lithuania, in 2005. When it was forced out of Belarus, Jonathan Fanton, president of the MacArthur Foundation at the time, supported its efforts to open a university in exile.

4.   See Prologue in this volume.

5.   Ira Katznelson, "Aristide R. Zolberg, 1931–2013," *Social Research* 80, no. 1 (Spring 2013): xx.

6.   Unless otherwise noted, the biographical sketch of Aristide Zolberg comes from a personal interview, fall 2008.

7.   See, for example, Aristide R. Zolberg, Astri Suhrke, Sergio Aguayo, *Escape from Violence: Conflict and the Refugee Crisis in the Developing World* (Oxford: Oxford University Press, 1989); Aristide R. Zolberg, *A Nation by Design* (Cambridge: Harvard University Press, 2008).

8.   T. Alexander Aleinikoff served as Deputy High Commissioner for Refugees at the United Nations between 2010 and 2015. For the current list of the institute's faculty and programs, see Zolberg Institute on Migration and Mobility at blogs.newschool.edu/zolberg-center#.

9.   Unless otherwise noted, the sketch of Ágnes Heller comes from personal interviews in 2007, 2013, 2014 and from Ágnes Heller, *A Short History of My Philosophy* (Lanham, Md.: Lexington Books, 2011).

10.   Yirmiyahu Yovel, "Laudatio for Ágnes Heller," delivered when Ágnes Heller received the Hermann-Cohen Medal for Jewish Culture-Philosophy in 2006 from the Hermann-Cohen-Akademie für Religion, Wissenschaft und Kunst, Buchen/Odenwald, Germany and reprinted in Katie Terezakis, ed., *Engaging Agnes Heller: A Critical Companion* (Lanham, Md.: Lexington Books, 2009), 11.

11.   Ágnes Heller, *A Philosophy of Morals* (Cambridge, Mass., Blackwell, 1990), xiii. In consultation with Ágnes Heller, the translation of the text quoted here is slightly different from the one published in the Blackwell edition.

12.   Ágnes Heller, *The Theory of Need in Marx* (London: Allison and Busby, 1976); Ágnes Heller, *Everyday Life* (New York: Routledge & Keegan Paul, 1984).

13.   Paul Hockenos, "84-year-old Philosopher Rallies Opposition to Hungary's Hard-Line Government," *Chronicle of Higher Education*, December 8, 2013, http://www.chronicle.com /article/84-Year-Old-Philosopher/143491. Republished in the international edition of *The New York Times*, December 9, 2013, as "A Scholar Is Back Home and Defiant in Hungary," https:// nytimes.com/2013/12/09/world/europe/a-scholar-is-back-home-and-defiant-in-hungary.html.

14.   Gergely Szakacs, "George Soros's Hungary University Signs Deal to Open Campus in Vienna," Reuters, April 9, 2018, https://www.reuters.com/article/us-hungary-election-university/george -soross-hungary-university-signs-deal-to-open-campus-in-vienna-idUSKBN1HG2T2.

15.   Jean Cohen and Andrew Arato, *Civil Society and Political Theory* (Cambridge, Mass.: MIT Press, 1992). Among the many accolades they have received, Jürgen Habermas has stressed the importance of Cohen and Arato's book. Jürgen Habermas, *Between Facts and Norms:*

Contributions to a Discourse Theory of Law and Democracy, trans. William Rehg (1992; Cambridge, Mass.: MIT Press: 1996), 367. Arato's recent work on constitutionalism includes *The Adventures of the Constituent Power: Beyond Revolutions?* (Cambridge, Mass.: Cambridge University Press, 2017); and Andrew Arato, *Post Sovereign Constitution Making: Learning and Legitimacy* (Oxford: Oxford University Press, 2016).

16. Elzbieta Matynia's most widely cited work on the subject is Elzbieta Matynia, *Performative Democracy* (New Haven, Conn.: Yale University Press, 2009). She is currently working on a book on South Africa. The New School for Social Research–Europe was founded in Wroclaw, Poland, on July 18, 2014.

17. Jeffrey Goldfarb, *Civility and Subversion: The Intellectual in Democratic Society* (Cambridge: Cambridge University Press, 1998). Since then Goldfarb has written extensively about the role of media and culture in democratic societies. More information on the Public Seminar is available at www.publicseminar.org.com.

18. Harold Clurman, *All People Are Famous* (New York: Harcourt Brace Jovanovich, 1974), 300. Joseph Greenbaum, spring, 2010, personal interview; Arien Mack, summer 2008 and winter 2018, personal interview.

19. In recent years the *Social Research* conferences have taken place under the umbrella of the Center for Public Scholarship, also directed by Arien Mack, see https://www.newschool .edu/cps/conference-series/.

20. Bob Kerrey cited in Richard Paddock, "Bob Kerrey's War Record Fuels Debate in Vietnam on His Role at New University," *New York Times*, June 2, 2016. See also J. Robert Kerrey, *When I Was a Young Man: A Memoir* (New York: Harcourt Books, 2002); Marc Santora and Lisa W. Foderaro, "New School Faculty Vote No Confidence in Kerrey," *New York Times*, December 10, 2008.

21. The New School's Strategic Plan 2013–2018, https://www.newschool.edu/about/university -resources/strategic-plan/.

APPENDIX A: EXTENDED NOTES AND COMMENTARY FOR CHAPTER 6

1. Peter M. Rutkoff and William B. Scott, *New School: A History of the New School for Social Research* (New York: The Free Press, 1986), 37.

2. Thorstein Veblen to Andrew Veblen, January 22, 1925, cited in Joseph Dorfman, ed., *Thorstein Veblen: Essays, Reviews and Reports, Previously Uncollected Writings*, (New York: Augustus M. Kelley, 1973), 224.

3. Dorfman, *Thorstein Veblen and His America*, 452.

4. Dorfman, *Thorstein Veblen: Essays, Reviews and Reports*, 224–29, at 275.

5. *Rutkoff and Scott, New School*, 37. Rutkoff and Scott refer the reader to three sources to substantiate their claim that Johnson fired Veblen: Johnson, *Pioneer's Progress*, 282–83; Dorfman, *Thorstein Veblen and His America*, 449–96; John Everett, president of the New School, 1978, personal communication. Neither Johnson nor Dorfman supports what they say.

6. Johnson, *Pioneer's Progress*, 283–83; Dorfman, *Thorstein Veblen and His America*, 449–96.

7. John Everett, Interview, *Lithopinion* 7, no. 2 (Summer 1972).

8. Robert Heilbroner, *Worldly Philosophers* (1953; New York: Touchstone, 1999), 213–47.

9. Heilbroner, *Worldly Philosophers*, 213–47.

10. Russell H. Bartley and Sylvia E. Bartley, "In Search of Thorstein Veblen: Further Inquiries Into His Life and Work," *International Journal of Politics, Culture and Society* 11, no. 1 (Fall 1997), 129–73.

11. "Professors Resign: Mystery on Midway; Five Men Quit University Faculty in One Day—Economy Hinted At," *Chicago Record-Herald*, June 6, 1906.

12. H. P. J-L to Mr Abraham Flexner, April 1,1919, Judson's Papers, University of Chicago.

13. Brander Matthews, "Mr. Veblen's Gas Attack on Our Colleges and Universities," *New York Times*, March 16, 1919.

APPENDIX B: EXTENDED NOTES AND COMMENTARY FOR CHAPTER 7

1. Tables 1 and 2, RAC, "The Refugee Scholars: A Retrospect," October 1, 1955, 4, 11, RG1.1.S200, B47F42, RAC.

2. Gemelli, *The "Unacceptables,"* 14; Krohn, "American Foundations and Refugee Scholars Between the Two Wars," 42–43; Krohn, *Intellectuals in Exile*, 72.

3. Alvin Johnson to Thomas Mann, January 4, 1939, box 5, Thomas Mann folder (1938–1951), Alvin Johnson Saunders Papers, Yale.

4. See note 21 in chapter 7.

5. Ruth Benedict to Alvin Johnson, March 31, 1933; Franz Boas to Alvin Johnson, March 30, 1933, NSA.

6. Descriptions and quotes are from Johnson,"Report to the Trustees of The Graduate Faculty," 6–9.

APPENDIX C: EXTENDED NOTES AND COMMENTARY FOR CHAPTER 9

1. Bruehl, *Hannah Arendt: For Love of the World*; Jerome Kohn, personal communication during August 2015.

2. Bruehl, *Hannah Arendt: For Love of the World*, 203.

APPENDIX D: EXTENDED NOTES AND COMMENTARY FOR CHAPTER 18

1. Unless otherwise noted, the biographical sketches of Arnhold and Gellert come from personal interviews held in spring 2015 and fall 2017 for Arnhold, and in spring 2015 with Gellert. Although I spoke informally many times with Walter Ebertstadt, the biographical

details I use in this portrait come from his memoir, Walter Ebertstadt, *Whence We Came, Where We Went* (New York: W. A. E. Books, 2002).

2. Eberstadt, *Whence We Came*, 21.

3. David Philipson, "The Breslau Rabbinical Conference," *The Jewish Quarterly Review* 18, no. 4 (July 1906): 652–53.

4. Eberstadt, *Whence We Came*, 21.

INDEX

Photo images are indicated by p and the plate number.

AAAE. *See* American Association for Adult
    Education
AAU. *See* Association of American Universities
AAUP. *See* American Association of
    University Professors
Abbott, Berenice, 70, 225
Abrams, Floyd, 325, 326
academic freedom/freedom of expression, ix,
    xvi, 4, 34, 349; AAU on, during McCarthy
    period, 200–201; AAUP report on in 1918;
    AAUP and, during McCarthy period,
    198–200; Charles Beard and, 3–4, 22, 32–33;
    Dewey on, 6, 23, 29, 30–31; Everett and,
    257–59; Hovde and, 192–93; A. Johnson
    on, 180–81, 202; Katznelson and, 321–22;
    Mitchell and, 49; New School bylaws on,
    194–95, 321–22; Orbán's Hungary and, 349;
    Robinson and, 3–4; Shipherd College and,
    202; Simons and, 194, 202. *See also* artistic
    freedom; Columbia University; dissident
    intellectuals in East and Central Europe;
    Fanton, Jonathan; National Endowment
    for the Arts (NEA), New School lawsuit
    against; *New Republic, The*; University in
    Exile
ADA. *See* Americans for Democratic Action
Adler, Alfred, 67

Adler, Stella, 71. *See also* Studio Theatre and
    Dramatic Workshop
Alexander, M. Jacqui, 303–4
American Association for Adult Education
    (AAAE), 62
American Association of University Professors
    (AAUP), academic freedom report of
    1918, 30; on communist professors during
    McCarthy period, 198–201; Dewey and,
    6, 23, 29
American Jewish Committee, 96
American Jewish Congress, 96
American Scholar, The, A. Johnson and, 90,
    123
Americans for Democratic Action (ADA),
    Hovde and, 193
American Sociological Association (ASA),
    Vidich and, 288
Ames, Joseph, 97–98
Amherst College, Meiklejohn and, 11–12
anniversary celebrations for New School: of
    School of Continuing Education, x, 228,
    233, 238; of University in Exile, x, 228–29,
    233, 235, 246, 249, 250, 283–84, 306, 329,
    331–33, of Social Research, 351. *See also*
    Johnson, Alvin, birthday celebrations
Ansley, Clarke, 65

anti-Semitism: A. Johnson on, 98, 113, 115, 307; New School faculty and, 385n12, New School trustees and, 307; Rockefeller Foundation and, 114. *See also* Arnhold, Henry; Eberstadt, Walter; Gellert, Michael; Hitler, Adolf; University in Exile; Arato, Andrew, p19, 327–29, 330, 350. *See also* Cohen, Jean; Democracy Seminars with East European dissidents; Heller, Ágnes; Lukács, Georg; Michnik, Adam

Arendt, Hannah, xvi, p10; Bernstein and, 273–74, 284; Cohn-Bendit and, 266–67, 426n20; death of, 283, 284; dissident intellectuals in East and Central Europe and, 335; Mack and, 350; Michnik and, 333, 335; at New School's Continuing Education, 366; *Origins of Totalitarianism* by, 146, 365–66; private papers of, xii; on political violence, 267; on student movement, 265–68

Armistice Day, Founding of Ecole Libre and; 155

Arnheim, Rudolf, 224, 242, 275. *See also* Gestalt Psychology; Wertheimer, Max

Arnhold, Henry: on Board of Trustees, 308, 351, 370; education and career of, 369; family history in Germany before 1935, 367, 369; Fanton and, 308, 370; fleeing Nazis, 369; WWII army service, 369; University in Exile Scholar Program and, 370; Zolberg Institute and, 370

artistic freedom: Fanton and, 322–27; Helms and, 323–25, 433n10; NEA and, 323–27; New School's Matsunaga exhibit and, 322–25; *Miller v. California* and, 323–24. *See also* academic freedom/freedom of expression

arts, at the New School. *See* murals; Parsons School of Design

ASA. *See* American Sociological Association

Asch, Solomon, 234, 275. *See also* Gestalt Psychology; Wertheimer, Max

Ascoli, Max (Mayflower professor of University in Exile): on Hovde, 174; in Italy, 362; A. Johnson and, 164; Neumann on, 146; as New School professor and trustee, 112, 118 174, 250; in Washington, D.C., during World War II, 150

Association of American Universities (AAU), on communist professors during McCarthy period, 200–201

Austill, Allen, 289–92, 294–95

Bacon, Caroline, 40, 58

Baldwin, Ruth Standish, 41

Barnard College: Putnam as dean of, 41; Robinson as dean of, 39

Barnes, Harry Elmer, 47, 56, 63–64, 385n25

Baruch, Bernard: A. Johnson relationship with, 13–14, 85; War Industries Board, and, 13, 14, Wilson and, 12–13

Beard, Charles A.: academic freedom and, 3–4, 22, 32–33; Butler and, 21–22; on facilities of New School, 44; on founding of New School, ix, 20, 55; A. Johnson on, 50, 386n23; Wesley Clair Mitchell on, 50, 386n23; reception to *An Economic Interpretation of the Constitution*, 26; resigning from New School, 51, 57, 59, 60–61, 81; vision of New School, 39

Beard, Mary, 39, 386n23

Becker, Carl, 42, 64

Belafonte, Harry, 186. *See also* Studio Theatre and Dramatic Workshop

Belarus, 344

Benedict, Ruth, 47, 361. *See also* Parsons, Elsie Clews

benefit dinners, 74, 126, 133. *See also* anniversary celebrations for New School; Johnson, Alvin, birthday celebrations

Bennington College, 144–45

Benton, Thomas Hart: mural painted by, 75–76; selling of mural of, 213

Berger, Peter, 263, 265, 292–93, 350

Bernstein, Richard, 273–74, 316, p9

Bick, Sally, 68

Billikopf, Jacob, 307

Bloch, Ernst, 122

Bloch, Marc, 153, 411n5

Board of Directors/Trustees of New School (1919–1933): founding members of, 383n34;

Clara Mayer on, 61, 62; new facilities on Twelfth Street and, 71–75; resignations from, in 1920s, 51, 55, 60, 61; students and, during 1920s, 61–62

Board of Trustees of New School (from 1933): anti-Semitism and, 115, 307; Arnhold and, 308, 370; Ascoli and, 174; David and, 241–49, 277; Donnelley and, 305; Eberstadt and, 308, 368; Everett and, 255–56; Fanton and, 301–3, 321–22; Gellert and, 308, 369; Graduate Faculty and in 1950s, 230–31; in late 1970s, 287, Hirshon and, 305–6, 313, p12; Hovde and, 174–75; Jews and, 307–8; A. Kaplan and, 239; J. Kaplan and, 249, 250, p9; Kerrey and, 351–52; Landa and, 256, 279; V. List and, 245, 249, 250, 278, p12; MacIver and, 248; MacLeish and, 185; A. Mayer and, 242; Clara Mayer and, 62; Milano and Orozco murals and, 179–80, 207, 210, 212, 215; R. Rockefeller and, 284; Schaffner and, 246; Simons and, 175, 176, 179–80; students and, 211–12; founding of University in Exile and, 89, 94, 103, 114, 126, 132, 194, 361; Walker and, 235; Ward and, 295, 299, 300. *See also* Johnson, Alvin

Boas, Franz, 95, 229, 361, 396

Bonnet, Henri, 154, 160, 234. *See also* Ecole Libre des Hautes Etudes

Borah, William, xii–xiii, xiv

Bourne, Randolph: death of, 79; *The New Republic* and, 18, 78; pacifism of, 78–79; E. Cornell and, 78–79; A. de Lima and, 78–79; A. Johnson and, 78–79

Boutmy, Emile, 35

Bowman, Isaiah, 133, 405n33

Brando, Marlon, 186. *See also* Studio Theatre and Dramatic Workshop

Brandt, Karl (Mayflower professor of University in Exile) p4; in Germany, 109–10, 361; at New School, 109, 113, 234; in Washington, D.C., 234

Brandt, Willy, 283–84

Brecht, Arnold (Mayflower professor of University in Exile), p11; arrest in Nazi Germany, 109; early life of, 107; family of,

109, 129–31; on fascism, 128; government positions in Germany before 1933, 107–8, 362; Germany trips in 1930s, 126–28; Heuss and, 262; Hitler and, 106–8, 128; A. Johnson's relationship with, 125, 126–28, 131–32; A. Johnson's seventy-fifth birthday and, 132; Luther and, 128–29; recruitment to University in Exile, 106, 109–11, 125; service to U.S. government, 130–31

Brecht, Bertolt, 184–86

Brod, Max, 360

Broun, Heywood, 189

Broyard, Anatole, 224. *See also* students

Bruère, Henry, 37

Bruère, Robert, 37–38

Bruner, Jerome, 300

Bry, Edith, 209–10

Bryn Mawr College, A. Johnson teaching at, 10, 11

Budapest School of Philosophy, 346–47

Burgess, John, 23, 380n10

Butler, Nicholas Murray: C. Beard and, 21–22; Carnegie Endowment for International Peace and, 20–22; Cattell's Faculty Club memo and, 27–28; firings of Cattell, Dana, L. Fraser; on founding of New School, 5–6; on Hitler's Germany, 135–36; Nobel Peace Prize, 21; as pacifist, 20–22

Byers, Hilary Paley (daughter of Dorothy Hirshon), 305

Cadoret, Michel, 235–36, 397n45

Cage, John, 225, 352

Califano, Joseph, 305; Byers and, 305–6; Fanton and, 305–6, 430n19; Hirshon and, 305–6

Canfield Fisher, Dorothy, 144, 145

Carnegie Endowment for International Peace, 20, 21, 149. *See also* Butler, Nicholas Murray

Cattell, James McKeen: AAUP and, 27, 30; at Columbia, 25–28; Columbia firing of, 3, 28–31; Committee of Nine and, 26–29; Dewey and, 27, 29–30; Faculty Club memo by, 27–28; lobbying congressmen, 28, 30; New School and, 41; Seligman and, 26–27; *University Control* by, 25

Cather, Willa, 74, 78

Causeway, James, 168, 170

Central European University (CEU): Ignatieff and, 343; Kis and, 343; Soros and, 343, 349; threat of closure of, 349

Chicago, University of. *See* University of Chicago

City University of New York (CUNY): Everett at, 255; open admissions at, 268

Civil Service Restoration Act, Germany, 87–88, 91, 104

Clay, Lucius D., 130

Clurman, Harold, 70, 350

COFRAT. *See* Committee on Freedom of Research and Teaching

Cohen, Gustave, 154, 157. *See also* Ecole Libre des Hautes Etudes

Cohen, Jean, 271–73. *See also* Arato, Andrew

Cohen, Morris Raphael, 63, 64

Cohn-Bendit, Daniel (Dany): Arendt and, 266–67, 426n20; de Gaulle and, 267; Michnik and, 330, 333

Cold War. *See* Communist Party; Red scare

Colm, Gerhard (Mayflower professor of University in Exile) p4; attacked by Nazis, 107; conversion to Christianity, 113; in Germany before World War II, 107, 113, 361, 401n92; in postwar Germany, 231; at the New School, 117, 125, 148, 250. *See also* Wald, Haskell

Columbia University: AAUP and, during World War I, 29–30; Everett at, 255; A. Johnson at, 10–11; E. Johnson at, 80; Katznelson at, 310–11, 313, 340; refugees from Institute of Social Research at, 99, 146–47; Swift on Extension Program at, 218–19; University in Exile's General Seminar and, 122; University of Heidelberg's 550th anniversary and, 135–36. *See also* Butler, Nicholas Murray; Beard, Charles A.; Committee of Nine; Dana, Henry Wadsworth Longfellow; Dewey, John; Fraser, Leon; Luther, Hans; Mitchell,

Wesley Clair; Robinson, James Harvey; Seligman, Edwin R. A.

Committee of Nine, 24; Cattell and, 27–29; Dewey resigns from, 29; Seligman and, 27–29

Committee on Freedom of Research and Teaching (COFRAT), 288. *See also* ASA

Communist Party: AAU in McCarthy period and, 200–201; AAUP in McCarthy period and, 198–201; A. Brecht and, 108; B. Brecht and, 184–86; *Chicago Tribune* on New School's faculty and, 188–89; Eisler and, 183–84; Gwathmey and, 193–96; Hook and, 181, 191 199, 202; Hovde and, 192–93; Hutchins and, 201; A. Johnson and, 180–88, 190, 209–10; Meiklejohn and, 202; Olgin and, 57, 181; Piscator and, 186–87; professors fired for being members, 198–200; Graduate Faculty's original policy on, 147–48, 178–79. *See also* dissident intellectuals in East and Central Europe

Communist Party of the United States of America (CPUSA). *See* Communist Party

Continuing Education: cartoonists and, 250–51; David and, 241; Fanton and, 303; fortieth anniversary of, 233–34; Graduate Faculty and, 224–25, 232; Landa and, 277; New School founders and, 37–39, 45; outside evaluators and, 218–19, 230

Copland, Aaron, 68

Cornell, Esther, 392n54; Bourne and, 78–79, A. Johnson's affair with, 78–81; A. de Lima and, 78–79

Cornell University, 11–12

Cowell, Henry: contributor to *Encyclopaedia of the Social Sciences*, 69–70; Clara Mayer and, 95, 225; at New School, 68, 95, 225, 242, 391n32

CPUSA. *See* Communist Party of the United States of America

Croly, Herbert; founding of New School and, ix; A. Johnson and, 12, 16–18, 51; leadership style of, 37; resigning from New School, 51, 57, 60; T. Roosevelt and, 16

Cultural and Scientific Conference for World Peace: Hovde and, 190–92; New School colleagues and, 191, 416n37

cultural pluralism, Kallen and, xiii, 6

Cummings, E. E., 225

CUNY. *See* City University of New York

Curtis, Tony, 186. *See also* Studio Theatre and Dramatic Workshop

Dana, Henry Wadsworth Longfellow, 3; AAUP and, 30; Columbia firing, 30, 31, 32; member of faculty at New School, 32, 63; political work of, 31–32

David, Henry: Board of Trustees and, 241–49, 277; Continuing Education and, 241; as dean of Graduate Faculty, 237; finances under, 243–44; Greenbaum on, 256; A. Johnson and, 239–40, 243, 305; Levin and, 245–46; Clara Mayer fired by, 241–43; as president of New School, 239–41, 256; resignation of, 248; Vidich on, 292

Day, Edmund, 102

de Gaulle, Charles: Cohn-Bendit and, 267; Ecole Libre and, 154–57; F. Roosevelt and, 155, 159

de Lima, Agnes, p3; anniversary year and, 228–29; daughter and granddaughter of, 78, 80–82, 105, 226, 393n53; death of, xi; as director of publicity, ix, 77–78, 82, 215–16, 219, 227–28; early life of, 78; on Ecole Libre, 157–58; on Eisler, 179; emancipated life of, 78; relationship with A. Johnson, ix–x, xii, 77–82; letters from A. Johnson to, 77, 88, 95, 96, 97, 100, 104, 116; McFarlane and, 81; Orozco murals and, 209, 211; Reed and, 209; retirement of, 256; on Simons, 175–76

de Lima, Sigrid (daughter of A. Johnson and A. de Lima), 78, 80–81; letter from A. Johnson to, 105; at New School, 226. *See also* Greene, Alison de Lima

de los Ríos, Fernando, 151, 158. *See* Ibero-American Center

Democracy Seminars with East European dissidents, 333–37; origin of, 333

Dewey, John: as advocate of educational reform, 52–53, AAUP and, 6, 30; on Beard, 6; Catell and, 27, 29; Committee of Nine, resignation from, 29; founding of New School and University in Exile and, 6, 63, 97, 377n10; A. Johnson and, 121 on pacifism, 30–31

Deyrup, Astrith, at New School, 80–81

Deyrup, Felicia, at New School, 80–81, 293

Deyrup, Mark, 373n54

Diamond, Stanley: critique of European colleagues by, 264–66; hiring of, 263–64; on rebuilding of Graduate Faculty in 1980s, 300; on 1970 student mobilization at New School, 258–61, 264–69. *See also* Nell, Edward

Dissent (magazine), Howe and, 196, 213

dissident intellectuals in East and Central Europe: Arendt and, 335; East and Central Europe program at Graduate Faculty and, 336–38, 340–41; Fehér as, 346, 349; Á. Heller as, 316, 329, 344, 346–49, p20; Journal Donation project for, 337–38, 351, p17; Kuroń as, 332–33, 335, 435n31; Lipiński as, 332; Mack and, 335–38; Matynia as, 334, 336–40; Michnik as, 329–37, 343; *Social Research* on, 335–36; Szacki on, 334; velvet revolutions and, 327, 332, 336

doctoral program evaluations. *See* McGrath, Earl James; Middle States Association of Colleges and Secondary Schools; Swift, Arthur; Ward, F. Champion

Donnelley, Strachan, 305, 430n18. *See also* Jonas, Hans

Duffy, Roger, 352

Duggan, Stephen, 91, 351. *See also* Emergency Committee in Aid of German [Foreign Displaced] Scholars; Institute of International Education; New University in Exile Consortium

Duke, Doris: as donor to New School, 169, 360, 413n3; A. Johnson on, 168–69; Staudinger and, 168

Eberstadt, Walter: on Board of Trustees, 308, 368; education and career of, 368; family history in Germany before 1935, 308, 367–68; Fanton and, 308; fleeing Nazis, 368; serving in British army, 368

Ecole libre des sciences politiques (Sciences Po): founding of, 35; idea for New School and, 35–36

Ecole Libre des Hautes Etudes (Ecole Libre): Hovde severing ties with, 161, 172; A. Johnson on, 154–55, 163–64; *Renaissance* journal and, 162–64; Rockefeller Foundation and, 152, 156–57, 411n10. *See also* Armistice Day; Fosdick, Raymond; de Gaulle, Charles; Kittredge, Tracy

Egas, Camilo, 70, 210, 213–14

Einstein, Albert, 91, 96, 99

Eisler, Hanns, 179, 183–84

Ely, Mary, 62

Emergency Committee in Aid of German [Foreign Displaced] Scholars, 91–92, 116, 133, 351

Encyclopaedia of the Social Sciences (Seligman and A. Johnson), 85, 93, 181; arts and, 69–70

Endowment for New School: Everett on, 257; A. Johnson on, 55, 133, 175, 249, 305, 376n5; Landa and, 277; Swift on, 221. *See also* "Save the School" campaign

Eugene Lang College, 302, 321; Fanton and, 303;

Everett, John: academic freedom and, 257–59; accomplishments under, 256; administrative team of, 256; Board of Trustees and, 255–56; W. Brandt and, 283–84; career background of, 256; at Columbia, 255; Greenbaum fired by, 289–90; Parsons School of Design and, 281–82; presidential appointment of, 255; retirement of, 256–57; Vietnam War protests and, 257–59, 261

facilities, of New School: in Chelsea, 44, 71–72, 384n1; C. Beard on Chelsea facilities, 44; Eleventh Street building, 227–28, 236, 325; Graduate Faculty building, 256, 277–79; Mills College buildings as, 282; Urban's building on Twelfth Street, 71–75; 81, 117–18, 174, 175, 213, 227, 325, 387n28, 392n46, p1; University Center, 352. *See also* murals, at New School

Fancher, Edwin, 225

Fanton, Jonathan, p12, p15; and academic freedom/freedom of expression, 303–4, 320–27; achievements at New School, 304; background of, 301, 434n22; Califano and, 305, 430n19; Continuing Education and, 303; dissidents in Eastern Europe and, 327–33, 336; Eugene Lang College and, 303; Helsinki Watch and, 328; Hirshon and, 305, 308–9; A. Johnson's influence on, 302, 304, 320; Jonas and, 302; Katznelson and, 309, 313, 320; Lowe and, 302; presidential appointment of, 214, 301–2, 308–9; resignation of, 350, 352

Federal Bureau of Investigation (FBI): Gwathmey and, 195; A. Johnson and, 182–83, 188

Fehér, Ferenc, 346, 349

Feiler, Arthur (Mayflower professor of University in Exile), p4; in Germany, 362; at New School, 123, 150

Ferenczi, Sándor, 67

Festinger, Leon, 319

Fine, Benjamin, 202, 215–16; Louis. S. Weiss Memorial Award in Adult Education and, p6

Flexner, Abraham, 99, 101, 357

Flexner, Bernard, 140

Focillon, Henri, 154, 155. *See also* Ecole Libre de Hautes Etudes

Fogelman, Raymond and Stella Sweeting, 279

Fosdick, Raymond, 152. *See also* Rockefeller Foundation

founders, of New School, 41, 42, 383n34; educational reform and, 48; resignations of, 51, 57–59, 60–61, 81; women and, 40–41. *See also* Beard, Charles A.; Croly, Herbert; Johnson, Alvin; Mitchell, Wesley Clair; Putnam, Emily James; Robinson, James Harvey; Sorchan, Charlotte Hunnewell (Martin); Straight, Dorothy Whitney

Frank, Lawrence, 81

Frank, Waldo, 67

Frankfurter, Felix, 41, 53, 97, 129, 233–34, 408n16

Fraser, Leon, 24–25

Fraser, Nancy, 304

Freedom House rally, 191

freedom of expression. *See* academic freedom/ freedom of expression

Free School, 50; Croly and, 35–36; A. Johnson on, 36–37

French structuralism, Ecole Libre des Hautes Etudes and founding of, 159. *See also* Lévi-Strauss, Claude; Jakobson, Roman

Fry, Varian, 92

fund raising, 132; alumni donors and, 305; Arnhold, 308, 346, 351, 370; Benton murals and, 213; Causeway and, 168; corporate foundations and, 261–62, 283, 317–18; David and, 243–44; Donnelley, 305; Duke and, 169; in early years, 40, 51, 55, 58, 60, 65–66, 71–74, 208, 383n28; Eberstadt and, 308, 368; for Ecole Libre, 154–55, 158, 164; Everett and, 256; Fogelman, 279; founding of New School and, 40, 51, 55; Gellert, 308, 369 Halle and, 99–101, 133; Jewish donors and, 307–8; Hirshon and, 305, 396; A. List and, 278–79; V. List and, 249–50, 338; 1945–1964, 168–69, 216–17, 227, 243–48; Milano and, 303, Orozco murals and, 208, 213; "Save the School" campaign and, 246–48; Schaffner and, 246; for School of Continuing Education, 228, 233; Simons and, 227; student enrollment and, 51, 53, 65, 72, 76–77; for University in Exile/ Graduate Faculty, 88–89, 94, 96, 97–101, 133, 154, 275, 279–80, 300, 317–18, 360; for Urban facilities, 71–76

Gellert, Michael: on Board of Trustees, 308, 368; education and career of, 368–69; family's history in Czechoslovakia before 1938, 368; Fanton and, 308; fleeing Nazis, 368

Gestalt Psychology. *See* Arnheim, Rudolf; Asch, Solomon; Henle, Mary; Wertheimer, Max

Ginnott-Cohn, Alice, 430n18

Giraud, Henri, 156, 161, 162, 411n6

Graduate Faculty (GF). *See* University in Exile

Goldenweiser, Alexander, 47, 64

Goldfarb, Jeffrey, p15, 327–29, 332, 333, 337–39. *See also* dissident intellectuals in East and Central Europe; Matynia, Michnik

Goodnow, Frank Johnson ("Mr. X"), 23, 380n10

Goodrich, Lloyd, 206–7

Gordon, David: Gordon-Rapp proposal for rebuilding Graduate Faculty in early 1980s, 293–95; Hirshon and, 306; as Marxist economist and teacher, 270–71

Graham, Martha, 70–71, 76

Great Depression: construction of Twelfth Street building and, 74; Keynes and, 119; founding of University in Exile and, xv, 88, 90

Green, Murray, 293. *See also* Jonas, Hans

Greenbaum, Joseph: xii, 226; A. Brecht and, p11; Everett firing of, 289–90; faculty workload and, 276; Mack and, 350; MacIntyre, Alasdair and, 287; Rorty and, 286–87

Greene, Alison de Lima (daughter of Sigrid de Lima and Stephen Greene), 80, 373, 375n2, 393n54

Grégoire, Henri, 154, 162–64. *See also* Ecole Libre des Hautes Etudes; *Renaissance*

Gruening, Ernest, 235

Gurwitsch, Aron, 263, 265, 273–74, 283

Guthrie, William D., 23

Gwathmey, Robert: Communist Party and, 193–96; FBI and, 195; New School and, 193–95

Habermas, Jürgen, 262, 273

Hadamard, Jacques, 154. *See* Ecole Libre des Hautes Etudes

Hagemann, Harald, 398n53, 399n63

Halle, Hiram, 246; founding gift for University in Exile, 99–101, 133; friendship with A. Johnson, 100–101; library named for, 100–101; translation of *Mein Kampf* and, 137–38, 140; Schaffner and, 100

Harner, Michael, 264
Haydn, Hiram, 226
Hecksher, August, 184, 186
Hegemann, Werner (Mayflower professor of University in Exile), 86, 363
Heilbroner, Robert, p18, 215, 256, 430n18; on Enabling Committee, 300; on future of Gradate Faculty in late 1970s, 290–91; on history of University in Exile/Graduate Faculty, 229–30, 284; as teacher, 270
Heidelberg on 12th Street, 284; Mann and, 134
Helms, Jesse, 323–25
Heimann, Eduard (Mayflower professor of University in Exile), p4; conversion from Judaism to Chritianity of, 114; in Germany, 120, 362; at New School, 117, 263
Heller, Ágnes, 346–49, p20; father of, 347; at Graduate Faculty, 316, 329, 344, 346, 349; Hungarian Revolution and, 348; Lukács and, 316, 348; New Left and, 348; Orbán's government and, 362; Philosophers' Trial and, 348; World War II and, 347–48; Yovel on, 347. See also dissident intellectuals in East and Central Europe
Heller, Pál, 347
Helsinki Watch, 328
Henle, Mary, 292–93. See also Gestalt Psychology
Hett, Benjamin, 87
Heuss, Theodor, 261–62
Hirshon, Dorothy, p12; on Board of Trustees, 305–6, 313; Califano on, 305–6; Everett and, 313; Fanton and, 308–9; A. Johnson and, 305, 306; Katznelson and, 313
Hitler, Adolf: A. Brecht and, 106–8, 128; Schumpeter on, 103; Staudinger's *The Inner Nazi* and, 137–38. See also *Mein Kampf* (Hitler), English translations of; University in Exile
Hobsbawm, Eric, 315, 431n31
Hofstader, Richard, 310
Hofstadter, Albert, 286, 288–89
Hook, Sidney: as anticommunist, 191, 199, 202; as member of Communist Party, 181; Freedom House rally and, 191

Horkheimer, Max, 99, 121, 146, 148. *See also* Institute of Social Research (Frankfurt School)
Hornbostel, Erich von (Mayflower professor of University in Exile), p4, 362; Cowell and, 68; family of, 113; in Germany, 68, 95, 113, 362; Johnson on, 184, 362; Wertheimer and, 69, 95
Horney, Karen, at New School, 67, 123
Houghton Mifflin, 139–44
House Un-American Activities Committee (HUAC): B. Brecht and, 185, 415n20; Eisler and, 181, 183–84; Gwathemy and, 195; Johnson and, 181, 188; Piscator and, 186
Hovde, Bryn, 178, 238; academic freedom and, 192–93; anticommunist rhetoric of, 189; on Conference for World Peace, 192; controversial decisions of, 172–73; critics of, 193; Cultural and Scientific Conference for World Peace and, 190–92; Ecole Libre and, 161; A. Johnson and, 170–71, 174–75, 189–92; O'Dwyer attacking, 192–93; refugee scholars and, 216; resignation of, 174, 217
Howe, Irving: *Dissent* and, 213, 350; on Orozco murals, 212–13
HUAC. *See* House Un-American Activities Committee
Humphrey, Doris, 70
Hutchins, Robert M.: academic freedom during McCarthy period and, 201–2; founding of University in Exile and, 97, 98–99
Huxley, Julian, 64, 66

Ibero-American Center at New School, 151, 158. *See also* de los Ríos, Fernando; Lévi-Strauss, Claude
IIE. *See* Institute of International Education
ILGWU. *See* International Ladies' Garment Workers Union
Inner Nazi, The (Staudinger), 137–38
Institute of International Education (IIE), 89, 90–91, 351. *See also* Duggan, Stephen; Emergency Committee in Aid of German [Foreign] Displaced Scholars; New University in Exile Consortium

Institute of Social Research, 99; New School and, 146–49. *See also* Frankfurt School

Institute of World Affairs (IWA), 179, 220; Ibero-American Center and, 151; A. Johnson on, 150–51; Lowe and, 150; Rockefeller Foundation and, 150, 360; Staudinger and, 169

International Ladies' Garment Workers Union (ILGWU), 52

IWA. *See* Institute of World Affairs

Jakobson, Roman, 155, 159. *See also* Ecole Libre des Hautes Etudes

Jay, Martin: *The Dialectical Imagination* by, 147; Speier and, 147–48

Jewell, Edward Alden, 75–76

Johns Hopkins University, 97, 133, 200, 229

Johnson, Alvin, p2, p4; birthday celebrations of, 132–33, 228, 233, 236, 249; daughter with Agnes de Lima (Sigrid), 78, 80, 81, 105, 226; death of, xi, 284. *See also* De Lima, Agnes; Johnson, Edith

Johnson, Alvin, career of: on *The American Scholar* editorial board, 123; Ecole Libre des Hautes Etudes, founder of, 235; *Encyclopaedia of the Social Sciences* associate editor of, 69–70, 85, 93, 181; Enemy Alien Hearing Board member of, 187–88; *The New Republic*, senior editor of, 9–20, *Social Research*, founder and editor of, 116, 122–25; professor of economics, 11–12; Spanish-American War, soldier in, 9–10; War Council Committee Against Discrimination and the Committee for the Equality of Education, head of, 402n97

Johnson, Alvin, retirement and after, 161, 164, 167, 170; attacks on, during McCarthy period, 189–92; fundraising for New School, 234, 246–50, 306; pushing out successors, 174–75, 245–46

Johnson, Edith Henry (wife of A. Johnson): academic training of, 80; children of, 80–81, 299; home-schooling and, 79–80, on husband's affairs with other women, 79–80

Jonas, Hans, p5; at GF, 223–24, 231, 263, 265–66, 272; Fanton and, 301; Habermas on, 263; retirement of, 283. *See also* Donnelley, Strachan; Greene, Alison de Lima

Judt, Tony, 327

Junior League, 56–57

Kafka Was the Rage (Broyard), 224

Kähler, Alfred (Mayflower professor of University in Exile), 120, 284, 363

Kahn, Julius, 28

Kallen, Horace, p6; on cultural pluralism, xiii, 6; as dean of GF, 169, 309; and first Red scare, 180; at fortieth anniversary of GF; on *Mein Kampf*, 142; and early days of New School, xiii, xxvi, 47, 63, 64, 66; and early days of University in Exile/GF, 97, 112, 118, 121

Kantorowicz, Hermann (Mayflower professor of University in Exile), 114, 362

Kaplan, Abbott, 238–39, 249

Kaplan, Jacob, p9, 249, 250

Katznelson, Ira, p13, p19; at Columbia, 310–11, 340; as dean, 313–17, 340–41; early life of, 309–11; East European dissidents and, 320; Fanton and, 313, 320; on founding of New School and University of Exile, 6–8, 340–41; Hirshon and, 313; student protests and, 310–11; A. Zolberg and, 314, 317, 344. *See also* Columbia University; University of Chicago

Kent State University, 258, 259

Kerciu, Ray, 250

Kerrey, Bob, 351–52

Keynes, John Maynard, 18, 318n21; German reform economists on, 119

King, Martin Luther, Jr., 250, 310

Kis, János, 343, 350

Kittredge, Tracy, 156–57. *See also* Rockefeller Foundation

Koch, Ed (mayor), 213–14

Kohn, Hans, 228

Korean War, impact on New School, 216

Koyré, Alexandre, 154, 159, 161, 163, 411n15. *See also* Ecole Libre des Hautes Etudes

Krohn, Claus-Dieter, xvi, 148–49, 360, 394n16, 400n75

Król, Marcin, 335

Krutch, Joseph Wood, 70, 228

Kunstler, William, at New School, 259–60

Kuroń, Jacek, 332–33, 335, 435n31

Kurzweil, Edith, 430n18

Landa, Albert, 256; Continuing Education and, 277; 65 Fifth Avenue building and, 277–79; Parsons School of Design and, 280–81

Lang, Andrew, 80

Langevin, Paul, 91. See also Einstein, Albert

Laski, Harold, xv, 34; A. Johnson on, 197–98

Lederer, Emil (Mayflower professor of University in Exile), p4; conversion to Christianity, 113; as first dean of University in Exile/Graduate Facutly, 103–4, 106, 120, 123; as editor, 120, 123–25; founding of University in Exile and, 88–89, 103–5; Frankfurt School refugees and, 146–48; in Germany, 85, 123, 362; on Keynes, 119; Neumann on Lederer's State of the Masses, 146; on rise of Hitler, 85–86, Schumpeter and, 101, 103; Speier and, 106, 146.

Le Gallienne, Eva, xiii, 71

Lehmann, Fritz (Mayflower professor of University in Exile), 363

Lerner, Max, 251

Levin, Nathan, 239, 244; David and, 245–46

Lévi-Strauss, Claude, 155, 159–62, 411n15. See also Ecole Libre des Hautes Etudes

Levy, David C., 281, 433n10. See also Parsons School of Design

Lindenbaum, Shirley, 264

Lipiński, Edward, 332

Lippmann, Walter: The New Republic and, 15, 18; at New School, 233–34; telegram to A. Johnson, 18; on Wilson 15

List, Albert: background of, 278; 65 Fifth Avenue Building and, 278–79

List, Vera, 249–50, 338, p12. See also Board of Trustees; "Save the School" campaign

Littauer, Rudolf (Mayflower professor of the University in Exile), 363

London School of Economics (LSE), 34; founding of, 35

Lorenz, Lee, 250–51

Lowe, Adolph, p5; in England, 150; Fanton and, 302, 329; and Frankfurt School, 148–49; in Germany, 120 121; 150; IWA and, 150; Nazis and, 106, 399n63; at New School, 150, 160, 250; 265–66, 329; recruitment to University in Exile, 104–5; Schumpeter and, 103; Staudinger and, 169. See also Heilbroner, Robert

LSE. See London School of Economics

Lubbe, Marinus van der, 87

Lukács, György (Georg): Arato and, 328; Á. Heller and, 316, 346, 348; Lederer and, 123

Lukashenko, Alexander, 344

Lusk Committee. See New York Committee to Investigate Seditious Activities

Luther, Hans, 128–29, 396n35; 550th anniversary of University of Heidelberg and, 129; A. Brecht and, 128–29; A. Johnson on, 97

Lyman, Stanford, 292–93

Macaulay, Frederick, 64

MacIntyre, Alasdair, 287, 294, 295

MacIver, Robert: as acting president, 248, 250; on Board of Trustees, 248; as chancellor, 255–56; A. Johnson letters to, 93, 122

Mack, Arien, 289, p.17; dissident intellectuals in East and Central Europe and, 335–38; Greenbaum and, 350; influence at Graduate Faculty of, 350–51; Journal Donation project of, 337–38, 351; New University in Exile Consortium and, 351; 353; sexism and, 350; Social Research and, 125, 273, 335–36, 350–51

MacLeish, Archibald, 184–85

Malina, Judith. See Studio Theatre and Dramatic Workshop

Malinowski, Bronislaw, 361

Mann, Thomas: Brod and, 360; University in Exile and, x–xi, 133–34. See also Speier, Hans

Mannheim, Karl, 104–6, 120, 121, 398n61

Mapplethorpe, Robert, 324

Maritain, Jacques, xv, 154, 161–63, 169, 236, 335, 411n15. *See also* Ecole Libre des Hautes Etudes

Marschak, Jacob: founding of University in Exile, and, 104–5, 361; in Germany, 120; at Graduate Faculty, 150, 359, 360–61; Schumpeter on, 103; at University of Chicago, 99

Matthau, Walter, 186. *See also* Studio Theatre and Dramatic Workshop

Marx, Karl: Budapest School of Philosophy and, 346–47; A. Johnson on, 180–81

Marx, Werner, 293

Marxist thought and New School students, 181, 257, 263, 264. *See also* student activism at New School; Cohen, Jean; Pollin, Robert

Matsunaga, Shin, 322–25

Matynia, Elzbieta, p19; life in Communist Poland, 339–40; East and Central Europe Program/ Transregional Center for Democratic Studies run by, 336–38, 350; Goldfarb and, 339, 350 Kalwinska fellowship for, 339–40; New School for Social Research–Europe network and, 350; as political exile, 340; student of Szacki, 334

Mayer, Albert (brother of Clara), 73, 76; resigns from Board of Trustees, 242

Mayer, Carl (Mayflower professor of University in Exile), 120, 231, 363

Mayer, Charles (brother of Clara), 73, 76

Mayer, Clara, on Board of Directors, 62; on construction of Twelfth Street building, 76–77; David firing, 241–43; family of, 74, 76–77, 242, 307; on Hovde, 173; A. Johnson on, 62–63, 242–43; McCarthy period and, 188, 193, 195; as New School administrator, 53–54, 81, 169, 173, 188, 239; as New School student, 61, 62

"Mayflower" professors of University in Exile, 361–63. *See also* Ascoli, Max; Brandt,Willy; Brecht, Arnold; Colm, Gerhard; Feiler, Arthur; Hegemann, Werner; Heimann, Eduard; Hornbostel, Erich von; Kähler, Alfred; Kantorowicz, Hermann; Lederer,

Emil; Lehmann, Fritz; Littauer, Rudolf; Mayer, Carl; Salomon, Albert; Simons, Hans; Speier, Hans; Staudinger, Hans; Wertheimer, Max; Wunderlich, Frieda

McCarthy period at New School, xv, 173, 177–79, 193–95, 199–200; Hecksher and, 184; A. Johnson on, 182, 190–91 202, 220. *See also* Brecht, Bertolt; communism; Eisler, Hanns; Gwathemy, Robert; Orozco, José Clemente; Red scare; Simons, Hans

McFarlane, Arthur, 81

McGhee, Paul, 239, 244, 248

McGrath, Earl James, 230–33

Meiklejohn, Alexander, 11–12; on founding of New School, 42–43

Mein Kampf (Hitler), English translations of, 136, 137, 138–44; copyright law and, 140, 145; court decisions on, 141–44, 365; Halle and, 101, 137–38, 140; Houghton Mifflin and, 139–44; profits from, 142–45; Reynal & Hitchcock, 138–40, 142–44, 366, 407n10; royalties for, 365; Stackpole and Sons, 140–43, 365–66, 408n10, 408n17; Trading with the Enemy Act and, 144

Mellon Foundation, 317–18

Meyer, Julie, 425n16

Michnik, Adam, 337, p15, p19; Arato and, 330; Arendt and, 333, 335; Cohn-Bendit and, 330, 333; contacts of, 333–34; Goldfarb and, 333; honorary doctorate for, 329–33; in prison, 331–32, 334, 336

Mickiewicz, Adam (*Forefathers' Eve*), 310

Middle States Association of Colleges and Secondary Schools (Middle States), 174, 217, 238, 240

Milano, Robert, 303, 431n24

Milberg, William, 371, 403n10

Miller, Arthur, 186. *See also* Studio Theatre and Dramatic Workshop

Miller, James, 257, 260

Mills College, 282

Milner, Joe, 77

Mirkine-Guetzévitch, Boris, 154, 163, 411n15. *See also* Ecole Libre des Hautes Etudes

Mitchell, Lucy Sprague, 48, 49

Mitchell, Wesley Clair, 12, 27, 355; academic freedom and, 49; at Columbia, 50; courses taught by, 6, 12, 47, 49, 50; founding of New School and, 4–6, 50; on idea for New School, 50; Midwestern home of, 4–5; resigning from New School, 51, 57; University in Exile, 50, 101–3; Veblen and, 356, War Industries Board and, 12, 13, 48

Mumford, Lewis, 65

Munson, Gorham, 67

murals, at New School: Benton and, 75–76, 213; Cadoret and, 235, 397n45; Egas and, 213–14; Orozco and, p7, p8. See also Orozco murals, at New School

Nagel, Thomas, 316

National Endowment for the Arts (NEA), 323–24; Congress and funding for, 326–27; New School lawsuit against, 325–27

National Guardian, 211

Nation by Design, A (A. Zolberg), 346

Nebraska, University of: A. Johnson at, 6, 9, 11; E. Johnson at, 79–80

NEA. See National Endowment for the Arts

Neisser, Hans: attacked by Nazis, 107; conversion to Christianity, 107; in Germany, 120, 395n16; on Keynes, 119; at New School, 231–32; Schumpeter on, 103

Nell, Edward: critique of European colleagues by, 264–66; hiring of, 264; on student movements, 258–61, 264–69. See also Diamond, Stanley

Neumann, Franz: on Ascoli, 146; on Lederer, 146–47; on New School, 146, 148; Rockefeller Foundation and, 148; on Speier, 146

New Left, 257, 263, 320–21, 348

New Republic, The, 78, 196; early history of, 15–16; financing, 40, 59; idea for New School conceived at, 34; A. Johnson writing for, 12, 14, 16–18, 51, 123; Lippmann and, 15, 18; New School and, 14–15, 378n21; New School lecturers and, 378n21; on U.S. entering World War I, 20; Wilson and, 18–19

New University in Exile Consortium (founded in 2018), 351, 353

New York Committee to Investigate Seditious Activities (Lusk Committee), xiv, 57

New York University (NYU): adult education program of, 218–19; New School trustees consider merging with, 244–248

Norton, William Warder, 62. See also students

NSSR. See University in Exile

O'Dwyer, Bill, 192–93

Olgin, Moissaye J., 57, 388n47; CPUSA and, 181

Oram, Harold, 280–81

Orbán, Victor, 349

Organization Committee, 42; men on, 41; women on, 40–41

Origins of Totalitarianism, The (Arendt), 146, 365–66

Orozco, José Clemente: fresco painting of, 206; A. Johnson and, 203

Orozco murals, at New School, 75–76, 179–80, p3; Board of Trustees and, 179–80, 207, 210, 212, 215; covering, 208–13, 227, p3; criticism of, 204, 205; A. de Lima and, 209, 211; financing for, 208; Goodrich on, 206–7; Howe on, 212–13; A. Johnson on, 203–10, 214, 418n8; Koch and, 213–14; New York Times on, 205, 211–12; panels of, 206–7; Reed and, 205–11; students on, 211–12

Overstreet, Harry, 63

Parsons, Elsie Clews: Benedict and, 47; A. Johnson and, 8, 81; on marriage and free love, 78

Parsons School of Design, 213, 303, 351; Landa and, 280–81; Matsunaga exhibit at, 322–25; merger with New School, 280–282. See also Levy, David; Oram, Harold

Pearson, Lester Bowles, 234

Piscator, Erwin: Communist Party and, 186–88; in Europe, 186; A. Johnson and, 186–87, 225; Studio Theatre and Dramatic Workshop at New School, 71, 169, 172, 186

Pollin, Robert, 269–71, 430n18

Pound, Roscoe, 53, 129

Powell, Thomas R., 29–30

Prague Spring, 310–11

presidents, of New School. *See* David, Henry; Everett, John; Fanton, Jonathan; Hovde, Bryn; Johnson, Alvin; Kaplan, Abbott; Kerrey, Bob; Simons, Hans; Van Zandt, David; MacIver, Robert

Prewitt, Kenneth, 372

Putnam, Emily James, 40, 41, 74

Quinton, Anthony, 286, 288

Rapp, Rayna, 293–94

Rauschenberg, Robert, 250

Red scare, first, xiv–xv, 56

Red scare, second, xvii; communist professors fired in, 198–99; A. Johnson on Enemy Alien Hearing Board in, 187–88; Laski and, 196–97; New School and, 167–68, 173, 180, 188–91. *See also* communism; McCarthy period

Reed, Alma: A. de Lima and, 209; on Orozco murals, 205–11

reform economists, in Weimar Germany, 119–20

refugees. *See* Ecole Libre des Hautes Etudes; Rockefeller Foundation; University in Exile

Renaissance (journal of Ecole Libre des Hautes Etudes), 162–64

renaming of New School for Social Research, 215, 219–220; Johnson on, 220; University in Exile, 118, 220 renaming of University in Exile, 118, 220

Reynal, Eugène, 142–44

Reynal & Hitchcock, 138, 142–44, 366, 407n10; editorial sponsors and, 139; royalties for Hitler from, 140

Riezler, Kurt, 262; government work in Germany during World War I, 121–22; head of Goethe University during Weimar period, 120; Heuss and, 262; Jewish wife of, 122; Lenin and, 121; at New School, 121; Weimar Constitution and, 122

Rivera, Diego: A. Johnson on, 203–4, 209; at Rockefeller Center, 204; E. B. White on, 204

Robinson, James Harvey, ix; Board of Directors of New School and, 42, 55–56; Columbia resignation of, 3–4, 41; on World War I, 20, 43; resigning from New School, 57, 59, 60–61, 81; vision of New School for, 34, 37, 38–39, 45, 50, 58–59, 66.

Rockefeller, Nelson, 285; Rivera and, 204

Rockefeller, Rodman, 284

Rockefeller Foundation, 116, 284; Day and, 102; Ecole Libre and, 156–57, 411n10; Fosdick at, 152; Germany and, 114; IWA and, 150, 360; Neumann and, 148; Rockefeller Archives and, 359; University in Exile and, 89, 90–91, 112, 148–49, 394nn15–16

Rockwell, Lee (great nephew of A. Johnson), 402n97

Roosevelt, Eleanor, 74

Roosevelt, Franklin D., 150; de Gaulle and, 155; Good Neighbor Policy of, 151; Koyré and, 159. *See also* Ecole Libre des Hautes Etudes

Roosevelt, Frank, 430n18

Roosevelt, Theodore, 15; Croly and, 16; Lippmann and, 15; and *The New Republic*, 15–16

Rorty, Richard, 286–87

Roseberry, William, 264

Rosenberg, Bernard, 293. *See also* Salomon, Albert

Rosenthal, Michael, 135–36

Rumsey, Mary Harriman, 41, 56, 307

Russell, Bertrand, 34, 63

Rutkoff, Peter, and William Scott, xvi, 56, 138, 193, 398n61, 413n21

Salmon, Lucy, 4, 78

Salomon, Albert (Mayflower professor of University in Exile), 120, 263, 293, 363

Sandburg, Carl, 225, 234–35

Sarton, May, 391n32

"Save the School" campaign: A. Johnson and, 246–48; Staudinger and, 246

Schaffner, Joseph, 100, 234, 246, 397n45; H. Halle family ties to, 234; Save the School and, 246; Staudinger's family ties to 246

Schapiro, Meyer, 225

Schneider, Alexander, 233, 234, 251; honorary doctorate for, p4

Scholte, Robert (Bob), 264

Schüller, Richard, 425n16

Schumpeter, Joseph, 120; Hitler and, 103; University in Exile and, 101–3

Schurman, Jacob Gould, 134

Schürmann, Reiner, 315–16

Schütz, Alfred, 221–23, 312

Sciences Po. See Ecole libre des sciences politiques

SDS. See Students for a Democratic Society

Seeger, Charles, 68–70

Seligman, Edwin R. A.: AAUP and, 27; Cattell and, 26–27; as chairman of Committee of Nine, 27–28; as dean of School of Political Science at Columbia, 24, 50; Dewey and, 29; as editor of Encyclopaedia of the Social Sciences, 69–70; founding of University in Exile and, 94–95, 97; A. Johnson and, 10, 69, 94

Shaikh, Anwar, 270–71

Shipherd College, 202

Shuster, George, 138–39, 141–42, 144, 157

Sitwell, Edith, 225

Simons, Hans (Mayflower professor of University in Exile), p6; academic freedom and, 194, 202; Board of Trustees and, 167, 170, 175, 176, 179–80; expanding campus of New School and, 226–28, 237; as dean of School of Political Science (Continuing Education), 169; as faculty member of Graduate Faculty, xi, 131; Ford Foundation and, 237; in Germany after 1945, 173–75; in Germany before World War II, 175–76, 363; Hovde and, 174–75; Jewish wife of, 174; Orozco mural covering and, 208–13, 227; Middle States Association and, 238; resignation of, 237–38; in Washington, D.C., 176

Smith, Daniel Cranford, 73

Smith, Emma Peters, 45, 46, 55, 61; New School firing, 81

Social Research, 116, 122, 146, 159, 229; A. Brecht and, 131; contributors to, 124; on dissident intellectuals in East and Central Europe, 335–36; on Hitler, 146; A. Johnson on, 124–25; Mack and, 125, 273, 335–36, 350–51

Sorchan, Charlotte Hunnewell (Martin), 40, 55, 431n23; as architect of New School's first campus, 44; as feminist, 78; as founder and early funder of New School, 40, 55 58, 383n29, 383n34

Soros, George, 336; CEU and, 343, 349

Spanish-American War, A. Johnson and, 9–10

Speier, Hans (Mayflower professor of University in Exile) p4; B. Brecht on, 109; founding of University in Exile and, 106, 109; Frankfurt School and, 147–48; in Germany, 106, 120, 362; IWA and, 148, 150; on Jay, 147–48; Jewish wife of, 401n94; Lederer and, 106, 146; Mannheim and, 106, 120; Nazi propaganda research of, 150; Neumann and, 146, 148; on psychoanalysis, 123, 148; at University in Exile/Graduate Faculty, 117, 174, 284, 329

Stackpole and Sons, 140–43, 408n10, 408n17. See also Mein Kampf, English translation of

Stanford University: Johnson at, 11, 12, 64; Veblen at, 64, 79, 355, 357

State of the Masses: The Threat of the Classless Society (Lederer), 146

Staudinger, Hans (Mayflower professor of University in Exile), p5; as codirector of Institute of World Affairs (IWA), 150; as dean of Graduate Faculty, 229–32, 235, 246; Duke and, 168; in Germany, 106.120, 131; The Inner Nazi by, 137–38; Jewish wife of, 138; A. Johnson on, 168; Lowe and, p5, 150; Nazis and, 106; as professor at Graduate Faculty, 131, 137–38; "Save the School" campaign and, 244–47; University in Exile's twenty-fifth anniversary dinner and, 235. See also Schaffner, Joseph

Steiger, Rod, 186. *See also* Studio Theatre and Dramatic Workshop
Stein, Gertrude, 70
Stein, Leo, 68
Stern, Fritz, 86
Stieglitz, Alfred, 67
Straight, Dorothy Payne Whitney: as early board member and funder of New School, 40, 41, 60, 71, 307; as funder of *New Republic*, 16, 40; and Junior League, 41, 56; as progressive, 78; widowed Mrs. Willard Straight marries Leonard Elmhirst, 60
Straight, Willard, 16
Strasberg, Lee, 70. *See also* Studio Theatre and Dramatic Workshop
Strauss, Leo, 99, 174, 231, 293, 346, 359. *See also* University of Chicago; White, Howard
student activism at New School: in defense of doctoral programs, 289, 293, 294; freedom of expression, 322–24; McCarthy period, 194, 197, 210, 211; postcolonial and women's studies, 303–5, 430n16; Vietnam War period, 257, 258–61. *See also* Alexander, M. Jacqui; Diamond, Stanley; Nell, Edward; New Left
student financial aid at New School, 52, 53, 66, 67, 274–77, 318, 432n42; GI Bill and, 169, 171, 224, 226; profile of, 38, 45.46, 49, 52; registration (1919–1933) 45, 46–47, 51, 76; registration (1933–1945), 116, 117, 118, 158; registration (1946–1963), 216, 220, 243, 274, 277; registration (1964–1982), 287, 289; registration (1980s), 318, 432n41
student political movements (1968). *See* Arato, Andrew; Arendt, Hannah; Cohn-Bendit, Daniel; Katznelson, Ira; Michnik, Adam; Miller, James; Prague Spring; Students for a Democratic Society; Vietnam War protests; Weather Underground
student profiles at New School, x, xiv, xv, 6, 37, 38, 39, 45, 46, 51, 52, 53, 54, 63, 65, 97, 105, 151, 154, 160, 160, 171, 181, 223–26, 229, 251, 257, 261, 263, 265. *See also* Berger, Peter; Broyard, Anatole; Cage, John; Cohen, Jean; de Lima, Sigrid; Donnelley,

Strachan; Ely, Mary; Fancher, Edwin; Ginnott-Cohn, Alice; Heilbroner, Robert; Green, Murray; Kurzweil, Edith; Marx, Willy; Norton, William Warder; Pollin, Robert; Roosevelt, Frank; Smith, Daniel Cranford; Studio Theatre and Dramatic Workshop, famous students of; Styron; *Village Voice*; Wald, Haskell; White, Howard
Students for a Democratic Society (SDS), 257–58
Studio Theatre and Dramatic Workshop, 70–71, 169, 172–73, 186, 187, 225; famous students of, 225. *See also* Adler, Stella; Piscator, Erwin
Sundiata, Sekou, 323
Sweezy, Paul, 269–70
Swift, Arthur, 218–21
Szacki, Jerzy: Goldfarb and, 339; Matynia and, 334; Michnik and 334, 335; as professor in communist Poland, 334, 335
Szent-Györgyi, Albert, 216

Templin, Wolfgang, 336
Texas, University of, A. Johnson at, 11
Theodor Heuss Chair, 262–63, 283
Tillich, Paul, 122
Tilly, Charles, 315, 317
Tilly, Louise, 315, 317
Truman, Harry S., Executive Order 9835 (1947 loyalty security program), 188
Twelfth Street building, 71, 73–76, 81, 189, 213, 227–28, 277–78, 284, 325, 387n28, p1; concerts at, 233, 251; A. Johnson office at, 174, 175; mortgage on, 168; University in Exile inauguration at, 117–18. *See also* Orozco murals, at New School

Universal Oil Products (UOP), Halle and, 99
University Control (Cattell), 25
University in Exile; founding of1933, p. 4; Katznelson on history of, 7, 341. *See also* anniversary celebrations for New School; Heidelberg on 12th Street; Mayflower professors of University in Exile

University of Chicago: AAU at, 201; A.
Johnson at, 11; Katznelson and, 313, 314;
University in Exile and, 97, 98–99; Veblen
at, 79, 357; Ward at, 295, 311. *See also*
Hutchins, Robert M.; Marschak, Jacob;
Strauss, Leo
UOP. *See* Universal Oil Products
Urban, Joseph, 71–76; as architect of Twelfth
Street building, 73–75, 391n38

Van Zandt, David, 352
van Zeeland, Paul, 154, 160, 161. *See also* Ecole
Libre des Hautes Etudes
Veblen, Thorstein, 93; on academic institution
reform, 5; as Big Four, 49; as faculty at New
School, 49, 64–65, 355; finances of, 355–56;
Mitchell and, 356; at Stanford University,
79, 357; sexual allegations against, 79, 355,
357; at University of Chicago, 357
velvet revolutions, 327, 332, 336
Versailles Treaty, 19, 119; German economy
and, 85
Vidich, Arthur, 288; on hiring at Graduate
Faculty, 292–93; rebuilding campaign and,
300; on student movements, 269
Vietnam War, 351–52
Vietnam War protests, xvii, 262; Diamond and
Nell on, 258–61; Everett and, 257–59, 261;
high school students and, 259; Katznelson
and, 310–11; Kent State University and,
258, 259; Kunstler at, 259–60; rock band
at, 260–61
Village Voice, 225

Wagner, Robert, 227–28
Wahl, Jean, 152–53. *See also* Colm, Gerhard;
Ecole Libre des Hautes Etudes
Wald, Haskell, 231
Walker, Ralph, 235
Wallas, Graham, 46–47, 53, 382n5
War Council Committee Against
Discrimination, 402n97
War Industries Board, 12, 13, 14, 48; Baruch
and, 12, 13, 14; A. Johnson and, 12, 13, 14,
Mitchell at, 12, 13, 48

Ward, F. Champion: as acting dean of
Graduate Faculty, 295; Enabling
Committee and, 311–12; Katznelson and
311; MacArthur Foundation and, 295;
recruitment plan for GF, 299–300; at
University of Chicago, 295; Ward Report
for rebuilding GF, 295, 312
Watson, John, 63, 66, 67
Weather Underground, 260. *See also* SDS
Weber, Max, 93, 123
Weil, André, 154, 161. *See also* Ecole Libre des
Hautes Etudes
Weizsächer, Richard von, 330
Welles, Sumner, 151
Wertheimer, Max (Mayflower professor of
University in Exile), p4; disciples of, 275;
Frankfurt School and, 148, in Germany,
69, 114, 362, Gestalt Psychology, founder
of, 69, at New School, p4, 117, 121, 123, 263,
121, 362. *See also* Arnheim, Rudolf; Asch,
Solomon; Henle, Mary
White, E. B., 204. *See also* Rivera, Diego
White, Howard: as dean of GF, 241, 250; as
GF student, 231, 292, 293; as Riezler's son-
in-law, 293
Wiggerhaus, Rolf, on political leanings of New
School, 147
Williams, William Carlos, 225
Williams, Tennessee, 186. *See also* Studio
Theatre and Dramatic Workshop
Wilson, Thomas Woodrow, 21; Baruch
and, 12–13; Lippmann and, 15; *The New
Republic* and, 18–19; Versailles Treaty
and, 19
Winters, Shelly, 186. *See also* Studio Theatre
and Dramatic Workshop
Wise, Stephen, 96
Wittels, Fritz, 67
Wolf, Dan, 225
Wolfe, Alan, 340
Wolfe, Don, 242
Wolfle, Dael, 258
Wolman, Leo, 64–65
World War I (Great War). *See* Baruch,
Bernard; Columbia University; Mitchell,

Wesley Clair; *New Republic, The*; War Industries Board
World War II. *See* Hitler, Adolf
Wright, Frank Lloyd, 70
Wunderlich, Frieda (Mayflower professor of University in Exile), p4; in Germany, 362; at New School, 117, 125, 150; Schumpeter and, 103

Yale University, 301, 302; A. Johnson papers at, xii; Malinowski at, 361

Yourdan, Philip, 186. *See also* Studio Theatre and Dramatic Workshop
Yovel, Yirmiyahu, 347

Zolberg, Aristide, p5, 315; education of, 345–46; Katznelson and, 314, 317, 344; *A Nation by Design* by, 346; in World War II, 344–45; Zolberg Institute on Migration and Mobility and, 346
Zolberg, Vera, 314, 317

CPSIA information can be obtained
at www.ICGtesting.com
Printed in the USA
JSHW021416210423
40684JS00003B/41